SOUTH ATLANTIC OCEAN
OCEAN
PARAGUAY
URUGUAY
ARGENTINA
CHILE
ANDES
Pampas
Gran Chaco
Entre Ríos
Patagonia
Tierra del Fuego
Falkland Is. (U.K.)
Stanley
S. Georgia (U.K.)
South Sandwich Is. (U.K.)
South Sandwich Trench
S. Orkney Is. (U.K.)
Elephant I. (U.K.)
Antarctic Peninsula
Cabo de Hornos (Cape Horn)
Estrecho de Magallanes
(Magellan's Str.)
Peru Chile Trench
Tropic of Capricorn
S. Felix
S. Ambrosio (Chile)
Islas Juan Fernández (Chile)
Santiago
Buenos Aires
Montevideo
Asunción
Córdoba
Rosario
Mendoza
São Paulo
Rio de Janeiro
Curitiba
Porto Alegre
Ushuaia
Punta Arenas
Río de la Plata (R. Plate)
Golfo San Matías
Golfo San Jorge
Bahía Blanca
Bahía Grande
Relief
Feet
Metres
16404
5000
9843
3000
6562
2000
3281
1000
1640
500
656
200
0
Sea Level
Land Dep.
656
200
13123
4000
22966
7000
Scale 1:25 000 000
0
200
400
600
800
1000 Miles
0
400
800
1200
1600 kms.
Lambert Azimuthal Equal Area Projection
© Collins ◇ Longman Atlases Cbi

POLITICAL AND ECONOMIC ENCYCLOPAEDIA OF SOUTH AMERICA AND THE CARIBBEAN

Other recent current affairs and economics titles from Longman Group UK Limited include the following:

OPEC and the World Energy Market: a Comprehensive Reference Guide (2nd edition), edited by Gavin Brown (1991)

The Annual Register (1990), edited by Alan J. Day

Political Scandals and Causes Célèbres since 1945: An International Reference Compendium (1990)

Political and Economic Encyclopaedia of Western Europe, edited by CIRCA Ltd (1990)

World Guide to Environmental Issues and Organizations, edited by Peter Brackley (1990)

Communist and Marxist Parties of the World (2nd edition), edited by Roger East (1990)

Youth Movements of the World, by William D. Angel (1990)

Political and Economic Encyclopaedia of the Soviet Union and Eastern Europe, edited by Stephen White (1990)

The European Parliament, by Francis Jacobs and Richard Corbett, with Michael Shackleton (1990)

Anti-Nuclear Movements: A World Survey of Opposition to Nuclear Energy, by Wolfgang Rüdig (1990)

The Broken Mirror: China after Tiananmen, edited by George Hicks (1990)

The British Trade Union Directory, edited and compiled by Wolodymyr Maksymiw (1990)

Employers' Organizations of the World, edited by Martin Upham (1990)

World Development Directory, compiled and edited by Roger East, Miles Smith-Morris and Martin Wright for CIRCA Ltd (1990)

Political and Economic Encyclopaedia of the Pacific, edited by Gerald Segal (1990)

World Directory of Minorities, compiled by the Minority Rights Group (1990)

Religion in Politics, edited by Stuart Mews (1990)

Western European Political Parties: a Comprehensive Guide, edited by Francis Jacobs (1989)

Trade Unions of the World, 1989–90 (2nd edition, 1989)

CPA World Directory of Old Age, compiled by the Centre for Policy on Ageing (1989)

Elections since 1945: a Worldwide Reference Compendium, general editor Ian Gorvin (1989)

Reuters Glossary: International Economic and Financial Terms, edited by the Senior Staff of Reuters Limited (1989)

POLITICAL AND ECONOMIC ENCYCLOPEDIA OF SOUTH AMERICA AND THE CARIBBEAN

Edited by
PETER CALVERT

With contributions by the following:

Dr Peter Beck (PB), Professor Jan Knippers Black (JKB), Dr Susan Calvert (SAC), Eduardo Crawley (EC), Professor Peter Flynn (PF), George Gelber (GG), Dr Richard Gillespie (RG), Mackie Holder (MH), Dr Darryl Howlett (DH), Professor Martin C. Needler (MCN), Jenny Pearce (JP), Lloyd Pettiford (LLP), Dr George Philip (GP), Rod Prince (RP), Lorimer Poultney (LP), Dr Colin Sage (CS), Dr Julian Saurin (JCJS), Dr Lewis Taylor (LT).

LONGMAN
CURRENT
AFFAIRS

POLITICAL AND ECONOMIC ENCYCLOPAEDIA OF SOUTH AMERICA AND THE CARIBBEAN

Published by Longman Group UK Limited, Westgate House,
The High, Harlow, Essex, CM20 1YR, United Kingdom.
Telephone (0279) 442601
Telex 81491 Padlog
Facsimile (0279) 444501

Distributed exclusively in the United States
and Canada by Gale Research Company
835 Penobscot Building, Detroit, MI 48226, USA.

DPA
DIRECTORY PUBLISHERS ASSOCIATION

ISBN 0-582-08528-4

A catalogue record for this book is available from the British Library

INTRODUCTION

The year 1992 is a significant one for both Europe and the Western Hemisphere. The first voyage of Christopher Columbus, 500 years ago, had profound effects on both. But for the Americas the legacy of Columbus is a dual one: for some, the real or imagined descendants of the conquerors, he is still admired and respected, but for many others his is seen as a legacy of subjection, colonization and death.

The 1980s have seen a strong and positive move towards democracy in the region. But the shift, though strong, has not been uniform. Moreover, economically the prospects are bleak. Most of the peoples of the bigger states of the region are worse off than they were a decade ago, and face at best an uncertain future in the 1990s. The smaller Caribbean island-states remain weak and insecure. The unification of the Single European Market, and moves to create a single trading bloc in North America, both threaten to erode their already weak position.

South America and the Caribbean traditionally have been seen as separate and distinct areas, and in international relations it is for some purposes helpful to think of them as separate. However they are linked by four factors. The most obvious is geographical proximity and a sense of separation from the "Old World" of Europe—though it must be remembered that the world is round, and that Rio de Janeiro, for example, is further from Washington DC, than it is from any European capital except Athens. The second is the pattern of Spanish and Portuguese settlement, and the way in which it has been subsequently shaped. This was dictated by the sea rather than the land, and it is still the sea and the air, rather than the land, that joins South America to the Caribbean. Thirdly, regardless of their subsequent divisions between the rulers of diverse European empires—the British, Danish, Dutch, French and Swedish, whose settlers were drawn by the magnet of sugar to the Caribbean islands and even, where they could get away with it, to the mainland—the independent states of the region today have all been colonies, and to that extent they share a common experience of colonial rule. Lastly they share, to a greater extent in the Caribbean, to a lesser extent in South America, a common awareness of their proximity to that global superpower, the United States, whose influence on all their lives can hardly be understated.

"Latin America" is still a useful term, as witness the fact that it is still used by Latin Americans themselves. But as a term describing 20 states, 18 speaking Spanish, one Portuguese and one French, it has always presented problems. As time passes the traditional distinctions between "Latin America" and the other cultural traditions of the Caribbean is being eroded. At the same time the geographical unity of the Caribbean Basin is increasingly reflected in a growing awareness of the economic and political factors that link the states in the region, despite their very diverse histories. The United States stands outside these perceptions, but without it they could not exist in their present form. The great challenge of the 1990s will be for the democratic states of the region to assume a greater degree of control over their own destinies, while at the same time enhancing this growing sense of a common purpose.

Organization. As with previous volumes in this series, the format is alphabetical. There are three types of entries: *country entries*, which contain data about each of the 47 territories covered, and are subdivided into a common pattern for ease of reference; *individual entries* on personalities, political parties etc. of special note; and *general entries*, which give an overview of problems or topics common to a number of countries or to the region as a whole. Cross references in each case are picked out in bold on their first appearance.

Peter Calvert

The Publishers would like to thank Harper Collins for permission to reproduce the maps on the endpapers of this book.

CHRONOLOGY

Early history

BC	
c.2300	Earliest villages in Peruvian highlands
c.2300	Earliest known pottery in Mexico
c.1500	Early Horizon period in Peru
c.1400	Olmec culture in Mesoamerica
c.1200	Chimú culture established in Peru
c.500	Monte Albán culture in Oaxaca
AD	Nazca culture in Peru
	Cuicuílco overwhelmed by volcano
c.400	Classic Maya period
c.650	Teotihuacán at peak of influence
c.800	Tikal, Palenque and Copán abandoned
c.900	Toltec culture consolidated in Mexico
c.1150	Collapse of Toltec dominance
1325	Foundation of Tenochtitlán
1438	Pachacuti Inca: Incas obtain ascendancy in Cuzco

Colonial period

1492	First voyage of Christopher Columbus; landfall at Watling Island, Bahamas; discovery of Cuba and Hispaniola
1493	Papal Bull *Inter caetera* divides the world into Spanish and Portuguese spheres
1493–96	Second voyage of Columbus
1494	*Treaty of Tordesillas* establishes Line of Demarcation
1496	Foundation of Santo Domingo, first European city in the Americas
1500	Pedro Alvares Cabral "discovers" Brazil while on the way to India
1508	Conquest of Puerto Rico by Juan Ponce de León
1511	Conquest of Cuba by Diego Velázquez
1513	Vasco Nuñez de Balboa crosses Isthmus of Panama and sights Pacific
1519–21	Conquest of Mexico led by Hernán Cortés
1521	Fall of Tenochtitlán (Aug. 13)
1523–24	Conquest of Guatemala by Pedro de Alvarado
1529	Settlement of Venezuela begins
1531–35	Conquest of Peru
1533	Fall of Incas
1534	Foundation of Spanish capital at Quito
1535	Foundation of Lima
	First Viceroy of New Spain (Mexico) appointed
1535–37	Expedition to Rio de la Plata of Pedro de Mendoza; foundation of Buenos Aires 1536
1536–38	Conquest of New Granada by Gonzalo Jiménez de Quesada
1538	Foundation of Bogotá
	First university established in the Americas at Santo Domingo
1540–41	Conquest of Chile by Pedro de Valdivía
1541	Foundation of Santiago de Chile
1542	*The New Laws of the Indies*; first Viceroy of Peru appointed
1549	First governor-general of Brazil appointed
1551	Universities established at Lima and Mexico City

1552	First African slaves shipped to Brazil
1563	Royal *Audiencia* created at Quito with jurisdiction over present-day Ecuador
1567	Foundation of Rio de Janeiro
1572	English attacks on Spanish settlements in the Caribbean (also 1585, 1595)
1580	Portugal under the Spanish Crown Second foundation of Buenos Aires by Juan de Garay
1621	Dutch establish government in the "Wild Coast" (Guianas)
1623	English settle in St Kitts (St Christopher), first English colony in the Caribbean
1624–25	Dutch seize Salvador, capital of Brazil
1625	English conquer Barbados
1630	Dutch seize Olinda
1632	English conquer Antigua and Montserrat
1635	French settle Guadeloupe and Martinique
1640	Portugal regains independence
1654	Dutch expelled from Brazil
1655	English capture Jamaica
1670	*Treaty of Madrid*: Spain recognizes English sovereignty in Jamaica Danish settlements in Virgin Islands
1670–71	Henry Morgan's attack on Panama City
1684	Bermuda becomes a British colony
1695	Brazilian gold rush begins (Minas Gerais)
1697	*Treaty of Rijswijk*: Spain cedes western Hispaniola to France; renamed Saint-Domingue Tayasal (Guatemala) falls to Spaniards
1703	*Methuen Treaty* between Britain and Portugal
1713	The *Asiento*: British allowed to trade slaves in Spanish America
1759	Expulsion of Jesuits from Portuguese territories
1762–63	British capture Havana
1763	Rio de Janeiro becomes capital of Brazil
1765	First British settlement in Falkland Islands (forces withdrawn 1774)
1776	Viceroyalties of New Granada and Rio de la Plata established
1778	Free trade established within the Spanish Empire
1780	Nelson nearly loses life in Nicaragua
1784	Swedes gain St Barthélémy from French
1791	Slave rising in Saint-Domingue
1803	The United States buys Louisiana
1804	Haiti gains independence from France
1807	Napoleon invades Portugal; Portuguese royal family transfer capital to Rio de Janeiro
1808	Napoleon invades Spain, deposes Carlos IV; Spanish War of Independence
National Period	
1810	"Grito de Dolores" of Fr Miguel Hidalgo in Mexico. Cabildo Abierto forms government in Buenos Aires
1811	Paraguay becomes the first Spanish territory to declare independence successfully
1814	*Treaty of London*: Britain obtains Demerara, Essequibo and Berbice which become British Guiana in 1831
1815	*Treaty of Vienna*: Britain gains Trinidad, Tobago and St Lucia, and confirms possession of British Guiana
1816	United Provinces declare independence at Tucumán
1816–19	United States annexes Florida
1817–18	General José de San Martín crosses Andes and defeats Spaniards at Chacabuco (Feb. 12, 1817) and Maipó (April 5, 1818)
1819	Simón Bolívar liberates New Granada at Battle of Boyacá (Aug. 7)

1820	Liberal revolution in Spain
1821	Venezuelan independence secured by Battle of Carabobo (June 24)
	Dominican Republic declares independence but is absorbed by Haiti (1822)
1822	General José de Sucre liberates Quito
	Prince Pedro of Braganza proclaims independence of Brazil (Sept. 7)
1824	Liberation of Peru achieved by Bolívar and Sucre at Battles of Junín (August) and Ayacucho (December)
1825	Independence of Bolivia, former Upper Peru
1828	Uruguay gains independence from Brazil
1829	Abolition of slavery in Mexico
1830	Ecuador secedes from Gran Colombia
	Death of Bolívar
1833	British establish rule over the Falkland Islands.
	Act of Emancipation—slavery ended in British Empire
1836	Texas defeats Mexican forces at Battle of San Jacinto
1838	Guatemala secedes from Central America; break up of Federation
1844	Dominican Republic secedes from Haiti
1845	Texas annexed by the United States
1846–48	The Mexican War (The War of 1847); USA defeats Mexico and annexes over half its national territory by *Treaty of Guadelupe Hidalgo* (1849)
1849	Congress of Lima
1857–60	War of the Reform in Mexico
1862–67	French intervention in Mexico
1865–70	The War of the Triple Alliance (the Paraguayan War)
1865–66	Spain at war with Peru, Chile and Bolivia
1868	Fall of the monarchy in Spain; end of Spanish imperial pretensions on mainland
1878–88	The Ten Years War in Cuba
1879	The War of the Pacific; Peru occupied, Bolivia loses Antofagasta
1888	Abolition of slavery in Brazil
1889	Fall of monarchy in Brazil; republic proclaimed
1889–90	First International Conference of American States, Washington, DC
1895	Liberals under General Eloy Alfaro in power in Ecuador
1895	José Martí lands in Cuba to seek independence

Rise of the United States 1898–1930

1898	Spanish–American War: USA occupies Cuba and Puerto Rico
1901	USA annexes Puerto Rico
1902	Independence of Cuba
1903	Independence of Panama; Hay-Bunau Varilla Treaty
1906	Second US occupation of Cuba (until 1909)
1910	Fifth International Conference of American States, Buenos Aires: Pan-American Union formed
	Outbreak of the Mexican Revolution (Nov. 20)
1911	US "Legation Guard" in Nicaragua
1914	USA occupies customs house in Vera Cruz, Mexico.
	Bryan–Chamorro Treaty
	Panama Canal opened (August)
1915	US Marines occupy Haiti (until 1934)
1916	US occupation of Dominican Republic (until 1924)
	The Columbus Raid and Pershing Expedition
1917	United States purchase Danish Virgin Islands
1919	Assassination of Emiliano Zapata
1920	Fall of Carranza in Mexico; emergence of the "Sonora Dynasty"
1926	US forces (withdrawn 1925) return to Nicaragua; Augusto Sandino begins guerrilla resistance
1928	Lindbergh flies from Washington to Mexico City
1929	Party of the National Revolution (PNR—now PRI) created in Mexico

Events 1930–60

1930	General Rafael Leonidas Trujillo, commander of the US-trained National Guard, seizes power in the Dominican Republic (Feb. 23) and rules as a dictator until his assassination (1961)
	Fall of Yrigoyen in Argentina (Sept. 6)
	Revolt in Rio Grande do Sul brings Vargas to power in Brazil (Oct. 30)
1931	Jorge Ubico elected President of Guatemala (Feb. 14)
	Maxmiliano Hernández Martínez becomes President of El Salvador (Dec. 2)
1932	The "Socialist Republic" in Chile (June 4–Sept. 13)
	Outbreak of Chaco War between Paraguay and Bolivia (June 15)
	Peruvian troops capture Colombian town of Leticia (Aug. 31)
	The "Matanza" (killing) in El Salvador
1933	Franklin D. Roosevelt proclaims "Good Neighbor" policy (March 4)
	Gabriel Terra dissolves Uruguayan Congress (March 31)
	Machado overthrown by student revolt in Cuba (Aug. 12)
1934	US abrogates *Platt Amendment* (May 29)
	Lázaro Cárdenas becomes President of Mexico (Dec. 1)
1935	Truce in Chaco War (June 14)
	Peru and Colombia settle Leticia dispute by ratification of *Protocol of Rio de Janeiro* (1935)
	Death of Gómez in Venezuela (Dec. 18)
1936	USA and Panama sign Treaty modifying status of Canal (March 2)
	Anastasio Somoza García seizes power in Nicaragua (June 2)
1937	Nationalization of oil in Bolivia (March)
	Railways put under workers' control in Mexico (June 12)
	Vargas proclaims *Estado Novo* in Brazil (Nov. 10)
	Massacre of Haitians in Dominican Republic
1938	Moyne Commission on living conditions in British West Indies
	Nationalization of oil by Mexico (March 18)
	Paraguay and Bolivia sign peace treaty ending Chaco War (July 21)
	Declaration of Lima on subversion from outside hemisphere (Dec. 24)
	Inauguration of "Popular Front" government in Chile (Dec. 24)
1939	Outbreak of war in Europe (Sept. 3) and First Meeting of Consultation of American Foreign Ministers, Panama (Sept. 23)
1940	Second Meeting of Consultation, Havana (July 21)
	UK–US "Destroyer-bases deal"
	Inter-American Peace Committee established (Dec. 4)
1941	Fighting between Peru and Ecuador in Marañón region (July 5); Ecuador forced to cede territory to Peru
	USA attacked by Japan (Dec. 7): Central American states, Panama, Cuba, Haiti and the Dominican Republic declare war on Japan (Dec. 8)
1942	Declaration of the United Nations (Jan. 1)
	Protocol of Rio de Janeiro ratified (March 31) settling Peru–Ecuador boundary dispute
	Mexico (June 1) and Brazil (Aug. 22) declare war on Axis powers
1943	Bolivia (April 7) and Colombia (Nov. 28) declare war on Axis powers
1944	Mass uprisings topple governments in Guatemala and El Salvador
1945	Ecuador declares war on Japan (Feb. 11); Paraguay (Feb. 9), Peru (Feb. 12), Venezuela (Feb. 16), Uruguay (Feb. 22) and Argentina (March 27) declare war on Axis powers
	Inter-American Conference on Problems of War and Peace, Mexico (Feb. 21–March 8); Act of Chapúltepec
1946	Election of Juan Domingo Perón (1946–55) in Argentina
	French territories in Caribbean become Overseas Departments (*Départements d'Outre-Mer*)
1947	Signature of *Inter-American Treaty of Reciprocal Assistance* (Rio Pact) (Sept. 2)

1948	United Nations Economic Commission for Latin America (ECLA) established
	Ninth Inter-American Conference, Bogotá (March 30–May 2)
	Assassination of Gaitán in Colombia (April 9); the *Bogotazo*
	Revolution in Costa Rica; establishment of "Second Republic" (April 19)
	Nicaragua invades Costa Rica (December)
1950	Outbreak of Korean War (June 25); Colombia sends troops
1952	Abolition of presidency, conciliar government in Uruguay (March 1)
	Batista seizes power in Cuba (March 10)
	Bolivia nationalizes tin mines (October)
1953	Rojas Pinilla assumes power in Colombia (June 13)
	Moncada uprising in Cuba (July 26)
	Britain suspends Constitution of British Guiana and lands troops (October)
1954	Tenth Inter-American Conference, Caracas (1–28 March); Declaration of Caracas
	Fall of Arbenz in Guatemala (June 27)
	Suicide of Getúlio Vargas in Brazil (Aug. 24)
	Dutch territories in Caribbean receive autonomy under Royal Charter from Queen Juliana
1955	Costa Rica–Nicaragua boundary dispute (January)
1956	Fidel Castro and the crew of the *Granma* land in Cuba
1957	Dr François Duvalier elected President of Haiti
	Nicaragua invades Honduras (May)
	Soviet Union launches first earth satellite (Oct. 4)
1958	West Indian Federation established
	US Vice President Nixon mobbed in Caracas (May 13)
1959	Fall of Batista in Cuba (Jan. 1)
	Fidel Castro becomes Prime Minister of Cuba (July)

Recent events

1960	Capital of Brazil transferred to Brasília (April 21)
1961	President Kennedy announces Alliance for Progress (March 16)
	The Bay of Pigs (April 17)
	Assassination of Trujillo in the Dominican Republic (May 30)
	US forces dispatched to Dominican Republic to eliminate Trujillos (Nov. 18)
1962	Break-up of West Indian Federation: Jamaica (Aug. 6) and Trinidad and Tobago (Aug. 31) independent
	Cuban Missile Crisis revealed (Oct. 22)
1963	Outbreak of communal violence in British Guiana
1964	Brazilian Revolution, fall of Goulart (April 2)
1965	Civil war (April 25) and US intervention in the Dominican Republic
1966	Oil discovered in eastern Ecuador
	Independence of Guyana, former British Guiana (May 26) and Barbados (Nov. 30)
	Military seize power in Argentina (June 29)
1967	Che Guevara killed near Camiri, Bolivia (Oct. 9)
1968	Military seize power in Peru (Oct. 3)
	XIX Olympic Games opened, Mexico (Oct. 12)
	"Rodney Riots" in Jamaica
	French Space Centre, Kourou, Guyane, opened
1969	"Football War" between Honduras and El Salvador (July 14–30)
	Anguilla repudiates rule by St Kitts; UK sends troops
1970	Protocol of Buenos Aires reforms OAS
	Black Power rising in Trinidad
	Cuba: Harvest of the Ten Millions
	Salvador Allende (1970–73) elected President of Chile (Sept. 16)

1971	Jean-Claude Duvalier succeeds his father on his death (April 21) and rules as an autocrat
1972	Norman Manley (1972–80) elected Prime Minister of Jamaica (Feb. 28)
	Chaguaramas summit (Oct. 7)
	Managua earthquake (Dec. 23)
1973	Independence of The Bahamas (July 10)
	Uruguayan Congress dissolved (July 27)
	CARICOM founded (Aug. 4)
	Military *coup* in Chile (Sept. 11); death of Allende
	Perón again becomes President in Argentina (Sept. 23)
1974	Independence of Grenada (Feb. 7)
	Death of Perón (July 1) who is succeeded by his wife, María Estela ("Isabel") Martínez de Perón, Latin America's first woman president
1975	Venezuelan iron ore industry (January) and petroleum industry (Dec. 31) nationalized
	Cuban troops in Angola (October) and Ethiopia (December)
	Independence of Suriname (Nov. 25)
1976	Guatemalan earthquake (Feb. 4); beginning of military campaign against the Indians
	Social Constitution of Cuba (Feb. 24)
	Military seize power in Argentina (March 24); beginning of the Process of National Reorganization
1977	*Panama Canal Treaties* between USA and Panama (Sept. 7)
1978	Referendum in Chile (Jan. 7)
	Assassination of Pedro Joaquín Chamorro (Jan. 10); outbreak of Sandinista revolution in Nicaragua
	Beagle Channel crisis between Argentina and Chile (Jan. 25)
	Panzós massacre, Guatemala (May 29)
	Independence of Dominica (Nov. 3)
1979	Independence of St Lucia (Feb. 22)
	Grenadian Revolution (March 13)
	New Ecuadorean Constitution enfranchizes illiterates; return to civilian government (April)
	Fall of Anastasio Somoza Debayle in Nicaragua (July)
	Independence of St Vincent (Oct. 27)
1980	Military *coup* in Suriname (Jan. 25); Lt Col Desi Bouterse seizes power
	Assassination of Archbishop Romero of San Salvador (March 24)
	Cubans take refuge in the Peruvian Embassy (April 4)
	Eugenia Charles elected Prime Minister of Dominica (July)
	Military Constitution of Chile approved in referendum (September)
	Edward Seaga (1980–89) elected Prime Minister of Jamaica (October)
	Anguilla leaves St Kitts (Dec. 19)
1981	Ecuador–Peru boundary clash (Jan. 29–Feb. 2)
	Patrick John plot in Dominica (March)
	Independence of Belize, formerly British Honduras (Sept. 21)
	Independence of Antigua and Barbuda (Nov. 1)
	President Reagan authorizes 'contras' against Nicaragua (Nov. 23)
	Leopoldo Galtieri assumes power in Argentina (Dec. 22)
1982	South Georgia incident (March 19)
	General Rios Montt seizes power in Guatemala (March 23)
	April 2: Argentina invades Falkland Islands, which are recovered by a British task force (May 1—June 14)
	Restoration of civilian government in Bolivia (Oct. 10)
	Onset of the "Debt Crisis"—nationalization of banks in Mexico (Sept. 1); Mexico defaults (December)
1983	Independence of St Kitts–Nevis (Sept. 19)

	Military *coup* (Oct. 13) and US intervention (Oct. 25) in Grenada
	Restoration of civilian government in Argentina (Dec. 10)
1984	*Boland Amendment* (July 26) prohibits US military aid to contras in Nicaragua
	Treaty of Peace and Friendship between Argentina and Chile
1985	Restoration of civilian government in Uruguay (March 1)
	Restoration of civilian government in Brazil (March 15)
	Death of Tancredo Neves (April 21)
	Guerrillas seize Supreme Court building in Bogotá, Colombia; President of the Supreme Court killed by army (Nov. 6)
1986	Popular uprising in Haiti; fall of Jean-Claude Duvalier (Feb. 7)
	"Iran–contra" scandal breaks (Nov. 25)
1987	Visit of John Paul II to Argentina; "Easter rising" (April)
	The Arias Plan for peace in Central America (June 25–26)
1988	Ecuadorean voters reject "free market" candidate (Jan. 31)
1989	Michael Manley re-elected Prime Minister of Jamaica (Feb. 9)
	Execution of General Ochoa Sánchez in Cuba (June 12)
	Resignation of Alfonsín; Carlos Menem becomes President of Argentina (July 8)
	Patricio Aylwin elected President of Chile (Dec. 14)
	US intervention in Panama (Dec. 20)
1990	Canada joins OAS
	Popular revolt in Haiti (March 11); Ertha Pascal-Trouillot provisional president
	Violeta Chamorro elected President of Nicaragua; takes office April 25
	Muslim uprising in Trinidad
1991	Belize and Guyana become members of OAS

A

ALEMAN VALDEZ, MIGUEL. As President during 1946–52, it was Miguel Alemán who took Mexico decisively down the path of capitalist development and alliance with the United States. Despite this fact, there was nothing in his background to mark him out as particularly conservative. As governor of Veracruz under **Lázaro Cárdenas**, Alemán took the initiative in mobilizing all state governors behind the President following the oil nationalization of 1938. Later, as Secretary of *Gobernación* under Avila Camacho, he developed particularly close ties with organized labour. Nevertheless his policy orientation as president was decisively right-wing.

Alemán appointed several businessmen to Cabinet positions — an unprecedented step in post-revolutionary Mexico — and purged the official unions of left-wing leaders, instead imposing more quiescent figures. He sharply slowed down the distribution of land and encouraged new export agriculture. He also stimulated the rapid urbanization of **Mexico City**. He also took a line on Cold War issues which was very supportive of the United States.

Late in his term of office he aroused fresh controversy by appearing to suggest that he might accept a second term in office. Although the precise mechanisms are still obscure, it is clear that senior figures within the "revolutionary family" pressured and persuaded him not to do so. In the end he supported Adolfo Ruiz Cortines, a benign middle-of-the-road figure, as his successor.

After leaving office Alemán devoted the considerable fortune which he had amassed during his political career to business ventures. He became a major figure behind the development of Acapulco as a luxury tourist resort; the Alemán family are now among the leading business interests in Mexico. Moreover while not participating openly in politics, Alemán used his influence in the direction of resisting any leftward moves.

GP

ALFONSIN, RAUL. President of **Argentina** 1983–89, Raúl Alfonsín was born on March 13, 1926. As a youth he joined the **Radical Civic Union** (*Unión Cívica Radical*—UCR), and at the age of 24 he was elected to his first public post, that of municipal councillor in his home town of Chascomús, in the province of Buenos Aires. He was later elected to the chamber of deputies in the national congress, and in 1965 became president of the UCR in Buenos Aires province, the country's largest electoral district.

As the visible leader of the party's left wing, he strongly opposed the military *coup* that deposed president Arturo Illia in 1966. Alfonsín dissented openly with what he saw as party leader Ricardo Balbín's excessively tolerant attitude towards the military regime, and to his rapprochement with the Peronists (**Justicialist Party**). The internal faction which he created in 1972, *Renovación y Cambio* (Renewal and Change), failed, however, in its bid to dislodge Balbín from the leadership.

When the military again took power in 1976, Alfonsín was one of the few mainstream politicians to speak out openly against their repression of the opposition and their abuses of human rights. He was also among the few leading politicians to criticize the military for occupying the **Falklands/Malvinas** islands by force in 1982. That same year, Balbín died. When elections were held in 1983, Alfonsín led the UCR to victory—the first time the Peronists had been defeated in a fully free contest.

His presidency was hallmarked by the trials and subsequent imprisonment of the military leaders who directed the "dirty war" of the mid-1970s; the only such instance on record in Latin America. His government introduced a new currency, the *austral*, as part of a wider, but unsuccessful attempt to stabilize the economy. By mid-term popular opinion had begun to turn against Alfonsín, and in the 1989 elections his party was defeated by the Peronists.

Faced with a worsening economic situation, Alfonsín decided to cut short his mandate by six months. In July 1989 he became the first elected president of Argentina to hand over power to an elected successor in 61 years.

EC

ALLENDE, SALVADOR. Salvador Allende Gossens (1908–1973) was a founder of the Chilean Socialist party in 1932. A medical doctor, Allende was Minister of Health in the Popular Front government of 1939; general secretary of his party from 1943 to 1970; and a senator from 1945 to 1970. He ran for president in 1958 for the FRAP, a left alliance, and would have won but for his poor showing among women voters; in 1964 he was beaten in a straight fight with the Christian Democrat, Eduardo Frei. As president from 1970 to 1973, Allende was plagued by divisions among the parties that made up his Popular Unity coalition, ranging from the centrist Radical Party, through the Communist party — a force for moderation at that time — to the far left of his own Socialist party. Allende was a traditional politician of deep humanitarian convictions, a skilled political operator and a convinced legalist but these qualities were no substitute for a single consistent political strategy. Allende killed himself in the Moneda Palace on Sept. 11, 1973 rather than be captured and shipped off into exile by the military.

GG

AMAZONIA. Brazil accounts for almost 5,000,000 sq km. of Amazonia's total area of some 6,500,000 sq km., making up about 55 per cent of Brazil's national territory. Official estimates of the population of Amazonia Legal in 1990 were of 14,500,000, almost 10 per cent of national population, or about 70 per cent of the people of Amazonia. Amazonia Legal includes the states of Acre, Amapá, Amazonas, Mato Grosso, Pará, Tocantins, Rondônia, Roraima and the western half of Maranhão.

One area in which the **Collor** government in Brazil broke new ground, and won respect and support, both at home and abroad, was in its environmental policies, especially towards Amazonia, but also towards other areas such as the *Mata Atlántica*, the Atlantic forest, now reduced to only 5 per cent of its former size, and the Pantanal, the beautiful swamplands of western Brazil. Here Collor took a sharply different line from his immediate predecessor, **Sarney**, and from the governments of the old regime.

The building of **Brasília**, inaugurated in 1960, and of the Belém-Brasília road, which was started in the same year, brought new interest in, and people to, the interior, as was the government's intention. The mixture of concern for "development" and to fill supposedly empty spaces, in the interests of "security", gave further priority to areas such as Amazonia under the military governments. Castello Branco launched Operation Amazonia (*Operaçâo Amazônia*), in a speech in Manaus in 1966, which included more road-building, the granting of "free port" status to Manaus, and the creation of a new federal agency, (*Superintendência do Desenvolvimento da Amazônia* — SUDAM), the Superintendency for the Development of Amazonia. Extremely favourable tax incentives were given to companies which would develop projects in Amazonia, including a 100 per cent tax rebate for 12 years. In addition, half a company's tax liability for up to 12 years could be invested in existing projects in the region, turning, in effect, tax revenues into venture capital. There were also lavish federal funds available and very cheap credit.

Between 1967 and 1973, land values in Amazonia shot up, by as much as 100 per cent, in real terms, annually, in eastern Amazonia. Large investors cleared land, with scant attention to the feasibility of the projects involved, and there began a series of increasingly violent land conflicts, between newcomers and the Indians and *caboclos* already on the land, and between different types of newcomers.

The Médici government (1969–74) introduced a second programme, in 1970, Programme of National Integration *Programa de Integração Nacional* — PIN), with explicitly social goals. It aimed to restructure the process of land occupation and to develop an integrated set of projects connected to the Transamazon highway network. A slogan of Médici was: "Land without people, for people without land", seeking to relieve pressures on areas such as the north-east. The government also created the National Institute of Colonization and Agrarian Reform (*Instituto Nacional de Colonização e Reforma Agrária* — INCRA), aiming to settle 100,000 families, with titles, on land, by 1980. The results were quite the contrary, dislocating both people and land markets.

Under Geisel, emphasis shifted, stressing the role of large investors, as exemplified by the Association of Amazonian Entrepreneurs (*Associação dos Empresários de Amazônia* — AEA). This coincided with the discovery of important mineral reserves, as at Carajás. It was also when ambitious hydroelectric projects were launched, such as Tucuruí, run by Electronorte. This was all stimulated by POLAMAZONIA, started in 1975. There was also investment of US$1,500 million, over half from the World Bank, in road-building, livestock and timber projects in western Amazonia, in a programme named *Polonoroeste*.

All through the military period, governments generally disregarded the plight of Brazil's Indians. An investigation by the Ministry of the Interior, in 1967, into the Indian Protection Service, (Serviço de Proteção ao Indio — SPI), found fraud and even murder. In 1969, SPI was replaced by the National Indian Foundation, (*Fundação Nacional ao Indio* — FUNAI), but this was underfunded. Its major failing was not to demarcate and protect Indian lands.

The Sarney government saw the situation become worse, except that some important pressure groups emerged. One was the Union of Indigenous Nations (*União das Nações*

Indígenas—UNI), founded in 1980. Another, in 1985, was the National Rubber Tapper Council *Conselho Nacional dos Seringueiros*—CNS), led by Chico Mendes.

The Catholic Church and the National Confederation of Agricultural Workers (*Confederação Nacional de Trabalhadores Agrícolas* — CONTAG), helped to organize smallholder communities. A reaction was the growth of the Democratic Union of Landowning Interests (*União Democrática Ruralista*—UDR), which helped to emasculate the agrarian provisions of the 1988 constitution.

The land crisis was not tackled by the new civilian government. Violence and land disputes multiplied and inflation fuelled the speculative market in land in Amazonia. In Rondônia, between 1984 and 1986, helped by road-building, land prices, in real terms, went up by 250 per cent.

The murder of Chico Mendes, in December 1988, focused world attention on Amazonia and its problems. So did the threat to Indian populations from the *garimpeiros*, especially to the Yanomami on the border of Roraima with Venezuela. This especially followed the appointment, by Sarney, of Romero Juca Filho to be governor of Roraima. He, with Sarney, managed to break up Yanomami lands, in September 1988, and, within three months, there were up to 100,000 miners in what had been Yanomami lands. The 8,000,000 hectare Indian and forest reserve, created in the 1950s, had been the home of the Yanomami, whose position now was desperate. The Yanomami question presents a major test for Collor and his advisers.

Another major issue, fundamental to all others, is deforestation, with Brazil holding 3,500,000 sq km. of tropical forest, or about 30 per cent of the world total. Estimates of deforestation vary, but a cautious estimate of destruction in Amazonia Legal, up to 1991, is at least 8.5 per cent, varying considerably in extent across the region, being worst in Southern Pará, Rondônia and Mato Grosso. The main causes of deforestation are ranching, road-building and land speculation, with much destruction coming from the expansion of the agricultural frontier since the 1960s, directly linked to road-building.

Again, the Sarney government did almost nothing about this basic problem. Its main contribution to Amazonian development was through a military-inspired programme, Calha Norte, which was important in showing the influence which the armed forces still exerted. Sarney also sought to reactivate the Amazon Co-operation Pact, signed, in 1978, by Bolivia, Brazil, Ecuador, Peru, Colombia, Venezuela, Guyana and Suriname. He and the armed forces tried to use it to express nationalist resistance to international concern for Amazônia, as in the Manaus Declaration, in May 1989.

Throughout the 1980s, the environment became ever more central to national political debate, second only to the economy. This was partly due to international interest, but also to the activities of effective pressure groups. There is a small Green Party (*Partido Verde*—PV) but more important were bodies such as the Ecumenical Centre for Documentation and Information (*Centro Ecuménico de Documentação e Informação*—CEDI) a Catholic research institute, based in São Paulo. There have also been important inputs from the Workers' Party (*Partido dos Trabalhadores—PT*), the Socialist Party (*Partido Socialista Brasileiro—PSB*) and the Workers' Central (*Central Unica dos Trabalhadores—CUT*) and, since 1986, the Alliance of Forest Peoples (*Aliança dos Povos da Floresta*—APF). This was mainly the result of co-operation between Indians and rubber-tappers, greatly helped by Dr José Lutzenberger, who later was to become Collor's Environment Secretary.

One achievement which seized international attention was the meeting of Indians and non-Indian groups at Altamira in February 1989. This largely caused Sarney to convoke an inter-ministerial working group on the environment, which on April 1, 1989 allowed him to announce a new programme, *Nossa Natureza*, "Our Nature". This diagnosed most of the problems, but did not set targets for solving them. Its main result was the creation of the Brazilian Environmental Agency (*Instituto Brasileiro de Meio Ambiente*—IBAMA), to be responsible for the environment, to control illegal deforestation and to enforce related laws.

It was in this context that Collor emphasized the importance of the environment in his inauguration speech, appointed Lutzenberger and Dr José Goldemberg, and created the Secretariat for the Environment (*Secretariado do Meio Ambiente*—SEMA). The environment was at the top of the political list, and remains there. Already, in December 1989, Collor had asked an environmentalist, Hélio Setti, to draw up an action plan for the first 10, 100 and 1,000 days of his government. All the recommendations for the first two periods were implemented.

There are still areas to be decided, including hydroelectric development, ranching, and agrarian reform to regularize land occupation: but there have been commitments to remove intruders from Yanomami areas, though, whether these are seen as pre-1988 or the 19 separate proposed reserves, is not clear, and to stop the construction of charcoal-fired pig-iron smelters along the Carajás-Itaquí railway.

SEMA is to be adequately financed, unlike Sarney's *Nossa Natureza*, largely through a World Bank loan of US$117,000,000, made in March 1990, as Collor took office. There is firm evidence that deforestation has slowed down in 1990, to about two-thirds of the rate in 1987. Some of this reduction has been caused by firmer government policy; some by lack of liquidity for ranchers and farmers after the **New Brazil or Collor Plan**, and some by a wetter burning period.

Reference to hydroelectric development is a reminder that there are points of disagreement between Goldemberg, who favours it, when properly controlled, and Lutzenberger, who does not. Questions have also been asked about the likely political survival of both these Secretaries: so far they seem to have full presidential backing.

Opposition to Collor's own position is likely to come from some of those who most supported him in his presidential campaign, but who are suspicious of his environmentalist conversion. These include lobbies in Amazonia, and elsewhere, who see regional development as a higher priority than protecting the environment. Reaction can often be vehement, as in the case of Gilberto Mestrinho, who, in 1990, was elected as governor of Amazonas, for a third time. Also, Ottomar Pinto, who won Roraima, partly by promising to open up Yanomami land to *garimpeiros*. Jader Barbalho, who won Pará, in the second round, is a landowners' candidate. In Acre, a right-wing candidate, supported by the UDR, beat a **PT** candidate linked to the rubber tappers.

If Collor's political hold slackens, he may have to come to terms with regional political bosses. Even if he remains in a strong position, he can expect no support from local agencies or courts. Meanwhile, there is no reason to doubt the sincerity of his commitment to the environmental issues, especially in Amazonia.

PF

AMERICAN POPULAR REVOLUTIONARY ALLIANCE Alianza Popular Revolucionaria Americana — APRA (Peru). The grandiosely named American Popular Revolutionary Alliance was founded in **Mexico** in 1924 by Victor Raúl Haya de la Torre (1895–1980), a student leader who had been exiled from **Peru** the previous year. Its philosophy combined Marxist ideas with *indigenismo*, the notion of the primacy of the indigenous inhabitants of the Americas, which led Haya to term the region "Indoamerica", and the concept of "historical space-time", by which he sought to apply the concept of relativity to social development. Works in which he expounded his views include *A dónde va Indoamérica*? (1936) and *Y después de la guerra qué*? (1946). On his return to Peru in 1930 Haya founded the Peruvian Aprista Party (Partido Aprista Peruano—PAP), which was suppressed in 1932 following the Trujillo revolt, the first of many revolts which made Apra (as it remained generally known) a major political force but brought it the unrelenting hostility of the Peruvian armed forces.

After Odría's *coup* in 1948 Haya was forced to spend six years as a prisoner in an annexe to the Colombian Embassy. On the fall of the dictatorship, he was released, but despite the loss of much of his fire, in 1962 he came close to winning the Presidency, only to be deprived of his victory at the last moment by military intervention. In 1979 he was elected President of the Constituent Assembly that wrote the Constitution of 1980 and returned the country to civilian government after he had died of old age. The fact that it was the first modern Peruvian Constitution to enfranchize illiterates and that the military government itself had carried out the expropriation of the great coastal estates and redistribution of lands to the Indians and made Quechua for the first time an official language equal with Spanish was a testimony to Haya's far-sightedness rather than to his influence. In 1985 Alan García was the first Aprista to be elected President and to be allowed to serve.

Apra's "maximum programme" for "Indoamérica" had five points: action against Yankee imperialism; the political unity of Latin America; nationalization of industry; internationalization of the **Panama Canal** and solidarity with all peoples. No other Aprista parties were ever founded, but populist parties of a similar kind include **Acción Democrática** in **Venezuela**, the Authentic Cuban Revolutionary Party (*Partido Revolucionario Cubano Auténtico*) in **Cuba**, the Revolutionary Action Party (*Partido Acción Revolucionario*) in **Guatemala** and the **Partido Febrerista** in **Paraguay**.

PARC

ANDEAN PACT (Acuerdo de Cartagena/Grupo Andino). The Andean Pact group, originally the Andean Subregional Integration Agreement, takes its Spanish name from the Treaty of Cartagena signed by the governments of Bolivia, Chile, Colombia, Ecuador and Peru on May 26, 1969. In February 1973 Venezuela joined the organization, but Chile decided to withdraw from the organization on Jan. 21, 1977, officially because of its hostility to foreign capital but in practice because of the other members' hostility to the dictatorial regime of general Pinochet. Even after the Mandate of Cartagena in May 1979, which called for greater political and economic co-operation, regional issues continued to disrupt the working of the Group; Bolivia briefly withdrew in 1980–81 after the seizure of power by General García Meza and Ecuador suspended membership in 1981 after a border clash with Peru.

The purpose of the Group was and is to promote economic integration between the member states by progressive elimination of tariff barriers and the co-ordination of industrial development, and since its formation intra-group trade has grown significantly. The supreme authority of the Group is the Commission, made up of one ambassador from each member state. Foreign Ministers meet annually or as required to formulate external policy. The Andean Parliament (Parlamento Andino) of five members from each state has a purely advisory role but the Court of Justice established in 1984 settles disputes arising under the Treaty.

PARC

ANGUILLA. *Population*: 7, 019 (1984). *Area* 96 sq km (Anguilla 91, Sombrero 5). GDP: US$20,800,000 (1987). *Top five trade partners*: USA, Puerto Rico, Trinidad and Tobago, US Virgin Islands, EEC (UK). *Education spending* 9.3 per cent of GNP. *Birthrate*: 23.5 per 1,000.

Geographical background. Anguilla, the most northerly Leeward Island, territorially includes the Island Sombrero, 48 km to the north, and other uninhabited islands. Its sub-tropical climate brings average temperatures of 27 degrees centigrade and 36 inches of rain per annum. This, with clear sea water and sandy beaches, has led to a growing tourist industry.

Socio-political background. Arawaks and Caribs originally inhabited Anguilla, a British colony from 1650 to 1657 and administered as part of St. Kitts (St. Christopher) Nevis from 1825. Anguillans have always fought this union, petitioning for separation in 1875 and 1958 and rejecting rule from St. Kitts when the union became an Associated State in February 1967.

Outline of political history. Anguillans wanted the internal independence of associated state status (Britain retained control of defence and external affairs). Led by Ronald Webster, head of the People's Progressive Party (PPM), then the lone political party, Anguillans took a stand against the St. Kitts – Nevis pact in May 1967. The impasse led to Britain sending in troops in March 1969. British Metropolitan Police remained on Anguilla until 1972, when the Anguilla Police Force was set up.

The Anguilla Act, passed by Britain in July 1971, allowed Anguilla to remove itself from the St. Kitts–Nevis–Anguilla state if independence was sought. Anguilla separated in December 1980, becoming a British Dependent Territory, finally becoming a separate dependency under the Anguilla Constitution Order 1982. On April 1, 1982 a new constitution became operational.

Ronald Webster became Anguilla's first Chief Minister following elections to the Legislative Assembly in March 1976. Emile Gumbs replaced him in February 1977 following a successful no-confidence motion. Webster won the 1980 elections with the newly-formed Anguilla United Party (AUP). This government collapsed in 1981 following the dismissal of the Minister of Agriculture in May and the resignation of another minister. Webster however won the resulting June elections with yet another new party, the Anguilla People's Party (APP). The party lost heavily at early elections in March 1984, with Webster losing his seat and being replaced by Emile Gumbs of the Anguilla National Alliance (ANA) which in 1980 abolished its former People's Progressive Party (PPP) name.

Recent developments—political. The 1984 election signalled the demise of Webster's political career. He resigned from the APP, renamed the Anguilla Democratic Party (ADP). His reborn AUP won two seats in the seven member elected House of Assembly, but Webster was rejected at the polls at the February 1989 election, also won by Gumbs.

Gumbs has turned Anguilla from a fishing and agricultural community to tourism and offshore financial services developments. A review of the Anguilla Constitution began in October 1985, and became effective in May 1990. One important development has been the appointment of a Deputy Governor with the Governor responsible for offshore banking.

Outline of economic development. Tourism accounted for 29 per cent of GDP in 1987, with the USA the principal market. The encouragement of international financial business has seen some 45 offshore banks registered by the start of 1990. These are seen as the major growth areas.

Traditional activities remain central to Anguilla's economic stability. Agriculture satisfies local demand, with the fishing sector a vital export earner. Some 10 per cent of GDP is contributed by this sector. Lobsters (64 per cent) and fish (35.6 per cent) were the main merchandise export earners.

Current economic development. Anguilla's industry revolves around boat-building and the export of salt, mostly to Trinidad for use in its oil industry. Manufacturing, fish processing and the building of schooners, increased by 29.8 per cent in 1987.

Prospects for development. Anguilla is thought to have a stable future, with especially tourism growth, based on its dependent status. Financial services and its niche-filling exports are all expected to continue the economic growth of the 1980s.

MH

ANTARCTICA. The seventh continent of Antarctica is often perceived as both "a pole apart" and "the world's last great wilderness" on account of its marginal location, geographical isolation, tardy discovery, unknown character, and pristine features. Traditionally, it has been interpreted as a peripheral area largely ignored by policy-makers, a trend encouraged by the manner in which most world maps either omit the region altogether or show merely a small coastal section. It is easy to overlook not only the intrinsic importance but also the vast size of Antarctica, whose area of 14,000,000 sq km exceeds the combined extent of either the USA and Mexico or Argentina, Brazil, Chile, Peru and Uruguay. However, the major South American nations adopt a rather different view towards what might be described as their "Near South".

The management of Antarctica. At present, Antarctica is "governed" by the so-called Antarctic Treaty System (ATS), a term employed to describe the complex of arrangements centred upon the 1959 Antarctic Treaty, which became effective in June 1961 and was signed by the 12 governments — these included Argentina and Chile — involved in the Antarctic programmes of International Geophysical Year (IGY). The treaty was intended to safeguard the peace and stability of Antarctica through prohibitions on military and nuclear activities, international scientific collaboration, special conservation measures, and a freeze of the troublesome sovereignty question. Indeed, an appreciation of the friction arising out of the Anglo–Argentine–Chilean rivalry for the same part of Antarctic real estate (e.g. the 1952 Hope Bay incident) provided a key stimulus for the conclusion of the agreement.

The management function was vested in the original signatories, which were described as Consultative Parties (ATCPs) and meet biennially at Consultative Meetings (ATCMs) held by rotation in member states (e.g. 1981 Buenos Aires, 1987 Rio de Janeiro). Specific issues can be considered by special ATCMs, as evidenced by the meeting held at Viña del Mar, Chile, at the close of 1990. The Antarctic Treaty, lacking any time limit, may last indefinitely, even if a review is permitted during or after 1991. This provision has often caused a mistaken belief that the treaty expires in 1991, and even influenced attitudes and actions, as evidenced by the post-1987 escalation of Peruvian involvement in Antarctica in the wake of press statements advocating government action to safeguard the country's interests before the "end" of the treaty.

The ATS over three decades — three key trends. The ATS has been characterized by three basic trends during its lifetime. In the first place, there has been increased participation. The original 12 ATCPs have been joined by a further 14 ATCPs — this status requires parties to perform "substantial" research in Antarctica (i.e. a permanent scientific base and programme) — and 13 non-ATCPs, which merely accept the treaty's principles and exercise observer status at ATCMs. The regime's current membership of 39 states, though comparing unfavourably with that (160) of the UN, includes not only the world's major states (e.g. USA, USSR, China, India, and most EEC states) but also governments accounting for about 70 per cent of the world's population.

Latin American states are well represented (Table 1) and perform an influential role in the operations of the treaty regime. They have figured prominently in the enhanced level of participation. Argentina and Chile, two original parties, have been joined as ATCPs by Brazil, Ecuador, Peru and Uruguay; thus, 20 per cent of the ATCPs derive from South America. Cuba and Colombia are non-ATCPs. In fact, accession to the treaty as a non-ATCP is often employed as a staging post before fulfilling the expensive research criteria required for ATCP status; for example, Colombia, having signed the treaty in 1989, is already aspiring to ATCP status. In practice, there has occurred a kind of Latin American "domino" effect in the sense that Brazil (accession 1975; ATCP status 1983), Uruguay (1980; 1985), Peru (1981; 1989), Cuba (1984); Ecuador (1987; 1990) and Colombia (1989) followed Argentina and Chile into the ATS. These dates imply Antarctica's increased perceived importance during the 1980s, when the participation of Spain (1982; 1988) was also relevant given Ibero–

Table 1: Latin American Antarctic Treaty Parties

Original signatories	Date of signature	Ratification
Argentina*	1 December 1959	23 June 1961
Chile*	1 December 1959	23 June 1961
Additional ATCPs to treaty	**Date of becoming ATCP**	**Date of accession**
Brazil*	12 September 1983	16 May 1975
Uruguay*	7 October 1985	11 January 1980
Peru*	9 October 1989	10 April 1981
Ecuador*	15 September 1987	19 November 1990
(Spain*	21 September 1988	31 March 1982)
Cuba**		16 August 1984
Colombia**		31 January 1989

* Consultative Parties (ACTPs)—original signatories and states adjudged to perform "substantial research activity" in Antarctica entitled to a decision-making role at Antarctic Treaty Consultative Meetings.

** Non-Consultative Parties—accession involves a recognition of the validity of the Antarctic Treaty's principles and entitles a party to observer status at meetings. It is often used as a stepping-stone towards ATCP status.

American political and scientific linkages on the topic.

The second theme concerns the ATS' evolution in response to changing circumstances and needs, as shown in 1980 by the Convention for the Conservation of Antarctic Marine Living Resources (CCAMLR). Conservation has proved a prime preoccupation for ATCMs, and a proposal for a comprehensive environmental protection convention is currently under discussion. In 1988 a minerals regime was negotiated, but this convention, though signed already by Argentina, Brazil, Chile and Uruguay, faces an uncertain future because of the opposition of certain ATCPs led by Australia and France. **Tourism** remains a matter for future action.

A third trend concerns the heightened international interest in the affairs of Antarctica, a development focusing upon the ATS' merits as a management mechanism as compared to an alternative UN-based common heritage regime. During the 1980s Antarctica, though never acquiring mainstream status on a par with the East–West or Middle East questions, emerged as a region which could no longer be ignored. The United Nations has conducted annual debates on the subject since 1983, while other international organizations, including the Non-Aligned Movement (NAM), the Organization of African Unity (OAU), the OECS (Organization of Eastern Caribbean States) and **CARICOM**, have assumed a sporadic interest in the region. The successive UN debates, in conjunction with the lobbying conducted for and against the ATS, meant that other South and Central American governments were forced to consider Antarctica for the first time. Costa Rica, Guatemala, Honduras, Nicaragua, Paraguay and Venezuela have responded at one time or another in a manner supportive of the ATS approach to the management of Antarctica. By contrast, one small Caribbean state, Antigua and Barbuda, performed a prominent role in the anti-ATS critical lobby alongside Malaysia in initiating and developing UN discussions on the topic.

The South American Antarctic. It is difficult to make generalizations about South American states and Antarctica, but there are certain areas of consensus, most notably, regarding a belief that the "South American Antarctic" occupies the quadrant between 0° and 90°W and represents a geographical and political continuity with the mainland. Argentina and Chile, glossing over their Antarctic rivalries and seeking hemispheric support against British claims, played a prime role in the formulation and evolution of this concept through the 1947 **Rio Treaty** (Inter-American Treaty of Reciprocal Assistance)—its area of coverage was defined to extend to the South Pole—the 1948 Donoso–La Rosa Declaration, and the 1978 Act of Puerto Montt.

Latin American nations, though sharing a feeling of hemispheric and developing state solidarity in support of the South American Antarctic concept, lack a coherent approach towards Antarctica because of differing geographical positions, traditional rivalries, and varying political, strategic, legal, economic, environmental and other concerns. Even those governments represented

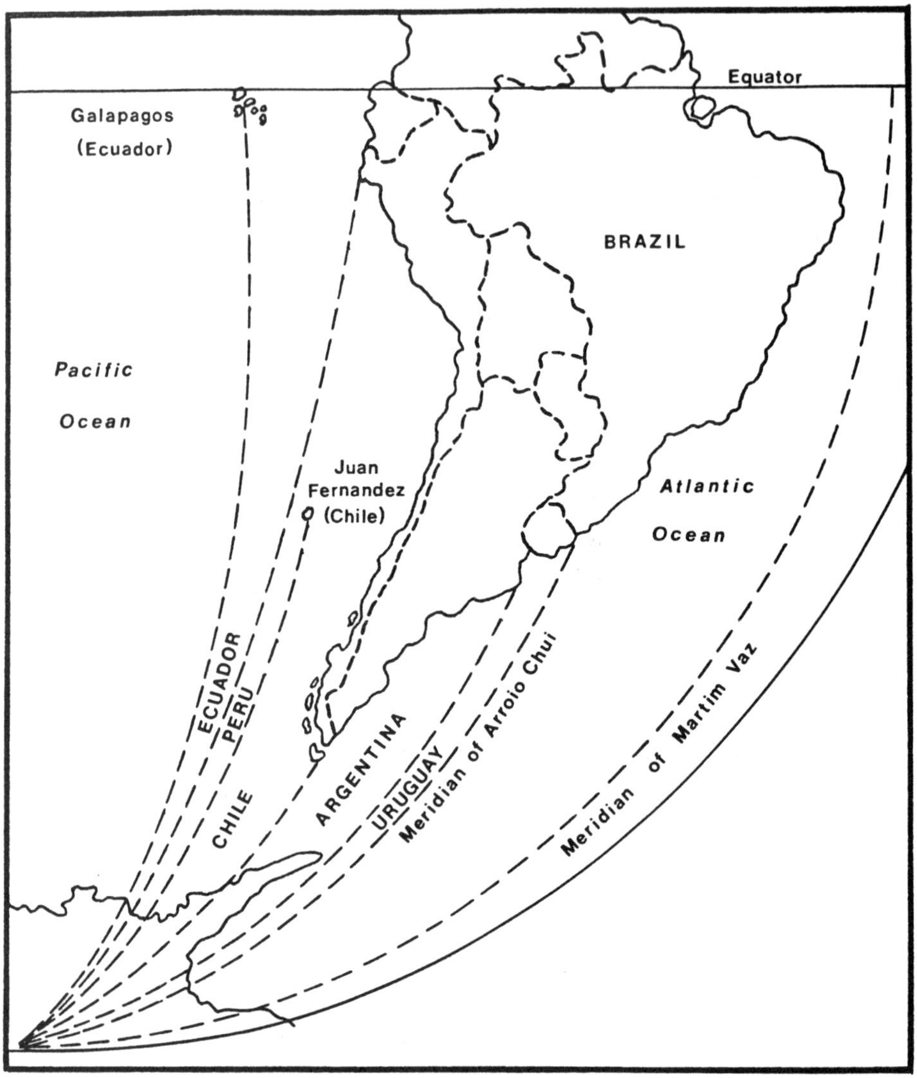

Figure 1: The frontage concept and Antarctica

within the ATS have different interests according to whether they are ATCPs or non-ATCPs, claimants or non-claimants, and exploiters or conservationists. Argentina and Chile claim a large part of the sector (i.e. 25°W–90°W), and their joint support for the South American Antarctic concept, the ATS as a management mechanism, and Antarctic scientific collaboration cannot disguise their continuing disagreement about the ownership of the area between 53°W–74°W south of 60°S (Figure 1).

South American interests in Antarctica. **Argentina** and **Chile** possess a long-standing interest in the geographically proximate polar region, which occupies a prominent role in their respective histories and includes national sovereign territory depicted on maps as a continuation of the mainland. The Antarctic territorial dimension contributes to national images of power, since both countries extend in effect from just above the tropic of Capricorn south to the South Pole. Geopolitical frameworks of thinking mean that their respective polar territories — *Antártida Argentina* and *Territorio Antártico Chileno*—possess a wider significance related to strategic, economic and other considerations, including their perceived Atlantic and Pacific Oceanic roles.

Both Argentina and Chile attach particular significance to the region, whose visibility has been fostered by a series of propagandist activities. For example, President **Pinochet** travelled to Antarctica twice, and his second visit during 1984 undertook "the sovereign Chilean act of founding of the first Antarctic city" at Teniente Marsh, South Shetland Islands. The word "city" was a somewhat exaggerated description for what was in reality a small family settlement, but the episode highlighted Chile's traditional effort to remind its people and the wider world about the existence and extent of its claim. Argentina's approach has often proved more blatant, as evidenced by the performance of symbolic acts interpreted domestically as strengthening the claim, including presidential visits, the erection of name plates, the conduct of weddings, the establishment of a "school", and the birth of babies presented as "citizens of Argentina and the Antarctic". The first of these Argentine Antarctic citizens, Emilio de Palma, was born at Esperanza base in 1978.

Science proves the basic currency of Antarctic laws and politics. Argentina and Chile operate six and three Antarctic bases respectively, while each of the other South American ATCPs maintain one base. Science is the prime method through which countries record, maintain and develop their individual polar interests, even if a significant proportion of Antarctic research tends to be of a co-operative nature. In this connection, there is evidence of an evolving South American research

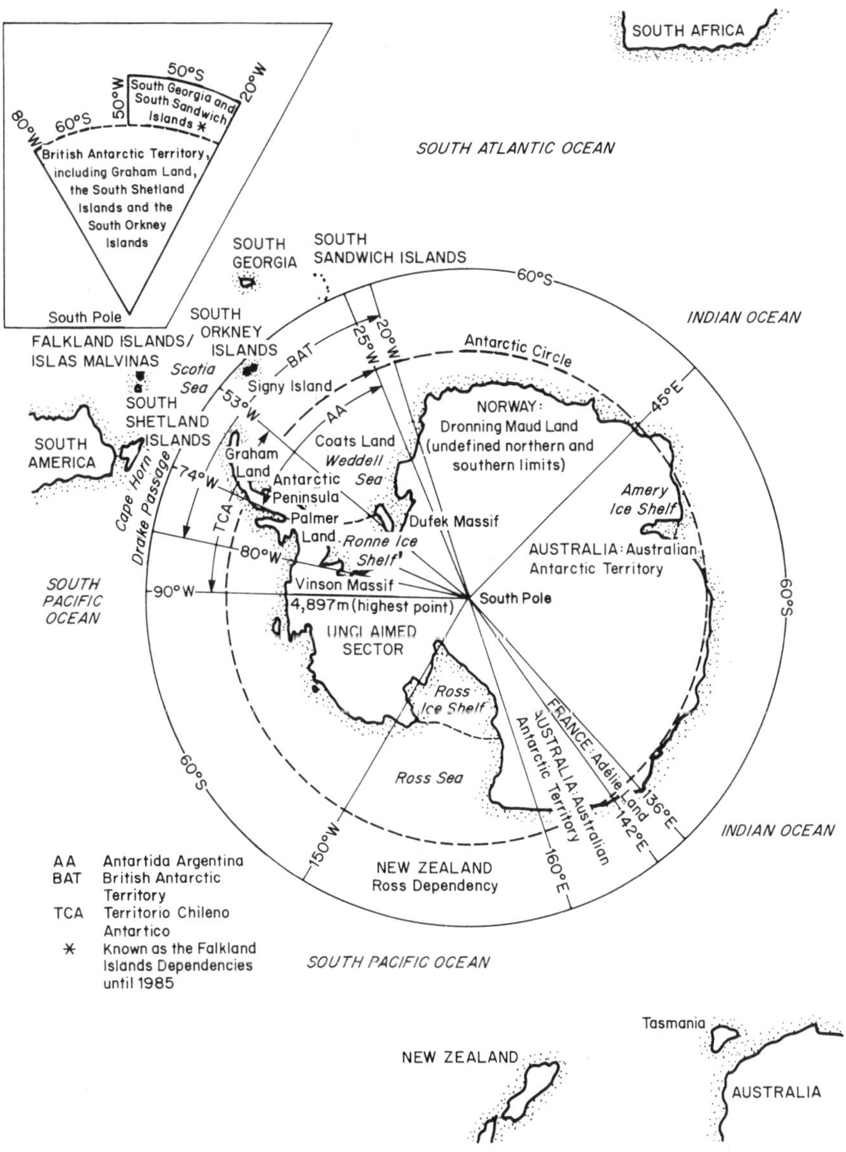

Figure 2: Antarctic territorial claims

network, although there exist also numerous scientific programmes involving collaboration with other parties like Britain and the USA (e.g. the long-running BIOMASS programme on krill and the 1987 Airborne Antarctic Ozone Experiment involved Argentina, Britain, Chile and the USA).

Other South American countries have a lesser and more recent interest lacking a sovereignty element. But this does not necessarily mean that Brazil, Ecuador, Peru or Uruguay treat Antarctica as a low priority issue. Brazil, though a non-claimant, has been associated *unofficially* with the "frontage" (*defrontação*) legal theory, which suggests basing claims upon meridians extending to Antarctic from mainland/insular boundaries and provides a rationale for Brazil, Ecuador, Peru and Uruguay to claim territorial rights in Antarctica (Figure 2). Naturally, neither Argentina nor Chile welcome the frontage concept, whose official implementation would scale down the extent of their claims. Inevitably, the ABC countries perform the main Latin American role in Antarctica, although the polar role of Ecuador, Peru and Uruguay should not be underestimated.

In many respects, an Antarctic role is perceived as a feature of Brazil's role as a regional power and a prerequisite of advance to great power status. To some extent, this aspect was accelerated after the Falklands War of 1982, when Argentine weakness suggested the need for Brazil to fill the resulting gap. Traditionally, Antarctica represented a further element of Argentine–Brazil rivalry, whereas more recently Antarctica has become an aspect facilitating integrationist trends in their relationship. Antarctica's status as a zone of peace links up well with the recent Argentine–Brazilian initiative for an adjoining South Atlantic Zone of Peace.

Conclusion. Any discussion of South America and Antarctica needs to consider points of difference alongside shared interests. In practice, the ATS has tended to moderate disagreements and to accentuate a common concern about the peace and stability of an adjacent polar region. In general, Latin American interest and activity in Antarctica has been confined to the South American quadrant, although participation in the ATS and international scientific programmes has fostered a broader continental perspective. For outsiders, like Britain and the USA, these trends have possessed both confrontational and co-operative implications, even if after the 1982 war the ATS offered one of the few points of meaningful contact between the Argentine and British governments until diplomatic relations were resumed in 1990.

PB

ANTIGUA AND BARBUDA. *General background*: Population: 77,000 (1987). *Area*: 441.6 sq km. *GDP*: EC$641.8 million. *Trade volume*: EC$605.3 million. *Top five trade partners*: USA, UK, Canada, Caribbean, Yugoslavia. *Defence*: 700-man defence force. *Urban population (centres over 20,000) as percentage of total*: 47; St. John's (capital) 36,000. *Birthrate*: 14.3 per 1,000.

Geographical background. Antigua, 280 sq km, Barbuda, 161 sq km, and uninhabited Redonda. 1.6 sq km, comprise this territory in the Leeward Islands. Barbuda is 40 km north of Antigua, Redonda is 40 km to the south-west. The country averages 80 degrees F like other West Indian countries, but rainfall is lower than the average, 1,000 mm per annum. St. John's, the capital, is home for 36,000 Antiguans, nearly half the 77,000 population. Some 1,500 people live on Barbuda.

Socio-political background. Britain colonized Antigua in the seventeenth century and added Barbuda in 1860. The country was pooled with other neighbouring English colonies as part of the Leeward Islands. In 1951 elections under universal adult suffrage were held and Antigua joined the **West Indies Federation** in January 1958.

On the collapse of the Federation in May 1962, Antigua was among colonies mooting an East Caribbean Federation. This failed, and Antigua opted for associated status, gained in February 1967. A 17-member House of Representatives was established and the Progressive Labour Movement, (PLM), led by George Walter, formed the first Antiguan government as an associated state, winning the February 1971 elections by gaining 13 seats.

Antigua and Barbuda became independent on Nov 1, 1981. It is a constitutional monarchy. Barbuda which strenuously opposed independence as part of Antigua, has one representative in the House, must be allowed at least two senators and has its own nine-member Barbuda Council.

Outline of political history. Antigua had in the, eighties, and continues to have the most consistently controversial political developments in the democratic English-speaking Caribbean. One reason cited for this has been the domination of Antiguan politics by the Antigua Labour Party, (ALP) and the Bird family, led by *Vere Bird Sr.*

Apart from the five year period 1971–76, the ALP has held power since 1946. Vere Bird Sr. is the Caribbean's longest serving leader. One son, Lester, became Deputy Premier in 1976, and another, Vere Jr. a senior minister responsible for transport. Both have been the subject of investigations. The Bird family and the ALP still remain dominant.

In 1976, the ALP campaigned against independence and won 11 seats. By 1978, the ALP claimed the country was ready and in an early election in April 1980, won 13 seats. This led to the first rift with Barbuda, which opposed independence as part of Antigua. In March 1981, the Barbuda People's Movement, (BPM), advocating secession from Antigua, won all the seats on the Barbuda Council.

Independence was gained on Nov. 1, 1981 as part of Antigua, but Barbuda has had an uneasy alliance with the larger country. The BPM, which lost council elections in March 1985 to the Organization for National Reconstruction (ONR), a party linked with the ALP, won the Barbuda seat in 1989 and has continued to campaign for separate status.

Recent developments—political. The BPM now holds all nine Barbuda council seats. The Government has refused to consider constitutional amendments but has agreed to talks with the Council. The BPM called for a review, to be conducted by the Commonwealth Secretariat, in October 1989.

The ALP, despite winning successive elections, has been characterized by internal strife. in 1984, opposition rivalry led to the ALP winning all the 16 seats, those on Antigua, it contested. In 1985, a new opposition party, the National Democratic Party, (NDP), was formed, merging with the UPM to form the United National Democratic Party, (UNDP), led by Dr. Ivor Heath.

A major crisis arose in November 1986 over improvements to V.C. Bird Airport. The project, handled by Vere Bird Jr., estimated at US$0.5 million, ended up costing US$11.5 million. A Cabinet reshuffle did not stem the damage and an official enquiry led by former Chief Justice of Grenada Sir Archibald Nedd found that while there was no criminal act, Vere Bird Jr. had acted improperly by awarding part of the contract to a company of which he was chairman and legal adviser.

Eight ministers, including Lester Bird, demanded the resignation of Vere Bird Jr. By 1988, further allegations of corruption centred on Lester Bird and the award of air routes to British Airways, among other things. Barbuda was also increasingly dissatisfied with treatment by Antigua and in March 1989 Barbudans blocked the unloading of 200 llamas from Chile. The Government had given US interests permission to establish a wildlife park and quarantine shelter without consulting the Barbuda people.

The ALP mended fences for the March 1989 general elections, winning 15 of the 16 seats it held previously. The UNDP won more than 30 per cent of the votes, but only one seat. It challenged seven results and started legal proceedings. One result was declared invalid and the other six ALP members who won the disputed seats resigned to contest August by-elections. The UNDP called for electoral reform first, while its ally, the Antigua Caribbean Liberation Movement (ACLM), said it had no funds for another campaign. The ALP members were thus declared elected in August.

British jurist Louis Blom Cooper concluded another highly critical enquiry into corruption allegations involving Lester Bird in November 1990. No action has been taken so far. The Bird government attempt to prosecute journalist Tim Hector who linked it with the murder of an American woman, failed after British Law Lords of the Privy Council found that the laws under which he was initially charged were unconstitutional. Antigua has also had a rocky relation with especially Trinidad and Tobago over its failure in 1988 to designate BWIA, Trinidad's national airline, Antigua's carrier. This impasse led to each country placing each other's goods under trade licences, but it was resolved in March 1988 after Antigua allowed BWIA landing rights.

More recently, Antigua, which is a member of the Organization of East Caribbean States, (OECS) and participated in the US-led Grenada intervention, has come under fire for strongly opposing closer political union in the OECS or the Caribbean Community, (CARICOM).

Outline of economic development. **Tourism** dominates Antigua's economy, contributing 12 per cent directly to GDP in 1981 and 40 per cent indirectly. Known for its 365 beaches, Antigua's main markets are the USA, Canada and the UK. Despite high tourist earnings, more than 50 per cent is sent back overseas.

Efforts have been made to diversify the economy. Cucumbers, and pumpkins were exported in 1988, as well as cotton (70,000 tonnes in 1985) and fruit, mainly mangoes and the Antiguan Black pineapple. Self-sufficiency in livestock farming has been encouraged. This, like crop production, was devastated by Hurricane Hugo in 1989.

Apart from an oil refinery, Antigua's manufacturing consists mainly of electronic assembly for re-export. Manufacturing accounted for 3.7 per cent of GDP in 1987.

Current economic situation. Antigua's GDP has increased by nearly six per cent annually up to 1988. The country however has high unemployment and heavy debt repayments. Further tourism development is seen as the way to support the country's two health schemes and education system.

MH

ARGENTINA. *General background. Population*: 32, 900,000 (1990). *Area*: 2, 780, 092 sq km. *GDP*: US$67,800. *Trade volume*: $14,680 million. *Top five trade partners*: United States, Brazil, Germany, USSR, The Netherlands. *Defence spending*: $1,117 million. *Education spending (percentage of GDP)*: 3.3 *Urban population (centres over 20,000) as percentage of total*: 86. *Birth rate*: 20 per 1,000. *Life expectancy*: 67 (men); 74 (women).

Geographical background. Argentina is roughly shaped like an isosceles triangle, with its base, 1,460 kilometres wide, straddling the Tropic of Capricorn, and its apex, 3,700 km further south, on the rim of the Antarctic circle. A little more than a third of its land borders is formed by the Andes mountains, which separate Argentina from Chile. The rest separate Argentina, in the north, from Bolivia and Paraguay, and in the east from Brazil and Uruguay. The country also has 4,500 km of coastline on the Atlantic. It must be noted that Argentina claims as its own the **Falklands/Malvinas** archipelago, the arc of islands running south-eastward of Tierra del Fuego (of which the largest are the South Georgia and South Orkney groups), and a section of **Antarctica** which is a projection of the width of continental Argentina towards the South Pole.

Apart from the foothills of the Andes, which spread far into the west-central and north-western provinces, major elevations are only found in the sierras of the central province of Córdoba and of Tandil, in the south of Buenos Aires province. Most of the southern half of the country, known as Patagonia, is covered in arid steppes that descend from the Andes to the Atlantic. The largest river system is that of the River Plate Basin, formed by the Paraná and Uruguay rivers and their tributaries, born outside Argentina, to the north, and traversing the eastern section of its territory southwards to the Atlantic. Three other large rivers cross Argentina from the Andes to the Atlantic: the Colorado and Negro in northern Patagonia, and the Chubut in central Patagonia.

This extension and diversity of terrain makes for a wide variety of climates, from the subtropical through the temperate to the sub-Antarctic. Large areas are hostile to human habitation: much of the Andean foothills, the Chaco bush in the north, the huge salt flats in the centre-north, and most of the Patagonian steppes in the south.

The country's agricultural map is dominated by the broad expanse of fertile sedimentary plains on the centre-east, known as the Pampas, whose suitability to cattle-ranching and grains production long provided the bulk of Argentina's export trade. Dominant crops elsewhere are sugarcane in the north-west, cotton in the north, and fruit both in the eastern Mesopotamia (mainly citrus) and along the northern Patagonian river valleys (mainly apples). Sheep farming, for wool, is the main farming activity in most of Patagonia. The central Andean provinces of Mendoza and San Juan have developed one of the world's largest wine industries.

Argentina has a wide variety of minerals, though not so far found in the huge quantities of the trans-Andean mining countries. Oil and natural gas have been found in abundance, in the south both onshore and offshore, in the west-central province of Neuquén, and in the far north-west.

Despite the extension of its territory, most of Argentina's population has long been urban (just under half the population live in cities of more than 100,000 inhabitants), and settlement has tended to concentrate in and around Buenos Aires, currently home to around a third of the country's entire population. The next most populous area, home to another third of the population, is the industrial belt which stretches from Buenos Aires to Córdoba, Rosario and Santa Fe.

Socio-political background. The massive turn-of-the-century influx of European immigrants, mainly from Spain and Italy, has given the population a markedly European complexion. By the end of the 1980s it was estimated that 85 per cent of the population was of European origin, and the remainder mestizo or Amerindian. The dividing lines between each of these groups is not too clear. Amerindian organizations, which have only recently become active, claim that there are in existence 14 identifiable aboriginal groups with a combined population of 1,900,000, or just above 6 per cent of the population.

Assimilation of the immigrant groups has been the rule, though several communities retain a distinct identity of their own, most notably the Arabs, the Jews, the British and the Germans.

Politically, Argentina is a federal republic, composed of 23 provinces and the Federal District (the most recent province, Tierra del Fuego, was created in 1990). Each province has its own constitution, and there are slight local differences in the ways they have organized their governments. The federal government is divided into three powers: a presidentialist executive, a bicameral legislature, and the judiciary. Elections are staggered as a result of the varying lengths of mandates: six years for the president, four years for members of the chamber of deputies (their terms overlap, so that half the chamber is renewed every two years), and three years for the senators. Appointments to the judiciary are made by the executive, but must be confirmed by the senate.

Formally, the jurisdiction of the federal executive is limited to little more than the conduct of foreign relations and the oversight of inter-provincial affairs: even the collection of income tax is a provincial prerogative "ceded" by treaty to the federal government. In practice, the federal executive holds the purse-strings (through its power to redistribute the taxes collected on behalf of the provinces) and enjoys wide powers to "intervene" a province (remove the elected provincial authorities and replace them with a federal trustee).

Outline of political history. Argentina began to be settled in 1543, in the extreme north-west of its present territory. This remained the most populated part of the country, and the hub of its political and economic activity, until 1776, when Buenos Aires, until then a minor trading port, was made capital of the newly created Vice-Royalty of the River Plate. From that point onwards Buenos Aires would increasingly become the centre of everything.

Argentine historians trace the beginning of the break with Spain to 1806–1807, when the *criollo* population resisted, and eventually defeated, two English invading forces. These events are seen as providing the native-born with the self-confidence necessary to depose the Viceroy and replace him with a local *junta* three years later, on May 25, 1810. Though there was a pro-independence party among the "May revolutionaries", this first action is more correctly seen as a local counterpart of the *junta* movement in Spain, against the imposition of a government headed by Joseph Bonaparte.

Spanish attempts to quell the rebellion led to the protracted "wars of independence", in which an important role was played by **General José de San Martín**, the military leader who is considered the *libertador* (liberator) of Spain's southernmost dominions, in the same way as Simón Bolívar is considered the Liberator of the northern half of South America. San Martín's campaign took him across the Andes, where he first helped Bernardo O'Higgins defeat the Spaniards in Chile, and then, in what was perhaps the first major amphibious operation in military history, in Peru.

The "United Provinces" formally declared their independence from Spain on July 9, 1816. There followed a period of struggle for ascendancy between the "unitarians", who wished to establish a single national unit ruled from Buenos Aires, and the "federals", who wanted the provinces to share power in a confederation. Ironically, it was a "federal" strongman from Buenos Aires province, **Juan Manuel de Rosas**, who in the two decades in which he directed the foreign relations of the confederation, first achieved something resembling the "unitarian" aspiration. And the later "unitarian" campaign to unseat Rosas, with the assistance of the provinces, was what actually achieved the unification of the country. Rosas was unseated in 1852, and a year later, in 1853, Argentina's first truly national constitution was adopted, though it would take another decade, and more internecine conflict, to bring the powerful province of Buenos Aires into the republic.

By this time, the territory ruled from Buenos Aires was considerably smaller than the old Viceroyalty of the River Plate: Bolivia, Paraguay and Uruguay had been established as separate units, while the new Argentine Republic had gained those territories of the old Captaincy-General of Chile that lay east of the Andes. In real terms, moreover, Buenos Aires only held sway over the northern half of the remaining territory. There was an internal "Indian frontier" which roughly ran in an arc from the south of the province of Buenos Aires to the south of the province of Mendoza. Beyond this frontier control remained in the hands of the nomadic Pampas Indians, who frequently raided the cattle ranches along the coastal strip.

General Julio Argentino Roca's "Desert Campaign" of 1876–79 finally rolled back this internal frontier, adding almost 400,000 square kilometres of Pampas farmland to the national economy, and bringing such isolated enclaves as the Welsh settlement in Chubut under central government control. Politically, Roca was also responsible for defusing much of the old contest between capital and interior by giving the elites of the richer provinces, such as Córdoba and Santa Fe, a share of the power previously held almost exclusively by Buenos Aires. With a national government now consolidated and control established over most of the territory, the "Generation of the Eighties" launched an ambitious programme of modernization, a key feature of which was the attraction of large contingents of immigrants from Europe. At the time the constitution of 1853 was adopted, Argentina had a population of barely more than one million; by 1914 their numbers had increased almost eightfold. Within a single generation the newcomers had become assimilated, and together with the middle classes spawned by this rapid expansion, soon began to demand a voice on the political stage, challenging an "enlightened" conservative elite which kept the franchise restricted and frequently resorted to electoral fraud in order to retain their grip on power.

The Unión Cívica Radical (UCR), a party founded in the 1890s, became the instrument for the aspirations of the new middle classes. Their basic demand was universal male suffrage and secret balloting. In pressing for it the UCR adopted a policy of "intransigence", refusing all offers from their adversaries, even those involving a share of power, which fell short of that demand. On several occasions the UCR became involved in armed uprisings which, though unsuccessful, finally helped persuade the government to give way. In 1912 President Roque Sáenz Peña promulgated an electroral law containing the provisions the UCR had campaigned for. Four years later, in 1916, the UCR's candidate, Hipólito Yrigoyen, was elected President by an overwhelming majority. He was succeeded in 1922 by a candidate from the "anti-personalist" wing of his own party, and in 1928 was again elected President.

Yrigoyen's second presidency was cut short, in September 1930, by a military *coup* which Argentine historians see as marking the beginning of an era of periodic military intervention in politics. The military, however, did not retain power. Instead they engineered the return of the conservatives, who through resort to electoral fraud remained in power until 1943; the period known as the "infamous decade". That year, in what was widely seen as a move to prevent the government from shifting from neutrality to a pro-Allied position in the World War, the Army staged another *coup*. The leader of the group of colonels who were the real driving force behind the coup, **Juan Domingo Perón**, at first took a second-line position in the new government, as head of the Labour Department. From there he built up a strong political base among Argentina's trade unions, using his powers to secure settlements of disputes in favour of his sympathisers, and displacing Communists and Socialists from union leadership. He then began to take more influential positions in government, first as War minister, later as Vice-President—until in 1945 his rivals within the army, backed by much of the traditional political establishment, desposed him and confined him on the island prison of Martín García.

A mass demonstration by the unions of Oct. 17, 1945 (henceforth to be celebrated by his followers as the "Day of Popular Loyalty") forced his release. Resigning his positions, Perón began to campaign as the presidential candidate of a coalition of parties created for that purpose. In 1946, running against another coalition representing most of the established parties, he was elected President.

His first term of office was marked by the adoption of pro-labour social legislation, the nationalization of foreign (mainly British) companies, and a determined attempt to foster industrialization. His charismatic wife Eva (*Evita* to the masses) ran an *ad hoc* social welfare system based chiefly on government largess. In 1949 he reformed the constitution, adding to it sections guaranteeing an array of social "rights", and allowing the re-election of the President.

He was re-elected in 1951. Without Evita's appeal to the masses (she died in 1952), and facing a severe economic crisis, his government turned increasingly authoritarian. Perón successively lost the support of the Church and of the armed forces. In 1955 Perón was ousted by a military *coup* and fled into exile.

Most of the ensuing two decades of Argentine politics were hallmarked by attempts to destroy, emasculate or co-opt the Justicialist **(Peronist) Party**. Elections called in 1958 were won by Arturo Frondizi, on the strength of a deal he had made with the proscribed Peronists; he was overthrown by a military *coup* in 1962 after allowing the Peronists to contest, and win, gubernatorial elections in the province of Buenos Aires. Elections were again held in 1963; with the Peronists proscribed, victory went to the candidate of the UCR, Arturo Umberto Illia, who attempted the slow re-integration of the Peronists to legal political life by fostering the emergence of "neo-Peronist" parties. Illia was deposed by a military *coup* in 1966.

The military who took over named their government the "Argentine Revolution". Unlike previous coups, which had overtly aimed at the restoration of a "purified" democracy, this one set itself the task of completely reshaping the political system. Parties were disbanded, and no time limit was set on the permanence of the military in power. The first phase, under corporatist-leaning General Juan Carlos Onganía, collapsed after a series of protests riots in 1969 (which also marked the appearance of urban guerrilla organizations in Argentina). His successor, General Roberto Marcelo Levingston, lasted only a few months before being eased out by General Alejandro Lanusse, who reversed the earlier policy and promised a return to elected rule. Lanusse tried to negotiate with the Peronists a phased return to full participation in politics. Perón replied by encouraging the left wing of his movement, including the Montoneros guerrillas, to create an atmosphere in which proscribing his movement would have meant risking a major insurgency. Though Lanusse effectively contained the *Montoneros* (and their Trotskyist counterparts of the *Ejército Revolucionario del Pueblo*, ERP), he finally allowed the Peronists to run under their own colours in elections held in March 1973.

Peronist candidate Héctor Cámpora won by a landslide. The inclusion of prominent members of the Peronist Left in his government, and the early blanket amnesty granted to imprisoned guerrillas, soon led to open conflict between these and the right wing of Peronism. The latter fostered the emergence of death squads, of which the most notorious was the "triple A", to wage a clandestine war against the Left. As abductions and assassinations multiplied, Perón returned to Argentina. Cámpora was forced to resign, and new elections were held in Sept. 1973. Perón became President, and his third wife María Estela, better known as *Isabelita*, Vice-President.

Perón sided with the Right; the government was purged of left-wingers, and Perón soon publicly dissociated himself from the *Montoneros*. The "dirty war" increased in intensity, and shortly after Perón died, in July 1974, political killings were running at an average of two a day. The presidency went to María Estela Perón, who proved unable to cope with the violence, particularly when it was aggravated by a severe economic crisis. In early 1975 the military were given a free hand to fight the ERP; by mid-year they had been given complete control of counter-insurgency operations. In March 1976 the military ousted the government.

Like their predecessors in 1966, the new military rulers (who baptised their government the "Process of National Reorganization") set themselves the task of reshaping Argentina's political system, extirpating left-wing "subversion" and imposing an indefinite moratorium on political activity. This was to be accompanied by the adoption of free-market policies, opening up the economy to competition from abroad.

Though they gave themselves draconian repressive powers, the military chose to conduct their campaign against "subversion", which soon came to mean any activities suspected of leaning left-of-centre, in secret. The methods of the earlier death squads were taken over and continued by the state: opponents were abducted, often tortured, and in most cases secretly executed. At least 9,000 people "disappeared" in this way (see **human rights**).

Their economic policies, fuelled by heavy borrowing from abroad, stimulated financial speculation rather than growth, and by 1981 the economy was collapsing. Political and labour dissent became more open, and pressure grew for a prompt return to elected rule. This was briefly arrested in early 1982 when the military suddenly occupied the British-held **Falkland/Malvinas** archipelago—a longstanding aspiration of Argentines from across the political spectrum. Support for the military government evaporated when they proved unable to prevent the British from recovering the islands, which they did in only 70 days. Defeat in war was followed by a swift political collapse: after only fainthearted attempts to control the transition, the military gave way and called free elections in 1983.

The 1983 elections were the first time the Peronists were defeated in a free contest. The candidate of the UCR, **Raúl Alfonsín**, won with a majority historically comparable only to those of Yrigoyen in 1916 and Perón in 1946. His government embarked upon a course of action unprecedented in Latin America: to investigate fully the crimes committed by the military while in power (usually referred to as "human rights abuses"), and to take those responsible to court. By the end of 1985, five of the military leaders of the "dirty war" had been convicted and sentenced. The Alfonsín administration also set about reducing the influence of the armed forces in the body politic, drastically reducing defence expenditure and curtailing the term of mandatory conscription.

During this first phase, not only was Alfonsín's popularity running high; a deep split took place in the ranks of the opposition Peronists, between the "orthodox" leadership and an emerging "renewalist" faction which advocated the reorganization of the party along more democratic lines. The crisis within the opposition peaked at the time of the 1985 legislative elections, when a divided Peronism saw its support fall to the lowest level ever. The outcome was twofold: within Peronism the "renewalists" won the party leadership, while a strengthened Alfonsín administration was able to launch an ambitious economic programme, the Plan Austral.

Though initially successful, the Plan Austral soon began to falter, eroding popular support for the government. At the same time, unrest began to fester in the armed forces, where a nationalist faction, led by officers who had held field command positions during the Malvinas/Falkland war (of which the most prominent were Colonel Mohamed Alí Seineldín and Lieutenant-Colonel

Aldo Rico), began to lobby for an end to the human rights trials, a public vindication of the "dirty war", and increases in military pay and defence budget appropriations.

Alfonsín gave way to military pressure and in December 1986, through the *punto final* ("full stop") law, limited further prosecution of the military on human rights charges. Nonetheless, the group of right-wing nationalist officers staged a mutiny in Easter 1987, following which the government, through the "due obedience" law, called virtually all remaining trials to a halt. Even this failed to satisfy the military rebels (popularly known as *carapintadas*, "painted faces", for their habit of daubing themselves with camouflage paint), who staged two further mutinies, in January and December 1988, overtly aimed at replacing the military high command.

When legislative elections were held in 1987, the ruling UCR was soundly defeated, and the Peronists recovered much of the voter support they had lost since 1983. As the economic situation worsened, the popularity of the government fell further, and so did the prestige of the "renewalist" wing of Peronism, which came to be seen as not differing greatly from the ruling UCR. When the time came for the Peronists to pick their candidate for the 1989 presidential elections, the nomination was won by a man closer to traditional Peronist populism: the governor of the province of La Rioja, **Carlos Saúl Menem**. Come the elections, Menem won by a wide margin—and so far had the state of the economy worsened that Alfonsín decided to cut short his mandate and hand over power six months early.

Recent developments—political. Far from signalling a return to traditional Peronist policies, upon taking office Menem adopted a drastic programme of liberalization more akin to the policies long advocated by Argentina's small conservative parties. This afforded him the support of the right-wing Democratic Centre Union (*Unión de Centro Nacional*—UCeDé) and of the provincial conservative parties represented in the national congress. By the same token it alienated many traditional Peronists and led to the division of the umbrella labour confederation, the CGT, into pro- and anti-Menem factions.

Menem also moved swiftly to restore diplomatic relations with Britain, which had been interrupted since the Malvinas/Falklands war of 1982. He sought to establish a special relationship with the United States; a policy most vividly expressed by his decision to send Argentine warships to support the UN blockade of Iraq—against the opposition of most of the population.

This combination of policies distanced Menem from the army's *carapintadas*, whom he had patronized during his election campaign—promising, among other things, that he would pardon the leaders of the "dirty war" who were serving prison sentences. In December 1990 the *carapintadas* staged an uprising, which Menem ordered harshly repressed. Nonetheless, at the end of the year Menem did fulfil his promise to pardon the "dirty war" leaders (together with *Montonero* leader Mario Firmenich). This triggered a wave of popular dissent. Menem's popularity deteriorated further in early 1991, first as a result of a scandal over widespread corruption in his administration, then over the sudden worsening of the economic situation, events which led to two successive cabinet reshuffles, and even to speculation that Menem might not last out his full mandate.

Outline of economic development. In early colonial times, the centre of economic activity in what is now Argentina lay in the north-west, which acted as a provider of goods and services for the large mining operations in the Alto Perú (now Bolivia). Buenos Aires, initially a minor trading post, later began to grow in importance as a result of two factors: (i) as capital of the Viceroyalty of the River Plate it appropriated the customs revenues of the Alto Perú mining operations; and (ii) its position as an Atlantic port made it an ideal point of entry for the smuggling that would eventually break the Spanish monopoly on trade with the Americas.

For a long time even after independence, cattle-ranching in the immediate hinterland of Buenos Aires remained a primitive affair: free-ranging cattle were literally hunted, and then chiefly for their hides. Salting beef for export began to emerge as an industry as a response to an outside event: the Civil War in the United States. More systematic cattle-ranching would have to await the end of the "Desert Campaign" of 1876–89, the subsequent introduction of barbed wire which allowed the enclosure of farmland, and the appearance of refrigerated sea transport, which enabled the establishment of a meat-packing industry.

The boom of the post-1880s coincided with the mass immigration and modernization policies fostered by the "Generation of the Eighties". The last decades of the nineteenth century witnessed the building of railways, urban infrastructure and modern port installations, and the introduction of extensive cultivation of grains in the pampas. These central plains came to dominate an economy based on a simple pattern of exchange: the country exported beef and grains, and imported manufactures. In both directions, the dominant partner was Britain—which was also the source of most of the foreign investment in Argentina. The formula was so successful that by the early twentieth century Argentina ranked among the most prosperous countries of the world.

It would not hold this position for long. The interruption of supplies during World War I highlighted the vulnerability of an economy lacking a manufacturing base of its own. The crisis of the early 1920s found Argentina, because of its geographic position and its political isolation, at a disadvantage in a world whose trading patterns had been dramatically altered by the opening of the two great canals, those of Panama and Suez.

The outbreak of World War II, a larger-scale reprise of the first in its impact on the Argentine economy, found the country still unprepared, and with most of the larger foreign enterprises run down through lack of investment. The nationalist military coup of 1943, and it successor, the first Perón government, were largely a response to this situation. The state took over the foreign companies and embarked upon a programme of rapid industrialization, financed out of the reserves built up during the war years and the export earnings of the farm sector.

Under heavy protection, import substitution was pursued simultaneously "at both ends"; from the finished products backwards, and from such "basic" industries as steel and oil forwards—which made the process increasingly expensive. Moreover, the rapid expansion of industry *vis-à-vis* the slower growth of agriculture inevitably led the country into a cycle of balance-of-payments crises.

The brief Frondizi administration (1958–62), under the banner of *desarrollismo* ("developmentalism") attempted to break out of this cycle through recourse to foreign investment. It did achieve a marked increase in growth, but not having changed any of the other factors ended by aggravating the cycle. In the period of military rule known as the "Argentine Revolution" an attempt was made to open the economy to outside competition and pursue export-led growth, while retaining the state's dominant role in the economy. This succeeded in weakening much of the country's industrial base, without achieving the principal aim, as Argentina began to find the markets for its traditional export goods, beef and grains, progressively constricted.

Diverse mixes of these policies were essayed, without much success, until the next military government, that of the "Process of National Reorganization" (1976–83) tried to combine a more drastic opening to outside competition combined with heavy recourse to borrowing abroad, but again while retaining the state's huge presence in the economy (apart from the public services, the state controlled the oil, steel and petrochemical industries, and a considerable portion of industry was under the direct control of the military). The policy mix adopted by the military stimulated financial speculation more than productive investment, and triggered a brief boom-bust cycle that ended up, through a series of bail-outs, by actually expanding the state sector.

When elected rule was restored in 1983, the civilian government inherited a heavily indebted country, with a much weakened industrial sector, inflation running close to an annual 1,000 per cent, and little to show for the efforts to achieve export-led growth save the emergence of soya as a new major export crop.

Recent economic developments. The Alfonsín administration first essayed a "gradualist" strategy to contain inflation at minimal social cost, but by mid-1985 decided to change tack and adopt a more drastic approach. The "Austral Plan" introduced a new currency, the austral, pegged at 0.80 to the US dollar, froze prices and wages, imposed stringent monetary policies and spending cuts intended to bring down the fiscal deficit from 12 per cent to 4.1 per cent of GDP. The plan, which though harsh enjoyed much popular support, succeeded in bringing down inflation and in creating the conditions for Argentina to reschedule US $13.4 bn of its external debt. GDP growth in 1986 reached 5.3 per cent—though by then the country was experiencing the difficulty of coping simultaneously with a large debt-servicing burden (both domestic and external) and the reduction of the public deficit in the virtual absence of external financing.

Starved of investment and with the scarcity of foreign exchange aggravated by a bad agricultural year, economic growth slowed down considerably in 1987, and inflation began to accelerate again. By 1988 the economy was in clear decline, which a new economic programme based on a "social pact" with business and labour, the "Spring Plan", only briefly arrested. A further adjustment effort just before the May 1989 elections also failed, and by June that year inflation was running at a monthly rate of 114.5 per cent.

The new government headed by Carlos Menem adopted shock policies to bring the country back from the brink of hyper-inflation. The currency was devalued by 54 per cent, stringent monetary policies starved the market of liquidity, public-sector rates and tariffs were increased threefold. A sweeping reduction of the state's role in the economy was announced, to be achieved both through drastic spending cuts and wholesale privatization of state assets (going much further than the divestment policies of the Alfonsín administration, which the Peronists had blocked in congress).

Within a few months inflation had been brought down to a monthly 10 per cent, but by the end of the year a rush on the exchange markets forced a further 35 per cent devaluation of the austral (to 1,000 per US dollar). The Menem government faced much resistance, even from within the administration, to its retrenchment and divestment policies, and it took the better part of a year before the first major privatizations (the state telephone company, Entel, and the flag air carrier, *Aerolíneas Argentinas*) were completed. The planned reduction of the state's payroll took even longer to begin in earnest.

Efforts to keep inflation in check demanded five successive adjustments of the Menem government's economic programme. The emphasis on curbing inflation and the maintenance of an overvalued austral conspired against the reactivation of the economy (GDP grew by only 1.5 per cent in 1989 and fell by 0.5 per cent in 1990). In early 1991, with the monthly inflation rate back into two digits, another marked devaluation of the austral took place, to just under 10,000 per US dollar.

EC

ARMED FORCES. The activities of the Latin American military can be divided into three categories: (i) combat against the armed forces of other countries and preparation for such combat, i.e. "national defence"; (ii) use in domestic policy implementation: in "maintaining internal security," in regional and local administration, managing state corporations and staffing non-military government functions, and work in construction and "development" projects; and (iii) involvement in national politics, up to and including the seizure of political power.

This last activity, which of course contravenes formal constitutional norms, has traditionally been regarded as especially characteristic of the Latin American military establishments, although it has become equally characteristic of African and Asian countries at a similar intermediate stage of development, on the long and winding road between stable monarchic or colonial government and stable constitutional democracy. Some military forces, particularly that of Brazil, have tried to maintain that the particular wording of the tasks assigned to the armed forces in the country's constitution implies a "guardianship" role that can legitimately extend to the actual assumption of the power to govern.

International conflict. It is often said that the Latin American armies have no real national defence function, but this is no more true of the region's armed forces than it is of those of other regions. Actual military clashes do occur — between Argentina and Great Britain in 1982, between Ecuador and Peru in 1981, between El Salvador and Honduras in 1969 — to give some recent examples. A series of border disputes remain outstanding, which could plausibly be expected to lead to actual fighting; several of these are longstanding conflicts inherited from the Spanish colonial era. A list of only the principal ones would include those between Guatemala and Belize; Colombia and Venezuela; Venezuela and Guyana; Peru and Ecuador; Peru and Chile; Chile and Argentina; and Chile and Bolivia. Because of the tendency of neighbouring countries to bear old grudges against each other, there is something of a checkerboard pattern of understandings and co-operative arrangements among the region's military establishments. To grasp the scope of these, let us begin with the rivalry between Argentina and Brazil for influence in the small countries with which both have borders: Uruguay, Paraguay, and Bolivia. Most recently, reflecting their relative economic strength, Brazil has had the upper hand in this relationship, and has also pulled far ahead of Argentina in the competitive arms build-up in which the two countries have long engaged. Moving west and north around South America: Chile, which has disputes with Argentina over their long border along the crest of the Andes, and over competing Antarctic claims, is therefore an ally of Brazil; Peru has also scores to settle with Chile, thus sympathizes with Argentina; Ecuador's and Colombia's grievances against Peru, to which they lost Amazonian territory, ally them with Brazil and Chile; Venezuela, which has territorial disputes with both Brazil and Colombia, is in the Argentine camp. These sympathies became manifest in the **Falklands War**, when Brazil and Chile gave lip service to the idea of Latin American solidarity with Argentina, while covertly giving assistance to Great Britain. This substructure of parallelisms of interest is reflected in military schooling patterns, so that, for example, Ecuador's pilots are often trained in Brazil and her naval officers in Chile.

These differing training and arms supply arrangements used to extend to the use of foreign training missions, with France and Germany competing, early in the century, for invitations from Latin American armies, while British naval training was sought after. Since the end of World War II, however, all this has become ancient history, as the United States has come to dominate in all such relationships: training missions, invitations to short courses and familiarization visits in the USA, and arms supply, for all service branches and almost all countries of the region. There are several whole or partial exceptions: Mexico has traditionally held aloof from "security" entanglements with the United States, which is after all her neighbour and ancient military nemesis; Cuba under **Fidel Castro** regards the United States as posing the principal military threat, and has established security arrangements with the Soviet Union, revolutionary Nicaragua looked to Cuba and the Soviet Union for military assistance after the United States induced its Western European allies not to honour Nicaragua's requests for military material; the Soviet Union also became the principal arms supplier of Peru during the 1970s, when a reformist military regime there fell afoul of the United States.

The military tulelage of the USA in the region extends to security doctrine, the intellectual rationale for a country's armament, force structure, and contingency planning. With differing degrees of reluctance, since, among other reasons, the several militaries were primarily concerned with their traditional regional rivalries, the USA succeeded in imposing its vision of an ideological conflict with the Soviet Union and Communism in the region. Institutional dependence through grant assistance and arms sales on concessionary terms (supplemented by covert stipends to key individuals) has underpinned US hegemony in the region. This means that Latin American governments do not normally take actions that contravene US political and economic interests or objectives. In the last analysis this hegemony is made good through US influence on the armed forces in their political interventions—somewhat as Soviet influence in Eastern Europe used to function through the medium of the ruling Communist parties.

Domestic policy implementation. Some countries have traditionally used active-duty military officers as administrators and managers in areas related to their technical specialties—in communications, for example, or roadbuilding. The Argentine military has for a long time run the state arms-manufacturing corporations directly. In Mexico military zone commanders form a secondary regional administrative system in the federal–state relationship, and zone commanders are frequently appointed as interim state governors when incumbents resign or are removed.

The major domestic policy task handled by the military, though, is maintenance of "internal security". Generally, militaries are initially reluctant to take on internal security tasks, regarding them with distaste; they do not fit the favoured image of the heroic soldier, gallantly defending national honour against foreign enemies; they entail grubby police work, and tend to make the armed forces unpopular. These duties are normally assigned primarily to police forces, some of which, like the Chilean *Carabineros*, are organized nationally as a fourth branch of the armed forces. Where insurgent forces are organized and active on a quasi-military basis, however, the army itself, however reluctantly at first, eventually becomes involved. Even though insurgent movements are normally—though not always—put down, cases of this kind are usually disasters for the country, since the army tends to act as it would against a foreign enemy, typically killing and maiming many more civilians than combatants, widening the scope of the conflict, and failing to draw crucial distinctions between actual armed insurrection, militant industrial action, and legitimate political dissent. The 1960s and 1970s, especially, witnessed, in country after country, "dirty wars", in which dissidents, suspected dissidents, and hapless bystanders were tortured and killed. Such tactics may be totally counterproductive, alienate the population, and even help the insurgent movement come to power, as in Cuba and Nicaragua. In El Salvador, by the end of the 1980s, a stalemate between government and insurgents had been reached; while in Peru the ferocious Maoist Shining Path movement, **Sendero Luminoso**, seemed still to be gaining on the hapless government forces.

The military in politics. Even in the most democratic and constitutional of countries the military, like other bureaucratic entities, gets involved in politics in the sense of attempting to get its budget increased by arguing the growing need for the services it renders. A second major objective is defence of its institutional autonomy, so that elected officials do not interfere in promotions and duty assignments, at least below the very top level. The attempt to do so by President Arnulfo Arias of Panama provided the occasion for his removal by the 1968 military *coup* led by Omar Torrijos after Arias had served only 11 days in office.

A further degree of involvement in politics occurs as the military leadership makes clear that certain lines of policy are unacceptable to them. Such a military veto is imposed not only in matters closely related to military concerns, i.e. in foreign and international security affairs. Under the "national security doctrine", successfully propagated by the United States within Latin American militaries from the 1960s on, the chief threat to security was taken to be from

Communist subversion, which was thought to flourish especially in conditions of social and economic underdevelopment; so that all kinds of domestic economic policies could relate directly to military security functions and thus become the occasion for armed forces pressure and even seizures of power.

The military seizure of power. This characteristically Latin American event, the ultimate stage in military involvement in politics, occurs more frequently at certain times, under specific circumstances, and in particular countries. Mexico, for example, has not witnessed the successful overthrow of an incumbent government since 1920. This appears to be because in Mexico there has been no vacuum of power, since government has been in the hands of a strong and well-organized dominant political party. Moreover, there has (at least until very recently) been no vacuum of legitimacy, as the ruling party claims descent from the leadership of the **Mexican Revolution** of 1910, and thus takes credit for major popular structural changes, such as the land reform, nationalization of the oil industry, and universal basic education; and it used to win elections by incontestable majorities. The tremendous legitimacy conferred on Fidel Castro's rule by his leadership of the 1959 Revolution in Cuba, similarly, made a military overthrow of his government highly unlikely. Countries where military seizures of power are more likely, by contrast, are those where ruling elites lack both popular support and a single unquestioned leadership.

There are also "contagion effects" and "habit-forming effects" that contribute to the likelihood of military seizures of power. Successful *coups* in other countries encourage military conspirators, as does a national tradition of successful *coups*. *Coups* are also more likely to occur close to election times and when economic conditions are deteriorating. There are various, and contrasting, putative reasons why this should be so, however, and the identification of probable occasions for *coups* is not the same as explaining the motivations and purposes of those who organize them.

These may prove on examination to be more complex than appears at first sight in journalistic accounts of the events. Communiqués by leaders of successful insurrections are primarily public relations exercises and feature noble and public-spirited motivations. But even "inside" journalism often misses the point in recounting the actual motives for the *coup*, since the conspiracy involved putting together a coalition of key actors, who may have had quite different motivations, so it may be quite misleading to talk of a single set of motives that were responsible.

The necessary participants in a successful military *coup* vary from country to country, but generally include the officers with direct command of tank forces in, or close to, the national capital; if possible, the officers nominally in top command and staff positions; and any officers with particular personal prestige, such as surviving war heroes. Commanders of the national military academy, similarly, are usually prestigious individuals whose collaboration in the *coup* is helpful. The ranking officers may themselves start off as neutral towards the conspiracy, or even opposed, but may end up going along with it if it is going to occur anyway and their opposition would only succeed in dividing the armed forces, precipitating fighting, and then possibly ending their careers if the conspiracy prove successful. Thus participants in a *coup* may actually differ greatly in political orientations and motivations. There differences of opinion among the conspirators may prove significant after the *coup*, in the making of decisions such as whether to stay in power for some length of time, or simply to remain content with having removed an objectionable government, organize new elections, and return to the barracks as soon as possible. Enlisted men ("other ranks") are not normally a factor in a military seizure of power, and there seems no difference in propensity to *coups* between armies that use conscription (about half of the total in the region) and those consisting exclusively of volunteers. Other ranks are drilled and bullied fairly effectively into taking orders, even where—as in El Salvador—the mode of their conscription was an unceremonious press-ganging of hapless youths emerging from a movie theatre or football stadium.

The only clear case of a successful non-commissioned officer's *coup* seems to be that led by Master-Sergeant Fulgencio Batista in Cuba in 1933, which replaced the entire officer corps, except for the handful of very junior officers who participated in the conspiracy, with ex-sergeants newly commissioned colonels.

The decision to intervene forcibly may respond to wishes of outside forces, particularly the government of the United States, which sometimes acts directly through its diplomatic representation, sometimes through its own military officials, and sometimes through the covert contacts of the Central Intelligence Agency. In cases such as those of the military seizures of power in Chile in 1970 and Brazil in 1964, the personnel of the Department of State, which is supposed to conduct the country's foreign policy, but was thought less likely to support a military solution than the President wished, were not kept fully informed of these clandestine contacts nor made privy to the full intent of the US President's policies. At other times, military *coups* are solicited by representatives of conservative political parties or élite economic interests, and are designed to remove from power, or keep out of power, political leaders thought likely to engage in programmes of redistribution of wealth or income. This occurred so regularly in Peru during the middle third of the twentieth century, for example, that the Peruvian armed forces became known as "the guard dogs of the oligarchy", a role which they finally rejected in their anti-oligarchic *coup* of 1968.

Although the political interventions of the armed forces occur frequently on behalf of the economic élites or the hegemonic power, this is not invariably the case. The military act in their own interests, too, and these occasionally, albeit infrequently, indicate anti-oligarchic or even anti-US behaviour. The 1968 Peruvian *coup*, for example, expropriated the International Petroleum Corporation against US wishes, began a break-up of oligarchic landholdings, and reoriented arms purchases to the Soviet Union. Normally, however, the military's own interests are conceptualized as compatible with those of the economic elite and the friendly neighbourhood superpower; so that even when acting "objectively" as a tool of ruling class or imperialism, as Marxists would put it, the military still act subjectively in their own interests: in securing military assistance on concessionary terms; in maintaining "law and order" and fighting subversion; in ensuring that public money is spent on "national defence" and not social programmes; and in eliminating organized labour as a power *bloc* able to contest the military's monopoly of the use of force. Conservative politicians soliciting a military *coup*, for example, have to explain not how it serves the oligarchy's interest, but how it is in the military's own interest to take action; but this normally presents no insuperable problems.

Justification of military intervention. In intra-military discussions about whether to stage a *coup*, military interests can be cited against, as well as for, intervention, however. For example: action should not be taken if it is likely to divide the armed forces, or to weaken their popular support among the public generally. President Osvaldo Hurtado of Ecuador used to make a point of briefing military leaders on the economic situation, ostensibly to show how important he thought them, but actually to impress them with the fact that a government taking over from him would have to pursue unpopular economic policies.

Since the military are concerned to maintain their favourable image among the general public, a very popular government is much less likely to be overthrown than one elected only narrowly, or one headed by a vice-president who succeeded to power without an election, or one which has compromised its legitimacy by violating constitutional prescriptions. Thus questions of a government's legitimacy in this sense may be analyzed in intra-military discussions, when a *coup* has been proposed, just as much as in a law or political science class. In fact, when the military overthrow a government that has itself violated legal norms, they can claim to be restoring constitutional legitimacy and not violating it. The plausibility of such claims must then depend on: (i) the gravity of the violation of legality alleged; (ii) whether a constitutional remedy was available; and (iii) whether the *coup* is followed by the restoration of constitutional normality within the briefest possible period. Claims that a *coup* was constitutionally or morally justified would thus be at their weakest if the incumbent president's offences were trivial; if they could have been corrected or reproved by normal parliamentary or judicial action; and if the resulting military government itself rules arbitrarily and makes no attempt to schedule new elections.

Military government. Before the 1960s, it was common for the military to stage a *coup*, remove a government which had somehow offended, then immediately transfer power to an interim civilian president who would schedule new elections. After the "national security doctrine" took hold, however, and armed forces began to believe that the defence of national security entailed domestic anti-subversive campaigns and policies of economic development and pre-emptive social action, military regimes set themselves up to rule indefinitely. Draconian repression of labour unions enabled the military regimes in Brazil and, for a time, Chile to show some one-sided improvements in economic statistics, but the overall record of military governments in economic policy is no better than that of civilian governments. Praise for the performance of particular military governments is in any case always naive if it only assesses benefits and takes no account of the dreadful costs of such governments in human suffering. No-one doubts that the conferring of power without limit can make possible considerable achievements, after all. However, it must be expected that such power will be abused, and that is why civilized countries have developed rules of constitutional practice precisely to avoid anyone's having power of that kind.

The transitions away from military rule that took place across South America in the late 1980s responded not only to civilian appreciation of the shortcomings of military rule, but to belief by elements within the military that such regimes are themselves inimical to military interests, not only because they alienate the public from the armed forces by their policies, but also because soldiers who are busy deciding issues of public policy are neglecting their primary duty of training themselves for combat. The miserable performance of the Argentine army in the Falklands War in 1982 drove this lesson home. A military regime thus typically ends as it began, with a *coup* staged by officers who believe that the incumbent government—even though itself run by members of the armed forces—is damaging military interests, so that military interests can best be served by returning to the barracks and leaving government to the civilians.

Divergent political orientations. In their political activities, military officers differ among themselves. Some of these differences are individual, reflecting different personal histories, ideological commitments, and social backgrounds. Because the military service is such a total environment, however, typically an officer's individual social background is overshadowed by his military training and institutional loyalties. These loyalties are not only to the military as a whole but to the individual branch of service and military academy class. Loyalty to one's academy class, or *tanda*, is particularly notable in El Salvador, where classmates promote each other's military careers and cover up each other's wrongdoing—which has been particularly blatant since the long-drawn-out civil war under way since 1970 has attracted huge quantities of US assistance and created opportunities for all kinds of rackets.

Military racketeering is especially marked in the less developed countries. El Salvador's initial advance into Honduran territory in the "Football War" of 1969 was greatly facilitated because some of the Honduran divisions guarding the border were made up of "ghost" soldiers, unofficially discharged by their commanding officers, who continued to collect pay on their behalf. In Paraguay the concessions to handle different contraband items—cigarettes, Scotch whiskey, drugs—are divided up among the various service branches.

Although the subject has not been systematically studied, anecdotal tradition assigns different political orientations to different service branches. Perhaps because of the autocratic authority traditionally enjoyed by naval officers at sea, the vary is generally regarded as more élitist and more conservative in politics, with some nostalgia for the days of British power. Air force officers, belonging to a relatively new service with something of a glamorous and dashing image, and living with a high level of risk, are thought of as personalists and opportunists in politics and especially close to the United States. Of course, navy and air force officers are not as significant in politics, as a general rule, as are officers in the army. The army controls territory, it may get assigned to crowd control and policing, and it is the largest of the services. Thus it normally takes the principal role when the armed forces become involved in politics. For geographical and historical reasons, air force officers have played a larger part in the politics of Honduras and Bolivia than they have elsewhere. Naval commanders have occasionally played a significant role in *coups* by threatening to bombard shore installations from ships; this occurred in Argentina when Perón was overthrown, and when Marcos Pérez Jiménez was overthrown in Venezuela. After a *coup* has occurred and a ruling *junta* of the service commanders installed, a naval officer sometimes becomes chairman if the position is assigned by personal seniority in rank, as in Ecuador in 1963.

Most of the time, however, the army is the dominant service politically. Within the army, the various branches have their political reputations. The infantry, closer to the people, is thought to be more nationalist and populist; the cavalry, of course, is more aristocratic and conservative. Even though "cavalry" today is overwhelmingly "armoured cavalry", that is, tanks, officers have retained the *esprit* and traditions of the horse cavalry. Engineers are technocrats and close to the United States. Military intelligence is particularly close to US covert political operations, permeated by Cold War ideology, and associated with sinister repressive activities. The same reputation attaches to special counterinsurgency forces, where these exist as a separate branch.

Conspiratorial coalitions. A military seizure of power comes after the formation of a coalition among conspirators of differing motivations and political orientations. Thus the *coup* is often followed by factional splits and conspiracies within the new ruling group over policies to be followed and posts to be filled. One common pattern is for the original moving force in the conspiracy to have been a relatively junior officer, a lieutenant-colonel, say, who secured the collaboration of a general of some distinction and personal prestige to serve as the nominal leader of the movement, but who then continues to conspire after the seizure of power until he himself emerges as the leading figure. This was the pattern followed by **Juan Perón** in Argentina and Omar Torrijos in Panama (and of course, by Gamal Abdel Nasser in Egypt). Another characteristic split often takes place over economic policy, between those preferring a more nationalist policy of promoting industry behind a tariff wall on the basis of a domestic market expanded by higher wage levels—which tends to inefficient industry producing sub-standard goods, and inflation; and those preferring to open the economy to international competition—which tends to depress living standards, produce excessive fluctuations in levels of economic activity, and lead to placing control and even ownership of the national economy in foreign hands. There is a constituency within the armed forces for each position. The nationalist policy seems more in keeping with the fundamental military commitment to patriotism and the security of control in national hands of strategic economic sectors. The pro-internationalist officers (called pejoratively *entreguistas*, or "sell-outs") support free-market policies favored by the military's traditional allies, the United States and the landed oligarchy, which are arguably more likely to lead to continued economic growth and thus to greater national power.

Military conspiracies are rarely purely military. *Coups* are frequently solicited by civilian politicians, who remain a part of the conspiratorial group. Alternatively, civilian politicians may be recruited by military conspirators, to help prepare a favourable public opinion and plan post-*coup* policies. Sometimes different military factions maintain more or less permanent alliances with specific sectors of political opinion. Twentieth-century Argentine history illustrates this point: a military faction allied with the middle-class Radical party rebelled against the rule of the agrarian oligarchy early in the century; military elements allied with the oligarchy returned the country to Conservative rule in 1930; yet another faction of the military ruled in collaboration with labour unions and the industrial sector of the middle class between 1945 and 1955.

Life without an Armed Forces. Because the military forces of the region have so often provided support for dictatorship, with all of its attendant evils, it is not surprising that many have come to believe that the advantages of having a military service are far outweighed by the disadvantages. During the early years of the twentieth century the United States sponsored the replacement of the armies by constabulary forces designed only for police duties in a series of countries that had been occupied by the US Marines—Haiti, the Dominican Republic, Panama, and Nicaragua. While the Panamanian and Haitian "constabularies" stayed quite small after the Marines departed, the fact that they had been reorganized and trained on a professional, "non-political", basis did not inhibit any of the four from playing politics, and the Nicaraguan and Dominican commanders, Anastasio Somoza García and Rafael Leónidas Trujillo Molina, respectively, established long-lived dictatorships that ended, in both cases, only with the dictator's assassination. Since both were protective of US economic and strategic interests, however, the US accepted this apparent deviation from its programme. (In the words often attributed, probably wrongly, to Franklin D. Roosevelt, speaking of Somoza, "He may be an SOB,' but he's *our* SOB."[1])

In 1948, the new revolutionary government of Costa Rica abolished its military forces entirely, and the minimal police force retained has stayed out of politics; nor have the country's neighbours evinced any recent interest in taking advantage of Costa Rica's lack of an army to conquer and annex the country.

[1]"son of a bitch"—a highly derogatory epithet.

MCN

ARMS CONTROL. In the 1970s and early 1980s there was much speculation that the region of South America and the Caribbean was on the verge of a nuclear weapons arms race. Many of these concerns have now dissipated as a result of the introduction of several important nuclear arms control initiatives in the region. And although concerns about nuclear submarine and ballistic missile programmes shed a more ambiguous light on future developments, the portents for further arms control and confidence building measures in the region remain optimistic.

Nuclear arms control. There are two nuclear arms control agreements that affect South America and the Caribbean, the Treaty on the Non-Proliferation of Nuclear Weapons (NPT) and the Tlatelolco Treaty. The former Treaty is a broad-based international agreement designed to limit the spread of nuclear weapons around the world, the latter is a specifically regional treaty which seeks to keep South America as a Nuclear Weapons Free Zone. Both Treaties were negotiated in the 1960s and have thus far achieved mixed success as nuclear arms control initiatives in the region.

In South America and the Caribbean region, only four countries have major nuclear programmes underway. These are: Cuba, Brazil, Argentina and Mexico. Of the four countries, Mexico is currently the only one that has become a party to the NPT. Other countries in the region, such as Chile, have established nuclear research programmes but have yet to embark on a fully fledged nuclear programme. The focus for nuclear weapons potential has thus centred on Cuba, Argentina and Brazil.

Cuba has a smaller and less advanced nuclear programme than either Brazil or Argentina. Cuba has two nuclear power plants still under construction at Cienfuegos. These plants were supplied by the Soviet Union and both will be under safeguards administered by the International Atomic Energy Agency (IAEA), the organization responsible for monitoring the nuclear industry worldwide. So although Cuba has refrained from participating in either the NPT or the Treaty of Tlatelolco, the plants will still be regularly inspected by the IAEA to ensure that nuclear material is not diverted from civil to military use.

Brazil and Argentina, on the other hand, have the most sophisticated nuclear programmes in the South America and Caribbean region. Both countries embarked on major nuclear programmes in the 1970s, stating at the time that they needed nuclear power to meet predicted shortfalls in future energy needs.

Today, Brazil has one nuclear power plant (Angra I, supplied by the United States), and three small research reactors currently in operation. Two further plants are scheduled for start-up in 1995 and 2000, respectively (Angra II and Angra III, both supplied by Germany as a result of a 1975 transfer agreement). Also under construction is a jet nozzle uranium enrichment facility, which is not expected to reach industrial-scale production until the year 2000, and a more significant gas centrifuge uranium enrichment research projects at the Aramar Research Center, Ipero and at the Institute for Energy and Nuclear Research, São Paulo.

Argentina currently has two nuclear power plants in operation (Atucha I and Embalse), with a third (Atucha II) expected to come on line in the mid-1990s. Argentina also has five nuclear research reactors presently in operation. But where the major advances in Argentina's nuclear power programme are underway are in the areas of enrichment and reprocessing technology. At Pilcaniyeu, Argentina has constructed a gaseous diffusion enrichment facility which is already operational and at Ezeiza a small-scale reprocessing project is also underway.

Throughout this period of nuclear expansion concerns have been expressed that because neither country is party to the NPT nor the Tlatelolco Treaty, then neither have they made any formal commitment not to pursue nuclear weapons paths. Speculation has thus been rife about the intentions of Brazil and Argentina where military nuclear programmes are concerned.

Both Brazil and Argentina reject the NPT because they regard it as an inherently discriminatory treaty. The Treaty distinguishes between two categories of signatory state: those states that have tested a nuclear weapon before Jan. 1, 1967 are classified as Nuclear Weapon States (NWS); and those states which have not conducted such a test are classified by the Treaty as Non-Nuclear Weapon States (NNWS). Brazil and Argentina regard this distinction between NWS and NNWS to be discriminatory because it legitimizes the existing international distribution of power between nuclear "haves" and nuclear "have nots". The two countries have therefore declined to sign the Treaty and are considered unlikely to do so.

As a signatory to the NPT all parties are obliged to open all nuclear facilities operating within their territory to safeguards inspections by the IAEA. This provision, referred to as Full Scope Safeguards (FSS), enables the IAEA to maintain a comprehensive picture of all nuclear material activities taking place within the signatory state. On the basis of such safeguards, the IAEA can then ensure other signatories that no diversions of nuclear materials are taking place and that the signatory is fulfilling its NPT obligations not to pursue nuclear weapons.

Brazil and Argentina have similarly declined to become full parties to the Tlatelolco Treaty. Brazil has both signed and ratified the Treaty but it is not yet in force on Brazilian territory. This is because Brazil has exercised the right under Article 28 of the Tlatelolco Treaty to waive the entry into force provision. Argentina has also signed the Treaty but only indicated its intent to ratify.

Over the last few years, however, both Brazil and Argentina have taken a more favourable stance towards the regional arms control initiative than the NPT. It is therefore considered, that of the two Treaties, they would be more likely to become full parties to the Tlatelolco Treaty.

Because Brazil and Argentina are currently not party to either the NPT or the Tlatelolco Treaty (which would also require FSS to operate) there is no comprehensive safeguards coverage over their nuclear industries. Parts of the nuclear infrastructure in the two countries is under IAEA safeguards (as a result of obligations undertaken in past nuclear transfer agreements), but a few key installations remain outside any international inspection. It is the existence of these installations which has fuelled the international speculation about the potential for these facilities being used for nuclear weapons programmes.

In the mid-1980s a major nuclear *rapproche-*

ment began between Brazil and Argentina which has quelled many concerns about the region. In November 1985, the then respective Presidents of Brazil and Argentina, Sarney and Alfonsín, announced that the two countries were to further their co-operation in the peaceful uses of nuclear energy and to begin a programme of mutual inspection of each other's nuclear facilities. The announcement also stated that the results of the mutual inspections would not be made available to the IAEA.

Since that time the two countries have developed much closer nuclear links, including reciprocal visits by the respective heads of state to their most sensitive nuclear installations. Even when President **Carlos Menem** replaced President **Raúl Alfonsín** in Argentina, and President **Fernando Collor de Mello** replaced President **José Sarney** in Brazil these confidence-building measures in the nuclear sphere continued.

On entering office, President Collor stated that he would implement a strategy of nuclear "transparency" for Brazil's nuclear programme. This policy has included introducing greater civilian oversight of its nuclear programme and curtailment of a military nuclear programme, known as the Solimões Project, which President Collor stated had been underway since the late 1970s. In September 1990, President Collor subsequently closed the previously secret nuclear test site at Cachimba in the Amazon forest. And at the United Nations, President Collor also called for a ban on nuclear testing in South America and the Caribbean.

At the same time as the statements about Brazil's "parallel" military nuclear programme were made public, the President also announced that Brazil would begin implementing a stricter policy for the export of sensitive technologies to other countries. This statement, too, has considerable arms control significance for the future as Brazil is already a major supplier of advanced conventional technology and will soon be in a position to export several key items of nuclear technology as well.

In November 1990, this evolving policy of nuclear restraint in the region was given a further boost. It was announced that Brazil and Argentina would begin negotiations with the IAEA to establish an acceptable safeguards agreement between the two countries that will allow the IAEA to receive information about nuclear material activities within their territories. The precise details of this arrangement have yet to be formalized, but it is an indication of future intent which may eventually lead to the two countries becoming full parties to the Tlatelolco Treaty.

Nuclear submarines and arms control. Whereas several developments in the nuclear area have given cause for optimism in South America and the Caribbean, the continued expansion of nuclear submarine research programmes in the region has been greeted with less enthusiasm. This is because nuclear submarine propulsion programmes are exempted from IAEA safeguards inspections. Countries pursuing such programmes could thus gain access to nuclear materials outside of international inspection which could then be used in nuclear weapons programmes.

Brazil is reported to be the country with the most interest in the region for acquiring nuclear submarine capabilities for the future. Brazil already has a sizeable fleet of seven diesel-electric conventional submarines with newer models currently under development with assistance from Germany. But it is in the area of nuclear propulsion technology that Brazil has developed considerable indigenous expertise. Much of the future success of this programme will depend on Brazil being able to achieve the high levels of uranium enrichment (20%+) necessary for nuclear submarine propulsion. Recent statements by high ranking Brazilian Naval officials indicate that their S-NAC 2 nuclear submarine research and development programme is making considerable progress and that the crucial levels of uranium enrichment are being achieved.

President Collor has indicated that the nuclear submarine research programme will continue under his administration. Even then Brazil is not expected to have a fully operational nuclear submarine constructed before well into the next century. There will inevitably be concerns expressed prior to that date, however, that nuclear material produced as a result of this submarine programme may be diverted for nuclear weapons purposes.

Argentina is also reported to have shown some research interest in nuclear propulsion technology, though the major impetus is directed towards a highly advanced diesel submarine programme, which Argentina is also pursuing with German assistance.

Space and ballistic missile technology and arms control. In recent years there has been unease expressed about the growing number of ballistic missile programmes underway around the world. This has arisen because of the concern that there may be a direct association between the acquisition of ballistic missiles and nuclear or chemical weapons capabilities. Similarly, the linkages between space programmes pursued for peaceful purposes and ballistic missile programmes designed for military use has also been noted.

These developments have fuelled further arms control initiatives by some of the major technology exporters to slow the pace of ballistic acquisition around the world. In April 1987, Canada, the United States, the United Kingdom, France, Germany, Italy and Japan established the Missile Technology Control Regime. The impact of this initiative on the region is difficult to evaluate, but the indications are that it has slowed certain programmes and led to a re-evaluation of some missile-related export policies.

Countries may pursue space and ballistic missile programmes for reasons of security, for prestige or for the economic benefits accruing from their export potential. A combination of one or all of these motivations may account for the considerable investment that both Argentina and Brazil have placed in acquiring advanced ballistic delivery vehicle and space launch technologies.

Argentina had developed the Condor series of ballistic missiles with ranges up to 600+ miles, while Brazil has been developing two series of missiles, the MB/EE and SS- series, with ranges estimated up to 750 miles.

Of the two countries, Brazil appears to have placed more emphasis on space research than Argentina. Brazil has already developed the Sonda series of sounding rockets with plans underway for a Satellite Launch Vehicle (SLV) to be ready by the mid-1990s.

Some ballistic missile systems developed by the two countries may have already been deployed and reportedly sold for export. Newer more sophisticated systems are also soon to come on line. Whether these will also be transferred to other countries depends greatly on the future export policies pursued by Brazil and Argentina. This will therefore be a major arms control issue for the future.

The arms control situation in South America and the Caribbean region is thus currently at a watershed. The improving nuclear co-operation between Brazil and Argentina induces speculation that the two countries may be close to becoming full parties to the Tlatelolco Treaty. If this does occur it might then be possible to pursue further arms control initiatives in the region, particularly confidence- and security- building measures and even within the conventional sphere.

DH

AUTHENTIC LIBERAL RADICAL PARTY Partido Liberal Radical Auténtico — PRLA (Paraguay). The Liberal Party, organized in Paraguay in 1887 by a group led by Cecilio Báez, seized power in 1904 and maintained its dominance until 1936, after which it was gradually displaced by the **Colorado Party**. With the seizure of power by **General Gustavo Stroessner** in 1954 divisions emerged, and a small faction, the so-called "Renovation" wing of the party accepted the role of captive opposition and were granted 20 seats in Congress in 1963. After the decision to boycott the elections of 1978, the bulk of the party, denied recognition, reformed in exile as the Authentic Liberal Radical Party. In April 1987 its leader Domingo Laíno returned from exile and was imprisoned more than twenty times before, following the fall of Stroessner in February 1989, the PLRA was formally recognized and Laíno nominated as presidential candidate.

PARC

AYLWIN, PATRICIO. Patricio Aylwin Azócar (born 1918), a veteran politician from the centre of the Christian Democrat party, was a senator and president of his party before the military *coup* in Chile in 1973. Aylwin has publicly admitted that it was a mistake on his part to support the *coup*, a mistake shared by almost all Christian Democrats, who thought that the military would simply intervene to restore (what they saw as) constitutional government and return power to the civilian politicians. As president (1990 —), Aylwin has won approval for his non-sectarian attitude to the other parties making up the *Concertación*.

GG

B

BAHAMAS, THE. *Population*: 244,000 (1989). *Area*: 13,939, sq km. *GDP*: B$2,100 million (1989). *Trade volume*: B$1,320 million (1989). *Top five trade partners*: USA, Nigeria, Mexico, UK, Angola. *Defence spending*: B $77,700,000, including allocation to 2,000-strong police force (1988). *Education spending (as percentage of GNP)*: 22. *Urban centres with population of over 20,000*: Nassau: 135,437; Freeport: 24,423. Birthrate: 18 per 1,000.

Geographical background. The Bahamas are a group of 700 islands and more than 2,000 cays and rocks. Only 29 of the islands are inhabited. The biggest islands are Grand Bahama, Abaco, Andres, Inagua, Eleuthera and Exuma. Although tenth in size, New Providence is the most important island with some 60 per cent of the population of the Bahamas and the capital Nassau. The other islands are known as the "Family Islands", the most important being Grand Bahama, on which Freeport, the second largest town, is situated.

Socio–political background. A Commonwealth country, The Bahamas' Parliament dates back to 1729. There is now a 49-seat House of Assembly, enlarged by six for the last elections on June 19, 1987, and a 16-member, all nominated, Senate. The country has been dominated by the Progressive Liberal Party (PLP) which won the first elections under adult suffrage in 1967 and was returned for a fifth consecutive term with 31 seats at the last elections. As leader of the PLP, Sir Lynden Pindling has been the dominant personality in Bahamian politics.

In the current Parliament the Free National Movement (FNM) holds 16 seats and there are two independent members. There are two other registered political parties, the People's Democratic Force (PDF) and Vanguard Party.

Outline of political history. The Bahamas was a British colony which gained self-government status in January 1964. In the 1967 elections, the black-backed PLP led by Pindling and the white-backed United Bahamian Party (UBP) each won 18 of the 38 seats. Pindling was able to form the government with the support of another member, launching one of the most resilient political careers in the Caribbean.

The Bahamas gained more autonomy in May 1969, becoming independent in 1973. The PLP maintained its majority in the elections of 1972, which were dominated by plans for independence, and those of July 1977 and June 1982. Despite charges of widespread corruption during the 1980s, Pindling's PLP won 53 per cent of the votes at the last election.

With its wealth, The Bahamas has escaped the economic woes of other countries, and the political upheavals. The so-called drug economy is what has plagued the government and has led to widespread unemployment, at some 18 per cent in 1988. The chain of islands lead The Bahamas to being a major drugs trans-shipment centre and it is said that, in one way or another, everyone in The Bahamas is affected by drugs.

Current developments — political. Charges of government complicity in the drug trade and the use of Bahamian bank secrecy laws to aid money laundering led to the setting up of a Royal Commission in November 1983 to fully investigate the charges. Pindling, then not knighted, was revealed to enjoy a lifestyle far outside the bounds of his income and to have received millions in loans and gifts from various people, although the Commission said they were not drug related.

Two ministers implicated by the Commission findings resigned in October 1984. Assistant Commissioner of Police Howard Smith was charged with bribery and dismissed, and some 51 people indicted by October 1985. Deputy Prime Minister Arthur Hanna resigned after failing to secure Pindling's resignation, two other ministers were dismissed and the FNM staged demonstrations. Pindling, however, remains unshakeable.

Drugs again dominated The Bahamas in 1987 and 1988, with widespread violence on the islands and more charges of corruption, this time made in Florida, USA, by Colombian drug dealer Carlos Ledher who lived on various islands in The Bahamas before his arrest. Pindling and the new Deputy Prime Minister were accused of accepting bribes and the FNM charged that Sir Lynden and Lady Pindling's finances needed further investigation. The UK Privy Council, the final court of appeal for Commonwealth countries, rejected the charges against Pindling and his wife in May 1988 but ruled that offenders could be extradited if found guilty of importing drugs into the USA.

The Bahamas and the USA clashed over the latter's attempt to open up The Bahamas' tight laws governing banking in an effort, the USA claimed, to track drug traders. Caribbean countries saw this as an attempt at foreign management by the USA of their internal affairs and The Bahamas led a CARICOM protest in July 1988.

Outline of economic development. It is hardly surprising that the Bahamas has fought to protect its banking laws for its range of offshore banking services made the country one of the leading financial centres of the world and is a major contributor to the wealth of The Bahamas. While not employing much of the population, in 1988, services contributed US$1,341 million to the economy. There are more than 400 offshore banks with more than US$100,000,000 in deposits, and since 1983 The Bahamas has had one of the largest "open registry" shipping fleets in the world, an area it entered in 1976.

Current economic situation. Tourism is, however, the main sector of the economy, contributing more than 54 per cent of GDP and employing some 43 per cent of the population. The climate, beaches and sailing through the islands are attractions, but casino gambling is a lure for the mainly American traffic, which accounts for 90 per cent of tourists.

The Bahamas remains the Caribbean's main destination, with 3,100,000 visitors in 1988, despite increasing competition. Along with financial services, tourism has maintained The Bahamas position as the Caribbean country with the highest GNP. This was US$10,280 per head in 1988. Government has increased spending in the tourist sector and has been exploiting the European market to remove the lopsided dependency on tourists from the USA. Banking fees were also doubled in 1988.

Manufacturing in The Bahamas was based on petroleum refining, but the refinery closed in 1985. Grand Bahama remains an important petroleum trans-shipment centre, but manufacturing has declined and now is based on rum, pharmaceuticals and salt. This sector contributes less than 10 per cent to GDP.

More than 80 per cent of foodstuff was imported during the 1980s but this has been reduced by government initiatives. There are now exports of some vegetables and fruit. Agriculture still remains the smallest sector, employing the least number of people, some five per cent.

Prospects for development. The Pindling government has moved to fight the great drug problem in The Bahamas through co-operation with the USA. A new legal assistance treaty came into effect in June 1987, the USA has been giving naval assistance since May 1988 and there has been financial and institutional collaboration. In addition, the government has allocated record spending on the police and coastguard to fight trafficking.

In 1989, Pindling moved to stabilize his administration by reshuffling the cabinet and appointing three new ministers. Incentives have been offered to encourage light manufacturing and agriculture. Tourism and financial services will remain the lifeblood of The Bahamas and should maintain high levels of prosperity. It is also likely that Sir Lynden Pindling will remain Prime Minister in the foreseeable future.

MH

BALAGUER, JOAQUIN. Five times president of the Dominican Republic, Balaguer served as the last puppet president under General Rafael Leónidas Trujillo, won elections under US Marine supervision in 1966 and re-election without serious opposition in 1970 and 1974. Forced by US intervention to accept defeat in 1978, he regained power in a more open and competitive election in 1986 and was re-elected in 1990. A scholar as well as a politician, he has been praised by friends and enemies alike for his political acumen.

JKB

BÁNZER, HUGO. Following a military education, including training in Panama and Texas, Hugo Bánzer Suárez (b. 1926) was a colonel in the Bolivian army by the age of 35. He served as Minister of Education and Culture under Barrientos between 1964–1966, and was military attaché in Washington DC between 1967 and 1969. Bánzer seized power in a military *coup* in August 1971 and his regime was notorious for its ruthless suppression of political opposition. The economy was opened to foreign investment while government resources were channelled towards the development of agro-industry in the eastern lowlands and especially towards Bánzer's power base of Santa Cruz. Much of the country's external debt was acquired during Bánzer's administration. Under increasing pressure Bánzer held elections in July 1978 in which Gen. Juan Pereda stood as the President's candidate. Massive fraud led to the annulment of the result and Pereda staged a *coup* ousting his mentor. Bánzer then formed the Nationalist Democratic Action (ADN) party as an electoral vehicle and participated in the 1979 and 1980 elections in which he came third with between 15 per cent and 17 per cent of the vote. In 1985 Bánzer topped the poll with 28 per cent of the vote but without an overall majority Congress installed **Víctor Paz Estenssoro** as president. Following the elections of 1989 Bánzer, who had come second in the polls, entered into the "Patriotic Accord" with the third-placed candidate, **Jaime Paz Zamora**, in which the latter secured the presidency while the ADN took control of key ministerial posts.

CS

BARBADOS. *Population*: 253,881 (1987). *Area*: 430 sq km. *GDP*: Bds $3,097 million (1988). *Trade volume*: Bds $354,194,000. *Top five trade partners*: USA, UK, Trinidad and Tobago, Canada, Japan. *Defence spending*: Bds. $18,100,000 (1988/89). *Education spending (as percentage of GNP)*: 19.1. *Birthrate*: 14.7 per 1,000.

Geographical background. Barbados, just east of the Caribbean island chain, has enjoyed the most stable political history in the region. Unlike others, it remained a British colony until independence on Nov. 30, 1966 and has a parliamentary tradition dating back to 1639, the third oldest in the Commonwealth after the UK's and Bermuda's.

Socio-political background. Since universal adult suffrage in 1951, two parties, the Barbados Labour Party (BLP) founded by Sir Grantley Adams, and the Democratic Labour Party (DLP) have dominated politics in the island. At the last elections held on Jan. 22, 1991, the DLP, led by Erskine Sandiford, won with a smaller majority of 18 seats in the expanded 28-member House of Assembly. The BLP, led by Henry Forde, won the remaining seats, a total of just more than 3,000 votes preventing a BLP victory. The other party contesting the election, the National Democratic Party, (NDP), led by Dr Ritchie Haynes, the former Minister of Finance in the DLP government, was heavily defeated. Three former MPs who split from the DLP in February 1989 to form the NDP with Haynes lost their seats and only Haynes saved his deposit. There are two other registered political parties, the People's Pressure Movement (PPM) and Workers' Party of Barbados (WPB), both ineffectual. The House of Assembly is complemented by a 21-member appointed Senate.

Outline of political history. Barbados, a Commonwealth country, got ministerial government in 1954 when Sir Grantley Adams of the BLP, which had governed since 1951, became premier. He later became the only Prime Minister of the short-lived West Indies Federation. The country achieved self-government in 1961, and the DLP, a 1955 splinter group from the BLP, won, and Errol Barrow become Premier.

He led the country into independence in 1966 and won the 1971 elections, but was heavily defeated in 1976 by the BLP, led by J.M.G.M "Tom" Adams, son of Sir Grantley. Barbados experienced rapid growth under the Adams' administration and was returned to power in the June 1981 elections, winning 17 of the 27 seats.

Adams was a major backer of the United States' intervention in Grenada in October 1983. A defence force had been established in April 1978, after a Cuba airlines jet was blown up just off Barbados shortly after the BLP 1976 victory, and troops were sent to St. Vincent in December 1979 on stand-by, as the government of St. Vincent put down a rebellion on Union Island.

In 1983, Adams fired his Minister of Health, Dr. Don Blackman, who later joined the DLP for the 1986 elections. Adams died suddenly in March 1985. He was succeeded by Bernard St. John, the BLP leader before the 1971 elections, during which he lost his seat. St. John's stay as Prime Minister was short as the BLP suffered a massive 24:3 defeat in the May 1986 elections, St. John and all but one of the cabinet losing their seats.

Barrow once again became Prime Minister, imposing spending curbs. Now a strong critic of America, he announced a review of Barbados' participation in the USA-backed Regional Security System in June and in November called a halt of recruitment to the Defence Force. Barrow had also opposed the US-led Grenada intervention.

Current developments — political. Erskine Sandiford, the Deputy Prime Minister, became head of the government when Barrow died suddenly in June 1987. Sandiford's style of leadership and management of the economy was widely criticized and in September 1987, Dr. Haynes, Finance Minister, resigned, subsequently forming the opposition as the NDP with three other former DLP members.

The DLP victory in 1991 was seen by the party as support for Sandiford and his policies. However, the BLP, which had won 40 per cent of the votes in 1986 and three seats, polled nearly half of all votes cast. More significantly, for the first time many people failed to vote, some 33 per cent, indicating disillusionment.

Outline of economic development. Along with a stable political framework, Barbados has experienced steady economic growth. GNP measured US$5,530 per head in 1987, with a growth of GDP by 6.7 per cent in 1988. The country has a broad economy, dominated by services, of which tourism is the most important.

Barbados received 451,485 visitors in 1988 when tourism contributed 11.8 per cent to GDP, earned Bds. $918,500,000 and with trade employed 20 per cent of the work force. The UK, Canada and USA are the main markets, but Europe and other regions are being explored.

The Tom Adams administration instituted offshore financial services, and this segment earned Bds.$40,000,000 in foreign exchange in 1988. There are more than 650 offshore companies, including captive insurances, foreign sales corporations and international business companies and six offshore banks. Insurance, business and financial services contributed 13.5 per cent to GDP in 1988.

Industry and manufacturing have been encouraged by successive governments. A downturn in electronic manufacture has affected these sectors, but they remain important. Industry accounted for 19.2 per cent of GDP in 1988, while manufacturing contributed nine per cent and employed some 10 per cent of the work force. Furniture, garment manufacture and electronic parts assembly are important.

Barbados has moved away from a dependence on cane sugar agriculture to a more mixed economy, but agriculture remains important. The country is virtually self-sufficient in vegetables, root crops and fish, developed in the early '80s. Some root crops are exported, mainly yams and sweet potatoes. Sugar output has declined, but remains the main export, mainly to the UK. It contributed 2.5 per cent to GDP in 1988 when it earned Bds.$67,200,000, 28 per cent of exports.

Current economic situation. Barbados is expected to be affected by the single European market which comes into effect in 1992. However, its stability, excellent infrastructure and high education levels are expected to keep it well placed in the future. Further agricultural diversification is being examined, with sea-island cotton a priority, despite a 1990 fiasco which led to calls for the dismissal of the then Minister of Agriculture Warwick Franklin. Offshore services are being given further encouragement and there has been spending to improve tourist facilities and to maximize profits from the industry.

Successive Barbados governments have been at the forefront of regional integration, and the DLP is fully behind moves for deeper economic integration. Meanwhile, a number of bilateral arrangements have been made, particularly with Trinidad regarding fishing, a common regional airline and identical positions in international negotiations.

Prospects for development. Despite fluctuations in tourism and manufacturing, Barbados is expected to maintain its relative property.

MH

BATLLE Y ORDONEZ, JOSE. José Batlle y Ordóñez (1856–1929), Uruguayan statesman, successfully beat off revolt and took the first steps towards social reform in Uruguay in his first term as president 1903–07. Following a visit to Europe and in particular to Switzerland, where he obtained his vision of a peaceful state with a weak executive freed from the curse of militarism, in his second term 1911–15 he embarked on a radical programme of welfare legislation, establishing public welfare and co-participation of all political parties under a collegial executive as the twin principles of Batllismo, doctrine of the dominant **Colorado Party**. His sons Lorenzo and César Batlle Pacheco continued to campaign for decentralized government within his party; his nephew, Luis Batlle Berres, leader of the social reform faction of the party, was President 1948–51, and his mantle in turn was inherited by his son, Jorge Batlle, who unsuccessfully contested the 1966 and 1971 presidential elections.

PARC

BEAGLE CHANNEL (Canal Beagle). The islets of Picton, Lennox and Nueva, situated at the eastern entrance to the Beagle Channel, believed since the nineteenth century to be Chilean, were disputed by **Argentina**, and in 1977 an arbitral award by the International Court of Justice in favour of **Chile** was rejected by Argentina, and war averted by the offer of mediation by the Vatican. Following the restoration of civilian rule in Argentina, the mediation proposals (confirming the islands as Chilean but establishing maritime boundaries confirming under the "Two Ocean" principle that the meridian of Cape Horn would remain the boundary between the Argentinian and Chilean spheres of influence (and hence the eastern political boundary of the Pacific) were ratified by both states and confirmed by referendum in Argentina in 1984.

PARC/SAC

BELIZE. *Population*: 180,000 (mid-1988). *Area*: 23,000 sq km. *Life expectancy* 67.

Geographical background. Bounded by the Guatemalan tropical forest province of El Petén in the west, by the Mexican Yucatán peninsula in the north, Belize lies exposed to the Gulf of

Honduras and the Caribbean Sea to the east. It is a predominantly low-lying sparsely populated country, with a coastline indented by numerous bays and mangrove swamps and fringed by keys (islands).

Socio-political background. Belize's inhabitants are primarily of Afro–Caribbean and Amerindian descent. The national language is English. Until 1984 the country's political life had been dominated for 40 years by George Price's People's United Party (PUP) which oversaw the transfer to Belizean independence from the United Kingdom on Sept. 21, 1981 as an independent state within the Commonwealth with HM Queen Elizabeth II as head of state, represented by a Governor-General, currently Dame Minita Elvira Gordon. There is a two-chamber National Assembly, with quinquennial popular elections to the House of Representatives, and an appointed Senate.

Outline of political history. In 1984, Manuel Esquivel of the United Democratic Party (UDP) broke the PUP's governmental stranglehold. In September 1989 Price was returned to office once more.

Current developments—political. There is a significant refugee community in Belize, particularly of Salvadoreans (15,000) and Guatemalans (10,000) who have fled civil war and government repression in their own countries. Refugees may number over 25 per cent of the total Belizean population. At the same time Belizean emigration to the United States is accelerating rapidly.

Long-standing territorial claims by **Guatemala** over Belize are currently subject to a process of negotiation under a permanent commission established between the two countries in May 1988.

Outline of economic development. The Belizean economy relies almost exclusively on the export of citrus fruits, bananas, sugar and tropical hardwoods to the USA (under the preferential terms of the **Caribbean Basin Initiative**) and to the UK and EEC (under **Lomé Convention** quotas). Earnings on citrus fruit rapidly overtook those of sugar in the early 1980s. Ownership patterns conformed to the export basis of the economy and in 1966 over 90 per cent of private land in Belize was foreign owned. PUP governments succeeded in reducing this level to 60 per cent in 1984 by encouraging local control. However the powerful Citrus Growers Association is dominated by large farm interests, whereas some 90 per cent of its members are small farmers. The Esquivel government went some way to reversing the policy of encouraging the local ownership of agriculture.

JCJS

BERMUDA. *Population*: 58,000 (1987). *Area*: 53 sq km. *Trade volume*: B$425,545 million (1 B$ = US$1). *Top five trade partners*: USA, UK, Canada, Aruba, Japan. *Birthrate*: 15.7 per 1,000.

Geographical background. What is known as Bermuda is, in reality, 10 islands linked by bridges and causeways; part of some 150 islands properly called The Bermudas or Somers Islands. Isolated in the Atlantic Ocean off the US state of South Carolina, Bermuda is blessed with sea water and beaches typically Caribbean, but with a milder climate, making it a favoured tourist resort. Its British heritage and proximity to the USA gives it a peculiar blend of influences, from which Bermuda benefits fully.

Socio-political background. Bermuda, discovered by the Spanish, but British since 1609, is the UK's oldest colony. Another distinction is that it has the second oldest representative body in the Commonwealth, after Westminster, dating from 1620, and one of the oldest in the world.

The island got its Constitution in 1968 allowing internal self-government. Amendments were made in 1973, giving the Governor responsibility for external affairs, police, internal security and defence, in 1974, providing for the post of Premier and "Cabinet", and in 1979 allowing for closer consultation between the Premier and Opposition leader on various appointments.

Bermuda's Parliament consists of 11 appointed Senators and a 40-member (dual representation) House of Assembly. The defence strength is disproportionate to the size of the country. Some 11 per cent of Bermuda is leased by the US Armed Forces, including the lone airport, where 400 personnel are stationed. There is a 734-strong Bermuda Regiment and a solid police force.

Outline of political history. The United Bermuda Party, (UBP), now led by Sir John Swan, has ruled Bermuda since the first elections under the Constitution in May 1968. The UBP, following elections in February 1989, now holds 23 seats, reflecting a drop in support. The Progressive Labour Party, (PLP) holds 15 seats, with one each held by the National Liberal Party, (NLP) and Independent Environmentalist.

Despite the UBP's stranglehold, politics in Bermuda have been characterized by rioting, racial overtones and divisions over whether the country should seek independence from Britain. Some 60 per cent of the population are of African origin.

Racial tension and rioting at the first elections under the Constitution in 1968 again flared in 1972 and 1973 and led to the deaths of the Governor, Commissioner of Police and three more. British troops were flown to Bermuda in 1977 after the Governor's assassin and another convicted murderer were executed, and rioting again broke out.

The PLP, a mainly black party, campaigning for independence won 46 per cent of the vote at the May 1976 elections. The UBP, which supported dependence, lost ground, winning 26 seats. A Royal Commission on racial violence was established in February 1978. Its report in August recommended new constituency boundaries to give the PLP a better chance of winning. The PLP still lost, and four of its members later resigned after the 1983 elections, becoming independents and forming the NLP in August 1985.

Sir John Swan, then Minister of Home Affairs, became Premier in January 1982 on the resignation of David Gibbons, who continued as Minister of Finance. Gibbons resigned this post in April 1984. He had become Premier after Sir John Sharpe, UBP leader since 1975, resigned in August 1977.

Current developments—political. The 1978 Commission had recommended early independence for Bermuda and Sir John Swan, knighted in 1989, has supported eventual independence. In 1986 proposals for a referendum were laid in the Senate, but the British Government was said to have rejected the Bermuda Government's plans in May 1989. The Swan administration now see no debate on the issue in the immediate future.

Outline of economic development. Bermuda enjoys one of the highest per capita GNPs in the world, topping the world in 1987 with US$16,071. This has dropped since, but Bermuda still has an enviable economy, all the more so as it has a small manufacturing sector, dominated by construction, a smaller agricultural base and, in the context of its economy, negligible exports, mainly pharmaceutical and medicinal products.

The country is totally dependent on imports, from water to energy. Food imports amount to 80 per cent of all imports while exports only total six per cent of imports. Bermuda's no income tax, extensive social welfare and free education system is built on tourism and an extremely strong financial services sector.

In 1988, tourism earned 60 per cent of all foreign exchange, contributed 36 per cent to GDP, employed 25 per cent of the population directly and an estimated total of 65 per cent. Bermuda's tourist clientele is rich, mainly from the USA, and its market is rigorously protected.

A variety of financial services is the other bulwark of Bermuda's economy. In this sector it benefits from a special tax treaty with the USA and its status as a British Designated Territory. Bermuda is the fifth largest flag registration country in the world, a leading insurance centre with more than 6,300 exempted companies registered in 1988. The whole financial sector contributed 22 per cent of GDP and 40 per cent of foreign exchange in 1987.

Current economic situation. Growth has slowed in Bermuda, and there is growing concern that steps must be taken to maintain its economy. No hotels have been built since 1972 and the public bitterly opposed plans to build a new one in 1990. An area of concern is the high number of foreigners who work in Bermuda, more than 7,000. It is unlikely that Bermuda will suffer any great collapse in its economy, but growth in the financial services sector will become even more important in the future, as there is no room for expansion in any other sector.

MH

BETANCOURT, ROMULO. Rómulo Betancourt, Venezuelan statesman, was born at Guatire, in the State of Miranda, on Feb. 22, 1908. He came from a poor family and had to work from the age of 14. As a law student in 1928 he took part in a rising against the dictatorship of Juan Vicente Gómez and was first imprisoned and then exiled, meeting with other exiles in 1931 at Barranquilla, Colombia, to organize left-wing opposition to the dictatorship. In 1936 Betancourt returned to Venezuela and worked to put together a Popular Front government, but in 1937 left-wing activity was proscribed and the group went underground until 1941, when it re-emerged under its present name, Democratic Action (*Acción Democrática*—AD).

Following the *coup* of October 1945 Betancourt emerged as leader of the provisional government of 1945–48, which established a new Constitution (1947) and held the country's first true elections in 1947. AD was at the same time a reforming movement and Betancourt himself, as interim president, carried out several major changes. Above all in 1947 he established the principle that for the future the revenue of the government form the exploitation of the nation's oil resources should at least be equal to that gained by the oil companies—the so-called 50: 50 principle. He ended the practice of granting new concessions and proposed the formation of a national oil company. A major programme of ploughing investment back into agriculture and industry was also begun, doubling electricity generating capacity and starting middle-cost housing schemes.

Following the fall of the dictatorship (1958), Betancourt was chosen as President (1959–64) in free elections supervised by the armed forces. As President Betancourt was successful, against all odds, in establishing a democratic political system in which power has passed peacefully, by election, from one major group to the other. The bravery shown by Betancourt himself when he narrowly escaped assassination in 1960 and his personal commitment to the principle of democracy gave him a strong personal following, while his decision to form a coalition government gave him the consistent support of Rafael Caldera and COPEI. With the aid of COPEI he was able to withstand the loss of part of the AD's youth wing, attracted by the rising star of Fidel Castro, and who soon formed a new organization, the Movement of the Revolutionary Left (MIR) with a programme of carrying the armed struggle into the countryside. Yet ironically Castro's personal dislike of Betancourt in the end strengthened him against his own armed forces, to whom he offered a new role as a modern, professional organization, in which for the first time NCOs and men as well as officers would be properly paid and equipped, and the guerrillas were easily defeated.

Betancourt's government continued the programme of land reform of 1948 in a way which, though cautious, maintained its momentum. By March 1963 Betancourt was able to report to Congress that some 57,000 families had been settled on 1,500,000 hectares of land, and it had become clear that the revolutionary left were failing to make headway in the countryside. Meanwhile in 1960 a state oil company, PCV, had been established. With no more concessions being granted this organization was intended to take over existing ones as they started to expire in the early 1980s. At the same time Venezuela took the lead in setting up the Organization of Petroleum Exporting Countries (OPEC), of which it has been an active member ever since. The subsequent stability of Venezuela under his successors helped consolidate Betancourt's position as a leading democratic statesman in the Americas. In his later years he lived in Bern, Switzerland. Four volumes of speeches and documents relating to his second Presidency were published as *La revolución democrática en Venezuela* in Caracas in 1968.

PARC

BISHOP, MAURICE. Maurice Bishop, Prime Minister of Grenada 1979–83, was born in Aruba in 1944. The son of middle-class parents, it was while returning in 1970 from the study of law in London, where he had been strongly influenced by the "Black Power" ideology of the day, that he experienced the April disturbances in Trinidad. Soon he joined with Kendrick Radix to found a mass organization which fused with Unison Whiteman's Joint Endeavour for Welfare, Employment and Liberation (JEWEL) to form the New Jewel Movement (NJM) in March 1973. Bishop himself sustained permanent injury from a beating from Gairy's henchmen, and his father was killed by police in January 1974. While the NJM's original vague anti-colonial and anti-capitalist programme soon gave way to a revolutionary programme and Marxist organization, Bishop himself was elected to the legislative council and became Leader of the Opposition in 1976. Learning that the NJM was to be "liquidated" on the orders of **Sir Eric Gairy**, a group led by Hudson Austin seized power on March 13, 1979, with the loss of 3 lives, while Gairy was attending a meeting of the UN in New York.

Bishop became Prime Minister of a Provisional Revolutionary Government (PRG) promising to hold fresh elections. However his position became increasingly untenable as the promise was forgotten and he became instead the spokesman for a government of "socialist orientation". All power was vested in the Central Committee of the NJM, in which the Marxist Bernard Coard, who as Minister of Finance was implementing a cautious strategy of state led growth, increasingly came to represent those pressing for more radical measures. On Oct. 13, 1983, Bishop was placed under house arrest on the orders of his colleagues: on Oct. 19 he was freed by a large crowd led by Unison Whiteman and with his supporters marched on Fort Rupert, where, however, he was seized by military personnel and summarily shot dead.

PARC

BOLIVAR, SIMON. Simón Bolívar, "*El Libertador*", dictator and subsequently President of Colombia, protector of Peru, patron of Bolivia, statesman and political philosopher, remains one of the great political figures of all time. He was born in Caracas, Venezuela on July 24, 1783. Descendant of a Spanish noble family, he briefly served in the militia before resuming his studies. Between 1803 and 1806 he visited France and Italy, where he swore to liberate his native country. When the revolution of 1810, which he had been one of the first to support, failed, he took the bold decision to carry the battle into modern Colombia, before returning to native provinces where he was hailed as Liberator at Mérida on May 23, 1813. After the Royalist reconquest of New Granada he escaped to Jamaica where he issued his celebrated *Reply of a South American to a Gentleman of this Island* (1815) setting out his political philosophy. In gratitude for help from Haiti to renew the struggle, on his return to Isla Margarita in 1816 he decreed the abolition of slavery, before setting out on the reconquest of New Granada. Independence was effectively achieved in 1819 and the new Republic of Colombia (including modern Venezuela) had already been organized when its position was secured at the Battle of Carabobo on June 24, 1821.

Following the incorporation of Ecuador in the new Republic, he advanced on the last stronghold of Spanish power in South America, Peru. There Bolívar met the Argentine liberator of Chile, **José de San Martín**, who renounced his position as protector of the infant republic of Peru and went into exile. In his place the Peruvian Congress conferred the supreme command on Bolívar, and in conjunction with Antonio José de Sucre the forces of independence were victorious at Junín and Ayacucho (1824). In tribute to him Upper Peru asked him to give them a Constitution and renamed their independent state Bolivia (1825). The Constitution he proposed was popular and representative, with some innovative features. In 1826 he convened the first congress of independent American states at Panama and is thus honoured as the originator of the **Inter-American System**. Sadly, Colombia had already fallen into chaos before he resigned its Presidency for the last time in 1830. Before he could go into exile he died of tuberculosis at a *quinta* near Santa Marta, Colombia, on Dec. 17, 1830, a few days after both Venezuela and Ecuador had seceded.

PARC

BOLIVIA. *Population*: 7,113,000 (1989). *Area*: 1,098,581 sq km. *GDP*: US$4,009 million (1988). *Trade volume*: imports: $484,500,000 (1988); $850,000,000 (1990); Exports: $542,300,000 (1988); $919,000,000 (1990); (1990 figures are preliminary estimates). *Top five trade partners*: Argentina, USA, Brazil, Germany, UK. *Education spending*: 2.4 per cent of GDP (1985). *Urban population (as percentage of total)*: 51.4 (1990) (32 per cent in centres with over 20,000 1980). *Birthrate*: 42.9 per 1,000. *Life expectancy*: men 52.5 (1985); women 55.7 (1985).

Geographical background. Bolivia is one of two landlocked countries in South America and shares borders with Peru, Brazil, Argentina, Paraguay and Chile, to all of whom it has lost land since independence. It is conventional to divide the country into three distinct geographical regions, each of which possesses considerable physical diversity:

(1) The Altiplano: a high inter-montane plateau enclosed between the Western and Eastern Andean *cordilleras* with an altitude of 3,800 metres and a cold, dry climate. Despite its barren appearance the Altiplano has historically supported high population densities, especially in the area bordering Lake Titicaca. The eastern Andean *cordillera* has rich deposits of minerals, including silver, tin, lead, zinc, tungsten, antimony and bismuth, and mining has been a vital economic activity of this region.

(2) The Valleys: Between the high Andes and the eastern lowlands lies a geomorphologically complex region of intermontane valleys. Although steep and unstable slopes make communications difficult, the lower altitudes, temperate climates and alluvial soils make this region agriculturally productive and capable of supporting high population densities. To the east of La Paz lie the intensely-folded, semi-tropical Yungas, while further south the valleys are broader, cooler and drier.

(3) The Eastern Lowlands: comprising 70 per cent of national territory but previously only sparsely populated, much of the lowlands has experienced rapid transformation during the past 30 years. To the north of Santa Cruz rainforest and savannah have given way to agricultural colonization and cattle ranching along several broad fronts. South of Santa Cruz, however, the climate becomes increasingly arid, although in this region lie exploited natural gas and petroleum resources.

Socio-political background: Bolivia is a multi-ethnic, primarily Catholic society in which a Spanish-speaking white élite remains politically and economically dominant over a socially mixed population most of whom are native speakers of Quechua, Aymará or another indigenous language. A strong sense of regional cultural identity exists amongst a population of whom almost half are rural dwellers. There is also considerable spatial mobility for, in addition to rapid urbanization, large numbers of rural people move between the highlands and the eastern lowlands.

The metropolitan area of La Paz, the political capital of the country, has grown to over 1,000,000 inhabitants, while Santa Cruz de la Sierra in the eastern lowlands has around half this population and Cochabamba, located between the two, about one-third. Although planners have emphasized the growth potential of this development corridor linking the three cities, physical and financial constraints severely hamper the construction of a much-needed integrated transport network.

Beyond the cities Bolivia is a sparsely populated country where 40 per cent of its people live from small-scale farming and, with a poor level of services, possess the worst social indicators of development in mainland America.

Outline of political history. After a prolonged and bloody struggle, Bolivia achieved independence in 1825. Yet its weakness as a nation was best symbolized by the loss of territory to its neighbours, especially its coastline and rich nitrate fields to Chile during the War of the Pacific (1879–82). Although the country experienced mineral-led development from the 1880s, the 1930s saw it once again enter into conflict with a neighbour — this time Paraguay resisting Bolivian expansionism in the Chaco where oil deposits were a strategic factor. The Chaco War of 1932–35 proved enormously costly in human terms but it established many of the conditions of social discontent and political struggle that eventually led to the National Revolution of 1952.

An almost classical model of civilian rebellion involving armed insurrection and popular mobilization brought to power the Nationalist Revolutionary Movement (*Movimiento Nacionalista Revolucionario*—MNR) and installed **Víctor Paz Estenssoro** as president. While there were great expectations for the Revolution, particularly amongst organized labour led by the miners' union, its concrete achievements were effectively three-fold: the introduction of universal suffrage, the declaration of agrarian reform and the nationalization of a major part of the mining sector. The MNR, which increasingly moved away from the aspirations of labour, held power until late 1964 when it was overthrown by a military *coup* led by Gen. René Barrientos. This marked the onset of a cycle of military involvement and acute instability in political life that lasted until 1982.

Notwithstanding this period characterized by a "continuity of ruptures", Bolivia has remained a constitutional republic with executive power vested in a president and cabinet, elected by universal suffrage for a four-year term. The bicameral legislature comprises a 27-member Senate and a 130-member Chamber of Deputies. No candidate has been able to secure an overall majority at any presidential election since 1978, and consequently the choice has devolved upon Congress and this has resulted in complex and sometimes surprising alliances between parties.

Recent development—political. The elections of 1980 were won by a centre-left coalition the Democratic and Popular Union (*Unión Democrática y Popular*—UDP) headed by **Hernán Siles Zuazo**, previously president 1958–62. However, Siles was prevented from assuming office by a military *coup* headed by Gen. García Meza with the support of local cocaine barons and other extreme rightist elements. Although García Meza clung to power for one year, and three successor military regimes lasted a further 15 months before a negotiated return to civilian rule, the period marked a low point in the behaviour of *de facto* government, of which there had been seven other examples between 1964 and 1980.

Consequently, there was great popular anticipation when Siles eventually took up his mandate in late 1982. Unfortunately, such expectations soon foundered as the UDP coalition began to disintegrate in government. Besides the political opportunism of certain coalition partners, and continuous attacks by the myriad of parties and factions in Congress, the government was increasingly squeezed by non-parliamentary opposition. On the one hand, the demands of organized labour represented by the Central Organization of Bolivian Workers (*Central Obrera Boliviana* — COB), combined both an expression of economic discontent and outright political opposition from the largely trotskyist-prevailing leadership. On the other hand, the interests of capital were being increasingly and effectively presented by the Confederation of Private Entrepreneurs (*Confederación de Empresarios Privados de Bolivia*—CEPB). Attempting economic stabilization with a series of inconsistent policies that sought to placate both capital and labour, as well as the IMF, Siles presided over effective economic collapse as levels of production fell and hyperinflation spiralled to almost 12,000 per cent for 1985.

New elections were held in July 1985 and the right wing **Nationalist Democratic Action Party** (*Acción Democrática Nacionalista—ADN*) this time emerged with the largest share of the vote, although without an overall majority. As it fell to Congress to nominate the president, it was Victor Paz Estenssoro of the MNR, which had polled two percentage points fewer than the ADN, who emerged with the support of the left wing parties implacably opposed to **Hugo Bánzer**, the candidate of the ADN, who had seized and held power from 1971 to 1978.

Within three weeks of his inaugauration as president, Paz announced Decree 21060, which marked a dramatic break with the past model of state capitalism. It heralded a New Economic Policy of orthodox neo-liberalism, designed to establish fiscal stability at the price of stringent austerity. Economically orthodox but politically audacious, this central programme seized and largely maintained the political initiative for the MNR over its opponents. First, by adopting a programme promoted by the ADN in the elections it effectively left its rivals with little choice but to enter into a formal political pact with the MNR. Secondly, in its confrontations with labour the government withstood the general strike called in the immediate wake of the declaration of Decree 21060, and faced a defensive labour movement badly weakened by the restructuring of the mining sector and the massive redundancies which resulted.

The elections of 1989 also produced no outright winner and, as in 1985, it fell to Congress to elect a new president. On this occasion, however, while the MNR had received marginally the greater number of votes in favour of Gonzalo Sánchez de Lozada, the architect of the NEP, a "patriotic" accord robbed him of the presidential prize. This was reached between the ADN and the **Movement of the Revolutionary Left** (*Movimiento de la Izquierda Revolucionaria—MIR*), hitherto mortal political enemies, which had come second and third in the poll respectively. The MIR, which was formed in 1971 in opposition to the *coup de'état* of Gen. Hugo Bánzer, initially represented a youthful, highly radical line, but shifted increasingly to the right in pursuit of power. Such political flexibility was rewarded when **Jaime Paz Zamora** of the MIR was inaugaurated as president on Aug. 6, 1989 while the ADN took control of the key ministries of state. While the alliance appears to have held, it has deepened the sense of disillusionment felt by a broad sector of the population with the electoral process and the opportunism of traditional party politicians.

Hence, the late 1980s witnessed the rise of a new kind of populism represented by the likes of Carlos Palenque, a media "personality" who owns radio and television stations in La Paz. Palenque's party, Conscience of the Fatherland (*Conciencia de Patria*—CONDEPA) easily won the 1989 elections in the city of La Paz but took only 11 per cent of the national vote. Yet this was equal to the combined vote of the left-wing parties within the elections, which represented a considerable decline in the political fortunes of the left over the decade.

Outline of economic development. While tin reputedly provided much of what little strength the Bolivian economy possessed during the twentieth century, in truth it has been in decline since 1929. Dominated by the "tin barons" of Patiño, Hochschild and Aramayo until the National Revolution, the mining sector thereafter largely came under state control in the form of the Mining Corporation of Bolivia (Corporación Minera de Bolivia—COMIBOL). However, the lack of state investment in exploration and mechanization, combined with difficult geological conditions and low quality ores led to high costs of production in Bolivia. The collapse of world tin prices in October 1985 sealed its decline in status, from the world's second largest producer in 1979 with output in excess of 30,000 tonnes, to a minor producer of 8,000 tones by 1987. Such circumstances made the restructuring of COMIBOL a major part of the Paz Estenssoro government's programme to reduce the size of the public sector. This led to the redundancy of 23,000 miners from a workforce which numbered 30,000 in the early 1980s, and has been accompanied by government encouragement of the private mining sector and diversification into other non-ferrous minerals of which there are substantial known reserves.

During the 1980s, however, the export of natural gas became the country's largest single source of legal export revenue, with some 30 per cent of foreign exchange earnings generated by pipeline exports to the Argentinian border at Yacuiba. Alongside natural gas, oil production has been less important and output has fallen since the 1970s to less than 20,000 barrels per day, barely sufficient to meet domestic needs.

Agriculture provides about 20 per cent of GDP but its growth has been uneven especially in the small farm sector where drought and economic recession have had a considerable impact. It is from this sector that many have sought to benefit from the relatively high earnings available in the coca–cocaine industry, either through securing and planting land on the agricultural frontier, or as casual labourers employed in processing operations (see **Drugs**).

The scale of the drugs industry in Bolivia is difficult to evalute precisely, but it certainly softened the impact of recession and the social costs of economic stabilization during the 1980s. With some \$300–\$500,000,000 of repatriated profits either entering the unregulated banking system as foreign exchange, or returning to the country as contraband imports of both basic and luxury goods, cocaine earnings provided a fiscal prop to an ailing economy and a safety valve against social discontent. It may also have indirectly helped the country to stabilize its external debt which currently amounts to some \$4,000 million. This has been reduced through purchases on the secondary market of private foreign debt at 11 per cent of face value, and a debt-for-nature swop worth some \$650,000 for forest conservation.

Current economic situation. Since the inaugauration of President Jaime Paz Zamora in August 1989 economic policy has not merely followed the course steered by the previous administration. Rather the government has intensified efforts to privatize state corporations and encourage direct foreign investment in the mineral and hydro-carbon sectors. This is an initiative that has generated considerable political opposition in a country where "resource sovereignty" is highly valued. Naturally this programme, it is hoped, will continue the slow process of economic recovery following the acute recession and hyperinflation of the early to mid 1980s. So far the economy has grown by 2–3 per cent during each of the past three years, legal export earnings in 1990 were at their highest level since 1980, and at 17.7 per cent Bolivia enjoyed in 1990 the lowest rate of inflation in Latin America. Yet such modest economic growth is barely sufficient to match the rate of population growth and has had little impact on employment creation or in raising levels of household income. These remain vital objectives especially if there is to be a sustainable resolution of the drugs trade problem.

Currently Bolivia is believed to generate between \$1,200–\$1,700 million worth of coca derivatives, and under intense diplomatic pressure from the United States crop substitution schemes are being promoted to reduce the area under coca leaf. Yet an estimated 300,000 people are believed to secure some part of their livelihood from growing or processing coca, and it is in providing an alternative source of employment with adequate remuneration which remains a critical task.

Prospects for development. It is expected that natural gas will remain a major source of export earnings into the forseeable future although Brazil is likely to replace Argentina as Bolivia's most important customer. Argentina has discovered significant gas reserves of its own, and it is expected that the current contract for the purchase of Bolivian gas which expires in 1992 will not be renewed. However, a new gas pipeline to the Brazilian border is under construction, and this will form part of a proposed border industrialization programme also involving the exploitation of iron ore reserves at El Mutun.

Consequently it is anticipated that Bolivia will continue to conduct more than half its trade with the countries of the Southern Cone Common Market notwithstanding its own current membership of the Andean Pact. Given that trade with its Andean partners is worth barely five per cent of that which it does with the Southern Cone countries, it is possible that Bolivia will change affiliation in the future.

Much of Bolivia's future prospects, however, will depend upon world market demand for its products which are almost entirely composed of primary commodities. With a very high proportion of the world's known reserves of lithium together with its other natural resource endowments, Bolivia may hope to generate a new phase of mineral-led economic growth in the future. Let us hope that the exploitation of these resources will not undermine sustainable development for its people in the long term.

CS

BOSCH, JUAN. Professor Juan Bosch is one of the two "grand old men" of recent letters and politics in the **Dominican Republic**. A social scientist who spent most of the Trujillo era in exile, he helped organize the **Dominican Revolutionary Party** (Partido Revolucionario Dominicano—PRD) and led it to power in 1963, only to be deposed after seven months in office. "Constitutionalist" forces who sought his return to power in 1965 were defeated by conservative factions of the military backed by United States marines. Professor Bosch subsequently organized a new party, the Dominican Liberation Party (*Partido de Liberación Dominicana* — PLD), which was the most serious challenger to **Balaguer's** Social Christian Reformist Party (*Partido Reformista Social Christiano*—PRSC) in 1986 and 1990.

JKB

BRASILIA. On April 4, 1955 in an election speech in Jataí, Goiás, **Juscelino Kubitschek** added to the 30 basic aims of his *Programa de Metas*, the *Programme of Goals*, his intention to transfer the capital of the country from Rio de Janeiro to a new city, to be built in the *planalto central*, the central plateau or upland, of Brazil. This had been an often repeated aim for over 130 years, since the great Brazilian statesman, José Bonifácio de Andrada e Silva, had first proposed the idea to the General Constituent and Legislative Assembly, which was summoned soon after Independence in 1822, to its first meeting, in solemn session, in May 1823.

Many people, in 1955, thought that Kubitschek's statement of intent would not survive the presidential election of November, or would certainly be lost amid the more pressing business of the new government. There was general astonishment, when, in September 1956, with the approval of a somewhat dismayed Congress, he created the *Companhia Urbanizadora da Nova Capital*, the Urbanization Company of the New Capital, better known as *Novacap*, to take responsibility for the building of the city. Congressmen, and others, including civil servants and foreign diplomats, suddenly realized that, soon, they might be rudely uprooted from the civilized delights of Rio de Janeiro, to be transplanted, in some spot, as yet undefined, close to the centre of Brazil.

There still was hope that the project would come to nothing, that it could be protracted to outlive Kubitschek's presidential term, that its cost would prove prohibitive, or that it would be technically too difficult. Such, often cynical, musings reckoned without the drive and energy of Kubitschek, and the flair and imaginative brilliance of those whom he called to work with him on the project.

The building of Brasília was started in 1957, then continued, day and night, for seven days a week. Kubitschek took a close personal interest in the work, frequently visiting the site and sleeping in a simple wooden building, which still is preserved, about 15 kilometres from the present city centre.

On April 21, 1960, though still far from finished, Brasília was inaugurated, marking, once again in Brazil's history, a definitive shift of government and a new focus of national development. Kubitschek had confounded his critics.

The idea of transferring the capital of Brazil, away from the coast, to which one generation of Brazilians after another stubbornly had clung, went back as far as Pombal, the authoritarian prime minister of Portugal in the eighteenth century. It was also part of the demands of the *mineiro* nationalists, who, in the eighteenth century revolt against Portugal, known as the *Inconfidência*, had demanded that the capital should be transferred to São João del Rey. This colonial town was the birthplace of *Tiradentes*, who was hanged in 1792, for his part in the insurrection, and, in 1910, of **Tancredo Neves de Almeida**, who was also to be buried there, in 1985. It was appropriate, therefore, that a *mineiro* president, Juscelino Kubitschek, should, at last, realize this *mineiro* dream.

José Bonifácio, in the second decade of the nineteenth century, had suggested "Brasília" as the name for the new inland capital. Later, the historian, Francisco Adolpho de Varnhagen, who afterwards became Viscount of Porto Seguro, argued that its site should be on the central plateau. This area was also specified in Article Three of the republican Constitution of 1891, which led to a survey of the proposed area in 1892. Future maps of Brazil showed a spot in Goiás marked *D.F.*, the site of the future *Distrito Federal*, or Federal District.

The scepticism of those who smiled quietly at Kubitschek's proposal of 1955 was partly explained by the continued failure of governments to take measures to fill the box marked on the map. Article 4 of the *Constitution* of 1946 again said that the capital should be moved to the central plateau, that surveys should be done, and a removal date fixed, and that the current Federal District should become the new state of Guanabara.

One result, in 1946, was that a commission was formed, the *Commissão de Estudos de Localização da Nova Capital do Brasil*, the Commission for Studying the Siting of the New Capital of Brazil. This body had to recommend the most suitable site for the new capital, its main criteria being that the new city must be near the main demographic centre of the country, must have good communications, and, if possible, touch the borders of one or more states.

One proposal, in a minority report of this Commission, was that the new capital should include the town of Tupaciguara, in the Parnaíba valley, in the *triângulo mineiro*. This was an already fast-developing region, with good communications, near to the frontier of three states, São Paulo, Goiás and Minas Gerais itself. There was some resistance to this idea from north-eastern politicians, who were afraid of further strengthening São Paulo, Minas Gerais and the centre-south. The majority report recommended a site on the central plateau, about 200 miles further north. The rectangle chosen included two distinct areas. One was in good farming land, north of Anápolis, and at the end of the railway system. The other was a large area of *cerrado*, or savannah.

The Coelho Commission's report lay before Congress from 1940, under Dutra, until 1953, during the second **Vargas** government. Vargas already had emphasized his *Marcha para o Oeste*, the March to the West, in his first term of office. Measures were now taken to find a suitable site. This should be on level ground, with a good water supply and a healthy climate, be free from malaria, be near good agricultural land and near to hydroelectric power. It should have locally available building materials.

The task of locating such a site was given to the North American planning firm of Belcher Associates. They carried out aerial photography and field surveys. They specified five sites, none of which met all the criteria required. These were called Blue and Yellow, not far from Anápolis, in the west of the Coelho rectangle, and Brown, Green and Yellow, in the east, in the *cerrado*.

Most speculation favoured either Blue or Yellow, but, in April 1955, a federal committee chose Brown.

The Brown site, in the *cerrado*, had no existing communications, was on land not considered most suitable for agriculture, had no large water supply and no nearby source of hydroelectric energy or building materials. It was, on the other hand, relatively neutral politically, and about 40 kilometres south from Planaltina, a colonial town, on the old pack route from the mines of Goiás and Cuiabá to the coast. Just five kilometres outside Planaltina was the *Pedra Fundamental*, the foundation stone, laid in 1922 by President Epitácio Pessoa, to mark the site originally chosen for the new capital.

There was also a certain symbolic quality to the Brown site, in that, 10 kilometres outside Planaltina, in the direction of the proposed new city, were the *Aguas Emendadas*, at which point spring two streams. One flows north to the Amazon basin, the other south, to the Plate river system. Apart from such symbolism, there were inevitable rumours that the decision had been influenced in terms of who owned the land, the value of which would increase dramatically by the choice of site.

Despite all these preparations, few people thought that, at last, a president would take action, even after the setting up of *Novacap*, in September 1956. They forgot that Kubitschek had been mayor of a planned city, Belo Horizonte, which, in 1897, had taken over from Ouro Preto, the colonial gold mining town, as capital of Minas Gerais. There was, even more recently, the example of Goiânia, the beautiful capital of Goiás, again a planned city, which, in 1937, replaced Goiás Velho, another colonial gold town, which had been state capital since 1727.

The head of *Novacap* was to be Israel Pinheiro, a close associate of Kubitschek in Minas Gerais, who, also, was a man of formidable energy and determination. If any group could move the capital, it would be *mineiros*, whose land-locked state, for over two centuries, had been the most heavily populated of Brazil, till overtaken by São Paulo.

On Sept. 30, 1956 the *Diário Oficial* announced a national competition for the design of the new capital. Twenty-six projects were submitted to a panel of judges, which included Sir William, later Lord, Holford. Their choice, six months later, was Lúcio Costa, whose simple design sought to control industrial sprawl, speculative building and, the scourge of many modern cities, the motor car.

Costa's plan also defined limits to the city, set out in a shape which some saw as a bent bow and arrow, and others, as a swept-wing aeroplane. It was a happy ambiguity in a plan for the capital city of a country with an indigenous tradition stretching back for thousands of years, but which had been quick to seize the advantages of rapid air transport, to reach areas deep into its interior.

Costa belonged to a group of Brazilian architects who had been directly influenced by Le Corbusier, who had visited Brazil in 1936, when Costa and others were designing the building for the Ministry of Education in Rio de Janeiro, which was completed in 1943. This beautiful and, then, revolutionary, building is now almost completely hidden among towering multi-storey office blocks of no distinction and personality, ugly, pretentious monuments to that uncontrolled blight which Costa had sought to resist in Brasília.

Other young architects who worked on the Ministry of Education building were Jorge Moreira, Alfonso Reidy and Oscar Niemeyer. They formed part of a generation of Brazilians, most of them born in the first decade of this century, who brought a new flowering to Brazilian architecture, planning and landscape gardening, using new, flowing forms and new materials suited to the tropics, combined with devices and much older materials, derived from Portugal and from the Moorish architectural tradition.

Concrete pillars gave a lightness and grace to buildings, while also creating coolness and space in an urban context. *Brise-soleil*, copied from Moorish *moxarabí* screens, shielded the light. Tiles, again in the Portuguese and Moorish style of *azulejos*, brought a cooling surface, often set against fountains and banks of plants, leading from within the building to reposeful courtyards and gardens.

It was all part of a wider, conscious revolution, stretching back to the "modernist" movement and the *Semana de Arte Moderna*, Week of Modern Art, in 1922, in which Brazilian writers, painters, architects and musicians sought their own identity, drawing on their own richly varied traditions.

Costa in architecture, like Heitor Villa-Lobos in music, Roberto Burle Marx in landscape gardening, Carlos Diegues, Nelson Pereira dos Santos and Glauber Rocha in films, Graciliano Ramos, José Lins do Rego, Erico Verissimo, João Guimarães Rosa, Rachel de Queiros, and others, in literature, all were delivering a similar message. It was the attempt, as described by the distinguished Brazilian historian, Sérgio Buarque de Holanda, speaking as a young man in the 1920s, to draw on native sources, to listen to "the profound voices of our race", while also seeking new freedom of form and idiom and freshness of style and image.

Kubitschek's period of office, deliberately, yet, sometimes, also unconsciously, drew on this tradition, gave voice to a new confidence, to a mood of national self-assertion and new vigour. Brasília gave concrete form, quite literally, to this spirit of the age. Its supreme architect was Oscar Niemeyer.

Niemeyer had produced the controversial designs for Pampulha, when Kubitschek was mayor of Belo Horizonte. The two men became friends. Lúcio Costa, who had designed, in 1948, the flowing complex of the apartment buildings in the landscaped gardens of Parque Guinle, in Rio de Janeiro, was the ideal partner for the design of Brasília. Together, Costa and Niemeyer produced one of the outstanding urban and architectural achievements of the twentieth century.

Costa's sketch for Brasília provided an "arrow" or a "fuselage", depending on one's interpretation, eight kilometres long and 250 metres wide, the *Eixo Monumental*, Monumental Axis. The head of the arrow, or nose of the plane, points east. At the head of this axis, is the *Praça dos Tres Poderes*, the Square of the Three Powers, with the Congress building, the President's palace and the Supreme Court.

These gleaming white symbols of the three arms of government have the Congress buildings in the centre, with the Senate and Chamber in two balanced half spheres. The Ministries run, in symetrical form and equal height, along the two sides of the axis, away from the "Three Powers", with the cathedral, on the western side, designed as a crown of thorns, half sunk into the ground. The most beautiful of the ministries is that of the Itamaraty, Foreign Affairs, a peaceful harmony of glass, water and plants.

Residential areas lie along the curve of the bow, or wings of the plane, with schools, shops and services. The old bus station now lies across the axis, with hotel and business centres on either side. The president's palace, the Palace of the Dawn, is close to the man-made lake, near which are most of the embassies and ministerial residences.

Brazilian architects, partly for reasons of economy, because of the cost of structural steel, chose reinforced concrete as their principal medium, one which also suited the tropics, and gave new freedoms of plastic line and form. Niemeyer was given the unrivalled opportunity of designing all the major buildings of Brasília, including those of the Three Powers, the 11 ministries, the cathedral and the presidential palace. He seized his chance and years later designed the monument and tribute to the city's founder, Juscelino Kubitschek, the *Memorial JK*, where Juscelino stands, smiling, and waving, in characteristic gesture, to the city which he brought to life.

The definitive move of government and foreign representation to Brasília was considerably slower than that of its construction. It took 10 years, for example, for the Itamaraty to move into the magnificent creation of Niemeyer, the *Palácio dos Arcos*, set in the water garden designed by Roberto Burle Marx, one of those outstanding artists born in the first decade of the century. Foreign embassies, too, dragged their feet, but were firmly asked to be in Brasília for the 150th anniversary of Brazilian independence, on Sept. 7, 1972.

Brasília had, and has, its critics, especially those who believe that the money spent on it could better have been used to alleviate growing pressures in other Brazilian cities, including the former capital. There were reservations about its impact on inflation and over the wisdom of creating a city of administrators and politicians, 960 kilometres into the interior, away from the usual political pressures of industrial society. Life in Brasília, it was argued, might produce a class of politicians and civil servants remote and isolated from the harsh realities of the rest of Brazil.

There is substance to these criticisms; but, steadily, Brasília has established itself as a city with its own life and identity. Its politicians are as much in tune, or out of tune, with national life as if they were in Rio de Janeiro or São Paulo, or in their home states, where, in any case, they spend much of their time. Nor is the city completely cut off from normal urban pressures. Satellite towns around it play an increasing part in local politics, including the current demand to turn the federal district into a state.

In 1980, the population of Brasília was 1,202,000. The estimate for 1990 is 1,943,000. Slowly, but steadily, its impact on the region, and on regions further west and north, has grown. The Brasília–Belém highway, for good or ill, directly affected Amazonia. By 1972, when the Itamaraty, at last, moved to Brasília, there were, already, an estimated 2,000,000 people strung along or near the road.

Brasília has given stimulus to the growth of Goiás and to political as well as economic change, as seen in the division of the state of Mato Grosso, to produce Mato Grosso, with about 1,786,000 inhabitants in 1990, and Mato Grosso do Sul, with 1,817,000. More recently, in 1988, the splitting of Goiás produced the new state of Tocantins.

The rapid development of the interior and the centre-west, in part stimulated by Brasília and the programme of road-building associated with it, is, arguably, a mixed blessing. Development has brought a price, including damage to the environment and to the indigenous population. The mushroom growth of cities threatens to reproduce much of the misery of the centre-south of the country. How these issues should be handled is a problem for Brazil's newly restored democratic régime, currently headed by President **Fernando Collor de Mello**. The seat of that government, and the centre of decision-making, thanks to the imagination of Kubitschek, and the labour of the men and women who built the city, is now firmly set in Brasília.

PF

BRAZIL. *Population*: 147,000,000 (1989 estimate). *Area*: 8,511,965 sq km. *GDP*: US$364,000 million, *GDP per capita*: $3,271. *Trade volume*: exports $34,400 million (1989); imports $18,300 million (1989). *Top five trade partners*: exports (1989): USA (26 per cent) Netherlands (7.8 per cent), Japan (7.1 per cent), West Germany (4.3 per cent), UK (3.2 per cent); imports (1989): USA (20.7 per cent), West Germany (9.4 per cent), Japan (6.6 per cent), Argentina (4.6 per cent), UK (2.8 per cent), (Note: the two principal trading partners are the EC (28.1 per cent of Brazil's exports in 1989 and 21.5 per cent of imports) and the USA (26.0 per cent of Brazil's exports in 1989 and 20.7 per cent of imports). *Defence spending*: 1.19 per cent of GDP. *Education spending*: 2.9 per cent of GDP. *Urban population as percentage of total*: (1988) 75. The six major metropolitan regions in 1989 held about 40,500,000 inhabitants, or about 28 per cent of the national population. *Birthrate*: 28.6 per 1,000. *Death rate*: 7.9 per 1,000. *Infant mortality*: 63.2 per 1,000. *Life expectancy*: 62.3 (men); 67.6 (women). There are considerable regional and social disparities.

Introduction. Brazil is a country of superlatives, both good and bad. As the fifth biggest country in the world by area and the sixth in population, it makes up roughly half of South America in both land and people. It shares common frontiers with every country except Ecuador and Chile. It has 4,579 miles of coastline and roughly 27,000 miles of inland waterways, including 70 per cent of, by far, the greatest river system in the world, the Amazon. It disputes with Canada the position of being the seventh or eighth largest western economy and the tenth in the world. The GDP of São Paulo state, alone, is greater than that of Argentina, while that of Brazil is larger than the GDP of all the other South American and Central American economies combined.

Other figures are equally startling. There was the success, for example, of the so-called "Economic Miracle", when, from 1968 to 1973, economic growth averaged 10 per cent a year, falling from 1974 to 1980, but still with an average annual rate of over 5 per cent. After problems in the early 1980s, there was, again, a rise of 5 per cent in GDP in 1984, with 8.3 in 1985 and 7.5 in 1986.

Such performance, often in an unfavourable international economic context, has underlined Brazil's potential for development and for becoming a major actor in world affairs, especially in the western hemisphere. So, too, has its diversified economy and the impressive statistics generated by it: the world's largest coffee producer, second in sugar, soya beans and cacao, second, too, in cattle and third in maize; but with most of its exports now being in manufactured or semi-manufactured goods. Brazil has the world's seventh largest steel production and the ninth largest car production; it is the second producer of iron ore and the eighth of aluminium.

Coupled with the country's other known vast natural resources, in hydro-electric potential, in forestry, in mineral reserves, including substantial discoveries of gold and cassiterite, it is understandable that some observers have been quick to seize on Stefan Zweig's now consecrated description of Brazil as "the country of the future" (*o país do futuro*). During the apparently heady successes of the military-backed régime in the late 1960s, it was even claimed, by government apologists, that "the future has arrived". Brazil, at the time, was often hailed, together with Japan, as the great success story of rapid capitalist development. Others, by contrast, were less sanguine, commenting, rather sourly, that Brazil had always had a great future, and always would.

Socio-economic background. The reason for such doubt is the other, more negative and disturbing side to Brazil's development and growth over the last three decades or more. One of its greatest resources, though not always recognized, is its *people*, now numbering about 150,000,000 though no-one really knows, since the 1990 census was not carried out, because of, as the government claimed, lack of resources.

Brazilians are rightly famed for their ready humour and hospitality, for the colour and vitality of their music, and their formidable skills on the football field, all of which have won for them respect and friendship around the world, yet, about 60 per cent of the population live in poverty and drudgery, and many in what officially is described as "misery", less than two minimum wages a month, less than $80, in a country where prices are generally high.

An estimated 90,000,000 Brazilians are undernourished, with malnutrition affecting 55 per cent of children under five years old. Sixty per cent live outside the formal economy, dependent on the informal sector. Most of the population are also badly housed, again needing to depend on informal, self-help housing, often in the *favelas*, or shanty-towns, around the great cities of the centre-south and north-east. These conditions are also being replicated in **Amazonia** and other areas, where rapid migration has not been supported by necessary infrastructure, so leading to a drift to towns and cities, which now are home to the majority of Amazonia's population.

Other social indicators reveal a similar picture, of lack of adequate health care, with preventable disease spread by inadequate housing and lack of sanitation. Infant mortality, nationally, is 68 per 1,000, but 122 per 1,000 in the north-east. The ratio of doctors to population is 1:1,200, as compared with 1:500 in the USA; but, again, there is great variation between regions and between town and country.

It is calculated that, in 1985, at least 22 per cent of the adult population was illiterate, with the quality of education falling since 1980, because the states have had difficulty in paying teachers and maintaining infrastructure. Ninety per cent of children do not continue school after the age of 10. Meanwhile, a nation justly famous for its love of children, has an estimated 16,000,000 children abandoned on its streets. These are often abused, tortured and even murdered, sometimes by the very policemen whose responsibility it is to protect them. Such abuses have aroused concern and protest both in Brazil and abroad.

Both urban and rural violence are on the increase, a formidable challenge to both federal and state governments. Rural killings are often linked to disputes over land. Often they are carried out by, or on behalf of, landowners resisting demands for change, as in the case of Chico Mendes, the rubber-tappers' leader, who was murdered in Acre in 1988. There is a powerful political lobby, the Ruralist Democratic Union (*União Democrática Ruralista*—UDR) to protect landowners' interests.

Other minorities, too, apart from children, are threatened or neglected, even when formally covered by the law and the new **Constitution** of October 1988. They include many of the country's remaining Indian population, sometimes, as in the case of the Yanomami, endangered by illegal gold mining on tribal lands and by mercury pollution from mining entering their rivers and food chains.

These wildcat miners, the *garimpeiros*, are, themselves, further evidence of problems caused by lack of social reforms, and by an unequal pattern of distribution of wealth, calculated to be the worst in the world. They are among the millions of poor Brazilians struggling daily for a living and, too often, not finding it.

For those who do survive into old age, life is generally hard, with little state provision for social security or other help, despite legislation dating back to the first government of **Getúlio Vargas** in the 1930s.

All these problems have been made worse by governments which, too often, have given little, or no, priority to the mass of the people and their needs, not least under the military-backed governments from 1964 to 1985, which explicitly chose a "development model" which gave priority to growth over distribution. These problems have been deepened by a burden of foreign debt, still, in 1989, standing at $114,000 million, with demands for debt service of $16,000 million, which could not be met.

There is also the internal debt, which, by mid-1989, was estimated at over $100,000 million, with service costing $20,000 million, even heavier than on the foreign debt. This, in turn, has fuelled a huge public sector deficit, which, in 1989, the IMF was insisting should be reduced, by the end of the year, from 6 per cent of GDP to 2 per cent, another impossible task.

All this in turn has produced rampant **inflation**, which successive governments have failed to control, despite a series of dramatic Plans and interventions, especially since the return to civilian government in 1985. Inflation currently remains the greatest challenge to both economic development, social cohesion and political stability. The yearly rate for 1990, despite the **New Brazil, or Collor, Plan**, introduced in March, was an unprecedented 1,800 per cent, though the figure was partly distorted by extremely high rates for the first three months. A new issue is how far the Collor Plan, in its attempt to control inflation, may be pushing the country more deeply into dangerous recession.

Brazil's process of development in recent years is, then, at best, a mixed one, overhung, or overshadowed, by searching questions. Nor has its recent experience greatly been helped by the international financial and business community, which, too readily, has seen Brazil, like the "Third World" more generally, as a source of profit and quick returns, rather than a genuine partner in mutual development.

To a large extent, it may be argued, many of the problems facing Brazil in 1991 are a result of political priorities and policies in the recent past, partly, but not solely, the legacy of the military régime and the strategists. With the start of the

"New Republic" in 1985, there was general hope for new priorities and redefinition of policies. Under the government of President **José Sarney** (1985–1990) those hopes were sadly frustrated.

November–December 1989 saw the first direct elections for president since that of **Jânio Quadros** in 1960. The young, energetic president now elected, **Fernando Collor de Mello**, has promised a new start and has shown vigour and courage in trying to tackle the crucial issues he faces, above all, inflation, but others, too, such as the future of Amazonia, and protection of the environment. How his government succeeds may well determine how far Brazil can realise its enormous potential for development between now and the turn of the century. This is a critical decade for Brazil.

Geographical background. While many of the problems bequeathed to recent governments stem from the 21 years of military-backed régime, others have much deeper historical roots. One is the problem of regional balance and disparity, which has been made worse in the last few decades by massive internal migration, first from the economically troubled north-east to the much more prosperous centre-south and, more recently, from both the north-east and the south into the centre-west and the newly opened regions of Amazonia. In the 1970s alone, more than 24,000,000 people moved from the town of their birth.

The more recent move west and north into new agricultural regions in Mato Grosso, Rondônia, Acre and Pará has largely been that of families, moving along the new roads, looking for land to work, producing extremely rapid growth in population, including the towns and cities. The population of Rondônia, for example, has grown from 503,000 in 1980 to a projected 952,000 in 1990, while that of Acre has expanded from 307,000 in 1980 to a 1990 projected figure of 405,000.

The more long-term movement has been that from the north-east into the cities and urban areas of the centre-south. In 1960, 46 per cent of Brazil's population was urban, rising to 59 per cent in 1970 and 75 per cent by the census of 1980.

The north-east, from which the bulk of these migrants have come, in search of work and a better life, has long been the most troubled region of Brazil economically. It is made up of nine states, which with their population in 1980 and projected population in 1990, are: Maranhão (4,097,000; 5,215,000); Piauí (2,188,000; 2,692,000); Ceará (5,389,000; 6,741,800); Rio Grande do Norte (1,934,600; 2,318,900); Paraíba (2,823,300; 3,247,600); Pernambuco (6,261,100; 7,360,900); Alagoas (2,020,600; 2,420,400); Sergipe (1,162,000; 1,416,600); and Bahia (9,635,800; 11,738,000). The total of 42,800,000 represents 28.5 per cent of Brazil's currently estimated population.

The north-east has three main geographical zones. The first is the *zona da mata*, the fertile coastal zone, principally devoted to sugar. Second, is the *agreste*, an intermediate zone of mixed cultivation, which produces most of the region's vegetables. The third is the much drier *sertão* where *vaqueiros* (cowboys), in traditional leather clothing to protect them from the sharp, spiny *caatinga*, raise cattle, and where peasant families try to make a living from the harsh land.

Many of the social and economic problems of the north-east have been linked to natural disasters, especially the severe droughts which regularly scourge large areas, particularly the *sertão*. Others are rooted in Brazil's colonial past, especially in the sugar industry established by the Portuguese within a few decades of Brazil's official discovery in 1500. At first the country was prized mainly for its red-dyewood (*pau do brasil*, or *caesalpina enchinata*) much used in the European textile trade. King Manoel I (1498–1521) made it a monopoly of the crown and, while Portugal attached much greater importance to Africa and Asia, 1,200 tonnes of dyewood were sent to Lisbon in the first decade of the sixteenth century, mostly for re-export to Antwerp.

But it was sugar which dominated the economy of Brazil throughout the seventeenth and eighteenth centuries. By 1570 there were about 60 mills (*engenhos*), producing about 2,000 tonnes annually, with, already, 23 mills in Pernambuco and 18 in Bahia. Sugar attracted more Portuguese migrants. By 1630, there were 350 mills. Brazil was now the largest sugar producer in the Atlantic and, throughout the century, sugar represented 90 per cent of Brazil's export value. By the mid-seventeenth century, north-east Brazil was probably the richest region in all the Americas.

Sugar also left legacies which still persist, not least in the land-holding system and social structure of the north-east. Partly to resist the threat of French settlement, King João II (1521–57) introduced a system of 14 captaincies, dividing the whole coastline of Brazil, in bands of various breadths, which, notionally, extended indefinitely into the interior, well beyond the line of the Treaty of Tordesillas in 1494. These were to be given to hereditary *donatários*, with widespread jurisdiction over the land and its people, including the founding of towns and granting of land. Some of these "donatories" established the first successful settlements, notably in Pernambuco, around the new ports of Santos and São Vincente, and near Piratinga. Already there was the concept of concentrated holding of large tracts of land, one which was to persist throughout Brazil's history.

The most important direct legacies in the north-east come, however, not from the *donatory* system, but from the sweetness of sugar and the sweat of slavery. The nature of sugar production, with the need to have the mill near to where the crop was grown and harvested, required large capital investment. The owners of the mills, the *senhores de engenho*, became a white aristocracy, living on their plantations. Below them were other farmers, themselves slave owners, and a whole social system grew around the *casa grande*, the great house, and the slave quarters, the *senzala*.

The plantation society and sugar economy of the north-east was dependent on slavery. Black slaves were imported in the middle of the sixteenth century, with over 50,000 arriving from Angola between 1570 and 1600, with perhaps 3,000 to 4,000 in Bahia by the mid-1580s and up to 8,000 in Pernambuco. By the end of the century, 70 per cent of blacks in Brazil worked in sugar. About 4,000 to 5,000 were imported in the seventeenth century and over 1,000,000 in the next. By 1800, excluding forest Indians, one-third of all Brazilians were slaves, with over 60 per cent of the whole population black or mulatto and roughly one-third white.

The impact of sugar and slavery on the social, racial and cultural pattern of north-east Brazil is still tangible, combined with the contribution of the *caboclo* culture in other parts of the region. With the steady decline of the north-eastern economy, continuing to the present, repeated attempts have been made to stimulate growth and development, including government agencies, such as the Superintendency for the North-East (SUDENE) and various schemes of tax incentives, to stimulate industrial and other related development. Some of this work has been entrusted to skilled economists, such as Celso Furtado, in the 1960s. Other initiatives have reflected attempts by politicians, not least under the military régime, to develop a regional clientelistic base. The problems of the north-east figure large on the agenda of President Collor, himself from Alagoas, following in office a president from Maranhão.

Other important colonial issues, which still persist, are those which saw the development of the centre-south, especially in the modern states of Minas Gerais, Rio de Janeiro and São Paulo, resulting in a shift of population, wealth and political power from the north-east to this more temperate region, much of it just outside the tropics. Present population figures for the centre-south are:

	1980	1990
Minas Gerais	13,635,200	15,831,800
Espírito Santo	2,062,100	2,523,900
Rio de Janeiro	11,508,200	14,133,300
São Paulo	25,521,200	33,069,900
Total	52,726,700	65,558,900

One group important in this process of developing the centre-south, were the roving *bandeiras* or expeditions, made up mainly of *mamelucos* (European and Indian mixed-bloods). They were based in and around the town of São Paulo. This town, like many others, had sprung from Jesuit missionary activity throughout the country, especially the policy of creating *aldeias*, villages or mission settlements, equivalent to the *reducciones* (reductions) of Spanish America. The *bandeirantes* penetrated deep into the interior, including raids on Jesuit reductions in Paraguay, in search of Indian slaves.

The *bandeirantes* partly enjoyed government sponsorship, especially in search of minerals, mainly gold, silver and emeralds. At the end of the seventeenth century, they found gold in what soon became known as Minas Gerais (General Mines). A gold rush began, which rapidly drew men from the coast and the plantations, where sugar already was in decline, through competition from the Caribbean.

Immigrants came, too, from Portugal and the Azores. By 1775, Minas Gerais had a population of 300,000, half of them slaves, and about 20 per cent of Brazil's population. It was to remain the most populous state till well into the twentieth century, the only heavily populated interior state in a country where, even today, most people live within a few hundred kilometres of the coast.

The gold, and later, the diamond wealth of Minas Gerais, not only developed that state, with its wonderful legacy of baroque architecture and sculpture. It also stimulated agriculture, to feed the mining camps and the towns into which they were transformed, including ranching in the most southern region of Brazil, which was to become, as Rio Grande do Sul, one of Brazil's most politically important states, sharing the *gaúcho* culture of neighbouring Uruguay and Argentina.

Mineral wealth in Minas Gerais also brought the development of Rio de Janeiro as an outport for the rich exports to Portugal. In 1763, this city took over from Salvador da Bahia as Brazil's capital, an eloquent statement of a shift in wealth and power.

Gold production began to decline in the second half of the eighteenth century and gold exports never exceeded in value those of sugar; but the shift to the centre-south was already determined. The position of Rio de Janeiro was then strengthened by the arrival of Dom João VI and the Portuguese court in 1808, escaping from Napoleon's army.

After independence in 1822, and the start of the Empire, came an even more important impulse, in the form of Brazil's next major commodity boom and new economic cycle, led by coffee.

Coffee, originally centred in the Paraíba valley, then moved into the state of São Paulo, as the railways were built between 1852 and 1868, with the link to Santos, across the mountain range, in 1868. By the end of the century, Brazil had 66.8 per cent of the world's coffee production and coffee accounted for 50 per cent of the country's exports, produced and exported from São Paulo.

The enriched coffee oligarchy began to exercise political power commensurate with their economic role. They were an important element in ending slavery in 1888 and in the move to a republic in 1889. They also attracted important waves of European immigrants, especially Italians, and gave early direction to demands for industrialization. Throughout the "Old Republic", from 1889–1930, they largely shared power with Minas Gerais and, to a lesser degree, with Rio Grande do Sul.

The political influence of those three states has never really waned, and one of the principal issues now facing President Collor is his need to work with and conciliate the current political leaders of Rio de Janeiro, São Paulo and Rio Grande do Sul, opposition state governors elected in October and November 1990.

The wave of European immigration brought further profound changes to the centre-south and to the racial and social mixture of Brazil. Before 1850, only about 19,000 immigrants had chosen to seek work in a country still dependent on slavery. São Paulo private enterprise then began to attract immigrants with 60,000, in over 60 colonies, from 1847 to 1857. As the coffee boom grew, immigrants began to arrive at an average rate of about 15,000 a year, a movement which was to last until the 1920s. Many were northern Italians, hard-working, able people, who provided labour both for the coffee economy and São Paulo's nascent industrialization.

By the 1920s, São Paulo, the *cidade dos italianos* (the city of Italians) was the second biggest Italian city in the world, after Rome. These and other immigrants, notably Germans, also brought new energy, talents and traditions to other parts of southern Brazil, to Paraná, Santa Catarina, and Rio Grande do Sul. These were later to stimulate the timber industry in Paraná and, above all, coffee and, then, soya, and the mining industry of Santa Catarina. Other immigrants, too, were to make important contributions, such as the large community of Japanese in São Paulo, who now largely control market gardening, and the Italians in Rio Grande do Sul, who were to develop Brazil's wine production.

The political dominance of the centre-south has continued. In the presidential elections of 1989, out of a, recently, greatly enlarged electorate of over 82,000,000, the state of São Paulo had 16,800,000 voters and Rio de Janeiro 7,500,000. 44 per cent of voters live in these two states, plus Minas Gerais, while the six biggest states, these, plus Rio Grande do Sul, Paraná and Bahia, contain as many as 64 per cent of potential voters.

Meanwhile, for most of the time, the rest of Brazil, the north and the centre-west remained, and, to a degree, remain, marginal to the economic and political life of the country. These are the regions of vast tropical rain-forests and of the *cerrado*, savannah, most of which, till recent years, remained virtually outside the national economy. One important period of exception, in terms of the economy, was the Amazonian rubber boom in the nineteenth century, which brought short-lived, but dramatic, prosperity to Manaus and the rubber barons. At the high point of the rubber economy, it provided almost 40 per cent of national export earnings, almost as much as coffee.

Unfortunately, by 1913, the virtual monopoly control by Brazil of the world's rubber economy was destroyed by the impact of cultivated rubber in South East Asia. Despite many subsequent attempts, it has not proved possible, mainly because of environmental factors, to grow the *hevea brasiliensis* in plantations in Brazil. The exploitation of Brazilian rubber has, therefore, remained through individual and poor rubber tappers.

The main economic impact of the north of

	1980	*1990 est*
Rondônia	503,000	952,000
Acre	307,000	405,000
Amazonas	1,447,000	1,999,000
Roraima	82,000	125,000
Pará	3,506,000	4,910,000
Amapá	180,000	248,000

Brazil now comes from mining in its various forms but the region has yet to find an overall strategy for sustainable development, which, again, is one of the key issues facing the Collor government. Meanwhile, its population, already substantial in some states, is growing fast in others. Figures for 1980 and projected for 1990 are set out above.

With the changing role of state governors, again, since 1982, directly elected, and with the greater powers given to the states in the 1988 Constitution, it is probable that the north will want a greater say in its own future than previously was allowed. This, again, could be a problem for Collor, in this case, because of resistance he may meet towards his more enlightened environmental policies.

Finally, there is the centre-west, traditionally very thinly populated, and of little political weight. This, again, is a region of rain-forest and *cerrado* and contains the beautiful swampland, the *Pantanal*, the conservation of which, like that of Amazonia and the *Mata Atlántica* (Atlantic Forest), is a current political issue facing the Collor government. **Juscelino Kubitschek's** dream of creating **Brasília**, inaugurated in 1960, was partly to open up this region. Slowly, it is happening. Brasília, the Federal District, is now a fully functioning capital. Its population in 1980, of 1,202,000, is now about 1,943,000. Signs of political, as well as economic, stirrings in the region are reflected in the division of the state of Mato Grosso, in 1978, to produce Mato Grosso (1,169,000 and 1,786,000) and Mato Grosso do Sul (1,399,000 and 1,817,000) and the splitting of Goiás (3,967,000 and 4,983,000) in 1988, to produce the new state of Tocantins. This brings the number of states to 26, plus the Federal District, some of whose inhabitants wish to turn it into a state.

Meanwhile, the population of São Paulo state, alone, in 1990 is estimated at 34,000,000, while, in 1989, the six major metropolitan regions (Recife, Salvador, Belo Horizonte, Rio de Janeiro, São Paulo and Porto Alegre) account for 40,500,000 people, or about 28 per cent of the national total. In 1970, the census listed five cities of over 1,000,000 inhabitants: by 1987 there were 11.

It is in these great urban centres that many of the new government's problems lie, of poverty, unemployment, housing, education, public health, public transport, and public security, without exhausting the list. How it may respond to them has to be seen in the context of Brazil's earlier political and economic experience and within the constraints which President Collor and his government may be expected to work.

Outline of political history. Brazil is not a "new nation", a newcomer on the world stage. It was a nation state, with a liberal constitution, only a few decades after the USA, and well before some European countries, such as Italy or Germany, had achieved political integration. None of the issues of contemporary debate is new in Brazil, though the terms used to describe them may now be different.

By the early nineteenth century there was informed discussion of the nature of representative democratic government, of the balance between different branches of government, of the party system, of the proper role of the armed forces or the church. There was debate, too, throughout the century, on the nature of the labour force, on inflation, and on the relations between Brazil and the international economy. This included the due response to foreign investment and the weight which should be allowed to foreign economic interests in influencing the shape of exports or the exchange rate.

One of the major legacies of the nineteenth century was *coronelismo*, a system of rural boss politics. The name came from the fact that, in many *municípios* of the interior, a predominant landowner or political boss was often "colonel" of the National Guard, a largely ceremonial force created in 1831. The *coronel* was the local pivot of a well-articulated process of political control, based on patronage, which ran throughout the political system. He provided services for his clients, who, in turn, delivered the vote. The heads of political clans then gave support to representatives at provincial and national level, gathered in a two-party system of Liberals and Conservatives. There was little to distinguish the two parties. If there were a deadlock, the Emperor, using the "moderating power" conferred on him by the Constitution of 1824, could arbitrate between them, dissolve Parliament, and avert the threat of anarchy or violence. In the twentieth century, the armed forces tried to abrogate to themselves this "moderating power", alleging that it was their responsibility to hold the ring for democracy, as defined by them.

Under the military regime, when the normal "bargaining" of democratic politics was suppressed, as allegedly, being "corrupt", there arose, in its place, an interlocking system of state-directed patronage. Former military officers received directorships, to steer companies towards government favours. Government ministers seeded their political careers by building clientage networks. One of the main barriers to redemocratization, even when pursued by government, was the entrenched interest of those whose patronage and power would be threatened by such a change.

Coronelismo still persists, in modified form. Sometimes, direct services are commuted into money payments, but not always. *Cabos eleitorais*, "electoral bosses", still bargain for votes, not just in the interior, but also in big cities. One of the principal, justified criticisms of the **Party of the Brazilian Democratic Movement** (*Partido do Movimento Democrático Brasileiro*—PMDB) under the "New Republic", after 1985, was that it was riddled with *coronelismo* and with *fisiologismo*, the scramble for office in return for political support. A much commented feature of the Congressional elections of October 1990 was how they revealed the persistence of the old political class, direct personalist appeal and clientelist traditions.

Another legacy is the political power of the **armed forces**. By contrast with Spanish America, the armed forces in Brazil did not play a major role in achieving independence. Their status was relatively low until the Paraguayan War, the War of the Triple Alliance, (1864–1870). This brought an increase in numbers, salaries, and training and a rise in prestige. The war was an important turning-point in terms of the politicization of the armed forces and their perception of their due political role, which was to be a major factor in the political life of the nation.

The army contributed to the abolition of slavery, mainly by refusing to hunt down runaway slaves, and, increasingly, the officer class began to see itself as "modernizing", under the influence of Comtean positivism, taught in the Escola Militar, the Military College. The officer class generally disparaged civilian politicians, whom they regarded as, at best, inept and often corrupt. They became something of a class apart and cultivated the notion that they had some sort of privileged Rousseauesque insight into the needs of the nation. They also developed an idiosyncratic idea of democracy.

Army leaders were responsible for deposing Emperor Pedro II in November 1889, and introducing the Republic. The first two presidents were army officers. In July 1922, a brief revolt of young officers, the *tenentes*, was ended, when they were shot down on the pavement above Copacabana beach. Their ideas and aims were vague, but were developed by other officers, critical of the oligarchy and demanding reform. In July 1924, *tenentes* rebelled and held São Paulo before setting off on a "long march" through the interior.

Their "Column" was led by Miguel Costa and Luís Carlos Prestes, later to be head of the Brazilian Communist Party (Partido Comunista Brasileiro—PCB), and generally is known as the *Prestes Column*. The march lasted two years and covered about 14,000 miles. It focused public attention on the rebels' demands and reminded the coastal, urban élite of the poverty and misery of the interior, but did not seriously threaten the government. What did, eventually, in 1930, end the First Republic was a disagreement among the political élites, largely under the pressure of the Great Depression. The revolution of 1930, formally led by the governor of Rio Grande do Sul, **Getúlio Vargas**, was successful, when, as in 1889, the leaders of the armed forces decided that they should support him.

Getúlio Vargas (1930–45) The Republic of 1889 to 1930 was held together by a working pact among the richest and most powerful states, especially after 1906. Till then São Paulo had dominated national politics with three successive presidents since 1894. There was now a working alliance between São Paulo and Minas Gerais, which, in effect, lasted till 1930, the so-called *café com leite* (coffee with cream) system, named after the two states' main products, coffee and cattle. Of the 10 presidents from 1894 to 1930, five were from São Paulo and three from Minas Gerais. One of the features of the 1930 revolt was opposition from the north-east and Rio Grande do Sul, demanding a fuller political role.

Politics in the "Old Republic" were governed by the Constitution of 1891, which gave considerable autonomy to the states, especially in fiscal matters but also in allowing state armed forces, which in, for example, São Paulo and Minas Gerais, were better trained, paid and housed than the federal army garrisons. Especially in terms of taxation, the states in Brazil had more jurisdiction than their equivalents in the USA. There was a constant tension between the states and the federal government, which still continues. The Constitution of October 1988, as the most recent expression of this tussle, has redressed the earlier centralist imbalance, imposed after 1964, by giving more weight and resources to the states and *municípios*.

Vargas, coming from a centralist, authoritarian, Comtean tradition, in Rio Grande do Sul, at once sought to curb the powers of the states as enjoyed under the "Old Republic", seen in a ceremonial burning of state flags. The state armed forces were reduced in power and status and the federal army greatly strengthened. He tried to introduce a national civil service, based on merit, and greatly enlarged the economic role of the federal state, partly, in the belief that the only way out of recession was through State investment and State control. In this, he was also influenced by the military and theorists. This central role of the State, as an engine of growth, development and national security, was to continue for, at least, the next half century.

The repressive authoritarian president against whom the *tenentes* revolted was Artur Bernardes (1922–26), a *mineiro* (i.e. coming from Minas Gerais). Presented with demands for change, he replied that the "social question" was one for the police. The *tenentes*, at least, had focused attention on the growing social tensions, urban as well as rural.

Others who now were demanding social and economic reforms and wider political participation included many European immigrants, coming from a different political tradition in, for example, Spain or Italy. There had been stirrings of working class demands, even in the nineteenth century. In 1891 stevedores in Recife founded a union and the following year were on strike. In 1903, 25,000 textile workers in São Paulo were on strike for 20 days, causing the federal government to pass a law the following year, allowing the expulsion of foreigners. This was partly in reply to the activity of foreign anarchists in the early organizations, especially in São Paulo. The Socialist Party, founded in São Paulo in 1902, had its newspaper in Italian, *Avanti*!

Of all direct political legacies to contemporary Brazil, that of Getúlio Vargas and his first 15 years in power is the most evident. Vargas and his government touched Brazilian life at every point and much of what followed was, in large part, a response or reaction to Vargas.

The Revolution of 1930 was much more than a quarrel among political élites responding to economic crisis. The political crisis came first. Vargas came to power with broad support in all social classes, a fact recognized by the armed forces' leaders.

Throughout his political career, Vargas never stopped learning, but, equally, he always reflected his *gaúcho* background from Rio Grande do Sul, with its strong, centralized executive, a concern for "progress", but, also, a sensitivity to social issues and the need for change. His first government was heavy with fellow *gaúchos*. One such was Oswaldo Aranha who had largely directed the revolution of 1930. Another was Lindolfo Collor, one of the author's of the "Liberal Alliance" programme of 1929–30. He was trained in pharmacy, then in the social sciences, had written a study of Garibaldi in Brazil and, from 1923, edited *A Federação*, the leading political paper of Rio Grande do Sul. His father's name was João Boeckel, but after his father's death, he took the name of his stepfather. He was a Protestant, who spoke German. He had served as a Federal Deputy on the Foreign Relations Committee of the Chamber of Deputies. He knew about European corporatism and was deeply concerned about social issues. He was the maternal grandfather of Fernando Collor de Mello. Vargas chose him to head the new Ministry of Labour, Commerce and Industry, popularly called the "Ministry of the Revolution".

Lindolfo Collor's legacy was two-fold. His two years in office saw the introduction of far-reaching social and labour legislation. This represented welcome recognition of the State's responsibilities in these areas and, on paper, gave Brazil advanced social welfare and labour legislation. In practice, it provided the means for more direct government control of workers and their actions, a major step towards the corporatist system which formally was adopted in the *Estado Novo* of 1937.

The new union legislation, in particular, severely limited any self-generated action from the working class. Now only one union was allowed for each trade, so that, of the 1,494 unions existing before 1930, only 364 were recognized by the new Ministry. This reflected, as Collor said of Decree No. 19,770 of March 1931, "the government's determination to incorporate the trade union movement into the state and the laws of the Republic". Later legislation greatly increased such "incorporation", including the introduction of a trade union levy (*impôsto sindical*), by which a worker had to pay the equivalent of one day's wages into a fund administered through the Ministry of Labour to the unions. The fund could not support strike action. In due course, the trade union movement come to be best understood almost as an arm of government, rather than as an autonomous organization of the working class. Their leaders were popularly known as *pelegos*. A *pelego* is a sheepskin which goes under the saddle, to give a more comfortable ride. The *impôsto sindical* continued into 1990, when it was ended by Lindolfo Collor's grandson, as part of the more general disengagement of the state.

The corporatist nature of the trade union movement was one of the most important political legacies of the 1930s. Another notable development was the appearance of mass political movements, both of the right and left, aiming at political mobilization at a national, rather than a state, level. One early attempt, after 1930, was the "Revolutionary Legion", a project cultivated by Oswaldo Aranha and other civilian and *tenente* leaders. This was strongly nationalist and authoritarian. It sought a "Brazilian" solution to Brazil's problems and, in São Paulo, claimed, at its peak in 1931, a membership of 17,000. It clashed with state political machines and fell apart with the São Paulo revolt of 1932.

The driving ideas behind the Legion still persisted, reshaped in a movement which had substantial appeal and support, the Brazilian Integralist Action (*Ação Integralista Brasileira*—AIB), formed in 1932, by a right-wing intellectual, Plínio Salgado. Drawing on European fascist models, it rejected any idea of class conflict, as a derivative of foreign political influences alien to Brazil. Its aims had substantial support among white-collar workers, the middle class, army officers, some clergy, and the middle-aged.

The other mass movement was the **National Liberation Alliance** (*Aliança Nacional Libertadora*—ANL), organized in 1935, as Brazil's version of the Popular Front. The *Integralistas*, too, were outmanoeuvred and defeated. Throughout 1936 and 1937, the Federal army was strengthened at the expense of the state forces, and a political threat from Rio Grande do Sul was defused. In part, this was linked to reaction to an alleged Communist plot, the "Cohen Plan", which was part of a wider move to cancel the presidential election of 1936. The *coup* was set for Nov. 15, but brought forward to Nov. 10, when the *Estado Novo* was introduced, to exclude the electorate, shelve the presidential election and impose an authoritarian, corporatist constitution, backed by the power of a now greatly strengthened federal army. In May 1938, the *Integralistas*, frustrated in their ambitions to direct and control national policies, attempted a *coup* against Vargas: it failed, and, in June 1939, Plínio Salgado sailed to comfortable exile in Portugal.

Estado Novo. The *Estado Novo*, from 1937 to 1945, left indelible marks on Brazilian politics. Many of its theorists and supporters played an important role in the régime imposed on the nation in 1964. Much of its legislation, as well as its political culture, dominated the post-war period, still hindering the creation of a more genuinely open political system. Authoritarian corporatism had widespread support throughout the country, especially in the industrial and business community, who saw it as a means of producing, relatively rapidly, a docile labour force, while supporting a basically nationalist, protectionist industrialization process.

The *Estado Novo* greatly increased the personal power and patronage of Vargas and strengthened the role of the State, supported by the federal army and by the Department of Press and Propaganda, which provided widespread media censorship. Vargas also had his own appointed *interventors* who replaced elected state governors. Brazil's entry into World War II on the Allies' side, sending an expeditionary force to Italy, made it increasingly difficult to maintain an authoritarian corporatist system at home.

Vargas was quick to realize this unsustainable anomaly and prepared for change. He began to develop another line inherited from Rio Grande do Sul, namely *trabalhismo* ("labourism"), concern for the working class, their demands and their support.

This was not a sudden break with the past. In annual Labour Day speeches he had stressed the dignity of labour and the contribution made by workers to national development. He introduced the minimum wage and promised a new Labour Code and to raise health standards. At the same time, he rejected the idea of class struggle as an alien European import, urging class co-operation.

Helped by the Minister of Labour, Alexandre Marcondes Filho, he stressed the changes to be introduced after the war, drawing on the energies of the "organized working classes", "new people, full of energy and hope".

Still, criticism grew, with increased demands for elections, parallels being drawn between Vargas and the behaviour of **Juan Domingo Perón** in **Argentina**. Vargas promised elections, but still the chorus grew, especially, by April 1945, from a broad, right-of-centre, anti-Vargas coalition, the National Democratic Union (*União Democrática Nacional*—UDN), which included many of those who had broken with Vargas since 1930.

Vargas fixed the presidential election for Dec. 2 and announced the creation of two parties. One was to stem from Marcondes Filho's labour machine and its base in *trabalhismo*. This was the **Brazilian Labour Party** (*Partido Trabalhista Brasileiro*—PTB). The other would draw its support from the wide-ranging patronage system, attached to the federal *interventores* in all the states. The aim was to combine both urban, industrial and rural patronage. This second party was to be the Social Democratic Party (*Partido Social Democrático*—PSD). These three parties were to dominate political life from 1945 to 1964 and their influence persists.

Vargas then strengthened suspicion that he might still try to cancel the elections and seek to continue in office, as in 1937, possibly following the example of Perón, who, on Oct. 17, 1945 had been recalled to power by mass popular support. The end came when General Góes Monteiro, the Minister of War, and General Eurico Gaspar Dutra, two corner-stones of the *Estado Novo*, decided it should. Góes resigned on Oct. 29. An ultimatum was issued to Vargas next day, and on

Aug. 30 1945, he quietly left for Rio Grande do Sul, leaving office, as he had entered it, on the decision of the leaders of the armed forces.

That same influence was reflected in the fact that, in the first presidential election in 15 years, both candidates were senior military officers, General Dutra (PSD) and Brigadier Eduardo Gomes (UDN), who had been one of the survivors of the *tenente* rising in Copacabana in 1922. Dutra won, with 56 as against 34 per cent of votes, with nearly 10 per cent for the candidate of the newly legalized Communist party. The electorate was now about 7,000,000, men and women, as compared with 2,000,000 men in 1930. In the 1945 Congressional election, nearly 6,000,000 people voted. The UDN won 26.3 per cent, as compared to a combined total for the PSD and PTB of 53.4 per cent. One of the senators elected was Vargas.

Eurico Gaspar Dutra (1946–1950). The politics of the next 18 years, until the *coup* of 1964, were developed under the Constitution of 1946. It was a liberal document, which extended the vote to people over 18, with some exceptions, mainly illiterates and enlisted men in the armed forces. This excluded over half the population. It also retained, virtually intact, the whole body of social and labour legislation from the *Estado Novo*.

One of the main features of the period was a constant struggle between left and right, between reformers, seeking wider distribution of resources, and those who resisted such demands. Another was the political tension between civilians and the armed forces, with a growing body of army officers in favour of direct intervention, or, even a *coup*. Another, related, issue, was the growing influence of the **United States**, especially in the period of the "Cold War", which was also linked to the debate over "nationalist" control of the economy.

The period of Dutra's government showed that authoritarian responses died hard. Despite the high hopes expressed in 1945, and the new constitution of 1946, it was a time of reaction and repression. Anti-trust legislation, introduced by Vargas, was quickly repealed by the *interim* Linhares government, under United States pressure.

The electoral success of the PCB was confirmed in State elections in January and supplementary elections for Congress. Again the PCB won about 10 per cent of the vote, even though there were now 14 competing parties. Party membership was now estimated at about 200,000, with strong party influence in the Confederation of Brazilian Workers (*Confederação dos Trabalhadores do Brasil*—CTB) as it developed from September 1946. Such success alarmed the armed forces' leaders and the UDN.

The 1946 constitution allowed the exclusion of "anti-democratic parties". As a result of its success in democratic voting, the PCB was declared illegal in May 1947 and, in October, the Senate voted to remove all Communists from elected office. The measure won the approval of military leaders, the UDN, and commentators in the USA. It was followed by action against working class groups, notably the Confederation of Brazilian Workers.

Economically, the Dutra government favoured liberalism and free trade, allowing the free entry of consumer goods and their imports, which rapidly drained the foreign reserves of $800,000,000 with which the government had started in 1945. Stimulus to production for the domestic market, produced an annual growth rate for 1945 to 1951 of about 6 per cent. The negative side of the record was a steady decline in the real minimum wage, from 100 in 1944, to 58 in 1948 and to 50.9 in 1950. Resources were being transferred from the poor to the rich under a government committed to free enterprise and capitalism, under the strong influence of the United States. Here was a ready target for nationalist, reformist critics as the 1950 elections drew near.

Vargas ran a vigorous campaign, as the first candidate to fly all over Brazil. As candidate for the PTB with the support of the PSD, and having made sure that the army leaders would accept his candidature, Vargas identified himself with the new, urban, industrializing Brazil, especially its working population, as contrasted with social privilege and subservience to foreign interests, which, he alleged, characterized the UDN. He won 48.73 per cent of the vote, of an electorate numbering just under 11,500,000 namely, 22 per cent of a population of slightly less than 55,000,000.

Getúlio Vargas (1950–1954). In his second period in office, Vargas was especially concerned to redress the loss in real wages suffered under Dutra, to raise the standard of living of the mass of the people and to address the question of Brazil's relations with the international financial and business community. He promised no miracles and proceeded cautiously. Dutra had introduced a law limiting repatriation of capital and remission of profits, but it had been skilfully circumvented. Vargas, in January 1952, imposed a limit of 10 per cent on profit remittances. It was a modest intervention, surrounded by cautious language, but provoked fierce criticism from the right and from abroad.

A major issue was the structure and control of Brazil's **oil** industry. Again, Vargas was cautious and moderate, aware of the need for foreign investment and technology, but unwilling to lose too much control to foreign oil companies. His original bill, of December 1951, proposed a mixed corporation, with majority state ownership, but pressure from both inside and outside Congress, including some from military spokesmen, concerned over "national security", demanded more state control. The law establishing Petrobrás, in October 1953, provided state control of Brazilian oil, with Juracy Magalhães, an army general and now a prominent UDN leader, former *tenente*, as its first president. The decision was not, as his critics alleged, a narrowly nationalist gesture by Vargas.

In his election speeches, Vargas had appealed for unity behind a government which was not the tool of parties, groups, classes, or interest, but which would work for all classes, for all the people, a call which has a very contemporary ring to it. At the same time, Vargas was genuinely concerned over the fall in the minimum wage, which had not been adjusted since 1943, with its real purchasing power halved between 1945 and 1951. In December 1951, he raised the minimum wage, which, still, barely kept up with recent rises in the cost of living.

He also made easier the use of the right to strike, which had been curbed by Dutra's law of January 1946, requiring that strike attempts should be submitted to the Ministry of Labour, and he removed the "ideology test" (*atestado de ideologia*), imposed by Dutra on union elections. Vargas was concerned to allow fuller expression to an industrial working class which, between 1940 and 1953 had almost doubled in size, from about 750,000 to 1,500,000. These measures brought the question of wages, rewards and distribution to the forefront. One response to these enlarged freedoms for the trade union movement was an extensive strike in São Paulo in March and April 1953, which affected 300,000 workers, coming soon after the election of **Jânio Quadros** as mayor of São Paulo. The strike was spearheaded by 30,000 textile workers, but rapidly spread to steelworkers and many other categories. There were clashes in São Paulo between pickets and the Department of Political and Social Order (*Departamento de Ordem Política e Social*—DOPS), who asked for help from the *Força Pública* and the federal army. Employers offered rises of 20–30 per cent. Quadros spoke of the need for 100 per cent. Vargas was blamed for the strike by the right-wing press, by the UDN and by some military officers. The *Estado de São Paulo*, and other conservative papers, said that he wanted to foment trouble, in order to stage a *coup* to continue in office.

Such attacks grew in intensity, even when Vargas introduced moderate cabinet changes in mid-1953, including Oswaldo Aranha, a highly respected politician and statesman, as Minister of Finance. The aim was to curb inflation and solve an alarming balance of payments deficit, which, by June 1953, was $1,000 million, largely because of imports during the Korean War. Aranha's brief was to cut public spending, limit credit and impose stringent exchange controls, all of which were contained in the *Aranha Plan* of October 1953. Unfortunately, this very orthodox, responsible plan found little support from foreign backers or from the United States.

The appointment of Aranha could only meet with approval. By contrast, the appointment to the Ministry of Labour of **João Goulart** opened Vargas to bitter attack. Goulart, then aged 35, was a rich, *gaúcho* landowner, a neighbour and political associate of Vargas. His appointment was partly intended to strengthen PTB influence in the Ministry of Labour, to respond to dissatisfaction expressed in the São Paulo strike, and prepare the way for the elections, due in October 1954, for all federal deputies, one-third of the Senate and most state governors. Goulart would also have to deal with an increase in the minimum wage, to counter sharply rising inflation, which already had eroded the rise of December 1951.

Goulart's appointment brought charges from the right-wing press that he intended to create a "trade union" state, similar to that of Perón in Argentina, and that he would align this "syndicalized" Brazil with Argentina and Chile in a *bloc* hostile to the United States. The attacks were especially vivid in *Tribuna da Imprensa* of **Carlos Lacerda** and in the Chateaubriand group, *Diários Associados*, and *O Globo*. *O Estado de São Paulo* was more responsible, but no less hostile.

More seriously still, there was evidence of growing opposition from the armed forces. This already had been seen in 1952, in elections in the *Clube Militar* (Military Club), always a testing ground for military opinion. These saw a defeat for more "nationalist" officers and a victory for those critical of Vargas and hostile to his policies towards the unions. Hostility was also seen in a long memorandum to the Ministry of War in February 1954, signed by over 80 army officers, all lieutenant colonels or colonels. It referred, among other things, to a "crisis of authority" and "subversion". Much of the opposition to Vargas now was centred in the National War College (*Escola Superior de Guerra*—ESG) founded in 1949. This already was becoming an important feeding ground for right-wing opinion and many of its graduates were suspicious of Vargas' government and policies, not least towards the working class.

Two days after the publication of the memorandum, Goulart announced plans for an increase of 100 per cent in the minimum wage, bringing it to 2,400 cruzeiros a month in the Federal District, then Rio de Janeiro city area, equal to the salary of an army second lieutenant. To avoid political embarrassment, Goulart resigned, but on May 1, 1954, Vargas announced that the recommended rise of 100 per cent would be made, justified by rises in the cost of living. This, at once, was attacked as inflationary and aimed, irresponsibly, at the elections later in the year.

Amidst all the furore, a group of Vargas' supporters, including a member of his palace guard, tried to shoot Lacerda, killing an air force officer. Vargas offered full enquiries, but the opposition could not be halted. On Aug. 22, Eduardo Gomes and other air force officers demanded the president's resignation, a call taken up in the anti-Vargas press. Vargas agreed to a temporary leave of absence. When told, on Aug. 24 that the absence must be permanent, Vargas killed himself.

One of the impressive features of Vargas' second period in office in the early 1950s is that it contained virtually all the issues which were to face his successors and which still face the Collor government. After Vargas' death the presidency was taken over by the Vice-President, Café Filho, member of the relatively small Popular Socialist a Party (*Partido Socialista Popular*—PSP), who did not share Vargas' views. The congressional elections went off peacefully, but right-wing opposition, again made vocal by Carlos Lacerda, now a federal deputy, swiftly gathered against the PSD candidate for president in 1955, **Juscelino Kubitschek de Oliveira**, who had won the governorship of Minas Gerais in 1950. Lacerda again began a smear campaign, this time to discredit Kubitschek.

The UDN were increasingly uneasy over their chances of winning enough votes from an electorate which now numbered 15,250,000, growing by about 20 per cent every four years, and increasingly reflecting demands of the urban population. Support for the move to stop Kubitschek's candidature also came from powerful military leaders, with plans for a *coup* laid as early as June. Lacerda was determined that the *getulista*, namely pro-Vargas, forces defeated in 1954 should not return to power, even through the PSD, but his attack was mainly directed at the vice-presidential candidate, João Goulart.

Constitutionalist military forces guaranteed the presidential election, which Kubitschek won, but only with 31.79 per cent of the vote. The civilian – military crisis then deepened, and it required a pre-emptive *coup*, led by the Minister of War, General Lott, on Nov. 11, to guarantee the succession, seizing in the process Lacerda's *Tribuna da Imprensa*. It was only with military support, and after a major military crisis, that Kubitschek took office on Jan. 31, 1956. There was no doubt where ultimate power lay.

Juscelino Kubitschek de Oliveira (1956–61). In many respects, Kubitschek's period in office was a high point in Brazilian politics. He, still, in 1991, is the only directly elected civilian president since Artur Bernardes (1922–26) to hand over office peacefully to his successor, the only other possible exception being Dutra, who was not, strictly, a civilian politician.

As former mayor of Belo Horizonte and governor of Minas Gerais, Kubitschek was a seasoned politician and one of many successful businessmen in the PSD. His presidency was marked by confidence, style, daring and success, his *Programa de Metas* (Programme of Goals), being aimed at "50 years progress in five". He was left relatively free by the armed forces to get on with his job, two exceptions being revolts of air force officers in Amazonia, in February 1956 and December 1959, neither of which was a serious threat.

Coming from a planned city, Belo Horizonte, and from Brazil's most important interior state, Kubitschek did not hesitate to carry through the oft-repeated intention of building a new capital in the interior. The result was **Brasília**, inaugurated in 1960, reflecting a determination to possess and develop the interior of the country and attract population away from the coast.

Like Vargas, the new president was determined to give impetus to Brazil's industrial development. Based on a strongly nationalist development ideology, further refined in the Institute of Advanced Brazilian Studies (*Instituto Superior de Estudios Brasileiros*—ISEB), Kubitschek's government sought to harness the energies of the national bourgeoisie and the working class in a massive effort of national will and enthusiasm. Industry grew relatively slowly in 1956 and 1957, but expanded in 1958 by 16.2 per cent, in 1959 by 11.9 per cent, and in 1960 by 9.6 per cent. GDP increased by 3.2 per cent in 1956, 8.1 in 1957, 7.7 in 1958, 5.6 in 1959, 9.7 in 1960, and 10.3 in 1961. Growth was especially rapid in such key areas as heavy goods and state-owned industry, reflecting the high priority assigned to infrastructural development.

The nationalist fervour, coupled with Brazil's

triumph in the football World Cup, and Maria Bueno's victory at Wimbledon, produced a general atmosphere of success and achievement, which partly disguised other facts, such as a steady decline in the absolute value of the minimum wage, at a time when skilled wages were also declining in relation to unskilled. There was also the very high inflationary cost of rapid development, which resulted, towards the end of the presidency, in a sharp increase in strike activity. Kubitschek, in this respect, left office just before the honeymoon was over.

Another growing anxiety was over inflation, especially expressed by foreign bankers and international agencies. Kubitschek tried to co-operate, by seeking a stabilization programme compatible with the commitment to public spending contained in his Target Programme. He accepted an elaborate plan, drawn up by Roberto Campos, director of the National Economic Development Bank (*Banco Nacional de Desenvolvimento Econômico* — BNDE) and Minister of Finance, Lucas Lopes. This implied close collaboration with the IMF (International Monetary Fund) and other institutions. At first, he saw no difficulty in reconciling rapid growth and a tolerable degree of inflation, but the pressures were too great and the IMF became the target for nationalist criticism, not only on the left, but among business and financial circles in Brazil. There was widespread approval when, in June 1959, Kubitschek broke off negotiations with the IMF. It was a story which was to be repeated many times.

One of Kubitschek's biggest failures was his inability successfully to pass on executive power to a candidate of his own party or of the Vargas coalition, evidence that, with an electorate of 11,500,000, it was no longer possible to direct the vote. Jânio Quadros, previously elected mayor of São Paulo, then governor, won, in the presidential election of 1960, 48.26 per cent of the total vote, against 32.93 per cent for Marshal Humberto Texeira Lott, a worthy, but much less colourful, candidate.

Jânio Quadros (1961). If there is any historical precedent for Fernando Collor de Mello, it must be Quadros. He had no real party backing, winning in defiance of political machine politics. He had no programme, depending on a direct, reformist appeal to the people. His early affiliation was with the small Christian Democrat Party. Born in Mato Grosso, in 1917, he moved to São Paulo in 1930, was elected *vereador* (city councillor) in 1948, mayor of São Paulo in 1953, and, having left the Party, governor of the State in 1955. In 1958, he became federal deputy for Paraná, and, in 1960, president of Brazil: it was an astonishing electoral record. All the while, he swopped, or rejected, party labels, running as his own man, without wealth or political patronage, though, in 1960, he was chosen, after much hesitation, as the candidate of the UDN, with the backing of Carlos Lacerda.

The attraction of Quadros for the UDN was that he could win votes, while they had shown themselves to be a minority party, unable to win the urban electorate, especially in voting for president. He was the great hope of the right, and of Lacerda's presidential ambitions. His symbol was a broom, to sweep away corruption and inefficiency, a theme to be repeated by Collor 30 years later, and he promised to cut wasteful state expenditure. He also had a good, if idiosyncratic, administrative record in São Paulo and was linked to São Paulo industrialists and their economic policies.

Quadros' short time in office saw an attempt to curb inflation, by cutting subsidies on essential imports, such as wheat and petroleum: he put up the price of food and transport. He introduced a multiple exchange rate, in effect, devaluing the *cruzeiro* by 100 per cent, which gave new incentive to exports. He introduced a credit and wage squeeze which pleased foreign investors, who offered substantial new credits. He took a generally tough line with the trade unions and his legislation fell most heavily on the working class, whom he professed to support, partly in reaction to a series of strikes in the public sector.

Quadros' greatest weakness was his lack of party backing and sufficient congressional support, coupled with an apparent disdain for both parties and Congress. The PTB and the PSD still had a congressional majority, though they were divided over whether they should support Quadros, as was the UDN. Increasingly, the president seemed to be appealing over the heads of parties and Congress, directly to the people. He shocked some of his military supporters and others on the right by decorating Ché Guevara, and he quarrelled with Lacerda, but there was no real political crisis, as in 1945 or 1954, and no-one wanted one. Quadros, suddenly, produced the biggest crisis since the death of Vargas, by resigning dramatically on the anniversary of Vargas' death, in August 1961. He seems to have hoped to be recalled with fuller executive powers, to bypass Congress. His bid failed, and the political right, for whom Quadros had offered such promise, now found itself with the dreadful thought, for them, of Goulart as president. It was the mirror image of what was to happen, in 1985, with the death of **Tancredo Neves** and the succession of **José Sarney**.

João Goulart, 1961–1964. In late August 1961, there was a real threat of civil war between "constitutionalist" military leaders, willing to accept Goulart, and others, including military ministers, who saw him as a threat to national security. Eventually, he was accepted, but with reduced powers under a "parliamentary" system. The Prime Minister was Tancredo Neves de Almeida, a skilled *mineiro* politician, who had been Minister of Justice in Vargas' last term of office, a member of the PSD, but acceptable both to the PTB and to many further to the right. In January 1963, a plebiscite restored full presidential powers to Goulart.

During both the parliamentary period and the fourteen months till the *coup* of 1964, Goulart governed with greater moderation and astuteness than many of his critics allow. He tried to be conciliatory with the United States, even when his more radical supporters were provocative. In the *Plano Trienal* (Three Year Plan), drawn up by the economist Celso Furtado, he tried to treat both economic and social problems together, to reduce inflation, while maintaining growth and a necessary measure of distribution. He urged necessary reforms in the tax system, banking, housing policies and, above all, agriculture. To achieve this, he sought a working agreement with the trade unions, especially in the National Confederation of Workers in Industry (*Confedereção Nacional dos Trabalhadores da Indústria*—CNTI) and the General Commando of Workers (*Comando Geral dos Trabalhadores*—CGT). With hindsight, perhaps only Goulart, or a politician with a sound basis among working class organizations, could have produced the "social pact", between government, employers and workers, which has proved so elusive, and which the Collor government still seeks.

Such a programme needed support, both in Brazil and abroad, which was not given. The stabilization programme was resisted by bankers and financiers, especially when accompanied by a rise in minimum wages of 60 per cent. The United States government was suspicious, or even hostile, refusing the help which was asked, while the IMF wanted guarantees with regard to further wage increases. The inflationary spiral provoked further demands and concessions, with, for example, 70 per cent rises for civil servants and the armed forces in July 1963. Critics on the left accused Goulart of trying too hard to conciliate foreign interests: from the right he was seen as subversive, identified with associates such as his brother-in-law, **Leonel Brizola**, who, in October 1962 had been elected as federal deputy for Guanabara, with more votes than any other Congressional candidate had ever received.

Inflation continued to rise, by 25 per cent in the first three months of 1963, as compared with a target of not more than that same figure for the whole year, and pressures grew on every side. Industrial growth-rate fell, from an average of 9 per cent from 1945 to 1957, and 11 per cent from 1958 to 1961, to under 8 per cent in 1962, and virtually nil in 1963. The balance of payments dropped from a surplus of $622,000,000 over the next two years. Brazil had to sacrifice $136,000,000 of gold reserves and take on trade debts of $177,000,000. Social and political movements in the north-east, notably the Peasant Leagues often linked to the church, demanded limited, much-needed reforms, but were painted as centres of extreme left-wing, internationally inspired subversion.

One constant problem was tension between the executive and Congress, the president being more reformist, both in programme and support. This was seen in the rejection of very modest plans for agrarian reform in October 1963. Goulart sought special powers, to impose a "state of siege", but neither right nor left would agree. Opposition from the right now coalesced. Some was deep-seated, going back to Vargas and the revolution of 1930, as in the case of the Mesquita family and the *Estado de São Paulo*. The *Escola Superior de Guerra* provided a coherent critique and an alternative strategy. Businessmen, financiers and politicians organized an opposition network through the Institute of Social Studies and Research (*Instituto de Pesquisas e Estudos Sociais* — IPES), a powerful pressure group, founded in 1961, working, too, with the Brazilian Institute of Democratic Action (*Instituto Brasileiro de Ação Democrática*—IBAD) organized in the 1962 elections. They all knew that they had the support of the United States, whose officials knew of their plans.

The crisis came to a head in March 1964, sharpened by a mass rally, addressed by Goulart, in Rio de Janeiro, on March 13, which received highly coloured press reporting, and a revolt of sailors and marines, from March 25–27, perhaps, in part, provoked by the right, which Goulart appeared to condone. This pushed previously loyal officers into opposition. The revolt started on March 31: Goulart took stock of his support and, on April 4, flew to Uruguay. One again, as in 1889, 1930, 1945 and 1954, the armed forces were in control.

Humberto Castello Branco (1964–1967). The *coup* of 1964 was an important political watershed, even if it did not merit the enthusiastic acclaim of the United States' ambassador, Lincoln Gordon, as being "one of the major turning points in world history, in the middle of the twentieth century", a perception reflected in the United States' recognition of the new regime, even before Goulart had left the country. Goulart probably could have survived, had he been willing to reach a compromise with those who threatened a *coup*. His refusal to abandon his colleagues, or to risk civil war, was a measure of his concern for Brazil, not matched by many of those who opposed him.

The victors of 1964 looked to a new era, seen as an end to the Vargas heritage and as a further opening of Brazil to free market capitalism, under the influence of the United States. The first military president, Humberto Castello Branco, was an able, much respected officer, who always had distanced himself from politics and his *golpista* colleagues. He had been Chief of Operations for the Brazilian Expeditionary Force, then Director of Courses at the Command and General Staff School, and Sub-Commandant at the ESG. He was a man of great personal integrity, whose eventual support for the anti-Goulart movement, in late 1963, strongly influenced other officers in their decision. Castello Branco was also highly regarded in the United States embassy, partly through his association with the military attaché, Colonel Vernon Walters, a senior intelligence officer with whom he had worked in Italy.

The Castello Branco government was probably the most able of the whole period of military-backed control from 1964 to 1985. It included General Golbery do Couto e Silva, founder of the National Information Service (*Serviço Nacional de Informações*—SNI) and head of the "research institute" which had largely co-ordinated the movement against Goulart. He represented the well-established intellectual strain in the Brazilian officer corps. His writing on geopolitics had a strong influence on military thinking, which still persists. He became an *éminence grise*, not just in the Castello Branco government, but, later, under Geisel, and for much of the term of Figueiredo. An even more prominent figure was Roberto Campos de Oliveira, formerly head of the National Bank for Economic Development (*Banco Nacional de Desenvolvimento Econômico*—BNDE), who now became Minister of Planning and virtually Prime Minister. He, too, was to influence the shaping of the political economy, as economist, diplomat and politician, for many years to come. The Minister of Finance was Octávio Gouvêia de Bulhões, another highly regarded economist, who was especially concerned with fiscal reform. Overall, the new government presented a formidable team, drawing strongly on men linked to the ESG and on right-wing economists and social theorists. The policies to be followed also owed much to ESG debates, being shaped, in the main, by civilians, rather than military officers.

The primary aim of the new government was to strengthen the economy, introducing an effective stabilization programme and encouraging foreign investment, while seeking to end the drift to "subversion", which, allegedly, had been evident in recent years. A general strategy already was available from discussions in the ESG, where, the key issues of "security" and "development" had been carefully examined. On April 9, an *Institutional Act* provided "the means... for the... economic, financial, political and moral reconstruction of Brazil". Next day, 40 members of Congress were deprived of their political rights, with several hundred more on April 14, including some of Goulart's ministers, labour leaders and, even, members of the UDN. Pro-Goulart officers and others in the armed forces were retired or stripped of political rights. The most prominent victim was Juscelino Kubitschek. It was the start of a process of authoritarian control and repression which was to become ever more harsh over the next few years.

The change of government brought a new wave of foreign investment and support, from Europe, the United States and Japan, and credits and loans from the IMF, the International Bank for Reconstruction and Development, and the Inter-American Development Bank. Foreign interest was further rekindled by an amendment to the Profit Remittance law of 1962, removing the 10 per cent annual limit on remittances and allowing the "capital investment" base to be adjusted for reinvested profits and for inflation. Roberto Campos also prepared a comprehensive 10-Year Plan, combining economic, social and political elements, based on a system sufficiently stable to allow planning to work, while also seeking the necessary degree of political consensus.

Castello Branco was the prime representative of the "Sorbonne group" within the armed forces, men linked to the ESG usually with experience in Italy during the war, seeing military intervention in politics as, sometimes, necessary, but to be as limited as possible, before returning to the barracks. He allowed, against opposition, direct elections for mayor in São Paulo, in March 1965, and for governor in 11 states in October 1965. The results of the October elections were widely interpreted as a defeat for the government, an exaggerated view, which nevertheless, provoked further political intervention, in *Institutional Act No. 2*, which gave greater powers to the president, extended government control, and ended direct elections for the president.

A later *Complementary Act* of Nov. 20 dissolved existing political parties. These were to be replaced by only two heterogeneous groups. The first, the National Renovating Alliance (Aliança Renovadora Nacional—ARENA) included most government supporters, while the other, the Brazilian Democratic Movement (Movimento Democrático Brasileiro—MDB) united most of the opposition. These two groupings were to last until 1979, maintaining at least the formality of party politics, expressed in Congress. The government now further tightened its control. In February 1966 *Institutional Act No. 3* decreed that state governors should no longer be elected directly, but chosen by state legislatures. It also ended direct elections for mayors of capital cities.

The military régime was meant to end political bickering and division. Ironically, it was divisions within the military leadership which frustrated one of the main programmes of the Castello Branco government, the Ten-Year Plan of Roberto Campos. Opposed to the "Castellista" group of officers and civilians was another, the so-called *Linha Dura* or "hard-line". The military element in this, mostly, had not served in Italy, had not gone through the ESG, was more closely associated with troop command, and took a more "nationalist" stance in relation to foreign involvement in politics and the economy. In civilian terms, it frequently had close ties to Carlos Lacerda and his political ambitions.

Older officers in the "hard line" insisted that the régime installed in 1964 should not repeat the cardinal mistake, as they understood it, of 1930, that the armed forces should not too quickly hand back power to the civilian political class which recently had been defeated. This view ran contrary to the perception of Carlos Lacerda and the other civilian politicians involved in the anti-Goulart conspiracy, who had hoped for a quick military *coup*, which might install in office the leaders of the UDN, with the armed forces withdrawing from power. This "hard line" opposition coalesced around General Artur da Costa e Silva, the Minister of War, supported by officers in the *Vila Militar*, the military garrison near Rio de Janeiro, and in the Officer Specialization School, (*Escola de Aperfeiçoamento de Oficiais*—EAO) the college for junior officers, in Rio de Janeiro. This more radical, nationalist movement also found a spokesman in General Alfonso Augusto de Albuquerque Lima, who wanted greater priority for social reforms, and less subservience to the United States.

Tension came to a head on the night of Oct. 5, 1965, with troops prepared to move against Castello Branco, to deprive him of office, a movement led by Albuquerque Lima. The crisis was resolved by General Costa e Silva, coming to an agreement with officers in the Vila Militar. Open disagreement, even conflict, was avoided, but at a price, which included that Costa e Silva would succeed Castello Branco, as the second president of the military régime. This, in turn, implied that the "Castellista", "Sorbonne" strategy for a return to liberal democracy was called in question, and that the elaborate, coherent 10-Year Plan of Roberto Campos, almost certainly, would be abandoned. On Oct. 3, 1966, Costa e Silva was chosen, in indirect election by Congress, as the next president of Brazil.

Artur da Costa e Silva (1967–1969). Costa e Silva, the first of three successive *gaúcho* military presidents, was a deceptively able officer, who allowed, or even, encouraged, a softer public image, to cover strong, often harsh, policies. He claimed that he wanted to "humanize" the military-backed régime, to achieve a new degree of legitimacy and support. Such aims contrasted strongly with the fact that, in order to ensure his smooth succession to power, yet more federal deputies were deprived of their political rights, in October 1966, and that, on Oct. 20, troops were ordered to surround Congress, closing it till after the elections of Nov. 15. In those elections, of a population of about 84,700,000, there were now 23,000,000 registered voters. Just over 17,250,000 turned out to vote, many deliberately spoiling their ballot sheets, in protest against increased authoritarianism, which, by October 1966, had purged Congress of about 20 per cent of those elected in 1962.

The Costa e Silva Cabinet reflected the strength of "hard line" officers and politicians. The new Minister of the Interior was Major General Alfonso Augusto de Albuquerque Lima. Now aged 57, he was a *nordestino*, who, previously, had been head of the National Department of Anti-Drought Works (*Departamento Nacional de Obras Contra as Secas*—DNOCS), then Director of Military Engineering. He had been in the ESG, but was mainly supported by more nationalist officers and civilian *técnicos*, suspicious of the recently enlarged economic and political role of foreign and multilateral interests. He was particularly concerned to win greater priority for regional development in the north-east and Amazonia. If he were to be a serious contender for presidential succession, he needed to be promoted to four-star general.

Another possible presidential contender, a *gaucho*, was General Emilio Garrastazú Médici, who had worked closely with Costa e Silva, before taking over from General Golbery do Couto e Silva as head of the SNI. Like others associated with the new president, he had opposed Marshal Lott and his "constitutionalist" stand in favour of Kubitschek.

The authoritarian character of the government was also strengthened by the appointment, as Minister of Justice, of Luis Antônio da Gama e Silva, a former rector of the University of São Paulo, who was to be instrumental in depriving former academic colleagues, among others, of their political rights. He was one of eight civilian ministers and eight military "hard-liners" in the new government.

Of the civilian ministers, the most important, in defining economic strategy and related social priorities, was Antônio Delfim Neto, the 38 year-old former Secretary of Finance for the state of São Paulo. He now re-established the primacy of his ministry above that of Planning, which had been raised to new importance under Roberto Campos. Delfim Neto was now able to build on what Campos had achieved by his orthodox stabilization policy, easing credit restrictions to industry and providing stimulus for economic growth, seeking to end the serious industrial recession produced by 1966. In both 1967 and 1968, he increased the money supply by over 40 per cent. He also continued the policy of keeping wage increases lower than the rate of inflation.

Between 1964 and 1967, the real value of the minimum wage had fallen by 20 per cent and industrial wages only somewhat less. By 1967, the average real minimum wage was 15 per cent lower than in 1955. Under Delfim Neto the cost of growth continued to fall most heavily on the working class and the poor, with growing inequalities between social groups. From 1960 to 1970, the real income of the bottom 5 per cent of the working population went up by 1 per cent, while that of the top 5 per cent rose by 72 per cent.

This was accompanied by growing regional inequality of distribution, with, for example, the north-east's share of gross domestic income falling in the decade and a disproportionate percentage of government spending going to the south-east. This pattern was the direct result of a deliberate strategy, which gave explicit priority to economic growth rather than to distribution, which established as a "basic priority the accelerated growth of the GNP, accepting as a short-term liability the corollary of an appreciable imbalance between individual rates of income".

By the clever use of a series of devices, including monetary correction, indexation and the "crawling peg", a regular series of mini-devaluations, the strategy was, within its own terms, remarkably successful, for a time. Exports shot up, from a very low base, to about $4,000 million in 1972, of which $1,000 million came from industrial exports, one-third of which had been developed over the last three years. By 1973, exports increased by 55 per cent on the previous year, to nearly US$6,200 million, with industry contributing about one-third.

By the end of 1974 the value of exports reached $8,000 million, a further increase of 25.8 per cent as compared with 1973. Delfim Neto could point to real growth rates from 1968, averaging about 10 per cent, with inflation, officially, contained at about 20 per cent, a balance of payments surplus of $2,377 million and foreign currency reserves of $6,417 million. This was 53 per cent more than at the end of 1972, making Brazil one of the half-dozen countries in the world with the highest foreign currency reserves. Then, just as Delfim was leaving office, came the international oil crisis.

Such performance entailed costs. One was the need to reassure the international financial and business community with regard to the régime's firm political control. Direct foreign investment had fallen off after its peak in the 1950s, with most transnational corporations preferring currency loans as the means to finance new capital outlay, since they could then repatriate both profits and the capital sum, but foreign participation in the dynamic sectors of the economy was high.

By 1975, for example, the top 12 largest firms (in terms of assets) in the consumer durables sector were all foreign-owned, as were 13 of the largest 20 in the non-durable goods sector, and 10 of the largest 18 in the capital goods sector. As early as 1967, the top 12 advertisers were all foreign-based firms, able to exert a powerful influence on the media to which they brought so much business. The need for foreign capital, to fuel the development model, also meant that successive governments encouraged increasing internationalization of the economy.

This sensitivity to foreign opinion and response was one source of the increasing authoritarianism and political repression under Costa e Silva and his successor. The need to exercise control was contained in the logic of the development model, including, too, the *arrôcho salarial*, the suppression of wage levels, holding them behind inflation. To impose wage settlements, through a government-determined formula, required political control of trade unions and workers' organizations, including strike activity. This control then had to be extended to other groups, including those within Congress, who might challenge the sacrifices which Delfim's strategy required.

The move towards a more authoritarian State also reflected the régime's response to a series of challenges to its power and policies. One came from Carlos Lacerda, who now urged the formation of a *Frente Ampla*, or "Broad Front" of civilian opposition, including leaders whom previously he had vigorously opposed, such as Kubitschek and Goulart. He offended the officer corps by being associated with a scurrilous press attack on the late President Castello Branco, who was killed in an air crash in July 1967.

Lacerda was now forbidden to appear on television, rejected by many of the "hard line", who earlier had supported him. In September, he went to Montevideo, to talk with Goulart, making his position at home worse, following this visit with a series of even more extreme accusations against the armed forces, of corruption and of defending a decadent oligarchy. In April 1968, Costa e Silva gave in to outraged military feeling and forbade any further activities of the *Frente*, which by now had associated with it protests from students, churchmen and a broad opposition. In December 1968, Lacerda was deprived of his political rights by the military régime which he had helped to bring to power.

Students presented one of the most public sources of opposition, with marches and demonstrations growing in strength throughout 1967 and 1968. Students were killed and many hurt by soldiers and military police reacting with extreme violence, especially in June, when 4,000 troops faced a student demonstration in Rio de Janeiro. Though banned in July, the demonstrations reached new heights in August, paralleling events in Paris, with some support from workers' delegations. The régime saw evidence of widespread subversion, and a threat to "national security", especially when there was also a wave of bombings and, in September, the publication of a document by Carlos Marighela, the former PCB federal deputy, advocating urban guerrilla warfare.

Most students were motivated simply by opposition to the military government, without the coherent Marxist ideology with which the régime generally credited them. They were largely middle class, the children of those who benefited from the policies of Delfim. Many were influenced less by Marxism than by the growing critique from the **Church** of the social policies of the government.

This call for change generally stressed that peaceful means should be used, as in the conspicuous case of Dom Helder Cámara, Archbishop of Olinda and Recife, who, preaching peace and justice, became a thorn in the side of the régime. Such criticism provoked stern, often violent, reaction, with clergy and laity arrested, frequently abused and, even, tortured or killed. There were divisions within the Church, including the hierarchy, but, by 1968, the régime, one of whose ostensible aims had been to defend a Western, Christian tradition, found itself increasingly asked, both at home and abroad, to show how its policies might square with Christian teaching.

Others in Brazil, partly influenced by the example of guerrilla war elsewhere, believed that peaceful resistance was not enough against a State which had the monopoly of violence and was willing to use it against its people. Those who took part in armed resistance generally claimed that their decision came only after peaceful means for change seemed to be closed. There was, in fact, little armed resistance in the wake of the *coup* with the first attempt to set up rural *focos* only in 1967. Various groups then were formed in 1967 and 1968, often splitting and re-grouping.

Two of the most important were the National Liberation Action (*Açao Libertadora Nacional*—ALN), led by Carlos Marighela , and the Popular Revolutionary Vanguard (*Vanguardia Popular Revolucionaria* — VPR), joined by Carlos Lamarca, a former army officer. The best known of the guerrillas, especially the urban guerrillas, was Carlos Marighela who, born in Bahia in 1911, joined the PCB within five years of its foundation in 1922 and remained active within it till his expulsion in September 1967, because of his criticism of party strategy. He became internationally famous for his writing on urban guerrilla resistance. He was ambushed and killed by police in São Paulo on Nov. 4, 1969. Lamarca was killed in Bahia in 1971.

The régime's response to criticism and opposition was *Institutional Act No. 5*, of Dec. 13, 1968, a "*coup* within the *coup*". This ended any pretence of "controlled democracy". It gave far-reaching new powers to the president of the Republic, who now could decree the recess of Congress and state and municipal assemblies, could "intervene" in states and *municípios* and suspend the political rights of any citizen for 10 years. Congress was now closed indefinitely and critics of the government, including Lacerda, lost their political rights.

In February 1969, the mandates of 33 congressmen were cancelled, including 11 from ARENA. Other *cassações* followed, so that, within three months, the MDB opposition in the Chamber was reduced by 40 per cent. Important state legislatures, including Guanabara, São Paulo and Pernambuco, were declared to be in recess and all elections due to be held before November 1970 were cancelled. Further proscription lists followed, of academics, journalists and diplomats. Brazil's authoritarian, "national security" State was now well and truly established.

This harsh reaction helped to distract attention from persistent divisions within the armed forces, especially linked to the question of who would succeed Costa e Silva. This involved a struggle between different factions of the armed forces, one of which supported General Albuquerque Lima and a more "nationalist" development strategy, sometimes compared to the new military government in Peru. This fight for the presidency was conducted in a context of increased opposition from urban guerrillas, who regrouped in July 1969 and produced a series of dramatic, if short-lived, successes, including the kidnapping of the United States' ambassador in September.

The government's answer was an increase in the use of torture and terrorizing tactics, with violence meeting violence. Costa e Silva still hoped to introduce a new constitution, on Sept. 8 to re-open Congress and "humanize" the régime, but faced overwhelming military opposition. He became ill on Aug. 29. His place was taken, not by his Vice-President, as the Constitution required, but by a military *junta*.

There then followed weeks of intense lobbying and discussions within the armed forces, concerning both the presidential succession and government strategy, destroying any myth of military unity. Albuquerque Lima had strong support, especially among more junior officers and in the air force, but the High Command of the Armed Forces made the apparently safer choice of Garastazú Médici, a four-star general, friend of Costa e Silva, former head of the SNI, and not likely to introduce a substantial change of direction. A compliant, politically weakened Congress agreed.

Emílio Garrastazú Médici (1969–74). After the crisis and uncertainty surrounding the succession, the Médici government essentially continued the policies of Costa e Silva, with Delfim Neto remaining at the Ministry of Finance. One difference was that repression became even more severe, combined with an extensive public relations policy to soften the government's image and win support, in Brazil and abroad.

The power of the president and the federal government were now further extended at the expense of the legislative branch, both at federal and state level, as were those of the Superior Military Tribunal, all in the name of national security. There was also a massive, ruthless reply to armed opposition, with many of the leaders killed in 1969 and 1970, with widespread arrests of people suspected of supporting or being part of the guerrilla movements. Torture was routinely and indiscriminately used on those arrested and, despite some dramatic successes in kidnapping diplomats, by the end of 1971, many of the guerrilla leaders were dead and many guerrillas were in prison or had been forced to leave the country.

While still further weakening Congress, appointing state governors and riding rough-shod over civil society, the government launched a massive publicity campaign to laud Brazil's economic success and growth, linking it to the brilliant performance of the national team in the 1970 World Cup in Mexico. This became one of the themes for the next carnival, with the government publicity department producing songs, jingles and slogans, while still censoring sambas and any artistic performances critical of the régime and its social priorities.

Many Brazilians looked on with weary cynicism and resentment, reflected in the elections for Congress in November 1970. In many areas, null and blank votes reached a startling 50 per cent. In a still emasculated Congress, ARENA won over 70 per cent of seats in the Chamber and 40 of the 46 senate seats contested. ARENA now had 220 federal deputies and MDB only 7.

In the midst of such cynical manipulation and political violence, Delfim Neto was named "Man of Vision, 1970" by the periodical *Visão*, cheered by politicians of the right, by businessmen and international financiers, and by many of the middle class, who had done so well out of his time in office. Meanwhile, military promotions in July and *Clube Militar* elections in May all underlined the defeat of the nationalist officers and the triumph of internationalized interests. The point was driven home, when Albuquerque Lima was passed over for promotion to four-star "general of the army".

Partly as a response to international criticism, the Médici government introduced a limited programme of social and regional development. One such was the Brazilian Literacy Movement (*Movimento Brasileiro de Alfabetização* — MOBRAL), headed by the able, right-wing economist, Mário Henrique Simonsen. Its budget for 1970 was $13,000,000: its stated aim was to provide basic literacy for about 4,000,000 people in two years. Another project, launched in 1970, was the Social Integration Programme (*Programa de Integraçâo Social* — PIS). This claimed to give workers a share in the product of industry, mainly through a "participation fund", controlled by the National Savings Fund, to which over 1,000,000 firms were supposed to contribute.

Another project aimed at the development and settlement of Amazonia. This was the National Integration Scheme, started in September. The plan was to open up Amazonia, moving colonists from the north-east and providing stimulus for the commercial and industrial development of Amazonia. This hinged on the building of two great roads. One, the Transamazonica, was to be about 3,200 miles long, running from the coast to link with the road system of Peru, and, eventually, the Pacific coast. The other would cut at right angles from Cuiabá, in Mato Grosso, to Santarém, at the junction of the Amazon and the Tapajós Rivers. There would also be spur roads north to Boa Vista, leading on to Guyana and Venezuela. New towns were to be built along the roads, attracting population and development.

Unfortunately, the schemes were ill thought out and ill-executed, damaging to the environment and indigenous people, without benefiting the colonists. Some of the main beneficiaries were large, often transnational corporations, such as Liquigas, Volkswagen and Swift Armour, or individual entrepreneurs, such as David K. Ludwig or Donvall Kniphoff.

PRORURAL, the Rural Worker's Aid programme, was meant to bring rural workers within the net of social security. It was to be part of a wider concern for agrarian reform, expressed in the National Institute for Colonization and Agrarian Reform (*Instituto Nacional de Colonização e Reforma Agraria* — INCRA), which was now expanded. This, in turn, was to co-ordinate with the *PROTERRA* Programme for the Redistribution of Land and the Stimulus of Industry in the north and north-east. It was all meant to tackle the desperate problem of rural poverty and deprivation. Unfortunately, there was no real political will to challenge the vested agrarian interests, most of which were embedded in the régime,

In his final *Mensagem* (Message to the Nation) of 1974, Médici looked back with pride to this time in office, faithful to the fundamental objective (of the "March Revolution" of 1964); "prosperity between 1969 and 1973 reached the highest levels of our history". He did not say to whom that growth and prosperity had been directed, or at what heavy social and political cost.

Ernesto Geisel (1974–79). Geisel's career had followed a pattern common among the Brazilian officer corps, a mixture of military and quasi-civilian postings. He came from a German Protestant family from Rio Grande do Sul. In the 1950s, he was on the staff of the National Security Council, then, from 1955–56, was Superintendent of the President Bernardes Refinery. In 1957, he represented the War Ministry on the National Petroleum Council, then headed the intelligence section of the army general staff. Before becoming president, he was Director of Petrobrás, the biggest company in Brazil. His brother, Orlando, was Chief of General Staff of the Armed Forces in 1969, during the crisis of Costa e Silva's illness, and then Minister of the Army under Médici.

Geisel came to office just as Brazil's economy was hit by the international oil crisis and as demand grew for an end to authoritarian controls and political repression. Even before the change of government, international bankers had voiced their concern over Brazil's rising foreign debt and the capacity of the economy to sustain it. The response of Delfim and his associates, such as Mário Hénrique Simonsen, himself a spokesman for international capital, was almost dismissively confident. Brazil's economy, especially its export performance, was sufficient reassurance. By 1974, when Simonsen had succeeded Delfim in the Ministry of Finance, that ringing, bell-like, confidence had a cracked tone.

An 11.4 per cent expansion of GDP took place in 1973, the highest growth rate of any major country in the world, with an increase in the last five years of 63 per cent.

The $2,300 million surplus in 1973 led the Central Bank to expand the money supply by 47 per cent. This produced demand inflation, aggravated by cost push, resulting from the oil crisis. The result, in the first six months of 1974, was that the general price index increased, at an average monthly rate, of 3.5 per cent, equivalent to an annual inflation rate of 51 per cent. At the same time, while exports rose to US$8,000 million, imports rose faster, to US$12,500 million.

Brazil, by contrast with 1973, no longer had a balance of payments surplus, but a trade deficit of $4,500 million. When everything was calculated, there was a total deficit in the balance of payments of $1,000 million. Meanwhile, total foreign debt rose to $16,700 million, which, set against foreign reserves of $9,200 million, resulted in a net foreign indebtedness of $11,500 million.

Over the next two years, the country plunged even more deeply into debt. It needed to import more than three-quarters of its oil requirements, added to large capital-goods imports. By 1976, the foreign debt was about US$25,000 million, as compared with US$12,900 million in 1973: by the end of 1977, it was around US$35,000 million. Foreign reserves in 1976 dropped to $3,500 million, contrasted with just under US$6,500 million in 1973. Compared with the growth levels for 1968–73, there was a forecast of zero, or, even, negative growth rates for 1976. By then, it was estimated, debt repayment and interest would consume about 44 per cent of the country's export revenue, at a time when inflation was running at about 50 per cent.

One of the big problems was Brazil's dependence on oil imports. By 1974, about 45 per cent of the country's energy consumption came from oil, needing about 900,000 barrels a day, of which the domestic oil industry produced only about 180,000 barrels daily. The sudden rise in the price of oil, combined with price rises on wheat, capital goods and steel imports, was a severe blow to the economy. In 1975, Geisel showed his authority and the pragmatism which had characterized his time at Petrobrás, when, for example, he concluded an oil prospecting agreement with the Ba'ath government in Iraq, just one week after Baghdad had expropriated the British Iraq Petroleum Company. In October 1975, he pushed through a decision to allow "risk contracts" to foreign oil companies to search for oil in Brazil. This cut across the long tradition in which Brazilian control of oil was a major touchstone of nationalist commitment. There now also began a feverish search for alternatives to petroleum, mainly in the form of alcohol produced from sugar.

The 12 months of 1974 not only marked the end of the "Brazilian Miracle" but also the start of the long process of dismantling the authoritarian system, of *distensão*, the relaxing of control, which, in due course, would lead to *abertura*, the "opening-up" of the system. This too, was partly a pragmatic response, to growing criticism from all sides, including from within the armed forces, the Church, lawyers, writers, students and politicians, of the steady descent into political repression. Other criticism questioned the efficiency, purely in terms of capitalist development, of a closed system of decision-making, not open to scrutiny and debate. Soon after taking office, Geisel spoke of the need for a slow, gradual and secure relaxation, a phrase which raised hopes for change. Some of those hopes were too high, not paying enough attention to the qualification "secure", namely, that political change must not only be gradual, but controlled, still firmly within the overriding priority of "national security".

At the same time, Geisel belonged squarely within the "Castellista" tradition of the officer corps, which had always seen the military intervention as a temporary incursion, which, as soon as possible, would hand back power to politicians in a democratic system. In this he had powerful support from General Golbery do Couto e Silva, who now became head of the president's civilian household. Golbery had retired from active service, rather than serve under Goulart, and had directed IPES. When working with Castello Branco, as head of the SNI, he had almost daily meetings with the president's Chief Military Aide, General Ernesto Geisel. He now came back to government as Geisel's chief political advisor. He had reflected deeply on the shaping of politics since the *coup* and was convinced that changes must be made.

Both Geisel and Golbery were aware of the opposition they would face, stemming from deeply entrenched vested interests, not only in the armed forces, but in the social and political system more generally, not least from former officers now installed in well paid positions, because of their previous links within the régime. The reacton to *distensão* came fast. Often, it was violent, including the bombing of premises of those who asked for change. Often, too, this stemmed from the "intelligence community" that Golbery largely had created.

A major test of *distensão* came in the elections of November 1974. The government permitted wide-ranging debate on issues which previously had been forbidden, including the worsening pattern of distribution of wealth. The results of the elections provided a genuine political watershed, startling the régime and surprising the opposition. The electorate, now over 31,000,000, had to vote for one third of the Senate, for 364 federal deputies and 787 state deputies. Of the 22 senate seats in dispute, MDB won 16, giving them 20 seats in the new Senate. MDB won 61 per cent of senate votes, as against 39 per cent for ARENA. In the Chamber, before the elections, MDB had only 87 deputies: now the party elected 172, compared with 192 for ARENA.

In the state assemblies, MDB previously had held only Guanabara. It now won six states, including São Paulo, Rio Grande do Sul and what, in March 1975, was to become Brazil's second most important industrial state. This was the greatly enlarged state of Rio de Janeiro, resulting from the joining of the existing state of Rio de Janeiro with that of Guanabara, the former federal district, mainly made up of the city of Rio de Janeiro.

The message from the elections was crystal clear. The people wanted change. They saw MDB as the party which might provide it, while ARENA was identified with a discredited régime. MDB support especially came from the main centres of economic activity, both industrial and agrarian, and from the principal urban centres. ARENA's vote was largely based on rural clientelism in the interior, the so-called *voto do cabresto*, or "herd vote", a pejorative term from the "Old Republic".

Electoral success for the opposition brought more reaction from the right, blaming the Geisel government for weakness. The charge was misdirected. Geisel and his advisors rightly judged the need for change and the régime's dangerous lack of support. The principal, very important conclusion which they drew from the 1974 elections was that it was dangerous to allow, in effect, regular referenda on the régime's performance, with protest votes attaching themselves to one opposition party, MDB. This realization was important for the shaping of *distensão*.

Part of the political relaxation involved an attempt to reach a better relationship with the Church and the trade unions. In May 1975, there was a rise of 41.4 per cent in the minimum wage, which, by April 1974, had fallen to about 44 per cent of its real value in 1964. The whole question of wages and of distribution of wealth became an issue of national debate, as did the need to expand the internal market, which also had implications for wages policy.

Another subject which seized popular interest was the continuing use of torture, especially when a leading *paulista* journalist, Vladimir Herzog, died under torture, followed by a metal-worker, Manoel Fiel Filho. There was a swift, angry public reaction. Geisel dismissed the head of the 2nd Army in São Paulo, General D'Avila Melo. These deaths were another milestone in mobilizing civil society against the repressive State.

The unpopularity of the régime contrasted visibly with the wave of sympathy over the death of Kubitschek, on Aug. 22, 1976, in a motor accident, and for Goulart in December, when shops in Rio de Janeiro quietly closed in respect. Meanwhile, Geisel resisted strong pressure from the right, including a speech by ex-President Médici, in July, to cancel the municipal elections due in November. These, in any case, were a limited test for the régime, since MDB could not field candidates in many *municípios*: the odds were also against the opposition, granted that, in 1972, ARENA had elected 3,349 mayors and 29,331 *vereadores* (councillors), as compared with MDB's mere 436 mayors and 5,936 vereadores.

Geisel was willing to face the test, made harder by an inflation rate of over 40 per cent, growing criticism abroad of Brazil's rising foreign debt, and further damaging evidence of political violence in the countryside, especially against priests, church activists and *posseiros* (squatters), seen in the shooting of the Jesuit priest, João Bosco Penido Burnier, in October: he and a local bishop, by chance, went to a village, where police were torturing three women. When Burnier and the bishop protested, police accused them of being "subversives" and 'Communists': they beat Burnier with rifle butts and shot him in the head.

Despite this background of criticism, protest and violence, the elections of November 1976 were largely indecisive. ARENA, as expected, won in the countryside and MDB in the larger urban areas: both sides claimed victory. The more important fact was that the elections had proceeded smoothly and that *distensão* was still in place. This seemed to be called in question a few months later, when the government suddenly announced changes affecting voting and representation. The *Pacote de Abril*, the "April Package", determined that there would not be direct elections for governors in 1978: they would be chosen by electoral colleges made up of state deputies and delegates from municipal councils.

The number of state deputies, once again, would be decided by the population of the state, not by the number of voters, so strengthening more conservative states, with large populations and high levels of illiteracy, so that relatively few voters would return a disproportionate number of deputies. The "Package" tightened control of the media during elections and extended the presidential term from five to six years. It also sought to maintain control of the Senate, reacting to the elections of 1974, by decreeing that half of the 44 senate seats due to be filled in 1978 should be decided by indirect elections. These soon were to be known, in typically Brazilian fashion, as the "bionic senators".

The "April Package" was rightly seen as a means of influencing the elections of 1978, but it was not just a move to curb the opposition. It was part of a wider strategy, which also was aimed at the right and at resistance to *distensão* within the armed forced. This "hard-line" resistance was largely being led by the Minister of War, General Sílvio Frota, who, throughout 1977, was conducting, in effect, a presidential campaign, seeking both military and civilian support. The "Package" was partly to reassure the right that liberalization would not go too far or too fast. Geisel then followed this up by removing General Frota from the Ministry of War on Oct. 12, acting on information from the SNI, and without even consulting the army High Command.

The strength of Geisel's position, within the army as well as the government, was also seen when he nominated as his successor General João Batista de Oliveira Figueiredo, director of the SNI. Figueiredo was still only a three-star general, but was rapidly promoted. His candidature was accepted at the ARENA convention, though it provoked protest from some hard-line officers, including General Hugo Abreu, head of the president's military staff. There was also, for the first time since 1964, an alternative candidate for the indirect election to the presidency. He was General Euler Bentes Monteiro, a former director of SUDENE, who now received the somewhat reluctant backing of the MDB convention. There was even an election campaign of sorts, but on

Oct. 24, 1978, the electoral college, controlled by ARENA, chose Figueiredo, by 355 votes to 266.

The congressional elections of November 1978 showed the effect of the "April Package", with an ARENA majority in both the Chamber and the Senate. MDB won majorities in only eight states and one territory, though the direct votes for senators were much higher for MDB candidates. With the elections guaranteed, Geisel was able, paradoxically, to introduce more liberal measures. He abolished *Institutional Act No 5* and a range of other repressive powers, as from January 1979. He also revoked orders banishing over 120 political exiles. He had kept his promise to start the return to democratic government, however slowly, gradually, and within the boundaries of national security.

João Batista de Oliveira Figueiredo, 1979–85. Figueiredo had links with both the "Castellista" current in the officer corps and with the harsher line represented by Médici. He had worked with Golbery in the SNI after 1964, became head of the of the presidential military staff under Médici, then head of the SNI under Geisel. One clear indication that he intended to carry on the process of *distensão* was that Golbery do Couto e Silva continued in his post, working closely with the new Minister of Justice, Petrônio Portela, an ARENA senator from Piauí. Golbery and Portela were the two main strategists directing the whole process of redemocratization. Their aim was always that it should be controlled, with its shape and pace directed by the régime, as Golbery explained in a lecture to the ESG in July 1980.

It was this strategy which lay behind the *New Organic Law of Political Parties*, of December 1979, which put an end to the two political groupings, ARENA and MDB, imposed in 1965. Formally, this marked the return to multi-party government, which 92 per cent of MDB congressmen and 85 per cent of ARENA said that they wanted. More immediately, it was a move to stop the electorate persistently rallying around MDB as a form of anti-régime referendum: it was a policy of *divide et impera*.

The main party supporting the régime was now the **Social Democratic Party** (*Partido Democrático Social*—PDS): 89 per cent of its members came from ARENA. Leaders of the MDB sought to keep its former title, becoming the **Party of the Brazilian Democratic Movement** (*Partido do Movimento Democrático Brasileiro*—PMDB). At first it lost nearly half of its original 189 MDB deputies, but gradually recovered ground, so that, by 1982, it was the major party of opposition. A third party was the Popular Party (*Partido Popular*—PP), a centre-party, which, initially, attracted some former ARENA members, including eight former ARENA governors, and some notable MDB figures, including Senator Tancredo Neves, from Minas Gerais. It had strong support from bankers, the financial community and the liberal professions. In late 1981, in response to changes in the electoral laws imposed by the régime, most of its members joined the PMDB.

An old party label now reappeared, the Brazilian Labour Party (*Partido Trabalhista Brasileiro*—PTB). This attracted only 23 of the former 52 ex-PTB deputies in Congress and only one senator. Golbery also arranged that the old name should not go to the party now forming around Brizola, just returned from political exile, but to another, rival group, led by Ivette Vargas, the great-niece of Vargas. It was a bitter blow to Brizola.

The new party furthest to the left was the **Worker's Party** (*Partido dos Trabalhadores*—PT). It was the one rooted in the "new unionism" centred in São Paulo. This was a movement, mostly of younger workers, which rejected the corporatist trade unionism bequeathed by Vargas, with its *pelego* tradition and its links to the Ministry of Labour. Its most prominent leader was **Luís Inácio da Silva**, or "Lula", president of the Metalworkers' Union of São Bernardo, an important industrial centre in São Paulo, especially for the motor industry. The new trade union movement produced the first strikes of Geisel's presidency in 1978, followed by others in 1979, and 1980, under Figueiredo. A major strike in March 1979 brought over 200 arrests, but continued till late April.

Lula was, by now, a political figure of national importance and the growing links between the unions and the Catholic Church pointed to a new challenge to the authoritarian State. Originally, in 1979, a new party needed 42 deputies and 7 senators, but this requirement was relaxed, to allow "temporary party blocs" without minimum support. After much hesitation, Lula, other union leaders and a group of intellectuals, formed the PT. By 1981, it had four deputies, but Lula and 11 other labour leaders were having to appeal against three-year prison sentences for their part in strikes in 1980. These eventually were quashed before the key elections of 1982.

The restructuring of the party system gave further stimulus to political debate and mobilization throughout 1980 and into 1981, but *distensão* suffered a major blow, in January 1980, with the death, from a sudden heart attack, of Petrônio Portela. He had presented himself as the most viable civilian candidate of "conciliation", with the Partido Popular as the party of "transition".

His death forced régime strategists to reconsider their position in preparation for the vitally important elections of 1982, when, according to SNI analysis, the PDS might win only three states, all in the north-east.

This re-thinking closely followed a change in economic policies. During Geisel's term, Delfim Neto was sent to gilded exile as ambassador to France, from where he carefully monitored developments in Brazil. Figueiredo moved Mário Henrique Simonsen, Finance Minister under Geisel, to a "super-ministry" in the Ministry of Planning. Simonsen believed that it was necessary to cool down the economy, especially as inflation rose from the 1978 annual rate of 40 per cent. One of his principal critics was Delfim, now returned as Minister of Agriculture. In August 1979, Simonsen resigned, to be replaced by Delfim, to the applause of the São Paulo business community. Delfim produced a new National Development Plan, which, in effect, promised to reproduce his performance of 1968 to 1974, aiming at similar rates of inflation of between 15 to 20 per cent. There was special emphasis on improving agricultural production, both to push up exports and reduce inflation. A growth rate of 6.8 per cent occurred in 1979, but inflation shot up to 77 per cent. Deficit on the current account rose to $7,000 million in 1978. Delfim's response was a maxi-devaluation of 30 per cent in December 1979, followed by publication of proposed devaluations and indexation changes for 1980 to head-off future inflationary pressures.

Throughout 1980, following the death of Portela, there was further evidence of right-wing reaction to *distensão* or *abertura*. This now took violent form, with the bombing of newstands which sold material critical of the régime, and letter-bombs to supporters of *abertura*, including the OAB, the Brazilian Bar Association, the former president of which, Raymundo Faoro, was one of the most effective critics of authoritarian controls. The current president, Seabra Fagundes, believed the bomb, which killed the secretary who opened it, had come from DOI-CODI, (Detachment of Operation and Information, and Centre for Internal Defence Operations), created by Médici to counteract terrorism.

These, together with the CIE (Army Information Centre) were the main intelligence organs, co-ordinated by the SNI providing an "intelligence community" which was virtually a state within a state. Estimates, at the time, of SNI personnel were as high as 50,000. It was linked to a system of entrenched interests, including the "golden parachute", which provided well-paid jobs for officers retiring from active service. Golbery later identified such interests as one of the main sources of opposition to *abertura*.

While right-wing violence grew more intense, there was also increasing disagreement within the régime on the political strategy to be adopted in the run-up to the elections of 1982. This was only one point of dispute between Delfim Neto and Golbery do Couto e Silva. Delfim favoured a series of coalitions, with the PP in rural areas and with the PP, PTB or PDT in urban centres. Golbery disagreed, but found himself under ever greater attack from Delfim and from General Octâvio Medeiros, Director General of the SNI, who already was seen as a likely successor to Figueiredo, not least since both Médici and Figueiredo had come to the presidency from heading the SNI.

The struggle came to a head after April 30, 1981, the eve of "Labour Day". An army captain and a sergeant of DOI-CODI, in civilian clothes, were about to plant a bomb in the Rio Centro, a concert and exhibition hall, where a Labour Day concert was being planned. The bomb exploded in their car, killing the sergeant, while also providing direct evidence of the involvement of the intelligence services in right-wing terrorism.

Golbery, among many others, wanted a full enquiry, but the régime attempted a crude cover-up of the affair. On Aug. 6, Golbery resigned as head of the *Gabinete Civil* (Civilian Staff). *Abertura* had now lost its two main strategists and Figueiredo was deprived of his most skilled political advisor, a loss from which he, and the régime, never recovered. It seems that part of the price for not being prosecuted for the Rio Centro affair, was that those behind it should no longer resist the elections scheduled for 1982.

The disagreement between Golbery and Delfim also involved the economy. Golbery wanted limited changes to the social security system, and stimulus to industry and employment, all with a view to the 1982 elections. This ran counter to Delfim's reversion to a far more cautious economic strategy than that which he had adopted on retaking office and in his maxi-devaluation of December 1979. In 1980, inflation reached the unprecedented level of 110 per cent.

A deficit of $3,500 million had to be covered by drawing on foreign reserves, GDP growth was 7.2 per cent, but only at a high cost. 1981 saw a fall in GDP, of 1.6 per cent, for the first time since 1942, with falls in industrial production and trade. In 1982, inflation fell slightly, to 95.0 per cent, but, by the start of the year, the foreign debt had jumped to $61,400 million, with debt servicing now the equivalent of 65.6 per cent of the value of exports. Delfim's answer was to dig deeper, to take on even more loans, even in the teeth of recession, which brought with it massive dismissals of workers, including within the motor industry.

One of Delfim's main concerns, in a major exercise of political cynicism, was to hide the painful truth about the economy from the electorate until after the elections of Nov. 15. Once the elections were over, and the régime was, in any case, faced with a massive opposition victory, the real scale of the problem was revealed. The current account deficit had gone up from $11,700 million, in 1981, to $16,300 million in 1982. Mexico, in August 1982, had declared that it could not service its foreign debts: now Brazil became the focus of world attention.

Even before the debt crisis was made known, Brazilians had given their verdict on the military-backed régime. Apart from Portela and Golbery do Couto e Silva, another politician seeking to direct *abertura* was João Leitão de Abreu, head of the Civilian Presidential Staff under Médici. He and Golbery had been involved with a North American professor of political science, Samuel Huntington, and with Brazilian academics, including Cândido Mendes de Almeida and Wanderley Guilherme dos Santos, in 1972 and 1973, in analyzing Brazil's move from an authoritarian to a more open political régime.

This resulted in a series of political interventions, sometimes called *casuismos* in Portuguese, rather crude attempts at political manipulation or engineering. Leitão de Abreu, another *gaúcho*, took over from Golbery in August 1981, returning to his former post, in charge of the Civilian Household. Trying to maintain control, the régime now introduced yet another political "package", in November 1981, relying on the *decurso de prazo*, whereby a legislative proposal sent to Congress by the president, with a 60-day limit for approval, became law, if not passed by Congress within the allotted time.

The new electoral rules forbade coalitions to elect governors. Every party now had to field candidates for all offices in all *municípios* to be contested: otherwise, it could not take part in the election in that *município*. This meant that opposition candidates must fight each other, to the benefit of the PDS. The most important provision was that voters must vote for candidates of the same party, from local councillor right up to governor (*voto vinculado*, the tied or linked vote). This again, in 1982, was meant to help the government, PDS party, which was better organized at local level, so that local, clientelistic choices should determine the result of direct elections for state governor, the first since 1965.

One, unexpected, result of this requirement was that the PP, unable to field candidates right across the country, decided to dissolve itself to merge with the PMDB, in the hope that this would strengthen its chances of providing a government of "transition". Another was that many voters who favoured the PT decided that they had no chance of electing a governor, as, for example, in Rio de Janeiro: they, therefore voted for Brizola, whose party, the PDT, benefited from the *voto vinculado*, since Brizola drew along with him other candidates, who, on an individual basis, would not have been elected. The overall result was a substantial victory for the opposition, though the *voto vinculado* did help the régime in the interior, especially in the north-east. The electorate was now more than 45,000,000 the biggest in Latin America.

The opposition won 59 per cent of the vote, taking 10 of the 23 states, with 50 per cent of Brazil's population and almost 80 per cent of GDP. Nine PMDB governors were elected, 13 PDS and one PDT, the other governor, of Rondônia, still being appointed. In Rio de Janeiro, the SNI tried to falsify the returns, to keep out Brizola, an effort which back-fired when, soon, it was made public. In Congress, the PDS had only a simple majority in the Chamber, but an absolute majority in the electoral college, which would choose the next president, and a two-thirds majority in the Senate, because of its 18 "bionic" senators elected in 1978.

The fact that state governors once again were directly elected, for the first time since 1965, introduced a change in the balance of power between the federal and state governments, especially in the most important opposition-led states of São Paulo, Rio de Janeiro, Minas Gerais and Paraná. Franco Montoro in São Paulo and Tancredo Neves in Minas Gerais were both politicians of the centre, but Brizola was still considered by many people within the régime as a serious challenge from the "subversive left" against whom the 1964 *coup* had been directed.

Brizola tried to be reassuring, both to the Figueiredo government and to the armed forces. His Secretary of Finance, César Maia, was an able economist and businessman, who introduced strictly orthodox, even austere, policies, but the PDT state government received no support from Delfim Neto for any of its development plans, in contrast to the experience of Tancredo Neves in Minas Gerais. Despite this, Brizola introduced an imaginative scheme to build hundreds of new schools. Designed by Oscar Niemeyer, the architect of Brasília, these were prefabricated, all to the same design, and could rapidly be built.

They were the idea of the anthropologist, Darcy Ribeiro, now elected as Brizola's vice-governor. The aim was to give full-time education to poor children, combined with school meals, shower facilities and medical and dental care. Apart from educating the children, these Centres of Integrated Education for the People (*Centros Integrados de Educação Popular*—CIEPs), also kept the children off the streets and from drifting into crime, drug running or prostitution, as well as freeing parents for full-time work to increase family income. The programme was given the highest priority by Brizola: it was very popular with the poorer communities and envied by others.

Another important programme was in the area of housing, especially in giving land titles and in a major effort to upgrade some of the *favelas*, accepting that this self-help housing was there to stay, not a passing phenomenon. One aim was, at least, to show what could be done in this area which previous governments had neglected, provided that resources were made available.

This, unfortunately, was a crucial problem. Brizola's government did not have adequate resources and the federal government, itself, quite apart from its hostility to Brizola, was struggling to cope with a major recession. The general lack of money, in all the states, was one reason why newly elected governors were not able to exert greater pressure on the federal government, of which they were, still, largely clients. This situation encouraged state governors of all parties to form lobbying blocks towards the President and Federal government.

Apart from the sharp jump in oil prices in 1974 and 1979, Brazil was faced with almost a doubling of Eurodollar interest rates, from 8.7 in 1978 to 17 per cent in 1981. Like the rest of the Third World, it was severely affected by the United States' change in monetary policy in 1979, producing an international recession, which lowered demands for Brazilian exports.

With great reluctance, Brazil turned to the IMF, with a "letter of intent" in January 1983, a severe setback for Delfim and his team. This involved the usual IMF recipes of tight control of the money supply and credit, cuts in public spending and in subsidies, and resistance to demands for wage increases. Private bankers, in the wake of Mexico's default in August 1982, now looked to the IMF for a lead on future policy. Brazil had a choice: hold back on its foreign commitments in the face of a world crisis, in part produced by its creditors, or accept IMF conditions and sink further into recession. More radical and nationalist voices urged the first course, but there was no solidarity or co-operation between the debtor countries, including Mexico and Argentina, and the government feared the long-term consequences of not meeting current obligations.

Brazil's recession deepened throughout 1983. There was an unprecedented fall in GDP of 5 per cent, with industrial production down by 7.9 per cent and capital goods by 23 per cent. There was a sharp rise in unemployment, especially in the industrial sector in São Paulo and Rio de Janeiro, and a steady decline in real wages throughout 1983 and 1984. The lower paid workers were especially badly hit, often unemployed, with real wages falling, while inflation for 1983 rose to over 200 per cent, over twice the rate in the previous year. The only positive indicator was a balance of trade surplus of $6,500 million, with exports of $21,900 million (down from $23,700 million in 1981) and imports of $15,400 million (from $22,100 million in 1981).

Figueiredo himself and the Delfim team became increasingly unpopular and discredited, and, with them, the whole basis for the régime, which earlier had sought legitimacy, especially from the middle classes, by its record of economic success. One major source of criticism now became the indirect election for president. A widespread campaign began for "*diretas-já*", "direct elections, now", aimed at the election of 1985. Such a change required a constitutional amendment, which must have the support of a two-thirds majority in Congress. This amendment was proposed in March 1983, by Dante de Oliveira, a PMDB deputy.

The "*diretas-já*" campaign, leading to the congressional vote on April 25, 1984, represented a major advance in terms of mobilizing civil society within the process of *abertura*. Politicians, churchmen, artists, lawyers, the media, and huge crowds of Brazilians of all classes attended massive rallies across the country in huge political demonstrations, far bigger than any seen before 1964, when the population, in any case, was much smaller: 500,000 in April 1983 in Rio de Janeiro, 200,000 in Goiânia and in Pôrto Alegre and over 1,000,000 people in São Paulo. The demand for the direct presidential vote pulled together all the resentment against the régime and expressed the nation's hope for the future. On April 25, 1984, the amendment failed to win the necessary two-thirds majority, but the message of the "*diretas-já*" campaign was clear: the people wanted change.

This unprecedented expression of political demand further alarmed many PDS politicians, who already were worried over the régime's failure to deliver the vote in 1982. Many were looking for a new patron, whom they thought they had found in **Paulo Salim Maluf**, a rich *paulista* businessman, a member of the increasingly influential Lebanese community, wealthy in his own right, through the Eucatex building materials firm, and by marriage to a member of the Lutfalla family.

The presidential succession question tore the PDS apart in 1984. Figueiredo, unlike Geisel, was unwilling, or unable, to indicate his preferred successor. There were bitter attacks on Maluf, especially from Antônio Carlos Magalhães, a former governor of Bahia, who resented Maluf's use of patronage within Bahia and the north-east. Another contender, Colonel Mário Andreazza, also had built up support, especially in the north-east, through the use of state-directed patronage, first as Minister of Transport under Costa e Silva and Médici and, now, in the powerful Ministry of the Interior.

The crisis came to a head in June, in a confrontation in the National Committee of the PDS, between supporters and opponents of Maluf. The committee's president, Senator José Sarney, and others who wanted to stop Maluf, abruptly resigned, forcing the definitive split within the party of the régime. That this was a calculated break rather than a spontaneous crisis, was seen in the speed with which the dissident group reformed, establishing a break-away faction, the Liberal Front (*Frente Liberal*—FL).

The PFL included, in addition to Sarney, Marco Maciel, an ambitious young politician from Pernambuco, and Aureliano Chaves, a former governor of Minas Gerais, now Vice-President to Figueiredo, whom he had replaced, as acting-President when Figueiredo was ill in 1981 and 1983. He was still generally regarded as a presidential candidate, but, unknown at the time, he had made an agreement with his fellow *mineiro*, Tancredo Neves. This was that, whoever won his party's nomination would have the other's support.

Meanwhile, the PMDB also turned to Tancredo Neves, as the ideal candidate of "conciliation". He had been federal deputy for the Vargista PSD over three decades, Minister of Justice in the second Vargas government, in 1953–54, and Prime Minister in the "parliamentary" period under Goulart. In August 1984, the PMDB convention chose Tancredo, now governor of Minas Gerais, as its candidate for the indirect presidential election of January 1985.

Earlier, in private conversation, Golbery do Couto e Silva had said that, if his overall strategy were to go awry, his preferred fall-back candidate for President would be Tancredo Neves, even though in 1984, he now supported Maluf. Tancredo Neves was widely respected by the leaders of the armed forces and among the dissident members of the PDS, now in the FL. As a shrewd *mineiro* politician, he would not have given up his long-coveted governorship of Minas Gerais, unless victory in the presidential election were guaranteed, a point endorsed by leading FL businessmen and politicians, in confidence, in September 1984.

In August, Maluf easily won the the PDS nomination as presidential candidate, by 493 votes to 350, but the "king-makers" of the régime already had rejected him. There was a threat of a military *coup* in September, but Tancredo Neves won the endorsement of those who mattered most, including the tacit, but public, support of former president, Ernesto Geisel.

Again, there was a price to be paid. It included agreement not to prosecute members of the armed forces who had been involved in torture or abuse of human rights, and a political deal concerning the proposed Constituent Assembly. This would not be elected independently, so producing a more radical body, but would consist of the Congress, due to be elected in 1986, which, because of the electoral system, would be relatively conservative.

In the indirect elections for president on Jan. 15, 1985, the electoral college elected Tancredo Neves and his Vice-Presidential candidate, by 480 votes, out of 686, while Maluf won only 180. The future Vice-President, reluctantly accepted by the PMDB, was José Sarney, who, only a few months before, had led the PDS, the party of the régime, which Tancredo now was being elected to replace.

The indirect election of Tancredo Neves, the first civilian president for 21 years, was greeted with jubilation, with carnival music and dancing. This was a new beginning, a "New Republic", full of promise. Swiftly and tragically, the laughter turned to tears, as Tancredo fell ill on the eve of his inauguration, in March 1985. The nation watched in compassion and sorrow, a people at his bedside, till the new president, who never would take office, died on April 22, the day of "Tiradentes", another *mineiro* hero.

Current developments—political (José Sarney 1985–90). The death of Tancredo Neves threatened to produce just that political crisis which he, as the candidate of conciliation, was meant to avert. His constitutional successor, José Sarney, was resented by many people on the right, both civilian and military, for having betrayed, they believed, the PDS and the régime. Among the PMDB, and on the left more generally, there was bitter dismay that the first civilian president under *abertura* should be the former leader of the government party, who, as recently as April 1984, had voted against the Dante Oliveira amendment to allow a direct vote for president.

Sarney was a seasoned politician, a former member of the more liberal *bossa nova* group in the UDN, former governor of Maranhão, and a senator; but he did not have the political stature of Tancredo Neves and, like Quadros in 1961, lacked strong party and congressional support. The evident danger was that, again, like Quadros, he might try to appeal directly to the people or become too dependent on the support of the armed forces. His smooth succession to the presidency owed something to the shock felt at the sudden loss of Trancredo Neves, but, even more, to the support of the leader of the PMDB, **Ulysses Guimarães**, who insisted that the democratic process should be respected.

From March to July 1985, there was a virtual revolt of the PMDB, one result of which was the failure to support a proposal that mayors appointed in 1982 might be eligible to be elected in newly restored direct elections for mayor in capital cities. This meant that Mário Covas, of the PMDB, appointed as mayor in São Paulo, was ineligible. In the elections of November 1985, the left made important gains, especially in the PDT and the PT. Brizola's candidates won in Rio de Janeiro and Pôrto Alegre and came close in Curitíba, Florianôpolis and Recife.

The PMDB also did well, but suffered a major setback in São Paulo, where Senator Fernando Henrique Cardoso, one of the party's most vigorous intellectual spokesmen, was defeated by only 138,000 votes (3.4 per cent). The victor was Jânio Quadros, the former president, who was supported by 38 per cent of the 4,800,000 electors. His campaign had been carefully planned and lavishly financed by the right, to produce a damaging blow not just to Cardoso, but to governor Franco Montoro's presidential ambitions and to the PMDB at national level. The success of Quadros in São Paulo and Saturnino Braga, of the PDT in Rio de Janeiro, pointed to the polarization of national politics which the indirect election of Tancredo Neves aimed to prevent.

By late 1985, it was clear that the PMDB was too heterogeneous a coalition to stay together for long, and that it could not provide the stable "party of government" which Brazil's new democracy evidently needed. Sarney's personal position was strengthened by the elections of November 1985, as shown in his new ministry, of February 1986, which gave office to the PFL element in the Democratic Alliance and to Sarney's old associates from the UDN and ARENA. Everything pointed to an early split within the PMDB, providing a new, more radical party of the left.

Important PMDB leaders began to distance themselves from Sarney, who was strongly criticized for lack of coherent policies, especially to contain inflation, now running at almost 250 per cent a year. Then, on Feb. 28, 1986 came the bombshell, a sudden, sharp, shock to the economy, which had been prepared, in almost total secrecy, for several months, under the guidance of the PMDB politician and São Paulo businessman, Dilson Funaro, the Minister of Finance. This was the **Cruzado Plan**, announced on television to an astonished nation by Sarney, surrounded by all his ministers. Sarney spoke of "a life or death struggle against inflation", which could reach 500 per cent by the end of the year. He called on the people for help.

One undoubted success of the Cruzado Plan was in guaranteeing support for the PMDB in the gubernatorial, congressional, and local elections of November 1986. The PMD won 22 of the 23 state governorships and elected majorities in the Chamber (53 per cent) and Senate (63 per cent) with 54 per cent in the Constituent Assembly. Among the losses was Darcy Ribeiro, Brizola's candidate for governor in Rio de Janeiro. He was beaten by an anti-Brizola coalition, losing to Wellington Moreiro Franco. The defeat owed much to Brizola's criticism of the Cruzado Plan.

The PDS fared worst of all the parties, reduced from 235 deputies in 1983 to only 35, while the PT grew from 6 deputies in July 1986 to 16 by February 1987. Having swept the board, the government then revealed a measure of opportunism and cynicism for which many Brazilians never forgave either Sarney or the PMDB, by dismantling the Cruzado Plan even while votes still were being counted.

A persistent concern throughout 1986, in the run-up to the elections, was the relative weakness of political party programmes and of party loyalties, as the political system tried to adjust to *abertura* and the process of transition. The PDS was in disarray and the PMDB was threatened both from the right and from its own internal divisions. The Democratic Alliance, which had served to defeat Maluf and elect Tancredo Neves, now seemed to have outlived its usefulness. A stern critic of the *Cruzado Plan*, the distinguished lawyer Raymundo Faoro, said that the continued use of decree laws showed that "this is no longer a régime of parties and Congress".

Politicians readily moved between parties, often leaving those under whose label they had been elected, while others with political ambitions, discussed which of several parties they might use as a vehicle for their plans. A startling example of this, in 1986, was Antônio Ermírio de Morães, head of *Grupo Votorantim*, the biggest private conglomerate in Brazil. In 1984, he had refused an invitation to be the Vice-Presidential candidate of Tancredo Neves, which, already, if accepted, should have brought him to the presidency. In 1986, he decided to seek election as governor of São Paulo, so looked around for a party. He would have been accepted as candidate by several, but finally opted for the PTB. Meanwhile, he made clear his distrust of "professional politicians" only interested in the spoils of office ("*fisiologia*"). Such attitudes justified the questions which Senator Fernando Henrique Cardoso, among others, posed in 1986: how could there be democracy without political parties?

The Congressional elections of November, which also produced the Constituent Assembly, did little to answer this question. In formal terms, the PMDB was the strongest party in Congress, while, despite the relatively poor performance of the PFL, the combined strength of the Democratic Alliance, of PMDB and PFL, went up from 72 to 78 per cent. Closer analysis, however, showed that the party with most representation in the Constituent Assembly was the former pro-government ARENA, some of whose members, often defectors from the PDS and PFL, had joined the PMDB up to the deadline of May 15, 1986. In other words, the Constituent Assembly was considerably less reformist than, at first, it had appeared. In this respect, it responded to the hopes of the military leaders in their pact with Tancredo Neves, that by making the Constituent Assembly coincident with Congress, rather than being independently elected, they would produce a more conservative body.

Throughout most of 1987, and 1988, attention largely focused on the deliberations of the Constituent Assembly, on the government's continued efforts to restrain inflation and on the related issue of pressures from the trade unions to produce a satisfactory wages policy. Once the constitution was, at last, promulgated, on Oct. 5, 1988, the main source of interest became the municipal elections of November 1988, seen as a major test for the Sarney government and its performance.

Closely linked to the problem of inflation was that of the foreign debt. Dilson Funaro, all through his term of office, as Minister of Finance, failed to win a sympathetic hearing from foreign private banks or foreign governments. On Feb. 20, 1987 Sarney again used nation-wide television to announce a moratorium on interest payments on part of the foreign debt. Using typically emotive phrases, such as "national security" and "betrayal of the country and of patriotism", he explained that national reserves had fallen from $6,800 million, two years before, to a current figure of $3,962 million, and that, "in the last five years, Brazil has paid $55,800 million in interest alone". The central point was that which also underlay the *Cruzado Plan*, when it was made clear that Brazil could not go on paying 4–5 per cent of GDP in interest payments, almost twice what had been asked of Germany after Versailles, when Keynes had feared for the whole international financial system.

The partial moratorium caused excitement abroad, but, at home, was generally seen as evidence of the failure of recent policy. It also reflected increasing pressure within the economy and the political system, in the form of wage demands and strike action. In February and March, there were serious strikes among port workers and in the petroleum industry, when, for the first time under the "New Republic", the government mobilized troops and armoured vehicles, to contain workers' protests and demands.

A further sign of tensions within the government was the resignation of João Sayad, as Minister of Planning, on March 17. He had tried to reconcile stabilization, including a partial price freeze over three months, with some larger measure of distribution and further acknowledgement of the need for social reforms, as part of the whole "transition" process. Funaro, too, was being criticized by employers and businessmen, accused of not being sufficiently sensitive to the danger of recession and of the need for a free market, as well as over his attitude to the IMF. These were all issues which were to run and run, till the end of Sarney's term and that of his successor.

The opposition to Funaro was carefully orchestrated. He had been a conscientious and imaginative minister, struggling with cancer, accused of being too much of an idealist. The São Paulo business community turned against him, supported by such spokesmen as ex-President Figueiredo. They pointed to an inflation rate for April 1987 touching 20.9 per cent in the month, with an accumulated record since the *Cruzado Plan* of 125 per cent. Funaro found scant support from the left of the PMDB and, on April 24, 1987, after 600 exhausting days in office, resigned.

The weakness of Sarney's position was seen in his failure to impose his own candidate, Tasso Jereissati, governor of Ceará, as successor to Funaro. Jereissati also had strong support in the business community, but the PMDB, through Ulysses Guimarães, vetoed the choice. The new Minister of Finance was to be Luiz Carlos Bresser Pereira, a distinguished academic economist, who also had long experience in both the private sector, through the *Pão de Açucar* supermarket group, and in government service in São Paulo.

Overruled in this choice, Sarney, now deeply unpopular, was criticized over other policies, including his plan to build a railway, the *Ferrovia Norte-Sul*, linking the Federal District to Goiás and to his own home state of Maranhão, at an estimated cost of $2,400 million. Sarney seemed to want to emulate Kubitschek, to leave a lasting mark on Brazil, but the project was open to charges of corruption, concerning the tenders involved, and it met considerable public derision, as the "railway of shame", "railway of *marajás*", (over-paid public servants) or *"ferrovia faraônica"* (railway of Pharaoh-like expense).

In May, Sarney tried, without success, to outwit one of his main critics, Leonel Brizola, the ex-governor of Rio de Janiero, who was preparing a national television broadcast for the PDT. Sarney anticipated the programme, by announcing that, in face of the problems currently facing Brazil, he would renounce the six years in office to which, he said, he was constitutionally entitled, but would continue for five. His attempt at a *"white coup"* failed, but the next bout of influenza to hit Brazil, as always, given a popular name, was known as a *"gripe José Sarney"*, the "flu which refuses to go away".

A more important initiative, on June 12, 1987, was yet another economic package, the *Novo Cruzado*, introduced by Sarney and Bresser Pereira, more generally known as the *Bresser Plan*. Sarney, now, in less than three years, had had three Ministers of Finance, four Presidents of the Central Bank, and five different economic projects. Again, it was meant to provide shock treatment. Prices and wages were frozen for 90 days: the "wage-trigger" (a mechanism by which, under the Cruzado Plan, wages were adjusted in relation to price-rises) was ended; the *cruzado*, again, was devalued. One predictable result was the impact on wages. These, it was calculated, had fallen by 30 per cent in real terms since the Cruzado Plan, and might fall by another 20 per cent, or more, in the next three months.

As before, the Plan did not have enough political backing, not just from the business community, but even from the President and the PMDB. Bresser Pereira became ever more politically isolated. In October, a survey showed that 15 per cent of respondents thought the Plan a failure and 67 per cent blamed it for a fall in purchasing power. Attempts to bring about better terms for debt repayment were also rejected by foreign bankers, and Bresser was unable to come to an agreement with Argentina to make a joint stand. On Dec. 18, 1987 he resigned, to be replaced by Mailson da Nóbrega, who had served in senior economic positions under Geisel and Mário Henrique Simonsen. His appointment was seen as a victory for conservative critics of recent economic policy.

Other indications of the same trend included pressures on the new Minister of Planning, Annibal Teixeira, who had replaced Sayad, especially in relation to proposed, relatively moderate, plans for agrarian reform. This was especially seen in the influence of the Democratic Union of Landed Interests (*União Democrática Ruralista*—UDR), an increasingly aggressive, even violent, pressure group, which sought to protect landowners' interests. The agrarian reform programme was substantially reduced by Teixeira, to provide "more realistic" goals. The government's first, ostensible, aim was to distribute land to 1,400,000 landless families, between 1986 and 1989. By mid 1987, less than 20,000 families had been resettled. In view of this derisory achievement, Teixeira reduced the 1987 target from 300,000 families to 200,000. This was in a country with an estimated 4,500,000 landless families working the land. Political "trimming" could scarcely go further.

Against this background of failure to contain inflation, or to achieve a more equitable agreement on debt repayment, or wages policy, or to tackle some of the country's most compelling social problems, including agrarian reform, the Constituent Assembly went about its work, always under the scrutiny of the armed forces, to whom Sarney, ever more, was under tutelage. To compensate for his lack of party and congressional support, the president unashamedly used every form of patronage and persuasion at his disposal. Even the less hostile of his critics, said that he was trying to run Brazil as if it were Maranhão, using a mixture of coercion and clientelism familiar in the politics of the north-east.

The Congress/Constituent Assembly, already heavily weighted to the right, too often responded to these pressures, especially through the *Centrão* (the large centre group). In May 1988, it effectively emasculated proposals for a modest degree of agrarian reform, with UDR supporters whooping in victory along the corridors of the Congress building. Already, in March, it had overturned a proposal to introduce a parliamentary form of government to curb presidential powers, which brought charges of the corrupt use of patronage by Sarney, to sway the vote. In June, it, at last, agreed to allow Sarney five years in office: well-informed calculations of how much was spent to achieve this vote went to dizzying sums.

The new Constitution was a long document, of 245 articles and 157 pages. Politicians on the Left, especially in the PT, thought it was deficient in important areas, but, despite such reservations and the supine, even venal, behaviour of the *Centrão*, it was generally seen as a major advance in terms of the transition to democracy. It finally got rid of the *entulho* ("rubbish") of the repressive legislation of the old régime.

The next major item on the political agenda in 1988 was the municipal elections of Nov. 15. Various developments in the preceding months promised to have a determining effect on these. One was the long-predicted split in the PMDB, which, finally, came in July 1988, quickened by the vote over Sarney's term of office. Dissident party members now formed the Party of Brazilian Social Democracy (*Partido da Social Democracia Brasileira*—PSDB). This avoided confusion with the PDS, but the new party quickly became better known as the *Tucanos* (the Toucans). It was especially strong in São Paulo, containing such influential figures as the former governor, Franco Montoro, the two São Paulo senators, Mário Covas and Fernando Henrique Cardoso, and the former Finance Minister, Luiz Carlos Bresser Pereira. It urgently needed to find a popular base of support and a national identity and platform, if it were to become the authentic, modern, social-democratic party of the Centre-Left, to replace the PMDB, which its founders hoped.

A more serious and more immediate challenge to the Sarney government than that of the *Tucanos*, came from the trade union movement and workers' wage demands. In February and March 1988, troops had been mobilized against strikers, but, still, protests and strikes increased, as wages and salaries were eroded by inflation, which, by October, was running at a monthly rate of 27 per cent, threatening to reach an annual rate of 1,000 per cent. Sarney, travelling abroad, stressed a record trade surplus of US$18,000 million, an increase of 1 per cent in industrial production, which had been expected to fall by 10 per cent, and record agricultural harvests for the second year running; but he did not mention the public deficit or inflation, rapidly threatening to become hyperinflation.

The one life-raft for workers was the *Unidade de Referência de Preços*—URP, a unit for adjusting wages in relation to price rises. Originally, this was meant to be used every three months, but already, in the private sector, was being applied monthly. Since at least May, there had been a running battle, in the public sector, between certain categories of workers and the government, which said the URP should not be applied to these workers.

In October 1988, during Sarney's absence abroad, resentment exploded. Across the country, 800,000 civil servants stopped work, involving 15 out of the 26 ministries and 21 other federal organizations. One reply from the government was the threat of violence: another was a further attempt to reach a "social pact", an agreement between government, employers and workers, a stock response, when faced with trade union demand, which, in recent months, had produced 304 strikes in industry, 85 in transport, and 11 in banking. Altogether there were 983 strikes, involving an estimated 3,500,000 workers.

At the end of October, the government called a meeting of employers' and workers' representatives. The employers were represented by Mário Amato, president of the Federation of Industries of the State of São Paulo (*Federação das Industrias do Estado de São Paulo*—FIESP). The CGT, now representing about 29,000,000 workers, was willing to discuss a wage freeze. The CUT refused, saying that the workers had no more sacrifices to offer. On Nov. 4, an agreement was signed in the Ministry of Labour. The main aim was to keep wages below the rate of inflation, while prices for 93 basic products would also be kept below the inflation rate. No-one was optimistic of success.

Then came a major crisis. Just under a week before the elections in over 4,000 *municípios*, striking steel workers occupied the National Steel Company's complex at Volta Redonda. On Nov. 8, the plant was surrounded by troops and, in the evening of Nov. 9, they opened fire, killing three young workers and wounding at least twenty-three. The officer in charge referred to urban guerrillas, and he and his colleagues were, subsequently, decorated for their action. A simple memorial to the dead was built by workers, only to be blown up, in May 1989, by right-wing extremists. For many working people, this symbolized their relations with the Sarney government.

The municipal elections of Nov. 15, 1988 showed a rejection of the PMDB and, above all, of the Sarney government. There was massive support for the left, with the most exciting success going to the PT. In São Paulo, the PT candidate was a woman from the north-eastern state of Paraíba, Luiza Erundina. She did not have full backing from her party leaders, yet defeated Paulo Maluf, the rich former mayor and state governor. The PT also won in the major industrial cities (the ABC cities) of São Paulo state, and did exceptionally well elsewhere, winning Pôrto Alegre and Vitória, capital of the state of Espírito Santo, while also coming second in both Rio de Janeiro and Belo Horizonte.

The PDT did less well. Its candidates won in Rio de Janeiro and Curitíba, but, in the large capital cities, Brizola's party polled just over 8,000,000, as against the PT, with over 11,500,000. The biggest loser was the PMDB, in stark contrast, just two years before, to the elections of 1986. Because of its nation-wide organization, it won most votes across the country as a whole, but with a huge vote of no-confidence in the principal urban and industrial centres. As with ARENA and the PDS before it, the PMDB now was winning only in the more rural and less economically dynamic areas of the country.

Compared with the heady popularity of 1986, Sarney and his government now were shown as lacking both legitimacy and credibility. One major problem for Brazil, was that, because of his successful manipulation of Congress, to allow him a fifth year in office, Sarney still had another year to go, yet, increasingly, people realized that no effective solutions to the nation's problems could be found as long as he remained in office.

Bereft of congressional support, Sarney was coming more than ever under the influence of the armed forces, especially of the Minister of War, General Leônidas Pires Gonçalves, and the head of the SNI, General Ivan de Souza Mendes. General Leônidas was especially alarmed at the growing strength of the Left, even before the elections of November 1988. He joined those who urged that one more major effort must be made to curb inflation. Otherwise, he believed, a drift into hyperinflation, in 1989, would simply give the candidates of the Left a walkover in the presidential election towards the end of the year. At the end of 1988, inflation for the year was a shade under 1,000 per cent with the monthly rate for December touching 30 per cent. The former Minister of Finance, Bresser Pereira, said that the best that could be hoped for 1989 was that the country might avoid hyperinflation and come safely through to the presidential election in November, which would mark the formal end of the transition to democracy. The implied fear was that, in 1989, as in 1889, the crisis might get out of hand.

The result of such anxieties was the Summer Plan of Jan. 15, 1989, a further major effort by the Sarney government to curb inflation. By the middle of 1989, inflation was up to 29 per cent, rather higher than it had been when the Summer Plan was introduced in January. It was clear that even more urgent measures were needed.

Apart from inflation, other problems, too, were plaguing the economy. The most immediate political issue was reaction from the unions. The trade union leaders who had negotiated the "social pact" said that Sarney had "torn it up" by his Summer Plan, and, throughout 1989, relations between the unions and the government worsened. There was a sharp increase in strikes, up in February 1989, as compared with February 1988, by 58 per cent. They were also becoming longer and more violent. In March, a call for a one-day "national strike" affected all regions of the country, paralyzed several state capitals, and involved, at least, 43 per cent of the economically active population. It was, by far, the most successful of the 11 such strikes called in the history of Brazil.

Sarney and the military leaders grew more apprehensive, when, in March 1989, the number of strikes reached a record figure of 479 in the month, and by April 25, there had been 408. On April 27, the President spoke on television of a "calamitous situation". He then sent to Congress *Medida Provisória No 50* (Provisional Measure 50). This sought to restrict the right to strike, which only seven months earlier had been guaranteed in the new Constitution. The proposal caused an uproar, and was rejected by Congress: but it served to show how far the Sarney government had lost both control of the economy and the respect of the people. All eyes now turned to the elections for president in November 1989.

Fernando Collor de Mello, (1990–). The municipal elections of November 1988 brought, as already noted, sweeping victories for the Left and underlined widespread dissatisfaction with the Sarney government. Approximately 75,800,000 electors chose 4,300 mayors and 43,600 municipal councillors. The success of the PT and PDT meant that their candidates for president in 1989, Lula and Brizola, started the new year, not just as clear favourites, but with one or other of them virtually assured of victory. Lula was just marginally ahead in popular polls, but Brizola had a far stronger electoral and political record. By contrast, it was difficult to see a candidate of the Right who had the remotest chance of winning.

There also seemed little hope for the principal PMDB candidate, the much respected president of the party, Ulysses Guimarães, but there were other potentially strong centre-left candidates, including Orestes Quércia, the PMDB governor of São Paulo, and Senator Mário Covas, leader of the *Tucanos*. Further left, at least formally, was Roberto Freire of the PCB.

A possible candidate of the so-called "New Right" was Guilherme Afif Domingos, of the Liberal Party (*Partido Liberal*—PL), a former president of the Commercial Association of São Paulo, ex-Secretary of Agriculture in the state government of Paulo Maluf and, since November 1986, federal deputy. Maluf, himself, recently defeated in the contest for mayor of São Paulo by Luiza Erundina, was now something of an outsider, as was, even more so, Jânio Quadros, though, after the elections of November 1988, he began to present himself, with feigned reluctance, as a potential candidate of the Right, to save the country from left-wing extremism. There were also, on the Right, Ronaldo Caiado, leader of the UDR, the powerful landowners' pressure group. Another possible choice for the right was Jarbas Passarinho, leader of the PDS, a respected politician and former army officer. From within the army, itself, a potential candidate was General Leônidas Pires Goncalves, Minister of War.

The political right was desperately looking for someone who could stop both Lula and Brizola, without much hope of finding him. Over the horizon, charged Fernando Collor de Mello, hastily scrambling together a tiny party, the sole function of which was to act as a vehicle for his candidature. This was given the resounding title of Party of National Reconstruction (*Partido de Reconstrução Nacional*—PRN), a title which, at once, carried criticism of the past and a message for the future.

Collor's rise in the polls was extraordinary. In February 1989, the month following the *Summer Plan*, he was nowhere. As early as April, with a showing of 13 per cent, he had overtaken Brizola (12.3 per cent) and Lula (10.2 per cent). This was the first time that Brizola had not led the field since Gallup began its surveys of presidential candidates in September 1987. In May 1989, Collor's percentage share was 17 per cent; in June, a massive 43 per cent; in July, down, slightly, to 39 per cent. By the end of August, 41 per cent and, by early September, just before free television time began, still 40 per cent, as compared with 14 per cent for Brizola, and only 6 per cent for Lula. The political right, as so often in Brazil's history, was threatening to outplay and confound its opponents.

Collor's main attractions were his youth, energy, his vehement criticism of corruption, inefficiency and of the Sarney government, and a promise of a fresh start. He presented himself as a new force in politics, different from the old political class represented by his opponents. A major advantage was his family's wealth and his access to the media, especially television. In fact, Collor was part of that political class which he derided, going back, at least, to his grandfather, Lindolfo Collor, though this link to the Vargas tradition was not highlighted in the campaign, probably because his publicity advisers knew how notoriously short was historical memory in Brazil.

Collor's campaign throughout 1989 was a simple repetition of demands to end corruption and inefficiency and criticism of Sarney's government and of the other candidates. It was also marked by violence, as Collor marched his supporters through the streets, his fist clenched in the air, making much of his claim to be a karate black belt. Like Quadros, he was to be a new broom, but there was little positive content or programme to be found. In June, he decided to make a European tour, to try to establish some form of international image. During his time in Europe, he spoke in general terms about privatization, said there were too many military ministers, and that he would curb the power of the SNI. He praised free enterprise and promised to curb the role of the state and reduce inflation. On the foreign debt, he said he favoured negotiation with individual creditors on a case by case basis.

After repeated criticism for his lack of policy, his advisors, late in the campaign, produced a *Diretrizes de Ação de Governo Collor de Mello*, an action plan for government, but this, too, was mostly couched in general terms. He also refused to take part in television debates with other candidates before the first round of voting, saying there was no point in debating with candidates who were so far behind him. At the same time, he spent money lavishly on his campaign, apparently not even dismayed, when, in June, his cousin, Eduardo, said that he thought the campaign of the PRN would probably cost "only" about $1,000 million, "because most of it is being done, and will be done, through voluntary work".

The person who really did depend on voluntary work was "Lula", candidate of the Brazilian Popular Front (*Frente Brasil Popular*—FBP), mainly made up of the PT, the PSB, the Green Party (*Partido Verde*—PV) and the Communist Party of Brazil (*Partido Comunista do Brasil*—PC do B).

Lula's standing in the opinion polls was slow to rise, moving from only 5 to 6 per cent in early September; but he performed well in television debates, emphasizing ideological issues and substantive policies. By late September, he moved from 7 to 10 per cent in the opinion polls, now in third place, beginning to alarm some members of the business community, including the President of FIESP, Mário Amato. He said that a victory for Lula would result in 800,000 businessmen, financiers and industrialists (*empresários*) leaving the country: Lula replied that this was nonsense. From Oct. 18 to the elections, Lula and Brizola were neck and neck, with 14–15 per cent support in the opinion polls, but Lula was confident that he would get into the second round and was already looking for broad left-wing backing.

When registration of candidates closed in July 1989, there were 24. Of these, 11 merited serious attention, and five had a chance of reaching the presidency, though the behaviour and eventual support of the other six could be important in determining the final result. There was some concern, too, that the long list of names of candidates and parties which, unlike in some other countries, did not have symbols on the ballot sheet, might cause confusion, not least among the 7,500,000 illiterate electors, or more, who now were voting for the first time in a presidential election, in accordance with the 1988 Constitution.

By October, or even earlier, it was clear that Collor would attract most votes, though, almost certainly, not the majority required to win on the first ballot, on Nov. 15, and that he would be joined in the second round, on Dec. 17, by either Lula or Brizola.

The Brazilian electorate in 1989 was facing its first direct presidential election since October 1960, when Jânio Quadros won, with 48.26 per cent of the vote. Voters, then, under the Constitution of 1946, had to be over 18 years old, which meant that, by 1989, only people over 47 could previously have voted in a direct election for president. The electorate, in 1960, was about 15,500,000 registered voters, out of a national population of just over 71,00,000. By November 1989, the electorate was over 82,000,000. The state of São Paulo, alone, had over 2,080,000 electors, more than all those registered in 1960, while Rio de Janeiro had 7,500,000. Of those, perhaps as many as 80 per cent had never previously voted in a direct election for president.

This huge electorate was also predominantly young. The 1988 Constitution determined that registration and voting should be obligatory for citizens over 18 years old, and optional for those aged between 16 and 18, or over 70, and for illiterates.

The extension of the vote to 16 year olds meant that about 4,000,000 of the electorate were voting for the first time for *any* public office. As many as 19 per cent of the electorate were under 22 and another 28 per cent were aged between 22 and 30. This meant that almost 50 per cent of the electorate was under 30. Roughly 38 per cent (about 30,000,000) were between 31 and 50, with only 15 per cent (12,000,000) aged over 50.

This young electorate knew little, if anything, about the period before 1964, and even less about the Vargas tradition, to which some candidates, such as Brizola, sought to appeal. Even the widely respected resistance of Ulysses Guimarães to the régime installed in 1964 was part of a misty past. What mattered was the here and now, still flickering on a television screen, intellectually undemanding, but rich in promise. This did not, of itself, imply an unsophisticated or malleable electorate. Its recent record had shown a remarkable degree of perception concerning policies and politicians, as seen in 1986, with response to the Cruzado Plan and the subsequent electoral reaction to its cynical dismantling. One incalculable factor was the vote of illiterates, estimated to be between 7,500,000 to 10,000,000 voters; but it was generally understood that one did not have to be literate in order to calculate political, especially short-term, advantage.

At the same time, the electorate was generally ill-educated and poor. It was estimated that about 68 per cent had never finished primary education, that 75 per cent earned less than two minimum wages, that 25 per cent did not know the name of the current President of the Republic, and that 90 per cent did not belong to unions.

The electorate was also geographically concentrated, mainly in the centre-south of Brazil. Some 44 per cent lived in the three biggest states, in terms of population, São Paulo, Minas Gerais and Rio de Janeiro, while the six biggest states, namely, those three plus Rio Grande do Sul, Paraná and Bahia, contained no less than 64 per cent of potential voters. This concentration of the electorate helped to explain Brizola's eventual defeat, in the first round, by Lula.

Brizola, before the election, was estimated to have about 45 per cent support in Rio de Janeiro, the third most important "electoral college" in the country, and about 50 per cent in Rio Grande do Sul. Other states were also important sources of Brizola votes, such as Ceará (12 per cent), Pernambuco (10 per cent), and Paraná (10 per cent). Brizola, also, contrary to what often was alleged, had a good spread in terms of social class, with 12 per cent in Class A, 15 per cent in B, and 12 in C.

His weakness, often noted over the years, but not sufficiently attended to, was in Minas Gerais, the second "electoral college", where he was only in fourth place in the poll surveys, with about 6 per cent of votes, and, above all, in São Paulo, where he was trailing in sixth place, with only 2 per cent of votes in the polls. If Brizola were to beat Lula in the first round, it was estimated that he would need only 5 per cent of *paulistas* and 8 per cent of *mineiros* to vote for him, since every percentage point in São Paulo was worth 80,000 votes and, in Minas, 90,000. Unfortunately for Brizola, it seems that his campaign teams, even as late as October, thought that they could leave their major effort in São Paulo and Minas Gerais to the second round, being confident of victory in the first.

The electorate of 1989 was also mainly urban. In 1960, when Quadros was elected, 30 per cent of the population lived in towns or cities, and only 5 per cent watched television: by 1989, at least 70 per cent watched television, the great majority living in urban areas. This electorate was also known to be disenchanted with politicians, with the Sarney government since 1985, and with the PMDB, which was fatally associated with Sarney. In April 1989, a public opinion poll found that 74 per cent of respondents had trust in the Church, 61 per cent in residents' associations, 56 in trade unions, 51 in the armed forces, 34 in businessmen, 29 in Congress, 25 per cent in the federal government, 24 in political parties, and only 14 per cent in politicians. A massive 81 per cent had no trust in politicians, and 70 per cent, none in political parties or the federal government. Yet, at the same time, 87 per cent of respondents said that they wanted to vote in the presidential election of 1989.

A large, young, poor, ill-educated, urbanized electorate, strongly influenced by television, disenchanted with politicians, parties and the political system, yet eager to participate in elections and in the political process. Here was the ideal breeding ground for the "anti-politician", calling a plague on all politicial parties, repeatedly and deliberately distancing himself from the present political scene, presenting himself as the archetypal "Mr Clean", whose broom would clean out the political stables. The times produced the man, Fernando Collor de Mello.

In the first round of the presidential elections, on Nov. 15 1989, Collor won 28 per cent of the national vote, Lula just over 16 per cent and Brizola well over 15 per cent, just 0.53 per cent less than Lula. It was a paper thin difference. Reliable sources said that it was helped by the right-wing media boosting Lula as a viable candidate in the final stages of the campaign, to exclude Brizola from the second round. The Right was, with reason, more afraid of Brizola's electoral chances.

The second round of the election was fiercely fought. The Left rallied round Lula, the Right round Collor, though both candidates sought to win the middle ground. Lula's support grew rapidly, so that, on the eve of the election, opinion polls showed almost equal backing for him and Collor. The vote, on Dec. 17, 1989, showed how close a run it was. With an electoral turn-out of 85.6 per cent, Collor won 35,089,998 votes (42.75 %), Lula, 31,076,364, (37.86%), with blank and spoilt votes (4,024,339) just exceeding the difference between the two candidates (4,013,634). The null and blank votes, in many cases, reflected continuing mistrust of politicians and the redemocratization process, but there are very few countries in the world in which a candidate can be defeated after polling over 31,000,000 votes. If he had won, Lula would have been the first working class candidate ever to have been elected as president in Latin America, and one of the few working class heads of state anywhere in the world. In this respect, at least, the election of 1989 was a measure of how far Brazilian democracy had come.

Collor's strength in taking office, in March 1990, was the legitimacy conferred upon him as the first directly appointed president in 29 years. The votes both for him and Lula were an expression of hope for the future, for youth and change. The biggest hurdles he faced were his inexperience, lack of an adequate party and of support in Congress. It was also expected that he would be faced by strong trade union opposition and close, if not hostile, scrutiny from the 57 per cent of voters who had not supported him.

The first positive signal came in Collor's choice of government, which was imaginative and, sometimes, surprising, providing an able, well-balanced team. The president's lack of party commitment left him free to take soundings across parties. He was reported to have had discussions with Senator Fernando Henrique Cardoso and Federal Deputy José Serra, both of the PSDB, the *Tucanos*, and with Federal Deputy César Maia, of the PDT, three of the most able men in Congress. He decided to form a new super-Ministry of the Economy, incorporating the existing ministries of Finance, Planning and Industry and Commerce. This was given to a 38 year-old economist, Zélia Cardoso de Mello, who had worked with Collor in Alagoas. She was part of the Campinas group of economists: her earlier political allegiance had been to the Left. Among her early statements, she said that she would not penalize the working class "which up to now has had to foot the bill for all the plans to fight inflation". Her related aims included an attack on inflation, reduction in the number of State employees, and privatization.

Another appointment, further to the Left than might have been expected of Collor, was that of Bernardo Cabral to the Ministry of Justice. He started his career as Secretary of the Interior and Justice in Amazonia, in 1958. His mandate as state deputy was revoked after the *coup* of 1964, and that of Federal Deputy in 1968, with suspension of his political rights for 10 years. He was chief *rapporteur* for the new Constitution of 1988 and a member of the PMDB until just before the second round of voting in 1989. He then defied the PMDB's executive direction to vote for Lula, opting, instead, for Collor.

A less surprising appointment was that of Margarida Maria Procópio Toledo as Minister for Social Action, having been state secretary in the same role in Alagoas, when Collor was governor. She promised to "combat the misery affecting 30,000,000 Brazilians". Her priority areas, she said, would include housing, with emphasis on homes for the poor, and basic sanitation, especially to prevent epidemic diseases, above all in children.

Two appointments caused both surprise and satisfaction, not least abroad. The first was the appointment of Brazil's best known conservationist, Dr José Lutzenberger, the foremost critic of previous lack of policies for the environment, to head a new Environment Secretariat (*Secretariado do Meío Ambiente*—SEMA). Such implied concern for the environment pointed to a head-on clash with some of Collor's principal supporters in Amazonia. The second was the appointment of Dr José Goldemberg, as Secretary of Science and Technology. He was previously Rector of the University of São Paulo, the leading university in Brazil, which trains half of the country's graduate students. A physicist, he helped to shape Brazil's science policy throughout the 1980s. His appointment, like that of Lutzenberger, gave weight and added credibility to the Collor government, while also providing evidence of the president's readiness to appoint the best people to the job, across traditional political boundaries.

Before taking office, Collor said that he would wage war on inflation. His first massive broadside came, without warning, within twenty-four hours of his inauguration on March 15, 1990. This was the *Plano Brasil Novo*, the **New Brazil Plan**. This was far more radical than any of the other stabilization plans which had preceded it, since the Cruzado Plan of 1986. It sought to provide an even sharper shock than ever before. Again, it was an authoritarian intervention, a packet of *medidas provisórias*, provisional measures, aimed at reducing liquidity as a precondition of cutting back inflation, and to reduce the public deficit, the primary motor of inflation.

Effects of the New Brazil Plan. The immediate, overwhelming reaction was admiration for a bold decisive move to end inflation, which by March 1990, had reached the unprecedented rate of 84 per cent for the month, or a calculated yearly rate of 4,653 per cent. For the first two months of Collor's government, March and April, a sense of crisis brought the president and Congress together, helped by the fact that Congress was reluctant to oppose a president recently endowed with the legitimacy of direct election. The honeymoon period soon ended, as attention turned to the elections in October, for Congress and governors. period soon ended, as attention turned to the elections in October, for Congress and governors.

One mistake was that Collor set too high targets, in attempting to reduce inflation, cut the deficit and public spending, and sack civil servants. More modest, more realistic goals would have been more effective: but that was not Collor's style, nor what the electorate expected. More seriously, he, and his advisors, underestimated the difficulty in "fine-tuning" the economy. He dismissed fears of recession by saying that liquidity could be turned on again, as required, like a tap. It was not so simple: too slow a rate of liquidity growth would produce recession; too fast would lead to rapid inflation, even to hyperinflation.

He also underestimated the ingenuity of his fellow-countrymen in finding ways of unfreezing their funds. The *New Brazil Plan* sought to be humane and flexible, with reasonable concessions, for instance, to charities and pensioners. These concessions were commonly abused, as was the practice of overpaying back taxes, in *new cruzados*, in order to receive a substantial refund in *cruzeiros*. It was a paradise for accountants. The result was that "total liquidity as measured by M4 (money in circulation and demand deposits, together with federal bonds in private hands and time and savings deposits) had returned to 85 per cent of pre-package levels by early June".

Meanwhile, inflation, again, began to rise up to 12.9 per cent a month in September and 14.2 in October. Minister Zélia Cardoso de Mello blamed both workers and businessmen for pushing up wages and prices, but most of her criticism was aimed at the business community and the abuse of cartels. The government already had counterattacked, with further curbs on the money supply expansion and lower borrowing limits for local and state governments. It brought back the *Letra de Tesouro Nacional* (LTN), a short term treasury bill, with a pre-fixed monthly interest rate, again to mop up liquidity. It also used a financial operations tax on short-term financial transactions, mainly to encourage funds to move from the overnight market into longer-term savings accounts and government paper. The Collor government was making every effort to keep inflation under control.

The difficulties were considerable. On July 17, 1990, for example, came the first issue of privatization certificates, also aimed at absorbing liquidity. Originally, it was hoped to shed one company a month, starting in July, but the programme had to be revised, hoping to start with *Usiminas* in October. This meant that the $7,000,000 which the government had hoped to raise from privatization in 1990 would not be met, which, together with other problems in raising government revenue, lessened the chances of making cuts in the public sector deficit.

There was also, as expected, strong resistance to attempts to cut the federal payroll by dismissing civil servants. By the end of June 1990, the government claimed that 60,000 had gone: other estimates said 40,000. One source of confusion was that many people were protected from dismissal by the Constitution, so had to be kept at home "on availability", on reduced pay. The number involved was, in any case, nowhere near the target of 360,000 by the end of June. In addition, many of those who were dismissed, not surprisingly, were at the lower end of the salary scale, so that savings were much less than had been hoped.

From the start, it was realized that a major test for the New Brazil Plan would be, as with its predecessors, the question of the wages and salaries, not least in view of the CUT's support for Lula and the general suspicion of Collor among trade union members. Real wages had risen after the return to civilian government in 1985, and after the Cruzado Plan in 1986. They then slipped in 1987, when the New Cruzado or Bresser Plan in June did away with the *gatilho*, the wages' trigger, of the Cruzado Plan. The Bresser Plan determined that wages should be adjusted every three months, measured by the national consumer price index. By this time, it was estimated that real wages had fallen by 30 per cent since the Cruzado Plan at the end of February 1986.

Over the next two years, strikes in key sectors of private industry pushed up real wages by 12.1 per cent in 1988, and 13.6 per cent in 1989. The Summer Plan de-indexation of wages, introduced in January 1989, lasted only five months, being overturned by rapid inflation and union opposition. Collor's New Brazil Plan, at first, "prefixed" wages, allowing rises in line with government projections of future inflation rates: in May, 1990, the government decided that wages should be negotiated freely, between employers and unions.

In May 1990, the question of wage increases came to a head in Congress, now in direct disagreement with Collor. This stemmed from a Labour Court ruling that wage losses in the year to March 1990, when Collor came to office, were about 166 per cent, so that appropriate adjustments should be made in new pay awards. Collor than issued a Provisional Measure (*Medida Provisória 185*), to override this ruling. This *Measure* was rejected by a joint session of Congress in May, but by only 149 to 133 votes. Collor immediately produced another *Provisional Measure*, reasserting his control over wage and salary increases. This head-on struggle was resolved, when the Attorney General, Aristides Junqueira Alvarenga, successfully appealed to the Supreme Court. It was an acid test of presidential and congressional power, underlining, though also, probably exaggerating, the issue of wages and salaries in the fight against inflation.

This tussle left the government with the need to find a solution which would satisfy the unions, without a return to wage indexation, especially when, in June 1990, negotiations between government, employers and unions broke down. Minister Zélia Cardoso de Mello now produced an ingenious proposal. This was the factor for salary or wage adjustment (*Fator de Recomposição Salarial*—FRS). In simple terms, this was a formula by which wages and salaries might be adjusted, so that, by August 1991, the losses in the year before Collor took office might be made good. At the end of June, the first adjustment, for July 1990, was announced, as 9.6 per cent. Everyone was rather confused, and no-one very pleased. These adjustments could not be passed on through price increases, which annoyed employers, while workers were suspicious of a distinction between projected and real inflation.

Despite such suspicion, and despite the victory of a right-wing president, the trade unions remained relatively quiet. There was a series of strikes, mainly in the public sector, especially in docks, oil refineries, steel mills, and companies scheduled for privatization. Still, the Ministry of Labour reported that, in the first seven months of 1990, the total number of workers involved in strikes was half that in the same period in 1989. In January to July, 1989, there were, it said, 10,409,792 strikers, 2,829 stoppages, and 23,823 days lost. In 1990, in the same period, there were 5,218,799 workers in 1,521 strikes, with a loss of 11,392 working days. The precise figures may be questioned, but the trend is clear, largely reflecting workers' fear of recession and unemployment.

On June 12, 1990, the CUT called for a general strike. The response was poor, except among the metal-workers of São Paulo. Workers feared loss of jobs and the impact of inflation, especially on food prices, which directly and tangibly hit their families. An exception was the strike of six weeks at Ford's São Bernardo de Campos plant. By late July, losses had reached $300 million. The company closed the plant.

The relative lack of union militancy is not just a result of fear of recession or unemployment. It reflects a genuine understanding of the threat of inflation and hyperinflation, the impact of which is immediately felt when doing the weekly shopping and trying to square the family budget. Fear of hyperinflation haunts and, to a degree, unites all classes. This partly underlay the government's attempt, yet again, in September 1990, to achieve a "social pact", an agreement between government, employers and workers' leaders, which, previously, was sought, in vain, most recently under Sarney, in late 1988, just before the introduction of the Summer Plan in January 1989. Talks went on for weeks, but, on Sept. 19, 1990 Collor had a meeting with Jair Meneguelli, leader of the CUT, in the Planalto Palace in Brasilia. Meneguelli presented a list of 13 demands, including a real increase in wages, a stop to the privatization of State companies, agrarian reform, to be managed by rural unions, and the non-payment of foreign debt. Collor already had fought to resist a return to wage indexation and was still insisting on his privatization policy. The negotiations, still, had a long way to go.

Discussion over wages could not be separated from the question of prices. The government aimed to end virtually all price controls by the end of July 1990, reversing a decision, in March, that, from the end of April, it would be setting maximum price increases for each month. The end of price controls was, however, still to be linked to a rigorous policing of companies, with a sample of 463 representative companies being forced to submit monthly reports on salary and production costs, profit margins and prices charged. These had to be sent to the supply and production department of the Ministry of the Economy, with the threat of firm action against prices which were judged to be "abusive".

Wages and prices also worried the leaders of Brazil's business community, who were generally concerned over the government's part in producing a deep recession. Critics of the government included Mário Amato, president of the Federation of Industries of the State of São Paulo (*Federação das Indústrias do Estado de São Paulo*—FIESP), Ricardo Semler, winner of the "Businessman of the Year" award, and Antônio Ermírio de Morães, president of Votorantim, the largest private group of companies in the country. They complained of high interest rates, unrealistic exchange rates and restricted demand. Abílio Diniz, president of Pão de Açúcar, Brazil's largest chain of supermarkets, complained that no company in the world could afford real interest rates of 32 per cent of a month.

A study by the *Instituto Brasileiro de Geografía e Estatísticas* showed industrial production in the first nine months of 1990 to be 8.1 per cent below that for the same period of 1989, predicting a fall of 8.1 to 8.5 per cent for the year as a whole. The National Confederation of Industries (*Confederaçao Nacional de Indústrias*—CNI) also predicted a fall in GDP of 4 per cent. The CNI's president, Albano Franco, foresaw widespread collapse of companies, unless demand picked up.

In September, when faced with renewed inflation, back up to 12.9 per cent for that month, the government hit back. The president of the Central Bank, Ibrahim Eris, recognized as being one of the most able of the Collor appointments, now reacted vigorously by imposing a further fierce liquidity squeeze, amounting to 950,000 million *cruzeiros* ($12,600 million). This involved forcing banks to keep new higher compulsory reserves in the Central Bank and preventing access to assets blocked under the original Collor Plan, to pay debts with cruzeiros.

When September's trade figures showed that the surplus had fallen by one-third against the previous year's figures, the Central Bank reversed its exchange rate policies, devaluing the *cruzeiro*, to help exports: previously, it had sold massive amounts of gold, to buy dollars with which it flooded the parallel market, pushing up the *cruzeiro* against the dollar. Traders estimated the amount of gold sold between June and September at over $2,500 million. The purpose was to reduce the differential between the official and parallel rates.

The credit squeeze, resulting from the high interest rate introduced in July and the second monetary squeeze of September, also forced people to bring in dollars from abroad, again keeping the parallel rate within 5 per cent of the official. October's figures proved to be the worst since January 1987. The projected surplus for 1990 was now down to $10,000 million, as compared with $16,000 million in 1989. The government, at last, listened to exporters and, in late November 1990, agreed to devaluation.

One area in which Collor broadly continued the policies of the previous government was over foreign debt. He continued to insist that service payments should be linked to overall economic recovery and to Brazil's foreign exchange reserves. In effect, he continued the "white moratorium". Minister Zélia Cardoso took a persistently tough line with the bankers. So, too, did Brazil's chief debt negotiator, Jório Dauster. Towards the end of the year talks still had to be conducted with both "Paris Club" creditors and the commercial banks. Everyone understood that discussions with the banks would be complicated and that, in any case, new arrangements would require Congressional approval. Dauster said that during talks with the bankers Brazil would not make even token payments on interest in arrears to the banks. It had not been paying interest since September 1989. It was estimated that, by the end of 1990, there would be an outstanding figure of $10,000 million. These negotiations with the banks would continue into 1991, when both sides hoped that some agreement might be found.

Both in terms of its foreign debt and the rest of its programme, the Collor government, by the time it reversed its exchange policies and agreed to devaluation in November, already had passed what always had been regarded as its first major political test, the elections of Oct. 3, 1990 for Congress and governors. They were to elect 27 state governors, 31 senators (one third of the senate), 503 federal deputies and 969 state deputies. For candidates for governor who did not get a majority vote in the first round, there would be a second election on Nov. 25.

Throughout the campaign, Collor cleverly refused to become involved or to allow the elections to become a referendum on his government's record, as had happened under the military régime. He would not give his support to any particular candidate, not even in his home state of Alagoas. He was also helped by the fact that his own party, the PRN, was still tiny, so that there was no question of a large protest vote turning away from the government party, as had happened to the PMDB in the recent past.

By the end of the first round of voting, on Oct. 3, it seemed that this strategy largely had worked and that Collor had even been strengthened by the elections. Only 11 candidates for governor won enough votes to be elected in the first round. Of these, only one, Leonel Brizola, in the state of Rio de Janeiro, was a firm opponent of Collor and his policies.

Early analysis of the new Chamber of Deputies also suggested that the president should be able to find sufficient support in the future. Less than 40 per cent of the former deputies were re-elected, but, as predicted during the campaign, the composition of the Chamber was still heavily to the Right, reflecting the persistent strength of clientelistic politics. One calculation put 257, out of the total of 503, into a broadly right-of-centre grouping, including Collor's PRN, the PFL, the PDS, PTB, PL and PDC. There were then 146 PMDB and PSDB (*Tucanos*), and a further 100 which had declared their opposition to the government, the PT, PSB, PDT, PCB and PCdoB.

In practice, such calculations mean little, since the parties do not fall into clear programmatic or ideological camps. The PMDB remains, to the surprise of some observers, the largest party, with 109 deputies, as compared with its previous 130, but it is still very heterogeneous, with many representatives to the right of centre. The PFL is in second place, with 92 as compared with its previous 90. Despite its origins as a break-away group from the PDS, in 1984, it is not clear how the PFL will behave. Some of its leaders, such as Marco Maciel, are said to favour a formal pro-government bloc in Congress: others are likely to want to retain greater autonomy for the party, waiting to see how Collor and his government perform in the longer term. They also want to avoid opening a confrontation with the PMDB, which also, apparently, is the view of the new Minister of Justice, Jarbas Passarinho, who replaced Bernardo Cabral.

Collor will need to negotiate carefully to win congressional support, with a substantial measure of concession and conciliation. He will require a great deal of skill, if he is to get his policies through, as already was seen in the row over wages and salaries in May 1990. This is where he will need all the experience and influence of a man such as Jarbas Passarinho. Although the congressional results of Oct. 3 were generally favourable to Collor, he still remains dangerously vulnerable through his lack of strong party support and a solid reliable base in Congress.

These questions were made sharper by the second round of voting for governors on Nov. 25, 1990 which were altogether less favourable to Collor than the first round. In his own state of Alagoas the polling was cancelled, because of alleged electoral fraud, while, in São Paulo, his strong supporter and political patron, Paulo Maluf, was beaten by Luiz Antonio Fleury, of the PMDB. This, in large measure, reflected the influence and record of the current governor, Orestes Quércia, who now will be a strong contender for the federal presidency in 1994. The result was a bitter disappointment for Maluf, the fifth election he had lost in six years.

Elsewhere, too, four governorships went to candidates who are in opposition to Collor, while eight more may give, at best, grudging support. This is at a time when the power of state governors has been increased by both direct election and the provisions of the 1988 Constitution. The patronage of the president and his control of federal funds are still powerful levers, but his position must be weakened by the fact that he can count on the certain support of only 14 state governors.

Growing disenchantment with the government and the political system was also seen in the relatively low electoral turn-out in 1990. In 1989, it was 85.6 per cent. A year later, it was well below 80. Throughout the campaign there was evidence of a growing weariness among the electorate, tired of so many elections and increasingly mistrustful of politicians' ability to live up to their promises. In a poll taken just before the October elections, more than 50 per cent of respondents said that they would not vote, if they were not legally obliged to do so; yet they are faced with an electoral timetable of seven more elections, plus a referendum, before the end of the decade.

The person who has emerged most strengthened from the elections of October and November 1990, is without any doubt, Leonel de Moura Brizola. He had a personal triumph in the first round, sailing through to election, for the second time in eight years, as governor of Brazil's second most important and wealthy state. In doing so he beat Jorge Bittar, the candidate of the *Frente Popular*, formed by the PT and the PSB. Among other things, the victory was a vindication of his first period in office, from 1983 to 1987. He then went on successfully to support candidates in the south in the second round, establishing himself as the most effective leader of the Left in Brazil. He now begins his third term as governor of a major state. He is fiercely opposed to Collor.

Now, again, there is talk of an alliance between the PDT and the PT. The PT did better in the 1990 elections than many people had predicted, doubling its representation in the Chamber of Deputies, from 17 to 34. The performance was all the more striking in that it was achieved in spite of a generally perceived crisis of confidence within the party. Lula decided that congressional politics did not really suit him and that he would not stand again for Congress. There were also public divisions and arguments, including among intellectual theorists of the party, such as Florestan Fernandes and Francisco Weffort, disagreeing, in the *Folha de São Paulo*, over the nature of class struggle and Marxist theory.

It was not easy to pinpoint the source of the *malaise*. It seemed to reflect a certain crisis of confidence in parts of the Left after the swift changes in the USSR and Eastern Europe. It owed something to the fact that Lula seemed to find it harder than, for example, Brizola, to recover from the defeat of 1989. So did many members and supporters of the PT. They did not seem to realize just what an extraordinary performance Lula's campaign was in 1989, or appreciate the importance of the support which it generated. The amazing thing was not defeat, but that the PT came so near to victory, after only nine years in existence.

Whether the PDT and the PT can unite in effective opposition still remains to be seen. Brizola has said that he would like to unite all the forces of the Left, though expecting difficulties with the PT. What seems certain is that opposition to Collor will grow, not just from the Left, and that increasing pressure will be put on him to modify his policies. In which direction, then, will Brazil move?

Outline of economic development. Economic policy in Brazil cannot be understood except in its political context, within the framework of the political economy as a whole. Equally, the political capacity of the government, under the "New Republic", as before, is circumscribed and, to a degree, determined by the performance of the economy.

Inflation was the main focus of internal political debate in the months of the presidential election campaign of 1989, directly linked to the question of wages, but eclipsing equally severe problems, such as the foreign debt, the internal debt and the fiscal deficit.

Critics of the Summer Plan of January 1989, such as Carlos Sant Anna, who was appointed president of Petrobrás in April 1989, complained of its damaging impact, causing an enforced cutback on investment. They failed to accept how much of Brazil's massive deficit was attributable to state companies, or the degree to which they contributed to the sharply rising internal debt. There was severe criticism of the high level of internal interest rates, which, by March 1989, were up to as much as 27 per cent a month for "overnight" bank deposits, though this was cut to 23 per cent at the end of the month. The reduction simply represented the government's concern that industrialists and farmers might turn to investments in securities, rather than stocks.

Servicing the internal debt was one of the government's main worries. By the middle of 1989, internal debt already had passed $100,000 million, and was still rising: it promised soon to exceed the foreign debt, then amounting to about $120,000 million. The government, by then, was spending more on servicing its internal debt than its external, spending $20,000 million on the former, and $16,000 million on the latter.

The president of the Central Bank, Elmo Camões, estimated, in May 1989, that with the current rate of inflation and public expenditure, the country, by 1990, would need to spend about $40,000 million to service the internal debt. By mid-September, as the presidential race became more intense, militant bank workers, among others, were calling for a halt to the servicing of the internal debt, to accompany an undeclared, but *de facto*, moratorium on foreign debt repayment.

By mid-September, it was calculated that a moratorium on commercial foreign debt would represent a saving of 1.9 percentage points of GDP, which, though substantial, would not cover a budgetary "gap", expected to reach 6.5 per cent of GDP. By now, the cost of servicing the internal debt was seen as the factor most likely to lead to hyperinflation.

Still, the burden of the foreign debt lay heavily across the country, though foreign bankers, taking their tune from Brazil, began to realize, throughout 1989, that nothing really could be done until

Sarney had finished his term of office. They, too, wanted a peaceful electoral campaign, hoping for a new start under a new government. By mid-1989, the *Banco Central's* quarterly publication showed that the total external debt had fallen to $112,300 million, namely, $7,300 million less than at the end of 1987, largely because of formal and informal debt swaps (about $6,200 million), amortization, and liquid capital flows. A bank spokesman thought it might fall by a further 2 per cent by the end of the year, to $110,100 million. This was little enough comfort to Brazil, having paid about $10,000 million in interest every year, for the last 10 years.

The main worry focused on September 1989, when payments to creditors of about $3,700 million were due. This, in turn, drew attention to the level of foreign exchange reserves and to the possible release of funds due to Brazil, which were being withheld. In early June, came reports of a possible moratorium, with Mailson da Nóbrega explaining that Brazil was expecting new funds from abroad: if these were not forthcoming, it would be necessary "to prevent the erosion of reserves". The simple argument was that Brazil, with reserves of $6,300 million in February, could not pay $3,000 million, or more, in September, without receiving new money. The government was still waiting for loans, already signed, but not yet received, from abroad, of $4,200 million. It was an exercise in arm-twisting.

One source of relief was to accept a form of "debt-for-nature" swaps, a modification of debt-equity swaps, related to the conservation of Amazonia and other threatened areas. Sarney, strongly influenced by armed forces' leaders, would not hear of it. The Amazon area was Brazil's, "even to destroy". Nor could Brazil expect much help under the "Brady Plan" when its economy was not meeting already agreed requirements, as with the IMF. It had a public deficit of 4 per cent of GDP, when the Fund was demanding no more than 2 per cent.

In the second half of 1989, Brazil began to implement its threat to suspend payment to protect reserves. The first victims were the "Paris Club" creditors, who failed to receive payments of $812,000,000, due on July 1. The *Banco Central* explained that, if it were to pay, reserves would be down to $4,800 million, or just over the equivalent of three months' worth of imports, which was considered to be too low.

The government then put further pressure on the IMF. It decreed the centralization of all exchange operations in the *Banco Central*, again to protect the level of international reserves, but also to curb the remittance of profits and dividends by transnational corporations. It was made clear that this "white moratorium" was no more than a postponement of payment.

It was a cat and mouse game, with an announcement, in July, that Brazil would renew payments to the "Paris Club", but would need to "ration" them, to avoid depletion of its reserves. At the same time, came a warning that there might have to be an "undeclared" moratorium in September, when a substantial number of interest payments ($3,000 million), would come due at the same time. Representatives of the creditor bankers seemed to take this news calmly. In August 1989, a team of Brazilian officials went to Washington, seeking "transitory" agreements with the IMF. At the same time, Brazil's quotation on the secondary stock market, went up from 30–31 per cent to 33–34 per cent. This was linked to an increase in reserves, by the end of July, to $6,500 million, equal to about four months' exports.

When, also in August, John Reed of Citibank visited Brasília he said that he believed the threat of hyperinflation could be avoided and that Brazil's creditors could accept delay in some interest payments, to keep international reserves above the "safe" limit, equivalent to four months' imports. Like everyone else, he was treading water, waiting for the election of a new president, when business might be resumed.

One persistent problem was that the public sector accounted for about 89 per cent of medium- and long-term debt, and State companies were responsible for more than half the loans granted to the public sector. Debt service also varied from year to year, since about 75.3 per cent of it had been contracted at floating rates (48.5 per cent at Libor), so that the country was very susceptible to changes in interest rates. Whoever was to be elected in 1989, had to confront these problems.

There was also the more general worry about recession, which was clearly threatening by April 1989, with GDP in 1988 having fallen by 0.3 per cent: this would be the third time in the decade that the IBGE had recorded a negative growth rate, the other years being 1981 and 1983. The decline was mostly in industry, down 0.4 per cent, while *per capita* GDP, as a whole, at 640 new cruzados, was 2.3 per cent lower than in 1987.

There was some good news. In the first quarter of 1989, the accumulated trade surplus reached $4,300 million, and the foreign trade department of the Banco do Brasil, *Cacex*, expected a surplus for the year at about $16,000 million. Agriculture, too, was performing well. The soya crop was expected to reach 23,500,000 tonnes, or about 31 per cent up on 1988. Maize was forecast at

26,000,000 tonnes, an increase of 6.5 per cent. These two crops accounted for about two-thirds of the total grains harvest, which, in 1988, had reached 66,000,000 tonnes.

Gold, too, in 1989, was showing increased production, even though 1988 had provided a record of 100.4 tonnes, 19.5 per cent up on the 84 tonnes of 1987. Of this *garimpeiro* miners, in 1988, produced 78.5 tonnes, 11.3 per cent more than the 1987 figure of 70.5 tonnes, though these were only the official, recorded production figures.

A worrying question, as the presidential election campaign became both more vigorous and more uncertain, was capital flight. A Central Bank forecast, in May 1989, suggested that capital repatriation by foreign companies could be, at least, $840,000,000 for the year, 10 per cent highter than the record, in 1986. Dividend and profit remittances by multi-national companies were also sharply up: the Central Bank had estimated $2,000 million for the year, but, from January to May, the figure already had reached $1,200 million. There were no reliable figures for illegal capital outflow, but this was expected easily to exceed the estimate for 1988, of $7,500 million, which, in turn, was 134 per cent more than in 1987. A general estimate was that Brazilians had between $35,000 million to $40,000 million deposited abroad, equivalent to about 10 per cent of GDP. Alleged reasons for this included inflation, deepening economic uncertainty, and worry over the presidential elections in November, especially in the light of left-wing successes in the municipal elections of November 1988.

There was still, too, in 1989, the perennial question of the level to be set for the minimum wage, which, again, found the President and the government at loggerheads with Congress, following earlier confrontation over the proposed change to the law on strikes. The Constitution of 1988 said that Congress should establish a minimum wage sufficient to satisfy the "basic needs" of a worker and his family, legislation which affected at least 20,000,000 workers and 10,000,000 pensioners.

In late May, the Chamber of Deputies voted an increase, as from June 1, from the equivalent of about $74 to US$109, at that time. This vote had to be approved by Senate and promulgated by the President. The government vetoed the proposal, because of the impact it would have on the deficit. The row lasted for weeks, till a compromise was reached, which favoured the Congressional proposal. Meanwhile, Congress revealed a sense of deepening crisis, worried about the adequacy of the budget which would be inherited by the new president, whoever he might be. This concern brought together economists from different parties at the end of July 1989, expressing a congressional initiative in reaction to a discredited, stubborn and irresponsible president.

The key concept was simple. There must be tax increases, especially on the very rich, on those, for example, who had made huge profits on the stock exchange, or in agriculture, who currently paid very little, combined with a reduction of 50 per cent in fiscal incentives. The new fiscal package was set out in five bills (*projetos de lei*). It was modest in scale, such that, if accepted, it might produce about NCz$2,000 million, or 0.4 per cent of GDP, when roughly twice that amount was needed to balance the budget of 1990, which had to be presented by the Executive to Congress by the end of August 1989.

What was being asked, with the approval of the Minister of Finance, was the application of the Law of Budgetary Directives (*Lei de Diretrizes Orcementárias*—LDO), approved by Congress at the end of the first semester. This was largely the work of the *paulista* PSDB deputy, José Serra, a specialist in fiscal reform and former Secretary of Finance in the Montoro government in São Paulo. His broad aim was to impose rigorous control of public spending up to the change of president in March 1990, with a tightening of budgetary procedures, to provide a responsible basis from which the new President might start. Sarney, fearing even further unpopularity, refused to sanction new taxes in his last year in office.

This presented yet another difficulty for his successor, as Sarney well knew, since the Constitution of 1988 did not allow taxes to be made effective in the year in which they were introduced: changes had to be agreed before Aug. 31. Sarney refused to co-operate, even when urged by General Ivan de Souza Mendes, head of the SNI. The August deadline came, and went. The new President, therefore, inevitably, would be faced with major problems in balancing his budget, in reducing the fiscal deficit, in curbing inflation, and in dealing with the issues of internal and foreign debt.

These were just some of the specific issues in store for the man who was to win in November, or perhaps December, 1989. What, more generally, was the wider profile of the economy? A fundamental problem was that of the deficit, which, because of lack of support in the country and in Congress, the government, throughout 1989, was unable to reduce. The money supply and inflation shot up, ending the year with a record inflation rate of 1,864 per cent. Still, despite fears earlier in the year, the economy grew. The years 1968 to 1973 had seen average growth rates of over 10 per cent a year: 1974 to 1980, an average of over

5 per cent. In 1981, there was a fall in GDP of 4.4 per cent and growth of only 0.6 per cent in 1982, a difficult year for many Latin American economies. In 1983 came another negative growth rate, of 3.5 per cent, but exports and expanded agricultural production brought a GDP increase, in 1984, of 5 per cent.

This performance was bettered in both 1985 and 1986, when GDP grew by 8.3 and 7.5 per cent, helped by export growth and domestic demand, because of the *Cruzado Plan.* This domestic demand fell away in 1987 and 1988, as a result of the decline in real wages and investment, as government policies faltered. Even so, 1987 saw growth of 3.6 per cent, thanks to agriculture and the exports of manufactured goods. There was no real advance in 1988, but in 1989, partly because of an increase in real wages, the growth of GDP, to some considerable surprise, was 3.6 per cent.

This growth, over the decade, was led by consumption rather than investment. Throughout the 1970s, investment had averaged more than 20 per cent of GDP, derived from both the public and private sectors. The pattern of the 1980s was different, with a collapse of direct foreign investment after 1982, and public sector commitments to debt service and other priorities.

International trade also played a relatively small role in economic growth, with exports never accounting for much more than 10 per cent of GDP, as in 1988, when they made up 10.2 per cent with imports 5.1 per cent. The relative percentage of expenditure on GDP for 1988 was: government consumption, 12.1; private consumption, 61.1; gross fixed capital formation, 21.7; exports, 10.2; imports, −5.1. In the same year, the percentage origin of GDP was: agriculture, 7.9; mining, 1.7; manufacturing, 39.5; construction, 7.2; trade, 8.8; transport, 3.6 and government, 7.1. The real, percentage growth rates, by sector, were: agriculture, 1.5; industry, −2.6; trade, −2.6; finance, 0.3; government, 2.1; transport, 4.2; and communications, 11.2.

The figures for employment in Brazil, by the end of the 1980s, showed a move away from agriculture, though still the biggest employer of labour, towards industry, construction, retailing, and the service sector. The labour force grew, according to official figures, from some 17,100,000 in 1950, to 61,030,000 in 1986, or about 44.5 per cent of the total national population, with 61.4 per cent of this within the working age category of 15–64 years old. Whereas, in 1950, about 60 per cent of the work force was in agriculture and primary activities, this figure had fallen to 26 per cent by 1987. The occupational structure of the civilian labour force by 1986 was, by sector: agriculture, 25.8 per cent (about 14,300,000); manufacturing, 16.2 per cent (9,000,000); building/construction, 6.5 per cent (3,600,000); trade and services, 11.4 per cent (6,300,000); transport, etc, 3.6 per cent (2,000,000).

Leaving aside non-civilian employment, at least 32–25,000,000 people, by 1988, were involved in the informal sector, though these figures, almost certainly, are an underestimate, not least because, many people worked in both the formal and the "black" economy. The same is true, or even truer, of the female share of the labour force, which, officially, went up from 18 to 34 per cent, from 1960 to 1986. This figure severely underestimates the role of women in the service and agriculture sectors, but is completely overwhelmed, when set alongside the millions of women working, without any official "work cards", in the informal sector. Similarly, official figures give no indication of the scale of child labour, which is massively evident in the informal sector.

Looking at various sectors of the economy, one of the most important growth points in recent decades has been the manufacturing industry, which has generally grown far more quickly than GDP as a whole. There was a cumulative decline of 15 per cent in the early 1980s, from 1981 to 1983, because of the recession, but renewed growth from 1984 to 1987, now mostly based on the domestic market rather than exports. The collapse of this demand in 1987 and 1988 contrasted with the consumer boom which had followed the Cruzado Plan in 1986, adversely affected manufacturing, but there was growth of 3 per cent in 1989, as opposed to a fall of 3.4 per cent in 1988. The growth rates for different branches of the manufacturing industry in 1989 were: capital goods, 0.4 per cent; intermediate goods, 2.6; construction goods, 3.7; durable goods, 2.4 and non-durables, 4.0 per cent. The division between major industries was: chemicals—0.3 per cent; metallurgical, 5.3; mechanical, 4.4; foodstuffs, 1.3; vehicles, −2.8.

Within the manufacturing sector, the State plays a preponderant role, with State-owned corporations sometimes taking on initiatives which private sector entrepreneurs are reluctant to do, or to preserve Brazilian control in certain areas, such as informatics and petrochemicals. One estimate suggests that, by 1982, the State accounted for 70 per cent of activity in the manufacturing sector, with 52 government companies amongst the top 200, ranked by sales, in 1988. Aircraft manufacturing is exclusively State controlled, through Embraer, and the State has the greatest share in the country's defence industries, with an estimated total annual production of between $4–6,000 million.

One area in which the State has played a major role is the steel industry, making Brazil the world's seventh largest producer, taking advantage of its rich deposits of high quality iron ore. Production throughout the 1980s went up from just under 18,000,000 tonnes in 1982 to nearly 18,300,000 in 1985, which represented a rise of 25.3 per cent as compared with 1984, to over 25,500,000 in 1988, 10 per cent up on 1987, and to over 25,000,000 in 1989. Most Brazilian steel is for domestic consumption, but, in 1988, because of a fall in domestic demand, and for the domestic market: most of the north-east's produce goes for export. In 1989, sugar exports were 1,100,000 tonnes, worth $305,500,000.

Like the IBC, the Institute of Sugar and Alcohol (*Instituto de Açúcar e Alcool*—IAA) was abolished by the New Brazil Pian in March 1990. The alcohol market was deregulated, prices now being allowed to float. Subsidies and price differentials between alcohol and petrol were also now to float, so that alcohol had to take its chance. Already, under the Sarney government, production of alcohol had been influenced by changes in international oil prices: in 1986, the price of alcohol was 47 per cent less than that of petrol, dropping to only 25 per cent in 1988. The Gulf War in 1990 to 1991 brought renewed interest in alcohol fuel, but its future is unclear.

Brazil, after the USA, is the world's biggest producer of soya, and is the biggest exporter of soya meal. The production of soya beans went up by about 15,500,000 tonnes, in 1984, to over 24,000,000 in 1989 (1985: 18,279; 1986: 13,330—down by 27.1 per cent; 1987: 16,969; 1988: 18,021). In 1989, soya and soya derivatives' exports earned $3,650 million. A major centre of production is now the *cerrados* (savannah) in Mato Grosso do Sul, with 47 per cent of national total in 1989. A negative aspect of soya bean production is the fear that it may replace other more staple foodstuffs, used for domestic consumption, especially beans and rice, is a conflict between a valuable export crop and food needed at home, not least to combat inflation fuelled by food prices.

Oranges, in recent years, have provided another major source of export earnings. São Paulo, the main supplier, has about 150,000,000 trees, the rest being grown mainly in Sergipe, Rio de Janeiro and Minas Gerais. Brazil now provides about 85 per cent of the world market for orange juice concentrate, with exports valued at $1,100 million in 1988, and a further $1,000 million in 1989.

Bahia produces 86 per cent of the country's cacao, which, since 1977, has experienced a fall in world prices. The government encouraged production for both exports and domestic consumption, but, while in 1988, exports earned $513,600,000, in 1989 there was a fall of 36 per cent, to $329,600,000.

Export performance, in some areas, has to be set alongside the fact that, from the early 1980s, Brazil has become increasingly self-sufficient in foodstuffs. In 1983, the country imported $1,300 million worth; in 1988, $602,000,000, with cereal imports, for example, down from $1,100 million, in 1983, to $300,000,000 in 1988. Figures of food output for domestic consumption include: rice, up from 7,460,000 tonnes in 1970, to 11,040,000 tonnes in 1989. Equivalent figures for the same two years are: beans, 2,210,000 to 2,320,000 tonnes; potatoes, 1,580,000, to 2,140,000; wheat, 1,840,000 to 5,300,000; cassava, 30,250,000 to a lower figure of 23,700,000 tonnes.

Looking at other statistics which affect domestic food consumption, as well as exports, Brazil's beef herd in 1988 was about 134,100,000 head, mostly in Minas Gerais, Goiás, Rio Grande do Sul and Mato Grosso do Sul. The Cruzado Plan in 1986 contributed to some serious distortions in terms of pricing, but eventual adjustments brought increased slaughter rates and milk production in 1987 and 1988. In 1985, beef exports were about $844,000,000, but pressure from the domestic market brought a reduction in exports, which only reached about $263,000,000 in 1989. To meet domestic demand, it has even been necessary to import beef.

The pig population, about 33,000,000 in 1980, is mainly in the south. Production of pork was down by 3.2 per cent in that year, and by a further 10.7 per cent in 1989, when total production was 624,000 tonnes. Chicken production is aimed at both the Brazilian and foreign market. It rose by 11 per cent in 1987, dropped sharply in 1988, because of the price of chicken feed, then went up again, by 6.3 per cent, in 1989.

The forestry industry is making an increasing contribution to the economy, though not as much as might be expected in view of the wealth and diversity of Brazil's forests. These reserves have also been squandered and depleted. In 1980, official estimates were that 68 per cent of Brazil, about 5,800,000 sq Km., was covered in forest. The following decade saw the destruction of about 13 per cent of this forest cover, by squatters, mining and smelting corporations, farmers, and timber companies. Government policies and programmes have also contributed to this loss, with virtually no effort at conservation. The first evidence of official concern only came after March 1990, when president Collor created a

Secretariat of the Environment (*Sema*), funded by a World Bank Loan of $117,000,000 with promises to prevent the burning of the forest.

Hardwoods are mainly used for the flourishing domestic furniture industry. The softwoods in the south are more important commercially, with the commercial reserve of the pine forests estimated at 420,000,000 trees, despite heavy felling. The export of pinewood, though important, is worth much less than that of timber products, such as plywood, compensated and planed woods, which earned $309,000,000 in 1986. Paper production, for the domestic market and for export, has grown substantially over the last decade, together with that of woodpulp. Paper and cellulose exports in 1989 were $1,300 million. Increasing demand is reflected in large plantings for commercial purposes, of eucalyptus and American pine, and of hardwoods, such as jacaranda and peroba. Other important forest products include palm hearts, carnauba wax, babaçu kernels, brazil nuts and oiticica oil.

The fishing industry is less developed and makes a smaller contribution to the economy than might be expected in a country with such an extensive coastline and river system. As late as 1983, 51.3 per cent of the national catch of 880,696 tonnes, was made by local fishermen, 23.3 per cent of it from fresh water sources. A commercial fishing industry has been slow to develop, mainly in the form of exports of crab, shrimp and lobster, from the north-east, especially to the USA and the EC.

Another sector of the economy which remains relatively underdeveloped in relation to the country's resources is *tourism*. There was a spurt of growth in the 1970s helped by special flights from the USA and Europe, but over 50 per cent of tourists were from other Latin American countries. These were affected by the economic downturn in the 1980s, especially in Argentina and Uruguay. In 1986, 1,900,000 foreigners visited Brazil, 1,200,000 from Latin America, 371,000 from Europe and 259,000 from North America.

A major tourist attraction is the carnival in Rio de Janeiro. Special internal air fares allow tourists to see the whole country, including its beautiful colonial towns. A more recent development has been ecotourism in Amazonia and, to a lesser degree, the Pantanal. Internal tourism has been encouraged indirectly by exchange restrictions. Unfortunately, a major disincentive to foreign tourists is the violence and lack of security in cities such as Rio de Janeiro or Salvador, which have been given widespread, perhaps exaggerated, publicity abroad, especially in the USA.

Brazil's air transport system offers all the necessary infrastructure for tourism, as for other sectors of the economy, serving more than 150 cities and towns. Brazilians were among the pioneers of air flight and the aeroplane had been a major factor in unifying the country, especially in the absence of an adequate railway, or, in some regions, road system. There are 29 major airports. The main airline, *Varig* (*Viação Aérea Riograndense*) is one of the best in the world. In 1989, it flew 16,100 million passenger-km, of which 11,200 million were international. The two other major operators, for internal flights, are *Vasp* (the São Paulo state airline) and *Transbrasil*, based in Curitíba, the state capital of Paraná.

The roads of Brazil still provided a completely inadequate transport system in the 1950s, but have been greatly improved over the last four decades, to provide the necessary infrastructure for the country's most important form of transport. In 1987, there were 1,675,040 kilometres of roads in use, of which only 8 per cent were paved. In 1988, there were 12,600,000 units of total road vehicles, 10,300,000 cars and 2,300,000 commercial vehicles.

The railway system, as in most of Latin America, was designed to get exports to the coast, rather than to link cities. It remains inadequate, as priority has been given to roads and motor vehicles within Brazil's overall development, and it has suffered from lack of investment. In 1980, there were 29,237 kilometres of track, and 29,901 kilometres in 1987. By 1983, only 6.7 per cent of track was electrified, while freight transport, which, in 1977, was 132,000,000 tonnes, was down to 75,000,000 in 1983. The Sarney government built a "steel railway", a new freight line, between the iron ore mines of the Minas Gerais "Quadrangle" and the steelworks at Volta Redonda and the port of Sepetiba, in Rio de Janeiro. In 1988, a new line was completed between the Carajás mines and the port of Itaquí, in Maranhão. Work on Sarney's other planned railway, between Brasília and São Luís, in his home state of Maranhão, was abandoned in 1989.

Ports at Itaquí and Tubarão (Espírito Santo) have been provided with specialized handling facilities, especially for iron ore and aluminium. The other most important ports are Rio de Janeiro, Santos, Paranguá, São Sebastião and Rio Grande, which in 1982, handled 280,000,000 tonnes of cargo. On Feb. 18, 1991 President Collor signed legislation to deregulate Brazil's ports and end restrictive laws which had been in force since 1934. Exporters, importers and shippers had long complained about monopolies, cartels, corruption and bureaucracy. They pointed to the fact that, in 1990, 47,000 people moved 320,000,000 tonnes of cargo throughout the national system, while 2,000 people in Rotterdam moved 292,000,000 tonnes. The dockers' union leaders blame archaic equipment and lack of investment. The stevedores' unions are determined to resist the proposed reforms and the 60,800 port workers have strong backing in Congress.

Throughout the 1970s, governments aimed to reduce spending on services, to increase the autonomy of national shipyards, and to build up the country's own shipping. In 1973, the national fleet consisted of 565 vessels, totalling 2,900,000 tonnes. By 1983, it was up to 1,452 vessels, and 9,300,000 tonnes. The main emphasis was on building dry cargo vessels and tankers, mainly for long-distance, international and coastal routes. Financial problems in the 1980s have slowed down this programme to nationalize the Brazilian fleet.

The last two decades have also brought rapid change in terms of mass communications. Together with the aeroplane, one of the most influential factors in national integration and communication, has been the radio, especially the transistor radio. Over 80 per cent of Brazilian households own radios, so that an important football match will be heard from the borders of Venezuela to the frontier with Uruguay. There are over 2,000 radio stations, most of them local. The most influential is *Rede Globo*, the Globo network, owned, and closely controlled, by the right-wing octogenarian, Roberto Marinho.

Radio stations can also draw on services provided by well-established, high-quality newspapers, such as *Jornal do Brasil* or the *Estado de São Paulo*. One of the best newspapers in the country is the *Folha de São Paulo*. Newspaper readership is relatively small, especially for the higher quality newspapers and for weekly magazines, such as *Veja*, *Istoé Senhor*, or *Visão*, which stand comparison with the best news magazines world-wide.

Brazil's publishing business, too, is vigorous and of high quality, with 40 major firms, but, by far the most important medium of mass communication is television. There are six principal networks, serving 177 stations, mostly in the south and south-east: the most powerful is *Rede Globo*, one of the five largest in the world. Over 50 per cent of Brazilian households own television sets. The moulding of a television image is one of the most important requirements for political candidates, as was clearly shown in the presidential election of 1989, when *Rede Globo* committed itself to the campaign of Fernando Collor de Mello. His family owns a television station in Alagoas: his father has close links with Marinho and *Rede Globo*.

All these developments are intricately linked to the country's financial system, characterized by the fact that the government is the main source of long-term capital and by the need for external finance. Continuing fiscal deficits have led to rapid monetary expansion and inflation. The government's borrowing requirements have also kept interest rates high, causing problems for business and affecting the operations of financial institutions. The Sarney government introduced changes in public finances, ending the *Banco do Brasil's* ability to issue currency: the *Banco Central* was now to be the only monetary authority. Domestic investment, as a proportion of GDP, went up from 15.3 per cent in 1984, to 17.0 in 1985, 19.2 in 1986, 22 in 1987, 21.8 in 1988 and 22.4 in 1989. Domestic savings, in the same proportion, were 15.3 per cent in 1984, 16.9 in 1985, 17.3 in 1986, 23.0 in 1988 and 22.5 per cent in 1989. Foreign savings were 0.1 per cent in 1985; 1.9 in 1986; 0.5 in 1987; −1.2 in 1988; and −0.1 per cent in 1989.

A major problem in terms of public finance has been the gap between revenue and public spending, which cannot be covered by non-inflationary means. Looking at the federal fiscal budget: federal fiscal revenues, in real terms, grew by 6.9 per cent in 1988, but fell by 8.0 per cent in 1989. This was caused by a fall in consumption and industrial production and by the elimination of some taxes in the new constitution of October 1988. The federal fiscal budget, including income tax, tax on industrial products and tax on financial transactions in millions of *New Cruzados* (Ncz mn.), from 1984 to 1989, was: 1984, 35; 1985, 130; 1986, 394; 1987, 1,203; 1988, 8,282; 1989, 112,593. Total expenditure for the same year, and the balance, were: 1984, 34 (balance, therefore, 1.); 1985, 121. (balance, 9); 1986, 500 (−106); 1987, 1,392 (−189); 1988, 15,511 (−7,229); 1989, 217, 523 (−104,930.)

Almost twice the size of the federal fiscal budget, in revenue and expenditure, is the State enterprise budget, which covers the spending and borrowing of the 560 State companies. Government control of this has been substantially tightened since 1985, by comparison with previous years. The size of this budget reflects the decision of governments in the mid-1970s to direct resources to this sector, to try to sustain growth. Major State corporations then built up debt borrowing heavily abroad, the service cost of which was greatly increased by the devaluation of February 1983 and subsequent currency adjustments. Capital expenditure, as a proprotion of the total, therefore, fell from 36.5 per cent in 1982 to 12 per cent in 1988. This was made worse by price freezes imposed by the Cruzado Plan in

1986 and by its successors, as well as by the removal of subsidies. State enterprises' share of the nominal deficit rose from 3.5 per cent of GDP in 1979 to 30.4 per cent in 1989. At the same time, the borrowing requirements of state and municipal governments also went up, from 2.7 per cent of GDP in 1986, to an estimated 18.9 per cent in 1989.

The budget system, including the monetary budget, now located in the Treasury secretariat, is complex. Trying to deal with it, the government and the IMF produced a definition of an "operational public sector budget deficit", namely, the borrowing requirement of the non-financial public sector, less the sum of monetary correction on the stock of domestic public debt. This was brought down from 4.3 per cent of GDP in 1985, to 3.6, in 1986, but revenues fell, and the government, in 1987, failed to reduce public spending. The deficit for 1987, went up to 5.5 per cent of GDP. In 1988, there was an attempt, as seen already, to freeze wages of public employees, largely in order to reduce the deficit, which was brought down to 4.3 per cent of GDP, but, again, it rose, by the end of 1989, to over 12 per cent, frustrating both government and IMF demands.

Overall control of monetary policy is the responsibility of the National Monetary Council (*Conselho Monetario Nacional*—CMN). This includes representatives of government business and financial interests. The role of the *Banco Central* in the implementation of monetary policy was strengthened by the emphasis on liquidity control in the New Brazil Plan of March 1990. This made the Central Bank responsible for converting *new cruzados*, withdrawn from circulation, into *cruzeiros*, and for the buying and selling of foreign currency on the domestic market. Until 1990, foreign operations and control of foreign trade was the responsibility of the Department of Foreign Trade—Cacex (*Carteira do Comércio Exterior*). The Collor government shifted this function to the *Co-ordinaria de Intercambio Comercial*—CIC (Commercial Trading Co-ordination), part of a new department of foreign trade in the Ministry of the Economy.

Throughout the 1980s, the money supply grew quickly, partly to meet domestic requirements and partly because of loans to the rural and export sectors. Sales of foreign currency, resulting from exports between 1984 and 1989, also played a part, together with foreign debt conversions.

Interest rates, until 1986, and the *Cruzado Plan*, were supported by *Obrigaçoes Readjustáveis de Tesouro Nacional*—ORTNs (Indexed National Treasury Bonds). Rates of interest were geared to the real rate of currency depreciation against the dollar, plus the dollar interest rate. After the Cruzado Plan, in February 1986, interest rates began to rise, especially towards the end of the year, in line with monthly inflation. After late 1987, interest rates were determined in accordance with the *Letras Financeiras do Tesouro*, described already.

Monetary correction has played an important part in Brazil's economy, ever since 1966, when first it was introduced. The it took the form of a pre-fixed interest rate, to compensate for inflation, and post-fixed rates, applied to an interest-earning financial instrument, adjusting the principal. The post-fixed rates were decided monthly, by a calculation which related the rate of inflation to the national consumer price index. Monetary correction was built into mortgages and agricultural loans and to the taxation system. It was also used to attract money into the *cadernetas de poupança*, savings accounts, used by the government to attract money into particular projects, and to encourage savings. Monetary correction became one of the most prominent features of monetary policy, and one of the motors of inflation. It was a principal target of the Cruzado Plan, seeking to cut "inertial inflation". It reappeared, in the form of the National Treasury Bond (*Obrigação de Tesouro Nacional*—OTN), which was ended by the Summer Plan of January 1989, only to be replaced by the National Treasury Bonds, (*Bônus de Tesouro Nacional*— BTN), another measure of indexation.

The banking system, required to support these financial movements, is of three kinds, investment, commercial and development. Investment banks, in practice, mainly issue 180-day working capital loans. Commercial banks supply short-term capital, mostly in the form of discounted trade bills. Development banks fund high priority projects and underwrite stock and bond issues. The government has also tried to promote savings, for which the most important bank is the *Caixa Econômica Federal*—CEF, together with finance houses, insurance companies and pension funds. The main source of long-term lending is the National Bank for Economic and Social Development (*Banco Nacional do Desenvolvimento Econômico e Social*—BNDES). Other banks which provide capital for regional development include the Bank of North-East Brazil (*Banco do Nordeste do Brasil*) and the *Banco da Amazônia*. There are also development banks financed by states.

Of the 20 biggest commercial banks, in terms of deposits, in 1989, seven were owned by federal or state authorities. Eleven were privately owned and two were under foreign control. The most important was the *Banco do Brasil*, with $6,600 million of deposits. Of the private banks,

Bradesco (*Banco Brasileiro de Descontos*) had deposits of $6,300 million, and *Itaú*, $3,600 million. Among 102 commercial banks, in 1988, 22 were foreign-owned or had foreign equity affiliation. Foreign ownership has increased as banks have run into difficulties, especially with loans to the public sector.

Brazil's *foreign trade* has shown impressive trade surpluses over the last decade, with imports sharply restricted. From 1982 to 1984, export performance was strong, helped by government incentives and domestic recession. It then fell, by 17.1 per cent, in 1984 to 1986, as domestic demand grew, commodity prices fell, and as the country found itself facing protectionist reaction from its principal trading partners. It rose again in 1987 and 1988, partly in reaction to a slacker domestic market, in contrast to the boost provided by the Cruzado Plan of February 1986. In 1989, an overvalued *new cruzado*, a reduction in export incentives and credit revived domestic demand, and a fall in commodity prices again reduced exports.

A remarkable feature of foreign trade is that 200 big firms produce over 75 per cent of export earnings, and even fewer account for 80 per cent of imports. Since March 1990, the Collor government has eased import controls, mainly in an effort to make domestic industry more competitive. Most trade is with the USA and the EC, with most exports being in manufactured goods. Exports to Japan are mainly in primary products. Trade with the **Latin American Integration Association** (*Asociación Latinoamericana de Integración*—ALADI), founded in 1980, fell away in the early 1980s, but has recovered since 1986, when a trade agreement was reached with Argentina. This was strengthened in 1990, aiming to establish a full common market by 1994. The New Brazil Plan, of March 1990, substantially lowered tariffs and brought an end to the list of prohibited imports.

Foreign direct investment in Brazil is still relatively small. As a percentage of GDP it was 0.7 in 1984, 0.6 in 1985, 0.1 in 1986, 0.4 in 1987, 0.9 in 1988 and 0.2 in 1989. The percentage stock of foreign direct investment by sector, at end of year book value for 1988, was: manufacturing, 74.0; services, 16.0; trade, 4.5; mining and oil, 2.5; other, 3.0. The stock of foreign direct investment, by source, was, for the same year: USA, 28.4 per cent; Japan, 9.6; Germany, 15.7; France, 4.3; UK, 6.2; other, 35.8. The share of the USA has dropped in recent years, while reinvestment of profits from Japan, Italy, the UK and the Netherlands has grown.

There has been a substantial fall in reinvestment in the more important Latin American countries since 1982. Measured in 1985 dollars, the average annual reinvestment dropped from $2,300 million to $1,500 million in 1983–1989, a decline of 32 per cent. This was especially notable in Brazil and Mexico: in the case of Brazil, annual average foreign reinvestment, in millions of 1985 dollars, fell from 1,094, for 1976 to 1982, to 570 for 1983 to 1989. This is an especially significant figure, when reinvestment can often account for almost half of investment in a given year.

The transfer of profit and dividends, already discussed, has been a central issue of political debate, ever since, at least, the second Vargas government, from 1950 to 1954. It is determined by the *Foreign Capital Law, No. 4131*, of 1962, passed by the Goulart government, which was amended, in 1964, by *Law 4340*. The *Banco Central* must authorize remittance of profits, royalty payments, dividends and the repatriation of capital. Remittances are taxed at 25 per cent. When they rise above an average of 12 per cent of registered capital on reinvestments over three years, there is a supplementary tax rate of between 40 and 60 per cent.

Investment through the Brazilian stock exchange, for foreign portfolios, must be done through a national securities house. The *Banco Central* has to sanction the application of foreign loans for capital purposes. Foreign firms can only use local credit to meet cash flows: official lending is normally made only to nationally owned firms.

The 1986 agreement with Argentina is only one indication of Brazil's closer commitment to a system of Latin American economic integration. Brazil was a signatory, in 1960, of the Latin American Free Trade Association (*Associación Latinoamericana de Libre Comercio*—ALALC), established by the Treaty of Montevideo. The other 10 countries which signed this were Argentina, Bolivia, Chile, Colombia, Ecuador, Mexico, Paraguay, Peru, Uruguay and Venezuela. In 1978, they advocated more free trade throughout the region, and, in 1980, through the Montevideo Treaty, created ALADI.

Between 1981 and 1986, intra-regional trade fell by 37 per cent, but recovered strongly in the last four years of the decade. In 1987, intra-regional exports were $8,500 million; in 1988, $9,700 million, and, in 1989, $10,900 million. Partly in reaction to the proposed European single market, there was further stimulus to Latin American regional integration in 1989, with Brazil making the running. In December 1989, Ministers from Brazil, Argentina, Colombia, Mexico, Peru, Uruguay and Venezuela, now known as the Group of Rio, deliberately excluding Panama from the former Group of Eight, decided to eliminate non-tariff barriers to reciprocal trade, and to improve the regional tariff preference system. Brazil is also a partner to the *River Plate Basin Charter*, signed in April 1969, together with Argentina, Bolivia, Paraguay and Uruguay, the principal aim of which is to co-ordinate efforts for infrastructural development in the River Plate region. In the same spirit, Brazil seeks to co-operate with neighbouring countries in the *Amazon Pact*, signed on July 3, 1977 in agreement with Bolivia, Colombia, Ecuador, Guyana, Peru, Suriname and Venezuela. Brazil has about 70 per cent of Amazonia, in both land and people. Sharing common frontiers with every South American country except Chile and Ecuador, it is, inescapably, a regional power, however reluctant it may be to shoulder that responsibility.

Prospects for development. The immediate future of the Collor government and its overall programme depends on the success of its economic measures, above all, the fight against inflation. Already, in the immediate aftermath of the second round of voting for governors, Collor admitted, in late November 1990, that some changes might have to be introduced to his stabilization programme. With inflation moving towards 19 per cent a month, the president still talked of reducing it to 3 per cent within several months. He blamed the recent rise in inflation on an increased oil import bill, caused by the Gulf crisis, producing extra costs of $300,000,000 a month. He was seeking, once again, some kind of "social pact", to which a main stumbling block was disagreement over wage indexation, which the workers and Congress wanted, but which the government saw as a key factor in fuelling inflation.

By Feb. 1 1991, as the country prepared for carnival, with inflation for January at over 20 per cent, the government introduced a new package of firm measures, Collor Plan II, imposing a freeze on prices and wages. The new measures included a 47 per cent increase in fuel prices and up to 71 per cent on utility charges. All banks and financial markets were closed for the day, a Friday, to prevent panic buying. It was the fifth austerity package in five years. Minister Zélia Cardoso de Mello insisted that this was just a "deepening" of the Collor Plan of 10 months earlier, but, since the government had previously rejected a price and wages freeze, a general assessment was that this marked the end of the Collor Plan, calling into question the government's credibility.

Collor, speaking to the nation, said that he had been left with "no option, but to use the 'surgical instrument' of price controls", and, like Sarney before him, urged the public to co-operate, to cut consumption and act as watchdogs for price rises. The president squarely blamed the business community for his failure, so far, to defeat inflation, speaking of his earlier plan as seeking to counter "the immense resistance of those who always had intolerable privileges... that this government is ending". He said inflation was a virus, which enriched those with money, but worsened the poverty of the workers. "The future of Brazil is at stake. Don't leave me alone in this—I need you." It was a direct appeal to the mass of the people, rather than to the business class which was being held to blame for continuing inflation.

Despite the appeal, the *Folha de São Paulo* found that 52 per cent of people were unhappy with the new package, which was accused of fixing prices in the shops at a higher level than previously was being charged, while freezing wages too low. Another survey showed only 30 per cent support, with only 21 per cent of those interviewed thinking it would benefit them.

The new package also has serious implications for government ministries, whose budgets were cut by 90 per cent, and for the state governors who take up their posts in March 1991. Under the Constitution, states should receive 50 per cent of federal revenues. Governors fear that they will not even be able to maintain public services, let alone develop new programmes. This is just the situation which seemed likely, after the November elections, with critical, or hostile, governors able to put severe pressure on Collor. He is said to be distancing himself from the new "package", giving it about three months to work, by which time he may have to introduce changes in his government. Minister Zélia Cardoso is currently in, at once, a powerful and vulnerable position.

A change of economic team still would not solve the underlying problems. Continuing inflation means that pressure will grow in Congress to reintroduce wage indexation, which, according to government analysis, is one of its primary causes. An attempt by Collor to veto such legislation, as he did in June, July and, again, in December 1990, would make even worse his relations with Congress, business and labour. Despite the relatively favourable results of the Congressional elections, there are still rich sources of tension and dispute with Congress. The trade unions, mainly through the CUT, are also demanding re-adjustment of wages, of the order of 493 per cent, to make up for losses which they claim have occurred since Collor took office. The mechanism for this adjustment again involves indexation. They also want a real increase of 100 per cent in the minimum wage, which again would be pegged to inflation.

Meanwhile, the recession continues, with gloomy initial estimates for the economy's performance in 1990: GDP percentage growth, −4.6; GDP per capita, −5.9; industrial output, −4.8; steel output, − 18.1; vehicle output, −9.7; agricultural output, −3.4; services, −0.3 per cent. The country's balance of payments deficit, according to the Central Bank's quarterly report, in mid-January 1991, widened to $5,370 million for the first nine months of 1990, from $1,990 million for the same period in 1989.

One particularly hard-hit area was car production, down by 9.7 per cent on the 1989 figure of just over 1,000,000 units with domestic sales falling by 6.4 per cent. Production of tractors and heavy farm equipment fell to only 27,400 units, with output, in December 1990, the lowest since January 1968. Autolatina, which controls 50 per cent of the domestic market, said that falling sales would mean voluntary redundancies.

At the same time, the CNI calculated that about 200,000 workers, or about 10 per cent of the workforce, in the industrial sector of São Paulo, lost their jobs in 1990. *Dieese*, the trade unions' research department, estimated unemployed workers in the metropolitan area of São Paulo totalled 789,000 at the end of November 1990, an increase of 34.3 per cent on the 1989 figure. Even the Ministry of Labour, in a study which appeared in late December 1990, reported an estimated loss of 312,613 jobs in the first 10 months of the year, with 58,437 in October alone. It rightly notes fear of job losses as a factor in the decline in the number of strikes, falling, in the first 10 months of 1990, to 2,097, as compared with 3,708 in the same period of 1989.

The trade surplus, by comparison, was relatively cheering. At just over $11,000 million, it was 31.6 per cent lower than in 1989, and well under the government's target of $11,000 million. This had to be set against the liberalization of imports in the Collor Plan, and the rise in the oil bill, because of the Gulf crisis, up from $3,400 million, in 1989, to $4,300 million in 1990.

Imports in 1990 rose by 11.5 per cent, to just below $20,400 million; exports fell by 8.7 per cent, to $31,400 million. Exports to Iraq fell by $233,000,000, or 68 per cent, because of the embargo following the invasion of Kuwait: but exports to Iran were up from $286,000,000 to $525,000,000, and to Saudi Arabia, rising by $85,000,000, to $290,000,000.

Elsewhere, there was a continuity of trench warfare, notably in the discussions between government officials and creditor banks on the issue of debt arrears. In December 1990, Minister Zélia Cardoso de Mello had announced a partial lifting of the 18 month-old debt moratorium, saying that Brazil would start to pay some of the interest on its $63,000 million debt with the banks. The suggested figure was $489,000,000 to be paid over the first three months of 1991, namely 30 per cent of the interest falling due in the first quarter.

In addition, Brazil would pay $900,000,000 of the accumulated arrears, about 15 per cent of the $6,400 million in arrears owed on direct loans to the government, but excluding almost $2,000 million owed on loans to others. The banks wanted payment of $2,500 million, and a further 50 per cent of the overdue interest by the end of the first quarter, the rest to be covered by five-year bonds.

Talks started again on Jan. 14, 1991, with banks offering slight concessions on the bonds payment, but Brazil stuck to its position that payment of arrears could only be made after a broad debt restructuring agreement had been made with the banks.

The discussions still continue, with an offer, later in January, from the banks' advisory committee to reduce by $2,000 million to $5,700 million the interest to be paid in the next three years. Brazil's negotiator, Jório Dauster, welcomed the move, but repeated Brazil's intention to pay only $2,400 million in arrears in that period. Brazil's efforts to link these questions to the wider issues of the economy are understandable and coherent. At the same time, a workable agreement on the whole foreign debt issue could greatly strengthen confidence in Collor's government in business and financial circles, especially at home, but also abroad, and may lead to that quickening of investment and resumed growth which is so badly needed.

One element of the Collor Plan which still remains in force is the privatization programme, which has taken much longer than expected to develop. A list of 22 companies was issued in August 1990, the aim being to raise $7,000 million. The programme was finally launched only in January 1991, still with the same figure in mind for this year, but $1,800 million for next. It needs foreign support, since Brazil's small stock market, especially in a recession, could not cope with its requirements. It expects to raise most funds from debt-equity swaps. Its director, Sérgio Zendron, speaks of $100,000 to $110,000 million being available. Of this $45,000 million is in foreign debt titles. The rest is in internal debt, $30,000,000 in blocked *cruzados* (frozen in the Collor Plan) and $5,000 million from compulsory purchase of privatization certificates by banks. Internal debt will be converted at face value. A decision is still awaited on conversion of foreign debt.

As many as 100 state companies may be in line for privatization. Foreign capital can be as much as 100 per cent of private companies, but foreign voters may hold only 40 per cent of voting shares. The first company to be sold will be Usiminas. Most will be in the steel, petrochemical and transport sectors. It is intended to use money raised to reduce the $120,000 million foreign debt, so as not to increase liquidity and hinder the anti-inflation programme.

The slow rate of progress of the privatization programme has meant that the government's aim to reduce the public sector deficit from 7 per cent of GDP to 1.1 per cent by the end of the year has fallen far short, not least since the public sector contributes so greatly to the deficit. The recession, too, has affected tax revenues, so that this basic problem still remains to be addressed. It continues as the most important motor of inflation.

The country's monetary base expanded by 58 per cent in December 1990, mainly due to increased demand for paper money, stimulated by the introduction of new rules governing investments. IMI went up by 41.4 per cent, so that the Central Bank exceeded by 89 per cent the monetary base targets set for the second half of 1990 by the National Monetary Council. It seems most unlikely that the target for the first quarter of 1991 can be met, since it was calculated on a 10 per cent inflation rate.

What all these figures mean in practice and in daily living, especially for the poor is reflected in a recent study by IBGE, based on its 1989 National Household Survey (*Pesquisa Nacional por Amostra de Domicilios*—PNAD) with data on representative samples of 86,000 households. This shows that the gap between the rich and poor widened throughout the 1980s. In 1982, the earnings of the top 5 per cent of the population accounted for 33.4 per cent of the national total: by 1989, it was 39.4 per cent. At the same time, the share of the poorest 30 per cent of the population dropped from 5.3 to 4.2 per cent. The study shows that this concentration of wealth grew\more quickly after 1987, in line with rising inflation.

The figures are worst for the north-east, where the share of total earnings of the richest 10 per cent was 55.7 per cent, and that of the poorest 10 per cent only 0.6 per cent. In the southern states, by contrast, Rio Grande do Sul, Paraná and Santa Catarina, the share of the wealthiest 10 per cent was 14 per cent, and of the poorest 10 per cent, 1 per cent.

Figures for the north-east are generally the worst for the country. The average wage is the lowest: 45 per cent of the population earns the minimum wage, or less. It has the highest illiteracy rate, 36 per cent, compared with a national rate of 18.2, with more than one third of the 24,000,000 Brazilians who cannot read or write living in the north-east. The level of education is the nations's lowest, with only 15 per cent of children finishing primary school. Infant mortality is the highest (136 of every 1,000 born die before the age of five years). 48.7 per cent of the population has no running water, 31 per cent no electricity.

Another study, financed by *UNICEF* again carried out by the IBGE, recently showed that half of Brazil's 58,000,000 adolescents are poor, while 17,000,000 live in absolute poverty. Seven millions Brazilians aged between 10 and 17 have to work, with 58.1 per cent earning less than $25 a month, with only 33.5 per cent of them having a legal work contract. Despite this, 12.7 per cent of those working contribute more than 30 per cent to the overall family earnings. The homes of 56 per cent of Brazilian children and adolescents lack toilets, only 33.1 per cent of this same group have running water, and 37.6 per cent have no electricity. More positively, the percentage of children aged from 5 to 6 attending school rose form 22.5 per cent in 1981, to 46.3 per cent in 1988. Attendances by children of seven to nine rose from 70.7 per cent to 83 per cent and by those of 15 to 17 from 63.1 per cent to 66.1 per cent.

The IBGE's 1989 Household Survey found that 42 per cent of Brazilians are now less than 17 years old. Of these, 24.1 per cent belong to families with average earnings, per person, equivalent to half the minimum wage, in other words, about $30 a month. Figures such as these explain why most Brazilians, whether they voted for Collor or for Lula in 1989, were voting against the old order, demanding change, and new priorities in government, voting for youth and a better future. They also explain the persistent support for Brizola, based on his programmes for education and housing.

Collor is right, though he is not the first, to say that inflation falls heaviest on the poort and the working class. This was evident in the street-filled enthusiasm for the Cruzado Plan and the massive pro-PMDB vote in 1986. Inflation, in itself, is only a symptom of more profound problems, but it hurts most immediately in the shopping basket and is more tangible in day-to-day living, than the public deficit, an over-blown money supply, or foreign debt.

The immediate danger is hyper-inflation. Brazilians have lived with it for, at least, the last two years. Now they are really worried about what will happen if the Collor Plan fails completely. What would this imply? It could mean, as in Argentina, the "dollarization" of the economy, which Brazil has tried to avoid in the past, where the United States dollar becomes the unofficial unit of the economy. Even this, in Argentina, did not end inflation or sufficiently relieve pressure on the political system.

A more pessimistic body of social analysis sees hyperinflation as leading to massive unemployment, further recession, widespread strikes and general social dislocation. This, it is argued, is the only set of conditions which could induce the armed forces, once more, to take power. The last group in Brazil, in 1991, to want this, must be the armed forces. They know that they, by themselves, have no solutions to the nation's problems. They, also, want to see a strong democratic system in Brazil.

This more apocalyptic scenario is, in fact, unnecessary. Brazilian democracy and its political system are as able to withstand severe inflation, recession, high public deficit, and social and economic tensions as most others. Brazil is by no means alone, at present, in feeling such strains. The more likely outcome is that it will muddle through, as long as others do not meddle.

It is very possible that the next major electoral tests will produce a left-wing government. Its most effective leader, on present evidence, would be Brizola, perhaps in co-operation with Lula and the PT and a broader left-wing coalition with the PDT; but crystal ball gazing is notoriously obscure in Brazil.

One thing is important. In considering current economic difficulties or social pressures, it is necessary to keep a sense of perspective, to set the present, admittedly difficult, situation in the context, not just of Brazil's enormous potential, but its very considerable achievements throughout this century, and longer. Its economic growth has been impressively consistent, grafting a diversified industrial economy on to an agrarian base, which also has become more diverse in recent decades. It has a sophisticated infrastructure for future development, most of the energy resources which it will need, and it has more than shown its ability to trade in world markets.

Brazil, unlike many other societies, has no tribal divisions and no deep ethnic or religious cleavages. Its people are rightly famous for their tolerance of how their neighbours conduct their lives. These qualities, too, are very positive assets for the future.

Much still needs to be done, above all, in redressing economic and social inequalities, which remain the most serious obstacle to national development: but these are now firmly on the political agenda. Brazil's new democracy will allow its people to keep them there, for action, now, and in the future.

PF

BRAZIL: FOREIGN RELATIONS. Brazil, physically, culturally and in terms of historical development, is closer to Europe and Africa than it is to the USA. The United States' influence, though important in the years after 1945 and the *coup* of 1964, is a relatively recent phenomenon. It is less profound and, almost certainly, less long-lasting than some United States officials would like to suggest. Rio de Janeiro is closer to any European capital, except Athens, than it is to Washington DC. For over four centuries, with the major exception of its indigenous population, its people came from Europe or Africa. Europeans, including English-speaking Europeans, commonly feel more at home in Brazil than they do in the United States. Brazil is, in no sense, in the "backyard" of the United States. It resents the sometimes rather crude attempts at arm-twisting, which may work in Central America or the Caribbean, though, even there, with difficulty, but which are totally unsuitable in dealing with the largest power in South America.

This sense of identification with Europe, Africa and the "Third World" lay behind the shaping of Brazil's "independent foreign policy" throughout the presidencies of **Kubitschek**, **Quadros** and **Goulart**. This was marked by a refusal simply to go along with the economic and political priorities of the United States, exemplified by the break with the IMF, a flexible approach to Cuba and a sympathy with "Third World" issues, especially in Africa, following an independent line, which already had been seen in Brazil's refusal to be drawn in to the Korean War.

The *coup* of 1964 brought Brazil closer to the United States, expressed in the famous remark of Juracy Magalhães, former *tenente*, later general, then ambassador in Washington, under Castello Branco: "what is good for the United States is good for Brazil". The geo-political thinking stemming from the ESG turned on such concepts as "Fortress America", on the notion of ideological frontiers and a lessening of conflict with the United States. The new government of Castello Branco broke off diplomatic relations with Cuba, sent troops to the Dominican Republic, in a show of solidarity, in 1965, and reaffirmed a mutual concern to end "subversion".

Yet, even in this immediate, post-*coup* period, there were tensions, stemming from the intrinsic challenge contained in Brazil's aims for rapid development and a share of world markets. The concepts of "security" and "development" within the ESG were intrinsically linked to that of "nationalism", which pointed to a conflict of interests between Brazil and any power which sought to confine it to a subordinate or clientelistic role.

After the change of government, in 1967, Costa e Silva's Minister of Foreign Relations, the *mineiro* Magalhães Pinto, again stressed the link between development and security, noting how genuine security depended on development. The result was emphasis on winning wider export markets, without political or ideological constraint, a policy reiterated by able spokesmen within the Itamaraty (the Brazilian foreign ministry), such as the ambassador in London, Dr Sérgio Corrêia da Costa.

A sharper nationalist stance on the part of the new government accompanied a return to greater solidarity with the "Third World", while, increasingly, there were signs of tension between Brazil and the USA, especially as US lobbies tried to impose limits on the import of Brazilian shoes and instant coffee. This issue of protectionism was to continue over the next decade, provoking particular resentment when combined with demands to repay foreign debt, while Brazil was not being allowed to trade freely to earn the means to pay.

There were political disagreements, too, as at the Geneva Conference of 1968, where Brazil joined such countries as India and the United Arab Republic, in opposing the joint US–USSR project to limit nuclear testing, while later refusing to support the Nuclear Proliferation Treaty, despite State Department pressure. Brazil's view was that access to nuclear energy was a necessary condition for development, and that attempts to exclude developing countries from its use was, simply, a new form of dependency.

Throughout the presidencies of Garrastazú Médici and Ernesto Geisel, the need for Brazil to find new foreign markets, and to diversify its trade, brought further tensions in Brazilian–US relations. The United States' share of Brazilian imports fell from 13.8 per cent in 1974 to 11.0 in 1975 (from a peak of 53 per cent in the early 1940s). The percentage of Brazilian exports to the USA also fell, to 23 per cent in 1972, then to less than 20 per cent, while Western Europe accounted for 43 per cent of exports in 1971 and 45.6 in 1972. From 1974 to 1980, exports to Western and Eastern Europe were more than double those to the USA. The role of the EC has continued to grow. From 1975 to 1985, Brazil's exports to Western Europe grew from about $4,000 million to $8,000 million.

During the presidencies of Ernesto Geisel and João Figueiredo, Brazil's trade both grew in volume and shifted direction. Exports to Africa increased from $407,000,000 in 1975 to $1,900 million in 1985. To Asia, Australasia and the Middle East, they rose, in the same period from $1,300 million to $4,600 million, with the balance of payments, in all these areas, favouring Brazil.

At the same time, Brazil showed a readiness to adopt an independent line on international political issues, often in defiance of Washington. In 1974, it quickly recognized revolutionary governments in Angola, Mozambique and Guinea-Bissau. In 1975, it made a nuclear agreement with West Germany, when the country offered a better technological package than the United States would allow. In 1977, it cancelled the military agreement with the United States, again seeking access to wider markets.

Under the Figueiredo government, with Saraiva Guerreiro as Minister of Foreign Affairs, Brazil moved even further back towards the independent foreign policy of the late 1950s and early 1960s. It refused to go along with United States' pressure on Nicaragua and El Salvador, unwilling to be drawn into the US Central American policy, even when, later in the decade, there were threats to make negotiation over the foreign debt even harder, unless Brazil gave more support in Central America. In part, the refusal reflected the concern of some military leaders in Brazil over the degree of logistical dependence on the USA which closer involvement would imply. This concern had been expressed as early as 1965, during Brazil's involvement with the Dominican Republic and had been deepened during the **Falklands/Malvinas** dispute.

In part, because of commercial interests, Brazil lent support to Angola and Mozambique in their disputes with South Africa, but did not support sanctions against South Africa: both De Beers and Anglo-American have big interests in Brazil. It has also adopted an independent line on the Middle East. It sold arms to both Iran and Iraq during their bitter war. During the Falklands/Malvinas conflict, it maintained good relations with both sides, capably handling Argentine affairs in London.

At the same time, Brazil is actively pursuing its role within Latin America, an inevitable consequence of economic weight in the region and its common frontiers with all South American countries except Chile and Ecuador. Within Latin America, Brazil is, itself, a creditor and its influence can be felt, to varying degrees, all around its borders. One eloquent example is the influence exerted on **Paraguay** by means of the huge Itaipú hydro-electric complex, the biggest in the world, costing $15,000 million. It has the world's highest dam, at 600 feet, and the largest, at 5,000,000 m^3. It aims to have a total of 18 turbines, each generating 700 MW, with a peak capacity of 12,600 MW. This joint programme with Paraguay has greatly increased Brazilian presence in eastern Paraguay, including Brazilian land ownership and settlement.

An agreement with **Argentina** was signed in July 1986. **Uruguay** came into it in August, and it continues to be taken seriously, on all sides, provoking considerable interest throughout the region more generally. It would have proceeded further and faster, but for the economic problems of the signatories. The protocols on capital goods drew special attention. Intra-regional trade, after falling by almost one-third, as seen already, from 1981 to 1986, has grown steadily over recent years, with the idea of regional integration receiving stimulus from the proposed European single market.

The main source of dispute for Brazil, has been over *informática* and the computer industry. The **Collor** government has eased these strains by starting to phase out the "market reserve". It has ended quantitative restrictions on computer imports, and the aim is to end the reserve completely by 1994. Until then, the Special Informatics Secretariat will continue. This is all part of a more general reform of trade policy, the most far-reaching since the 1950s, in order to make domestic producers more competitive. Quantitative restrictions on imports were abolished as of July 1990. Tariffs on imports of raw materials, machinery and parts, which have no locally produced equivalent, also have been ended, and textile tariffs halved. There is to be a general reduction of import tariffs, in four annual stages, up to 1994. By then, the top rate should be reduced from 105 per cent to 40, and the average rate cut from 35 per cent to 20.

The Collor government also, in May 1990, lifted curbs on remittances of profits and dividends and on capital transfers abroad. In July, it unblocked transfers in the pipeline, aiming to clear a backlog of some $1,800 million, held by the Central Bank, by December. All these moves were welcomed by multinationals, pointing the way to renewed foreign investment. Another change, in the administrative system, was the abolition of *Cacex*, the foreign trade department at the *Banco Central*. Its functions were transferred to the Trade Co-ordination Office (*Coordenaria de Intercámbio Comercial*—CIC) part of a new department for foreign trade within the Ministry of the Economy. These changes, together with a promise by Brazil to introduce legislation to protect pharmaceutical patent rights, brought a response from the USA, in the withdrawal, in June 1990, of trade sanctions imposed in October 1988. These had consisted of 100 per cent retaliatory duties on paper products, consumer electronics and drugs.

There was general agreement that, in terms of trade, relations between Brazil and the USA were better in 1990 than for several years previously. How long this might last was open to doubt.

PF

BRAZILIAN COMMUNIST PARTY (Partido Comunista Brasileiro—PCB). In 1906, socialists formed the Brazilian Workers' Confederation, with its paper at first in Italian, *La Parola dei Socialisti*, followed, in 1912, by the first Portuguese-language socialist paper, *A Voz do Trabalho*. The year 1922 saw the founding of the PCB, accepting the principles of the Third International, so gaining admission to the Comintern.

The leadership of the PCB was notably élitist and there was a strong foreign element in most left-wing movements. Partly, this reflected the small size of the urban working class, estimated from the 1920 census only at about 275,000, which by the middle of the next decade had grown to around 700,000. There was, nevertheless, a new political force with which politicians and government had to reckon.

The best-known leader of the PCB was Luis Carlos Prestes, who had led the famous Prestes Column on its long march of about 14,000 miles through the interior of Brazil from 1924 to 1926. After the revolution of 1930, Prestes became a Communist and went to Moscow. On his return to Brazil, he became one of the most prominent figures in the **National Liberation Alliance** (*Aliança Nacional Libertadora*—ANL). He was arrested after the so-called "Communist conspiracy", *Intentona Comunista*, of Nov. 15, 1935, and the PCB was declared to be illegal.

The party was again given legal status in 1945. In that year, its presidential candidate won 10 per cent of the vote, when the National Democratic Union (*União Democrática Nacional*—UDN), the main party of the right, won only 26.3 per cent. This electoral success was repeated in state elections in January 1946 and supplementary elections for Congress, when, again, the PCB won 10 per cent of the vote, even though there now were 14 competing parties. Party membership now was estimated at about 200,000, with strong influence in the Confederation of Brazilian Workers (*Confederação dos Trabalhadores do Brasil*—CTB) as it developed from September 1946. The 1946 Constitution allowed for the exclusion of "anti-democratic parties". In May 1947, the Dutra government declared the PCB illegal and, in October, the Senate voted to remove all Communists from elected office. Among those removed were Jorge Amado, one of Brazil's most distinguished novelists, who had been elected as federal deputy from Bahia, and Carlos Marighela, also federal deputy from Bahia, who, two decades later was to lead one of the most important urban guerrilla groups, having, by then, broken with the PCB.

Although legally proscribed, the PCB remained an important force in politics in the 1950s and 1960s, especially through the trade union movement, playing an active part in organizing strikes, mainly in the public sector, in the early 1960s. It also helped to develop some of the Peasant Leagues in north-east Brazil. It mobilized public opinion in the "nationalist" camp throughout the post-war period, then became one of the main targets of those who carried through the *coup* of 1964.

After the military seizure of power in 1964, the PCB was severely divided in terms of its analysis of what had gone wrong. A common charge was that it had become too élitist and "bourgeois" and that it had compromized its revolutionary tradition. One important rival group was the **Communist Party of Brazil** (*Partido Comunista do Brasil*—PCdoB), which followed a Marxist line. Among other prominent critics, who broke with the party, was Marighela, who now advocated direct action and violent resistance. Luís Carlos Prestes, in exile, remained the Secretary-General of the party.

The PCB remained illegal after the reorganization of parties in 1979, but later was reinstated in a general amnesty. Prestes, back in Brazil, found himself in disagreement with other leaders and, in 1984, after more than 50 years at the head of the PCB, was expelled by the party, though remaining, till his death, a powerful, coherent advocate of the need for radical reforms. The PCB has not had the resurgence of support which it, and others, expected in the 1980s. It did relatively poorly in the presidential elections of 1989 and the congressional and other elections of 1990. It has suffered from a notable decline in morale following the changes in Eastern Europe. It has been generally overtaken on the left by the PT and, within the trade union movement, by the CUT. If it is not entirely a spent force, it shows little sign of real energy.

PF

BRAZILIAN LABOUR PARTY (Partido Trabalhista Brasileiro—PTB). This was one of two parties founded by **Vargas** in preparation for the presidential election scheduled for Dec. 2, 1945 the other being the Social Democratic Party (*Partido Social Democrático*—PSD). The PTB especially found its base of support in *trabalhismo*, the Vargista "labour" tradition stemming from Rio Grande do Sul and theorists such as Alberto Pasqualini (1901–1960). This was developed throughout the 1930s, first by Lindolfo Collor, as head of the new Ministry of Labour, Commerce and Industry after 1930, then by other Ministers of Labour, notably Alexandre Marcondes Filho. The PTB also had close links with the corporatist trade union movement, providing many of the so-called *pelegos*, trade union leaders linked to the Ministry of Labour.

The PTB came to power with Vargas in the election of 1950, when he won 48.73 per cent of the vote, with *trabalhismo* providing the basis for his second period in government, when **João Goulart** was made Minister of Labour. After the death of Vargas, the PTB won 14.9 per cent of votes in the Congressional election of 1954, as compared with 13.6 in 1950 and 10.1 in 1945. The PSD won 22 per cent and the UDN, 13.6 per cent. Together with the PSD, the PTB provided the congressional support for **Kubitschek**, elected in October 1955 as the candidate of the *PSD*.

After the resignation of **Quadros** in 1961, the PTB again provided the president, in **João Goulart**, but suffered a major defeat with the *coup* of 1964, after which many of its leaders were deprived of their political rights. In 1965, with the creation of only two party *blocs*, most *PTB* congressmen joined the Brazilian Democratic Movement (*Movimento Democrático Brasileiro*—MDB). With the return to multi-party politics after 1979, the PTB reappeared, but the *sigla*, or party acronym, was deliberately refused to **Leonel Brizola**, who had tried to claim it after his return to Brazil. It was awarded, instead, by the electoral authorities, to Ivette Vargas, a niece of Getúlio, to break the claim of Brizola and his supporters to be the main heirs of the Vargas tradition.

The PTB remains relatively strong in Rio Grande do Sul, but, generally, has been outdistanced on the left by the **Worker's Party** (*Partido dos Trabalhadores*—PT) and by the Democratic Labour Party (*Partido Democrático Trabalhista*—PDT) of Brizola. It is perceived as having moved to the right and, in 1983, formed a short-lived coalition with the pro-government PDS. By the elections of 1989, it was still the fourth largest party in Brazil, but was divided into four main groups, so that its presidential candidate, Affonso Camargo, had no chance of success.

PF

BRITISH VIRGIN ISLANDS. *Population*: 12, 197 (1987). *Area*: 153 sq km. *GDP*: US$101.5 million (1987). *Top five trade partners*: USA, US Virgin Islands, Puerto Rico, UK. *Birthrate*: 21. 6 per 1,000.

Geographical background. The British Virgin Islands comprise a number of small islands in the Leeward Islands in the Caribbean Sea, to the east of Puerto Rico. The islands were first settled by Europeans in the mid-seventeenth century and became a British possession in 1672.

Socio-political background. Under the terms of the 1967 Constitution, amended in 1977, the British government appoints a governor for the islands who is responsible for defence and foreign affairs, internal security and certain administrative and financial matters. Other matters are the responsibility of the Chief Minister and the Executive Council. The governor acts as chairman of the Executive Council, which is responsible to the Legislative Council comprising nine elected and two ex-officio members. The Chief Minister is the person who can command a majority of the elected members.

Outline of political history. Since the introduction of greater internal autonomy in 1967, political power has alternated between the two main political parties, the Virgin Islands Party (VIP) and the United Party (UP), often with an independent holding the balance of power. In 1983 the VIP and UP each won four seats, the remaining seat going to an independent, Cyril Romney. Romney became Chief Minister, forming a government with the UP. In elections in 1986 the VIP gained a majority and Lavity Stoutt (who had served as Chief Minister between 1967 and 1975) returned as Chief Minister. Both parties are based more on personal following than on ideological differences and both seem committed to continued dependent status.

Recent developments—political. In March 1988 the Deputy Chief Minister, Omar Hodge, was dismissed for trying to obstruct a report of an inquiry into a bribery charge against him. Hodge joined the UP and in 1989 announced the formation of a new political party, the Independent People's Movement.

Although foreign policy is the preserve of the colonial power, the British Virgin Islands has been encouraged to extend links with neighbouring territories, becoming an associate member of the Organization of East Caribbean States (OECS) in 1984 and of CARICOM in 1990.

Outline of economic development. The island's economy is closely linked with that of the neighbouring United States Virgin Islands (USVI), since a large proportion of the workforce are employed in the USVI and the majority of the islands' limited exports are shipped there. The US dollar is also used as the British Virgin Islands' currency. Agriculture and fishing provide most of the value of exports, but this is vastly outweighed by the large cost of imports, mostly of food, machinery, building materials and fuel. This is offset by earnings from tourism and the offshore financial sector.

Current economic situation. During the 1980s tourism has grown rapidly on the islands, although poor communication links have limited the number of arrivals. To compensate for this the islands have concentrated on upmarket and sea-borne tourism, particularly from yachting. Another sector of the economy which has developed significantly in recent years is the offshore financial sector. Legislation passed in 1984 allowed the tax exemption of locally registered companies and the number of foreign companies registered in the islands has increased from 10,600 in 1988 to 13,000 by the end of 1989. Income from licence fees totalled $4,000,000 in 1989. Problems in Panama and promotions in Hong Kong were estimated to have increased this registration figure to over 23,000 by late 1990. Fears about the possible misuse of these companies for fraud or for the laundering of drug profits has increased attention on monitoring and regulation. The islands are self-financing, with the government estimating a surplus of US$2,460,000 on the recurrent budget for 1990, but aid for capital projects is still provided by Britain.

LP

BRIZOLA, LEONEL DE MOURA. In the elections for state governors in **Brazil** on Oct. 3, 1990 only 11 candidates won the majority vote necessary for election in the first round of voting. Of these, only one was in direct opposition to President **Collor de Mello**. He was Leonel Brizola, now being elected, in a massive victory, for the second time, as governor of the state of Rio de Janeiro, a position to which he previously had been elected in 1982. Brizola's election and his authoritative, successful, support for the **Democratic Labour Party** (*Partido Democrático Trabalhista*—PDT) candidates in the second round of voting again marked him as the most influential leader of the political left in Brazil and, arguably, in South America.

Brizola was born in 1922 in Rio Grande do Sul. He had some early training as an engineer, then was elected as state deputy for the **Brazilian Labour Party** (*Partido Trabalhista Brasileiro*—PTB) in 1950. In the same year, he married Neusa Goulart, the sister of **João Goulart**, Vargas' protégé and future president of Brazil. Vargas was his best man. In 1952, Brizola became state Secretary of Public Works and, in 1954, was elected federal deputy for the PTB with the highest number of votes, till then, recorded in Rio Grande do Sul.

In 1955, he was elected Mayor of Porto Alegre, capital of Rio Grande do Sul, with more votes than all the other candidates put together. In 1958, still only 36, he was elected as state governor (1959–1962). He won a reputation as a vigorous administrator and social reformer, and was one of the leading spokesmen for Brazilian nationalist interests.

In 1962 he was elected governor of the former Federal District, with almost 300,000 votes, almost one-third of the total, the highest vote ever recorded, till then, in such an election. Brizola saw himself as being in the full *trabalhista* (labour) tradition of Vargas, but won a reputation as one of the more radical influences on Goulart. He was the prime target of those who brought down the Goulart government in 1964.

Brizola advocated resistance to the *coup*, but went to Uruguay and remained in exile until after the amnesty which allowed his return to Brazil in 1979. In 1981, he founded the PDT and, in 1982, won the governorship of Rio de Janeiro. Again, despite federal government hostility and lack of resources, he ran an effective administration. His programme for the CIEPs and for housing, were, in effect, part of an eventual programme for national government. From 1982, right through to 1989, he was always seen as the leading candidate for the presidency, with his chances further increased by the PDT successes in the elections of November 1988.

Throughout the campaign for the presidency in 1989, Brizola was anxious to win the middle ground, presenting himself, as during his term as governor of Rio de Janeiro, as a moderate reformer of the Centre Left. Steadily, both he and Lula were overtaken by Collor, with Lula just beating Brizola into second place in the first round of voting in November. Brizola's cardinal failure was not to win sufficient support in São Paulo and Minas Gerais, which, together with Rio de Janeiro, contain 44 per cent of the national electorate. Brizola recovered quickly from this setback, continuing his trenchant criticism of Collor and his programmes, right through to the Congressional elections and those for governor in October 1990 and into the second gubernatorial round in December.

On March 15, 1991 Brizola was inaugurated, for the second time, as governor of Rio de Janeiro. How he succeeds in this office will largely determine his own political future and, perhaps, by implication, that of Brazil. He and the PDT may be able to form an effective left-wing alliance with Lula and the **Worker's Party** (*Partido dos Trabalhadores*—PT). Even without such support, Brizola currently presents the most serious challenge, and possible alternative, to the Collor government.

PF

BURNHAM, LINDEN FORBES SAMPSON. As leader of the **People's National Congress** of **Guyana** from its foundation in 1957 to his death on Aug. 6, 1985, Forbes Burnham came to power in 1964 after a violent crisis had overwhelmed the government of the then British Guiana, led by his marxist opponent, **Cheddi Jagan**. Prime Minister of the independent Guyana until 1980, and then executive President, Burnham imposed an autocratic style of government, leaning towards Cuba, the USSR and the Non-Aligned Movement, while pursuing statist economic policies, under which export production and public finances entered into a prolonged crisis, while Burnham himself lived in considerable luxury. He was persistently accused of holding on to power through rigged elections, and was widely held responsible for the death of **Walter Rodney**, a leading historian and political opponent, in 1980.

RP

BUSINESS ORGANIZATIONS. Under the world-wide influence of American examples, Chambers of Industry and Trade are widely established throughout South America and the Caribbean. Inevitably such organizations have a significant political weight at local level and in support for political parties and groups dedicated to the maintenance of capitalism and the principle of free enterprise; an example being a major umbrella organization of agriculturalists and businessmen generally, such as the **Co-ordinating Committee of Agricultural, Commercial, Industrial and Financial Associations** (*Comité Co-ordinator de Asociaciones Agrícolas, Comerciales, Industriales y Financieras* — CACIF) in Guatemala.

However, a much more significant role at

national level is played by the powerful national producers'organizations necessitated by a policy of maintaining world prices in primary commodities by the maintenance of a constant supply through the application of quotas; e.g. by coffee producers, such as the National Federation of Coffee Producers (*Federación Nacional de Cafeteros*) of **Colombia**. Alternatively this role may be played by a state agency such as the Brazilian Coffee Institute (*Instituto Brasiliero do Café*) in **Brazil**, but in the latter case the agency is often "captured" by its clientele.

Mexico. It is compulsory in **Mexico** for all business to register with one of the registered business chambers. There are many of these but the most important are CONCAMIN, CANACINTRA and CONCANACO. These liaise both formally and informally with Mexican politicians; however they are fairly independent and not subject to serious political control.

Nevertheless some business élites have found it necessary to set up genuinely independent business associations. The CCE was set up in 1975 to respond to the strong sense of threat felt by many businessmen at the policies of **Luís Echeverría**. Coparmex has emerged more recently as the main voice of business neo-conservatives who favour free trade, a smaller role for the state and a more open political system.

The system itself has until recently regarded the open political respresentation of business interests with considerable ambivalence. Until 1970 most contacts between government and business took place through informal channels, with overt political statements by business leaders being firmly discouraged. After 1970 tensions between government and business grew and businessmen increasingly wanted to express themselves independently. In 1987 the **Miguel de la Madrid** government appeared to accede to this and began a set of negotiations with all business groups as part of the government's "Pact of Economic Solidarity". This Pact was renewed under President **Carlos Salinas** and remains in force.

Mexico therefore appears to be moving toward the kind of corporatism which exists in Austria and parts of Scandinavia in which business organizations negotiate over policy at arm's length with government.

PARC, GP

C

CACIQUE. The word *cacique* is a corruption of the Arawak word *kassequa*, which means boss. It seems to have been first used by the Spaniards to apply to any Indian chief. However the present-day meaning in Mexico corresponds more to "boss" in the US city politics sense, though with some important differences. The definition of a *cacique* would be someone who successfully mobilizes informal and to some extent extra-legal resources in order to enjoy social and political power, generally of a localized nature. Post-Revolutionary Mexico relied on local power holders to impose a degree of order (often without law) in a turbulent and at times almost ungovernable country: these power holders generally commanded or at any rate had access to irregular armed forces and could impose their will locally at the point of a gun. Subsequently political authority strengthened and power came to be centralized in the presidential office in Mexico City. Thus whereas during the 1920s local *caciques* really did wield great local power, the pattern is now greatly modified although it has not been completely abandoned.

Today a *cacique* is still likely to command extra-legal sources of money and possibly force, but will certainly not exclude perfectly legal forms of political action such as inducing a group of followers to vote in a certain way. He will be the dominant force in a small group of activists, quite possibly kinsmen, and will use the consequent resources to ally with some local power groups and fight others. His ultimate objective may be political power, but is more likely to be money. The analogy with a political boss in the United States is accurate in some respects but misleading in others; the most important difference is that the "no re-election" rule in Mexican politics makes it difficult for political office, as such, to provide the formal resources to consolidate informal sources of power. Instead the Mexican *cacique* is likely to try to control office-holders rather than running for office directly.

GP

CALDERA, RAFAEL. Rafael Caldera, Venezuelan statesman, was born at San Felipe-Yaracuy on Jan. 24, 1916. As a student he was a delegate to the International Congress of Catholic Youth at Rome in 1934 at which the idea of founding Christian Democratic parties was actively pursued. In 1936 Caldera formed the *Unión Nacional de Estudiantes* (National Union of Students), a breakaway from the *Federación de Estudiantes de Venezuela*, and nucleus of the future *Comité de Organización Política Electoral Independiente*, later **Comité Pro-Elecciones Independientes (COPEI)**, which emerged as a political party in 1946, and of which he was Secretary-General from 1948 to 1968. Between 1945 and 1969 he was a professor of sociology at the Universidad Central de Venezuela.

As COPEI's first Presidential candidate he ran a good second to Rómulo Gallegos in 1948. A signatory of the Pact of Punto Fijo, he contested the 1958 elections but ran a bad third, despite which he subsequently held to his promise to go into coalition with **Acción Democrática (AD)** and thus performed a crucial part in consolidating democracy in Venezuela. Candidate again in 1963, and by then well-known as a writer, he led the *copeyanos* to victory for the first time in the Presidential elections of 1968. Despite a successful term of office (1969–74), in which he consolidated Venezuela's position as an economically stable country and a significant actor in regional politics, Caldera himself was unsuccessful in seeking re-election in 1983, after the constitutional ten-year interval. He is the author of *Andrés Bello* and of numerous other works on law and politics.

PARC

CAMARILLA. There are several different words in Latin American Spanish that refer to largely the same thing. The Mexican word, *camarilla*, refers to a small team of figures who hunt together in the jungles of politics and the bureaucracy.

Mexican administration is based on a spoils system. The President chooses his Cabinet; members of the Cabinet will be left largely free to choose their own team. These will then choose their subordinates, and so on until the most humble posts in the administration are filled. It is therefore rational for semi-hierarchical "teams" of would-be office holders to remain together. This is especially so because in Mexico there are few sources of institutional power outside the Presidency and the public administration; incoming presidents will therefore choose Cabinet ministers largely from among their own entourage, and will eventually select their successors from the cabinet itself. Political friendships are therefore paramount in determining an individual's advancement or otherwise.

There is nothing to stop an individual from leaving a *camarilla*, either by choice or through some form of expulsion, but Mexican political history shows that political friendships can be astonishingly consistent and durable. Betrayals and defections do of course occur, but they tend to arouse a greater sense of shock in Mexico than in many other countries In Mexican politics people devote their loyalties more to other people than to ideologies or government functions.

There are no hard and fast rules relating to how *camarillas* form, although they tend to recruit new members from quite young adults. In the 1920s and 1930s a crucial recruiting function was played by university teachers at the national university. Today foreign study is more common, at least for the aspiring élite, and the role of Mexican universities is less. Students at a particular foreign (especially US) university may form political friendships. What is clear is that, despite the far more technocratic style of contemporary Mexican politics, *camarillas* continue to form and play an active part in political recruitment.

GP

CANADA. Canada has had a significant trade and economic presence in Latin America since the late nineteenth century, when the Canadian entrepreneur Fred Stark Pearson built the tramway system of Rio de Janeiro, among others. However seeing its role rather as part of the "North Atlantic Triangle" of Britain, Canada and the United States, and taking an active role in World War II from its beginning, it did not choose to join the **Organization of American States (OAS)** until 1990, and in the intervening years has held aloof from any form of political involvement in Central or South America. It became popular in the Caribbean as a generous aid giver which made few if any demands on the recipients of its assistance.

PARC

CÁRDENAS, CUAUHTÉMOC. Cuauhtémoc Cárdenas was only a moderately prominent figure when he emerged as one of the leaders of the "Democratic Tendency" of the PRI in Mexico in 1986. The essential premise of the Democratic Tendency was a simple one. Most political activists within the PRI, including Cárdenas himself, supported a form of nationalism on economic issues and a moderate socialism on social ones. Meanwhile the government of de la Madrid was pursuing policies of liberal capitalism. It was therefore desirable for supporters of the PRI to make their own preferences clear and influence policy in the desired direction.

Once it had become clear that the Democratic Tendency was failing to influence presidential policy—the nomination of **Carlos Salinas** to be the successor to **Miguel de la Madrid** provided evidence of this failure—the Democratic Tendency abandoned the PRI altogether and Cuauhtémoc launched an independent candidacy for the presidency. He was quickly supported by some moderate left-wing parties and later the Marxist candidate—Heberto Castillo—stepped down in favour of Cárdenas. Given a clear run on the left, Cárdenas mounted a formidable challenge to the PRI. According to official figures, he carried the Federal District and four other states of Mexico; he was given 32 per cent of the vote to Salinas' 51 per cent. Cárdenas himself continued to assert that he was the victim of fraud and that honest elections would have resulted in his own outright victory.

An obvious reason for the strength of Cárdenas' candidacy was the strength of the family name; as the son of **Lázaro Cárdenas**, he enjoyed immediate public recognition. He retained a power base in Michoacán, where he had once served as governor. He was also in a good position to claim to represent the "authentic" ideas of the Revolution against the economic liberalism represented be de la Madrid and Salinas.

Since the 1988 elections Cárdenas has acted effectively as the leader of the Mexican opposition. He has travelled abroad and campaigned within Mexico itself. However he has so far proved unable to make much of an impact against Salinas, though any further division in the ruling party will undoubtedly work to his advantage.

GP

CÁRDENAS, LÁZARO. Lázaro Cárdenas was born in 1895 in the western Mexican state of Michoacán. He grew to manhood during the Revolutionary years, and rose to become a general. He remained loyal to Obregón and Calles during the 1920s and early 1930s, while cultivating some popular support of his own, and was rewarded when Calles accepted him as presidential candidate for the Revolutionary party in 1934.

The Cárdenas presidency marks a turning point in Mexican political and social history. In social terms, the period was one of radical reform. There was a vast redistribution of land which finally broke the power of Mexican landlords. Trade union activism was encouraged; even quite militant union activity was not discouraged. The effect was to achieve a considerable redistribution of income toward Mexico's poor. However by the end of Cárdenas' term, in 1940, middle class and business discontent was beginning to take on a threatening aspect and Cárdenas began to consolidate his reforms from around the middle of 1938. In fact the oil expropriation of March 18, 1938 appears to have been the high water mark of his radicalism.

In political terms, Cárdenas built up the all-powerful six-year presidency with no re-election but with the outgoing president choosing his successor. In 1935 and 1936 he confronted and defeated Calles, who sought to maintain control through manipulating the political system. He did so by building up and strengthening the "mass organizations" (the **CTM** and **CNC**) which greatly increased the direct institutional resources open to the presidential office. Toward the end of his term he resisted demands for a more open choice of successor, by imposing his own candidate upon the official party and then ensuring that this party then won the elections. He hoped to avoid renewed polarity and upheaval, but the effect was to strengthen the authoritarian dimensions of Mexican politics.

After leaving office in 1940 Cárdenas continued to play an active part in Mexican politics; he served in the cabinet of his successor, and subsequently sought to play an international role. Cárdenas was generally out of sympathy with the rightward drift of Mexican politics after 1946; if anything he seems to have moved to the left after leaving office. He received the Stalin Prize in 1955 and became an enthusiastic early supporter of the **Cuban Revolution**. However despite maintaining some degree of local influence in Michoacán, Cardenas never enjoyed as much impact on the national scene as he had hoped. He was largely a victim of the extreme presidentialism which he had done so much to devise.

GP

CARIBBEAN BASIN INITIATIVE (CBI). The Caribbean Basin Initiative was an economic plan for the Caribbean region, announced by President Ronald Reagan in January 1984. Its purpose was to extend US access to Caribbean products by giving preferential access for certain regional products to the US market. Countries wishing to receive assistance under the scheme had to be approved as politically acceptable to the **United States**, to declare their commitment to American-style free enterprise and to enter into bilateral agreements with the United States embodying specific economic conditions. Among these conditions were: tax concessions for investors, the right to repatriate profits from their investments and guarantees that their holdings would not be nationalized.

PARC

CARIBBEAN COMMUNITY AND COMMON MARKET (CARICOM). The Caribbean Community and Common Market was created by the Treaty of Chaguaramas signed in Trinidad in July 1973, and replaced the Caribbean Free Trade Association (CARIFTA) created in 1965. Present members are Antigua and Barbuda, Bahamas, Barbados, Belize, Dominica, Grenada, Guyana, Jamaica, Montserrat, St Kitts-Nevis, St Lucia, St Vincent and the Grenadines and Trinidad and Tobago. The purpose of the organization is to promote intra-regional trade and development; however its work in this regard has been much hampered by unilateral decisions of member states and by lack of funds. The Caribbean Development Bank (headquarters at St Michael, Barbados) is an associate institution of CARICOM.

Subject only to decisions of the Heads of Government Conference, which has met regularly since 1982, the work of the Common Market is directed by the Council, consisting of a minister of government from each member state. The secretariat is located at Georgetown, Guyana.

PARC

CASTRO, FIDEL. Fidel Castro, Prime Minister of **Cuba** 1959–76 and President since 1976, has been a significant actor in world politics for over 30 years, during which time as leader of a small Latin American country he has maintained his defiance both of Cuba's neighbour, the United States, and of his ally the Soviet Union.

Fidel Castro Ruz was born at Mayarí in the Oriente Province of **Cuba** on Aug. 13, 1926. He was the second son and third child by his second marriage of a wealthy sugar planter, a self-made immigrant from Galicia in northwest Spain. He was educated at Jesuit schools in Santiago de Cuba and Havana before enrolling in Havana University as a law student in 1945. Soon drawn into student politics, in 1947 he joined the Cuban People's Party–Orthodox (*Partido del Pueblo Cubano–Ortodoxos*) led by the charismatic Eddy Chibás. A keen sportsman at basketball and baseball, it was not long before his liking for physical activity led him to join an abortive expedition to overthrow the Trujillo régime in the **Dominican Republic**. As a delegate to a student congress during the Inter-American Conference of 1948 he was a witness of the Bogotazo in **Colombia**.

Having graduated as a lawyer in 1950, Castro ran for Congress in 1952, but the elections were cut short by Batista's *coup*. The following year, reverting to direct action, he led an attempt to seize the Moncada Barracks in Cuba's second city, Santiago, on July 26, 1953, and was lucky to escape arrest until the immediate reprisals had died down and he could surrender to a former classmate. Sentenced to a term of imprisonment, he was released under a general amnesty in 1955 and after several months went into exile in Mexico City to plan his return. It was there that he met and recruited **Ernesto Che Guevara** for his expedition.

At the end of 1956 Castro and his followers set sail from Tampico on the *Granma* to liberate Cuba. They were ambushed on the shore and Castro and his brother Raúl were again lucky to escape. With only 13 followers they managed to make their way to the Sierra Maestra, which Castro knew well from hiking expeditions. It was not for another two years that they were ready to announce their presence and with the Declaration of the Sierra Maestra to cement their alliance with other insurgent groups, promising land reform to the workers on the cane fields. After the opening of a second front at Escambray in mid-1958 confidence in the Batista régime began to wane, and on Jan. 1, 1959 the dictator fled. Two days later Castro entered Havana in triumph at the head of the insurgents and formed a provisional government with his former judge, Manuel Urrutia Lleo, as President.

There followed a period of brilliant improvization as Castro became impatient with the government he had created and assumed effective power. As Prime Minister and leader of the revolution, he ruled without constitutional restraints, making decisions and communicating them to the masses through long speeches carried nationwide by television. In face of the increasing hostility of the United States administration, he sought support from the Soviet Union, which had signalled its arrival on the world scene as a superpower only two years before by launching the world's first earth satellite. The Soviet Union agreed to replace the United States as a market for Cuban sugar, to supply it with oil and to arm its forces. In 1961 the incoming Kennedy administration sponsored an unsuccessful attack on the régime by a force of exiles trained in Guatemala. The invasion was a complete failure, and on Dec. 1, 1961 Castro proclaimed his new allegiance with the stirring but inaccurate phrase: "I am a Marxist-Leninist and always have been".

Less than a year later, Soviet missiles being deployed in Cuba were detected by US spy planes, and in a confrontation between the superpowers the Soviet Union backed down and agreed to remove the missiles. As part of the bargain, however, to which Cuba was not party, the United States agreed not to make a second attempt to overthrow Cuba's increasingly socialist government. As far as possible, however, Cuba was isolated from the rest of Latin America, though not from the rest of the world, and between 1961 and 1965 strenuous but futile attempts were made to increase its industrial base. As a final attempt to escape increasingly strong Soviet pressures to conform to their model of economic growth, an attempt was then made to increase agricultural output, culminating in the "Harvest of the Ten Millions" in 1970. Though a record amount of sugar was produced—-8,300,000 tonnes—it fell short of the much heralded goal, and was achieved only at the cost of diverting all other efforts to the one aim. Castro offered his resignation but this was rejected by large crowds.

In 1975 Castro was finally forced to bow to Soviet pressure and accept a Soviet-style Constitution. On the promulgation of the new Constitution, Osvaldo Dorticós Torrado, who had held the post as a figurehead since July 1959, was pushed aside and Castro himself assumed the post of President. Since that time Castro's tenure of power has been secure. As President of **Cuba**, Fidel Castro is head of state and head of government. He is also First Secretary of the **Cuban Communist Party** (**PCC**). His brother, Raúl, whom he nominated as his successor in June 1985, is a Lieutenant-General, Minister of the Revolutionary Armed Forces and Second Secretary of the PCC.

By 1975, however, Cuba had already become established as a member of the Non-Aligned Movement, and in that year Castro had the opportunity to pay his debts to the Soviet Union when the new Marxist government of Angola was attacked by armed forces sponsored by the government of white South Africa. In *Operación Carlota* Cuban forces were rushed to Angola and with the assistance of the latest Soviet weapons were decisive in stemming the tide and propping up the pro-Soviet government. A few months later Cuban forces were in action again in Ethiopia under the command of a Soviet general helping the pro-Soviet government drive back a Somali attempt to recover the Ogaden. Around the same time the Latin American consensus disintegrated and Cuba resumed some regional trade. By the beginning of the 1980s Cuba was giving technical assistance to the friendly governments of **Grenada**, **Jamaica** and **Nicaragua**. The incoming Reagan Administration in 1981 saw its hand, and that of the Soviet Union, behind all the troubles of the region. Though they hesitated to attack Cuba itself, in the US invasion of Grenada in October 1983 a number of Cuban civilian technicians were killed. Meanwhile the Cuban economy began increasingly to show the signs of wear and tear after the long embargo imposed on it by the US government.

With the coming of "perestroika", however, Castro refused to follow the Soviet line, which he regarded as a betrayal of socialism. In a "rectification campaign" announced at the 1986 Party Congress the first hesitant moves in that direction were reversed on the orders of Castro himself. In 1989 the collapse of communism in Eastern Europe left Castro's Cuba more exposed than at any time since 1961. However Castro remained securely in control, his charisma seemingly as strong as ever and the mechanism of party rule intact. Though in fact on a number of occasions since 1961 both the United States and Cuba have in turn made efforts to initiate a dialogue, Castro has always in public maintained the uncompromising line that if there are to be any concessions, they must be made by the United States. On the other hand, the original revolutionary fervour has long since worn off and not since the loss of Che Guevara in Bolivia in 1967 has there been any serious attempt to turn the Andes, as he had once hoped, into "the Sierra Maestra of South America". But he has given Cuba, a small island with a small population, a role in world politics out of all proportion to its size and become one of the few Latin Americans of the twentieth century to gain an international reputation. In the last analysis he has been able to count on the United States not wishing to incur the substantial casualties that would follow a direct military intervention, and, to date, his calculation has proved correct.

PARC

CAYMAN ISLANDS. *Population*: 26,400 (1989). *Area*: 259 sq km. *GDP*: $429 million. *Trade volume*: $231.5 million. *Birthrate*: 17.2 per 1,000.

Geographical background. The Cayman Islands comprise three low-lying islands (Grand Cayman, Little Cayman and Cayman Brac) situated in the Caribbean Sea to the south of Cuba. The islands have poor soils and scrub vegetation and became a dependency of Jamaica in the early eighteenth century and remained so until Jamaican independence in 1962 when they reverted to the status of a British dependent territory.

Socio-political background. Under the terms of the 1959 Constitution, revised in 1972, the British government appoints a governor who is responsible for defence, foreign affairs, internal security and the public service. The islands' executive body, the Executive Council, consists of the governor as chairman, three ex-officio appointed members and four elected members of the Legislative Council. The Legislative Council comprises 12 elected members and three appointed members.

Outline of political development. There are no formal political parties on the islands, with political loyalties centred around personalities, although there have been informal "teams" of candidates in recent general elections. All candidates have usually committed themselves to uphold continued dependent status and work for economic growth. In elections in 1984 nine seats were won by independents and three by the Dignity team led by Benson Ebanks. In elections in 1988 24 candidates contested the 12 seats. Five new members were elected, two of whom were chosen to join the Executive Council. Ebanks and Norman Bodden were re-elected as the two senior members to join the Executive Council.

Current developments—political. During 1990, however, the elected members of the Legislative Council began to make their feelings heard against some decisions of the Executive Council, opposing a number of measures. A series of disputes, particularly during the budget debate when a change in the composition of the finance committee was forced through, strengthened calls for a review of the existing constitutional arrangements. In response, the Foreign and Commonwealth Office promised a review of the constitution to be carried out during 1991, possibly leading to a more developed system of executive government, with a chief minister, a cabinet drawn from the elected representatives and an outside non-partisan speaker in the Legislative Council.

Outline of economic development. Since the early 1970s the Cayman Islands have developed a thriving economy based on banking, financial services and tourism, giving the islands one of the highest levels of gross domestic product (GDP) per capita in the region at US$16,800 in 1988.

Legislation introduced gradually since the 1960s developed the Cayman Islands into an attractive tax-free haven, particularly for funds from the USA. By the end of 1989 the Caymans had 538 banks, representing 60 different countries and making the Caymans the world's fifth largest banking centre. Over 20,000 foreign companies were registered in the islands in 1989 and 357 captive insurance companies. Registration fees, licences and stamp duty provide an important part of the government's revenue. The potential for fraud in the offshore financial sector was significantly reduced after pressure from the US authorities in the early 1980s had prompted a review of bank secrecy laws. In particular this had involved the locally registered subsidiary of the Bank of Nova Scotia which had refused to give information about accounts to US investigators tracing the "laundering" of profits from trafficking in illegal drugs. In 1984 the Caymanian government signed an agreement with the USA allowing access to information in certain cases. This was reinforced by a mutual assistance treaty signed in 1986 and ratified by the US Senate in 1990.

The government has also promoted tourist development strongly, leading to a construction boom on Grand Cayman. The number of tourist arrivals has increased sharply during the 1980s and the islands have also become a major cruise ship stop. Construction has included not only hotels, but also condominiums and offices and the infrastructure to service such expansion. In contrast to Grand Cayman, the other two islands have remained relatively unaffected by construction development. The population has also grown significantly, as the Caymans attract migrant workers, in particular from Jamaica and Haiti. This has led some Caymanians to worry about the fall in the proportion of Caymanians in the islands' population. Immigration controls are already strict. In 1987 a constitutional amendment passed by the Legislative Council and approved by the Privy Council changed the qualifications for voting in elections to protect the rights of Caymanians.

Current economic situation. The boom in banking and tourism contributed to continued economic growth during the 1980s, with an increase of 16 per cent in GDP in real terms during 1988, leading to some fears of possible overheating in the economy. Government revenues, mainly derived from customs duties, remain buoyant, contributing to a surplus of US$19,000,000 in 1989.

LP

CENTRAL AMERICAN COMMON MARKET—CACM (Mercado Común Centroamericano). The Central American Common Market (generally CACM, sometimes CACOM) was founded by the General Treaty for Central American Economic Integration, signed by the Central American states of Costa Rica, El Salvador, Guatemala, Honduras and Nicaragua at Managua on Feb. 13, 1960. Policy is formulated by ministerial meetings of the five member states' Ministers of Central American Integration, and meetings of other ministers, presidents of central banks etc. The Permanent Secretariat (*Secretaría Permanente del Tratado General de Integración Económica Centroamericana*—SIECA) in Guatemala City supervizes the working of the Treaty and arranges meetings as required. There are several associated regional institutions, including the Fund for Economic Stabilization founded in 1969.

Between 1962, when the Treaty came into effect, and 1969, when its operations were disrupted by the so-called "Football War" and the consequent withdrawal of Honduras in 1970 from the work of the organization, there was a considerable increase in intra-regional trade, despite the largely similar nature of the five economies. In 1973 Honduras made bilateral arrangements with the other three states, but by the time that diplomatic relations with El Salvador were restored in 1980 civil war had broken out there and that and the Nicaraguan crisis led to a steep decline in intra-regional trade.

An agreement to establish a Central American Monetary Union was signed in 1984 but has yet to be implemented.

PARC

CENTRAL PLANNING BOARD (Junta Central de Planificación — JUCEPLAN) (Cuba). Founded in March 1960, the Central Planning Board of **Cuba** (with its president a member of Politburo after 1976), was responsible for the research, development and co-ordination of macro-economic policy and programmes. It therefore operated through and with the various state enterprises and ministries. JUCEPLAN became the central organ of the planned economy, whilst at the same time the increasing target of criticism for its insensitivity to economic needs, especially in matters of distribution and allocation of resources. Following the rectification announcements, sweeping changes in JUCEPLAN resulted in numerous dismissals, but more importantly it lost considerable directive influence although it is open to question whether the economic problems faced by Cuba during the 1980s were attributable to errors in JUCEPLAN or inherent to a planned economy.

JCJS

CEREZO AREVALO, VINICIO. Mario Vinico Cerezo Arévalo, President of **Guatemala** 1986–90, was formerly Secretary-General of the **Christian Democratic Party** of Guatemala (*Democracia Cristiana Guatemalteca*—DCG). A black belt at karate, throughout his political career he has travelled with a small arsenal of weapons, all of which he knows how to use. Assassination attempts on him began shortly after his choice as secretary-general of the new party, the first in April 1975, the day after he had telegraphed the then president to ask for an investigation into the circumstances of the death of the secretary general of the Guatemalan Labour Party (*Partido Guatemalteco del Trabajo*—PGT) the previous December. In 1984, after President Mejía Victores had called for elections to a Constituent Assembly, Cerezo, noting the upsurge in death-squad violence that followed, said: "A section of the army does not want democratization at any price". Despite this he received the support of the larger part of the army to become Guatemala's first civilian president for 16 years, and proved unable to mount any effective investigation into the appalling **human rights** record of his predecessors.

PARC

CHACO WAR. The Chaco War (1932–35) was the most serious conflict in South America in this century. Ironically the two countries involved, **Bolivia** and **Paraguay**, had much in common. Both had been the victims of wars in the nineteenth century, in which they had lost strategically important territory and both were landlocked, dependent on trade routes running through the territory of watchful neighbours. Both believed that the Chaco Boreal, or northern Chaco, part of an upland plain which stretches from Brazil in the north southward across the Rio Pilcomayo into northern Argentina, might conceal important oil resources.

To avert the threat of Bolivian troops being stationed on the other side of that river, close to Asunción the national capital, the Paraguayan army had built forts in the Chaco, an area of featureless semi-desert which turns to swamp when the rains come, stretching from the foothills of the Andes to the Rio Paraguay, to assert its claim to possession and the Bolivians had done the same. Under Hernando Siles, President of Bolivia 1926–30, the Bolivian claim to the region was set far beyond anything that had been claimed before, beyond the line provisionally agreed between the two countries in 1913 and the actual line of Paraguayan defence, and from 1928 on there were armed clashes in the region.

Paraguay sought to bring the question of the Chaco before the League of Nations, which called for a ban on the supply of arms to either side. Learning that Bolivia was importing arms with the support of Chile, however, the Paraguayans, with the support of Argentina, were the first to open formal hostilities in mid-1932 by attacking a Bolivian advance guard on the near side of the Chaco. The League branded Paraguay an "aggressor". Eventually it lifted the arms ban in favour not of Paraguay but of Bolivia, but not before superior Paraguayan forces had driven the Bolivians back into the foothills of the Andes. There, within sight of the oilfields of southern Bolivia, with their lines of supply over-extended, they were forced to stop in 1935, while Bolivia hastily agreed to a truce. The peace signed in 1938 disguised the concessions made by both sides as a so-called "arbitral award", the terms of which had in fact been agreed in advance.

The consequences of the war were considerable. Paraguay left the League in 1935 and initiated its final collapse as a serious international body. It gained almost as much territory as it had lost to Argentina and Brazil in the War of the Triple Alliance (1865–70), but only at the cost of reactivating military intervention in politics. In Bolivia the war exacerbated the division between the country's military leaders and the Indian workers, and ultimately was the principal causal factor of the Revolution of 1952.

PARC/SAC

CHILE. *Area*: 756,629 sq km. *Population*: 12,748,000 (1988). *GDP*: $18,321 million (1988). *Trade volume*: exports : $7,052 million (1988); imports : $4,833 million (1988). *Top five trade partners (1987)*: exports : USA, Japan, West Germany, Brazil, UK; imports: USA, Japan, Brazil, West Germany, Venezuela. *Defence spending*: $583,000,000 (3.6 per cent of GNP—1986). *Education spending*: $833,000,000 (5.2 per cent of GNP—1986). *Urban population as percentage of total (centres over 20,000)*: 85 (1988). *Birthrate*: 23 per 1000 (1988). *Life expectancy*: male: 68 years (1988); female: 75 years (1988).

Geographical background. Chile is a strip of land, 2,600 miles (4,160 km) long, between the Andes mountain range and the Pacific Ocean, averaging 110 miles in width. The northenmost mineral-rich provinces were acquired in the War of the Pacific (1879–83) against Peru and Bolivia. Chile's climates vary from the arid northern Atacama desert, the driest place on earth, to the cold and windswept lands of Tierra del Fuego.

Chile also claims a substantial sector of **Antarctica**, overlapping with both the British and Argentine claims. Most of the population is concentrated in the central valley, stretching from just north of the capital, Santiago, to Concepción, some 322 miles (515 km) to the south, which enjoys a Californian climate—a short winter and a long, dry summer of warm days and cool nights. Further south, the climate becomes much wetter, sustaining a burgeoning forestry industry and northern European-style agriculture. Still further south, beyond Puerto Montt, 656 miles (1,050 km) from Santiago, Chile becomes an archipelago, obliging the land traveller to cross over into Argentina to reach the southernmost town of Punta Arenas.

Outline of political history. Chile is a country of long democratic traditions. Before the military *coup* of Sept. 11, 1973, Chile had enjoyed 41 years of democratic rule under the constitution of 1924, and before 1932 there had been only brief periods of military rule. The *coup* overthrew the socialist president, **Salvador Allende**, who had been elected with a little over a third of the popular vote in 1970, installing the military government headed by **General Augusto Pinochet** which lasted until March 1990.

The most lasting changes made during the 16-year period of military dictatorship are economic. The incoming Christian Democrat president, **Patricio Aylwin**, has been left a legacy which other democratically-elected presidents in Latin America might envy—high growth, external debt brought under control, low inflation and a healthy balance of trade surplus. This economic transformation, however, could not have been achieved without the draconian repression, that is, the violation of fundamental **human rights** as an instrument of policy, which marked General Pinochet's rule. The benefits of economic growth have gone overwhelmingly to the rich and the middle class while the numbers of poor people have increased significantly. At the same time the new government has inherited a "social deficit", the product of 16 years of under-investment in public health, housing and education, which enjoyed rapid expansion under the governments of Salvador Allende and Eduardo Frei, the Christian Democrat president who preceded him. There is agreement between the political forces which united to vote against General Pinochet (Christian Democrats, some moderate right-wingers and a majority of the left) that programmes to correct this social deficit must not fuel inflation and must be determined by the resources which the government can make available.

The military took power to crush the threat of "communism" in Chile at a time of widespread leftist agitation and rebellion in Latin America. They left power as the real communism of the USSR and Eastern Europe was being revealed as ideologically and practically bankrupt. Not surprisingly the changes on the left have been most marked. The Chilean left has had 16 years in which to evaluate its dramatic three years in government under Salvador Allende and to absorb the lessons of persecution and exile. Today the great majority of the left have rejected past ambiguous attitudes to "bourgeois" democracy and have accepted the straitjacket imposed on its hopes of social and economic change by the international triumph of market economics. President Aylwin and his government were elected under rules imposed by a constitution drawn up by General Pinochet and the miliary junta and approved in a highly questionable plebiscite in 1980. This constitution provided for another plebiscite in 1988 in which the people would be asked to vote YES for a presidential candidate proposed by the military junta, General Pinochet himself in other words, or NO. A YES vote would have meant that Pinochet himself would have continued as president until 1997, when he will be 82 years old. A NO victory, on the other hand, would trigger an election for president as well as a Chamber of Deputies and Senate.

After the failure of various political and civic alliances to force Pinochet from office and after a failed attempt on his life in 1986, mounted by the Manuel Rodríguez Patriotic Front, the armed wing of the Communist Party, the Christian Democrats came to the conclusion that, despite severe limitations imposed on open politics, the plebiscite offered the best chance of a return to civilian rule. They were joined in early 1988 by a grouping of Socialists who formed the *Partido por la Democracia* (Party for Democracy—PPD) specifically to participate in the plebiscite campaign. In the end 17 different political groups came together to form the *Concertación* (Coalition) to contest the plebiscite. The Communist Party was the last opposition grouping to urge its members to vote NO in the plebiscite.

The opposition, recognizing that the chances of a YES victory increased with the number of citizens registered to vote, mounted a vigorous voter registration drive. The Catholic church organized its own civic education campaign to the same end. When the electoral register closed on Aug. 30, 1988, the day that Pinochet was nominated as the official candidate of the junta, 7,435,913 Chileans over the age of 18 had registered to vote, a record 92.1 per cent of eligible voters.

The Pinochet government maintained its

almost total control of the media during the plebiscite campaign, opening up access to television only to the extent of giving the opposition 27 late-night television spots of 15 minutes each in the month before the plebiscite. The opposition withdrew one of these spots, dealing with human rights, rather than submit to government censorship. These opposition broadcasts made an enormous impact, especially outside the main urban centres, where people, and particularly the poor, had virtually no access to independent media of any sort. While the opposition stressed reconciliation and optimism in its appeal, the government used strident images of a threatened return to the violence, inflation and shortages which had preceded the 1973 *coup*, images which would have meant little to the many Chileans who were too young to remember the Allende years.

The plebiscite was held on Oct. 5, October 1988. The mechanics of voting were largely copied from the pre-*coup* era. The multiplicity of voting *mesas* (tables), 22,131 in all, and the presence of hundreds of observers from abroad and the opposition's own poll watchers, made any massive and systematic fraud impossible. The result gave the opposition NO camp 3,967,579 votes (54.71 per cent of the total) and the Pinochet YES camp 3,119,110 (43.01 per cent), opening the way for the presidential and congressional elections which were held 14 months later on Dec. 14, 1989.

Current developments—political. The NO victory in the plebiscite ushered in a period of frenetic political activity. Presidential, senate and assembly candidates had to be designated and political parties of all sorts had to be effectively organized. For the anti-Pinochet camp, with the experience of its successful plebiscite campaign, it was important to maintain the unity of the *Concertación*, which duly became the Coalition of Parties for Democracy (*Concertación de Partidos por la Democracia*). Patricio Aylwin of the Christian Democrat Party (PDC) was selected as the presidential candidate.

On the right the two major parties were *Renovación Nacional*—RN (National Renovation) and the *Unión Democrática Independiente*—UDI (Independent Democratic Union), closely identified with Pinochet and the free market economic model. The parties were forced to make alliances and run as lists by the electoral system adopted by the Pinochet government.

Pinochet did not stand himself, stepping aside to let his finance minister, Hernán Büchi, represent the official right. These two candidates were joined by an independent rightist, Javier Francisco Errázuriz. Having decided not to stand and foreseeing an opposition victory, Pinochet's main interest was in ensuring that any future government could not unravel the economic and political system which he had created. The main means of securing this end was the 1980 constitution. It created an independent Central Bank, a National Security Council with veto power, nominated by Pinochet and including ex-officio the heads of the three branches of the armed forces and nine nominated members of the Senate out of a total of 36 members. In the unlikely event that Pinochet himself should relinquish the position of commander-in-chief of the armed forces, he would automatically become a senator-for-life. Previous reforms had restricted trade union activity, privatized social security and much of health care and given responsibility for education to local government. A new law gave civil servants security of tenure. At the time of the election it was estimated that only 519 posts in the whole of the public sector could be filled at the discretion of the incoming government. General Pinochet also ensured that he will remain as commander-in-chief of the army until 1997 with a place in the senate.

The electoral rules under which the election was held over-represented the right in those areas where it was in a minority, in effect, the major urban areas. Each constituency, both for senate and assembly, returned two members, though each voter had only one vote. Parties could make alliances to present lists of two candidates per constituency. If one list received more than twice the votes of the next-most-voted list, it duly elected its two candidates. If it received less votes, then it elected only one candidate, with the next list also electing one. Thus, in a constituency in which there were only two competing lists, it would be possible for the leading list to receive 66 per cent of the vote and still elect only one of its candidates, with the other seat going to the list with only 34 per cent of the votes. Under this system, the socialist leader, Ricardo Lagos, running as the PPD candidate for one of the Santiago senate seats, was number two on the opposition list with Andrés Aylwin of the PDC; he received 29.2 per cent of the vote (399,408 votes), but because his list received only 59 per cent of the total vote, the second senate seat went to Jaime Guzmán of the UDI whose list received 31 per cent of the vote and who personally received 223,302 votes (16.4 per cent).

In the event some of the restrictions contained in the constitution were relaxed after tough negotiations between Pinochet and the opposition: the Senate was expanded to 36 elected members; the National Security Council was deprived of its veto power; Article 8, outlawing "subversive" organizations, was repealed; and civilian authority over the armed forces was increased. The Pinochet government, under pressure from its own supporters to ensure continuity in economic policy, even agreed that the five-person governing board of the Central Bank should be constituted by two government nominees, two opposition nominees and headed by an independent president.

Patricio Aylwin won the presidential elections with 55.2 per cent of the vote. Hernán Büchi took 29.4 per cent and Javier Francisco Errázuriz 15.4 per cent. Aylwin's supporting coalition won 22 of the 38 elected Senate seats, with the PDC taking 13, the Socialists five and independents and Radicals four; in the assembly the coalition won 72 out of 120 seats. With a minority in the 47-member Senate, the government has to negotiate its legislative programme every step of the way. RN, the major right-wing party, with 29 assembly seats and six senators (who were quickly joined by eight senators elected as independents) has so far indicated that it is prepared to co-operate with the government, providing that it does not tinker with the free market system.

Under this constitution Aylwin, as the transitional democratic president, will have only a four-year term. Subsequent presidents will have an eight-year term. The priority for this government is to cement civilian institutions in place, maintain economic growth and to make an impact on poverty in Chile. It is not clear how the parties of the *Concertación* will choose to fight the next election. Activists in all parties see the *Concertación* as a necessary but essentially transitional device. The experience of working together, however, and a realistic appreciation of the limits of what can be done, have already eroded old ideological differences. The existence of a strong right-wing too imposes greater discipline on the *Concertación* and its allies. Right-wing parties polled 42.7 per cent of the total vote in elections for the Chamber of Deputies. This is significantly higher than the roughly one-third of the popular vote which the right enjoyed before 1973.

The Armed Forces remain powerful. Even after 17 years of military rule, however, the army retains its non-political Prussian traditions, that is, it respects military hierarchy and obeys the orders of its commander-in-chief. This tradition served General Pinochet well in the past, enabling him to rely on the obedience of the entire army and to weed out the relatively few potential dissidents among the officer corps. Now these traditions are working against his personal ambitions. The army is pledged to uphold the constitution, its own constitution. The other branches of the Armed Forces have made clear that they will not support any breach of constitutionality. The Head of the Air Force, General Matthei and the Head of the Uniformed Police (*Carabineros*), General Stange, were the first government figures to acknowledge Pinochet's defeat in the plebiscite, underlining their support for the constitution, eliminating any temptation on the part of the right or Pinochet himself to disregard the results.

Revelations in late 1990 that military personnel had colluded with members of the secret police to run a loan-shark operation, known as *La Cutufa*, provoked a wave of unease among the military. Although the allegations did not implicate Pinochet himself, he was forced to retire four generals and cashier 16 officers. Many other officers, tempted by the extraordinary rates of interest offered by *La Cutufa*, lost their life savings, giving a solid economic cause to military discontent.

Relations between Chile and its neighbours, Argentina, Peru and Bolivia have never been easy. Argentina and Chile came close to war in 1978 over the Beagle Channel dispute before it was settled in 1984 through the mediation of the Vatican. Peruvians complain periodically about the lands taken from them in the War of the Pacific and Bolivia persistently agitates for the return of its outlet to the sea. There is unlikely to be any major reduction in the armed forces establishment or budget. Chile's armed forces total 101,000, of whom 33,000 are conscripts. The army numbers 57,000, of whom 30,000 are conscripts; the navy 29,000 (3,000 conscripts); the air force 15,000; and the *Carabineros* 27,000. In 1989 the Ministry of Defence was responsible for 13.8 per cent of government expenditure in pesos and 15.4 per cent of foreign currency expenditure, down from over 20 per cent during the mid-1980s.

There is still a tiny minority of extreme left activists, and indeed extreme right-wingers, who have not renounced the use of violence to make their points, but they are rejected by an overwhelming majority of the population. They certainly do not justify an anti-subversion role for the Armed Forces. In April 1990 the Manuel Rodríguez Patriotic Front was responsible for an attempt on the life of General Gustavo Leigh, a former air force commander and a member of the junta formed immediately after the *coup*. At the time it was widely speculated that a right-wing group was responsible because the anti-democratic right is seen as the only possible beneficiary of a climate of violence. For the same reason many qualified observers suspect that armed left-wing groups have been heavily infiltrated by former members of the secret police who, as beneficiaries and fanatical adherents of the Pinochet regime, wish to destabilize the new democratic government.

It is too early to say whether Patricio Aylwin, who was 71 when he assumed power, will run for president in 1993. The future of the centre-left political alliance he heads and its constituent parts will depend on his success in tackling the problems of poverty in Chile. The government, refusing to embark on inflationary programmes, is asking the poor to be patient but recognizes that such patience will not last indefinitely. The Christian Democrats, however, are in a strong position. The present constitution provides for a run-off between the two leading candidates in an election in which no candidate secures an absolute majority of the votes. With their candidate virtually certain to be among the first two, the Christian Democrats, as a strong centre party, will be well placed to make an electoral pact with the left or the right. The second-round system will also free the left to run its own candidate without having to do a deal with the Christian Democrats beforehand.

Outline of economic development. Since the Popular Front government of 1939 created the state development corporation CORFO (*Corporación de Fomento*) to provide funding for industry, the state has been responsible for much of Chilean economic development. The Popular Unity (*Unidad Popular*) coalition headed by Salvador Allende completely nationalized the large US-owned copper companies, Anaconda, Braden and Kennecott, and extended the agrarian reform initiated by the Frei government. Using a little-known law still on the statute book which allowed the state to "intervene" in a company when the supply of an essential product was threatened, many companies were brought under state control. By 1973 the state was responsible for about 80 per cent of GDP. Meanwhile the Nixon administration in the United States had embarked on a campaign against Chile in the international financial institutions. The combination of deficit financing, mismanagement and economic destabilization at home and abroad, produced shortages and inflation—400 per cent between January and September 1973.

Pinochet and the military junta were deeply prejudiced against "dirty" politics—the fudging, the wheeling-and-dealing and the compromises—which are part of any democratic politics, and had long been a feature of the Chilean political system. Not without reason, they argued that this interplay of vested interests around an economically interventionist state, was a prime cause of inflation. They had no ready-made answers, however, to the economic crisis. The first two years of military government were marked by rivalry between the corporatist right, which had no objection to state regulation, and the advocates of the free market, known as the "Chicago boys", drawing their inspiration from the theories of Milton Friedman based at the University of Chicago. By late 1974 the Chicago boys had won undisputed control over the economic ministries.

The very high rate of inflation and the sense of an economy out of control were the factors which prepared the military government and its supporters for the "shock treatment", as the Economic Recovery Programme was called. Immediately after the *coup* the military government had removed price controls, allowing inflation to reach an annual rate of 600 per cent. In the course of 1974 the price of copper fell from 126 to 62 cents a pound. Copper production itself fell from 935,000 to 791,500 tonnes and, at the end of 1974, income from the export of copper had been halved and there was a balance of payments deficit of $375,000,000.

The Chicago boys prescribed across the board reductions in government expenditure, the selling off of the state sector of the economy and deregulation in almost every field. As the shock treatment took effect, causing an abrupt contraction of demand, firms began to go bankrupt and were bought up by the financial groups which controlled the banks. In 1975 GDP fell by 13 per cent and unemployment reached 30 per cent. The government also announced that the system of high protective tariffs which had been in existence for decades was going to be progressively dismantled, with the average tariff falling to 10 per cent by 1980.

Pinochet's economic advisers argued that Chile should abandon economic strategies which concentrated on meeting the needs of local markets, limited inevitably by the small size of the Chilean population, and specialize in products for which its natural resources gave it a comparative advantage: copper and mining products, fruit and vegetables, seafood and wine, timber and forestry products. The new "non-traditional" exporting industries were seen eventually as rivalling copper as earners of foreign exchange.

The economic team promised a self-regulating economy based on untrammelled market forces. A new labour code drastically reduced the power of the unions; pension funds and social insurance were transferred to the private sector; and they set about selling off public companies. In their anxiety to win international investor confidence, however, the economic team fixed the exchange rate of the *peso* against the dollar. Between June 1979 and June 1982 the *peso* was valued at 39 to the dollar at a time when inflation in Chile was running at over 30 per cent per year, over double the rate in the United States and Western Europe. Money flowed into Chile, mainly to finance consumer credit and imports. Medium- and long-term external debt more than doubled between 1978 and 1982, from $5.9 billion to $13.8 billion. By 1982 the total debt was $17.3 billion. With the *peso* so overvalued local producers could not compete, there was a wave of bankruptcies and in 1982 the crash came. GDP fell by 14 per cent in 1982 alone. The government had to step in to rescue Chile's bankrupt financial institutions, assuming more far-reaching control over the economy than the vilified *Unidad Popular* government had ever dreamed possible.

There was subsequently a more prudent return to free market economics which has brought Chile growth of 5 per cent a year since 1984, rising to almost 10 per cent in 1989. Tariff barriers were raised abruptly to 35 per cent, to be reduced by 1988 to the present level of 15 per cent. It was only in 1989, however, that *per capita* GDP surpassed that of 1981.

Current economic situation. The foreign debt, which reached $22 billion in 1987, has been brought under control by debt-equity swaps, re-negotiation and Chile's consistent ability to generate trade surpluses. Significant further reduction of the debt through debt-equity swaps is unlikely given that the investments acquired by foreign corporations in this way eventually augment the outflow of funds. The government has just successfully completed a re-negotiation which evens out the hump of debt falling due in 1991/2. Currently the external debt stands at $16 billion.

Copper remains Chile's single most important export and makes Chile the largest copper producer in the world. CODELCO, the giant corporation formed by the amalgamation in one state-owned company of the holdings of Anaconda, Braden and Kennecott is by far the largest producer. Liberalization of foreign investment regulations, however, has allowed mining multinationals such as Rio Tinto, Phelps Dodge and Broken Hill of Australia to open up new mines.

Although copper production has nearly doubled since the early 1970s, from 735,000 tonnes in 1973 to 1,413,000 tonnes in 1987, it now accounts for about 43 per cent of exports compared with 79 per cent in 1970. "Non-traditional" exports, such as grapes, apples, kiwi fruit, forestry products and seafood are responsible for an increasing proportion of exports. They have the advantage too that they are not subject to the large fluctuations in price to which copper is susceptible. In 1990 Alejandro Foxley, Aylwin's Finance Minister, predicted that non-copper exports will continue to grow at the rate of 12 per cent per year until the mid-1990s, boosting exports from their present 30 per cent of GDP to 35 per cent. If government predictions are fulfilled, Chile will overtake Argentina to become the fourth largest exporter in Latin America.

Manufacturing, concentrated in the processing of Chile's natural products, contributes about 21 per cent of GDP. Food processing, chemicals linked to Chile's rich mineral deposits and wood products, including paper and pulp, account for about 70 per cent of manufacturing output.

Stabilization was the keynote for the Chilean economy in 1990. Pinochet's pre-election tax cuts in 1989 fuelled inflation which peaked at an annual rate of just over 30 per cent in October 1990. Adverse factors are the expected slowdown in the world economy in 1991, which will effect the copper price and the Iraqi invasion of Kuwait and its effect on the price of oil. Chile imports over 70 per cent of its oil needs. Exports in 1991 are expected to be $8.33 billion, down from the record $8.5 billion of 1990, while imports are expected to rise by 8 per cent to $7.78 billion.

This export-led eonomic growth has been bought at the cost of low wages. Most of Chile's ("non-traditional") exports depend on an army of seasonal workers, *temporeros*, mobilized to pick fruit. The fruit-packers of the Central Valley are large employers of low-paid women. Today 80 per cent of Chileans earn less in real terms than they did 20 years ago. A study conducted at the end of 1988 in Santiago concluded that 50 per cent of Chileans were living in poverty, unable to afford the basic necessities for their families, compared to 30 per cent in 1969. Real wages in 1988 were scarcely more than they were in 1969.

The environment has also been another victim of the export drive. Marine species have suffered as high value shellfish and crabs have been scoured from the seabed. Hardwood forests of beech and oak have been converted into woodchips, mainly by Japanese companies, while the 1976 law approving subsidies for reforestation has led companies to burn down native forests in order to claim the subsidy for replanting.

The Aylwin government has introduced a number of measures to address the problem of poverty. Soon after assuming office, corporation tax was raised from 10 to 15 per cent and is now to be levied on all profits, not only distributed profits as before; higher earners will pay more tax; and Value Added Tax, reduced by General Pinochet in advance of the 1989 election from 20 to 15 per cent has been raised to 18 per cent. These increases are expected to generate $600 million a year for the government's social solidarity fund. The economic team see the first year of government as essentially defensive, bringing inflation under control before they can start to implement their own programme.

Prospects for development. After President Frei's "Revolution in Liberty" and Allende's Chilean Road to Socialism, Chile is once more being held out as a model to other countries in Latin America. This time the recommendation is being made by the UN Economic Commission for Latin America and is based on Chile's success as an exporter. Model or not, the prospects for Chile as it picks up the threads of its interrupted democratic tradition are good. All members of the present government, Christian Democrats and socialists alike, are convinced of the need to reconstitute pluralism and democracy in Chile. They are aware that this will be costly and that the poor, who have borne the brunt of the economic achievements of the dictatorship, cannot live on a diet of patience. They argue that social investment, in health, housing and education is needed if Chile is to maintain economic growth. They face a vigorous and self-confident right-wing opposition, however, which is reluctant to surrender the economic gains made under Pinochet. Moreover, there is no reason, politically, why the right should co-operate in ensuring that the *Concertación* is successful in carrying out its social programme.

GG

CHRISTIAN DEMOCRATIC PARTY Democracia Cristiana Guatemalteca — DCG (Guatemala). The Christian Democratic Party in Guatemala was established in August 1955 as a middle-class party committed to vehement anti-communism and opposition to organized labour despite the repression of the latter during the Castillo Armas government (1954–57). The growth of the DCG only occurred in the 1960s in parallel with the rise of Christian Democracy in other parts of Latin America and in particular with the incorporation of the politics of Catholic Action. From its foundation to 1985 all DCG presidential candidates were from the military, and put forward its historically most progressive platform including complete agrarian transformation prior to the fraudulent elections of 1974. The acceptance by the DCG of the National Opposition Front (*Frente Nacional de Oposición*—FNO) coalition candidacy of General **Efraín Ríos Montt** for the 1974 election confirmed its subordination to the oligarchical agenda and from this time onwards moved steadily to the right, fulfilling little more than a legitimating and mediating role in Guatemalan politics.

In the wake of successive repressive military regimes, particularly between 1977 and 1984, the DCG was identified by the government of the United States of America as constituting the acceptable face—or "civilized right" — of Guatemalan politics (much as the PDC under Napoleón Duarte in **El Salvador** received US approval). Moreover increased contacts and formal links with the **Comité Co-ordinador de Asociaciones Agrícolas, Comerciales Industriales y Financieras—CACIF** had brought the DCG support from important fractions of capitalism which was either being restricted by the growth in the economic power of the army or the structural constraints of the traditional agro-export basis of the economy. Whilst the election of the DCG government was of benefit to many CACIF sectors, little has been done to reduce human rights abuses or even investigate past abuses. Indeed Cerezo explicitly refused to overturn Decree 8–86 announced by General Mejía Victores before leaving office which gave all army personnel immunity and amnesty from prosecution for **human rights** abuses. Human rights abuses have escalated sharply since 1989, particularly during military campaigns invariably conducted without effective DCG government control. The US government cut military aid once again on Dec. 21, 1990 due to the failure of the DCG government to tackle the problem.

JCJS

CHRISTIAN DEMOCRATIC PARTY (Partido Demócrata Cristiano — PDC) (El Salvador). The Christian Democratic Party of **El Salvador** was established contemporaneously with the spread of Christian Democracy throughout Latin America, based as it was upon the growing body of Catholic social doctrine, anti-communism and technocratic strategies of modernization. Since its foundation in 1960 the PDC has drawn the bulk of its support from the urban middle classes (which gained most through the Alliance for Progress and **Central American Common Market** (CACM) period of the 1960s), traditionalist trade unions, and certain peasant associations. Throughout its history the fate of the PDC has been closely mirrored by the fortunes of its founder and principal architect José Napoleón Duarte who was elected as the PDC candidate for the mayoralty of San Salvador between 1964 and

1970, was defrauded of the presidency in 1972 (arrested, tortured and exiled to Venezuela), and, following the resignation of fellow PDC member Héctor Dada from the civil/military junta of February 1980, became the only civilian to remain on the junta. By December 1980 Duarte was made president (until August 1982) whilst the majority of the traditional PDC activists had left the party or been obliged to join illegal organizations—many into the Revolutionary Democratic Front (*Frente Revolucionario Democrático*—FDR)—due to the growing level of political violence and the rightwards move of the PDC.

The party's centrist image and the personal history of Duarte ensured that **United States** policy in El Salvador would be directed through active support for the PDC against the extreme right of the **National Republican Alliance** (Alianza Republicana Nacionalista—ARENA) and the leftist politics of the FDR and the **Farabundo Martí Front for National Liberation** (*Frente Farabundo Martí para la Liberación Nacional*—FMLN). In 1984 Duarte was elected president for the first time, but neither he nor the PDC controlled Assembly had *de facto* control of El Salvador. Duarte died on Feb. 23, 1990 of liver cancer, after several years of illness, shortly after leaving office.

JCJS

CHURCH. The history of Christianity in Latin America and the Caribbean has been dominated by the history of the Catholic Church. Still today, despite the rapid advances of Protestantism in the last 30 years, the confessional bias of Latin America and the Caribbean lies towards Catholicism which claims the faith of some 80 per cent across the region. Within this hegemonic regime however there are important regional and confessional variations. Foremost amongst these is the historically stronger influence of Protestantism in the English-speaking Caribbean and amongst former Dutch territories, and the more recent (i.e. twentieth century) Protestant proselytism in Central America. In addition, the region has been swept by evangelical **fundamentalism**, especially over the last two decades. Both in their own right and as a challenge to Roman Catholicism there have been the important pre-Columbian and African-derived faiths which have been inherited by specific groups or have become distinct but syncretic forms with Catholicism, i.e. beliefs that have often, if mistakenly, been labelled "folk religions".

The history and role of the Catholic Church in Latin America pre-dates the initial conquest of Latin America under the Spanish empire. Rights of conquest and colonization granted first to Portugal and then to Spain by the Papacy corresponded with the *jus patronatus* of the propagation of the faith. Colonization and evangelization became one enterprise initially confirmed to the Spanish monarchs in 1492, with reference to the *Reconquista*, by the papal bulls *Provisionis Nostrae* and *Dum ad illam* by which the Crown gained the right to name all bishops. This was followed in 1493 by the critical bulls, known as *Inter caetera* and *Eximiae devotionis*, which placed all newly discovered lands under the Crown, but also ceded the definition of diocesan boundaries, rights to tithes and tributes, and the posting of missionaries to the Crown. The conquest of Latin America was defined primarily as a crusade, and from the naming of the first Latin American bishops in 1512, through the consolidation of temporal and secular authority in the Supreme Council of the Indies in 1524, to the period following independence from Spain there was a remarkable unity of religious and secular authority, a bonding of Church and State. However since independence, particularly as a consequence of the specific outcome of each country's liberal–conservative conflict of the nineteenth century, the plurality of paths of development of each national church is striking.

It is important to recognize the distinct but often overlapping meanings attributed to the term Catholicism: the first refers to the universal and open religion of sinners, whilst the second pertains to the institutional and sectarian religion of the just (Enrique Dussel). Whilst most Latin Americans are encompassed by the former there remains ambivalence over a majority inclusion in the latter. Estimates of practising Catholics (as opposed to those baptized into the Church) vary wildly from 12 per cent to 25 per cent as a region-wide average of adherents, but the variation between each country is much greater; thus Cuba is accredited with only 1 per cent of Catholics actually practising. Formal baptism into the Church is not necessarily an accurate indicator of those who claim adherence to it, but four broad groups of states can be identified. First, states whose nominally Catholic population is 90 per cent of the total or over include **Argentina**, **Brazil**, **Colombia**, **Costa Rica**, **Dominican Republic**, **Ecuador**, **El Salvador**, **Paraguay**, **Peru**, **Venezuela**; second, states whose nominally Catholic population is 80 per cent to 90 per cent include **Bolivia**, **Chile**, **Haiti**, **Honduras**, **Nicaragua**, **Netherlands Antilles**, **St Lucia**; third, states whose nominally Catholic population constitute between 50 per cent and 80 per cent of the population include **Belize**, **Grenada**,

Guatemala, **Panama**, **Uruguay**; finally, those states in which nominal adherence to Catholicism is less than 50 per cent of the total population and/or comparable in size to various protestant denominations include **Cuba**, **Guyana**, **Jamaica**, **St Vincent**, **St Kitts**, and **Suriname**.

The broad triumph of the Liberals over the Conservatives throughout Latin America during the latter half of the nineteenth century and, in some cases the first decades of the twentieth century, saw the serious erosion, weakening and, in the case of Mexico, the complete subversion of the power of the Church. Invariably the anti-Church commitments of the Liberals resulted in, first, the alienation of Church lands to private owners thereby cutting away its source of economic power and, secondly, removing either wholesale or by degrees the virtual monopoly held by the Church over education, thereby removing a central pillar of its secular authority. In general terms, though not exclusively so, the deeper the triumph of the Liberals the weaker each respective national Church became. At one extreme the nationalization of Church property in 1859 and the failure to recognize the Church at all in the Constitution of 1917 and its prohibition from "political activity", suppressed the profile of the Mexican Church until the 1960s and 1970s culminating in the **Conference of Latin America Bishops** (*Conferencia del Episcopado Latinoamericano*—CELAM) held in Puebla in 1979 contemporaneously with the visit of Pope John Paul II. Nevertheless the Church in Mexico remains a relatively weak institution. On the other hand the political tradition following the Portuguese empire of Brazil led to a broader more firmly based, if diverse, Church. With 358 bishops the Brazilian episcopate is the largest in the world and had sufficient institutional strength to constitute the single biggest critic and opponent of military rule following the 1964 *coup*.

Of recent times, particularly in the years just prior to and in the aftermath of Vatican II, the principal problems facing all the national churches have been twofold. First, the nature, composition and function of the institutional Church vis-à-vis Catholicism in the national context. This had been both a major theological and political controversy. Second, and derived from the first problematic, the relationship between the national Church and the Vatican and the Papacy. Since the Second Vatican Council and the regional confirmation of its conclusions at CELAM's meeting in Medellín in 1968 there has arisen a tension—on occasions bitter and open quarrels—between sections of the Church hierarchy on the one hand and the so-called popular church and progressives in the episcopate on the other. This has been most dramatically characterized by liberation theology and the theological mission of the "preferential option for the poor", the proliferation of "Christian base communities" (*Bases de Comunidad Cristiana*—BCC), and the immersion of the Church into the burning questions of social and economic justice. The question of what is the Church for and for whom necessarily led to the question what was its nature to be. Indications of the types of response can be gained from Brazil, El Salvador and Argentina. In the former case the National Bishops' Conference (*Conferência Nacional de Bispos Brasileiros*—CNBB) under the inspiration of Dom Helder Cámara, Archbishop of the poverty-stricken province of Recife, supported opposition to the abuses of the military regimes, initiated a wide range of social and educational programmes, established the Pastoral Land Commission in 1979 (dedicated to the interests of the landless and rural poor), and encouraged the radical pastoral activities derived from the BCCs. During the 1960s and 1970s the progressives held the balance within the CNBB but since the late 1970s the balance has shifted to the bureaucratic conservatives with the active approval of the Vatican. Such a shift arose not only out of the deep conservatism of the Vatican under John Paul II, but because the direction that the Brazilian Church was moving in was deemed a threat to the ecclesiastical and theological authority of the Vatican. Since Latin American Catholics form the single biggest body of believers in the world, Vatican authority over its national Churches is of critical importance.

In the case of El Salvador the evolution of the Church in both its political and theological relations is instructive. An essentially conservative Church was plunged into a bitter crisis of civil and political society just as a conservative Archbishop, Oscar Romero, was appointed in 1977. The murder of close associates of Oscar Romero, such as Father Rutilio Grande, the generalized repression against the Church and the population was a catalyst to his appreciation of the theological centrality of the Church as witness. The assassination of Romero on March 24, 1980 while celebrating the Mass symbolized, if nothing else, the power of and fear held by the opponents of a Church rejuvenated by Vatican II.

Most national episcopates are divided into three broad groups, conservatives, progressives and moderates. Since 1979 there has been a strengthening of the conservatives, but this condition has been one which has historically characterized the Argentine, Colombian, Ecuadorean, Nicaraguan and Venezuelan Churches. In the case of Brazil under the current Pope there has been a marked rightwards shift. The liberal Helder Cámara has been replaced by the arch-conservative José Cardoso Sobrinho. The radical Archbishop of São Paulo, Evaristo Arns, has had his archdiocese divided into four and assigned a prosperous diocese thereby undermining his pioneering work. To strengthen Vatican control of the episcopate the conservative Archbishop of Bahia, Lucas Moreira Neves, was appointed to the College of Cardinals. These types of policies are slowly being applied across the region as a whole.

Mexico. The Church in **Mexico**, as elsewhere, was conservative in social and political terms until around 1960. Thereafter it has been less conservative and also less united; each of the political tendencies in Mexico today enjoys the support of part of the Church. Historically, the Mexican experience was complicated by the success of the anti-clerical Reform of the 1850s and the Revolution of 1910–17. Consequently, unlike most of the rest of Latin America, the Mexican Church found itself subject to political exclusion and, on occasion, persecution. Consequently the Church's association with powerlessness rather than power almost certainly strengthened its appeal to the majority of Mexicans.

The Mexican **Constitution** of 1917 contains a number of clauses which are directly restrictive of the Church's right to participate in politics, or even in open society. It is, for example, forbidden to wear religious garments (e.g. monastic clothing) in a public place—although this article of the Constitution is not strictly enforced. In fact there has been virtually no overt conflict between Church and State since 1940, and relations between the two have steadily improved. An important landmark was the visit of Pope John Paul II to Mexico in 1979. The government is content for the Church to continue with an active role in Mexican education—so as to supplement the rather limited resources which the state makes available in this area. Recently, indeed, the Salinas administration looked for ways of increasing the political role of the Church, but appears to have abandoned this initiative which enjoyed little popular support.

Indeed although the Right-wing opposition party—the PAN—is associated with a kind of political Catholicism, most Mexicans (according to public opinion surveys) prefer to see the Church kept separate from politics. Indeed the Catholic Church in Mexico is probably now in slow decline. Although the vast majority of the Mexican population considers itself to be Catholic, a diminishing number actively practice their religion. Among the educated, urban middle and upper middle classes, active Catholicism involves only a small minority. Moreover among the rural poor, Protestantism has been making increasing inroads.

Thus, although the state is increasingly well disposed toward organized religion—particularly in its more conservative and hierarchical aspect—Mexico is following other countries in which urbanization and the spread of higher education becomes associated with a decline in religious observance.

JCJS/GP

COLLOR DE MELLO, FERNANDO. Collor was 39 when, in December 1989, he became the first directly elected president of **Brazil** since **Jânio Quadros** in 1960. He and Quadros had much in common, both being elected on a populist platform, condemning corruption, inefficiency and the whole political class, and coming to power without strong party or Congressional support. One difference was that Quadros in 1960 had much more political experience, including the responsibility of office, than Collor had by 1989.

Fernando Collor de Mello began his political career in 1978, when, aged 28, he was nominated as the "bionic" mayor of Maceió, the capital of Alagoas, at the end of the Geisel government. In the elections of 1982, he was elected as federal deputy for the **Social Democratic Party** (*Partido Democrático Social*—PDS). In the Chamber of Deputies, Collor presented 11 projects, including one to reduce taxes on radio and television stations: none was approved. Collor voted in the electoral college's choice of president, in January 1985 for his "*padrinho de casamento*", the best man at his wedding, **Paulo Maluf**. Like Maluf, himself, who had married into the wealthy Lutfalla family, Collor also benefited through marriage, to a member of one of Brazil's wealthiest families, the Monteiro Aranhas. When the presidential candidates had to declare their wealth, in August 1989, the two wealthiest were Maluf and Collor.

Most of Collor's wealth came from his father, Arnan de Mello, a member of a distinguished literary circle in Maceió, capital of Alagoas, in the early 1930s, linked to Gilberto Freyre in Recife. He was a journalist and property dealer, who had benefitted through his connections in Rio de Janeiro with the Vargas family and with Roberto Marinho and the *Globo* group. He was governor of Alagoas, from 1951 to 1956, for the National Democratic Union (*União Democrática Nacional*—UDN). In 1962, he was elected senator for the Christian Democratic Party (Partido

Democrático Cristão—PDC), then moved into the National Renewal Alliance (Aliança Renovadora Nacional—ARENA) in 1965. In 1963, he was imprisoned for shooting and killing a colleague in the Senate, though not the man at whom he was aiming; but, later, he again took up his Senate seat. He owned both the *Diário Carioca* in Rio de Janeiro, and the *Gazeta de Alagoas*, plus two radio stations, and one television station, *Radios* and *TV Gazeta de Alagoas*. He maintained his close links with Marinho and *Globo*.

In 1985, like many other refugees from the Democratic Socialist Party (*Partido Democrático Socialista*—PDS), Fernando Collor de Mello joined the **Party of the Brazilian Democratic Movement** (Partido de Movimento Democrático Brasileiro—PMDB), against the will of Tancredo Neves, who said that if Collor were to be accepted, it would first be necessary to accept Maluf. His entry into the party was helped by Sarney. In the avalanche of PMDB victories in November 1986, swept along by the Cruzado Plan, Collor was elected governor of Alagoas. In 1987, he began his campaign as the scourge of the "*marajás*", the "maharajas", civil servants, who, through a loophole in the law, received wildly inflated salaries and privileges. He also began to cultivate his image as the "anti-politician", eventually creating the National Reconstruction Party (*Partido da Reconstrução Nacional*—PRN) as his personal electoral vehicle. He gave up the governorship on May 14, 1989, to be able to run as presidential candidate, in a campaign which swiftly brought charges of maladministration during his term of office.

In his first year in office, Collor showed imagination and courage, especially in his choice of ministers and in the **New Brazil** or Collor Plan, to curb inflation. By March 1991, he was again faced with inflation running at over 20 per cent a month, growing labour unrest and a general decline in the credibility of his programme and his government.

PF

COLOMBIA. *Population*: 30, 800, 000 (1988). *Area*: 1,141,748 sq km. *GDP*: US$31,940 million. *Trade volume (1988)*: exports: US$5,165 million; imports: US$3,794 million; *Top trade partners (1989)*: USA, West Germany, Holland, Japan. *Defence spending (as percentage of GNP—1986)*: 1. *Education spending as percentage of GNP*—1986): 2.8 *Urban population (as percentage of total*—1987): 69.1 *Birthrate*: 1.7 per 1,000 (1987). *Life expectancy*: 66 (men); 71 (women) (1988).

Geographical background. The country consists of three main geographical areas. The mountainous region of the west is cut by three mountain ranges of the Andes, separated by deep valleys, notably those of the two great rivers, the Cauca and Magdalena. This region covers 26 per cent of the country's surface area but is populated by 80 per cent of the country's inhabitants. It represents the heartland of the country's economic life. To the east lies a second region of flat lands, with huge savannahs or plains (*Llanos*) to the north and extensive forests to the south. Less than two per cent of the population live here. Finally, there are the Pacific and Caribbean coastal regions, some 19 per cent of all national territory and inhabited by 19 per cent of the total population, and the island group of San Andrés and Providencia.

Socio-political background. Colombia's social, political and economic development has been deeply affected by geography and climate. Most indigenous peoples had settled on the cooler highland areas and this settlement pattern was followed by the Spanish conquerors who built today's capital city, Bogotá, at over 2,600 metres on a plateau in the eastern mountain range. The settlement of the warmer, lower slopes and finally the eastern plains was begun during the nineteenth century as a result of population growth and pressure on the land and continues to this day. The process of colonization has been very conflictive between small peasant farmers and large-scale landowners.

The great size and physical barriers of the country have created considerable transport and communications problems. These hindered the development of a national market and created regional identities and political fiefdoms that have shaped Colombia's political as well as economic history. As late as 1949, a World Bank mission had concluded that inadequate transport facilities, particularly roads, were the greatest single obstacle to Colombia's economic development.

Over 70 per cent of Colombia's population is considered *mestizo* (mixed Spanish and Indian). The indigenous population which numbered about 3–4,000,000 at the time of the Conquest according to some estimates, was decimated in the fifteenth and sixteenth centuries and today constitutes only about two per cent of the population. The shortage of labour to meet the demand of the new Spanish rulers, led to the import of thousands of African slaves to work the gold mines of Antioquia and the large agricultural estates of the Cauca valley. About six per cent of the population today are estimated to be of

African descent. The final 22 per cent of the population are made up of those of European descent only.

Colombia underwent a process of rapid urbanization from the 1950s to the 1980s. Unlike many parts of Latin America, the 70 per cent who now live in urban areas are not concentrated in one major city. Colombia has three cities of over 1,000,000 people, two between 500,000 and 1,000,000, and 17 between 100,000 and 500,000. A considerable emphasis on birth control programmes has helped reduce the birth rate to 1.6 per cent a year, comparable with the developed world. It is also a comparatively well educated population, especially amongst the younger sectors who have benefitted from increased educational opportunities over the last few decades.

Economic and social changes in the 1960s and 1970s, have also witnessed the rise of one of the largest middle classes in Latin America. Colombia has a number of very well trained technicians and professionals. But while a sector of the middle class has gained genuine prosperity, a much larger group is neither prosperous nor impoverished, and mostly likely represent the relatively few who have access to waged employment rather than members of professions.

Income distribution remains highly unequal. In 1985 according to official government figures, the richest 10 per cent of urban families received a little less than 40 per cent of total income while 50 per cent of families received less than 20 per cent. The poorest 20 per cent gained less than five per cent of the total. A Department of National Statistics survey in 1988 of 13 towns with a total population of 11,419,378 found that 32.02 per cent lived in poverty and 4.36 per cent in total poverty. Over half the 13,000,000 Colombians who are officially recognized as living in poverty, live in the rural areas, and of these over 40 per cent live in absolute poverty.

Outline of political history. Present-day Colombia had been one of the most impoverished outposts of the Spanish empire. Its gold supplies were in no way comparable to the silver riches of Potosí's Cerro Rico in present-day Bolivia, and its agriculture remained technologically backward, with no plantation agriculture as in Venezuela to stimulate local economic development. The difficulty in finding a means of generating wealth remained a backcloth to the political troubles confronting the independent republic in the nineteenth century.

The *creole* or local born élite which dominated the post-independence years, were formally committed to constitutions, laws and elections, and even adopted European names for the two parties, Liberal and Conservative, which emerged to reflect the divisions amongst them. But, with the rejection of independence leader, **Simón Bolívar's** vision of a great confederation of the Andes based on strong central government, the élite broke into warring regionally based factions and the creation of a viable nation-state proved elusive throughout the nineteenth century.

Colombia's unique political culture was born in these years. On the one hand there was a vibrant political life, in which elections and electioneering were an important element, reported by a dynamic press. On the other, there was the frequent recourse to arms to solve disputes (in the wake of the 14 years of the Wars of Independence there were eight general civil wars, 14 local civil wars, countless small uprisings, two international wars with Ecuador and three *coups d'état*). There were no decisive victors from the many wars of the nineteenth century, establishing another element to the country's political tradition, that of élite negotiation and compromise. The potential for accommodation helped ensure the survival of Colombia's two political parties into the twentieth century when their deep antagonisms might otherwise have threatened their continued domination of Colombian political life.

The divisions between the two traditional parties did not reflect substantial disagreements except over the role of the **Church**, which the **Liberal Party** saw as a bastion of privilege and the Conservatives as a guarantor of social order and authority. Unlike in other Latin American countries at the time, where the Liberals usually succeeded in dismantling a great deal of Church power, in Colombia, an agreement was reached in 1887 between the two parties which recognized the authority of the Catholic Church. The Church continued to be a major political actor (on behalf of the Conservative party) for at least the first half of the twentieth century.

The signing of the Concordat of 1887 followed on the establishment of the ultra-centralist constitution of 1886 which is still in force today. The constitution strengthened the power of the President and inaugurated a short-lived period of modernization which saw the creation of a permanent army (the military school was opened in 1891) and infrastructural improvements. These were brought to an end by the Thousand Day War (1899–1902) which devastated the country and involved the death of some 100,000 people. The war reflected another long-lasting feature of the Colombian political system. The party wars involved the mobilization of large numbers of people around the regional leaders of each party. Loyalties to the parties were gradually sealed, literally, in blood as people saw their relatives killed by members of the opposing party.

These loyalties would form an important legtimizing factor for the nation state which began to be forged seriously in the early twentieth century. Coffee production and export was the basis for this process. Coffee production centred initially on the department of Antioquia and at last provided a means for financing a central state as well as generating economic development in other sectors, such as industry. By the 1930s, coffee provided 70 per cent of Colombia's export earnings.

The years 1885–1930 are known as the years of the Conservative Republic as that party dominated the state, mostly with support from a fraction of the Liberals. Social pressures built up in these years as urbanization and industrialization brought social changes and struggles over the land created many tensions in the rural areas. The government of the Liberal President, Alfonso López Pumarejo (1934–38, known as the Revolution on the March) sought to accommodate these pressures. He helped build a labour confederation, the Confederation of Colombian Workers (*Confederacíon de Trabajadores de Colombia*—CTC), whose members would depend directly or indirectly on the state and introduced legislation (bitterly opposed by landowners) to allow some redistribution of land.

The militantly conservative forces within the élite soon mobilized against these efforts to adapt to the process of social change. The Church and a sector of the Conservative party, influenced by Franco's Spain and led by Laureano Gómez, began to organize a "counter-revolution". In a climate of growing political polarization, a new leader had gained power within the Liberal party by 1946. Jorge Eliecer Gaitán was committed to mobilizing the "people" against what he called the "oligarchy" of both Conservative and Liberal parties. Gaitán's populist appeal to the masses grew rapidly in a society which was socially and economically as well as politically, extremely polarized. Amidst growing political violence, Gaitán was assassinated on Feb. 7, 1948.

Colombia now plunged into a prolonged period of civil war between the two parties, known as *La Violencia*. It cost the lives of an estimated 200,000 people. It is divided into two phases, 1949–53 and 1958–65, the latter being a period of social banditry carried out mostly by former Liberal party guerrilla leaders who had refused to accept an amnesty. Between the phases, the party leaders attempted to resolve their differences, first by supporting a *coup d'état* led by General Rojas Pinilla in 1953. When Rojas Pinilla attempted to create an independent basis to maintain him in power, they conspired to oust him and in 1958 they made their own agreement, the National Front, to alternate power between them.

The National Front pact was a formal agreement between the two parties to alternate the presidency between them for 16 years, and to divide all legislative bodies and public corporations (Senate, House of Representatives and departmental and municipal councils), cabinet offices, judicial posts and posts at all levels of public administration by agreement between the two parties. This enabled the parties to pre-empt the traditional source of conflict between them over access to the state and its resources. It also ensured that no third party could challenge them.

With political stability restored, the two traditional parties could now concentrate on the promotion of economic modernization and development. The years following the party pact were to witness substantial economic progress. But the pact created a whole new set of problems for the political system.

By guaranteeing the traditional parties access to government, the party pact allowed them to postpone the much needed organizational reforms which might have turned them into modern institutions with political programmes and internal democracy, capable of confronting the pressures of social and economic change. The parties remained largely in the hands of regional party bosses, with policies as well as presidential candidates decided by negotiation amongst an élite group of political leaders. Politicians increasingly mobilized their vote through clientelist practices of vote-buying and Congress became the locus of power struggles between party bosses.

Loyalties to the parties declined, particularly in the burgeoning cities, as people no longer felt the need to vote. Abstention rates at election time were very high, particularly for the legislature. Only two of the six presidential elections between 1966 and 1986 attracted more than half the eligible electorate and only three attracted more than half of those who had registered to vote. The decrease in loyalties to the parties was reflected also in two institutions of major importance to the country.

On the one hand, the Catholic Church in giving its blessing to bipartisan rule and burying its long hostility towards the Liberal party, began to lose its privileged position within the state, while increasing urbanization encouraged the secularism which would also undermine its authority. The army on the other hand, traditionally subservient to party political influences, began with the help of US training and assistance, to create its own increasingly autonomous and influential position. This has not involved political ambitions to control the state as such, but the army has insisted on its right to run its counter-insurgency campaigns without interference from elected civilian authorities, resulting in frequent accusations of abuse of its power and privileges. The Minister of Defence is appointed from the Army and is a powerful voice in support of the Army's interests within any government. The Army has grown in size, particularly from the late 1970s, when it increased from 80,000 men in 1978 to 135,000 in 1988.

In the second place, the party pact sealed the political system, so that expressions of grievance and discontent could find no channel within it. Even after the pact formally came to an end in 1974, power sharing arrangements continued. The first competitive presidential election was held in 1974, but parity in the Cabinet and public employment was retained formally until 1978. From that date, Article 120 of the Constitution required the majority party to offer "adequate and equitable" representation in the executive branch to the party with the second highest number of votes.

Some movements tried to challenge bipartisan government from within the two traditional parties. This is the case of Rojas Pinilla's attempt to create a new urban movement, the Popular National Alliance (ANAPO), which came very near to winning the 1970 election, indeed there were many accusations that they were deprived of victory by an electoral fraud. Other movements sought alternatives outside the bipartisan state and the electoral process as a whole.

There is a long history of guerrilla warfare in Colombia. But this has mostly been associated with the two traditional parties, particularly the Liberals. In the early 1960s, guerrilla movements emerged committed to ending the domination of the two traditional political parties. The Revolutionary Armed Forces of Colombia (*Fuerzas Armadas Revolucionarias Colombianas* — FARC) grew out of the Communist Party-led centres of peasant self-defence during *La Violencia*. It came virtually to control considerable regions of the country, particularly in the eastern plains. Two other movements, the Popular Liberation Army (*Ejército Popular de Liberación* — EPL) and the Army of National Liberation (*Ejército de Liberación Nacional* — ELN) were also formed in the early 1960s, influenced by Maoism and the Cuban revolution respectively.

Although these three movements were seriously weakened during the 1970s by the army's counter-insurgency campaign, they reorganized towards the end of the decade. Armed struggle had by then received a renewed impetus by the appearance of a new movement in the late 1970s, which grew from dissidents of the FARC and members of ANAPO disillusioned with the electoral process by what they believed had been an orchestrated fraud on April 19, 1970. This organization called itself the April 19 Movement and is known as the **M-19**. It distinguished itself early on from the other movements by its insertion in the cities rather than remote rural areas, in recognition of the demographic changes which had turned Colombia into an overwhelmingly urban country. Taking its inspiration from the national hero, **Simón Bolívar**, rather than foreign ideologies, it attracted considerable support from middle-class youth, who had benefitted from expanded educational opportunities but were frustrated when they were not matched by employment and career opportunities.

The challenge from these armed movements grew towards the end of the 1970s. At the same time, the state faced another, potentially more threatening challenge. This came from organized social movements which explicitly and for the first time in the country's history, rejected control by the traditional parties. The government of Carlos Lleras Restrepo (1966–70), one of the more innovative in recent Colombian history, had created a peasant organization in an effort to force the more traditional landowners to modernize their landholdings. This organization, the National Association of Peasant Users (*Asociación Nacional de Usuarios Campesinos* — ANUC) freed itself from state control and spearheaded a period of radical mobilization of the peasantry in the 1970s.

In addition, throughout the 1970s, trade unions independent of the two main confederations controlled by the two traditional parties (the CTC to the Liberal party and the Union of Colombian Workers (*Unión de Trabajadores de Colombia* — UTC) to the Conservative Party), began to gain increasing numbers of adherents amongst the working population. This was to culminate in 1986 with the formation of the United Workers Central (*Central Unitaria de Trabajadores* — CUT), the country's first independent workers' confederation and with a clear majority of the unionized labour force. In the small and medium urban centres of the country, another kind of movement emerged independent of all political forces. These civic movements challenged the state for its failure of provide basic services in the urban centres, and in particular drew attention to the corruption of local politicians.

Yet another challenge to the Colombian political order appeared in the late 1970s and grew throughout the 1980s. This was created by the enrichment of a new class of entrepreneurs associated with the cocaine trade. Colombia's cocaine mafia came to control the most lucrative part of the trade, its processing and distribution. The wealth they accumulated enabled them to build up a powerful network of influence within the Colombian political system as well as to threaten the functioning of key institutions of the state, particularly the judiciary. The cocaine mafia were able to further destabilize a political system already vulnerable to partisan and corrupting influences.

Recent developments—political. During the 1980s, the traditional politicians attempted to deal with these various political challenges. They were deeply divided on the appropriate course of action. A sector favoured reforming the political order, modernizing the political parties, strengthening the state and introducing urban and agrarian reform to meet at least some of the demands of the poorer sector of the population. Another group preferred to dig its heels in, support the army in dealing with popular unrest as well as guerrilla forces and even back various forms of "private justice" if the state failed to restore law and order.

President Belisario Betancur (1982–86) attempted to reach an agreement with the guerrilla movements as part of a political strategy to deal with the growth of violence and social unrest. The course of events which finally led to the breakdown of his peace plan is hotly disputed, but its failure to win the support of the army and key sectors of the Colombian élite were major factors in its demise.

Hostilities had resumed between army and guerrillas by 1985 and in November that year the M-19 took over the Palace of Justice. The army stormed the Palace killing 95 people, who apart from the guerrillas present, included 12 of the country's 25 supreme court judges and many members of the Palace staff; 14 people "disappeared", including eight members of the cafeteria staff, three casual visitors to the palace and three guerrillas. In October 1990, the Army Commander who had led the assault, General Jesus Armando Arias Cebrales—by then retired, was found guilty of a number of illegal actions during the attack and the Attorney-General ordered his dismissal from the army.

The events at the Palace of Justice drew international attention to the dangerous level of violence facing the country. With its long history of criminal and underground activities, Colombia already had a high level of street violence and crime. In 1973 its murder rate was one of the highest in the world (19.8 murders for every 100,000 inhabitants). By 1989 the Andean Commission of Jurists put the figure at 69 per 100,000 inhabitants. By the late 1980s, over 20,000 people were being murdered every year. This rise of the cocaine mafia hugely increased the level and nature of the violence and Colombia's legal system was totally unable to cope. In 1985 only 20 per cent of all crimes were reported in the 11 major towns and only one per cent of these resulted in a prison sentence.

In an effort to prevent the government succumbing to US pressure to extradite mafia bosses, the mafia engaged in assassinations of top-ranking officials and individuals, including the Minister of Justice, Lara Bonilla in 1984, Guillermo Cano, the editor of the leading daily newspaper, *El Espectador* in 1986, Jaime Pardo Leal, leader of the main opposition Patriotic Union (UP) party in 1987 and Attorney-General Carlos Mauro Hoyos in 1988.

The situation was further complicated by the tacit alliance which the mafia began to cultivate with some of the most conservative sectors of society in the army, industry and on the big ranching estates. This alliance involved the setting up of right-wing paramilitary death squads to eliminate left-wing activists, suspected guerrilla sympathisers and even "undesirable" social elements such as homosexuals and prostitutes. By the mid-1980s, the government acknowledged the existence of 140 such groups. The impunity with which these groups operated, including in areas of strong military presence led many to conclude that their presence was at least tolerated if not encouraged by the highest authorities.

President Virgilio Barco Vargas came into office for the Liberal party in 1986 at a critical political moment. More of a technocrat than a politician, Barco put great emphasis on strengthening the state and its capacity to deal with the many challenges. He hoped to bring back legitimacy to the government and restore faith in its institutions. For the first time, bipartisan government was abandoned and Barco governed with Liberal party support only. Barco introduced a number of reforms, agrarian, urban and constitutional, but ran into fierce and entrenched opposition within Congress from party bosses of his own and the opposition Conservative party (which in 1987 officially renamed itself the **Social-Conservative Party**). This reduced the effect of the reforms, and resulted after a long congressional struggle in the abandonment of the constitutional reform which had sought to eliminate Article 120, the last vestige of coalition rule.

The direct election of mayors did take place in 1988 as part of moves to decentralize and give greater powers to local authorities as well as make local politicians more responsive to the electorate rather than party bosses. But the level of vote rigging and buying was very high and only half the eligible electorate voted. And the elections were surrounded by an incredible level of violence. The total toll of deaths associated with these elections for 1988 was seven mayors, 28 candidates for mayors, 75 councillors and 19 candidates for the muncipal councils. In these circumstances, the fact that the elections took place at all was considered somewhat of a victory for the democratic process.

Barco also tried to strengthen the state's ability to deal with violence in a effort to stamp out the system of "private justice" which was now rampant in many parts of the country. But by enhancing the powers of the army through an anti-terrorist statute introduced at the beginning of 1988, many felt that the impunity with which the army operated its counter-insurgency campaigns had been encouraged. A state of siege has in fact been in force in Colombia almost continuously since the late 1940s, giving the President emergency powers. Barco sought to extend these powers even further.

But increasing reports of human rights violations began to damage the country's international reputation. In 1989, Amnesty International published a report highly critical of the role of the army in the violation of human rights. Human rights organizations based in the country, such as *Justicia y Paz* and the Jesuit research centre, CINEP, gathered data on killings from the press. Between 1986 and 1989, there were 8,000 killings for political, possibly political and social "clean-up" purposes. Most of the victims were peasants, but they also included trade unionists, politicians, particularly from the Patriotic Union (*Unión Patriótica*—UP) party, which by the end of 1989 had lost over 1,000 activists). There was also a macabre new phenomenon: the massacre. In 1988, 691 people died in 84 massacres (killings of four or more people), mostly carried out by right-wing paramilitary groups.

Barco's final months in office were particularly dramatic. In August 1989, Luis Carlos Galán, a reforming politician who was tipped to be the Liberal party candidate for the 1990 elections with a considerable chance of winning, was assassinated. The murder was carried out on the orders of the Medellín drugs cartel, and it alerted the political establishment to the extent to which the mafia had become a virtual "state-within-state", complete with private armies. President Barco had nine Ministers of Justice; most resigned after mafia threats to the lives of themselves and their families.

The murder of Galán led to the outbreak of a virtual "drugs war" between the government and the Medellín-based mafia. The United States immediately sent US$65,000,000 in emergency military assistance to the Colombian government and in December announced plans for a major increase in military assistance to the Andean countries trying to combat the cocaine industry. At the end of December 1989, the Colombian government scored a major victory with the killing of leading drugs baron Gonzalo Rodríguez Gacha. The operations of the mafia were badly hit and by February 1990 it was offering a deal to the government. This was rejected, although there were significant voices within the traditional parties in favour of a negotiated solution to the drugs war.

There was no indication that mafia power had been finally broken; it was the Medellín cartel that bore the brunt of the government offensive, other mafia bosses based in Cali who had always kept a lower, less brutal profile than their rivals, were virtually left alone. Evidence that the right-wing alliance, of which the Medellín cartel were a major part, remained active was seen in the run-up to the May 1990 elections. Two more candidates were gunned down: Bernardo Jaramillo of the UP (the UP subsequently withdrew from the elections), and Carlos Pizarro, leader of the M-19 guerillas who had accepted a peace aggreement with the government at the end of 1989 and formed a political party to contest the elections. There were 35 massacres between April and June 1990, leaving 150 dead and 45 wounded; 200 policemen had been murdered in the first six months of the year; in Medellín murders were reported at the rate of 32 a day in the first six months of the year, while throughout the country hundreds of civilians continued to die in mysterious and confused circumstances.

The first half of 1990, therefore, suggested that the Colombian government was still embattled, confronting a crisis of both legitimacy (the relationship of government and people) and authority (the challenge from the drugs mafia to its monopoly of violence and its institutional integrity). In the lead-up to the March 1990 elections for Senate and Congress, 73 activists of the UP were killed in 54 days. But, the second half of 1990 raised expectations that political shifts were taking place which would significantly alter the nature of the traditional Colombian political order.

The first sign of such shifts were the presidential elections of May. On the one hand they confirmed that very substantial sectors of the population remained deeply disillusioned with the political system. The abstention rate was one of the highest ever for a presidential election: 54 per cent of registered voters, 72 per cent of the eligible electorate. The climate in which they took place did not encourage faith in the process. At least two candidates spent the campaign holed up in secret underground bunkers, and it was fought mostly through the media. The Social-Conservative party candidate Rodrigo Lloreda, described it as "trying to conduct a love affair through letter writing".

Yet, amongst those who did bother to vote, the result reflected a number of surprising shifts. The most outstanding was the support for the **Democratic Alliance–M-19** (*Alianza Democŕatica*—AD–M-19), this alliance was dominated by the M-19 and included a number of other forces with a broadly speaking social-democratic perspective. The AD–M-19 won 12.5 per cent of the vote, not only the highest ever reached by a left-wing grouping, but the highest vote of any force outside the two traditional parties. They also defeated the official candidate of the Social-Conservative party, Rodrigo Lloreda. This party had split, and its right wing had formed the Movement of National Salvation with Alvaro Gómez Hurtado as presidential candidate. This movement had come second in the poll, showing that a substantial minority still favoured right-wing, authoritarian solutions to the country's problems.

But it was the centre-right candidate of the Liberal Party, César Gaviria Trujillo, who won the presidency, claiming to represent the reforming tradition of murdered candidate Luis Carlos Galán. His victory and the vote for the AD–M-19 suggested that substantial sectors of the middle-class, at least, were pushing seriously for institutional renovation and reform. This conclusion is supported by the vote in favour of calling a Constituent Assembly to discuss constitutional reform. The proposal was put to the electorate at the same time as the Presidential vote, and over 80 per cent of those voting, more than 5,000,000 people (about twice the number who had voted Gaviria into the presidency), supported it.

Gaviria prudently spent the best part of the three months before he officially took up office on Aug. 7 out of the country. On taking office, he boldly gave the leader of the AD–M-19, Antonio Navarro Wolf, the health portfolio. His government represented a generational shift in the political élite, with an average age between 40 and 45, and a move away from the old political "bosses" towards those with professional and technical experience.

The issue which dominated the first months of Gaviria's presidency was that of the Constituent Assembly which would have the task of drawing up a new constitution. The most organized sectors of the population were demanding an open Assembly with maximum representation of all sectors, including trade union and peasant organizations. The final composition of the Assembly was however determined by a negotiation between the major political groups, with the innovation that this now included the AD–M-19, not just the two traditional parties.

The agreement, reached in September, reduced the Assembly to 70 members and made all seats open to popular vote, rather than offering the popular organizations guaranteed seats as they had demanded. The Supreme Court after much debate, approved the Assembly but surprised everyone by maintaining that no issues should be excluded from discussion (the party agreement was to exclude the discussion of the armed forces or the question of extradition) and no pre-conditions on who could stand for election. The date of the election was set for Dec. 9, 1990, and the Assembly would convene in February 1991.

The election failed in the end to reverse the abstentionist trends, which reflected the deep disillusionment with the political system throughout Colombian society. Seventy-five per cent of registered voters abstained. The M-19 won 19 out of the 70 seats on offer, a very high number though not as high as some polls had predicted beforehand. A new political force had come onto the political scene to challenge the hegemony of the two traditional parties. But doubts remained as to whether it could bridge the yawning gap between state and civil society in contemporary Colombia.

Outline of economic development. Despite its turbulent political history, Colombia has been one of the more successful Latin American economies during the twentieth century, at least in terms of macro-economic statistics. This is partly due to the ability of the business sectors to distance themselves from the party political battles. The coffee sector for instance has operated as a more or less autonomous part of the economy in the hands of the National Federation of Coffee Growers (FEDECAFÉ). Other associations or *gremios* began to emerge in the 1940s to represent the interests of different sectors of the economy, almost all maintaining a bipartisan executive and deeply opposed to state intervention in the economy and ensuring considerable private sector influence over all aspects of economic policy-making.

Colombia embarked on a process of modernization and economic diversification in the years following the Party Pact of 1958. The World Bank-funded infrastructural programme facilitated the building of the Atlantic Railway between 1952 and 1961 cutting the journey from Bogotá to the coast from several days to 24 hours. This opened up previously inaccessible but fertile agricultural regions, such as the area round the middle Magdalena river, and stimulated commercial agriculture. Large-scale commercial farms expanded dramatically in the 1960s encouraged by government incentives, to meet the food needs of the growing population in the cities and to generate export earnings to finance industrial expansion. Sugar, cotton and rice production were soon producing exportable surpluses. Banana exports expanded in Uraba, while cut flowers found a favourable climate and a cheap, largely female labour force in the Bogotá savannah. By 1975, non-traditional agricultural exports made up 12 per cent of total exports.

By the late 1980s, Colombia was not only the second largest coffee exporter in the world, but also the second largest exporter of cut flowers, the fifth largest banana exporter, the third largest coal exporter, as well as the fourth largest oil exporter in Latin America.

Coffee provided less than 50 per cent of export earnings by 1980, compared to almost 79 per cent in the 1950–54 period. This is despite the fact that between the late 1950s and the first half of the 1980s, coffee production broadly doubled. This expansion of production was due to the arrival of modern methods and the introduction of the Brazilian *caturra* plant. This process of modernization was vigorously promoted by FEDECAFÉ. It enabled Colombia to regain its competitive position on the world market, particularly when in the mid-1970s, severe frosts affected the Brazilian crop. FEDECAFÉ reaped the benefits of the resulting bonanza in earnings, which controversially, the government refused to tax. The power of FEDECAFÉ is very great indeed. Through management of the Coffee Fund (originally set up to finance the witholding of coffee from the market when prices are low), income from coffee taxes, coffee exports and sales of coffee for domestic consumption, FEDECAFÉ has diversified its interests into finance, shipping, construction and other areas and is considered one of the biggest economic enterprises in the country. It has also funded development projects in the coffee-growing region, where health, education and service provision are noticeably higher and social unrest lower than in other parts of the country.

Industry grew at a high average rate of 8.5 per cent a year between 1967 and 1974 with continuing diversification favouring intermediate goods (textiles, wood, paper, rubber, chemicals), consumer durables and to a lesser extent capital goods. By 1968 three cities, Bogotá, Cali and Medellín, were responsible for over 68 per cent of national value added and over 60 per cent of industrial employment. By 1979, 65 per cent of foreign investment was also concentrated in this "golden triangle".

Industrial growth began to slow down in 1974 and between then and 1980 averaged 5.6 per cent a year. During this period Colombia's economy was liberalized and cheaper foreign goods allowed in to force greater efficiency on industry. Industrial exports which reached a peak of 46 per cent of total exports in 1974 began to decline with the partial ending of subsidies in 1975 and during the world recession of 1979 fell to 29 per cent of total exports. They were also hit by inflation and the distortion of the currency by the influx of dollars from the coffee bonanza and the illegal drugs trade.

Also, by the late 1970s, industrial firms had developed a fragile dependency on a financial system that had grown prodigiously and with insufficient regulation after interest rates were freed in 1974. Firms took on high-cost short-term loans and became dangerously indebted. When the recession hit they were unable to repay their loans creating a major crisis in the financial system in 1982. The state intervened to bail out the banks, taking over eight commercial banks representing 65 per cent of the system's capital. Import restriction and new export subsidies were introduced to help industry out of the recession. Industrial recovery was underway by 1984, with a period of sustained growth after 1986, though it did not match the high growth of the early 1970s.

The economic changes outlined had an immense social effect. Population movements had become intense during *La Violencia*, as people headed for the urban areas to escape the violence. Between 1951 and 1964, the urban population doubled. Economic modernization in the countryside fuelled further urban growth as small peasant farmers were forced off the land by the expansion of commercial estates. The urban population doubled again, from 9,000,000 to 19,000,000 people between 1964 and 1985 (census years) while the rural population grew by less than 10 per cent. This urban growth was not matched by increases in employment opportunities or the provision of fundamental services and housing. Although manufacturing industry overtook agriculture in terms of contribution to GDP, it had only created half a million jobs by 1985. By 1984, 56.6 per cent of employment in the urban areas was in the informal sector, which includes a wide range of activities, legal and illegal, but all unregulated by the state.

In the countryside, problems of landlessness and landhunger have generated much social unrest. As small peasant farmers have sought to colonize the remaining areas of the agricultural frontier, they have frequently come into conflict with large cattle ranchers intent on extending their grazing land. The state has failed to provide assistance to these peasant colonizers, either in the form of infrastructural support or credit to help their economic survival, or provide defence against the encroachment of the cattle ranchers.

Lack of job opportunities in the urban areas and the threatened collapse of the peasant economy in many rural areas, has fuelled Colombia's historically strong underground and criminal economy. Peasant colonizers for instance turned in the late 1970s to growing coca leaves, the basis of cocaine production, to ensure their survival and looked to the FARC guerillas for their protection against the state, the cocaine dealers and the cattle entrepreneurs. In the cities, cocaine became the basis of a flourishing underground economy during the 1980s.

During the mid to late 1970s, the Colombian cocaine traffickers came to control the most lucrative parts of the cocaine trade, the processing and distribution. They brought most of the raw material from Peru and Bolivia and processed it in laboratories in Colombia. The fortunes they have made are legendary. Between 1981 and 1988, net income accumulated from drug trafficking amounted to about US$14.2 billion. At the beginning of the 1980s, net income was estimated to be higher than 6 per cent of GDP, falling to about 2.5 per cent at the end of the decade, although that does not take into account the exports to Europe as opposed to the USA which could take the figure up to 3 or 3.5 per cent of GDP. A relatively small part of this has found its way back into Colombia. Two economists from the Colombian think tank, FEDESARROLLO, suggest that in 1988, for example, about US$800,000 to US$1,000,000 returned to Colombia, the rest remaining in foreign banks.

The cocaine mafia have spent their earnings on articles of conspicuous consumption: paintings, race horses, car imports, entertainment and especially real estate. They have also invested in land. Recent investigations (e.g. *Semana* Nov. 29–Dec. 5 and *Economía Colombiana*, Feb–March 1990) suggest that by the end of the 1980s they controlled about 4.3 per cent of productive land in the country, about 1,000,000 hectares of land. The lands are mostly dedicated to cattle ranching, using very advanced techniques involving high levels of capital investment. The degree to which the mafia have penetrated industry and banking is reputed to be considerable, though accurate information on this is not available.

Cocaine has had a considerable impact on the Colombian economy. At one level it has provided a huge number of jobs (an estimated 250,000 according to *Economía Colombiana*, Feb.–March 1990) and even social amenities in some of the poorest inner city areas. Its impact at the macroeconomic level is more controversial. The influx of dollars has helped the finance the external trade balance, but whether cocaine has really helped sustain the Colombian economy through the difficult years of the 1980s is a more complex issue. It has been noted that unlike most other Latin American countries, Colombia had had an uneven economic record in the 1980s, but avoided the crisis experienced by most of its neighbours. It has managed, for instance to continue servicing its external debt, which had reached US$16,500 million by 1988 and cost 7 per cent of GNP that year. But cocaine is only one factor in explaining the country's economic performance. Other factors include the fact that coffee prices fared rather better than other commodities in the 1980s, and enjoyed a bonanza in 1986. Another important factor is the role of Colombia's energy resources.

In 1980, Colombia's coal output stood at 4,000,000 tonnes, while by 1986 this had risen to 11,500,000 almost all the increase coming from the Atlantic coast, where a huge new mine, the El Cerrejón project, had begun to come on stream. Projections for 1990 indicate an output of 22,600,000 tonnes. Colombia is also thought to have other promising sites for large-scale coal production. Colombia also has extensive oil deposits, and in the 1980s became an oil exporter, producing 302,000 barrels a day by 1986 with production reaching 450,000 barrels during 1990. Considerable oil exploration is also underway in conjunction with foreign companies. The contracts signed with the companies have been very controversial, and the ELN has taken to blowing up oil pipelines to register its protests. Nevertheless, Colombia's future as an energy exporter is quite promising, and mining had replaced manufacturing as the major area of foreign investment by the end of the 1980s.

It was estimated that in 1990, oil exports would for the first time in the country's history generate more foreign exchange earnings than coffee, assisted by the rise in prices as a result ot the crisis in the Gulf. Coffee prices on the other hand, were very badly hit when the International Coffee Agreement collapsed in 1989. The losses from the collapse of the agreement were estimated at US$270,000,000 from September to December 1989.

Current economic situation. The political problems of the Barco government were mitigated by the country's healthy economic performance. GDP grew by 5.4 per cent in 1987 and was still relatively healthy in Latin American terms at 3.7

per cent in 1988 and an estimated 3.2 per cent in 1989. But problems were appearing in the last year of the administration which Gaviria would inherit. In particular, inflationary pressures grew during 1989, reaching 35 per cent for basic food items that year. Inflation had already reached 10.2 per cent in the first three months of 1990, and is expected to reach at least 30 per cent for the year as a whole.

President Gaviria made control of inflation a central objective of his new administration. In addition, he described four aspects of his economic policy: "modernization, internationalization, efficiency of the state and social transformation" (*El Tiempo*, Oct. 28, 1990). The policies have involved emphasis on international trade and competitiveness, trade liberalization, rapid reduction in public expenditure, the abolition of price subsidies and the continuation of a programme of privatization begun with the Barco administration. The programme has encountered strong popular opposition. Wage levels in real terms were estimated in September 1990 to be below their September 1984 level, while the rise in petrol prices and those of public services affected the poorer sectors of the population. Unemployment was also rising having fallen to single figures in the late 1980s, it was estimated to be back at 10 per cent by 1990.

Prospects for development. With its relatively diversified economy, wealth of natural resources, including huge potential reserves of coal, oil and natural gas, and history of sound economic management, Colombia remains one of the healthiest economies of Latin America. The country enjoys a strategic position as the gateway to South America, bordering on both the Pacific and the Atlantic. There is talk of building a canal to replace the Panama canal in the northern part of the country, while the Pacific coast is earmarked for major developments with considerable interest from the Japanese.

However, as with all the countries of Latin America, large numbers of people are excluded from the measured economy and there is little prospect that the pattern of economic development could provide jobs for more than a privileged few either in agriculture or industry. Social and political problems remain the greatest obstacle to development.

Of these, the drugs problem captures the headlines. Cocaine supplies continued to flow in 1990, despite the government offensive against the Medellín cartel. In one of his first acts in office, Gaviria retreated from Barco's extradition strategy, and on Sept. 5, 1990 promulgated Decree 2047 which allowed people accused of drug trafficking to turn themselves in, provide information on their accomplices and relinquish property earned illegally. The government in turn, offered immunity from extradition and a reduction by half of sentences imposed from Colombian courts.

The problem of violence also remained acute in 1990. The most notable government successes in this respect were the negotiations with the guerrilla movements. The M-19's reinsertion into the political arena, was followed by the opening of negotiations with other movements. Even the ELN, previously considered the most opposed to any deals with the government, began by the end of 1990 to express some willingness to enter into dialogue.

How far traditional members of the ruling élite will tolerate guerrillas-turned-politicians remains to be seen. The success of the AD–M-19 has greatly alarmed those who want to maintain the old, closed and exclusive political system, and the use of assassination against opposition figures is firmly entrenched in the political traditions of the Colombian right. As a result of such assasinations, the UP which had gradually become the leading left opposition movement of the latter half of the 1980s, was decimated and severely weakened politically. The ability of the AD–M-19 to attract the middle-class vote had by the end of 1990 turned it into a far greater threat to the traditional order than the UP had ever been, and a major test for the government policies of modernization would be the ability of its leaders to survive physically.

Human rights' violations remained another very serious problem. Evidence accumulated by international bodies was building up a strong picture of the involvement of official organs of the state in abuses. The government put much of the blame on the drugs mafia who were known to fund paramilitary groups. Barco took various measures to curb such groups during 1989 when it was apparent that they had grown extremely powerful, particularly in certain regions of great social conflict. He also promoted legislation to prevent the army from arming civilians and creating self-defence groups which many believed provided personnel for the paramilitary.

But the groups continued to operate in 1990, even when the drug barons associated with them had been forced on the run or in the case of Rodríguez Gacha, killed by the security forces. In January 1990, for instance, 42 peasants were kidnapped in Uraba by a 52-man paramilitary group. The peasants were taken in two trucks, accompanied by an estimated 30 armed men, according to a subsequent official investigation, through the roads of a heavily militarized area, patrolled by the Voltigeros Batallion based in Uraba. The 42 peasants were taken to the ranch of Fidel Castano, a landowner closely associated with paramilitary violence, where they were tortured and killed. Details of the massacre were provided by a deserter, and some of the bodies recovered in mass graves at two of Castano's ranches.

The failure to bring to justice members of the military implicated in human rights' crimes has been roundly condemned by human rights' organizations. The impunity with which the armed forces operate has undermined respect for the country's institutions and limits the effects of efforts to modernize the state and legitimize government. Another urgent task of government, is to restore the credibility of the legal system as a whole. Five judges were killed in 1988 and 12 in 1989, as well as many other members of the legal profession. The inability of the government to guarantee the safety of justice officials—judges, prosecutors, investigators—is just one of the critical issues facing any attempt to create respect for law and order in the country. The prospects for Colombia's future political stability, will rest on the capacity of the state to resolve some of these basic problems of the relationship of state to civil society.

JP

COLORADO PARTY— NATIONAL REPUBLICAN ASSOCIATION (Asociación Nacional Republicana—Partido Colorado, ANR—PC) (Paraguay). The Paraguayan Colorado Party was organized in 1874 by General Bernardino Caballero, who dominated politics behind the scenes for the next 40 years. It takes its name from the red ties traditionally worn by its supporters. In opposition 1904–40, the Colorados regained a footing in government under the dictatorship of General Higinio Morínigo (1940–48), and gained control of the Army after the unsuccessful Liberal–Febrerista revolt of 1947, when their militia, the *Py-nandu*, hunted down political opponents. In 1948 and 1953 the sole candidate for the Presidency was the Colorado nominee, and under **General Gustavo Stroessner** the party consolidated its position as the sole party of government. In 1967 the dissident populist wing of the party, the Popular Colorado Movement (Movimiento Popular Colorado—MOPOCO) went into opposition and was banned, and the now unified party, reorganized on a hierarchical basis, became the main vehicle for mobilizing political support for the regime, where necessary with the use of force. A constitutional amendment ensured it a permanent majority status in Congress, and party membership became compulsory for all civil servants and members of the armed forces. In 1985 its so-called "ethical" faction however allied itself with the opposition **Authentic Liberal Radical Party**.

PARC

COLORADO PARTY (Partido Colorado—PC) (Uruguay). The Colorado Party of Uruguay was originally the party of the middle-class liberals and followers of José Artigas who supported the country's first President, General José Fructuoso Rivera against General Manuel Oribe (1835–51). Returning to power with Brazilian support in 1865, it consolidated its position and has dominated Uruguayan politics in the twentieth century. It controlled government until 1958 when under the unique Consejo National de Administración the **National Party** finally won the elections after 93 years in opposition. With the restoration of the Presidency in March 1967 the Colorado Party returned to power with a majority of 100,000 votes and ruled until President Bordaberry effectively handed over power to the armed forces (1973). A Colorado President, Julio María Sanguinetti, was again elected in 1984, though with less than a third of the votes cast, and the National Party, under **Luis Alberto Lacalle Herrera**, won the 1989 elections that marked the real restoration of democracy. It is too soon, as yet, to say whether Colorado dominance has been broken in the post-military period.

Although the mass parties of Uruguayan politics have not been clearly tied to different social classes, Colorado support has traditionally come from the poorer and more urban sections of the population. Its vote has been strongest in the south-east, the north and the west. Under the leadership of **José Batlle y Ordóñez**, at the beginning of the century, the Colorado Party became associated with social reform. Policies included advanced social welfare programmes, the *colegiado* system of government and proportional representation.

Internal divisions based on personalities as well as policies are reflected in shifting factions within the party. These "sub-lemas" are associated with different lists at election times, which support different presidential candidates, e.g. that of Luis Batlle and his son Jorge (List 15) and of the Batlle Pacheco brothers and the late General Oscar Gestido (List 14), which has been reformed constantly in recent years. Some have inspiring names invoking political virtues such as loyalty and unity, but all claim to be "Batllista".

SAC

COMMITTEE FOR INDEPENDENT ELECTIONS (Comité Pro-Elecciones Independientes—COPEI) (Venezuela). Venezuela's alternative party of government, COPEI, was first registered under the electoral law of 1946 as the *Comité de Organización Política Electoral Independiente.* A Christian Socialist party, its economic position is close to that of the AD and it is no less nationalistic, but it emphasizes the dignity of the individual, the social function of property and the need for mutual harmony between Church and State.

It is affiliated to the Christian Democratic international and its labour confederation is affiliated to the *Confederación Latino-Americana de los Sindicatos Cristianos* (CLASC).

COPEI secured between 13.2 per cent and 21.1 per cent of the poll in the three elections of the Provisional Government of 1945–48, but its real rise to power began when it entered into coalition with **Democratic Action** in 1959. It was first successful under its founder Rafael Caldera in 1968, but the second COPEI President, Dr Luis Herrera Campins (1979–84), had the misfortune to lead Venezuela into the debt crisis and the party was unsuccessful in regaining its position in the 1988 elections, though it remains the major opposition party.

PARC

COMMUNISM. The crisis of communism was abundantly evident in Latin America and the Caribbean well before the announcement of *perestroika* in the Soviet Union and the collapse of communist regimes in Eastern Europe. It was seen in the failure of the Communist-endorsed "Chilean Road to Socialism" in 1970–73, in the movement's growing fragmentation and, in several countries, in the rise of new left-wing forces whose successes in political or trade union elections, or in the process of armed struggle, challenged the traditional communist party pretension to the role of revolutionary vanguard.

Diversification within the communist movement was catalyzed by the **Cuban Revolution** of 1959. While some communists reacted against the heterodoxy of the Cuban "model", others tried to incorporate "lessons" learnt from this triumph into their own strategies and tactics. Communist responses to the revolutions in **Grenada** and **Nicaragua** some 20 years later were more broadly sympathetic, although once again they defied traditional communist assumptions about revolution. It was the crisis of these revolutions, rather than the original triumph, that proved divisive. The "implosion" of Grenada's New Jewel revolution in October 1983 and the electoral defeat of the Sandinistas in the Nicaraguan election of February 1990 sowed tremendous self-doubt within the movement. Coming on top of the experience of harsh military rule in much of Latin America, these setbacks led many communists to advocate party renewal. Ironically, the main rallying point for the orthodox Marxist–Leninists was now that heretic of the 1960s: **Fidel Castro's** Cuba.

For some time after the Cuban revolution, it was legitimate to consider as part of the communist movement not only the parties descendant from the Comintern and their Trotskyist, Maoist, pro-Chinese and pro-Albanian offshoots, but also some Caribbean New Left groups and a number of revolutionary nationalist forces, whose genesis owed considerably, though by no means exclusively, to Castro's triumph in Cuba. Despite some fundamental differences over strategy, tactics, alliances and even ideology, these sectors were joined by a common commitment to Leninist vanguardism and democratic centralism, the espousal of socialist economic principles and an admiration for communist regimes.

Although historically communism has been the most internationalist of the political movements in the region, it is important to recognize the part played by regional and national influences in the recent diversification of the movement. Since communist polycentrism became a reality, the strongest international influences have been intra-regional, with Cuba, Grenada and Nicaragua having a greater impact than Vietnam. Moreover, there has been widespread national adaptation as communists have sought to acquire legitimacy through the invocation of nationalist heroes such as José Martí, Manuel Rodríguez, Francisco Morazán, **Simón Bolívar** and Augusto Sandino, or through support for nationalist political forces, as on occasion in Panama, Mexico and Argentina. The exploitation of national myths and symbols by many communist parties had evident instrumental motives, and was not just the result of communist acculturation. Nonetheless, it should not be construed as a mere subterfuge: although changes of party image and support for broad alliances are nothing new in the communist world, in the past they were the product of an international party line, whereas in more recent years they have been a response to national political exigencies and regional influences.

During the 1980s communist activitists were disappointed by the limited achievements of armed struggle and the collapse of broad communist-backed political alliances. At the start of the decade, guerrilla warfare had a compelling attraction for many communist party members, who did not want to be left on the sidelines, as their colleagues had been in the Cuban and Nicaraguan revolutions. In **El Salvador** and **Guatemala**, guerrilla veterans now headed organizations that enjoyed much stronger support then the orthodox communist parties. Hoping to retain some mass influence, communists both there and in **Honduras** belatedly joined their former rivals by engaging in armed struggle and by joining umbrella organizations in a subordinate capacity. The most effective of these co-ordinating bodies was the **Farabundo Martí National Liberation Front (FMLN)** in El Salvador, within which the communists constituted the fourth largest force out of five. The Chilean Communists also revised their attitude to armed struggle. Their policy of "armed popular rebellion" was the result of various factors: the failure of the left's broad front reformist approach in 1970–73, **Pinochet's** efforts to institutionalize and thereby prolong his military regime, the Christian Democrats' determination to exclude the Communist Party from a new opposition alliance, and the pressures for a more aggressive line emanating from the party's younger clandestine militants, including some shanty town activists.

By the mid-1980s, however, the insurgent movements in Central America could see that an insurrectional triumph as in Nicaragua was out of the question, given the level of US response, the effects of repression on the left, and the war-weariness of the civilian population. Increasingly, armed struggle was used by guerrillas in Central America and **Colombia**, no longer as a means to attain the "final victory" but as a means of securing concessions at the negotiating table. In Colombia, where the earliest peace settlements were reached between the government and sectors of the guerrilla movement, allowing ex-guerrillas to participate in the political system, the communist party became deeply divided over whether on not to suspend the armed struggle. The advantages of constitutional activity were counterbalanced by the hazards of participation as left-wing militants were targeted by right-wing death squads. Between 1984 and 1990, more than 1,000 supporters of the communist-backed Patriotic Union (UP) were assassinated, among them successive UP presidential candidates Jaime Pardo Leal and Bernardo Jaramillo. Divisions over the use of violence (and whether to unite with the Socialist Party) also became pronounced in **Chile**, where a majority of communists opted for a return to peaceful methods when civilian rule was restored in March 1990, but a minority persisted with violence, fearing that the democratic transformation would prove more apparent than real.

The only communist party to engage in armed struggle with any success has been **Sendero Luminoso**, an offshoot from the Maoist wing of Peruvian communism which sees itself as *the* Peruvian Communist Party and not a mere guerrilla movement. During the 1980s *Sendero's* influence spread from southern **Peru** along the Andean highlands to reach the principal area of coca cultivation, where pragmatic deals were struck with drug-traffickers, who received "protection" from the guerrillas in return for payments. From 1984 *Sendero* became increasingly active in Lima, and attempts to repress the movement had little success. However, even *Sendero* was exhibiting signs of crisis by 1990. Although the guerrilla movement had grown numerically and expanded geographically, its development had not gone according to the Maoist scenario of rural insurgency leading to the creation of a people's army in the countryside: indeed some peasant communities were turning against *Sendero* in reaction to its ruthless use of violence, while recruitment to the organization was strongest in the cities. This gave rise to a divisive discussion about whether *Sendero* should redirect its original strategy or devise a new one based upon its urban strength.

Communist experimentation in the 1980s also took the form of participation in broad left political alliances which included the far left. Maoists and pro-Soviet communists engaged in joint trade union campaigns in Honduras, but their rivalry hampered the formation of electoral alliances in **Ecuador**. In Peru, **Mexico** and **Argentina**, shared left-wing sympathies for Cuba helped to overcome the traditional antagonism between orthodox Communists and Trotskyists. A realignment of left-wing forces occurred in each of these countries, giving rise to new electoral alliances. Through them, communists were able to overcome their isolation, but again they often had to accept a subordinate role for themselves. Where they were able to lead such as alliance, in Argentina, the electoral performance was much more disappointing.

The most influential broad alliance was the "United Left" (IU) coalition in Peru. The official Peruvian Communist Party for a while exercised considerable influence within IU, due to its pivotal position between reformist and revolutionary groups therein, but in 1989 the balancing act became impossible and in 1990 the division of the alliance proved electorally disastrous. IU's share of the national vote fell from 21.3 per cent in 1985 to 6.9 per cent in 1990. None the less, IU's earlier electoral success, both parliamentary and municipal, encouraged attempts to form new left-wing alliances with communist involvement in **Bolivia** and Chile during the 1980s. In Bolivia, communists took part in electoral lists headed by the New Left in the shape of the Free Bolivia Movement, with only local success. In Mexico communist subordination went much further: after taking part in the creation of the Mexican Socialist Party, the communists quickly dissolved their new party into the national left Party of the Democratic Revolution (PRD), formed in 1989 by **Cuauhtémoc Cárdenas**, a populist and nationalist leader who had broken with the ruling **Institutional Revolutionary Party (PRI)**.

Virtually all of the communist parties of the region saw their unity undermined in the 1980s by disputes over reform or revolution, their choice of allies or relations with them, or the question of political violence. In the meantime, in many countries they saw their traditional social base decline — not, as in Western Europe, as a result of economic growth, but rather due to the collapse of industries amidst the region's economic decline. Communist forces were weakened by the numerical decline of national working classes and/or the ineffectiveness of trade unionism in conditions of high unemployment. Here, they suffered from their traditional "economism" and their future prospects are poor unless they manage to find ways of appealing to new social sectors and can intervene more effectively in new social movements.

With the exception of Cuba, communism has been far less of a mass phenomenon in the Caribbean than in continental Latin America. Institutionally it is far more tenuous in the anglophone and francophone Caribbean, its popularity often depending on partial trade union successes or the personal prestige of a leading intellectual, such as Trevor Munroe in **Jamaica** or Tim Hector in **Antigua**. The disastrous *dénouement* of the Grenadian revolution in 1983 undermined the electoral standing of the Caribbean left in general, and led many communist groups to re-examine old ideas and jettison some of them. On the one hand, there had been the spectacle of the hardline Stalinist faction led by Bernard Coard using the "People's Revolutionary Army" to fire on the people and to execute the popular Prime Minister, **Maurice Bishop**; on the other hand, the whole Grenadian experience had shown the impossibility of introducing "socialism in one island", especially so near to the USA.

In Grenada itself, the Coard faction's opponents created the Maurice Bishop Patriotic Movement in 1984 and gradually regained ground by becoming more moderate. They showed a greater readiness to collaborate with reformist sectors and they adopted a charismatic young leader when they chose Terrence Marryshow in 1988. Meanwhile, in **Guyana, Cheddi Jagan**'s **People's Progressive Party** adopted a much more pragmatic course in the aftermath of the Grenadian invasion; the party announced that it would not establish a communist regime if it were elected to office, and it even seemed interested in forming part of a national government. There was also a move to the right in response to left-wing unpopularity in **Dominica**, where the Dominica Liberation Movement Alliance united with centre-left parties to form the Labour Party of Dominica in time for the 1985 election. Even Munroe's Workers' Party of Jamaica, which had advised the Stalinist faction of the New Jewel Movement in the run-up to the Grenada crisis, and lost much support when this became known, abandoned some old concepts and claimed to be undergoing a patriotic and democratic transformation. Behind these signs of moderation were fears about the US reaction if the left were to gain power in the future, but also the response of orthodox communists to the Gorbachev revolution in the USSR, and a desire not to become isolated as **Michael Manley's People's National Party** moved from a left-wing position to the centre.

A shift to moderation in response to defeat was also seen in **Brazil**. Both in Brazil and in **Uruguay**, mainstream communists emphasized the need to consolidate new democratic regimes after years of military rule. Not only had the **Brazilian Communist Party** (*Partido Comunista Brasileiro*—PCB) suffered from two decades of military rule at home, it also reacted with circumspection to the 1973 defeat in Chile, where a number of Brazilian communists had resided as political exiles. Extreme moderation, almost to the point of losing its communist identity, helped the Brazilian party to recover its legal status in 1985, but left a political opening for the emergence of new left-wing rivals, chiefly the electorally much more successful **Workers' Party** (*Partido dos Trabalhadores*—PT).

Another dimension to the crisis of communism in the region has been the existence of policy differences between Marxist regimes. Cuban–Soviet differences came to light in 1983, both during the Grenada crisis, when Cuba supported Maurice Bishop while the Soviet leadership backed the usurping Coard faction, and in the course of a communist party split in **Costa Rica**, when again the more moderate faction was supported by the Cubans while the hardliners were backed by the (pre-Gorbachev) Soviet party.

Five years later, there was tension between the Cuban leadership and the Sandinistas. The Cubans deeply disapproved of the Nicaraguan response to the economic calamity resulting from the contra war: the austerity measures announced by the Sandinistas in 1988, and the Nicaraguan plans to strengthen the role of the market and attract foreign capital, were denounced by Fidel Castro as the "most right-wing" economic policies in Central America. While the Sandinistas supported the Gorbachev reforms in the Soviet Union and the changes in Eastern Europe, the Cuban leadership was moving in the opposite direction. Cuba had experimented with peasant markets earlier in the 1980s, but in 1986 had embarked upon a campaign of "rectification" of such "errors"; the latter were said to have given rise to social tensions, and there were government fears about the possible emergence of a conservative class of *kulaks*. Meanwhile, there was a clear contradiction between the one-party state in Cuba and the existence of pluralism and competitive elections in Nicaragua, institutionalized through the Constitution of 1987.

These divisions were deeply disorientating for Latin American and Caribbean revolutionaries who years earlier had been swept along by *fidelista* rhetoric about Cuba, Nicaragua and Grenada standing as three beacons, illuminating the way forward to victory for other left-wing movements.

Although the Cuban regime saw out the decade, and rallied the regional opponents of *perestroika*, its image was much tarnished by the purges of military and government personnel in mid-1989 and particularly the execution of former Angolan war hero, General Arnaldo Ochoa, who was accused of involvement in the drug trade. By refusing to strip Ochoa of the honours that the Nicaraguan state had bestowed upon him, the Sandinistas indicated that they did not believe the official allegations made against the victims. Some observers saw the events as an attempt by Castro to improve Cuba's relations with the USA by cracking down on drug-trafficking; others believed that Castro had acted to eliminate a faction that has its own plans for the leadership succession.

Although communist opinion was divided over Cuba's retrenchment, by 1990 it was difficult for the Cuban regime to continue serving as an ideal "model" for left-wing movements abroad. The cutting of Soviet subsidies to the Cuban economy, which had been worth approximately one-quarter of the island's GDP, brought a severe reduction in Cuban living standards and a threat to the revolution's twin flagships: the health and educational services. It was in these circumstances that Cuban soldiers were returning from Angola, expecting to be treated like war heroes.

Thus, by 1990 the regional communist movement was severely fractured and ideologically disorientated. The Mexican communist party had disbanded itself and tendencies within most other parties favoured either a profound renovation of their existing organization or an ending of the historical socialist–communist divide. In Nicaragua, there were proposals to seek entry of the Sandinista Front into the Socialist International, while in the Brazilian and Chilean communist parties there was a growing fascination with developments in the Italian Communist Party (PCI), which was changing its name and engaging in a fruitful dialogue with the German Social Democratic Party (SPD). Whatever the future of Cuba, it seemed clear that most communist forces in Latin America and the Caribbean faced the prospect of declining electoral and industrial influence in the 1990s. The key to survival seemed to lie in tactical and organizational adaptation to new circumstance, and ideological renewal, but whether either of these processes might lead to anything that was recognizably "communist" was open to doubt.

RHCG

CONFEDERATION OF MEXICAN WORKERS (Confederación de Trabajadores de México—CTM). The Confederation of Mexican Labour is not the only officially recognized labour confederation in Mexico. There are also the Regional Confederation of Mexican Workers (*Confederación Regional de Obrera Mexicana* — CROM) and the Revolutionary Confederation of Workers and Farmers (*Confederación Revolucionaria de Obreros y Compesinos* — CROC). All three are formally integrated into the over-arching Congress of Labour (*Congreso del Trabajo* — CT). However in terms of practical politics the CTM is by far the most powerful labour confederation in Mexico.

The power of the CTM is based on its political rather than its labour role. Many of its workers are organized in factories and industries where organized labour is not especially powerful. However since the Ministry of Labour has extensive rights to arbitrate labour disputes, industrial muscle is of far less importance that political contacts. The CTM is an affiliate of the ruling **Institutional Revolutionary Party** (*Partido de la Revolución Institucional*—PRI) and can exercise considerable influence in party matters as well as governmental ones.

The head of the CTM, Fidel Velázquez, was born in 1900. He played an active role in setting up the CTM in 1936 and took it over in 1947 following the resignation of Vicente Lombardo Toledano. Velázquez showed little or no sympathy with radical Left-wing politics, and was often accused by his critics of total conformism. Such an accusation, however, greatly distorts Velázquez' real role. He in fact turned the CTM into a patronage machine which offered extensive o portunities for social mobility to workers who showed loyalty to the party and the system. Moreover the advent of increasingly competitive party politics has changed the character of his political role. In the past he served as a bulwark against the Marxist Left; now PRI candidates who were nominated by the CTM are vulnerable to election defeat, but nevertheless the PRI itself would be even more vulnerable without the backing of the CTM. Velázquez has used his influence to slow down, without being able to prevent, the gradual liberalization of both Mexican politics and the Mexican economy since 1982.

It is presently almost impossible to assess the influence of the CTM separately from the role played by Velázquez himself. Velazquez' demise has been anticipated many times, but he remains obstinately in control. It seems fairly clear, however, that the influence of the CTM is in slow decline and this decline may accelerate when Velázquez is no longer on the scene.

GP

CONFERENCE OF LATIN AMERICAN BISHOPS (Conferencia del Episcopado Latinoamericano—CELAM). The Conference of Latin American Bishops draws together all the bishops from each national episcopate. It has held three General Conferences with the fourth Conference to be held in Santo Domingo in 1992. The first Conference was held in 1955 in Rio de Janeiro, but the critical Conference which formalized and indeed extended the findings of Vatican II was the second, held in Medellín, Colombia in 1968, in the presence of Pope Paul VI. CELAM II has been described as "the most significant event in the history of the Latin American Church and perhaps in the continent as a whole during the twentieth century". Not only did the Conference conclude with the preferential option for the poor as defining its mission, but initiated a new sense of purpose, regeneration and determination in the Latin American Church to deal with the growing immiseration of the regional population. It also established a degree of dynamic autonomy from Rome and proved to be the only organization capable of unifying Latin America. Although the theological and practical advances made after CELAM II were confirmed at CELAM III held in Puebla in Mexico in 1979 they were partially rendered ineffective and implementation was generally less enthusiastically implemented steps as the conservatism of the Vatican took hold. Nevertheless CELAM II continues to be the single greatest influence on the **Church** today.

JCJS

CONSTITUTION (Brazil). The Brazilian Constitution of October 1988 was generally seen by those who produced it as the final stage in freeing the country from the repressive powers accumulated by the régime in the years of military-backed governments since 1964. Members of the Constitutent Assembly, elected in November 1986, were particularly sensitive to the need for this, since one of the persistent problems in the period of civilian politics, from 1945 to 1964, was that the Constitution of 1946 had introduced a range of liberal measures, but had left the social and labour legislation of the Estado Novo and its Constitution virtually intact.

The new Constitution took up some of the themes which went back as far as the Constitution of 1824, such as the power to be given to the central government. The 1824 document had been much influenced by the Swiss French constitutional theorist, Henri Benjamin Constant de Rebecque. It emphasized strong central control, mostly through the Emperor. He was to have a special "moderating power", distinct from the legislative, executive and judicial, giving him a watching brief over all other branches of government, as "supreme head of the nation and its first representative".

With the start of the Republic in 1889, the pendulum swung the other way, so that the Constitution of 1891 gave considerable authority to the states, not only in fiscal matters, but in allowing the existence of state armed forces, which often were better trained and more effective than the federal army garrisons. In matters of taxation, the states under the "Old Republic" had more jurisdiction than their equivalents in the USA. After the revolution of 1930, the move towards creating a stronger central state was reflected in the Constitution of 1934 which greatly increased the powers of the federal government, with much enlarged responsibilities for social and economic policies. There was, at the same time, an attempt to limit the powers of the president, by comparison with the Constitution of 1891, and to reduce the influence of the major states, by providing federal deputies for every 130,000 inhabitants, but only one for every 250,000 after a total of 20 deputies from any one state.

The 1934 Constitution remained largely untested in practice, being overtaken by events and replaced by the Constitution of the *Estado Novo*, which was mainly the work of the *mineiro* right-wing politician, Francisco Campos who, much later, was also to provide the prologue and some of the articles for the first Institutional Act after the *coup* of 1964. The *Estado Novo* Constitution greatly strengthened the powers of the president. He would decide when indirect elections for a national assembly should be held. He would choose one of the two candidates for election to the presidency, the other being chosen by an electoral college. The Constitution enshrined the corporatist principles underlying the *Estado Novo*, explicitly forbidding strikes and lockouts, with only those trade unions which were recognized by the state being allowed to represent the interests of their members. Strikes were defined as being anti-social, part of that "class struggle" which the preamble to the Constitution explicitly rejected.

The persistence of corporatist social and labour legislation in the otherwise liberal Constitution of 1946 bedevilled national politics throughout the post-war period. This liberal document was then further rejected in the Constitution of 1967, introduced under the Castello Branco government. This was largely seen by the régime as bringing to an end the "first phase of the Revolution". It essentially pulled together the Institutional and Complementary Acts introduced since 1964. The great increase in the power of the central government was partly reflected in the change in the name of the country, from the United States of Brazil to the Federative Republic of Brazil.

The central government was especially strengthened in the field of economic planning, with powers to intervene in states which did not follow the directives of economic planning. The document also confirmed the enlarged powers of the executive in relation to Congress, and the authority of the military courts to try civilians in matters affecting national security.

By the time the Constituent Assembly met in 1987, the repressive powers of the "national security" state had been strengthened even further, notably through the notorious Institutional Act No 5 of December 1968, and the other powers associated with it. In the broad processs of redemocratization and transition, the role of the Constituent Assembly was seen to be crucial, even though many people regretted that, as a result of a secret agreement between **Tancredo Neves** and the leaders of the **armed forces**, it was not to be elected independently, but was to be the elected Congress of 1986, also acting as the Constituent Assembly. Despite these reservations and despite the pressures which **José Sarney** and others brought to bear, the Constitution of 1988 was generally seen as positive and enlightened. Its general provisions were that, within the Federative Republic of Brazil, the president should be elected for a term of five years. He should choose a cabinet of which he would be head, and in which he would have considerable residual powers. There was to be a two-chamber Congress, with a Senate, with 75 seats, made up of representatives of the 26 states, plus the federal district of **Brasília**. The Chamber of Deputies would have 490 members, directly elected.

Each of the 26 states and the federal district of Brasília was to have its own legislature and administration, and each state its own judicial system. There was also to be a system of courts to deal with disputes between states and with matters in which state courts were not competent.

The president remained strong, but there was a shift of power towards the legislature, with an end to decree laws. There were guarantees of extensive civil and human rights, including more adequate legal protection for women and minors, and minorities, including Brazil's indigenous population. The rights of workers, both urban and rural, were extended, including the trade unions' rights to organize, operate and strike.

There was now to be greater devolution of tax revenues to states and *municípios*. The fiercely debated economic sections restricted the definition of a company of national capital, imposed restrictions on mining operations, with provisions for foreign-owned companies to adjust to changing circumstances, and forbade new risk contracts for hydrocarbon exploration, though existing contracts might continue. These provisions were among those most criticized from the political right and from abroad.

The voting age was reduced to 16, with illiterates allowed to vote. Sarney's term was to end on March 15, 1990 with direct presidential elections, in two rounds, if no candidate won a majority in the first. The new presidential terms would be five years, ending on Jan. 1, with elections to be held 90 days before. Constitutional amendments would need 60 per cent of the vote in both houses of Congress, but there was provision for a plebiscite, in September 1993, to decide on the system of government, with a review of the Constitution, on the basis of amendment by an absolute majority of members of Congress in joint session.

One of the more controversial sections was that which still left extensive powers to the armed forces. They could only intervene as guardians of the civil law, at the request of one of the three constitutional powers, the president, Congress or judiciary; but their constitutional role, in other respects, reflected the effectiveness of the military lobby in the Constituent Assembly. Despite some concern over such provisions in the

Constitution, and deep anger over the way in which certain sections, such as those on agrarian reform, had been emasculated, there was general agreement that Brazil now had a constitution which would allow it to move more easily into its new phase of democratic government, with provision for important social and economic reforms. The next step was to ensure that these should be implemented.

PF

CONSTITUTION (Mexico). Mexico is still governed in theory by the Constitution of 1917, which has distinct similarities to the Constitution of 1857. The Constitution has been amended on many occasions since 1917. Between 1917 and 1984 the Constitution was amended no fewer than 369 times. However in order to change the Constitution, a two-thirds majority of Congress is necessary; at present the ruling **PRI** enjoys only a 60–40 majority in the Chamber of Deputies.

Although frequently referred to, however, the Constitution has a symbolic more than a practical legal importance. Mexico has no tradition of judicial review, and it is the President who has the final say on all important matters. Presidents themselves sometimes break the law, and cannot readily be called to account. Nevertheless the symbolism is itself important, and has given underpinning to many of the policy directions of governments since 1920, although Mexico's rulers have, since around 1982, been largely out of sympathy with some of the socialist and social democratic aspirations outlined in the Constitution. Nevertheless governments have rarely if ever directly challenged these aspirations, but have merely sidelined them. To take just one example, each of Mexico's 31 states is in theory autonomous but in practice the federal government has no difficulty whatever in controlling them, which it does covertly through the exercise of patronage.

GP

CO-ORDINATING COMMITTEE OF AGRICULTURAL, COMMERCIAL, INDUSTRIAL AND FINANCIAL ASSOCIATIONS (Comite Co-ordinador de Asociaciones Agrícolas, Comerciales, Industriales y Financieras — CACIF) (Guatemala). Established in 1957, the Chamber of Agriculture, Commerce, Industry and Finance in Guatemala was established to represent the interests of a broad range of economic actors. It acted more effectively to push the interests of "modernizing" capitalism than the Asociación Guatemalteca de Agricultores (AGA) and the Cámara de Comercio (CC). In particular, CACIF furthered the diversification of the economic base of Guatemala during the period of the **Central American Common Market (CACM)**. The Common Market served Guatemala most effectively of the Central American economies since its relatively larger manufacturing and processing base was able to exploit the lifting of barriers to intra-CACM trade and the development, however half-heartedly, of import substituting industrialization. CACIF's long-term importance has lain in the co-ordination of a constituency of non-traditional entrepreneurs who have been able to identify new markets. Firmly committed to *laissez-faire* capitalism CACIF has resented encroachments and abuse of institutional privilege by the army in significant growth areas of the economy which the urban-based bourgeoisie would otherwise be able to exploit. Implicit opposition to the army has meant that CACIF has tended to support the Guatemalan Christian Democratic Party (*Democracia Cristiana Guatemalteca* — DCG). CACIF is not, however, a homogenous and unified association and this is most clearly identified by divisions over the degree of committment to land reform and more particularly over tax structures which favour or harm the alliance of local with multinational capital. CACIF has benefited from the years of DCG rule and is likely to continue to back the party.

JS

COSTA RICA. *Population*: 2,600,000. *Area*: 51,000 sq km. *GDP*: US$4,310 million (1987). *Expenditure as percentage of central government spending*: defence 2.2; education 16.2; health 19.3. *Merchandise exports*: $1,155 million (1987). *Merchandise imports*: $1,377 million (1987). *Debt service as percentage of goods and services exported*: 12.1. *Urban population as percentage of total*: 45. *Life expectancy*: 71 (men); 76 (women). *Infant mortality*: 18 per 1,000.

Geographical background. Costa Rica lies between Nicaragua in the north and Panama in the south and has both Pacific and Caribbean litorals. In common with its neighbours the Caribbean coast is characterized by low lying and humid mangrove. The central *cordillera* continues the isthmian spine from its neighbours and the slopes of the mountains have provided a fertile and temperate climate ideal for the cultivation of coffee which has been the mainstay of the Costa Rican economy for a century and a quarter.

Outline of political history. Unlike the neighbouring republics, Costa Rica's conservative–liberal conflicts were not settled by the 1870s, but continued through to the first decade of this century. A firm constitution had been created in 1871 however, and despite the *coup* of 1917 was resilient enough to last until the Second Republic was declared following the brief civil war of March–December 1948, and a new constitutional settlement arrived at in November 1949. The more open political arrangements of the 1930s Costa Rica had allowed the growth of a relatively strong labour movement, particularly the Workers' and Peasant's Bloc, which was reformist in character and allied with Rafael Angel Calderón Guardia's National Republican Party (*Partido Republicano Nacional*—PRN) to support an innovative and progressive legislative programme of social welfare and labour protection. While underlying economic power was not threatened by such programmes a split in the PRN and the rise of José Figueres Ferrer's Social Democratic Party (*Partido Social Democrático*—PSD) led to the contest of the results of the February 1948 elections and the outbreak of civil war.

Figueres' war-making and peace-making capacities allowed his control of the *interregnum* period of 1949–1953 to set the terms of the second Republic and the hegemony of the reconstituted PSD, now the **National Liberation Party** (*Partido de Liberacíon Nacional*—PLN), for the next 37 years (between 1953 and 1990 PLN candidates were elected to the presidency for all but 12 of those years, and controlled the Congress for all but four years).

Throughout the PLN administration of Oscar Arias Sánchez (1986–1990) the president was heavily committed to the resolution of the regional conflicts, particularly of those in Nicaragua and El Salvador. Arias became the architect of a regional peace plan whose principal elements were the cessation of hostilities, cancelling aid to insurgents and the negotiated return to constitutional rule, which was supported and signed by the Contadora Group (Panama, Mexico, Venezuela, Colombia) and the Lima Group (Argentina, Brazil, Peru, Uruguay) in August 1987 and approved by the UN General Assembly in October 1987. This initiative has come to form the basis of United Nations ONUCA monitoring of the peace process in the region, whose units have already been deployed.

Current developments—political. The domination of the PLN was again broken during the February 1990 presidential and Congressional elections (both held every four years, the latter being a unicameral legislative assembly of 57 seats) in which the **Social Christian Unity Party** (Partido de Unidad Social Cristiana—PUSC) won 29 seats and its candidate, Rafael Angel Calderón Fournier (the son of the president of the 1942–44 period) was elected president on 51 per cent of votes cast. The margin over the PLN is nevertheless slight, with Carlos Manuel Castillo gaining 47 per cent of the vote and the PLN securing 25 seats in the Congress.

Outline of economic development. The stability of the post-civil war period, established largely through the extensive welfare programme and the abolition of the armed forces, began to be jeopardized during the 1980s largely as a consequence of falling terms of trade and its continued reliance upon coffee and bananas as primary foreign exchange earners. Throughout the post-1948 period Costa Rica possessed the smallest industrial base of the region but the highest level of public employment and greatest provision of public services. In so far as exchange earnings could support such programmes the development model was strong. But in the 1980s public debt which had enabled the expansion of the public sector combined with depressed agro-export prices brought Costa Rica into crisis (long term public debt was valued at 95.9 per cent of GNP in 1987). Devaluations of the *colón* from December 1980 (until then it was tied to the dollar at C8.60) became a constant feature during the 1980s such that by 1988 its value was only C75 to the dollar. Devaluation compounded the problems of the severe debt crisis which had hit the economy by 1980 when its public foreign debt amounted to $1,800 million and its service accounted for 25 per cent of foreign exchange earnings. While the debt service ratio has abated since the high of 40 per cent in 1985 it still remains at around 30 per cent for a total external debt of $4,650 million.

Current economic situation. The consequence of the Costa Rican debt crisis has been the deep cut in public expenditure as required under International Monetary Fund aid programmes. Both the governments of the PLN and the PUSC have pushed through tough austerity programmes including wage cuts, the removal of price controls, the elimination of subsidies particularly on food and transport, the reform of the tax system, and the breaking of the index-linking of public salaries. Relations with the IMF have been strained especially over the terms of the loans which have resulted in numerous strikes by labour organizations, opposition from within the PLN and condemnation by the Church. For example, in October 1981 an extended finance facility of $329,000,000 was suspended because Rodrigo Carazo Odio's National Unity (*Unidad*

Nacional—UN) government refused to remove import controls, and in May 1986 the PLN government had to suspend interest payments completely due to shortage of foreign exchange. The PUSC government's June 1990 austerity programme which pushed up utility costs by 30 per cent and cut a further 7,000 jobs in the public sector led to demonstrations of over 100,000 people in San José. Whilst labour militancy has increased and poverty has grown (the National Planning Ministry reported that 23 per cent of Costa Ricans lived in poverty) so PUSC popularity has declined significantly. Nevertheless Calderón has been able to secure approval from the IMF and the US Agency for International Development (USAID) for the re-scheduling of debts and further loans of $213,000,000 million despite the freezing of accounts in March 1990 when the government failed to meet the IMF target of reducing fiscal deficit to 2 per cent of GDP.

Outlook for development. Pressure to generate foreign exchange has boosted the tourist industry such that by 1988 it was the third largest earner behind coffee and bananas bringing in $164,000,000 per annum. A massive increase over the 1980s of an unwanted source of earnings has been the caused by the trafficking of drugs and the laundering of drug money through Costa Rica. Just one trafficking operation broken in May 1990 prevented the Cali cartel of **Colombia** from pushing 1,000 kg of cocaine per month through Costa Rica. Extensive co-operation with the US Drug Enforcement Agency is in place but the inability to deal with the scale of the problem is widely recognized especially when senior public figures are involved. Despite the recommendation of a presidential commission of 1989 that all those implicated in narcotics offences should be excluded from public office this is unlikely to deter such activity.

JCJS

CRUZADO PLAN. In August 1985, Dilson Funaro took over from Francisco Neves Dornelles as Minister of Finance of **Brazil** in the **Sarney** government. Dornelles was an orthodox economist, nephew of **Tancredo Neves** and one of the appointments inherited from Tancredo, when Sarney came to office. Funaro was a *paulista* businessman, but was one of a group of younger economists and politicians anxious to introduce new priorities with the arrival of the New Republic. He especially drew on the advice of economists in the Pontifical Catholic University, in Rio de Janeiro, and the University of Campinas in São Paulo, all linked in one way or another, to the **Party of the Brazilian Democratic Movement** (*Partido de Movimento Democrático Brasileiro*—**PMDB**). One of their shared characteristics was a mistrust of monetarism, especially in analysing the causes of inflation, and a consequent mistrust of the IMF and of remedies which might lower inflation, only at the cost of deepening recession.

By January 1986, the Sarney government was being widely criticized for its apparent lack of policies to deal with inflation and the economy more generally. The PMDB had also suffered a severe setback in the election for mayor in São Paulo in November 1985. Several prominent PMDB politicians were moving away from Sarney, critical of the Democratic Alliance, and there was widespread speculation over a split in the PMDB with the formation of a new left-of-centre party.

The Cruzado Plan of Feb. 28, 1986 abruptly ended such speculation. It was delivered as a sharp, sudden shock to the economy and society, a "right-cross", delivered wihout warning. It was said that only 15 people in Brazil knew what had been planned, since at least the previous September, shortly after Funaro took office.

The aim of the plan was to cut inflation at one blow, introducing a "life or death struggle against inflation" that might reach 500 per cent by the end of the year. Appearing on television, with all his Ministers, Sarney made a dramatic, emotional appeal for help to the whole nation.

The Cruzado Plan introduced monetary reform: it replaced the *cruzeiro*, then declining in value at the rate of nearly 0.5 per cent a day, with the *cruzado*, with one *cruzado* to equal 1,000 *cruzeiros*. This was to be a strong currency, with fixed parity in relation to the US dollar (13.8 *cruzados*). It attacked "inertial inflation", the vicious circle by which price rises were passed through the economy, by ending generalized indexation, which was seen as the principal means of transmitting inflation, through monetary correction. All prices were frozen, for an indefinite period, at the levels of Feb. 27, 1986 with a list of maximum prices, published to help maintain control. There was also a freeze on wages, after granting a wage rise of 8 per cent to all workers, and after also increasing the minimum wage by 8 per cent.

The Cruzado Plan won widespread support and applause, with only a few fierce critics, most notably, **Leonel Brizola**. It was seen as a courageous and imaginative intervention, drawn up by some of the country's best-trained economists. Sarney's popularity reached heights not seen before and, across the country, people responded to his appeal for help, forming watch-dog groups in supermarkets, to monitor prices. Most of the theorists behind the Plan came from the PMDB, so that it bound Sarney and the PMDB together, at least until the very important elections in November 1986, when the Congress to be elected would also be the Constituent Assembly. The trade unions, which had been planning strikes, found no support for opposition to a president riding high on a wave of support and admiration.

Critics of the plan, though relatively few, expressed concern at the president's overriding of Congress in a populist appeal to the people, using the discredited decree laws of the old régime. This, they said, would further weaken political parties and the still nascent democratic system. Brizola questioned whether, or for how long, the "dominant classes', especially bankers, industrialists and employers, would support the Plan, if they judged it to be working against their interests.

Sarney had introduced the Cruzado Plan at the end of February, earlier than the economists who designed it had advised. Looking at the experience of the Austral Plan in **Argentina**, of May 15, 1985 they believed that their "package" would also need adjustments within a few months. They advised Sarney to wait till perhaps April, so that changes would not have to be made before the November elections. Sarney decided to act in late February, because of mounting political pressure, criticism, and inflation.

By as early as May, it was clear that changes should be introduced, to stop an over-heating of the economy. Sarney, then enjoying his newly won popularity, refused, hanging on till November and the elections for governors, Congress and local office. The elections brought a resounding victory for the PMDB. Then, even while the votes still were being counted, the government began to dismantle the Cruzado Plan. Sarney later blamed the PMDB for the delay. Cruzado II was introduced on 21 November. This modified the inflation index and introduced large increases in payments to the National Housing Bank. It also raised prices for petrol, alcohol, public utilities and motor cars.

The rapid, cynical dismantling of the Cruzado Plan, once election success had been assured, caused widespread dismay across the country. It began the general disenchantment with Sarney, his government, and the PMDB, and made it harder to win support for future efforts to curb inflation.

PF

CUBA. *Population*: 10,580,000. *Land area*: 110,860 sq km. *Trade volume (1988)*: exports: 5,518 million *pesos*; imports: 7,579 million *pesos*. Total external debt: 11,009 million *pesos*. *Public expenditure percentage rates (1989)*: *defence*: 10.2; *health and education*: 21.4; *housing*: 6.3. *Urban population as percentage of total*: 70. *Life expectancy*: 70.9 (men); 74.2 (women).

Geographical background. Cuba is physically the largest and most heavily populated of the Caribbean islands. It lies some 180 kilometres south of Key West in Florida and its western extremity is at a distance of 210 kilometres from the Mexican Yucatán peninsula. Its closest neighbour, to the east, is Haiti, some 90 kilometres away, with Jamaica approximately 100 kilometres due south. What is known as Cuba is in fact an archipelago constituting the westernmost collection of the Greater Antilles and although the northern coast is fringed by a chain of numerous islands and keys (principally the archipelagos of Sabana and Camaguey), the second-largest island, formerly called the Isle of Pines, lies to the south of mainland Cuba and is now named the Isle of Youth (*Isla de Juventud*). The islands enjoy a subtropical climate and fertile soils. With the exception of three mountain ranges, the highest being the Sierra Maestra in the south east, Cuba itself is characterized by low hills. The southern coast is fringed by some areas of swamp.

Socio–political background. The population of Cuba is predominantly of Spanish descent with a large minority of African origin, the majority being of mulatto (mixed) population. The stratification and separation of populations along racial lines which typified colonial Cuba began to break down during this century, and has done so further since 1959. The appreciation of the African contribution to Cuban development has been a significant feature of the past 30 years. The indigenous Taino and Guanahatabeye population (circa 100,000 in 1492) were wiped out within a few decades of the Spanish "discovery" of the island by Christopher Columbus on his first voyage (1492). The current population of 10,580,000 is expected to reach some 11,700,000 by the year 2000. Largely as a consequence of the extremely high level of health care and welfare provision, population expansion has begun to level off in recent years at slightly under 1 per cent per annum growth.

Outline of political history. Cuba achieved independence from the Spanish empire as late as May 20, 1902 following the Spanish–American war of 1898 and was the last of Spain's American territories to achieve this status. It is widely recognized that Cuba inadvertently and unintentionally exchanged one imperial master for another as the economy and interests of the **United States** began to determine the nature and composition of post-independence Cuba. Only with the final overthrow of the regime of Fulgencio Batista on Jan. 1, 1959 by revolutionaries led by Dr **Fidel Castro**, did the hopes of José Martí, the Cuban nationalist hero of the 1890s, begin to be fulfilled.

The Spanish conquest and colonization of the Cuban archipelago did not begin until 1511 and effective resistance to occupation was over by the middle of the sixteenth century. The island did not offer a bonanza economy to Spain as did the precious metals of Mexico and Peru and Cuba's economic development was slow, hindered by the rigid trading monopoly demanded by Madrid. By the mid-seventeenth century enforced trade liberalization (as a consequence of imperial rivalry) led to the emergence of an agricultural export economy based upon slavery. Slaves were first brought to Cuba in 1526 and the institution of slavery was not abolished until, in practice, 1888. This period saw the expansion of the sugar, tobacco and coffee sectors which were to remain the central sources of income for the island to the present day. Economic control and ownership was marked by absentee landlords throughout the colonial period, and whilst the other Spanish American colonies secured independence around 1821, the plantation economy of "the ever-faithful Island" developed in a manner akin to that of the southern states of the USA.

Indeed the growing movement for Cuban independence from Spain during the nineteenth century was paralleled by the rise of a strong annexationist movement urging incorporation into the American Union. The tension between these emerged as early as 1869 when a premature "Cuban Republic" was declared by the Guaimato Assembly of 1869, and was followed by two further struggles, the Ten Years War (1869–79) and then the *Guerra Chiquita* (1879–90), before being resolved by the intervention of the **United States** in the War of Independence 1895–98.

The period of US dominance. It was during this war that the Cuban nationalist hero José Martí met his death (1896), after warning with great prophetic insight of the threat from the "colossus of the north". This whilst the Spanish–American War concluded with Cuba's independence from Spain it began a neo-colonial relationship with the United States. The Platt Amendment of February 1901 to the Act establishing Cuban independence gave the USA the right to intervene in Cuban internal affairs at its discretion. Only in 1934 was the Amendment rescinded.

The period 1902 to 1959 saw massive US investments in Cuba across all sectors of the economy with virtual monopolies in public utilities. US economic interests reached a peak prior to World War II but it was US support for Fulgencio Batista, head of the army in the uprising of 1933–34, which was critical in undermining the progressive government of Ramón Grau San Martín and giving Batista *de facto* control of Cuba until 1940, when he was elected to the presidency, and subsequently until his fall on Jan. 1, 1959 in face of the descent from the Sierra Maestra by Castro and his guerrillas combined with a general strike in Havana.

The Cuban Revolution of 1959. The political strength and organization that existed at the beginning of the year lay with Castro's July 26 Movement, the Revolutionary Directorate (*Dirección Revolucionaria* — DR), and the Popular Socialist Party (*Partido Socialista Popular*—PSP). Although the post-insurrection presidency was initially given to Manuel Urrutia Lleo and later transferred to Osvaldo Dorticos Torrado in July 1959, the real power of the provisional government lay with Castro in the office of prime minister.

The main political initiatives of the provisional government to the end of 1960 were the start of agrarian reform, the establishment of trade links with the Soviet Union, the creation of the **Central Planning Board** (*Junta Central de Planificación*—JUCEPLAN) and the expropriation and nationalization of foreign, principally US-owned businesses without compensation. Centralization of decision-making and national economic and political planning presaged the direction that the administration was moving in: this direction was further encouraged or necessitated by the opening of diplomatic relations with the USSR in May 1960, the complete embargo placed by the USA on Cuban trade in October 1960 and ultimately the breaking of diplomatic relations by the US with Cuba. The creation of popular organizations such as the Committees for the Defence of the Revolution—CDRs (*Comités para la Defensa de la Revolución*), the Federation of Cuban Women (*Federación de Mujeres Cubanas* — FMC), the Union of Communist Youth (*Unión de Juventud Comunista* — UJC) compensated in part for the absence of an organized mass party and became the generators of a form of organic unity for the new Cuban society. They played an ever more important role following the failed CIA-backed invasion at the Bay of Pigs on April 17, 1961 when the threat of counter-revolution and the return of the *ancien régime* became a reality. Only with the formal unification of the July 26 Movement, the DR and the PSP, into the Integrated Revolutionary

Organization (*Organización Revolucionaria Integrada*—ORI) was an embryonic "democratic centralist party" created.

The Bay of Pigs fiasco, the Cuban missile crisis and the implacable US hostility to the revolutionary regime in part provoked the consolidation of the rule of ORI and its transformation in 1963 into the United Party of the Socialist Revolution (*Partido Unido de la Revolución Socialista*—PURS). Castro's explicit dedication to a socialist project dates back only to April 1961 and acceptance of Marxism-Leninism to Dec. 1, 1961. It was not until October 1965 that the PURS finally metamorphosed into the **Cuban Communist Party** (*Partido Comunista Cubano*—PCC). The centrality of the PCC was not however formally confirmed until the approval of the 1975 Constitution. Until that time that Constitution of 1940 continued in operation, though extensively modified by the Fundamental Law of 1959. In turn the latter was subject to extensive modification and revision, reflecting the radical process of collectivization and public ownership of property and enterprise.

The chief characteristic of the 1960s in Cuban politics was the establishment of a comprehensive social, educational and health system upon which a firmer economy could be based. Major land holdings were collectivized in 1960, mass literacy campaigns commenced in January 1961, country-wide vaccination programmes began in 1962, and further and deeper agrarian reform continued from 1963 such that by 1968 even small farms were being taken into public ownership. Political conflict within ORI and then, post 1965, in the PCC was focused upon the differences between the "new Marxists" such as Castro and **Ernesto Che Guevara** and the old communists of the PSP, notably Aníbal Escalante and the "micro-factionists". The expulsion and eventual imprisonment in 1967 of the latter confirmed Castro's hegemony and the opportunity to pay undivided attention from then on towards the expansion and development of the economy.

The first Congress of the PCC was held in Havana in December 1975. Further Congresses were held in December 1980 and December 1985 (part deferred to December 1986). The fourth Congress is to be held in 1991. Until the first Congress was convened the Party had neither formal rules nor an explicit written programme. It was at this first Congress that Fidel Castro and his brother General Raúl Castro were elected First and Second Secretaries of the Party, posts which they continue to hold. At the same time elections were held for the National Assembly of Organs of People's Power, the central legislative and administrative machinery. Rulings made by the Council of Ministers, the executive, have equal standing to that of the National Assembly and given that the latter meets only twice a year the balance of power lies firmly within the Council of Ministers.

Although the institutionalization of the state was completed by the end of the 1970s, growing economic problems associated with inefficiency of production, basis of allocation and distribution, and narrowness of export base and market led to a political reassessment following the 1986 Congress. A return to the revolutionary consciousness of the 1960s and the appeal to moral incentives were cornerstones of the "rectification programme".

Foreign policy. Cuban foreign policy since the revolution has been marked by an increasing success and confidence but its prime point of vulnerability has throughout been its economic reliance upon the USSR. Its sponsorship of guerrilla revolution (*foquismo*) in Latin America during the 1960s was an uncompromising failure that ended with the death of Che Guevara in **Bolivia** in 1967. Since then, however, the Cuban government has supported revolutionary states and revolutionary movements in the Third World with great consistency and effect. Foremost in its success has been the military support lent to Angola over a 15-year period culminating in the Cuban defeat of South African forces at Cuito Cuenavale in March 1988, which helped secure not only Angola's integrity but the independence of Namibia on the basis of UN Resolution 435 of 1978. Over 100,000 troops have served overseas in at least 37 African and Middle Eastern countries, invariably in areas of conflict. In addition Cuban military advisers have been posted to **Nicaragua**, **Jamaica**, **Grenada**, and **Guyana**. In 1980 there were some 4,300 experts and technical specialists in Cuba, mainly from the socialist *bloc*, and over 11,000 Cubans (other than the military) providing development assistance to Third World countries. Since the mid-1960s Cuba has provided doctors, nurses, teachers, construction workers and technical advisers amongst others and received students into Cuba for similar training. Given its relatively weak material economic position but strong educational and human resources Cuban aid has invariably been given in this form. Such large and extensive deployments of the Cuban **armed forces** has meant that combat and organizational experience has been gained in both conventional and guerrilla operations.

Recent developments—political. Between April 21 and Sept. 26, 1980 over 123,000 Cubans left the island for the United States from the port of Mariel. The regime had permitted anyone wishing to leave the country to do so and also took the opportunity to transfer people who were criminals, mentally ill or otherwise regarded as "undersirables". By the time the "boat-lift" ended it was claimed that there were still 100,000 Cubans still wishing to leave. Indicative of the desire to leave Cuba have been repeated occupations of foreign embassies in Havana by would-be emigrants. Despite the restoration of the US–Cuban anti-hijacking treaty of 1973 in September 1980 (it had been suspended by Cuba in 1977) the Mariel exodus was followed by a series of hijackings. More serious was the refusal of the US government to accept about 1,500 of the "undesirables" although by December 1984 Cuba agreed to accept them back under an immigration agreement with the US due to take effect on Nov. 20, 1987. At this stage, there were still about 1,900 "*marielitos*" in federal prisons in the USA and 5,000 "excludable" Cuban aliens. However the immigration agreement was one of the first casualties of the US decision to allow, indeed encourage and sponsor, transmissions from an anti-Castro radio station based in Florida known as "Radio Martí". Although the station began broadcasting both commercial programmes and propaganda on May 20, 1985 the plan for the station had been announced in 1981. Cuba threatened retaliation with the building of a 500,000 watt transmitter which would interfere with domestic frequencies across the USA.

With the increased hostility of the Reagan and Bush administrations greater active preparedness has been called for by the Cuban government. Already in 1979 the Soviet Union had been accused of taking a series of measures which collectively aroused the concern of the Carter Administration: stationing a combat brigade, deploying 20 MiG-23s, constructing the Cienfuegos submarine base, and transferring 20 Antonov AN-25 military transport aircraft to the island. Despite the Cuban denial that the allegations were "completely groundless", the USA engaged in practice assaults at Guantánamo, while overflying Cuba with SR-71 spy planes. Fear of invasion recurred and in May 1980 locally organized territorial militias (MTTs) were created.

Cuba acted as host to the Sixth Non-Aligned Movement (NAM) summit in September 1979 and Dr Castro held the presidency of the Movement between 1979 and 1982. Although provoking some dissent and controversy Castro's address to the summit argued that the socialist *bloc* was the "natural ally" of the NAM, that the NAM should give greater support to such movements as the PLO, Polisario Front, SWAPO, the Patriotic Front (Zimbabwe) and that it should recognize the Heng Samrin regime in Cambodia and oust the Pol Pot representation at the United Nations. However Soviet intervention in Afghanistan in December 1979 alienated many non-aligned members both from the Soviet Union and from Cuba.

With the election of Ronald Reagan, relations with the United States further deteriorated, reaching their lowest point to date during the invasion and occupation of **Grenada** in October 1983. The Cuban government had in fact unreservedly condemned the military *coup* against **Maurice Bishop**, with the words that "no doctrine, no principle, no position proclaimed as revolutionary...can justify [such] savage methods". There is no evidence, therefore, for the US allegation that the *coup* was part of a Soviet–Cuban plot for power projection and domination in the Caribbean, nor was there, as alleged, a substantial Cuban military presence in Grenada. There were in fact some 784 Cuban construction and other workers on the islands and only 40 military advisers. The effect of the invasion was to increase Cuban security fears to the extent that the defence budget of 1985 was planned to rise by 26 per cent. The US government invoked the Trading with the Enemy Act of 1917 in July 1983 in an effort to tighten the economic noose around Cuba. However as the United States increased the pressure Cuban foreign relations with other countries were being steadily improved. Diplomatic relations with most Latin American countries, broken in the 1960s, were restored in the mid- and late 1980s, providing new and potentially crucial trade openings. Only one Latin American country constantly maintained relations with Cuba, namely **Mexico**. The **Organization of American States** (OAS) had suspended Cuban membership in January 1962 and placed a trade embargo on it in July 1964. Although in 1975 the OAS voted to accept Cuba once again it was up to each individual country to re-establish links, and in any case Cuba refused to re-join the OAS. Virtually all Latin American countries had re-established diplomatic links with Cuba by 1991, the principal exceptions being in Central America.

Whilst anti-Cuban rhetoric has not been as strident under the Bush administration as under Reagan, the policies have remained much the same, and the possibility of US aid to the USSR has been made conditional on the withdrawal of the latter's support to Cuba.

Outline of economic development. The Cuban foreign policy imperative of diversifying external linkages in so far as they corresponded with, or at least did not counter, the revolution's orientation, was made stronger by the economic weaknesses and strengths it inherited. Despite wanting to end its pre-1959 dependency on agro-exports, and above all on sugar, Cuba has not been successful in diversification; it has simply shifted its target market. Cuba still depends heavily upon the USSR, which imports its sugar at preferential rates and provides oil and oil derivatives at heavily subsidized prices. But supply by the USSR of additional oil for resale on the world market is to end at the end of 1991 and Cuban relations with the countries of the Council for Mutual Economic Assistance (CMEA or COMECON) have already been terminated by the political and economic turmoil taking place in eastern Europe. The only bright spot is that over approximately the last five or six years it has been successful in establishing new links within Latin America.

The initial post-revolutionary period was marked by the taking into public ownership of large sectors of the economy. The prime motivation in the first half of the 1960s was generating and consolidating popular support for the revolution through redistribution and expansion of consumption rather than through domestic capital accumulation. The most valuable Cuban asset, land, was controlled from the outset. The first Agrarian Reform Law of May 1959 limited private ownership to a maximum of 400 hectares, and the excess distributed to landless peasants and smallholders. By 1963 the maximum holding was reduced to 67 hectares under the terms of the second Agrarian Reform Law. Despite the benefits of land redistribution and an initial programme of reducing export agriculture, publicly owned land became overwhelmingly dedicated to sugar, beef and tobacco production. Foremost amongst these was the "Ten Million Ton" sugar production target to be reached by 1970. The failure of this plan and the costs of energy, technology and human resource inputs and the opportunity costs involved persuaded JUCEPLAN to abandon such concentrations of economic activity and reassert broad long-term planning. This abandonment was in part stimulated by the necessity to overcome the shortages of basic supplies caused by the US-imposed embargo and to develop the skill and human resource base following the exodus of skilled personnel after the revolution. On the other hand the obvious weaknesses of this centralized production effort raised calls to decentralize economic decision-making at the first Congress of the PCC.

Industry. Whilst concerted attempts at comprehensive import-substituting industrialization were abandoned as early as 1964, high level of investments in education and training did enabled the Cuban economy to develop a firm technical base. Returns on the educational and technical investments of the 1960s coincided with Cuba's accession to the CMEA in July 1972, and the period 1971–75 showed growth rates in the Global Social Product (GSP) of 7.5 per cent per annum, a period in which industry expanded by 43 per cent and agriculture by 12 per cent.

In 1959 between 80 per cent and 90 per cent of Cuban capital equipment was of US origin and thus following the embargo the economy was forced both to seek other sources, principally the USSR, and to develop domestic technologies of repair and refurbishment. Indigenously produced technologies reflected existing Cuban economic strengths and thus Cuba became world leader in sugar production technology. The value of a good technical back-up to agriculture can be seen from the fact that industrial growth from 1965 to 1985 was as rapid as the best Latin American country. Already by 1961 industry was 85 per cent collectivized; by 1968 it was almost all in public ownership.

Newer industrial exports were also developed. Nickel exports are currently valued at US$500,000,000. Again the USSR is the main market, and with Cuba holding the fourth largest deposits in world it plans to produce 100,000 tonnes per year by 2000. Once again due to the nature of the siege economy it has had to concentrate on import-substitution and production of basic industrial materials, in particular those which are necessary for broader economic expansion and in those areas which would otherwise consume valuable foreign exchange. As a consequence, for example, Cuba has made rapid advances in metallurgy and the engineering tool sectors as well as being a world leader in pharmaceutical and biotechnology.

The construction industry which employs 10 per cent of work force has received a boost in the late 1980s as increasing tourism demanded the construction or improvement of hotel and facility building and is likely to remain a key new area. Construction, particularly in house building is one of those areas which suffered in the squeeze in the early 1980s and despite the re-introduction of mini-brigades on a widespread basis as part of the rectification process shortage of housing remains probably the most serious single social problem in Cuba today. Notwithstanding a GSP growth rate of 7.3 per cent per annum in the period 1981–85 the economy suffered in the long-term, although different sectors — housing for instance — were worse hit than others, due to the high level of imports without parallel increase in exports. The balance of payments crisis generated from 1981 onwards as sugar prices fell was only partly helped by oil revenues from resale. Although as a result of Cuba's relatively successful renegotiation of external debt the exchange crisis eased in the second half of the 1980s, GSP growth never rose beyond 0.5 per cent per annum in the period 1986–90.

Agriculture. Expansion of agriculture was made possible both by internal economic changes and by the record prices on the world market for sugar in the early 1970s. Moreover the period 1970–74 was marked with the sugar value of total exports rising from 80 per cent to 90 per cent, as well as the conclusion of major sugar agreements with the USSR. Although land area turned over to sugar did not increase appreciably there was increased and widespread mechanization. Two-thirds of sugar is now cut by machine. The wholesale modernization of the sugar processing industry occurred from the early 1970s onwards and although private small farmers were generally more efficient producers of sugar per hectare, the discrepancy was gradually reduced in large part due to the irrigation programme which now covers over one-third of state sugar farms but which is not available to private farmers. Some 40 per cent of cultivable land is now dedicated to sugar production employing about 360,000 or 12 per cent of the labour force, as against 37 per cent of the economically active population in the sugar industry in 1960. The failure of the 1970 Ten Million Ton programme which was short by 15 per cent precipitated the mechanization of the industry, a record harvest being produced in 1975. In 1990 there were 2,000,000 hectares under sugar producing between 7,200,000 to 8,300,000 tonnes since 1982 and processed in 159 sugar mills. Typically between 3,400,000 and 4,000,000 tonnes is exported to the USSR. On occasions after poor harvests Cuba has had to buy sugar on the world market to meet the Soviet quota.

Other areas of agriculture have been similarly transformed: in 1959 73 per cent of the land belonged to 9.4 per cent of the population, now it is virtually all under public ownership. But of equal importance was that employment in agriculture prior to the revolution was variable, seasonal and underemployment was widespread. One of the first acts of the revolutionary government was to establish the National Institute of Agrarian Reform (*Instituto Nacional de Reforma Agraria*—INRA) in 1959. It de-emphasized agriculture for industrialization during the early 1960s and permanently absorbed much rural labour. In the period 1960–1985 26 per cent total investments equal to $11,179 million have been made in agriculture, highlighting its economic significance. Small farmers were brought under the National Association of Small Farmers (*Asociación Nacional de Agricultores Pequeños*—ANAP) in the wake of the revolution, but in 1977 supported the formation of co-operative associations (*Cooperativas de Producción Agropecuaria*—CPA) which reflected the commitment to decentralization and local initiatives brought forward at the first Congress of the PCC.

Following the legalization of peasant markets in 1980 in an attempt to supply the food market more effectively not only were the collectivist ideas of the CPAs threatened but the CPAs themselves were charged with being corrupted by growing capitalist practices. By May 1986 the parallel small farmers' markets were shut down as part of the "rectification process", with, it appears, no disastrous consequences. Although domestic use agricultural production has increased over the 1980s the problem of distribution especially to the major cities has not been overcome.

The 1980s was also a bad decade for tobacco production for export as drought and disease drastically reduced harvests. As part of the diversification of the 1970s and the need for foreign exchange citrus production was massively expanded. Now Cuba is the fourth largest exporter in the world, producing 506,000 tonnes in 1990. Once again the wish to generate foreign exchange on the one hand, and to preserve it on the other has led Cuba to export 50–60 per cent of the coffee produced and to engage in a substantial rice production programme initiated in 1968 to provide new staples. At the same time it still relies on imports of cereals and cotton.

Energy. Since 1984 as part of the efficiency drive of rectification all sugar mills have burnt cane waste to generate electricity, saving 1,400,000 tonnes of oil per annum. In order to reduce costs and external dependencies sources of energy have been diversified and in August 1990 an energy saving programme was announced with the intention of cutting petrol and diesel consumption by 50 per cent. Although currently Cuba only produces 718,000 tons of crude oil per annum, or 6 per cent of its needs, with the processing of Soviet oil in mind it has built four refineries, with a fifth under construction which, when complete will bring refining capacity to 260,000 barrels per day.

Currently under construction are two of four planned nuclear power stations, and it is hoped that nuclear generation will produce 50 per cent of the country's electricity needs by 2000 and thereby cut energy imports. Installed capacity of electricity generation is 3,500,000 kilowatts (1987) or 15, 200 million Kwh.

Finance. In the aftermath of the revolution the central bank, the *Banco Nacional de Cuba* (BNC) initially fell under the responsibility of Ernesto Che Guevara (who also headed the Industrialization Department of the Institute of Agrarian Reform, as well as being Minister for Industry) and with the abolition of the Ministry of Finance in 1966 secured a monopoly of financial control and national budgeting for the whole economy. The BNC is the sole domestic commercial bank and the last resort for international business and foreign exchange dealings. In so far as it has fulfilled a multiplicity of functions it has had to carefully balance domestic development budgets with the financing of external commitments. Thus, for example, the shortage of foreign exchange during the mid- to late 1980s restricted manufacturing industries' ability to import vital spare parts which in turn failed to generate sufficient and badly needed foreign revenue. The shortage of hard currency has been described as the "Achilles heel" of the Cuban economy. Since Cuba is neither a member of the World Bank nor the International Monetary Fund it has received no development aid from these and related multilateral agencies. Debt owed to the USSR is, on the other hand, estimated to be in the region of US$25,800 million whilst Cuba's total external debt for convertible currencies has almost doubled since 1984, from 5,964 million *pesos* to 11.009 million *pesos* in 1988. In 1982 a third of Cuban debt to the West was rescheduled; in 1983, 53 per cent; in 1984, 40 per cent; and in 1985, 29 per cent. In autumn 1990 "Paris Club" creditors were once again invited to consider rescheduling the debt, now amounting to US$6,100 million. Notwithstanding Fidel Castro's exhortations to other Latin American debtor states to halt payments to creditors, Cuba itself has been meticulous in meeting debt obligations if possible and in carefully renegotiating its debt if not. Only once, in April 1986 were repayments frozen for a period of 90 days and then only on the payment of principal and not interest.

Social and welfare. Above all, Cuba is rightly proud of its investment in social welfare. Infant mortality is now only 11.1 per 1,000 live births, there is one doctor for every 303 citizens. In the field of education, illiteracy is all but non-existent, day nurseries are widespread and access to higher education is unparalleled in the western hemisphere, including North America.

Current economic situation. Nothwithstanding the instability of the Soviet economy the 1990–91 Soviet–Cuban trade agreement envisaged an expansion in trade of approximately 8.7 per cent, but there is little likelihood that this growth can be sustained nor can the 12,000,000 tonnes of oil currently provided by the USSR be maintained indefinitely on current terms even if this agreement were to be renewed. (The resale of Soviet-supplied oil is a major foreign exchange earner but subject to dramatic fluctuation in prices, thus, for example, earnings from this source from 1985 to 1989 fell from US$600,000,000 to US$180,000,000). The export profile of Cuba by value is as follows (for 1988): sugar 4,124 million *pesos*, minerals and concentrates 360 million *pesos* (1987), fruit and vegetables 213,000,000 *pesos*, fishery products 146,000,000 *pesos* and tobacco 98,000,000 *pesos*. Eighty-six per cent of exports are directed to CMEA countries whilst 87 per cent of its imports are from these countries. This profile is likely to change substantially following the CMEA commitment to trade through convertible currencies from 1991. During 1988 Japan, Spain, Argentina, Mexico were Cuba's biggest non-CMEA trading partners. A joint venture law was passed in 1982 which allowed 50 per cent ownership, tax concessions, land grants and infrastructural support to foreign investors. Although the take-up rate was minimal in the early years, with the development of tourism in particular interest has increased.

Tourism may become the single most important economic and social development in Cuba during the 1990s. Already in 1989 there was a 32 per cent increase in tourist arrivals over 1988 amounting to 326,000. Intur, the state tourism board has promoted Cuba as a tourist destination particularly in **Canada** (which never broke diplomatic and trading links), West Germany and Spain. A new international airport was opened at Varadero, and new air routes are being planned (particularly in the light of Aeroflot's decision to abandon Havana as the hub of its Latin American operations in favour of Miami). The PCC is nevertheless aware of the dangers to the gains of the revolution, the orientation of the revolution and revolutionary consciousness of the influx of tourist dollars and tourist enclaves. By 1989 the tourism sector generated in the region of US$260,000,000 in hard currency.

Although over the 1980s government expenditure was increasingly deficit financed there is a 10 per cent enterprise tax, a sharply progressive personal income tax and sales taxes. In addition as a means of controlling non-basic goods, a tax known as the *impuesto de circulación* is placed on goods sold through the legal parallel market.

Still, the balance of revenue over expenditure in 1984 fell short by 76,000,000 *pesos* by 1987 it was short by 1,146 million *pesos* and projected figures for 1990 was a deficit of 1,980 million *pesos*. The main sectors of public expenditure in 1989 were composed as follows: production 4,798 million *pesos* (36.8 per cent); education and health 2,895 million *pesos* (21.4 per cent); cultural and scientific activity 2,300 million *pesos* (17 per cent); defence and public order 1,380 million *pesos* (10.2 per cent); housing 852 million *pesos* (6.3 per cent); and administration 528,000,000 *pesos* (3.8 per cent). It was in 1978 that a new national accounting method was introduced, known as the System of Economic Management and Planning (*Sistema de Desarrollo y Planificación Económico*—SDPE) and agreed at the 1976 Congress which reduced, though did not eliminate, the allocative inefficiencies of the planned economy. The return to a strict economic planning following the errors of 1970 resulted in a commitment to the first Five-Year Plan of 1976–80. By the Third Plan of 1986–90 and Castro's open and sharp criticisms at the Third Party Congress and the initiation of the rectification process, greater emphasis was placed upon guaranteeing external commitments and obligations and to austerity and efficiency measures at home. This involved not only administrative reorganization but the dismissal and demotion of incompetent and inefficient bureaucrats on the widest scale since the revolution.

JCJS

CUBAN COMMUNIST PARTY (Partido Comunista Cubano — PCC). The new Communist Party of **Cuba** was formally established in 1965. There had been a predecessor by the same name which had been formed in 1925 but which adopted the name of the Popular Socialist Party (*Partido Socialista Popular* — PSP). Outlawed by Batista its influence waned and became incorporated in the Integrated Revolutionary Organization (*Organización Revolucionaria Integrada*—ORI). The new Party was effectively a separate and original creation of Castro. The PCC is a democratic centralist party, the only legal party and institutionally secured by the 1976 Constitution which assigns it the role of the "highest leading force of society and of the state". The Party performs a directive function across the whole of society and over government, moreover decisions made at higher levels are binding upon all lower levels. The hierarchy runs from the membership to local work committees, to municipal and then provincial committees, then the Central Committee (currently comprising 225 members) and finally the Politburo (composed of 24 members). The elision of state and party means that both are divided regionally into 14 provincial units and 169 municipal administrations. However in an attempt to avert the fusion of party and government typical of the pre-1976 period, differentiation was encouraged through the creation of Organs of People's Power (OPP). Party membership stands at approximately 515,000. Over the last five years there has been a concerted effort to encourage younger members, women and blacks into senior party and government positions.

JCJS

CUBAN REVOLUTION. The Cuban Revolution was first and foremost a nationalist revolution, the expression of a movement of self-determination and anti-imperialist. The revolutionaries sought to allow **Cuba** "to live outside the entrails of the monster", to paraphrase José Martí. It was neither a communist-led nor a communist-inspired revolution. Only if one considers revolution to be an ongoing process rather than a brief series of events can Marxism be said to inform its progress, and then only from 1961 onwards.

Discontent with the presidency of Carlos Prío Socarrás of the Authentic Cuban Revolutionary Party—a progressive and reformist party—had led to the meteoric rise of the more radical Cuban People's Party (Ortodoxos) which, by the time of the 1952 presidential elections was favourite to win. However, General Fulgencio Batista, whilst already possessing significant *de facto* power staged a *coup* on March 10, 1952 which was followed by a widespread repression of all opposition movements and resulted in the deaths of at least 20,000 people. Following the attack on the Moncada barracks in July 1953 by the **Castro** brothers, the militarized anti-Batista movements became dominated by insurrectionists and not marxist revolutionaries. From December 1956 Castro's guerrillas operated from the Sierra Maestra and with increasing effect continued armed operations in Havana itself, eventually forcing Batista to flee and the regime to collapse. Whilst the corruption and repression of the Batista regime, the military success of the guerrillas, and the latent nationalist sentiment of the majority of the population served to support the nationalist programme of Castro, the pre-1959 period was not characterized by a clear, discernible and concerted political organization on the part of the guerrillas. The singularity of the success of *foquismo* as an insurrectionist strategy in Cuba between 1956 and 1959 was not to be repeated elsewhere in Latin America.

JCJS

CULTURE. The term "culture" has many meanings. To a sociologist, culture refers to the entire pattern of behaviour of a society. Marxists (in particular those of the Soviet Union) have in the past often argued for a rather simple economic determinism, in which culture forms only part of the superstructure of society resting upon the dominant economic base. However most modern marxists now accept that the culture of a society (in the sociological sense) also affects and shapes its capacity for economic production, an idea which has long seemed obvious to non-marxists. Comparison, for example, of the economic history of **Argentina** with the comparable instances of Australia and Canada, suggests that a mechanistic economic explanation is inadequate and that cultural differences, in the sociological sense, have to be taken into account if the differences in outcomes are to be adequately explained.

Confusion arises from the fact that the word "culture" is much more commonly and widely used to designate the evidences of specialized forms of self-expression such as art, music, **literature** etc. Culture in this sense, sometimes termed "high culture", is generally seen as being the particular province of **intellectuals**. However although this may to a considerable extent be true of much of South and Central America, culture in the rest of the Caribbean has a much more universal origin and appeal.

PARC

D

DA SILVA, LUIS INACIO, ("LULA"). In **Brazil**'s presidential election of 1989, **Fernando Collor** was the richest of the candidates: Lula was the poorest. Only four years older than Collor, Lula had seven brothers, all working men, and three sisters working as maids (*empregadas*). Of all the candidates, he was the closest to an electorate in which 70 per cent earned less than NCz$700 a month.

Lula came from the north-east to Santos, on a *pau-de-arara* ("parrot perch"—an open lorry) in 1952. In 1957, he went to São Paulo and in 1958 started working in a factory making screws. In 1969, he became active in the metal-workers' union, of which he was elected president in 1975, and re-elected in 1978. He was one of the principal leaders during the important strike in the ABC industrial towns in 1979, and, when the **Workers' Party** (*Partido dos Trabalhadores*—PT) was formed, in 1980, was elected as its first president, helping to form the Workers' Central Union (*Central Unica dos Trabalhadores*—CUT) in the following year. He ran in the election for the governorship of São Paulo in 1982, coming fourth, then was elected as federal deputy in 1986, with 650,000 votes. He played a major role in the PT's success in electing 10 mayors in November 1988, including those of São Paulo, Porto Alêgre and Victôria.

By the start of the presidential election campaign of 1989, the PT had 550,000 members, able to bring over 60,000 militants to a campaign rally. Its close links to the CUT, which controlled almost 1,000 unions, meant that Lula could count on the active support of about 100,000 people working for his election. This support included rural as well as urban, industrial workers, even in areas such as Acre, among the rubber tappers and their union. The PT also had close links to the **Church**, especially its more radical members in regions such as the north-east. Many intellectuals and artists also supported Lula, and many people working in the public sector and government service, as seen eventually, in the vote in Brasília.

Both Lula and the PT seemed to find it difficult to recover from the defeat by Collor in the second round of voting for president in December 1989. Many observers, by contrast, were greatly impressed by how close Lula came to victory and by the party discipline and energy which his campaign revealed. During 1990, Lula decided not to contest the Congressional election of Oct. 3, preferring to concentrate on winning support for himself and the PT for the future with speeches and meetings across the country.

It still remains to be seen how far Lula and his party can co-operate with **Leonel Brizola** and the PDT, and with other groups on the left, but he is firmly established as an able, widely respected politician of genuinely national stature. He is respected as a man of personal integrity, with a commitment to social and economic reforms and the improvement of the conditions of the working class and the underprivileged majority of Brazilians. Few candidates in any democracy can have failed to win the presidency after polling over 31 million votes, as Lula did. No other working man has come so close to being elected as president anywhere in Latin America. There is still time.

PF

DE LA MADRID HURTADO, MIGUEL. Miguel de la Madrid Hurtado was President of Mexico 1982–88. He is remembered mainly for his economic reforms, for it was he who changed the course of the Mexican economy from what he dismissively described as "financial populism" toward economic liberalism and free trade.

De la Madrid was born into a middle class family in Colima; in earlier days, these social origins would have seriously handicapped his ascent in Revolutionary politics. However he was one of the prime beneficiaries of a change in the pattern of political recruitment which promoted ascent through the federal bureaucracy rather than (as in earlier years) through regional politics. De la Madrid underwent part of his education at Harvard, and returned to Mexico with the necessary technocratic credentials to work in various economic and financial positions. In 1979 he was promoted to be Minister of Planning under José López Portillo, and in 1981 he was selected as the latter's successor. He was not especially close to López Portillo who chose him mainly because he believed that de la Madrid would reassure the business community.

De la Madrid's credentials as a technocrat were genuine; the quality of economic policymaking during 1982–88 was high. It was greatly to de la Madrid's credit that Mexico avoided the ruinous economic fate which looked likely when the price of oil collapsed at the beginning of 1986. De la Madrid also avoided engineering the traditional pre-election boom during 1987–88. When he left office the most difficult part of the transformation of the Mexican economy in the direction of free markets and lower inflation had been accomplished.

On the other hand de la Madrid's political management was relatively weak. Although personally honest, he had no real answer to the corruption which had become endemic in Mexican public administration by 1982. Nor did he really know how to deal with the challenge posed by a stronger electoral opposition; he was content to leave these problems to his successor.

De la Madrid in office was cautious and not at all power hungry. He tended to rely for advice upon a very narrow group of supporters. He was remarkably restrained in the face of adverse criticism. Since leaving office he has shown no desire whatever to play an active role in public affairs. In short he showed many of the characteristics that would have made him an excellent Central Banker or Minister of Finance, but lacked some of the more aggressively political qualities that might have slowed the decline of the **Institutional Revolutionary Party** (*Partido de la Revolución Institucional*—PRI) during his term in office.

GP

DEMOCRATIC ACTION (Acción Democrática—AD) (Venezuela). A social democratic party in **Venezuel**a, AD stood for civilian government, freedom of thought and expression, opposition to dictators, protection for workers and state-led economic growth. In recent years it has adopted a distinctively Third World position, accompanied by a degree of hostility to the United States and its policies. It is affiliated to the Socialist International and has fraternal relations with APRA in **Peru**, as well as other of the so-called "Aprista" parties.

Influenced originally by Marxism, from which it adopted its distinctive organizational structure, it was founded in Barranquilla, Colombia, in 1931 by exiles opposed to the dictator Juan Vicente Gómez. Dissolved along with all other political parties in 1937, until 1941 it led a clandestine existence under the title of the National Democratic Party, and when it re-emerged under the leadership of **Rómulo Betancourt**, AD had already lost its Marxist character. Between 1941 and 1945 it grew rapidly, so much so that its leaders co-operated with military officers to overthrow the imcumbent government and seize power.

As the provisional government of 1945–48, the undemocratic way in which it had come to power was initially to frustrate its intentions to establishing a truly democratic government, though it did carry out some substantive reforms and held the country's first free elections in which it obtained between 70 and 78 per cent of the vote. AD's first constitutional government (1948), led by the distinguished novelist Rómulo Gallegos, passed an Agrarian Reform Law and established the Instituto Agrario Nacional (IAN) to administer it, but was deposed after only eight months in a *coup* led by Colonel Marcos Pérez Jiménez, when AD was banned. When Pérez Jiménez siezed power personally he went even further in his efforts to extirpate AD; two of its general secretaries were killed and two imprisoned, one of whom died in detention. But the party survived through its strong organization based on the Leninist cell structure.

When, after the dictator's deposition, AD returned to power with Betancourt himself as constitutional President (1959–64), AD which had secured 49.45 per cent of the votes cast in the presidential election, governed in coalition with its main rivals COPEI and the URD. In 1964 Betancourt was succeeded by his old colleague. Raúl Leoni (President 1964–69), whose relative conservatism did not alienate the *campesinos* who formed the principal support of the governing party, with its main strength in Maracaibo and the *llanos*. But divisions over policy weakened its control, and as the oil price fell, the 1968 elections saw COPEI come to power for the first time. Since neither faction of AD would agree to join it in a coalition, it ruled alone and, despite a shaky start, it became the basis of a second grouping of parties capable of holding power. In 1973 that year AD and COPEI between them obtained three-quarters of the votes cast. However the steep rise in the price of oil as a result of the first oil shock of the 1970s came too late to prevent the return of power to AD in the 1973 elections with **Carlos Andrés Pérez** as their standard-bearer, and it was he who carried through the nationalization of oil and steel, only to be defeated at the polls amid charges of corruption in 1979. AD returned to power under Dr Jaime Lusinchi in 1984 and in 1989 President Pérez was returned for an unprecedented second term. It remains one of Latin America's most successful democratic political parties.

PARC

DEMOCRATIC ALLIANCE OF CIVIL OPPOSITION (Alianza Democrática de Oposición Civilista—ADOC) (Panama). Originally created to fight the 1984 elections (as *Alianza Democrática de Oposición*—ADO) in which its candidate Arnulfo Arias was fraudulently denied the Presidency in favour of Barletta the official Democratic Revolutionary Party (*Partido Revolucionario Democrático*—PRD) candidate. ADOC, with Endara at its head is now the ruling coalition after backing the National Civic Crusade (*Cruzada Civilista Nacional*—CCN) in 1987. Composed of the Christian Democratic Party (*Partido Demócrata Cristiano*—PDC), Arias' Authentic Panamenista Party (*Partido Panameñista Auténtico*—PPA), and the Nationalist Republican Liberal Movement (*Movimiento Liberal Republicano Nacionalista*—MOLIRENA). ADOC thus brought together the most powerful groups of the Panamanian political establishment with the sole purpose of overturning the power of the (Panamanian Defence Forces—FDP) and the Democratic Revolutionary Party (*Partido Revolucionario Democrático*—PRD) in general, and **General Manuel Antonio Noriega** in particular. Nevertheless ADOC required not just the financial support of the Christian Democratic Union and of President Bush, who authorized funding of ADOC to the tune of US$18,000,000 for the 1989 election campaign, but an invasion to propel it into power. Soon after it took office political conflict began to fragment the coalition. In September 1990 three coalition partners joined the opposition PRD, and government popularity in polls fell from 90 per cent in January 1990 to 32 per cent in October 1990 as it proved unable either to deal with the economic crisis or to assert its authority over that of the United States in Panama.

JCJS

DEMOCRATIC ALLIANCE–M-19 (Alianza-Democrática—M-19—AD–M-19) (Colombia). The main force of the AD–M-19 is undoubtedly the M-19. This Colombian guerrilla organization was founded in 1972 by a sector of Rojas Pinilla's Popular National Alliance (*Alianza Nacional Popular*—ANAPO) party and some former combatants with the Colombian Revolutionary Armed forces (*Fuerzas Armadas Revolucionarias Colombianas*—FARC). It took the name M-19 to commemorate the April 19 elections, when, they maintained, ANAPO had been deprived of victory by a fraud. The movement never belonged to any left-wing orthodoxy, but sought to build an anti-oligarchic and anti-imperialist mass movement with an armed wing. The organization's first public act was to steal the Independence hero, **Simón Bolívar**'s sword, in a symbolic gesture to place it in the nationalist tradition. In the late 1970s, it began to escalate its actions, building up strong support in some of the poor urban shanty towns. Government repression, which included the systematic use of torture on arrested combatants and sympathizers, made them popular heroes. Many imprisoned leaders were released in an Amnesty under President Belisario Betancur, which was widely criticized by the army. Belisario launched a peace plan which was fraught with problems. Days before an agreement was to be signed in 1983, a right-wing paramilitary group gunned down Carlos Toledo Plata, an M-19 leader who was living legally under the terms of the amnesty. Nevertheless, the M-19 commander, Carlos Pizarro, signed the agreement, although he too had been wounded in a police ambush on his way to the signing. The failure of the government to implement promised reforms, continued army attacks and death squad killings, led to a collapse of the peace agreement. in 1985, the M-19 took over the Palace of Justice which was stormed by the army. The events in the Palace severely weakened the organization. By the late 1980s, they were ready to make an agreement with the Barco government, and in March 1989 negotiations were opened. The negotiations were very tortuous, and did not result in agreement until March 8, 1990 when the group formally surrendered their weapons. This gave the M-19 only two days to campaign for the Congressional elections of March 11. Even so, Carlos Pizarro won 8 per cent of the vote for mayor of Bogotá. As his campaign for president gathered strength, Pizarro was assassinated. Nevertheless, Antonio Navarro Wolff, his successor as leader of the organization and presidential candidate for the alliance created with a number of other small left-of-centre groups, won 12 per cent of the vote and finished third in the May elections. Navarro Wolff became Minister of Health in the Gaviria government, but resigned to stand for the Constituent Assembly elections on Dec. 9.

JP

DEMOCRATIC CENTRE UNION (Union Del Centro Democrático — UCD) (Argentina). Conservative party was founded in Argentina by Alvaro Alsogaray to contest the 1983 elections. The UCD is the latest and most successful of the political ventures of Alsogaray, an army engineer who left the service to become a successful industrialist, and who served as economy minister during the government of Arturo Frondizi (1958–62).

The first of these, in the mid-1960s, was the Independent Civic Party (*Partido Cívico Independiente*—PCI), created to embody the "social market economy" ideas advocated by

Alsogaray; his own interpretation of the similarly named policies applied in post-war West Germany. It attracted only scant voter support, as did its successor, New Force (Nueva Fuerza) when if fielded Julio Chamizo as presidential candidate in 1973.

UCD, however, profited from the growing disenchantment with state intervention and protectionism that followed the debt crisis in the early 1980s, and began to attract a new, younger breed of conservative voters. The party's ideas found a welcome environment in the traditionally left-wing university student movements. This did not start to translate into substantial voter support until the latter part of the decade, when UCD succeeded in getting 11 representatives elected to the lower chamber of congress.

Its prominence was enhanced in 1989 when the recently elected president **Carlos Menem**, a sudden convert to the kind of economic policies espoused by the UCD, appointed Alvaro Alsogaray as his adviser on matters related to the external debt. Later, Menem also appointed María Julia Alsogaray (Alvaro's daughter and the best-known of the younger generation of UCD leaders) to manage the privatization of the state telephone company. In congress, the UCD *bloc* has acted as an ally of Menem's, making up for the defection of dissidents from the *bloc* of the ruling **Justicialista** (Peronist) party.

EC

DEMOCRATIC LABOUR PARTY (Partido Democrático Trabalhista — PDT) (Brazil). The party was founded by **Leonel Brizola** after his return to **Brazil** in 1979, which coincided with the re-establishment of multi-party government. At first, he wanted to take up the party title and initials (*sigla*) of the PTB, the **Brazilian Labour Party**, (*Partido Trabalhista Brasileiro*), one of the two parties founded by **Getúlio Vargas**. Brizola had been one of the most prominent leaders of the party up to 1964 and until the suppression of the party system in 1965. Taking up the old party label would have confirmed Brizola as being in direct political descent from Vargas.

Another faction, led by Yvete Vargas, the great-niece of Vargas, also claimed the party *sigla*. The Brizola faction had a better claim, in that, in the newly formed PTB *bloc* in Congress, made up of 22 ex-Brazilian Democratic Movement (*Movimento Democrático Brasileiro* —MDB) deputies and one Senator, plus one ex-ARENA deputy, Brizola had the support of 22 of the 23 deputies. The Superior Electoral Court (*Tribunal Superior Electoral*— TSE), awarded the *sigla* to the Yvete Vargas faction, largely as a tactic to prevent Brizola from taking up the Vargas mantle.

Brizola, though deeply disappointed, founded the PDT, incorporating the *trabalhista*, labour, title of the Vargas tradition. Other prominent politicians of the pre-1964 period who joined the party included Doutel de Andrade, Darcy Ribeiro and Neiva Moreira. It also attracted some of the younger political exiles returning from European universities.

By 1981, the original *bloc* was reduced to 10 deputies, the rest having joined the **Party of the Brazilian Democratic Movement** (*Partido do Movimento Democrático Brasileiro* — PMDB) the opposition party, which was formed from the MDB; but the elections of November 1982 brought a boost to the party's development. The imposition by the regime of the *voto vinculado*, the requirement to vote for candidates of the same party for every office on the ballot paper, meant that, in the state of Rio de Janeiro, candidates of the PDT, though perhaps little known to the electorate, won seats because of being linked to Brizola's candidature as governor.

The PDT, therefore, became the party of state government in Rio de Janeiro from March 1983 to March 1987. Overall, in the elections of 1982, it won 6.1 per cent of valid votes cast at national level, as compared with 3.7 per cent for the **Worker's Party** (*Partido dos Trabalhadores*— PT) 4.7 for the PTB, 41.5 for the **Social Democratic Party** (*Partido Democrático Social*—PDS) and 44 per cent for the PMDB. It now had one governor, Brizola, one senator, for Rio de Janeiro, Roberto Saturnino Braga, and 23 federal deputies.

The PDT government in Rio de Janeiro contained some very able people, such as the Secretary of Finance, César Maia, who brought discipline to the state finances, to allow Brizola to carry through some of his proposed programme. A persistent problem was the hostility of the federal government, first under Figueiredo, then under the civilian presidency of **José Sarney**.

In terms of the party, the period in office showed strains, arising from Brizola's own political style and from the different ideological positions of people within the PDT. Brizola proclaimed his adherence to a European form of social democracy and maintained contacts with European leaders and with the Socialist International. Within the party, by contrast, he was often seen as too insistent on imposing his own views and direction, very much in the *gaúcho* authoritarian tradition. His own political position was that of reformist *trabalhismo*, derived from Rio Grande do Sul and from Vargas. Others in the party, especially, but not exclusively, younger members, were more radical, more explicitly socialist and more ready to accept wider debate and democratic processes within the party. Brizola was even accused of not caring, essentially, for political mobilization through the party and party organization, but of seeing the party as his personal electoral and political vehicle.

In the municipal elections of 1985, Brizola's candidate, Saturnino Braga, won election as mayor in Rio de Janeiro supported by a popular Deputy Mayor, Jó Resende, who had well-established political links with grass-roots politics in the city, especially in the *favelas*. In Porto Alegre, the election was won by Alceu Collares, with Brizola's strong support, and PDT candidates did well in Curitíba, Florianopolis and Recife. One indication of strains within the party was that both Saturnino Braga, a highly respected socialist intellectual, and Jó Resende, subsequently broke with Brizola and the PDT.

Brizola's criticism of the **Cruzado Plan** partly accounted for the defeat of the PDT candidate for governor in 1986, Darcy Robeiro, though he was, too, a much less forceful candidate than Brizola and opposed by a strong anti-Brizola coalition, headed by Wellington Moreira Franco, whom Brizola had defeated as PDS candidate in 1982. The party suffered like others, in the sweeping victory of the PMDB, borne along by enthusiasm for the Cruzado Plan.

In the municipal elections of November 1988, the PDT candidate, Marcelo Alençar, was elected mayor in Rio de Janeiro, as was Jaime Lerner in Curitiba. PDT mayors were also elected in São Luís in the north-east, and almost tied with the PMDB candidate in Fortaleza, suggesting that the party was starting to have an impact at national level. In the cities of the industrial south, including São Paulo, the ABC cities, Santos and Porto Alegre, the party's performance was eclipsed by that of the PT, with its string of resounding victories.

The performance of Brizola in the presidential election campaign of 1989 depended on his personal appeal much more than on party support or programme. It also revealed the weakness of the party, and of support for Brizola, in the two vitally important states of São Paulo and Minas Gerais, which, together with Rio de Janeiro, contain 44 per cent of the Brazilian electorate. The six biggest states, namely, those three, plus Rio Grande do Sul, Paraná and Bahia, contain no less than 64 per cent of voters.

It was estimated that, for Brizola to beat **Lula** in the first round of voting in 1989, he needed only 5 per cent of the paulista vote and 8 per cent of the mineiro, since every percentage point in São Paulo was worth 80,000 votes and, in Minas Gerais, 90,000. Brizola's personal appeal was not able to make up for lack of party organization and a concentrated campaign effort in those two states. It has been suggested that, mistakenly, he was conserving scarce party funds for the second round after the first.

In the elections for governor and for Congress, on Oct. 3 and Nov. 25, 1990 Brizola emerged greatly strengthened, through his own success in being easily elected as governor in Rio de Janeiro and in his effective support for other PDT candidates. In the Congressional elections, the party dropped slightly in terms of its representation in the Chamber, falling from 49 to 46 deputies, but it was, still, in third place, after the PMDB, with 109 deputies, and the Liberal Front Party (*Partido da Frente Liberal*—PFL) with 92. The PDT was followed by the Party for National Reconstruction (*Partido da Renovacão Nacional*—PRN) Collor's party, up from 31 to 41, the PDS, up from 32 to 40, the PSDB, down from 60 to 37 deputies, and the PT, which doubled its representation, from 17 to 34 deputies.

The PDT is now caught up in the general restructuring of political parties and the political system, within which, the PMDB, after the elections of 1990, is still the strongest single party in the Chamber, but with its position greatly weakened by comparison with the first years of the "New Republic". One solution, in the short-term, may be an alliance with the PT and other parties of the left. If, however, the PDT is to play an effective part in this, or any other political, initiative, it must, in common with most other parties, more carefully define its identity and its programme. It must also establish a greater measure of autonomy and independence in relation to Brizola than, so far, it has managed.

PF

DEVELOPMENT. Development, even more than most terms in public discourse, is user-friendly; it has virtually as many potential meanings as potential users. If there is a commonality among its many uses, it might be in denoting enhancement, that is, increasing value or desirability; but that leads us once again to subjectivity. Metaphors aside, society is not an organism with a genetically programmed innate potential. We cannot say of a society, as a gardener might of a flower, that it has become what it should be.

What so complicates the study of international, or Third World, development, in particular, is that the most commonly adopted meanings (and thus explanations and strategies) do not simply differ;

from diagnosis to prescription, they are almost diametric opposites. Development is a standard borne by those who would promote the interests of the affluent and the powerful as well as by those who would serve the poor and the weak; by those who would expand the reach of the most industrialized states and those who would shield the least modernized from nefarious influences; by those who would stress the virtues of entrepreneurship and individualism and those who would nurture community and collective concerns; by those who would pursue strategies of top-down initiative and decision-making and those who advocate a bottom-up, or grassroots, approach; and finally, by those who would exploit and maim Mother Nature for the benefit of either business or labour in today's world, as well as by those who concern themselves with a bountiful and livable environment for future generations.

The divergence of interpretations begins with the diagnosis of the central problem. In the late 1950s and early 1960s, when international development assistance was becoming a major enterprise and the academic community was laying out the rationales that were to support it, it was generally assumed that traditionalism was the problem and modernization was the solution. Dealing now with the flotsam of modernization, more recent generations of theorists and practitioners are tempted to search for grounding in tradition.

Strategies and manifestations. For good and ill, many of the consequences of the general thrust of modernization and of the undertakings of the more developed states and international donor agencies in the name of development were manifest first and most dramatically in Latin America. The Latin American states were the first of the so-called Third World to gain formal independence. They were also the states most immediately and directly under the influence of the United States as it emerged extraordinarily rich and powerful in the aftermath of World War II. From that time until the onset of deep economic crisis in the early 1980s, Latin America was industrializing and urbanizing more rapidly than any other major region, and its population was growing at the fastest clip.

The approach to development that was undertaken by the United States and most major donor agencies in the 1950s and that in most particulars survived at least through the 1960s stressed the promotion of increased production and productivity, especially through macroeconomic planning; institution building; public investment in large-scale infrastructure projects (e.g., highways, dams); training and technical assistance, stressing First World technologies and bureaucratic procedures; and the facilitation of private trade and investment abroad.

Planning stressed attention to comparative advantage, which for most LDCs was seen to lie in the export of primary products, and to infrastructure projects that enhanced the feasibility of foreign investments. Foreign assistance was not normally tied to specific projects, but was often tied to the purchase of capital goods from the United States and to the elimination of tariffs or regulations viewed as obstacles to trade and investment. Development plans drawn up with US assistance often called for new taxes. The nature of the power structure in most client states meant that taxes would be regressive, and any new tax burden would be borne by the non-affluent. Resulting new revenues were not to be spent on the poor, however; it was argued that benefits would eventually "trickle down" to low income sectors, but that short-term requirements of capital accumulation called for the minimization of public spending on general services and social welfare.

A major overhaul of US foreign aid legislation in 1973 redirected attention to "basic human needs" but did not then or later redirect much in the way of resources. Meanwhile, overall outlays of US development assistance to Latin America were dropping in the 1970s. Most such aid was reclaimed in the 1980s for the promotion of security interests and private enterprise. Macroeconomic planning, infrastructure, and productivity were re-emphasized, along with export promotion and privatization.

It has long been an article of faith in the West that the underdevelopment of the Third World is a consequence of its failure to become—or delay in becoming—a part of the world system. Opinion leaders of the Third World have often been convinced that the opposite is the case—that their underdevelopment is a consequence of the nature of their relations with the West. Thus, while rarely lacking in advice from the First World, some Third World leaders, movements, and regional organizations have devised their own strategies for protecting their industries, expanding their markets and even competing with First World producers. Those strategies have included import substitution industrialization—implying state support and protection for domestically owned infant industries and emphasis on domestic market expansion; diversification of export products and markets; regional economic integration; associations of primary product producers; and multilateral bargaining with more developed states.

The Latin American states, in fact, got a head start in testing such locally generated strategies.

Some such strategies have been successful at some times and in some places. But over time First World powers have ordinarily found ways either to frustrate Third World initiatives or to turn them to their own advantage. Particularly for the Latin American countries, most of which were under authoritarian rule in the 1970s and virtually all of which sunk into deep recession in the 1980s, dependency and debt have made the pursuit of home-grown strategies impossible.

By the late 1960s and to a far greater extent by the beginning of the 1990s, the thrust of late industrialization and other manifestations of the diffusion of "modernism" had brought about dramatic changes throughout the Third World. In demographics, one of the most consequential changes was urbanization. Latin America, about 70 per cent rural in 1925, was almost 70 per cent urban at the beginning of the 1990s. In fact, one-half of the population is now in cities of over 100,000, and the region boasts of or frets about several of the largest cities in the world.

Another such change was the population explosion, which owed much to the spread of modern sanitation and medicine. After having grown at rates of up to three per cent a year for some two decades, Latin America's population growth began to slow in the 1960s and was down to about 2.5 per cent annually at the beginning of the 1990s. Still, population had increased from some 15,000,000 at the time of independence in 1820 to more than 425,000,000 in 1990, and it was expected to reach 600,000,000 by the turn of the century.

In social organization there had been in the post-war period a considerable breakdown of extended family or tribal ties and a partial regrouping in such organizations as unions and parties. Social structure was also transformed, as the expansion of commerce and the growth of government itself generated middle classes, and industrialization gave rise to urban working classes.

In political organizations, social and technological changes led generally to a weakening of regional *caudillos* and to a greater concentration of power in the central government of the state. New patterns of trade, new modes of production, and increased productivity transformed the traditional market basket, resulting in the availability of a greater quantity and variety of consumer goods. And changes in attitude were manifest in rejection of communal ties and values and the embracing of consumerism.

A harvest of mixed blessings. There is no denying that the diffusion, or recycling, of the products and attendant social features of the vanguard of technology has brought many blessings to the Third World generally and to Latin America in particular. But those are mixed blessings, to say the least, and the mix has often favoured only a minority. Although the provision of sanitation facilities and health care services remains woefully inadequate in most countries, modern medicine has truly changed the face of the earth, bringing about dramatic improvement in infant and maternal mortality rates and thus in life expectancy. In Latin America, infant mortality rates are the lowest of any Third World region (about 55 per 1,000) and life expectancy (about 64 years in the early 1980s) the longest. One of the upshots, of course, of this modern miracle is what has come to be known as the population explosion. The explosion is often allotted the lion's share of the blame for the failure of development, or the failure of development to benefit the teeming masses of the Third World. (It is usually overlooked that rapid population growth was probably a precondition for the rapid economic growth that is seen by so many as the primary goal and manifestation of development.) Population growth drops somewhat with urbanization, but urbanization, with all its attendant problems, is hardly to be encouraged. The only benign formula we know of for dramatically reducing the growth rate is widely shared prosperity with greater opportunities, in particular, for women.

Urbanization has made possible the provision of such amenities as electricity and running water and such service institutions as hospitals and public schools. Indeed, as in health, gains in education, and particularly in literacy, have been impressive. The frantic pace of urbanization, however, and the sheer size of some urban concentrations, has placed a severe strain on municipal governments, resulting in extensive pockets of urban anarchy. And the population explosion has meant that on a global basis, while the absolute numbers of well-fed, literate persons, rises, so do the numbers of the hungry and illiterate. It was estimated in 1990 that three-quarters of the population of Latin America was suffering from some degree or manifestation of malnutrition.

Urbanization, along with technological advances, has facilitated the spread of the communications media, enhancing the distribution of information, but also of misinformation and of propaganda. It has also led to traffic congestion, pollution, and street crime. Progress in curing such respiratory diseases as tuberculosis has been offset by the development of new respiratory ailments resulting from the constant inhaling of gasoline fumes and other pollutants.

Changes in social organization have weakened

the constraints imposed by family and community on individual behaviour, dissolving patron–client networks, mitigating such practices as nepotism, and freeing the individual to choose his or her own locales, associates, and professions. But the same change process weakens also the socialization and security provided by extended families and traditional communities without necessarily generating enough jobs or social welfare services to compensate for the loss. In fact, late industrialization, typically capital intensive, has scarcely begun to absorb the workforce so rapidly being pushed off the land or pulled by the attractions of the metropolis and swollen by the population explosion. The ratio of available urban jobs to job-seekers in Latin America was far worse at the beginning of the 1990s than it had been a half century earlier. Thus the new freedom may well be of the sort that means "nothing left to lose"—freedom to wander jobless, homeless, and hungry in alienated isolation. The streets of Bogotá, São Paulo, and so many other cities have become cruel homes and schools for untold thousands of urchins.

Socioeconomic changes have made possible new, more effective forms of political organization, resulting, in some cases, in the dissolution of feudal patterns; reinforced central governments have acquired greater capabilities for public service, but also, given the expansion of military, paramilitary, and police forces, for surveillance and repression.

The new consumerism may have accelerated production and the creation of jobs. In fact, such attitudinal change may have been a necessary concomitant to the expansion of domestic markets, but it also increased demands for imports and contributed to burgeoning debt. Furthermore, the spread of the new consumerism has not necessarily been reflected in the generation of a correspondingly large category of new consumers. The purchasing power of workets in Latin America has actually been declining since the early 1960s. The economic development strategy, popular in the 1950s and 1960s, that featured import substitution industrialization was generally characterized by a simple transfer of technologies and product lines from First World to Third. Technologies thus were capital intensive and product lines catered to the middle and upper classes. The combination of production geared for the few and increasing demand by the many fed inflation and frustration, and, in general, contributed to a climate of crisis.

Development planners might have met this crisis by increasing the range and volume of products to cater to the working classes and by taking other steps to accelerate the expansion of domestic markets, but the political and economic implications of such a commitment were threatening to élites. Thus, the most common reaction was that of dampening effective demand—in some cases so abruptly and by measures so harsh that military dictatorship seemed called for. Subsequently, planners, prodded by the International Monetary Fund (IMF) and other public and private creditors, turned again to an emphasis on production (often highly mechanized) for export, a strategy wherein the masses streaming into the cities were needed neither as workers nor as consumers. Meanwhile, land previously devoted to subsistence farming has been converted for export production.

Increasing landlessness is a particularly acute problem in much of the world, and development programmes have done little to remedy it; in fact, such programmes have sometimes made it worse. Richer farmers more readily have access to newly available products, technologies, and credit; and the enhanced value of the land tempts those richer farmers to buy out or push out their struggling tenants or neighbours. Some 90 per cent of the arable land in Latin America now belongs to 10 per cent of the landowners, a greater concentration than in any other world region of comparable size. The alienation of the land—whether by force of arms or by market forces—has led, in many countries, to scarcity of basic foodstuffs and inflation of food prices. It was estimated that in the 1970s population increase and agricultural production in Latin America had kept pace with each other, but such production was largely for export or for cattle feed, the benefits of which were narrowly distributed. A net exporter of foodstuffs, Latin America was nevertheless spending some 60 per cent more at the end of that decade than at the beginning to import food. The alienation of the land has also led to bloated urban labour forces, to ever larger and more desperate pools of migratory farm labourers, and, most dramatically of late, to insurgency, particularly in Central America. Finally, it has contributed, in more developed and less developed states alike, to the most profound kind of dependency, in which only a privileged or isolated few have the option of producing what they would consume or of consuming what they produce.

For many Latin American countries modernization has brought spurts of rapid economic growth. For a number of them it has brought about a major transformation in the nature of goods produced and exported, from unprocessed primary goods to processed ones, for example, or from primary goods to manufactured ones. **Brazil**, at mid-century heavily dependent on wildly fluctuating markets for coffee and primary goods, competes now with the major powers in the marketing of state-of-the-art military hardware and other high-tech products.

Even for the most successful competitors, however, modernization has been accompanied by chronic unemployment, chronic inflation, unpayable debts, denationalization of resources, environmental degradation, and a deepening of dependency. In the case of dependency, direct political ties between the United States and most of its Latin American clients may have become attenuated and economic ties of investment, trade and aid may have been diversified; but subsistence farming, almost everywhere under assault, threatens to go the way of subsistence hunting and fishing, and handicrafts have virtually become dependent on tourism for their survival. The world capitalist system has penetrated the steepest mountain ranges, the steamiest jungles, and the loneliest islands; and the community that does not depend for its livelihood on decisions made in faraway places by people unconcerned about its welfare is very rare indeed.

Latin America's lost decade. Along with truly impressive progress in public health care delivery, public education, and literacy during the first three decades of the post-war period, Latin America as a whole had been enjoying annual economic growth rates averaging 4 to 6 per cent. In 1982, however, for the first time since mid-century, Latin America's overall gross national product registered negative growth. Average per capita GDP for the region dropped by almost 8 per cent during the 1980s.

Even orthodox First World economists, pleased with the export promotion, privatization, deregulation, and austerity that have characterized recent economic policy in the region, speak of the 1980s as a "lost decade" for Latin America. The foreign debt, for the region as a whole, was approaching $500 billion in 1990 and claimed about half of the area's export earnings for interest payments alone. The debts of Brazil and **Mexico**, $114 billion and $94 billion, respectively, at the end of the decade, though dwarfed now in absolute terms by the US debt, were the highest in the Third World; and those of several other Latin American states were higher still in per capita terms.

Latin American economies had also been wrenched by inflation rates that averaged 437 per cent in 1988. As if to spite those economists who had posed a choice between inflation and unemployment, the latter was also rising. Official figures on urban unemployment showed a regional average of 11.2 per cent for 1986 and 1987; but most Latin Americans assumed that official figures were artificially low. Underemployment, furthermore, was far higher.

These problems, along with declining rates of investment, of production and of productivity, and declining real wages and salaries, were exacerbated by the sharp rise in energy costs and the global recession of the early 1980s, but they were in large part also a consequence of the modern international version of debt peonage and of the punishment creditors and their collection agency, the International Monetary Fund, were able to inflict on defaulters. That punishment had generally included currency devaluation, higher interest rates, lower wages and longer working hours, a slashing of government services, subsidies, and welfare programmes, and a veritable fire sale of government assets. As the rich made the usual choice as to whether or not to accept sacrifice, the additional load of sacrifice was being borne mainly by those who had no choice.

Even if reasonable rates of economic growth were to be resumed in the 1990s—and no-one seems to be predicting that—such growth would not qualify in the minds of many Latin Americans as development. To be meaningful to the long-repressed majority, development must encompass equity as well as accumulation, choices and opportunity as well as occupation and sustenance, a sense of self-worth and dignity as well as national pride, and some degree of control over personal, community, and national destinies.

JKB

DÍAZ ORDAZ, GUSTAVO. Gustavo Díaz Ordaz was president of **Mexico** 1964–70. He came from lower middle-class provincial origins, and began his ascent through becoming Senator for his home state of Puebla. Later he worked in Mexico City, in the Ministry of *Gobernación*, of which he served as Secretary 1958–64. However despite serving in what were at least nominally political roles during this period, he emerged as a somewhat old fashioned figure for the 1960s. By the end of his term as president he was seen by his enemies as the personifacation of the most authoritarian and despotic features of the Mexican state.

In some respects, however, Díaz Ordaz was less authoritarian than his critics believed. He made little attempt to intervene directly in local or regional government, or in the day-to-day process of economic management. He was content to leave active policy-making to others and rarely intervened arbitrarily. From a narrow technocratic viewpoint, indeed, Mexico was quite well governed during 1964–70. However Díaz Ordaz showed little or no interest in the politics of reform, and his most characteristic attitude to any form of political dissent was one of open hostility. This made him an unfortunate choice to be president during the 1960s when the currents of student radicalism, so characteristic of many countries in and around 1968, reached Mexico.

Díaz Ordaz was taken by surprise by the student movement in Mexico and greatly feared that his country's hosting of the Olympic Games, in which he took particular pride, would be threatened. He therefore decided to repress the student movement and on Oct. 2, 1968 troops opened fire on a demonstration in the Plaza de Tres Culturas at Tlatelolco in central Mexico City; several hundred people were killed.

Although Mexican politics were essentially quiescent up until this time, many well-placed Mexicans were shocked at the sight of Mexican soldiers killing students in the capital city in full view of the international press. Very few people publicly criticized Díaz Ordaz at the time, but his own chosen successor Luis Echeverría quickly and publicly distanced himself from the Tlatelolco massacre. Díaz Ordaz was evidently embittered by the way in which his policies were repudiated by his successor, but made no active attempt to intervene. His particular brand of political conservatism went to the grave with him.

GP

DOMINICA. *Population*: 94,200 (1989). *Area*: 751 sq km. *Trade volume*: EC$226,200,000. *Top five trade partners*: USA, UK, Japan, Trinidad and Tobago, St. Lucia. *Birthrate*: 21.4 per 1,000.

Geographical background. Dominica, once regarded as a Leeward Island but now as a Windward Island, is one of the Caribbean's most mountainous countries. As a result, it averages consistently high rainfall, 6350 mm in areas like Morne Diablo (1,447 m) and 1750 mm annually in coastal areas. This, in turn, has given rise to lush vegetation, forests covering 40 per cent of the total land area, 365 rivers and the export of drinking water. Dominica is also one of the very few Caribbean countries with a still relatively intact and large indigenous population. There are some 3,000 Caribs who occupy 2,835 ha and are mainly engaged in traditional skills such as weaving.

Socio–political background. The Commonwealth Republic of Dominica is led by Mary Eugenia Charles, the Caribbean's first female Prime Minister. Head of the Dominica Freedom Party (DFP), she has been ruling since July 1980. Elections to the 21-seat House of Assembly were last held in July 1990. There is also a nine-member Senate.

A British colony since 1782, Dominica became independent on Nov. 3, 1978. Patrick John, formerly of the Dominica Labour Party (DLP) became the island's first Prime Minister and Frederick Degazon, President. This marked a period of scandal and civil unrest which only stabilized under Miss Charles, and from which Dominica is still recovering.

Outline of political history. Until 1939, Dominica was a member of the Leeward Islands Federation, becoming a Windward Island in December 1959 when that association ended. It achieved separate status under a new Constitution in January 1960 and was a member of the short-lived West Indies Federation, 1958–62.

Edward LeBlanc's DLP won the first election under separate status and he became Chief Minister. Dominica became an associated state in March 1967 and LeBlanc became Premier in October 1970, after the DLP again won general elections.

LeBlanc retired in July 1974, to be succeeded by Patrick John. In the March 1975 elections, the DLP won 16 of the 21 seats in the expanded House of Assembly. Patrick John therefore became the island's first Prime Minister following independence in late 1978. Shortly after, the government sought to introduce legislation restricting trade union and media freedom. The social upheaval which followed eventually ended in the arrest, trial and sentencing of John and others, a process which took almost 10 years to bring to conclusion, and the disbandment of the Defence Force in April 1981.

In demonstrations against Government proposals the Defence Force killed two people. This gal vanized popular support against the Government, mobilized under the umbrella Committee for National Salvation (CNS), which demanded John's resignation. John refused and a 25-day general strike followed. His resignation came only after President Degazon had fled the country, finally resigning in February 1980, and all of the Cabinet Ministers resigned.

Backed by the CNS, Oliver Seraphine was elected Prime Minister and an interim government formed to plan for elections in six months. Seraphine headed the new Democratic Labour Party (DEMLAB) at the elections eventually held in July 1980. But both he and Patrick John lost their seats when Eugenia Charles' DFP swept to power winning 17 of the 21 House seats.

Miss Charles was faced with a country on the brink of anarchy. Allegations of the Defence Force's involvement in the marijuana trade led to its disarment in April 1981. A state of emergency was declared, but two *coup* attempts were led by former Defence Force members. A number of people were imprisoned, including Patrick John, who was implicated. John and others were acquitted at a trial in June 1982. However, at a retrial in October 1985 John and the former deputy commander of the Defence Force each received 12-year sentences. The former Defence Force commander was hanged in 1986 for the murder of a policeman during the second *coup* attempt while five other soldiers who had received death sentences had them commuted to life imprisonment.

Current developments—political. In 1985, a coalition of a new DLP, reactivated by John during his years of freedom, DEMLAB and the United Dominica Labour Party, united as the Labour Party of Dominica, (LDP) to contest elections held on July 1. Led by Michael Douglas, the LDP won five seats, failing to stop a return to power of the DFP, which won 15 seats. The other seat was won by Rosie Douglas, brother of Michael. Immediately after the election the LDP boycotted House sittings in protest against government's decision to halt live parliamentary broadcasts. But by July 1987, the DFP had gained two members, with the LDP reduced to four.

Miss Charles has had to deal with her share of protests in the 1980s, apart from the LDP boycott of the House. She was a major supporter of the 1983 Grenada intervention, been criticized for harsh economic measures and postponed city council elections, originally scheduled for November 1988, for a year. She, however, remains firmly in charge, forging close links with the USA and, uniquely for a Caribbean Commonwealth country, France. France helped to quell both *coup* attempts and has given Dominica much aid.

In the Caribbean, Dominica under Miss Charles has played its role in **CARICOM**, the regional grouping. The country is however more concerned with a smaller political union. It has backed fuller integration of the Organization of East Caribbean States (OECS) and is progressing with St. Vincent, Grenada and St. Lucia to form a political union called the Regional Constituent Assembly. Talks on this were last held in early 1991 in Kingston, St. Vincent.

Outline of economic development. Dominica, an agriculturally based economy, has a GNP of $1,650 per *capita*. Agriculture accounted for 31 per cent of GDP in 1988. Bananas dominate Dominica, accounting for 70 per cent of exports. The island's economy was devastated in 1979 and 1989 by Hurricanes David and Hugo respectively, necessitating much aid support. Despite the problems associated with such dependence on bananas, the island's topography does not lend itself to an economic alternative. The UK buys virtually all the banana production.

Current economic situation. Manufacturing has been encouraged, but remains small. Exports include soap and oils, based on the important coconut crop. The manufacture of timber and timber products is being encouraged and water is exported to countries such as Aruba. Dominica has reduced fuel imports to 6.6 per cent and it is expected that by 1992 all energy requirements will be supplied by hydroelectric power.

Prospects for development. Dominica's future remains tied to agriculture. Its terrain and volcanic sand beaches makes great tourist development unlikely, despite its great natural beauty. The Charles government has encouraged and overseen massive land reform, which has proved successful. It seems that to maintain its social welfare, education and other programmes the future of Dominica lies with some sort of union with other similarly easily disrupted countries in the region.

MH

DOMINICAN REPUBLIC. *Population*: 7,137,000 (1990). *Area*: 48,464 sq km. *GDP*: $3,216 million (1986). *Trade Volume*: Exports, $718,000,000; Imports, $1,400 million (1990). *Top trade partners:* imports: USA, Venezuela, Mexico, Japan; Exports: USA, Netherlands, Puerto Rico. *Defence spending (as percentage of GNP)*: 1.4 (1985) or US$22 per capita. *Education spending (as percentage of GNP)*: 7.8. *Urban population in centres over 20,000 (as percentage of total)*: 55 (1990). *Birthrate*: 33.6 per 1,000 (1980–85). *Life expectancy*: 61 (men); 65 (women) (1990).

Socio–political background. The Dominican Republic is a rich country populated by poor people. The national territory is blessed with fertile soils and rich mineral deposits, with plentiful fish and fowl and forests, and with an equable climate; but its people, ingenious and industrious though they be, have benefited little from nature's bounty.

Socially and culturally, the republic represents a blend of Latin American and Caribbean characteristics or, one might say, of Spanish and African influences. The population is predominantly mulatto, with little remaining trace of the pre-Colombian indigenous peoples. Spanish is spoken universally and Roman Catholicism is practised almost universally, although Protestant missionaries have made inroads and some elements of African religions have persisted or have been reintroduced from Haiti.

Although the country ceased be held formally as a colony in the nineteenth century, it has been, along with most other Caribbean states, economically appended and politically subordinated to some external power throughout its history. Since the turn of the century, the relevant external power has been the United States. The nature of the republic's dependence has meant that the most important decisions as to what would be produced, at what level of production, with what technology and mix of capital– or labour-intensity, and how and where major products would be marketed would be made beyond its borders and without reference to the needs of its people.

Geographical background. The island of Hispaniola, which the Dominican Republic shares with **Haiti**, lies to the south and east of Cuba, west of Puerto Rico. Occupying the eastern two-thirds of the island, the Dominican Republic is larger than all other Caribbean island states except Cuba. Its 19,000 square miles encompass a variety of ecological zones, from cool mountains to tepid plains and from tropical rain forests to scorching desert to balmy beaches. Its population is fast-growing, having more than doubled from 3,000,000 in 1960 to more than 7,000,000 in 1990.

The country is underdeveloped, with much of its human and material potential unrealized, but it is rapidly modernizing under the prod of governments and foreign investors. Subsistence agriculture has gradually given way, for example, to agribusiness—especially sugar production for export. Markets for primary products, however, and especially sugar, are highly unreliable. Consequently, despite occasional spurts of economic growth, the nation's economy is unbalanced and fragile. Although impressive advances have been make in the last two decades in industrialization and economic diversification, and some sectors—mining, manufacturing, tourism, and banking, for example—have become highly modern, the country remains heavily reliant on markets and prices it cannot control, on loans it cannot repay, and, increasingly, on imported food it cannot afford. Meanwhile, though emigration to more prosperous areas, particularly Puerto Rico and the United States mainland, has provided some relief for the now chronic problem of unemployment, the ranks of the unemployed continue to be swelled by illegal immigration from even less fortunate Haiti.

Outline of political histroy. Many modern nation-states have had to fight for their independence, but the Dominicans have had to fight repeatedly for theirs. Just as there have always been some among them who were willing to relinquish sovereignty for protection or to sell out the national patrimony for personal or factional advantage, there have been many others willing to risk everything to retrieve or secure independence for their small state. The very precariousness of independence and the experience of fighting for it from generation to generation have contributed a certain poignancy and intensity to Dominican nationalism.

As in the case of many other Latin American countries, the military campaigns that secured independence left the armed forces (or at least a variety of armed bands) in a power position that was wholly out of keeping with constitutional and legal clauses stressing civilian supremacy. Struggles in the nineteenth century against the would-be colonizers of Spain, France, and Haiti gave way at the turn of the century to a new kind of struggle against a new kind of threat. In this struggle the military, at least the largest or most successful elements of it, was to become a tool of the colonizer (the United States Marines, 1916–1924), and later, with the passing of direct occupation, of the hegemonic power in a neo-colonial relationship.

The 31-year dictatorship of General Rafael Leónidas Trujillo, who rose to power through command of the constabulary established during the US occupation, left no aspect of national life unscathed. No political institution had any domestic base independent of Trujillo and his thugs. Politicians like **Joaquín Balaguer**, who had associated themselves with the regime, were widely discredited, especially among the educated in urban areas. Those like **Juan Bosch**, who had fled into exile, remained untainted but also unschooled in the grisly reality of Dominican politics. After Trujillo's death in 1961, Balaguer, who was serving as puppet president, yielded to US and domestic pressures and stepped down. Elections in 1962 resulted in a solid victory for Juan Bosch and his centre-left **Dominican Revolutionary Party** (*Partido Revolucionario Dominicano*—PRD), but after only six months in office, Bosch was overthrown. The country's traditional reactionary forces—in particular, the oligarchy, the military, and the Church—had united to bring down the PRD government and to dominate the so-called Triumvirate government that succeeded it.

In April 1965, The Triumvirate was itself toppled by an uprising dominated by pro-Bosch, or Constitutionalist, forces. A civil war ensued, as reactionary elements of the military, encouraged by US military advisers, launched an attack against the Constitutionalists and their PRD civilian supporters in Santo Domingo's poorest neighbourhoods. Facing the prospect of a victory by the pro-Bosch forces, US President Lyndon B. Johnson sent in the marines. In elections in 1966, supervised by the US Marines and their military cohorts from a few other Latin American countries, Balaguer and his Reformist Party (PR) soundly defeated Bosch and the PRD. Balaguer was re-elected in 1970 and 1974 in elections boycotted by the PRD and most other parties.

During the long reign of Balaguer, virtually all political activists, including some now aligned with him, suffered death threats, narrow escapes, detainment and deportation. Thus it was a more cautious PRD that contested and won the elections of 1978. Even so, military officers seeking to block its accession to power backed down only after the Carter Administration interceded in support of the democratic process. As Bosch had defected to form another, more leftist, party, the Dominican Liberation Party (PLD), the PRD's standard-bearer this time was Antonio Guzmán, a wealthy rancher.

Guzmán opened up the system, eliminating restraints on civil liberties and urging respect for human rights. He also purged some of the most highly politicized and reactionary military officers and reorganized the armed forces. His political position remained weak, however, as he encountered fierce opposition from within his own party as well as from Balaguer's PR. And his assumption of power coincided with a steep economic decline. Sugar and most other exports were in low demand, and petroleum, all of which had to be imported, was scarce and expensive.

A bad situation was made worse by a devastating hurricane in 1979. Thus, social services continued to be neglected, and economic development programmes were sustained only at the expense of a sharply mounting foreign debt. Corruption scarcely abated. In fact, it is generally believed that it was embarrassment over his own daughter's involvement in shady deals that drove Guzmán to suicide shortly before the end of his term. Meanwhile, Senator Salvador Jorge Blanco had been elected to the presidency for the term beginning in 1982.

Jorge Blanco, a reputable lawyer-politican noted for defending victims of political persecution, pledged to maintain and strengthen the social and political liberalism introduced by his predecessor; to stem the tide of corruption; to trim the size of the bureaucracy, which had mushroomed under Guzmán; and to expand services and protection to the disadvantaged majority. Economic and political circumstances largely beyond his control, however, combined with the weaknesses of his own administration to discredit Jorge Blanco's presidency.

Jorge Blanco was even less acceptable to politically oriented officers than Guzmán had been. Having so much to overcome, Jorge Blanco was exceptionally generous with the military. Nevertheless, he never achieved the levels of control over and respect from the officer corps than Guzmán enjoyed. Facing the spectre of default on foreign debts, Jorge Blanco caved in also to the demands of the International Monetary Fund (IMF) for the imposition of austerity measures that severely penalized his own constituency and deepened the factionalism within the PRD. In particular, the *peso* devaluation of April 1984 resulted in sharp price increases for essential commodities and ignited riots in Santo Domingo that left more than 100 dead. His government never recovered from that episode, and it sunk ever deeper into unpopularity as charges of corruption mounted during its final months.

The PRD thus faced the elections of 1986 with a severely divided party, a reputation besmirched by corruption, and an economy in shambles. Running at the head of a newly constituted Social Christian Reformist Party, Balaguer took a plurality of some 41 per cent of the vote, leaving the PRD's Jacobo Majluta with 39 per cent and Bosch, heading the Dominican Liberation Party, with 18 per cent.

The fact that so many voters misremembered the era of Balaguer as one of general, rather than highly selective, prosperity owes much to Balaguer's legendary political acumen. Friends and enemies alike credit his intelligence, and even those who know him best describe him as enigmatic. Under the tutelage of Trujillo, he learned to listen and not to speak unnecessarily; he also learned how to reward and discipline supporters, co-opt the uncommitted, and punish his enemies. He was adept at combining authoritarianism with paternalism, but, always the pragmatist, he adapted with ease to operating in a more open and democratic system, building on his strengths in bargaining and conciliation.

Recent developments—political. Relative calm prevailed during the first half of Balaguer's fifth term, but beginning in the spring of 1988, public protests over low wages, the soaring costs of basic goods and services, and the scarcity of such amenities as electricity and potable water, became remarkably widespread. Eleven provinces were crippled by general strikes, and incidents of violence were reported throughout the country. At least ten protestors were killed and scores were injured in confrontations with riot squad police in the capital, Santo Domingo, and in Santiago, the second-largest city. Negotiations between labour and business leaders mediated by the Catholic hierarchy served to contain the unrest, but strikes were common throughout 1989 and riots erupted from time to time.

In the meantime, as Balaguer turned his attention to the construction of a mammoth lighthouse to commemorate the quincentennial in 1992 of Columbus's arrival in the new world, even middle class Dominicans were increasingly living in the dark. Daily powercuts, or *apagones*, interrupted supplies of running water as well as of light and caused spoilage of food and medicine. Small businesses were folding at an alarming rate.

The major beneficiary of the discrediting of the Balaguer government and the disunity of the PRD has been Bosch's PLD. Despite rapid growth, it remains by far the best organized party. New members are carefully trained and older members meet regularly for study and discussion of political issues. Although there is as yet no heir apparent to Bosch, there is a well-established echelon of mid-level leadership. Bosch himself is noted for his incisive commentary on social inequality and on US imperialism, even before audiences likely to react negatively to such themes. As the elections of 1990 approached, however, he trimmed his sails somewhat. Responding, perhaps, to the recent decapitalization and dismal mismanagment of some public enterprises, he even joined the chorus calling for privatization.

The main issue in the 1990 campaign, apart from the age and roadworthiness of the two major contenders, was the Balaguer government—or the lack of it. As during his earlier terms, Balaguer had done a great deal of building; but he had not given equal attention to what should happen inside the buildings—to ensuring that his new clinics and schools would have nurses and teachers. Government employees, in particular had been sadly neglected.

Throughout the campaign period, public opinion polls showed Bosch enjoying a strong lead, and on election day, May 16, he was favoured in early returns. Two days later, however, the central electoral commission reported that by a slim lead Balaguer had won another term. With foreign election observers supporting the PLD demand, Balaguer's PRSC agreed to a recount. Its results, announced after a tense two-week lapse, reconfirmed the earlier finding. Many Bosch supporters remained sceptical, however, about the validity of the process.

Outline of economic development. The Dominican economy has suffered in exaggerated form from the uncertainty and dependency and deterioration in the terms of trade for producers of primary products that have plagued the Third World generally and Latin America in particular. Sugar cane cultivation was introduced to the island by Columbus himself. Nevertheless the republic's economy was based essentially on subsistence agriculture until Trujillo transformed it for his personal advantage, leaving behind an export-oriented economy heavily dependent on sugar. Economic growth since the early 1960s has been erratic but substantial. Between 1960 and 1980 real per capita income rose from $513 to $1,050. After 1980 the Dominican economy, along with that of the United States and of much of the rest of the Western world, slipped into recession.

The collapse of the world sugar market in the early 1980s, followed in short order by a massive cut in the Dominican quota of the US sugar market, left the country economically destitute and terminally indebted. The tourist industry has since become the country's major foreign exchange earner. Non-traditional export crops grown on land formerly devoted to sugar cane and light industry in the proliferating duty free zones have also contributed to a measure of economic recovery. Nevertheless the country remains utterly dependent upon dollar remittances from the nearly 1,000,000 emigrants now living in Puerto Rico or the United States and on hard currency loans contracted at great cost to national sovereignty and social peace. By 1990, per capita income had climbed back only to $800.

Current economic situation. The Balaguer government's approach to the nation's very severe economic problems—printing *pesos* to cover public works programmes and to stimulate agricultural production—has generated new jobs but has also resulted in devaluation and accelerated inflation. The latter was pegged officially in 1988 and 1989 at about 60 per cent, but it was generally believed to be much higher. Perhaps the poor had learned to live with economic insecurity, but with the double shock of *apagones* and inflation, insecurity increasingly stalks the middle class as well. Meanwhile foreign reserves accumulated first of all from remittances from Dominican emigrants, second from tourism, and to an unknown degree from drug deals could not be expected to service adequately a foreign debt of some $4 billion. A new class of financiers, however, has learned how to profit from the country's economic prostration—through currency exchange deals and speculation in scarce commodities. This group competes for influence with another new rich sector, the *narcotraficantes* (drug dealers), some of whom are plying their trade in the Dominican Republic, while others are merely laundering their money earned elsewhere.

Prospects for development. The more things change in the Dominican Republic, the more some things stay the same. Politics at the highest level, for example, remains a *pas de deux*. Defying the odds of time and fortune, the two grand old men of letters, Joaquín Balaguer and Juan Bosch, the primary contenders for power when Trujillo was abruptly removed from the scene in 1961, continue to dominate the political arena at the beginning of the 1990s. Along with the two remarkably durable octogenarians, even the supporting cast of characters remains much the same as it was in the 1960s.

Another characteristic of Dominican life that has changed little over the years is the hardship of it for most Dominicans. The benefits of the **Caribbean Basin Initative (CBI)** of the 1980s, like those of the "economic miracle" of the 1970s and the Alliance for Progress of the 1960s, have mostly been siphoned off long before reaching the deprived majority of peasants and blue-collar workers or would-be workers.

The republic has weathered remarkably well the political and economic crises of the 1980s, but the calm that prevails as the country faces a new decade is an uneasy calm that should not be mistaken for stability. Considerable economic readjustment and diversification has taken place, but it is not clear that those changes, featuring disincentives to internal market expansion, will solve even the long-term problems of balance of payments and debt servicing; and they are not even addressed to the shorter-term problem of the economic insecurity of the majority of Dominicans.

JKB

DOMINICAN REVOLUTIONARY PARTY (Partido Revolucionario Dominicano — PRD) (Dominican Republic). The Dominican Revolutionary Party was an urban-based, left-of-centre, nationalist party that supported Professor **Juan Bosch** in 1962 in his successful bid for the presidency of the **Dominican Republic**. Under fragmented leadership, it survived Bosch's defection and a decade of repression to win presidential and congressional elections in 1978 and 1982, under the leadership first of Silvestre Antonio Guzmán (president 1978–82) and Salvador Jorge Blanco (president 1982–86). It has since slipped to third place, however, trailing the more nearly personalist parties of **Balaguer** and Bosch.

JKB

DRUGS. Undoubtedly the most important development issue facing many Latin American and Caribbean countries today is the production and trafficking of illegal drugs. The lucrative profits generated by this transnational industry have provided a financial cushion during the past decade of economic recession, and absorbed the labour of over 1,000,000 Latin Americans in a range of activities, not all of which should be presumed to be illegal. Producers of coca leaves, for example, can claim to be following an historically important cultural tradition. Although this cannot be said for casual labourers employed in processing operations, they have nonetheless sought to secure their livelihood amidst high unemployment. Indirectly the drugs trade has fostered a massive subterranean economy that provides such services as: the supply of precursor chemicals for refining cocaine; financial laundering involving foreign currency exchange dealing and the import of contraband goods; and the apparatus of violence that underpins the entire structure and challenges the legitimacy of state institutions.

The drugs connection linking producers in the south to consumers in the north has a long history, but during the last decade or so it has taken on an increasingly violent form. Rising demand for cocaine in the United States has led Washington to prioritize supply-side policies involving eradication at source.

This has increased the pressure upon Latin American governments to wage their own "war on drugs", with the United States offering military and logistical support and tying its disbursment of aid to the achievement of crop substitution targets.

This policy first appeared in the mid-1970s as the Mexican government began aerial spraying operations on marijuana and opium crops, a campaign that for many years was hailed as a successful example of crossborder co-operation. Yet this eradication programme served less to reduce demand for marijuana than to divert large-scale cultivation for the North American market to other parts of the Caribbean—principally **Colombia**, **Jamaica** and **Belize**. It also stimulated greater efforts within the United States to produce home-grown varieties such as *sinsemilla*.

While today the production of marijuana is thought to make it the second crop by value within the United States, it also generates vital sources of income for smaller producers. Jamaica, for example, has been reputed to earn more from the export of marijuana than from its traditional sources of foreign exchange—bauxite, sugar and tourism. Meanwhile, **Mexico**, an earlier "success" story of eradication, has not only resumed the production and export of marijuana and opium derivatives, but has also become a conduit for an increasing proportion of cocaine entering the United States. Finally, Colombia is still estimated to earn between $300–$500 million from marijuana, and lesser but growing amounts from the production and export of opium and synthetic drugs such as methaqualone. Yet these sums are small in comparison with the earnings derived from cocaine, on which we focus here.

The cultivation of coca leaf, its processing and refining into a powerful derivative and the international distribution to markets in industrialized countries illustrates many of the characteristics of a streamlined multinational business. At the pinnacle of the international cocaine industry are the rival Colombian cartels of Cali and Medellín, which have been engaged in murderous competition. These are followed by national "drug barons" in **Peru**, **Bolivia** and other countries who have used corruption and violence against the incumbents of political office and the judiciary to establish the degree of autonomy necessary to pursue their activities with minimal disruption. Yet at the base of the pyramid are the hundreds of thousands of peasants and urban poor who have sought a livelihood from the cultivation and processing of coca leaf amidst the severe economic recession that has wracked Latin America during the 1980s.

Coca. Coca (*Erythroxylum* spp.) forms part of the natural pharmacopoeia of the Andes and its use has been dated back into the third millenia BC. Coca leaves are widely used throughout the Andean region and Amazon Basin as a masticatory that serves as a mild stimulant and sustenance for work, and they possess a nutritional value providing essential vitamins and minerals. As the "sacred leaf of the Incas", coca performs an important sacramental role, and is a strong symbol of cultural identity amongst native Andean people. It is vital, therefore, to distinguish the traditional role of coca from the use of more powerful derivatives such as "crack" and cocaine.

Today approximately 300,000 hectares are planted to coca, of which Peru accounts for some 60 per cent, Bolivia 30 per cent, Colombia around 10 per cent with small amounts in **Ecuador** and **Brazil**. This represents almost a doubling of the area under coca during the last six years, and reflects the massive process of frontier expansion that has occurred, especially in the Chaparé region of Bolivia and the Upper Huallaga Valley of Peru, the two main coca growing areas. The dramatic increase in coca production during the 1980s can be attributed to two major factors.

First, the high price of coca compared to alternative crops: for example, in Bolivia in the mid-1980s its price advantage was between 4 and 24 times the returns on traditional food and cash crops. Secondly, the scale of the crisis affecting highland agriculture in Peru and Bolivia, in which drought and economic recession severely hit an already structurally impoverished rural population, encouraging outmigration in search of improved livelihood prospects. That many rural migrants headed for the coca-growing frontier underlines the importance of this sector as the main, if not only, source of economic growth and employment within Bolivia and Peru during the 1980s.

Much of the casual labour that has sought work on the frontier has been employed in refining operations in which coca leaf is turned into paste. This relatively simple process, using principally lime, kerosene and sulphuric acid, has become widely practised amongst small producers for several reasons. It avoids the wild fluctuations in price of coca leaves, it allows producers to retain more value-added from their labour, and it reduces the bulk of 500kgs of leaves to a more manageable 2.5kgs of paste which is then sold to merchants. Most of this paste then passes through two further stages of refining: the first yields cocaine sulphate (base); the second cocaine hydrochloride, its purest form. These two operations are performed by more specialised laboratories, most of which have hitherto been located in Colombia.

Profits. As with much legitimate international trade, profit margins increase as the product is refined and moves downstream, though in this case reflecting the risks of seizure and loss of capital. Thus it is estimated that less than 1 per cent of the value of the final product finds its way back into the hands of the primary producers. Providing that such figures, which have been drawn from a variety of sources, are treated with extreme caution and used only to indicate orders of magnitude, notional gross returns can be ascribed to each country participating in the international cocaine industry.

Bolivia, for example, is believed to generate around $1.5 billion of cocaine products based upon a growing indigenous expertise in refining operations and increasing autonomy from the Colombian cartels. Of this, some $500 million remains in the country with perhaps half finding its way into the hands of the primary producers. Meanwhile Peru is thought to earn around $2 billion per year, but it is much more dependent upon Colombian operations for the purchase and processing of its coca products. Finally, Colombia itself, as the fulcrum of the industry, has derived the greatest value-added through an effective, if weakening, monopoly over the refining and distribution of cocaine hydrochloride. Gross earnings have been estimated at between \$7–\$11 billion or more, of which some \$2 billion returns to Colombia each year for investment in urban real estate, cattle ranching and other speculative outlets.

Yet such sums are small when considered alongside the \$100,000 million plus gross value of retail street sales of cocaine in the United States. During the 1980s this total grew even as the wholesale value of cocaine entering the USA fell: from \$60,000 per kilo early in the decade to \$10,000 by the close. Crucially, more than 90 per cent of this massive turnover is laundered through the continental and offshore banking systems. This provides large profitable commissions for many of the best known North American commercial banks, as US Justice Department research has revealed. It also indirectly incorporates a tier of small Caribbean countries into the industry, with **Panama**, the **Bahamas** and the **Cayman Islands**, amongst others, taking advantage of the demand for financial services by providing laundering facilities for enterprises with surplus cash.

Violence. The growth of the cocaine trade has been accompanied by extensive corruption, violence and a direct challenge to the legitimacy of the state and the authority of its institutions. This has been most graphically demonstrated in Colombia where the cartels have waged a campaign of terror against political life, judicial process and civil society. The responsibility of the extreme right for these events contrasts sharply with the spectre of a left-wing narco-terrorist conspiracy which was a scenario promoted by US diplomats and policy-makers during the Reagan years. There are, nevertheless, examples of mutual tolerance and an occasional convergence of interests between rural guerrilla movements and drug dealers who otherwise subscribe to quite incompatible political projects. The Revolutionary Armed Forces of Colombia (*Fuerzas Armadas Revolucionarias de Colombia* — FARC), for example, operate in the coca-growing region of Caquetá, imposing taxes on the sale and movement of leaf and derivatives, and protecting peasant producers from the exploitation of drug intermediaries and abuse by the army. In Peru **Sendero Luminoso** has become entrenched in the Huallaga Valley, taking advantage of peasant opposition to forcible coca eradication schemes to carry out armed attacks on police posts and other targets representing the state. This has led to the region being placed under a state of emergency and where crop substitution and counter insurgency operations are inseparably entwined within an overall military strategy of low intensity conflict.

By comparison, there has there been relatively little violence in Bolivia, and this limited to a number of isolated incidents. Undoubtedly this derives from the strong historical tradition of trade union organization in the country. Bolivian coca growers are affiliated, through their local syndicate, into one of five federations which, despite their political differences, represent a powerful voice at national level. This has been most evident, for example, in their resistance to compulsory coca eradication schemes involving the use of chemical herbicides.

Alternatives. The United States has pressured Bolivia and Peru into drastically reducing their production of coca leaves as a way of stamping out the drugs trade. Yet its technical assistance, logistical support and aid programme overwhelmingly comprise the hardware and personnel of repression over a more flexible policy to develop crop alternatives. At the Cartagena Summit held in February 1990, George Bush promised the Andean region \$2.2 billion over five years in financial and military aid, yet Bolivia's own alternative development strategy will cost \$939 million per year for an indefinite period. This would not only guarantee income to coca producers during a transitional phase in which alternative perennial crops mature, but would stimulate economic recovery in general, creating jobs for much of the casual labour hitherto employed in cocaine processing operations.

There is currently considerable emphasis being placed on crop-substitution programmes in which producers receive a *pro rata* payment of \$2,000 per hectare as an incentive to destroy their coca. In 1990 Bolivia exceeded, for the first time, an eradication target of 6,000 hectares of coca and was rewarded with \$18,000,000 in aid. Yet this success was due to a downturn in the price of leaves that, for much of 1990, sold well below the estimated costs of production of \$30 per 100lb bale. Whether this will be the turning point in the strategy of agricultural reconversion, in which increasing amounts of land will be taken out of coca and turned over to alternative food and cash crops, is too early to say. There are several factors that need to be considered in conclusion, however.

First, the long-term success of crop substitution policies will not only depend on variable local prices of coca leaves but on the international price of cocaine sulphate and chlorohydrate. Thus efforts to reduce supply in the South must be accompanied by greater efforts to reduce demand in the North. Secondly, alternative crops must offer the prospect of reasonable and sustainable financial returns to small farmers. The current promotion of exotic crop species in Bolivia, for example, has yet to be accompanied by a clear identification of markets, creating the danger that there may be no demand for substitute crops and, hence, no profit in their cultivation. This may drive producers back into growing coca on the agricultural frontier continuing the process of tropical deforestation.

Thirdly, the need for economic growth to generate employment opportunities is vital if Latin America is to avoid a major problem with substance abuse and associated crime. Already it has been estimated that over 400,000 Colombians regularly smoke *basuco* (coca paste mixed with marijuana and/or tobacco) while in Brazil cocaine dealing is believed to be behind the current wave in urban violence. It should be clear from the above that the drugs issue is one that cannot be treated in isolation but needs to be placed alongside the other major development issues linking North and South.

CS

DUVALIER, FRANÇOIS. ("Papa Doc") Duvalier, trained as a physician, was elected president of **Haiti** in 1957 with the support of a black middle-class movement. His rule, until his death in 1971, was as nearly totalitarian as the country's low level of development permitted. Upon his death, the presidency passed to his son, Jean-Claude Duvalier ("Baby Doc"), then only 21, who maintained a somewhat more modern and less ghoulish, but nevertheless repressive, government until he was toppled by a popular uprising in 1986.

JKB

E

ECHEVERRIA ALVAREZ, LUIS. President of **Mexico**, 1970–76, Luis Echeverría Alvarez had served as Minister of *Gobernacíon* (Interior) under his predecessor, Gustavo Díaz Ordaz, and had held that office (with responsibility for the police) at the time of the Tlatelolco massacre in October 1968. His election campaign stressed strong law and order themes. Once in power, however, he sought to present himself as a left-wing President dedicated to reform and the extension of civic participation, but both domestically and internationally his initiatives created additional problems. By aligning himself with Venezuela and Cuba in the creation of the **Latin American Economic System** (*Sistema Económica Latino-Americana*—SELA) he signalled his intention of pursuing a non-aligned foreign policy independent of the United States, and in 1975 he broke off diplomatic relations with General **Pinochet**'s **Chile**, despite Mexico's long-standing policy of automatic recognition of all governments regardless of their political affiliation (the Estrada Doctrine).

His decision to vote against Israel on the Palestinian question, however, led to a US boycott of Mexico's tourist industry; his order to nationalize land holdings in Sonora in the last days of his Presidency precipitated the devaluation of the *peso* and a serious loss of business confidence; and his choice of his old friend and boyhood companion Gustavo López Portillo as his successor turned out to be a serious blunder. Despite this (or because of it) he received three votes for the post of secretary-general of the United Nations. A wealthy man, his purchase of *Excelsior* as an organ for his political views, was much resented by those who admired the way in which it had been able to maintain its independence.

PARC

ECONOMIC COMMISSION FOR LATIN AMERICA AND THE CARIBBEAN—ECLAC **(Comisión Económica por América Latina y el Caraïbe—CEPALC).** The United Nations Economic Commission for Latin America (ECLA) was established as part of the United Nations Organization in 1948 to co-ordinate policies for economic development in Latin America, and adopted its present title in 1984. Members are all independent Latin American and Caribbean states plus France, the Netherlands, Portugal, Spain, the United Kingdom and the United States. The directing Commission meets biennially in different member capitals. The Executive Secretariat has its headquarters in Santiago de Chile, and there is a sub-regional headquarters for the Caribbean. It has two sources of funding, the UN budget and additional voluntary contributions.

ECLAC has two purposes, to further the economic growth of Latin America and to strengthen the economic relations of the region with the rest of the world. This is achieved through studies, the preparation of reports and the publication of the *Economic Survey of Latin America*. From the beginning its work and that of its adherents, termed *cepalistas* from the initials of its title in Spanish (originally CEPAL), has been characterized by a distinctive position first outlined by the economist Raúl Prebisch in his *Economic Development of Latin America and its Principal Problems* (1949), which emphasized the need for the distribution of the fruits of development, and the consequent need to plan for the social aspects of development such as employment and income distribution. In 1962 it established the Latin American Institute for Social and Economic Planning (ILPES) at Santiago de Chile to provide training and advisory services for governments and their officials.

PARC

ECUADOR. *Population*: 10,700,000. (1990 est.) *Area*: 269,178 sq km. *GDP*: US$8.54 million. *Trade volume*: imports, $2.23 billion; exports, $2.02 billion (1987). *Top five trade partners*: USA, Japan, W. Germany, Italy, Brazil. *Defence spending*: $220 million. *Education spending (as percentage of GNP)*: 3.7. *Urban population (as percentage of total)*: 53.5. *Birthrate*: 36.8 per 1,000. *Life expectancy*: 59.8 (men); 63.6 (women).

Ecuador is a middle-sized Latin American country of great touristic charm, and considerable interest to the outsider on cultural, scientific, and political grounds, although its economic attractions are rather more modest. Its traditionally turbulent political life has appeared to settle down in recent years to an acceptance of peaceful electoral competition, although it would be rash to take the continuation of this state of affairs for granted. A great deal of social change, along with rapid population growth and urbanization, has occurred during the second half of the twentieth century. Exports have been principally of the primary products of agriculture, mining, and fisheries, although the mix shifts over time. Since the switch of the national currency unit, the *sucre*, from sterling zone to dollar zone in 1925, the economy has been clearly in the American sphere of influence. Overtly and covertly, the United States government has played an intermittent role, influencing developments in Ecuadorean politics, motivated primarily by concerns about "security" ranging from the hypothetical to the imaginary and metaphysical, growing out of the Cold War with the Soviet Union.

Geographical background. As the country's name signifies, Ecuador lies on the equator, which almost passes through the country's capital, Quito. The country is conventionally divided into four geographic regions: the sierra, that is, the high Andes and the intermontane valleys, in which lie Quito and a majority of the country's cities; the coast, the humid littoral along the Pacific, which contains the plantations producing for export, and also Guayaquil, the country's largest city and principal port—although it is located not on the ocean itself but inland on the Guayas river; the *oriente*, the tropical eastern lowlands sometimes referred to as the Amazonian region, although territory claimed by Ecuador that actually reaches the Amazon river was annexed by Peru a half-century ago; and the Galapagos Islands in the Pacific, referred to in official documents as the Columbus Archipelago (*Archipiélago de Colón*). Almost all of the country's population is concentrated, in approximately equal numbers, in just two of these regions, the coast and the sierra. The **Galapagos** are inhabited principally, and spectacularly, by exotic fauna; the inhabitants of the *oriente* are primarily only partially acculturated Amerindians, missionaries, and oil workers.

Socio–political background. These regional identities provide the basic framework of the country's politics. The highlands are the region, traditionally, of Indian villages and of large estates using Indian labour in a variety of un-free or semi-free forms, after the fashion of medieval Europe. Until very recently, the Indian population was politically quiescent, barred even from voting by the requirement of literacy for the suffrage. With only tenuous road and rail communications with the coast, the highlands were sleepy, backward, and very Catholic. Quito, the capital, was a slow-moving town of priests and soldiers, bureaucrats and craftsmen, destined to be dominated by the Conservative Party. The coastal region, on the other hand, was loyal to the Liberal Party. Oriented to export agriculture, its life was trade, commerce, and finance. Its population was a kaleidoscope not only of Indians and Hispanics, but of blacks, recent immigrants from Europe, and Lebanese. Its main city, Guayaquil, was bustling, exciting, and a little dangerous. To the oligarchy that ruled in the sierra, the coast was turbulent, irreligious, unreliable, and alien; to the élite of the coast, the sierra was backward, fanatical, arrrogant, and parasitical.

In this inter-regional rivalry, each contender had its strengths. The sierra held the seat of government, and was the region of origin of most army officers. The coast, on the other hand, generated most of the country's income, and, through tariff collections, the government budget. If government policy seemed too favourable to sierra interests at the expense of the coast, the merchants of Guayaquil could go on strike, close down the port, and dry up government revenues. With the discovery of oil in the 1970s, however, the government acquired a source of revenue independent of customs collections, and the power of the coast was weakened.

In national elections, however, the power of the coast is critical. Although there are about as many voters in each region, voters in the sierra tend to split among various candidates and parties, so that no candidate comes out of the highlands with much of an advantage. The more restless and rootless voters of the coast, on the other hand, without continuing loyalties to one party or another, are likely to swing drastically to a particular candidate, thus giving him the margin of victory.

The coast prefers theatrical and charismatic populists. These can be of left, right, or centre: the leftist rails against the oligarchy, the rightist complains about the bureaucrats of the sierra who get in the way of enterprise, the centrist denounces dishonesty in government. Of whatever stripe, these populists are Ecuador's curse. They may come to office, attempt to deliver on their promises with no understanding of economic logic, and create a disaster; they may win the election with the help of moneyed coastal interests, who expect to be paid back in contracts and graft; or they may frighten the proper gentlemen of the sierra into soliciting a military *coup* to keep the rabble from office; or, like José María Velasco Ibarra, they may manage to do all three.

As the suffrage has been extended, the Christian democrats (*Democracia Popular*, or Popular Democracy) and the social democrats (*Izquierda Democrática*, Democratic Left) have tried to form grassroots party organizations with a loyal following of ideologically conscious voters;

they have had some success in the sierra, reducing the old Conservative and Liberal parties to marginal status, but have made hardly a dent on the coast.

Outline of political history. Before the coming of the Spaniards, present-day Ecuador was a province of the Inca Empire, ruled from Cuzco, in Peru. Still today the predominant, although not the only, indigenous language spoken is Quechua, the language of the Inca Empire. For most of the colonial era Quito continued to be ruled from Peru—although the colonial capital was at Lima, on the coast—but for a short period it was transferred to the authority of the regional government at Bogotá in Colombia. Colonial rule was supported by a bureaucratic class of appointees sent out from Spain itself, by the clergy of a Catholic church given special treatment by the government, and by the merchants participating in the monopolistic arrangements for trade with the motherland. Dissident, or liberal, ideas took root among urban intellectuals dissatisfied with clerical control over the press, education, and the theatre; among merchants excluded from the trade monopolies; and among agriculturalists wanting to produce crops forbidden as competitive with the products of Spain.

Independence came, however, not altogether as a triumph of Liberal ideas. A Liberal government had come to power in Spain with the Revolution of 1820, and Conservatives were afraid of the legislation such a government should produce. Moreover, a host of opportunists—such as delinquent taxpayers—got on the independence bandwagon. The country became independent at first as a province in the Federation of Greater Colombia, under the leadership of **Simón Bolívar**. Ecuador began its independent national life proper only with the dissolution of the Federation in 1830.

Initially, Conservatives and Liberals agreed to alternate in the presidency; the agreement held for 12 years, after which the Conservative president, General Juan José Flores, reneged on the agreement and established a dictatorship. The revolt of March 1845 against Flores began a 15-year period of civil war, electoral fraud, and the adoption of several new constitutions; this period did, however, see the abolition of slavery, in 1852.

Order was restored by the iron-fisted rule of the arch-Conservative Gabriel García Moreno, regarded today as one of the great national heroes. Devoutly Catholic, ruthless, but personally honest, García Moreno stabilized the constitution and established the central institutions of government on a firm basis. He was assassinated in 1875, but the Conservatives remained in control for another 20 years.

The Conservative hold on power was broken in 1895 by a successful Liberal revolution lead by General Eloy Alfaro, who remains the great icon of the Liberal movement in the country. Although Alfaro himself served only two presidential terms, he was the dominant figure in government until his assassination in 1912. The Liberals nevertheless remained the dominant force in the country until 1944. The major achievement of the Liberal era was to separate church and state, a principle enshrined in the constitution of 1906, one of the more important of the 17 or 18 (the number is disputed) constitutions Ecuador has had.

The Liberal era was not brought to an end by the rise of left-wing parties, although the Ecuadorean Socialist Party (*Partido Socialista Ecuatoriano*—PSE) was founded in 1926 and the Ecuadorean Communist Party (*Partido Comunista Ecuatoriano*—PCE) in 1927. The Liberals happened to be in power when the boundary dispute with Peru gave rise in 1941 to a war which Ecuador lost, along with a large slice of its national territory (see **Ecuador–Peru Boundary Dispute**.)

The succeeding period, until the present day, has been marked by more or less fair elections in which the traditional Conservative and Liberal parties have competed with others of an *ad hoc* and personalist character. As the electorate has expanded to include groups of lower social and economic status, upper-status groups have no longer been able to count on ruling through the traditional parties, and have instead solicited military seizures of power in order to keep out of office, or remove from office, populist leaders who might have unacceptable personal traits, but more importantly threatened the established distribution of wealth and income. The most dominant figure of this period was the five times president Dr. **José María Velasco Ibarra**.

Recent political developments. Ecuadorean politics has experienced a phase change with the adoption of the Constitution of 1979, the first in Ecuadorean history to give illiterates the right to vote. This meant the final enfranchisement of the country's Indian population, although rapidly growing literacy had made the old prohibition ineffective, as the elections of 1979, held before the new constitution went into effect, showed. In the institutional framework established, the new constitution followed the traditional Ecuadorean pattern of a single-chamber legislature elected on a proportional representation basis by province; and a separation of powers in a unitary republic, with a president directly elected for a single unrepeatable 5-year term by those 18 and older.

In 1979, a young Guayaquil intellectual, Jaime Roldós, was elected as a stand-in for his uncle by marriage, Asad Bucaram, a populist of nebulous views whose candidacy was blocked by the incumbent military regime. Roldós was himself killed in a plane crash, but was succeeded by his progressive vice president Osvaldo Hurtado, a distinguished political scientist, leader of the Christian Democratic (Popular Democracy, *Democracia Popular*—DP) party. Although the projected reforms of the Roldós and Hurtado administrations were stymied by lack of funds, élite opposition, and bureaucratic sabotage, their regime marked the final decomposition of the old Conservative and Liberal parties, which were overshadowed by the Christian Democrats, and by the Social Democrats (known as the "Democratic Left").

However, the 1979 constitution called for a run-off if no presidential candidate secured an absolute majority, so that in 1984 the candidate of the Democratic Left, Rodrigo Borja, who secured the most votes in the first round, was narrowly defeated in the second round of voting by León Febres Cordero, a reactionary neo-liberal business leader who ran as a conservative in the sierra and a populist regional representative on the coast. In the tradition of reactionary populism, Febres Cordero's government was characterized by pandering to élite economic interests, chaotic administration, repressive acts, and general irresponsibility. Borja was however successful in the 1989 elections, defeating in the run-off the latest, and perhaps the craziest, of populist leaders from the coast, Abdalá Bucaram, nephew of the now defunct Asad. Borja's honeymoon was short-lived, as he faced an uphill battle against inflation, foreign indebtedness, and contracting demand for Ecuador's exports.

Suspending payments on the foreign debt but imposing an austerity programme anyway, Borja lost his legislative allies, *Democracia Popular*, in the ensuing wave of unpopularity. This left his Democratic Left party with only 31 of the 71 legislative seats. The Borja administration rapidly declined into the ineffectiveness characteristic of progressives attempting to rule democratically in élite-dominated, socially fragmented, and politically undeveloped Ecuador.

Outline of economic development. The primary economic activity in Ecuador has always been agriculture. This has predominantly meant the growth of grains, fruits, and vegetables in the sierra for local consumption, along with cattle and sheep raising. Although the mountainous terrain means that only a fraction of the land is suitable for use, there is a year-round growing season. Land on the coast was little utilized until the late nineteenth century, when advances in public health technique made it possible to bring under control the yellow fever and other tropical diseases that limited population growth. Since then the coast has been devoted to plantation crops for export. The tendency has been to over-respond to world market demand, so that there is a boom-and-bust cycle as many producers switch to the latest high return crop only to find that the market is saturated, whereupon the new crop is cut back and takes its place as only one in a range of products being exported. This has been more or less the pattern successively with respect to coffee, cacao, bananas, and African palm. A problem with agricultural exports is that Ecuador competes on disadvantageous terms with African producers who have traditional trade ties, and shorter supply lines, to Western Europe, with Central American producers, who face lower shipping costs to the United States, and with South East Asian areas that are closer to Japan.

Current economic situation. The traditional export-agriculture structure has been modified in recent years by several developments. Principal of these was the discovery of oil in the *oriente*, the eastern lowland area. Although exaggerated early hopes of wealth were disappointed, petroleum became the leading export, and Ecuador joined OPEC, the Organization of Petroleum Exporting Countries. Fisheries have developed into a major activity, with Japan being a good customer for Ecuadorean shrimp and tuna. However, the industry has been beset by disputes over fishing rights, especially between Ecuador and US flag vessels.

The third significant development in the economy has been the growth of manufacturing. The principal urban areas early on developed those beverage and food processing industries common to even the least advanced countries, and the highland towns have a strong tradition of craft production of basic necessities like clothing and furniture.

The Quechua-speaking Indians of the Otavalo valley have developed a major textile industry, with a large export sector, beginning with the traditional ponchos, but moving on to standard European items of dress. Otavalan traders can be found all over Latin America, and even in Europe. More recently, the Otavalans have commercialized the distinctive music of the highlands, which blends Indian and European influences and instruments, and one can now meet with musical groups from the valley touring

Europe and North America, and selling their recordings.

Under the favourable tariff arrangements of the Andean Pact, Quito became a centre for the manufacture of kitchen appliances for the whole region. The construction industry has experienced a boom with the use of government employee pension funds for mortgage financing. Great hydro-electric dams constructed with petroleum revenues have made it possible to supply electricity in adequate quantities all over the country.

One of the most striking developments of recent years has been the effective liberation of the Ecuadorean Indian from his traditional position of virtual serfdom. The Spanish conquerors had imposed labour service and special tax obligations on Indians, even those continuing to live in their own villages rather than as resident labourers on the great estates. After independence there was some movement in the direction of mitigation of these burdens, under the pressures of Liberal ideology and Christian conscience, although legal restrictions could usually be evaded. In 1833 the requisition of uncompensated labour service was made illegal; slavery was abolished in 1851; special Indian tribute obligations were abolished in 1857, and compulsory tithes to the Catholic church in 1889. Military governments in power in the 1960s and 1970s removed the last of the unpaid labour obligations, *huasipongaje*, labour in lieu of house-rent.

Prospects for development. Indians are now politically organized into a national federation, which in 1989 staged a major national strike in support of a set of economic and social demands.

MCN

ECUADOR – PERU BOUNDARY DISPUTE. During the Spanish colonial period, the territory of the Presidency of Quito amounted to over 1,000,000 square kilometres (400 square miles), but over the years so much territory had been ceded to **Colombia** and **Brazil** that when the dispute with **Peru** flared into warfare in July 1941 Ecuador's territory was only half what it had been in colonial times. Seeking easy popularity at home, the military government of Peru took advantage of the preoccupation of the great powers with the war in Europe to settle its ancient territorial claims (based on a tenuous reading of disputed colonial documents) by force. Favouring the claims of the stronger Peru, now in *de facto* control of the disputed territory, over the weaker Ecuador, the United States and the major South American powers forced the Ecuadoreans to sign the Protocol of Rio de Janeiro (1942), recognizing Peruvian ownership of the disputed territory and setting the southern boundary of Ecuador at southern latitude 4° 32"10'. This started in train the events that led to the overthrow of the then Ecuadorean president, Carlos Arroyo del Río.

The people of Ecuador have never accepted the loss of the Amazonian territory, and the Protocol of Río was formally denounced in 1960 by one of the governments of **José María Velasco Ibarra**. The territory seized by the Peruvians — still shown as Ecuadorean on Ecuadorean maps—was thought to contain petroleum, but ironically the petroleum that was discovered in the region lies in the territory still owned by Ecuador. This creates a dangerous stituation, since the border has never been finally demarcated, and further fighting is not outside the boundaries of possibility. It was when flying to a frontier town in the disputed zone, in which fighting had again broken out, to express his repudiation of Peruvian territorial pretensions, that President Jaime Roldós was killed in an airplane crash on May 24, 1981.

MCN

EL SALVADOR. *Population*: 5,200,000. *Area*: 21,393 sq km. *GDP*: US$4,750 million (1987). *Expenditure as a percentage of total government spending*: Defence 26.8; Education 17.1; Health 7.4 (1987). *Merchandise exports*: $634,000,000 (1987). *Merchandise imports*: $975,000,000 (1987). *Debt service as percentage of goods and services exported*: 19.4. *Urban population as percentage of total population*: 44. *Life expectancy*: 58 (men); 67 (women). *Infant mortality*: 59 per 1,000.

Geographical background. The smallest of the Central American republics, El Salvador is the only one without a Caribbean coast. To the northeast lies Guatemala, with Honduras forming the northern and eastern border. Nicaragua is separated from El Salvador however only by the Gulf of Fonseca.

Socio–political background. The high population density has in recent years become increasingly urbanized as agricultural modernization and intensification has entailed the expulsion and alienation of the subsistence peasantry from their lands. The four centuries of annihilation and incorporation of the indigenous population has meant that ladinization was virtually complete by the middle of this century. Only in the past 40 years has there been a systematic extension of the agricultural frontier and population expansion in the Pacific lowlands, before this the primary subsistence economy and agro-export economy was concentrated in the naturally fertile, hillier and more temperate inland areas.

The most recent Constitutional change was approved in 1983 by which an executive president would be directly elected every five years, with a 60 member unicameral Legislative Assembly elected triennially.

Outline of political history. El Salvador became independent from Spain along with the rest of the Captaincy-General of Guatemala in 1821 and following the break-up of the Central American Federation by 1838 was subjected to the typical conservative-liberal conflicts characteristic of the region. Liberal domination was established between 1871–1880 and despite a nominal commitment to constitutionalism *de facto* power remained, and continues to be largely held by, a landowning oligarchy.

With only partial exceptions—in perhaps the elections of March 1931 and February 1972, and immediately following the October 1979 *coup*—the system has appeared for many years one of political pluralism. However oligarchical domination of the legislature and the forces of order has ensured that political openings have been brief and resulted in severe repression. The military *coup* under General Maximiliano Hernández Martínez in December 1931 against the reformist government of Arturo Araújo resulted in the massacre of 32,000 peasants in January 1932 and then the consolidation of the military as the arbiters of political participation for the next 50 years. Between 1931 and 1979 the terms of political succession were set by the military, from 1948 onwards *continuismo* was exercised through a military-based party, in the form of the Revolutionary Party of Democratic Union (*Partido Revolucionario de Unión Democrática*— PRUD) and then from 1961 in its reconstituted form of the PCN. Throughout this period, however, effective economic and social domination lay within the hands of the landed oligarchy. Only with the October 1979 *coup* was *continuismo* and oligarchic control seriously threatened, and this was primarily a consequence of the strength of the wide range of opposition groups rather than the terms of the *coup* itself. The failure to mediate the polarization of Salvadorean society over the period of the civil/military juntas of October 1979 to March 1980 had as its consequence not only the final resort to civil or revolutionary war but the creation of an explicitly oligarchical party separate from the military, namely the **Nationalist Republican Alliance** (*Alianza Republicana Nacionalista*— **ARENA**). The continuous war since 1979 has cost the lives of an estimated 100,000 people, the majority of whom have been civilian non-combatants, and some 500,000 people have become refugees.

The latest crisis can be dated back to the effective collapse of the **Central American Common Market** following the four-day war (the so-called "Football War") between El Salvador and **Honduras** in 1969 which marked the expulsion from Honduras of Salvadorean peasants who had settled in Honduras (as many as 300,000) as a consequence of land shortage in El Salvador, and with their subsequent repatriation the compounding of an existing labour surplus as well as the importation of a wide and decisive experience of labour organization. The trade unions, peasant associations and political groupings established since 1969 initially pushed for genuine democratic representation, but in increasing recognition of the inherently corrupt nature of institutional rule and the failure by the régime to guarantee basic physical security, groupings not only broadened their demands but the popular armed movements grew in numbers and strength. The consolidation of the guerrilla movements in 1975, the failure of the minimal land reform programme of 1976, and the growing death squad activity had effectively polarized Salvadorean society by 1977, which despite the draconian repression of General Humberto Romero's régime on the one hand and the mediating attempts of Archbishop Oscar Romero (head of an increasingly persecuted **Church**) on the other were not able to overcome. The three juntas successively established after the *coup* of Oct. 15, 1979 were characterized by the progressive withdrawal of parties and unions as it became clear that fundamental reform would not be considered by the oligarchy. By January 1980 the Revolutionary Co-ordination of the Masses (*Co-ordinadora Revolucionaria de Masas*— CRM) was formed to unite the popular movements to follow the joint agreement of the guerrilla organizations. This civil–guerrilla alliance was later transformed into the **Revolutionary Democratic Front/Farabundo Martí Front for National Liberation** Frente Democrático Revolucionario/Frente Farabundo Martí para la Liberación Nacional (FDR/FMLN) civil/military opposition alliance which has formed the extra-legal opposition since 1981.

The civil war has been marked by periodic offensives by the FMLN with the guerrillas on occasions controlling as many as eight of the country's 14 departments including parts of the capital. It is widely acknowledged that without **United States** military and economic support, particularly during the FMLN "final offensives" of 1981 and 1989, the régime would have fallen. Negotiations between the government and the

FDR/FMLN have been conducted intermittently usually with the mediation of the Church, the regional governments or more recently through the auspices of the United Nations. FDR/FMLN conditions prior to the 1989 elections were the postponement of the presidential elections for six months, the confinement to barracks of the army and a cease-fire, the inclusion of the Democratic Convergence Party (*Convergencia Democrática* — CD) on the Central Electoral Council, the establishment of the supervisory electoral body, changes in the electoral code to include refugees and exiles, the neutrality of the United States. ARENA and the army rejected all such requests. Ongoing and regular negotiations have been held in Geneva, Caracas, San José and Mexico City to establish a common negotiating agenda. However, thus far, the fundamental demand of the FDR/FMLN of the demilitarization of Salvadorean society and guarantees of physical security have been vetoed by the army.

Current developments—political. Following the elections of March 19, 1989 the far-right ARENA party candidate, Alfredo Cristiani, was elected president with 53 per cent of the votes cast. The **Christian Democratic Party** (*Partido Demócrata Cristiano*—PDC) received 36 per cent, the National Conciliation Party (*Partido de Conciliación Nacional*—PCN) received 4.1 per cent, and the Democratic Convergence (*Convergencia Democrática*—CD) received 3.9 per cent of the 1,400,000 votes cast in an election with less than a 50 per cent turnout of registered voters, in which a further 500,000 electors had not received the required voting papers by election day, and where there was no attempt to conduct the poll in 21 of the 264 municipalities. Furthermore, although the principal popular opposition party Democratic Convergence, which reflects many of the strands of the FDR/FMLN, did contest the election at the final hour, the FDR/FMLN called for an election boycott and organized an effective countrywide transport stoppage on election day.

The ARENA presidency of Cristiani and the ARENA-controlled Legislative Assembly succeeded that of José Napoleón Duarte's PDC. Duarte had won the presidential elections of 1984 with 43 per cent of votes cast over the 30 per cent cast for the ARENA candidate Major Roberto D'Aubuisson. The integrity of the ballot was widely questioned and most of the centre and left parties failed to participate as a consequence of their proscription or due to violence and intimidation. They were also boycotted by the FDR/FMLN coalition. However the elections were the first under the new constitutional arrangement of 1983, and received substantial backing (in particular financial support for the "moderate" PDC) from the government of the United States as a demonstration of its active encouragement of the process of "democratization" in Latin America.

Current economic situation. The cost of the war on the economy has been profound: in addition to the collapse of coffee prices over 1986 and the worst coffee harvest for 30 years during 1988–89 (normally coffee generates some 50 per cent of foreign exchange earnings) and the general decline in terms of trade, the FMLN have increasingly targeted economic interests for attack in particular coffee warehouses and processing plants, generating and the electricity grid, and transport systems. The country's failure to fulfil even its ICO coffee quota has led to cuts in future quota levels. As well as the immediate costs of war, some 45 per cent of the budget has been dedicated to its prosecution in addition to the military and economic aid provided by the USA. Despite a decline of official bilateral US aid from a high of $370,000,000 in fiscal year 1986 to a $284,000,000 request for 1992 the economy is still dependent on this aid.

In accordance with the neo-liberalism of ARENA there has been an extensive programme of privatization and attempted reduction in public expenditure, particularly in the provision of food subsidies and increases in fuel and water prices. Inflation climbing above 25 per cent per annum and the impact of devaluation has exacerbated the economic crisis of the country particularly for the poor, and in the wake of the 1986 earthquake which left some 1,500 dead and over 300,000 homeless, over 50 per cent of the country's children are malnourished and some 85 per cent of the population is classified as living in poverty. Public finances are being increasingly dedicated to the servicing of the country's external debt, the ratio of which stands at approximately 23 per cent.

Prospects for economic development. There is little prospect of economic recovery without an end to the civil war.

JCJS

EUROPEAN COMMUNITY. The European Economic Community (EEC), comprising the Benelux countries, France, West Germany and Italy, came into existence in 1957 as a result of the Treaty of Rome of that year, which in turn built on the treaties establishing the European Coal and Steel Community (ECSC) and the European Atomic Energy Committee

(EURATOM) among the original six. The Community was enlarged in 1971 by the accession of Britain, Denmark and Ireland; Greece was admitted in 1981 and Spain and Portugal in 1986; while the applications of Turkey, Austria, Cyprus and Malta are still awaiting action. Since 1983 the term European Community (EC) has been used to mark the consolidation of the original three communities into one, which, with the implementation of the Single European Act which came into effect on July 1, 1987, is intended to become a single unified market by 1992.

The French Overseas Departments (*Départements d'Outre Mer*—DOM) and the remaining British and Dutch dependencies in the region are for many purposes treated as part of the Community and enjoy the highest levels of aid. Relations between the Community and the countries of the Caribbean area which were formerly colonies of Britain, France or the Netherlands are governed by the **Lomé Convention**, the latest in a series of multilateral trade agreements giving such countries (and some others) preferential trade rights. Separate from the Convention there are three protocols which give Caribbean countries preferential access to the European market: the Sugar Protocol, which guarantees access for agreed quantities of tropical sugar at the European intervention at a price determined by the Community—which has however historically been substantially above the world price; the Banana Protocol, which benefits principally the Windward Islands by maintaining a price above that accorded to Latin American bananas, whose access to Britain and France (though not to Germany) is thereby restricted; and the Rum Protocol, which is of limited value to both sides owing to the low demand for the product in Europe. A considerable amount of Community aid is also channelled into the Caribbean states, in general in proportion to their need, and both trade and aid policies appear in the main to have been beneficial from the point of view of the recipients.

Since 1975 the importation to the EC of many products from the Latin American states has been strictly regulated, and in the case of fresh chilled or frozen beef, formerly a major export of Argentina and Uruguay, prohibited altogether. However investment by Community countries in the region has become increasingly important, and with the accession of Spain and Portugal to the Community the Latin American states hoped in their turn to obtain a better trade deal. In 1987 both Haiti and the Dominican Republic applied for admission to the Lomé Convention, but were admitted in 1989 only after it had been made clear that the decision would not be a precedent for other countries of the region.

PARC

F

FALKLAND ISLANDS (Islas Malvinas). *Population*: 1,919 (November 1986). *Area*: 11,961 sq km. *Top trade partner*: UK. *Urban population as percentage of total (Port Stanley)*: 58.9. *Birthrate*: 15.0 per 1,000. *Life expectancy*: 67.3 (men); (women) 72.3.

Geographical background. The Falkland Islands consist of two large islands and a number of lesser ones, situated in the South Atlantic to the North East of Cape Horn. They take their English name from that given by Captain John Strong in 1690 to the shallow Falkland Sound which divides the two main islands, East Falkland and West Falkland. Both consist of hilly moorland much of which is boggy. A hard surfaced road runs from the capital, Port Stanley, on East Falkland, to Mount Pleasant Airport; otherwise there are no proper roads. Transport between the outlying islands is by light aircraft.

Socio–political background. Since 1833 the islands have been under British rule, which is disputed by **Argentina**, and the majority of the inhabitants are of British settler origin. They are administered by an Governor (currently Mr William H. Fullerton) assisted by an Executive Council of five members: two ex-officio and three elected by the Legislative Council. The Legislative Council consists of two ex-officio members and eight members elected by universal adult suffrage. Defence of the islands is maintained by some 1,600 British troops, consisting of one reinforced infantry company for airfield defence, one RAF squadron of Phantom jets, and a naval presence.

Outline of political history. British interest in the islands began with their sighting by John Davis in 1592. The Spanish claim that they were first sighted in 1504 by a deserter from Magellan's expedition is unverified. They do not appear on maps until shortly after 1700, when sailors from St Malo (hence the French name Isles Malouines, from which the Spanish Islas Malvinas) first started visiting them in search of fish and seals. Until the first colonizing expedition by France in 1764 the islands were uninhabited; their settlement, Port Louis, was transferred to Spain in 1767 and renamed Soledad (Solitude), and a Spanish garrison first established. An earlier British settlement (1765) was expelled by Spain in 1770 but allowed to return the following year after diplomatic protests; it was withdrawn three years later. The islands remained part of the Spanish Empire until the Spanish garrison was withdrawn in 1811. In 1820 Colonel Daniel Jewitt claimed the islands on behalf of the government of Buenos Aires, but when in 1829 the government of the United Provinces took steps to annex them, Britain protested on grounds of its prior claim, and on Jan. 3, 1833 Captain J.J. Onslow of HMS *Clio* formally took possession of them in the name of the British government.

After World War II Argentine claims to the islands were revived and in 1967 they were formally claimed as part of the Territory of Tierra del Fuego. After a series of diplomatic incidents Resolution 2065 (XX) of the UN General Assembly in December 1965 called on both sides to enter into talks to further the decolonization of the islands. Talks foundered on Argentine insistence that they should have sovereignty over the islands and the strong resistance to this on the part of the inhabitants. Publication of the first Shackleton Report in 1976 increased tension by strengthening hopes that the islands had an independent economic future, and when talks came to nothing Argentina invaded the islands (*see also* **Falklands War, 1982**.)

Recent developments—political. Diplomatic relations between Britain and Argentina, suspended in 1982, were re-established in 1990 under a formula which avoided discussion of the outstanding dispute. The 150-mile Falkland Islands Protection Zone (FIPZ), which had replaced the wartime exclusion zone, was then lifted, and joint measures taken by Britain and Argentina to conserve fish stocks, which were being depleted by unregulated fishing.

In January 1989, despite trade union demonstrations, the Bahamian registered freighter *Indiana I* was able to re-establish sea communications with the South American mainland, docking at Montevideo and Punta Arenas.

Elections for the Legislative Council held in October 1989 returned eight independent candidates pledged to a "no links with Argentina" platform. No members of the islands' only political party, Desire for the Right, founded in 1988, were successful.

Outline of economic development. Since the nineteenth century the islands have been divided into large sheep farms, and the production of wool, hides and tallow from more than 600,000 sheep remain the mainstay of an economy which (except for the war years) has been self-sustaining since the 1870s. Strong winds and the lack of ground cover have hitherto restricted agricultural diversification though most farms grow vegetables for their own consumption.

Current economic situation. After the 1982 war, a second Shackleton Report recommended the setting up of a Falkland Islands Development Corporation (FIDC) and a substantial revenue has been generated by the sale of fishing licences, estimated at £27,000,000 in 1987–88 and £34,000,000 in 1988–89. However the Falklands Government's own attempt to set up a fishing fleet was unsuccessful, and the collapse of the Anglo-FIDC Seamount Corporation with debts of some £10,000,000 contributed to the heavy losses reported by the FIDC in mid-1989.

Prospects for development. Despite this recent setback, it was expected that national income would exceed £45,000,000 a year by 1992.

PARC

FALKLANDS/MALVINAS. In conformity with established practice, where the sovereignty of a territory is disputed and the contending parties each have distinctive names for the territory concerned, international organisations commonly use both, thus: Falkland Islands/*Islas Malvinas*, and others may choose to do so if they wish. The British term **Falkland Islands** derives from the name Falkland Sound given to the narrow stretch of water between East and West Falkland by Captain Strong's expedition in 1690. The French term *Isles Malouines*, from which the Spanish and Argentine term *Islas Malvinas* is in turn derived, originated at the beginning of the eighteenth century among the French sealers and whalers who were the first to visit the islands on a regular basis, and reflects the fact that many of them came from the French port of St. Malo in Brittany.

PARC

FALKLANDS WAR, 1982. Following the assumption of power by General Galtieri in **Argentina** in December 1981 plans were made for a military seizure of the Falkland Islands. On April 2, 1982 an Argentine naval expedition landed, deported the Governor and established a military government. While a mediation attempt was made by the US Secretary of State, General Alexander Haig, a British task force was prepared, and sailed for the South Atlantic. On May 1, hostilities recommenced with an air attack on Stanley airport, followed by a series of air and naval engagements in which heavy losses (ARA *General Belgrano*, HMS *Sheffield*) were sustained on both sides. On May 21, troops landed at San Carlos Bay on Falkland Sound, and advanced first on Goose Green (recaptured on May 29) and on Port Stanley itself, where the Argentine military garrison under the command of General Menéndez surrendered on June 14. The war re-established British control of the islands at the cost of 255 British and 652 Argentine lives and some 3,000 wounded.

PARC

FARABUNDO MARTÍ NATIONAL LIBERATION FRONT (Frente Farabundo Martí para la Liberación Nacional — FMLN) (El Salvador). Named after Farabundo Martí, the founder of the Communist Party of **El Salvador** and victim of the massacre of 1932, the FMLN was formally created on Oct. 10, 1980 from all principal guerrilla organizations: the Popular Liberation Forces (*Fuerzas Populares de Liberación*—FPL), the People's Revolutionary Army (*Ejército Revolucionario del Pueblo*—ERP) and National Resistance (*Resistencia Nacional*—RN). Despite lack of co-ordination and internecine conflict in the mid-1970s these organizations had established a powerful guerrilla base by 1980, such that following the failure of the first and second post-*coup* juntas and the creation of the FMLN, the civil organizations of the **Revolutionary Democratic Front** (*Frente Democrático Revolucionario*—FDR) were provided with protection and armed strength against government forces. The alliance with the FDR was made easier by the earlier organic connection between the constituent parts of the FDR and the FMLN; thus, for example, the FPL's main support organization had been, since 1975, the BPR. It is clear that the Salvadorean armed forces cannot defeat the FMLN, nor does the FMLN have the decisive power to overthrow the regime. The war has become a war of attrition and the FMLN since mid-1989 has placed greater emphasis upon diplomatic initiatives along with the FDR.

JCJS

FEBRERISTA PARTY. (Partido Revolucionario Febrerista — PRF) (Paraguay). The Febreristas or "Men of February" originated in discontent among junior officers at the conduct of the Chaco War, and the failure to pay demobilized soldiers the social benefits they had been promised. In February 1936 a revolution led by Col Rafael Franco overthrew the Liberal government of Eusebio Ayala, but denied the support of the **Colorado Party** his short-lived government fell in 1937 though the Febrerista movement survived both this and its defeat in the joint Liberal-Febrerista revolt of 1947. Because of its military connections it survived as a legal opposition party under the government of **General Gustavo Stroessner**. A social democratic party, it is affiliated to the Socialist International.

PARC

FRENCH GUIANA. *Population*: 114,900 (1990). *Area*: 90,000 sq km. *Trade volume*: US$561.7 million. *Top five trade partners*: France, Trinidad and Tobago, USA, Japan, French Antilles. *Birthrate*: 27.9 per 1,000.

Geographical background. French Guiana (Guyane) lies on the north coast of South America between Suriname and Brazil. It is sparsely inhabited, with much of the interior of the country covered by jungle. The territory was first settled by Europeans in the mid-seventeenth century and became a French colony. In 1946 it became a department of France and in 1974 was made a region.

Socio–political background. Under the terms of the 1982 decentralization reforms the French government appoints a Government Commissioner (or Prefect) to oversee defence, foreign affairs, security and general administration. Daily executive power is in the hands of a directly elected 19-member General Council. Councillors serve a six-year term with half of the seats on the council being available for election every three years. Wider social and economic powers are in the hands of a 31-member elected Regional Council. French Guiana sends two deputies and one senator to the National Assembly in Paris.

Outline of political history. Politics in French Guiana in recent years have centred around the local federation of the Socialist Party (*Parti socialiste guyanais*—PSG), which has led the campaign for greater autonomy, and the separatist trade union, the Union of Guyanese Workers (*Union des travailleurs guyanais*—UTG). The PSG holds the majority on both the General and Regional Councils, but its tenure in power has been criticized for corruption and inefficiency. Divisions within the party during 1989 led to the expulsion of the chairman of the Regional Council, Georges Othily, from the party for working with opposition parties, although Othily was later elected to the National Assembly as a senator.

Outline of economic development. The economy of French Guiana is highly dependent on that of France. Many goods are imported, creating a large imbalance of trade. Local industries include shrimp fishing, logging and limited mineral extraction. The potential for development in the interior of French Guiana has been largely unexploited. A major plan of the development of the area (the *Plan vert*) proposed in 1975 by the then Secretary of State for Overseas Departments and Territories, Olivier Stirn, floundered after the initial enthusiasm and finances provided dissipated. By contrast, the development of the European Space Agency's base at Kourou has continued to grow. The success of the *Ariane* rocket (after a series of early setbacks), coinciding with the *Challenger* disaster for the US space shuttle programme, allowed the ESA to increase the number of satellite launches. By mid-1990 55 satellites had been successfully launched from Kourou.

Current economic situation. The population of French Guiana has risen dramatically during the 1980s from 75,000 to an estimated 114,000. Some of this has been encouraged by the government, such as the settlement of Hmong refugees from Laos. Other immigrants have been connected with the space programme at Kourou, where a new town has been built to house the centre's staff (mostly French). However, of the 30,000 foreigners estimated to have settled in French Guiana in the last decade over half are thought to be illegal immigrants from Haiti, the Dominican Republic and other Caribbean countries, and refugees and economic migrants from French Guiana's neighbours, Guyana and Suriname, where civil war and economic collapse have increased the numbers crossing the border. By the end of 1987 up to 8,600 refugees fleeing from unrest in Suriname were accommodated in camps in the west of the country around St Laurent-du-Maroni. The presence of refugees and illegal immigrants has exacerbated social tensions, particularly as French Guiana has a high rate of unemployment and many people emigrate to France to seek work. An increase in crime was attributed to the presence of the refugees and prompted a one-day general strike in September 1989 and the provision of reinforcements for the police force by the government.

LP

FUNDAMENTALISM. By far and away the fastest growing churches in South America and the Caribbean are those that can be described as "evangelical fundamentalist". While there are regional concentrations of activity, such as in Central America and the Caribbean as well as Bolivia, Brazil and Paraguay, there is a comprehensive spread of such types of protestant fundamentalism across the region as a whole. Although numbers of adherents are difficult to estimate, one respected authority has suggested that whereas there were only 12,000,000 Protestants (not necessarily evangelicals) in 1968 in Latin America, by 1980 this number had risen to 25,000,000 and by 1988 numbered around 35,000,000.

Protestant fundamentalism (which should not be confused with traditionally established Protestant churches affiliated to the World Council of Churches) can be characterized by several key elements which are necessary, if not sufficient, conditions for the use of such a label. One can treat in a similar way most Protestant denominations, Pentecostalist and independent churches as movements which have "rediscovered the gospel of the early church". "Born again" movements, according to Professor Michael Dodson, share the common belief that the second coming of Christ will be a real and temporal historical event, that the Gospels constitute the sole and irrefutable source of authority, and it is in this latter sense that the term fundamentalism gains meaning. The principal differences amongst fundamentalist sects arise from their interpretation of the second coming, namely, when will it happen and under what circumstances? Post-millenialists assert that Christ will return after the establishment of the kingdom of God on earth, whereas the much more dominant pre-millenialists consider the reverse sequence to be applicable. In Latin America the overwhelmingly most powerful and expanding sects are both pre-millenialists and tribulationists. Dodson explains the significance as follows: "A fundamentalist (pre-millenialist and dispensationalist) will typically ... embrace the notion of the Rapture in which Christ raptures all born again Christians, living and dead, into the air at the same time that he ushers in a seven-year period of tribulation. During the great Tribulation the Antichrist controls the world and all persons who subsequently convert to the faith in Christ are severely persecuted. At the end of the seven years Christ returns, good and evil do battle at Armageddon, and the millenial kingdom is established when the forces of Christ prevail". It is in the light of this apocalyptic vision, and its apparent imminence, that evangelical sects have interpreted the immediate and absolute imperative to engage in the missionary activity of saving souls.

The spiritual warfare of fundamentalism has been tied to the ideological and temporal warfare of anti-**communism** and in Latin America can be closely tied to the context of the second Cold War. Millenialism is in Dodson's words "indifferent or even hostile to the temporal world. Political action to make the world a better place... (is) regarded as futile". Thus as Catholicism moved left after Vatican II to take on the "preferential option of the poor", fundamentalism moved right to combat godless "communism". The majority of fundamentalist sects did not wish to challenge the temporal order since saving souls was their remit, and should intervention in Caesar's domain be necessary then salvation from materialistic atheism provided the spur and the terms of activity. It is for these and other reasons that fundamentalist sects have been associated with right-wing régimes and leaders throughout the region. Moreover a significant, though by no means full explanation of the growth of the sects in the 1980s has been the rise of the Christian Right in the USA and their support of right-wing organizations and régimes. Thus, for example, Pat Robertson, a major backer of the Bush presidential campaign and head of the evangelical "700 Club" in the USA, toured Central America in 1990 visiting **Guatemala, El Salvador** and **Honduras** whilst also distributing 1,500,000 pounds in weight of food across the three states as part of missionary activity. The born-again Christian Oliver North and numerous Nicaraguan contra leaders were regular guests on religious broadcasting channels such as those of the Praise the Lord Club, Church of the Word, and Christian Voice. The weight of the fundamentalist churches has been put behind the contras and anti-communist regimes in the region.

There is ample evidence of the use of humanitarian and developmental aid provided by the sects as means of "purchasing" the souls of the newly-converted. The country in which the sects have penetrated most deeply and effectively is Guatemala where the social dislocation and fragmentation as well as the economic insecurity caused by the civil war provided fertile ground for missionary activity. Former President Efraín Ríos Montt of Guatemala is a member of the Church of the Word and the current Guatemalan President Jorge Serrano is also an evangelical. Whilst the expansion of the protestant sects has been dramatic over the past decade—there are now 10,000 churches comprising 300 denominations of which at least 200 are independent i.e, evangelical sects according to Virginia Burnett—and is not unicausal, the power of "*anima por lamina*" ("souls for tin roofing") is significant. Thus the number of converts, estimated at 2,000,000 people, has to be treated with scepticism as must the depth of conversion and length of time of conversion. However the missionary activity, particularly in the predominantly indigenous areas, most often accompanied military campaigns against the guerrilla, and evangelical activity was often a central part of Rios Montt's "beans and guns" counter-insurgency operations. In so far as nominal conversion brings with it some guarantee of physical security from army violence and the provision of basic needs it remains an attractive option. Repression of the Catholic **Church** in Guatemala as it campaigned for respect for **human rights** and social justice has aided the expansion of evangelical sects.

Nevertheless the spread of evangelical fundamentalism is not confined to right-wing régimes and its attraction may well lie in the escapism of its other-worldliness especially as manifested in the pentecostalist or charismatic sects. The apparent failures of the Catholic Church to respond to the spiritual needs of the mass of the population may account for the conversion of the poor, but the sects are particularly strong amongst the middle-classes and ruling classes of various countries. This applies in Guatemala, Honduras, and **Costa Rica**, as well as in **Bolivia** and **Chile**. In the latter case some 15 per cent of all army officers are reputed to be members of evangelical churches, despite the deep Catholic traditionalism of the upper échelons of the armed forces, and this may be due to a rejection of the progressive nature of much of the Church following Vatican II: the dispute is therefore not primarily theological rather it is political and only later does it receive theological justification. There is no doubt that the Catholic Church, both traditionalists and progressive have found the rise of evangelical sects theologically disturbing and politically threatening and it is for this reason that analysis of numbers becomes so important and controversial. Thus a study on evangelical expansion in Costa Rica published in 1990 by the International Evangelical Institute argued that only 8 per cent of Costa Ricans were evangelicals and not the 25 per cent claimed by many evangelical leaders (for propaganda purposes) and suggested that Roman Catholic commentators exaggerated the numbers for political effect. Parts of the Catholic Church have responded with their own mass evangelization campaigns known as Evangelization 2000 and Lumen 2000.

Although the 1980s showed a dramatic rise in the membership of the sects in the region their presence dates back to the 1930s and that of the traditional Protestant churches to the mid-nineteenth century when they were encouraged by Liberal anti-clerical, anti-Catholic régimes intent on breaking Catholic hegemony. The activities of the Wycliffe Bible Translators were typical of the early independent missionary activities, but the more recent wave in Latin America began in the 1960s with missions such as Evangelism in Depth of the Costa Rican-based Latin American Mission, but it was in the 1970s that the more militant evangelicals, mostly US-based, such as the Assemblies of God, Church of the Word, Transworld Mission, Caribbean Christian Missionaries, World Vision and Disciple a Whole Nation began concerted crusades. To take but one example, the Roman Catholic National Conference of Brazilian Bishops (CNBB) has estimated that there are between 12 and 16,000,000 members of new evangelical sects. Of these sects the largest are the Assemblies of God (8,000,000), the Christian Congregation (2,000,000) the Brazil Church for Christ (1,000,000), God is Love and the recently founded Church of the Universal Reign of God with 500,000 adherents each. The CNBB believes that the sects will expand to some 30,000,000 by the end of the 1990s.

As in the rest of the region one of the principal means of conducting missionary work is through the broadcast media. The sects have used television and radio in a more co-ordinated and purposeful manner than the Catholic Church thus far. In **Brazil** the founder of the Church of the Universal Reign of God, Edir Macedo Bezerra, recently bought two radio stations and one television station in São Paulo to conduct evangelical crusades. Control of significant sections of both the broadcast and print media or the establishment of such media from new are amongst the first steps taken by the sects throughout Latin America. Use of these media has been facilitated in many cases by the North American origins of the sects where there is a highly financed and sophisticated electronic media network to draw upon. Not only have these methods been successful in themselves but they have been able to exploit the greatest weakness of the Catholic Church which suffers from a chronic shortage of clergy and a very poor proportion of priests to adherents. It is for this reason that the theologian Pablo Richard argued, through the Catholic Regional Centre for Ecumenical Information in Mexico, that the proliferation of Christian Base Communities was the most effective means of slowing and potentially halting the spread of the sects.

One important arena of influence increasingly utilized by the sects is education. Where the public provision of education is limited or non-existent the independent churches are one of the few sources of educational funding and Accelerated Christian Education programmes devised in the USA, for example, are transferred and utilized in fundamentalist schools in Latin America. A core teaching of the ACE curriculum is that Catholics are not proper Christians and Jews are not accepted by God, and that secularism and humanism are diabolical manifestations (Rose and Brouwer).

The comment made by the Archbishop of Lima, Augustus Vargas Alzamora, that the activities of evangelical sects in Peru are "an insidious campaign against our Catholic faith" is a view widely shared across the region by Roman Catholics, both progressives and conservatives. But in countries with high and growing numbers of sects the pressure is not insidious but open and increasingly institutionalized: Guatemala is the obvious example, but in Bolivia pressure from the Evangelical Association of Bolivia has been placed upon the government to re-interpret the Constitution to grant all Christian churches the same constitutional rights and privileges held by the Catholic Church. The Archbishop of La Paz, Luís Sáinz, criticized the Bolivian President for endorsing the activities of evangelical sects some of whom he accused of "provoking collective assassinations and genocide" including members of the Assembly of God who murdered six people in the Beni province of Bolivia in 1989 for allegedly being possessed by the devil. Criticism of the sects is not exclusive to the Catholic Church, but is also forthcoming from a wide variety of established Protestant churches.

Other fundamentalist sects in the region include the Unification Church (or "Moonies") which had over 1,000 adherents in **Paraguay** and close contact and support from the former President **Alfredo Stroessner**, the alliance of interests being based upon both parties' vehement anti-communism. Numerous small cults exist, perhaps the most notorious being the People's Temple cult whose 900-strong community in Jonestown, **Guyana** committed collective suicide. However their political impact is generally negligible. Notwithstanding the abortive *coup* attempt in Trinidad and Tobago in 1990 by Islamic fundamentalists such movements have little presence or importance in either Latin America or the Caribbean as yet.

JCJS

G

GAIRY, Sir ERIC. Eric Matthew Gairy, Prime Minister of **Grenada** 1972–79, was born of poor parents near Grenville in 1922. Introduced to union politics while working as a clerk in an Aruban oilfield, he began his climb to power by founding the Grenada Mental and Manual Workers Union (GMMWU) in 1950. Within a year it had conducted a successful strike in the sugar industry and obtained such support among other plantation workers that a general strike in 1951 forced its recognition, and in the same year swept his Grenada People's Party (GPP), soon renamed the Grenadian United Labour Party (GULP), to victory in the first legislative council elections held under direct suffrage. Defeated in 1957 amid accusations of corruption, Gairy returned to power in 1967 and led the country to independence in 1974. Despite his growing eccentricities and failure to address popular needs he was able to retain power in 1976 by the use of force, much of it directed by his personal shock-troops, the "Mongoose Gang". Overthrown in 1979, he was allowed to return to the island by the Americans after the **Grenadian Intervention** in 1983 and has continued unsuccessfully to contest elections in the hope of returning to power.

PARC

GALÁPAGOS ISLANDS. Named after the giant turtles that are only one of the many distinctive types of fauna that inhabit the islands, the Galápagos form an archipelago under the sovereignty of **Ecuador**, the coast of which lies 580 miles east of the island of the group closest to shore.

The islands are of volcanic origin, some very recent, and provide a fascinating study of the evolution of life on volcanic soils. Because of the isolation of the islands, which are strictly controlled as a national park, the birds and animals have no fear of human beings and can be observed from close up. Only one of the fourteen islands of the group has permanent inhabitants. Visitors to the others cannot stay on them overnight, but must stay aboard their vessels. The distinctive characteristics of the animal life on the islands are said to have influenced Charles Darwin, who visited them, in the writing of *The Origin of Species*.

The fact that the islands are Ecuadorean territory has given Ecuador jurisdictional claims to a substantial area of the Pacific, which has long contributed to disputes over fishing rights with tuna fleets, especially from the United States and Japan. The islands stretch over an area of 780 sq km (300 square miles).

MCN

GOULART, JOAO. Few Brazilian politicians have been more maligned than João Goulart, both by his contemporaries and by historians, too ready to impose easy labels. He has been described as inept, irresponsible, "populist" and part of the "negative left", whatever that may mean. In fact, he was none of these things. He was, however, too far to the left for some interests in Brazil and abroad, especially in the **United States**.

João Belchior Marques Goulart, or "Jango", as he was better known in his native Rio Grande do Sul and throughout his political life, was born in São Borja, the same *município* as **Getúlio Vargas**, on March 1, 1919. His father, Vicente Rodrigues Goulart, was a wealthy *estanceiro*, a rancher, raising cattle and sheep on two large estates, *Meio* and *Nossa Senhora*, as well as being a businessman and industrialist. He was one of the owners of the firm *Vargas, Goulart, Gomes & Cia. Ltda.*, together with Protásio Dornelles Vargas, a brother of Getúlio Vargas, and Saladeiro Itaqui, both of whom specialized in the production of *charque*, salted and dried beef.

Goulart's father, Vicente, was caught up in the civil war of 1923, when his estates were invaded, and, in 1930, he commanded troops in support of his neighbour, Getúlio Vargas. One of 'Jango's' sisters, Neusa, married **Leonel Brizola**.

Goulart, throughout his youth, showed more interest in farming than in academic work or politics. On his father's death, in 1943, he inherited 14,000 hectares and a herd of more than 30,000 cattle. His involvement with politics began in 1945, when Vargas, set aside by the leaders of the armed forces, returned to São Borja. Goulart, initially, favoured the **Brazilian Labour Party** (*Partido Trabalhista Brasileiro* — PTB) but helped Vargas in his support for Dutra and the Social Democratic Party (*Partido Social Democrático* — PSD). He then joined the PTB, and began his political career, supported by Vargas, who, after his election as Senator for the Constituent Assembly, retired to São Borja. Goulart was a close associate of Vargas in this period, becoming deeply enmeshed in the politics of the presidential succession and meeting the many politicians who sought out Vargas in São Borja. Goulart's estate became the hub of Vargas' political activities. It was there, on April 19, 1950, his birthday, that Vargas announced his candidature for the presidential election of Oct. 3, which he went on to win. While supporting Vargas in the campaign, Goulart was also a candidate as federal deputy for the PTB, and was duly elected.

Goulart then took leave of absence from the Chamber, to become Secretary of Interior and Justice in the new state government of Rio Grande do Sul, headed by Ernesto Dornelles, a cousin of Getúlio Vargas. He strengthened his political bases within the state and in the PTB across the country, and, in 1952, took over the national directorate of the party. In May 1952, Vargas called Goulart to Rio de Janeiro, where he took up his seat as federal deputy and developed a close relationship with the trade unions, which was to remain important throughout the rest of his political career.

Goulart already had a reputation as an able negotiator and became involved in reconciling labour disputes. In close collaboration with Vargas, he took responsibility for controlling the main posts in the institutes of social welfare, which, in turn, distributed jobs at local level. Goulart was now in a position to control a whole system of state-directed patronage. At the same time, he prepared a new political framework, to give more power to the trade unions, which, in turn, would allow them to give stronger support to the president, who was under sharp attack from the National Democratic Union (*União Democrática Nacional*—UDN) and the right more generally.

There were also pressures on the government from the working class and the trade unions, demanding substantial increases in wages to counter inflation and a rise in the cost of living between 1943 and 1951 of the order of 100 per cent. Changes in the laws concerning strikes led, among others, to the major strike of March 1953, centred in São Paulo, the so-called "Strike of 300,000", (*see* **BRAZIL**) and to a strike in the merchant fleet in Rio de Janeiro, Santos and Belém in June. The Minister of Labour, Segadas Viana, argued the need for changes in the labour laws, but, meanwhile, wanted to use a decree, passed during World War II, which would allow the government to treat the strikers as if they were sailors in military service. Goulart, as president of the PTB, and with good contacts in the unions, disagreed with this solution. The result was his appointment as Minister of Labour in June 1953.

The appointment brought renewed attacks from the right, especially from **Carlos Lacerda**, reviving charges that Goulart wanted to introduce a "trade union state", modelled on Perón's government in Argentina. They continued even when Goulart settled the strike in the merchant marine, reaching an agreement which satisfied most of the strikers' demands, but displeased Oswaldo Aranha, the Minister of Finance, who was trying to cut costs in the public sector, in which the strikers were mostly employed. Goulart also introduced changes in the laws relating to strikes, removing some of the controls introduced under Dutra and introduced changes in the leadership of the unions, some of which stemmed from Dutra's presidency.

In August 1953, as part of a general review of labour and social legislation, Goulart and the Ministry of Labour helped to organize, in Rio de Janeiro, the first *Congresso Brasileiro de Previdência Social*, (Brazilian Congress of Social Welfare). This provided a much needed forum to examine issues of fundamental importance to workers and for them to air their grievances. This, too, was attacked by the right as a "Peronist congress, preparing for social disorder".

Goulart was repeatedly accused of fomenting strikes and of being a "Minister of the workers", rather than a "Minister of Labour". He rejected such charges, arguing that his Ministry's good relations with the workers should be a source of reassurance for employers, not of alarm. He said that he and his Ministry were ready to support and applaud capitalists who used their economic power to create wealth, while bringing to their initiative a social, human and patriotic dimension.

When the strike in the merchant navy broke out again, in October 1953, Goulart was willing to sanction the use of force to end it, though he took care to be in the north of Brazil at the time, leaving the intervention to Hugo de Faria, head of the National Department of Labour. The incident was an exception to the more common pattern under Goulart, where he was able to reach agreement through conciliation and concession, as during a strike of bank workers in January 1954, when he was accused by bankers of conceding too much.

Apart from attending to the wage issue, Goulart, as Minister of Labour, introduced important changes in other areas, notably affecting social security and pension schemes, but his main concern was to reach a working agreement between government, workers and employers.

The crisis and confrontation reached a peak, as Vargas and Goulart expected, when, in January 1954, Goulart began to prepare a project to present to Congress, recommending that the minimum wage should be doubled, from 1,200 to 2,400 *cruzeiros*, the equivalent of the pay of a second lieutenant. Foreseeing opposition, Goulart put his Ministry at Vargas' disposal. There was outraged protest from the right. Lacerda continued to advocate a *coup* against Vargas. In Congress, a faction within the National Democratic Union, the "Banda de Música", (the "Band") organized a campaign against Goulart and his "subversion". In February, a manifesto from 82 colonels and lieutenant-colonels expressed concern at the proposed wage increases and a drift to subversion. On Feb. 22, Vargas accepted Goulart's resignation.

What Goulart largely achieved as Minister of Labour was a measure of that "social pact" which subsequent governments, including those of Sarney and Collor, sought to reach. He was making a careful and, on the whole, successful effort to deal with the demands of Brazil's increasingly industrialized working class, which now had the vote and could put pressure on both government and employers. He was having to do this in a period when inflation was quickly eroding wage increases. At the same time, he had to negotiate with employers and industrialists unused to the process of negotiation and, since the *Estado Novo*, unaccustomed to industrial action, which they were quick to label as "communist" or "subversive". He was also faced by an intensely hostile opposition, in Congress, in the armed forces, and in the media, who were determined to destroy Vargas and, with him, Goulart.

With the death of Vargas in 1954, Goulart at first withdrew from politics, then was defeated in the election for Senate in Rio Grande do Sul, later that year, by a coalition candidate. In 1955, he was elected Vice-President, when **Juscelino Kubitschek** won the presidency. As Vice-President, he was also President of the Senate and developed a special responsibility for dealing with the unions, an area in which Kubitschek was relatively weak. He unified various strands in the labour movement and allowed the government to maintain good relations with the unions, though these were becoming strained towards the end of Kubitschek's term, as industrial and real wages fell.

In October 1960, Goulart was re-elected as Vice-President, though he lost in Rio Grande do Sul, São Paulo, Guanabara and Minas Gerais. **Jânio Quadros** was elected as President. Goulart kept his distance from Quadros, disapproving, in particular, of the austerity stabilization programme, which fell most heavily on the poor and the working class. He was on an official visit to China when Quadros resigned.

Lacerda and the National Democratic Union, after three consecutive electoral defeats, had supported Quadros as a candidate who might bring power to the right and, at a more personal level, help Lacerda to reach the presidency. The resignation of Quadros, largely provoked by Lacerda's criticism, threw the right, and the whole political system, into turmoil, and almost led to civil war. The resultant compromise was the adoption of a parliamentary system, to curb Goulart's freedom of action, with provision for a plebiscite. At the age of 43 Goulart became President. His Prime Minister was **Tancredo Neves de Almeida**.

Such a choice of Prime Minister hardly suggested a radical or irresponsible programme. From September 1961 to January 1963, throughout the "parliamentary" period, the tone of Goulart's government was moderate and conciliatory. His cabinet of "national union" included, apart from Tancredo, other PDS politicians, notably, **Ulysses Guimarães** in Industry and Commerce, and centrist spokesmen, such as André Franco Montoro, of the Christian Democratic Party (*Partido Democrático Cristão*—PDC), now put in charge of Labour and Social Welfare.

The Ministry of Finance went to a banker, Valter Moreira Sales. The PTB had two ministers. One was Santiago Dantas at Foreign Affairs, the other, Estácio Souto Maior in Health. The UDN was not left out. It had Mines and Energy, with Gabriel Passos, and Transport and Public Works, with Virgílio Távora. It was a cabinet which included men of ability, high ideals and social conscience: its composition was neither "populist" nor "subversive".

The programme which Goulart began to set out followed his earlier letter to Benedito Valadares. It included periodic readjustments of wages and salaries, taking account of the rate of inflation, a continuation of the "independent foreign policy", nationalization of some foreign subsidiaries, and the so-called "base reforms" (*reformas de base*). These included reforms in the agrarian sector, banking administration, taxation, the electoral system and in the urban sector. He also stressed the need to expand access to education.

Proposals for agrarian reform met predictable opposition, and were especially held up by the question of the form of compensation to be provided for expropriated land. In Rio Grande do Sul, Brizola expropriated a subsidiary of ITT, but this was an exceptional measure, not part of a general wave of expropriations. In foreign affairs, Brazil re-established relations with the USSR, which had been broken off under Dutra, and, at the conference in Punta del Este, in January 1962, Santiago Dantas refused to be pressured by the USA into hostile policies towards Cuba.

Faced with severe financial and economic problems inherited from the Quadros government, Goulart knew that he needed support from the business and banking community, both at home and abroad. His stress on agrarian reform linked it to resolving social tensions across the country, just as he tied his "base reforms" to the provision of the fullest measures of security for the future. There was a rise in the minimum wage in October 1961, but this already was in the pipeline, and, at 40 per cent roughly in step with the rise in the cost of living of 38 per cent in Rio de Janeiro and 42 per cent in São Paulo. He made a serious effort to contain public expenditure throughout 1962. He stressed his commitment to stabilization and a readiness to work, within all reasonable limits, with the IMF and other financial agencies.

He especially stressed this during his visit to the United States in April 1962, looking for support for his programme, when he told Congress and President Kennedy that Brazil was opposed to the régime installed in Cuba and that it would pay adequate compensation for any United States assets appropriated, with those funds to be reinvested in Brazil. His mission was not successful. The IMF and other creditors were, in particular, not convinced of his commitment to a stabilization programme, while signals going back to the United States persisted in painting Goulart as an extremist, or as someone who was being used by forces further to the left of himself.

On his return, Goulart found that the economic situation and social tensions and violence in the countryside, especially in the north-east, had worsened, while a heavily conservative Congress continued to block his proposed reforms. At the same time, he was under growing pressure from the left to produce the promised reforms, especially agrarian reforms, which still only remained on paper.

In a speech at Volta Redonda, on May 1, 1962 Goulart began a campaign to win back executive power in relation to Congress and to bring forward the plebiscite on the system of government. He stressed the need to reform the Constitution of 1946, especially as that affected agrarian reform, which he said was indispensable for improving the standard of living of the people and for national development. This began a polarization of politics which was to last for the rest of his presidency, between the left and "nationalist" camp, demanding reforms, and conservative forces, both in Brazil and abroad, which showed themselves ever more hostile to Goulart. These now quickened moves to get rid of him. One sign of the growing tension was the collective resignation of Tancredo Neves and the whole cabinet on June 26, on the pretext of having legally to leave office now, in order to be able to run in the Congressional elections in October.

This produced a new crisis, when Goulart's nomination of Santiago Dantas, the former Minister of Foreign Affairs, as Prime Minister was rejected by Congress. A second nomination, more to the right, was, effectively, vetoed by the trade union leaders. Eventually, he was able to appoint as Prime Minister Francisco de Paula Brochado da Rocha, who had been ex-Secretary of Interior and Justice of Brizola in Rio Grande do Sul, a man further to the left than Santiago Dantas, whom Congress had rejected.

The key political issue now was the balance of power between a directly elected, reformist president, supported by the trade unions and broad public opinion, especially in urban, industrial Brazil, and a Congress, largely coloured by a more traditional, clientelistic vote in the interior, especially in the north-east. Pressure steadily grew to bring forward the plebiscite on a return to full presidential powers. Such a return was supported, not just by the unions, but by military ministers appointed by Goulart. There were threatening noises from Gen. Dantas Ribeiro, in Rio Grande do Sul, evidently backed, or even inspired, by Brizola. The new Prime Minister asked for special powers for the Council of Ministers, including important initiatives affecting agrarian reform, anti-trust laws and more extensive state controls. On Sept. 13, 1962 Congress refused to concede special powers to Brochado da Rocha. The Prime Minister and his Cabinet resigned on the following day. Again, Brazil was without a government. As one way out of persistent crises, Congress, on Sept. 16, agreed to a "popular referendum" on the parliamentary system, to be held on Jan. 6, 1963. The electorate, on that day, voted, overwhelmingly, to give full presidential powers to Goulart.

Once approval for the referendum was given, Goulart was able to put together a provisional Council of Ministers. This included Hermes Lima, as Prime Minister and Minister of Foreign Affairs, João Mangabeira in Justice, Eliézer Batista, Mines and Energy, Darcy Ribeiro, Education, and, as Minister without Portfolio, for Planning, the distinguished Cambridge-educated economist, from north-east Brazil, Celso Furtado. He was charged with producing a plan for Brazil's development. The result, announced on Dec. 30, 1962, was the *Plano Trienal* (Three Year Plan). This aimed to treat both economic and social problems in an integrated manner, a need brought home to Furtado by both intellectual reflection and his close experience of the north-east.

Furtado's recommendation was to stress the external sector as a source of recent inflation, noting Brazil's declining export capacity in the late

1950s and early 1960s, because of too great a dependence on primary products. He stressed the need for much faster industrialization, so that Brazil might share in the market for manufactured goods. He also stressed that inflation must be cut back, but not at the expense of growth, perhaps accepting 10 per cent inflation combined with 7 per cent growth, while, at the same time, giving priority to a strategy of wider distribution and social reform. It was an ambitious, difficult formula, eventually built into the Dantas–Furtado programme. It has been described as the most ambitious programme of any post-war Brazilian regime, and, this, under the so-called "populist", Goulart.

After taking up full presidential powers, in January 1963, Goulart named a new government, which reflected a further effort to keep a balance between contending political interests, seeking to win back some of the middle ground. His economic policy remained the Dantas–Furtado Plan attempt to reconcile stability, growth, distribution and reform within a democratic system, as he explained in his annual address to Congress, in March 1963, seeking "a high rate of development, but, at the same time, reducing its social cost and working for a more just distribution of the growing wealth of the country".

He stressed the need for structural reforms, required for development. These included changes in the tax system, banking, government administration, in housing policies, and, above all, the structure of Brazilian agriculture. He believed, he said, that it was the duty of his government, "inspired by the Christian and democratic spirit of the Brazilian people, to introduce a just agrarian reform".

Goulart's aims, in 1963, taken directly from the *Plano Trienal*, were founded in the best development theory of the day and in an attempt to reconcile contending social forces within a democratic, multi-party system. Ultimately, in 1964, he failed, pulled down by his political opponents, in Brazil, and abroad, especially in the USA, and, in part, by his own political miscalculations in the last weeks, days, even hours, before the *coup*. At the last moment, he could have saved his skin, by abandoning his friends and all for which he had worked. He refused to compromise, just as he was unwilling to engage in confrontation which would lead to civil war.

Goulart went into political exile in **Uruguay**, where he became involved, for a short time, with the Frente Ampla. His health was poor and he devoted himself, successfully, to business interests in Uruguay, **Paraguay**, **Argentina**, and Brazil. He died, of a heart attack, on Dec. 6, 1976 without having returned to Brazil.

Goulart has been maligned, misunderstood and misused both by the political right and left, and perhaps, even more, by historians. With a return to democracy in Brazil, and a search for new priorities, there should be a more informed and sympathetic understanding of João Goulart, and of what he tried to do.

PF

GRENADA. *Population*: 100,000 (est. 1987). *Area*: 344 sq km. *GDP*: US $104,300,000 (1987). *Trade volume*: $80,000,000. *Top four trade partners*: UK, Canada, United States, Caricom. *Education spending (as a percentage of GNP)*: 4.6 (1983). *Birthrate*: 25.1 per 1,000. *Life expectancy*: 69.

Geographical background. The State of Grenada consists of the island of Grenada, approximately 34 km long by 19 km wide, lying some 160 km north of Trinidad and some 105 km south of St Vincent, together with the largest of the Grenadine islands, Carriacou, and its neighbour Petit Martinique. Of volcanic origin, Grenada is very hilly, the highest point being Mt St Catherine in the Central Highlands—840 m (2757 ft), and the beaches of its heavily indented coastline are amongst the best in the Caribbean. The climate is tropical, with temperatures varying from 21 to 29 C, and annual rainfall from 1000 to over 5000 mm. The wet season is between June and December.

Socio–political background. At its discovery by Christopher Columbus on Aug. 15, 1498, Grenada was inhabited by Arawak Indians. In 1650 the Governor of Martinique purchased the island to establish a trading station, and it was formally annexed by France in 1674. In 1762 it was captured by British forces under Admiral George Rodney. It was recaptured by the French in 1779 but returned to Great Britain in 1783, and a French uprising in 1797 was suppressed. After the abolition of slavery in 1834 the cultivation of sugar which had formed the base of the colonial economy under both French and British rule was replaced by that of nutmeg, cloves, ginger and cinnamon. Some 97 per cent of the population are descendants of the African slave population, the small minority being Asians and Europeans; the largest religious group is Roman Catholic (60 per cent) followed by Anglican (20 per cent).

Outline of political history. In 1958 Grenada became part of the short-lived **West Indies Federation**, becoming an Associated State of the UK with full internal self-government in 1967 when the Federation broke up. City and town councils were abolished in 1969. Following elections in 1972, in which the Grenada United Labour Party (GULP) led by **Eric Gairy** won 13 of the 15 seats in Grenada's House of Representatives, the island attained independence on its own account of Feb. 7, 1974, despite widespread unrest and the resignation of the Governor, Dame Hilda Brynoe, in protest at the government's authoritarian style.

In 1979 Gairy's government was overthrown while he was abroad by a *coup* by the opposition New Jewel Movement. The Provisional Revolutionary Government (PRG) led by **Maurice Bishop** aligned itself with the Soviet Union and with **Cuba**, incurring the hostility of the United States. Factional conflict within the PRG then led to a military *coup*, in which Bishop was shot. These events, and the assumption of power by a Revolutionary Military Council under General Hudson Austin, commander of the People's Revolutionary Army, formed the pretext for intervention by the United States with the support of some of the Eastern Caribbean states (*see* **Grenadian Intervention, 1983**) and the appointment by the Governor General, Sir Paul Scoon, of an interim government under Nicholas Braithwaite. In December 1986 General Austin, Bernard Coard (former Deputy Prime Minister of the PRG) and 12 others were convicted of the murder of the former Prime Minister and sentenced to death.

Recent developments—political. At a general election in December 1984 the centrist New National Party (NNP) won 14 of the 15 seats in the House of Representatives, and a new government formed by Herbert Blaize. In 1987 three ministers seceded from the NNP to form the National Democratic Congress (NDC) and after further secessions in support of Braithwaite's candidature for Blaize's seat, the Prime Minister, already in poor health, was defeated for the chairmanship of his own party. When he died in 1990 he was succeeded as Prime Minister by his deputy, Ben Jones, previously Minister of External Affairs.

Outline of economic development. Grenada's economy is primarily agricultural and is heavily dependent on the growth for export of three crops, nutmeg (approx. 6,500 acres), cocoa (15,000 acres) and bananas (4,500 acres). One third of the economically active population is engaged in agriculture, mostly as small farmers. Much of the 8,000 acres of forest was destroyed by hurricane in 1955 and most has been replanted in Honduran mahogany and blue mahoe teak.

The second largest contributor to the national economy is tourism. It was to enable direct flights to the island by modern jet aircraft that the ill-fated PRG embarked on a project to build a new airfield at Point Salines using Cuban technical assistance, which the Americans claimed was a military facility. The government relies on tourism, as well as remittances from the many Grenadians who live overseas, to balance the endemic trade deficit. The balance of visible trade has consistently been negative since 1979, and was $46,100,000 in 1987. Total external debt stood at $80,900,000 in the same year. Industry is small-scale, confined to consumer products such as beer, oils, soap, furniture and clothing for the local market.

Current economic situation. The post-intervention governments have pursued conservative economic policies, and in his last budget, introduced in April 1989, Herbert Blaize claimed that revenue, increased by the imposition of a 10 per cent value added tax, would finally be equal to expenditure. Unemployment, under 10 per cent for males in 1970, was by 1990 running at an estimated 40 per cent.

Prospects for development. Further expansion of tourism offers the best prospect.

PARC

GRENADIAN INTERVENTION, 1983. In March 1983, while United States forces were on "manoeuvres" very close to Point Salines, President Ronald Reagan, in his celebrated "Star Wars" speech, linked Grenada specifically to an alleged "threat" to American security from the Caribbean. However it was the overthrow of **Maurice Bishop** on Oct. 13, 1983 that finally precipitated US intervention. On Oct. 20, the day after Bishop was seized by soldiers and shot, a naval task force, originally prepared for the Lebanon, was redirected towards Grenada, while the day after, following an indication from the USA that such an invitation would be welcome, in Bridgetown, Barbados, members of the recently formed Organization of Eastern Caribbean States (OECS), excluding Grenada, met and resolved to ask Washington to intervene "to restore order and democracy".

On Oct. 25, some 8,000 US troops launched a combined land, air and sea attack on the island. Owing to faulty intelligence, an obsessive but unfounded belief that the island was full of Cuban soldiers and over-reliance on technology it took three days to occupy the island and nine to end all resistance, in the course of which at least 111 people died and 644 were wounded, the vast majority of them Grenadans. President Reagan objected on Nov. 3, 1983 to the term "invasion" to describe the US intervention in Grenada; it was, he said, a "rescue" mission. In fact it was both an invasion and an intervention, and, indeed, the largest US military operation since Vietnam.

PARC

GUADELOUPE. *Population*: 386,600 (1990). *Area*: 1,780 sq km. *GDP*: $1,100 million. *Trade volume*: $1,363.6 million. *Top five trading partners*: France, Japan, Martinique, USA, French Guiana. *Education spending (as a percentage of GNP)*: 14.4 *Birthrate*: 20.4 per 1,000. *Life expectancy*: 66 (men); 72 (women).

Geographical background. The French overseas department of Guadeloupe consists of two islands joined by a bridge, with a number of small offshore islands, lying in the Leeward Islands of the Eastern Caribbean between Montserrat and Dominica. There are also two more distant dependencies (St Barthélémy and the French part of St Martin) to the north-west of Antigua. Guadeloupe was settled by Arawak and Carib Indians before the arrival of European settlers, led by the French, in the early seventeenth century. It remained a French colony, developing a plantation system of agriculture based on the labour of imported African slaves. Slavery was abolished in 1848 and in 1946 Guadeloupe became a department of France and in 1974 was made a region.

Socio–political background. Under the terms of the 1982 decentralization reforms the French government appoints a government commissioner (or Prefect). There is a 43-member elected General Council which is responsible for daily executive affairs and a 41-member elected Regional Council with wider social and economic and planning powers. The territory sends four deputies and two senators to the French National Assembly in Paris.

Outline of political history. Politics on Guadeloupe is dominated by the local affiliates of metropolitan political parties. The left-wing parties, (the Socialist Party (*Parti socialiste*—PS) and the Guadeloupe Communist Party (*Parti communiste guadeloupéen*—PCG) have traditionally been stronger in Guadeloupe than on Martinique and hold the majority on both the General and Regional Councils. In the most recent elections to the General Council in 1988 the left-wing parties increased their representation to 26 seats. The centre-right is represented by the Rally for the Republic (*Rassemblement pour la République*—RPR) and the Party of Guadeloupe (*Le Parti pour la Guadeloupe*—LPG), whose leader, Lucette Michaux-Chevry, was a minister in the Chirac government. The majority of popular opinion favours greater autonomy for the islands, but pro-independence sentiment also seems to be growing, particularly after the decision by the PCG in 1988 to pursue a policy of independence rather than greater autonomy.

Current developments—political. During the 1980s Guadeloupe was the scene of the majority of violent incidents related to extreme pro-independence groups. Demonstrations and strikes by pro-separatists in support of a detained member of a militant pro-independence movement led to rioting in the capital, Pointe-à-Pitre, in July 1985. The Popular Union for the Liberation of Guadeloupe (*Union populaire pour la libération de la Guadeloupe*—UPLG) has emerged as the main "anti-colonialist" pro-independence group, contesting local elections for the first time in 1988, but boycotting presidential and elections for deputies to the National Assembly.

Outline of economic development. The economy of Guadeloupe is similar to that of Martinique and marked by heavy dependence on France. French investment and social legislation have given the islands a higher standard of living and better infrastructure than their neighbours but have served to exacerbate the deep structural imbalances in the economy. The high level of imports creates a large trade deficit, offset by French aid and government transfers. The rate of unemployment is high, and there is extensive emigration to France (compensated by immigration of officials and others from France itself). Tourism is the main economic activity outside the service/administration sector. Agricultural production is in decline with sugar, formerly the main crop, now mostly being used for domestic rum production. Output of sugar totalled 76,100 tonnes in 1988. The two outlying dependencies (St Barthélemy and St Martin), by contrast, have developed vibrant economies based almost entirely on tourism.

LP

GUATEMALA. *Population*: 8,700,000 (mid-1988). *Area*: 109,000 sq km. *GDP*: US$8,100 million (GNP per capita: US$900). *Trade volume*: Merchandise exports (1988): US$1,074 million; Merchandise imports (1988): US$1,548 million. *Average annual rate of inflation* (1980–88): 13.3. *Debt service as percentage of GNP*: 4.4 *Urban population as percentage of total (centres over 20,000)*: 33. *Life expectancy*: 60 (men); 65 (women).

Geographical background. The Republic of Guatemala lies between Mexico in the north, Belize to the east, and Honduras and El Salvador in the south. Although possessing both Caribbean and Pacific coastlines, the former litoral on the Gulf of Honduras remains restricted by the territorial waters of Belize and Honduras. The central and northern areas of Guatemala are mountainous, becoming less rugged to the east, and giving way to a coastal plain in the west. The tropical rainforest province of El Petén juts boldly into Mexico in the north-east.

Socio–political background. It is in the highlands which cover over a third of the country that the surviving indigenous population of Guatemala concentrate. Official figures put the ethnic Indian population at approximately 2,750,000 of the population although most independent estimates are no lower than 3,700,000 people. The ethnic Indian population is in fact differentiated into 21 Mayan language groups. A series of military campaigns over the last two and a half decades, documented and condemned by the UN General Assembly, the UN Human Rights Commission, Amnesty International, the European Parliament and Americas Watch among others, has however resulted in over 150,000 killings and the cultural, social and economic dislocation of the indigenous communities. At the peak of the civil war in 1982 over 150,000 refugees, predominantly Indians, had additionally sought refuge in Mexico, and in 1990 Guatemalan refugees registered by the UNHCR numbered some 45,000.

The Constitution, confirmed in 1986, guarantees a unicameral legislative National Congress with 116 members elected every five years. The congressional elections of Nov. 11, 1990 gave the National Centre Union (*Unión del Centro Nacional* — UCN) 41 seats, the **Christian Democrats** (*Democracia Cristiana Guatemalteca*—DCG) 28 seats and six smaller parties the rest. The President holds executive power for five years, and is currently Jorge Serrano of the rightist Solidarity Action Movement (*Movimiento Acción de Solidaridad*—MAS) which holds 18 congressional seats. His election in the November 1990 election and January 1991 run-off means that for the first time in Guatemalan history a civilian president has succeeded another civilian.

Outline of political history. Historically the indigenous population had been subordinated to the economic, social and political structures established first by the Spanish colonists and then, following the independence of Guatemala in 1821 and the liberal reforms of the late nineteenth century, to the coffee exporting interests of the *ladino* (wholly or partly of Spanish descent) oligarchy. The presence of a large rural population afforded a permanent reserve of labour to be employed in the growing agro-export sector which has formed the basis of the Guatemalan economy. By 1913 coffee accounted for 84 per cent of export earnings. With growing agricultural diversification into bananas, sugar, and cotton particularly during the 1950s and 1960s, and a slowly growing manufacturing base the export profile had been modified by the end of the 1980s to one where agricultural exports accounted for some 59 per cent of exchange earnings.

Since the overthrow of the democratic government of Jacobo Arbenz in 1954, Guatemala was for more than 30 years ruled by a series of military administrations with the exception of the period 1966–70, when, under the presidency of Julio Méndez Montenegro, the military ruled from behind the scenes, as they have done since 1976. After the assassination of Colonel Carlos Castillo Armas in 1957, the February 1958 elections resulted in the choice of General Miguel Ydígoras Fuentes who in turn was ousted by a *coup* in March 1963 led by General Enrique Peralta Azurdia. Peralta's suspension of the constitution signalled the first planned, if discontinuous, military campaign specifically targeting the indigenous population. Regardless of the election of the civilian government of Mario Méndez Montenegro (1966–70), his accession to power was contingent on the recognition of the complete autonomy of the Ministry of Defence and the right of the army to pursue its own counterinsurgency strategy. As one leading commentator has remarked of the 1966 election. "Nowhere else in Latin America—except in El Salvador and Honduras—was a putative reversion to constitutional order matched by such a massive intervention by the military in the public sphere". In fact the long-running war against the indigenous population first became particularly severe in the period 1966 to 1968, when it was directed by Colonel Carlos Osorio Arana, who succeeded as President (1970–74). Violence declined under Colonel Eugenio Kjell Laugerud García (1974–78) only to erupt at a new level of intensity under General Romeo Lucas García in 1978. The repression was directed initially at the pro-Cuban Rebel Armed Forces (*Fuerzas Armadas Rebeldes* — FAR) principally based in the provinces of Izabal and Zacapa, which had been active since 1962, but as new guerrilla movements developed, making links with urban organizations, the main targets of internal war became the **Guerrilla Army of the Poor** (*Ejército Guerillero de los Pobres* — EGP) and the **Guatemalan National Revolutionary Unity**

(*Unión Revolucionaria Nacional Guatemalteca* —URNG).

The brutality of the repression and its indiscriminate targeting of the Indian population, forced President Reagan to continue President Carter's example of cutting off military aid to the Kjell Laugerud and Lucas García governments, as well as those of **Efraín Rios Montt** and Oscar Mejía Victores which followed. Alternative sources of arms and training were however afforded by Argentina, Israel, South Africa and Taiwan. Although the indigenous population were the subject of most of the repression, trade unionists, party members (including DCG members), human rights activists, church workers and community associations suffered disappearances, extra-judicial executions, torture and imprisonment. Eventually by 1984 the almost complete eradication of the armed opposition, the domination achieved by the army, pressures for greater economic stability, and international condemnation of the repression led to commitments by the army to civilianization.

The civilianization of Guatemalan politics occurred through a two-phase plan announced by General Oscar Mejía Victores following his *coup* in August 1983 ousting General Rios Montt. A new National Assembly was elected to re-write the constitution in July 1984 and in November 1985 presidential elections gave the Christian Democrat civilian Vinicio Cerezo Arévalo *de jure* power. The elections following so many years of wholesale repression, described by the *Financial Times* as "a line-up of four extreme-right parties and two right-wing parties, one centre-right with a token centre-left grouping, the Social Democrats . . . providing little more than window dressing", failed to transfer *de facto* power from the army which over the previous decade had succeeded in acquiring substantial economic concerns.

Outline of economic development. The army, especially middle and senior-ranking officers, had utilized the draconian law and operational conditions necessitated by the counter-insurgency campaigns to develop personal economic stakes in real estate, telecommunications, television, electricity, banking, air transport, and numerous parastatal agencies. One study estimated that by 1983 60 per cent of the Department of Alta Verapaz was owned by army personnel. By 1985 the army had come to challenge the economic power of the oligarchy traditionally embodied in the landowners and commercial organizations such as the Guatemalan Farmers Association (*Asociación Guatemalteca de Agricultores* — AGA), the National Coffee Association (*Asociación Nacional del Café* — ANACAFE), and the more modernizing **Co-ordinating Committee of Agricultural, Commercial, Industrial and Financial Associations** (*Comité Co-ordinador de Asociaciones Agrícolas, Comerciales, Indusriales y Financieros* — CACIF). The long-term consequences of the rise of these new and powerful economic interests in Guatemala are likely to be the structural constraints they place upon democratic and/or civilian governments to diversify the bases of economic power, to reform the distribution of land, to prevent the further alienation of indigenous lands, to permit the growth of organized labour and to encourage the pluralization of political representation. Any moves to alter the essential disposition of power by civilian governments has already been met with legislative retrenchment and the mobilization of institutional vetoes from CACIF or the army.

Obviously Guatemalan economic development has been distorted and retarded by the civil war. Again the economic, and hence social and cultural, well-being of the indigenous population has been undermined by the repression that has forced tens of thousands to leave their land for the capital. The condition of the poor had been further worsened by the effects of the February 1976 earthquake which affected 16 of the 22 departments killing 22,000, injuring 77,000 and making over 1,000,000 homeless. The inadequacy of the response of public aid in terms of the provision of health care and sanitation in particular, and the growth of shanty towns, of both underemployment and unemployment continues in its effects today.

Current economic situation. According to the latest **ECLAC** figures 87 per cent of the population are living in poverty, with infant mortality by the government's own figures as high as 135 per 1,000. The lives of the poor have been further troubled by rapidly increasing inflation throughout the 1980s, up to 177 per cent by the fourth quarter of 1988 but which currently stands at 90 per cent per annum. The economy has still not recovered from the dramatic slump in coffee prices during 1986–87 and with increasing oil prices is not likely to be able to fully service its external debt nor promote further economic growth. The largest budget item is the service of the country's $2,400 million external debt, which was so costly to service that payments to the World Bank were temporarily halted during 1990. Debt service problems have been compounded by recent devaluations of the *quetzal* (which had been held at par to the dollar since the 1920s), and have effectively undermined any minor gains outlined in Cerezo's "Five Hundred Day Programme" announced in August 1989 and the encouraging rates of growth reported in non-traditional export sectors during 1987 and 1988.

JCJS

GUERRILLA ARMY OF THE POOR (Ejercito Guerrillero de los Pobres/Unión Revolucionaria Nacional Guatemalteca — EGP/URNG) (Guatemala). The Guerrilla Amry of the Poor (EGP) is the main constitutive unit of the Guatemalan National Revolutionary Unity (URNG) and these continue to form the main revolutionary guerrilla organizations, and bear the brunt of army attacks. They both have the indigenous communities as their principal constituencies of support, although due to the degree of repression during the late 1970s and early 1980s visited upon the host populations and the substantial military defeats of the guerrillas popular support is much curtailed and guerrila activity much less effective.

Guerrilla warfare in Guatemala began in December 1962 following the creation of the Rebel Armed Forces (*Fuerzas Armadas Rebeldes*— FAR) and the alliance established with the communist Guatemalan Labour Party (*Partido Guatemalteco de Trabajadores*—PGT) which had recognized the necessity of armed struggle in April 1961. Political leadership lay with the PGT whilst the military campaign was conducted through two FAR front organizations, the 13th November Revolutionary Movement (*Movimiento Revolucionario 13 de Noviembre*— MR-13) and the Edgar Ibarra Guerrilla Front (*Frente Guerrillero Edgar Ibarra*—FGEI) which was led by two ex-army officers, Marco António Yon Sosa and Luis Turcios Lima respectively. The initial guerrilla strategy based on concentrated attacks (*foquismo*), was disastrous and led to the capture and execution of the majority of the FAR leadership by 1972. The EGP grew out of FAR dissidents who argued for a strategy of prolonged people's war building up community support both materially and ideologically over the long term. At the same time the area of organization had moved from the west of the country to the highland provinces of El Quiché, Huehuetenango and Chimaltenango. The second main constitutive unit of the URNG was the Revolutionary Organization of the People in Arms (*Organización Revolucionaria del Pueblo en Armas*—ORPA) which extended its support and operations less deeply but more extensively into the east and the capital. The EGP and ORPA joined in coalition with the remaining and regenerated FAR and PGT to form the umbrella URNG in February 1982 (although there had been coordinated military activity since 1980) So effective was guerrilla activity, in the light of the events of July 1979 in Nicaragua and the collapse in El Salvador at the beginning of 1980, that the Guatemalan state was in serious danger of downfall. The army's response was an explicitly and publicly announced scorched-earth policy and genocidal reply to the guerrillas. At least 50,000 people were killed during the period 1978–1984 and 440 villages in the highlands were wiped off the map.

Whilst the army's military campaign was successful in suppressing the guerrillas and forcing the withdrawal of support from the indigenous population through forcing it into exile, through terror, through the creation of "development poles" and "strategic hamlets", and through the establishment of civil patrols, the URNG still counts on some 1,500 to 2,000 armed forces. Periodic negotiations between the URNG and the government, most recently at El Escorial in Spain, have failed to agree on a timetable for a ceasefire, on reform of the army, and URNG participation in the 1991 Constituent Assembly elections.

JCJS

GUEVARA, ERNESTO "CHE". Ernesto Guevara de la Serna was born in Rosario in Argentina in 1928. Despite the asthma he contracted in his youth, which caused his parents to move to the highlands, he was a keen rugby player, and travelled extensively in the *altiplano* (highlands) while a medical student at the University of Buenos Aires, from which he graduated in 1953. Following his graduation he again travelled northwards, and being in **Guatemala** at the time of the fall of the Arbenz regime in 1954 had to take refuge in the Argentine Embassy, receiving safe conduct to exile in Mexico City, where he married Hilda Gadea. Soon afterwards he met Raúl Castro, who introduced him to his brother **Fidel**. Originally recruited as doctor to their expedition, the Cubans called him "el che"—the usual Latin American nickname for Argentines. After their flight to the Sierra Maestra, however, he emerged as a military leader, ultimately being entrusted with the second front in the Escambray mountains. On the success of the **Cuban Revolution**, he was made Minister of Industries, and given responsibility for agrarian reform and industrialization, as well as the Central Bank. But in 1965, as the failure of Cuba to industrialize became increasingly clear, he left Cuba to try to form an anti-imperialist front in Africa and in 1966, having severed his connections with his adopted country, returned to **Bolivia**, where his guerrilla force, lacking indigenous support was soon tracked down. On Oct. 9, he was captured near Vallegrande and soon afterwards shot, apparently on direct orders from the highest authorities. After his death he became a powerful icon of revolution for the student movements of the later 1960s, in Europe and the United States, as well as in South America.

PARC

GUIMARAES, ULYSSES SILVEIRA. Ulysses Guimarães, president of the **Brazilian Democracy Movement** (*Movimento Democrático Brasileiro*—MDB) and, previously, president of the Movement for Brazilian Democracy (*Movimento Democrático Brasileiro*—MDB) is one of the most highly respected men in Brazilian politics, especially for his leadership of the opposition to the military régime and for his role in guiding **Brazil** back to democratic government.

Born in Rio Claro, São Paulo, in 1916, Ulysses studied law and was elected, first, to the Constituent Assembly of São Paulo, for the Social Democratic Party (*Partido Social Democrático*—PSD) in 1947, then as federal deputy in 1950. He soon became one of the most prominent PSD members of the Chamber, one of the reformist Ala Moça, Youth Wing group. He was officially nominated as the party's candidate for the governorship of São Paulo in 1958, but failed to win the support of **Juscelino Kubitschek**, who was more anxious to conciliate the current governor of São Paulo, **Jânio Quadros**.

In the parliamentary period under Goulart, Ulysses became Minister of Commerce and Industry, then left the government with the Prime Minister, **Tancredo Neves**, and the rest of his Cabinet, in 1962. After the *coup* of 1964, he was one of several members of Congress who hoped that an Emergency Act might sanction some of the immediate aims of the *coup* leaders, to keep the initiative within Congress. The Supreme Command of the Revolution, especially the "hard line" military leaders, rejected the idea, being determined that the legitimacy of the new régime would come from the "revolution" itself, not from Congress.

This marked the start of Ulysses' battle to maintain the role of Congress within an increasingly authoritarian state, which gave ever more power to the executive, and it was during the period of the military-backed régime after 1964 that Ulysses Guimarães made his most important contribution to the political life of Brazil. After the ending of multi-party politics, following Institutional Act No. 2, in October 1965, he joined the MDB, was re-elected to the Chamber in 1966, and became leader of the MDB in 1971.

In 1973, Ulysses, now the leading parliamentary spokesman for civil society, agreed to be nominated as presidential candidate in the indirect election for president in January 1974. His candidate for Vice-President was Barbosa Lima Sobrinho, president of the Brazilian Press Association, a man from Pernambuco, a distinguished writer, who always had defended Brazil's national interests. Both knew that they had no chance of winning in the Electoral College rigged by the régime.

Many people in MDB thought that their candidature was wrong-headed, taking part in an empty charade. Ulysses disagreed. He argued that, as an "anti-candidate", he, at least, would have an opportunity publicly to draw attention to the nature of the political system and to issues too long excluded from open debate, such as, censorship, torture, and the costs of a development model imposed on the poor and the working class.

The Electoral College endorsed the régime's candidate, General Ernesto Geisel, whose brother, General Orlando Geisel, was Minister of War. The sureness of Ulysses' judgement was reflected in the anger of his opponents, especially in the armed forces, at his presumption and audacity in opposing the régime's nominee. It was also seen in the massive pro-MDB opposition vote in the elections of November 1974, in which Ulysses was re-elected to Congress.

In the opening phase of *distensão*, or political "relaxation", in 1973 and 1974, Ulysses Guimarães disagreed with some theorists of the centre-left and with a prominent North American political scientist, who recommended a gradual, controlled return to democracy. The Brazilian theorists were afraid of a backlash from the armed forces. The North American feared that the process of relaxation might get out of the "control of those who initiated it". Ulysses, knowing Brazil and its people, thought otherwise. He believed that the people of Brazil were fully ready for the responsibility of voting for their representatives, including, as in the past, unlike the system in the USA, a direct vote for their president. He also knew the depth of resentment against continued military tutelage.

Ulysses continued to be a thorn in the flesh of the military-backed régime, fiercely critical of Geisel's April Package of 1977 and of punitive measures against members of the opposition in Congress. He moved always with skill and refined political timing, putting himself out of reach of his political opponents, both civilian and military. With the return to a multi-party system in 1979 and the creation of the PMDB, he steered the early moves of the new party, becoming its leader in January 1980. He continued to oppose the stratagems of the régime to control the process of redemocratization, including the ruling, in the approach to the elections of 1982, that party coalitions would not be allowed, and that voters should choose the same party, (*voto vinculado*), for every office. The PMDB, with Ulysses at its head, won massive support in 1982, at local level, in Congress and in the vote for governors.

As more open political discussion was allowed, Ulysses, together with civil society as a whole, was able to contribute to debate which previously was confined to those who held state power. After the elections of 1982, Delfim Neto and the government were forced to admit the severity of the international debt problem, in the wake of Mexico. This pushed Brazil into the arms of the IMF, with its predictable formulae. Ulysses, in August 1983, was one of the first to stress that IMF solutions would cause great harm, advocating a moratorium on the payment, both of principal and interest, for, at least, three years.

The elections of 1982, and the whole move to more open government, swelled the demand for a return to democracy, one of the principal touchstones of which, in Brazil, was the direct election of the country's president. Ulysses Guimarães joined in the demand for *diretas-já*, "direct vote — now", in late 1983 and 1984, which brought millions of people, in peaceful demonstrations, into the streets. He, and other senior politicians, such as Tancredo Neves and Teotônio Vilela, gave weight and dignity to the campaign, even in its ultimate defeat on April 25, 1984, when men like **José Sarney**, president of the PDS, voted against the necessary constitutional amendment.

With the break-up of the PDS, the appearance of the PFL and the creation of the Democratic Alliance in 1984, Ulysses played a major rôle in guaranteeing the indirect election of Tancredo Neves in January 1985. He already had reached an agreement, with Tancredo, before the *diretas-já* vote, that, if the next presidential election were to be direct, Ulysses would be the candidate: if indirect, Tancredo. Ulysses worked unselfishly to support Tancredo's candidature.

The death of Tancredo Neves presented a major problem for Ulysses and the PMDB. At first, he was inclined to oppose the succession of José Sarney, being fully aware of the resentment felt in the PMDB towards a man who only months before had been leader of the pro-régime PDS party. Ulysses then decided that the overriding issue was to guarantee the return to a civilian presidency. His personal authority brought, at least, grudging acceptance from the PMDB.

Throughout the government of Sarney, Ulysses remained loyal, even when, before the *Cruzado Plan*, the president's stock was falling rapidly, and, again, after the success of the elections of November 1986, when the PMDB became tarnished, both by its association with Sarney and by the supine behaviour of too many of its members in the Congress/Constituent Assembly.

One of the saddest periods of Ulysses' career was when he saw the split in the PMDB, however much of this may have been expected, which produced the Party of Brazilian Social Democracy (*Partido da Social Democracia Brasileiro* — PSDB) in July 1988. The great highlight, by contrast, was when he promulgated the new **Constitution**, in October 1988. After years of struggle, threat and doubt, the cornerstone now was laid for Brazil's new democracy.

Ulysses Guimarães, better than most, knew the difficulties that still lay ahead. In the presidential election campaign of 1989, he worked hard to restore the fortunes of the PMDB. It was a forlorn hope, The party was too closely identified with the Sarney government and its lost chances. There was great sympathy and affection for Ulysses, but few votes. There was general acknowledgement that the party had not lived up to its leader. Many Brazilians still do not fully realize how much they owe their new political freedom to Ulysses Guimarães. Those who know him and his work appreciate his achievement.

PF

GUYANA. *Population*: 754,000 (1989). *Area*: 214,969 sq km. *GDP*: US$360,000,000 (1988). *Trade volume*: $466,000,000 (1988). *Top five trade partners*: USA, 31.9%; UK, 20.3%; Trinidad and Tobago, 7.8%; Japan, 5.4%; West Germany, 5.2%. *Defence spending*: $34,000,000 (1985). *Education spending (as a percentage of GNP)*: 10.1 (1987). *Urban population (as percentage of total)*: 31 (1987). *Birthrate*: 24 per 1,000 (1987). *Life expectancy*: 67.3 (men); 72.3 (women) (1990).

Geographical background. The Co-operative Republic of Guyana, a former British colony and the only English-speaking country in South America, lies on the Atlantic Ocean between Venezuela and Suriname, bordered to the south by Brazil. Much of the country is heavily forested and very sparsely inhabited; 90 per cent of the population live on the relatively narrow coastal strip, much of which lies below sea level and is protected by sea walls, A high rate of emigration contributed to a decline in population of about 5,000 between 1980 and 1989; approximately 50 per cent of the population is of Indian descent, 30 per cent African and 5 per cent Amerindian. Those of mixed origin, together with Chinese, Portuguese and other Europeans, make up the remainder. The main religions are Christian (46 per cent) and Hindu (37 per cent).

The coastal plain is the area of greatest agricultural production, with large-scale cultivation of sugar cane and rice, both for export and domestic consumption, and food crops. Cattle are farmed in the inland savannah area, notably the Rupununi in the south-west, and there is a timber industry, currently the subject of expansion plans, in the forest zone, where a long-planned road is under construction to connect Lethem on the Brazilian border with the capital, Georgetown, on the coast.

Bauxite is mined at Linden on the Demerara river, south of Georgetown, and in the eastern county of Berbice. Gold and diamonds are mined in the western county of Essequibo, and offshore exploration for oil is taking place.

The three settlements of Essequibo, Demerara and Berbice, established by Dutch settlers in the seventeenth century, were ceded to Britain by the Treaty of Utrecht in 1814 and amalgamated into the colony of British Guiana in 1831. The colony became independent under the name of Guyana on May 26, 1966; it became a republic on Feb. 23, 1970.

Guyana has outstanding border disputes with Venezuela and, to a lesser extent, with Suriname. The latter claims 15,540 sq km of territory in the New River area in the south-east, while Venezuela maintains a claim dating back to 1840 to the whole of the Essequibo, an area of 137,270 sq km, or almost two thirds of the country. The claim appeared to have been settled by an arbitration treaty signed in Washington in 1892, but it was re-opened by Venezuela in 1962, since when a number of efforts have been made to find a means by which the dispute may be solved.

The matter was referred to the United Nations secretary-general in 1983, and the two countries agreed in November 1989 to accept the Vice-Chancellor of the University of the West Indies, Alister MacIntyre, as "good officer", with the task of proposing procedures to the two parties. Relations with both Venezuela and Suriname improved considerably in the late 1980s; a bilateral commission was set up with Suriname to discuss approaches to a solution of the New River dispute.

Socio–political background. Under a constitution which came into effect in October 1980, Guyana has a government headed by an executive president, backed by a prime minister and a number of vice-presidents and deputy prime ministers. There is a single chamber of 65 members, elected every five years on a list basis under a form of proportional representation. The country is divided into 10 administrative regions, and there are six municipalities including Georgetown, administered by a mayor and town council. The country maintains a standing army, the Guyana Defence Force, together with a People's Militia and a youth training body known as the Guyana National Service; it was announced in 1990 that the defence force strength was being reduced.

Outline of political history. Politically, Guyana is a sharply divided country, with communal conflict a significant part of its history. A major crisis occurred before independence, when the 1953 general election, the first to be held with full adult suffrage, was won by the **People's Progressive Party** (PPP), led by **Dr Cheddi Jagan**, a marxist. After 135 days in office, the PPP government was removed from power by the Governor and the constitution was suspended, on the grounds that the colony was threatened by communist subversion from within the government.

In 1955, the PPP split into two fractions headed by Jagan and the party's first chairman, **Forbes Burnham**. With the support of other Afro–Guyanese (those descended from African slaves), Burnham founded the **People's National Congress** (PNC) in 1957, leaving the PPP largely composed of Indo–Guyanese, descended from the indentured labourers hired after the end of slavery in 1838. After the PPP came back into office in 1957, relations between the two parties worsened to the point of serious communal violence in 1963–64, in which hundreds of people were killed.

A constitutional conference in London led to the adoption of a system of proportional representation which allowed the PNC to take power in coalition with the United Force party, following the general election of 1964. After independence in 1966, the PNC consolidated its rule in the 1968 election, widely criticized as rigged. Persistent allegations of electoral fraud have continued ever since, but in October 1990, **President Desmond Hoyte** accepted proposals for reform for the elections due to be held in early 1991.

Outline of economic development. Under the regime of Forbes Burnham, which lasted until his death in August 1985, Guyana followed political and economic policies similar in many respects to those of the Communist bloc, although it did not become a one-party state. The government nationalized the bauxite and sugar industries, together with other properties of Booker's, the country's dominant conglomerate; the media were also brought under state control, and in 1974 a PNC congress decided that the party should assume "paramountcy" over the government, which it said was "merely one of its executive arms".

The heavy debt incurred through the nationalizations, estimated at more than US$250,000,000, was accompanied by a downturn in the economy as a result of the oil price increases of the early 1970s. From then on, production in the vital export-earning bauxite, sugar and rice industries showed a declining trend, aided by managerial inefficiency and corruption. Government finances went into deficit, and the current and capital accounts of the balance of payments showed heavy deficits throughout the 1980s. High inflation, a severe shortage of foreign exchange and a collapsing currency were accompanied by deterioration in services such as electricity and water supply, education and health. By 1989, the external debt amounted to US$1,300 million.

Current economic situation. Hoyte, who took over after Burnham's death, has put his economic policies into reverse, opening the country to foreign investment and accepting the former bauxite and sugar owners back to manage the industries. Long negotiations with the IMF and World Bank, backed by an international support group of donor countries, culminated in June 1990 with the repayment of arrears to the international agencies and the adoption of an IMF agreement to support the government's economic recovery programme. The government remained acutely short of foreign exchange, however, and the activities of smugglers and black market currency dealers remained largely outside its control, with the Guyana dollar standing in October 1990 at G$100=US$1, compared with an official rate of G$45. The year was expected to show a further decline in GDP, with inflation of about 50 per cent and unemployment of 27 per cent.

RP

H

HAITI. *Population*: 6,296,000 (1990). *Area*: 27,750 sq km. *GDP*: US$1,856 million (1986). *Trade volume*: exports: $191,000,000; imports: $326,000,000 (1990). *Top five trade partners:* imports: US, Caribbean, Japan, Canada, France. exports: US, Italy, France, Belgium, Caribbean; *Defence spending (as percentage of GNP)*: 1.6 (1985). *Urban population as percentage of total (centres over 20,000)*: 29 (1990). *Birthrate*: 35.4 per 1,000 (1980–85). *Life expectancy*: 51 (men); 54 (women) (1990).

Geographical background. Haiti occupies the Western one-third of the island of Hispaniola, but has virtually the same population—7,000,000—as the Dominican Republic, which occupies the other two-thirds. The population, 95 per cent black, descendants of African slaves, and 71 per cent rural, is the least well nourished, least literate, and by any material indices the most wretchedly poor of the Western hemisphere.

"Haiti", in the language of the almost annihilated Arawaks, means high land, and indeed most of the terrain consists of convoluted hills and mountains that were once cloaked in the rich foliage of a tropical rain forest. But the fertile valleys have long been claimed by domestic and foreign absentee landowners for commercial ventures, and the denuded and eroded hills stand as both cause and effect of rural poverty.

Socio-political background. Once the richest by far of France's sugar plantation colonies, Haiti was the first Latin American country to gain independence (1804) and the first state in the modern world to be born of a slave rebellion. As the colonial power and the landowning aristocracy had been one and the same, the rebellion dismantled the entire ruling class. French officials and planters were expelled (or killed) along with the military and religious institutions that protected and legitimized the rejected social order. Fifty years were to pass before Catholic priests again appeared on the scene.

After a couple of decades during which victorious armies of former slaves overran and terrorized Hispanic inhabitants of what is now the Dominican Republic, the Haitians retreated to their mountains and, ever conscious of being a Black republic in a predominantly white hemisphere, sought only to be left alone. That was not to be.

Among the island's misfortunes has been its proximity to the United States. In 1915, with war looming in Europe and instability threatening US investments in Haiti, the United States alleged German subversion and sent in the marines. When they finally withdrew in 1934, the black majority had been suppressed and power was in the hands of the small mulatto economic élite.

The country's dual culture—a French-oriented mulatto élite and a black African-oriented majority—continues to be reflected in all aspects of national life. The French-speaking élite, which looks to France for cultural inspiration, is highly literate. In fact, it has been estimated that on a per capita basis the country's writers are accredited with more book titles (mostly published in France) than those of any other country in the Western Hemisphere except the United States. The Creole-speaking majority is mostly illiterate, but also abundantly creative. African rhythms are pervasive at social and religious functions, and Haitian "primitive" painting has enjoyed world renown since the 1920s. The country is said to be 80 per cent Catholic and 100 per cent Voodoo. Given the reputed powers of the Voodoo *houngans*, or priests, few want to take chances.

Outline of political history. The dual culture is reflected also in the broad outlines of political competition. The black nationalist movement that came to dominate political life after World War II developed largely as a reaction against the co-operation of the mulatto élites with the United States occupation forces. The movement was spearheaded by a small and insecure black middle class that sought the support of, and claimed to speak for, the neglected masses.

François Duvalier, an early participant in the movement, was elected president in 1957. He succeeded early on in eliminating his rivals and in gaining control over the army—the only institution that had served as an autonomous centre of political power. Having established a network of armed bodies, each of which reported directly to him and served as a check on the others, and having convinced most of the believers in voodoo that he possessed supernatural powers, he achieved a measure of personal control over national life that was probably as extensive as the country's level of development permitted. Actively opposed throughout the period of his rule by the élites of his own country and at one time or another by the Vatican and the governments of Cuba, the Dominican Republic, and the

United States, Duvalier outmanoeuvered every enemy except death.

Having elected himself president-for-life, Duvalier, before his death in 1971, had the constitution revised so as to allow him to name his successor and to lower the age qualifications for the office from 40 to 18. His choice was his playboy son, Jean-Claude, who soon became known as Baby Doc. The official results of the referendum on the amendment regarding succession were about 2,500,000 votes in favour to one against.

Baby Doc curbed the most visible excesses of the security forces and constructed a governmental facade sufficiently modern to attract foreign aid, investment, and even tourism. But selective detention, torture, and execution, and wholesale corruption continued much as before. The culture of violence and its corollaries, generalized fear and suspicion, were sustained in large measure by the same body of thugs, known as the *Tontons Macoutes*, who had underpinned Papa Doc's ghoulish rule.

A popular uprising in 1986 finally rid the country of the Duvalier dynasty, but not of the network of corrupt military and protected thugs that had supported it. The military-dominated National Governing Council that moved into the vacuum freed political prisoners, unmuzzled the press, and promised a transition to a freely elected government. The leader of the Council, General Henri Namphy, soon proved, however, to have little vocation for democracy. The promised elections, which got underway on Nov. 29, 1987, yielded no new government, as the dreaded *Tontons Macoutes* attacked voters at the polls with guns, clubs, and machetes, killing more than 30 of them and wounding hundreds.

Anarchy alternated with tyranny through the end of the decade. Elections held under tense conditions in January 1988 gave the presidency to Christian Democrat Leslie Manigat, a scholar who had spent most of the Duvalier years in exile. But he was overthrown the following September, to be replaced by another politician in uniform, General Prospero Avril. After another popular uprising in 1990, the military stepped aside, leaving government in the hands of Supreme Court Justice Mme Ertha Pascal-Trouillot until elections could be scheduled again.

Recent developments—political. Manigat returned to the country in October with the intention of running again for the presidency, but his candidature was disqualified on a technicality. By November there were about a dozen declared candidates, the strongest of whom appeared to be Fr Jean-Bertrand Aristide, a Roman Catholic priest and "liberation theologian" who ministered to and campaigned among the poor of Port-au-Prince. He was challenged on the right by Roger Lafontant, former Minister of the Interior and "enforcer" of the deposed régime of "Baby Doc" Duvalier. The electoral season was not without several violent incidents, including one in which a grenade exploded at a rally for Fr Aristide, killing seven of his supporters. The tension was eased for the moment when the electoral commission nullified Lafontant's candidacy, again on a technicality.

The election, on Dec. 16, 1990, turned out to be a testament to Haitian courage, optimism and determination to rid themselves of the scourge of corrupt and violent government. Carefully monitored on this occasion by foreign and international observers, the election drew a turnout of some 70 per cent and gave a landslide victory to Fr Aristide. With 75 per cent of the vote counted Aristide had 68 per cent and led his nearest rival, former World Bank economist Marc L. Bazin, by some 54 percentage points. All major groups pledged to respect the outcome of the election, but few were confident that peace would reign long after the foreign observers departed. In the event, an attempted *coup* by Roger Lafontant was put down, and Fr Aristide sworn in without further incident.

Outline of economic development. Agriculture is the mainstay of the Haitian economy. Coffee is the major export crop, but sugar cane, rice, corn, and sorghum are also grown for domestic or export markets. Most farming is for subsistence only, and it is a measure of the desperation of Haitian peasants that while less than one-third of the already overworked land is considered arable, more than half of it is in fact farmed.

Each year some 30,000 peasants migrate to the unwelcoming cities. Urban unemployment was estimated at 40 to 50 per cent at the beginning of the 1990s. Tourism, sugar-refining, flour milling, cement and textile manufacturing, and light assembly industries offer employment for some, but wages are very low. The most dynamic sector of the economy in the 1980s was the assembly industry, particularly the making of baseballs for the US major leagues. The assembly industry generated some 50,00 jobs in the 1980s, mostly for women, but the political instability and open violence of the latter part of the decade put a damper on foreign investment and devastated the tourism industry.

Per capita income, a dismal $350, was nevertheless deceptive, since 90 per cent of the population was fortunate to earn half that amount. Services had always been neglected. Even in the capital, Port-au-Prince, where almost all of the national budget had normally been spent, 96 per cent of the population lacked running water. There were more Haitian doctors practicing medicine in Montreal than in all of Haiti, where the ratio was one physician for each 8,200 persons. A survey in the early 1980s, showed that for every secondary school teacher in Haiti, there were 189 security-force personnel; and for every secondary school there were 35 prisons.

Current economic situation. More than 1,000,000 Haitians have taken refuge—political or economic—outside the country, and hundreds more have died trying to reach foreign shores. Many who remain are quietly starving; 90 per cent of the children suffer from malnutrition.

Ordinary Haitians are extraordinarily rich in imagination and creativity, but in little else.

JKB

HERNANDEZ COLON, RAFAEL. Born in 1936, Hernández studied law. He was appointed attorney-general of **Puerto Rico** in 1965, and was president of the senate between 1969 and 1971. He served as governor between 1972 and 1976 and was narrowly defeated by Carlos Romero Barceló in the election in 1980. He regained the governorship in 1984 and was re-elected in 1988. He has fought to maintain a high profile for Puerto Rico, particularly at Washington, in defence of commonwealth status.

JKB

HONDURAS. *Population*: 5,100,000 (1989). *Area*: 112,088 sq km. (including inland water). *GDP*: US$1,310 million (1983). *Trade volume*: $1,815.55 million (1986). *Top five trade partners*: USA, Japan, Guatemala, Venezuela, Italy, *Defence spending*: $120,000,000 (1985). *Education spending (as a percentage of GNP)*: 4.3. *Urban population as percentage of total (centres over 20,000)*: 24. *Birthrate*: 44 per 1,000. *Life expectancy*: 63 (men); 67 (women) (1989).

Geographical background. The Republic of Honduras is a very mountainous country, being transversed by the *Cordilleras*, with peaks rising to between 1,500 and 2,400 m above sea level. There are lowland plains on both her northern (Caribbean) coastline and on her narrow outlet to the Pacific via the Gulf of Fonseca between Nicaragua and El Salvador.

The lowland areas are hot and wet. The mountains are drier and temperature varies widely due to altitude differences. The Carribbean coast lies in the hurricane belt. Around 682,000 hectares are cultivated but much of the soil is of poor and acidic varieties (except for the coastal plains of the north and some of the interior) so that large tracts of land remain uncultivated.

There are 15,006 km of roads but these are poor and only 1,809 are paved. Road construction is accelerating reasonably quickly. The rail network totals just 1,004 km and exists chiefly to serve the northern coastal banana belt around the Caribbean ports of Tela and San Pedro Sula. There is little river transport. In contrast there is a well developed air transport system which is important for both passengers and freight (there are three international airports and 33 smaller airstrips).

Population growth is high and has averaged over 3.1 per cent since at least 1960. Tegucigalpa (pop. 597,512) is the largest city with 13.7 per cent of total population. Comparatively speaking San Pedro Sula is large for a Central American second city (population 397,201).

Socio–political background. About 90% of the population are of mixed (*mestizo*) origin. Around 7 per cent are Amerindians, the principal indigenous groups being Carib, Opatoros and Sumo. Just 2 per cent are of African origin, living mainly in the Caribbean lowlands and known as Garifunas. There are also a small number of Europeans.

Spanish is the national language, though English is widely spoken, especially in the Caribbean region where it is the first language for some. A variety of Indian languages are still in daily use. The main religion is Christianity (95.1 per cent Roman Catholic). Primary education (7–13 year olds) is free and compulsory but non-attendance is a problem and only 70 per cent are enroled. Adult (over 15) illiteracy is 31.4 per cent. The national university is located in Tegucigalpa but it also has campuses in La Ceiba and San Pedro Sula. Education spending is about 30 times less than in Costa Rica. Major causes of death are the diseases associated with malnutrition and poor hygiene (in 1990 President Callejas admitted that 80 lower income children die each day during the rainy season due to gastroenteritis and other intestinal disorders). A total of 75 per cent of urban and 13 per cent of rural dwellings have piped water. In rural areas only 1 per cent has a proper sewerage system. Crude death rate is 10.1 per 1,000, Infant Mortality Rate (IMR) is 23 per 1,000. There is one doctor for every 3,120 people although this ratio has been slowly decreasing over time. Social security provision is limited. There is insufficient housing and most lack basic facilities in both rural and urban areas.

Outline of political history. Nominally a presidential republic with a unicameral Congress,

Honduras has been dominated by military leaders for much of its history, and was often a battleground for the ambitions of would-be leaders of Central America. In 1969 anger at immigration from overpopulated El Salvador was the pretext for the so-called "Football War", also known as the 100 hours war, which in actuality took 13 days, cost 5,000 lives, and very seriously disrupted, the Central American Common Market (formed 1961).

Recent developments–political. From 1981 Honduras was the base for the US-backed armed force, the so-called "contras", attempting to overthrow the government of Sandinista Nicaragua, and since 1983 US troops have been continuously stationed in the country. The stationing of foreign troops on its soil became a major issue in internal politics as Honduras came to be considered little more than a US aircraft carrier or "state for sale". A new opposition coalition grouping the Liberal Democratic Movement (*Movimiento Liberal Democrático*—M-Líder) concentrated criticism on this issue. Labour federations and *campesino* (farmworker) organizations began to demand not only jobs and land but also the removal of foreign troops. General Gustavo Alvárez Martínez, who as one of the United States' staunchest allies had helped organize the "contras" and had allegedly connived at death squads, was assassinated in Tegucigalpa on Jan. 25, 1989 by guerrillas of the newly formed pro-Cuban Cinchonero People's Liberation Movement (*Movimiento Popular de Liberación Cinchonero*—MPL-Cinchonero). Effects of the austerity drive of President Callejas will be unpredictable (see below); a banana strike of 1990 was settled forcibly by troops and with an agreement which fell well short of the workers' demands.

The current political parties are: **National Party** (*Partido Nacional*—PN), **Liberal Party of Honduras** (*Partido Liberal de Honduras*—PLH), Innovation and Unity Party (*Partido de Inovación y Unidad*—PINU), Christian Democratic Party of Honduras (*Partido Demócrata Cristiano de Honduras*—PDCH), Communist Party of Honduras (*Partido Comunista de Honduras*—PCH), Social Democratic Party of Honduras (*Partido Socialista Democrático de Honduras*—PSDH), Socialist Party of Honduras (*Partido Socialista de Honduras*—PASOH).

Outline of economic development. Honduras is the archetypal "banana republic" and was dominated for many years by the United Fruit Company (now United Brands) of Boston. Bananas still account for 30 per cent of exports. Coffee comes second on 22.7 followed by wood (4.7), sugar (3.4) and beef (2.8). Honduras is the fourth largest exporter of bananas in the world, after Costa Rica, Ecuador and Colombia and ahead of Panama and Guatemala. Exports of shrimps and lobsters are increasing. Other products are tobacco, beans, maize, rice, cotton, palm oil, sugar cane, cement and tropical fruits.

Current economic situation. An influx of US military aid during the 1980s improved infrastructure in the border region but at the cost of social problems. In 1988 the IMF declared Honduras ineligible to use general resources of the fund effective in light of overdue financial obligations of 20,000,000 Special Drawing Rights (SDRs). In 1989 Honduras also became ineligible for World Bank funds because of accumulated arrears of $80,000,000 and by 1989 total external public debt was estimated at over $3,600 million. In 1990 Honduras effectively went back on the list of countries eligible for lending by multilateral institutions when it concluded a $41,000,000 standby agreement with the IMF. This was accompanied in 1990 by a rescue operation which included a $245,700,000 bridging loan from the USA, Japan, Venezuela and Mexico. The Honduran government will seek to reschedule much of its external debt and seek new funds to pay back the bridging loan. Honduras' initial credit "blacklisting" came when former President Azcona refused to implement IMF policies. On assuming office President Callejas immediately implemented a policy of economic austerity leading to the lending agencies' change of heart. Honduras decided late in 1990 to abandon the long-time official exchange rate of US$1 to 2 lempiras. Such a move may lead to subsequent devaluation and inflation.

Prospects for development. There are largely constrained due to limited energy resources and a history of reliance on one or two agricultural export crops. Furthermore the private sector has not been willing to re-invest profits in Honduras.

LLP

HOYTE, HUGH DESMOND. A former teacher and lawyer, Desmond Hoyte became President of **Guyana** on the death of **Forbes Burnham** in August 1985, after 16 years as a government minister, for much of the time responsible for economic development and finance. He became a vice-president in 1981 and was named First-Vice-President and Prime Minister in 1984. Winning an election in December 1985 widely criticized for serious irregularities, Hoyte gradually manoeuvred to consolidate his position within the ruling **People's National Congress**, while dramatically reversing Burnham's economic policies by inviting foreign investment, privatizing state enterprises and seeking financial agreements with the IMF. Under his rule, harassment of political opponents and state control of the media was relaxed, and a "national dialogue" undertaken. In preparation for a general election in 1991, he agreed to measures of electoral reform.

RP

HUMAN RIGHTS. By human rights is meant those rights which every human being should have by the mere fact of their existence, and which it is the duty of all other human beings, regardless of their political, religious or other beliefs, to assure them. Universally accepted are certain fundamental rights that are *negative* rights, in that they require no special resources to achieve them, merely that the government of the country concerned should refrain from breaching them or allowing others to do so. Examples are the right to life; freedom of speech and of religion; equality before the law and the right to a fair trial. Other social and economic rights have been described as *positive* rights, in that they require the application of resources by government to make them possible: for example, the provision of adequate housing, food or health services. For this reason both traditional liberals and modern libertarians have been reluctant to attribute to these the status of human rights, on the grounds that they cannot be properly regarded as universal.

Breaches of human rights have occurred throughout Latin America's independent history, despite the existence of constitutional guarantees, but the first resolution on the defence of human rights in the Americas was not adopted until 1938. The Atlantic Charter (1941), which asserted the "four freedoms", affected all nations that took part in the conflict against Germany. It was notably influential in inspiring Central America's brief experiment with democratic government in the immediate post-War period. The signature on May 2, 1948 of the *American Declaration of the Rights and Duties of Man* and the adoption in December 1948 of the *Universal Declaration of Human Rights* for the first time established a yardstick against which to measure the conduct of governments.

However the reluctance of the Latin American states to sanction any kind of intervention in national sovereignty was maintained, despite various instances of the use of arbitrary detention and the very systematic use of torture under the dictatorship of Marcos Pérez Jiménez in **Venezuela**. Hence the question of human rights in the Americas did not become a major issue before the late 1960s, when the military dictatorships that had again begun to spread in the region in response to the threat presented by the **Cuban Revolution** faced the new challenges of urban terrorism, urban "guerrilla warfare", and the kidnapping of diplomats and businessmen. The kidnapping and subsequent death of the American police instructor Dan Mitrione in **Uruguay** in 1968 was alleged by the **Tupamaros** to have been a reprisal for the use of torture against their members, and between 1968 and 1972 the governments of **Brazil** and **Guatemala** were additionally accused of conniving at the operation of "death squads" against those suspected of terrorism.

The Inter-American Commission on Human Rights (IACHR), had been set up in 1960 as one of the principal organs of the **Organization of American States (OAS)**, in order to "promote respect for human rights". Visits were made by the commission to the **Dominican Republic** in 1965–66 to assist all parties in maintaining human rights in a state of civil war, and to both **El Salvador** and **Honduras** during and after the "Football War" of 1969. In the years that followed the Western Powers, led by Richard Nixon and Henry Kissinger, insisted that the Soviet Union subscribe to a declaration of human rights in the Helsinki Declaration. But the violent fall of Salvador Allende in **Chile**, and the purges that followed, were an unwelcome reminder that many "Western" states could not claim to be guiltless of human rights violations. Hence when in its reports on Chile, following visits both by the Executive Secretary and by a group of five commission members, the IACHR was able to name the names of those who had been tortured and, in many cases, vanished without trace—the 'disappeared' (*desaparecidos*)—both it and other organizations, notably Amnesty International, were attacked and condemned as misguided, wrong or communist-inspired by the right-wing governments they had criticized. Despite this in 1977 and 1978 formal invitations to the IACHR to visit their countries were issued by, among others, the governments of Panama, El Salvador, Haiti and Nicaragua.

Under the cloak of the "National Security Doctrine", by which the armed forces tried to justify in the name of national security both their own intervention in domestic politics and the widespread and flagrant breaches of human rights that accompanied it, the systematic and deliberate use of terror, brutality and torture reached a new peak under the "Process of National Reorganization" in **Argentina** after 1976, commonly known afterwards as the "dirty war" (*guerra sucia*). In the 1980s, when Latin

American states, looted and pillaged by their own armed forces, began once more to turn towards democracy, the armed forces found themselves confronted by the dilemma of how to get out of politics without running the risk of being held to account for their crimes. The outcome has taken a different form in each of the states most affected, though in no case have civilians been able effectively to hold their own armed forces to account.

Argentina. Between 1976 and 1979 the military government of Argentina waged a clandestine war of terror against guerrilla groups and all whom they believed might be their sympathizers. As early as 1980, the silent protests of the "Mothers of the Plaza de Mayo" against the arbitrary arrest, detention and disappearances of their loved ones began, but were broken up by force. In 1982, however, in the Falklands War, the Argentine army was discredited utterly by its inability to discharge the purpose for which it officially existed. Before handing over to the civilian government of Dr **Alfonsín** in 1983 they issued themselves a formal pardon, but it was overturned by the newly elected Congress. The new government appointed a National Commission on the Disappearance of Persons (CONADEP) with the distinguished writer, Ernesto Sábato, in the chair. CONADEP's report, *Nunca Más* ("Never Again") published in December 1984, documented more than 9,000 instances of arbitrary arrest, torture and death of individuals, identified detention centres and named many of those responsible, and was followed by legal action against the members of the military juntas that had held power between 1976 and 1983. On Dec. 9, 1985 ex-President Jorge Videla and Admiral Massera were sentenced to life imprisonment, and ex-President Viola, Admiral Armando Lambruschini and Air Force Brigadier Orlando Agostí to 17 years, eight years and four and a half years' imprisonment respectively. The Defence Bill passed by the Senate in October 1986 formally reversed the "National Security Doctrine" and reaffirmed the principle of civil control of the armed forces.

However, this was to be the high-water mark of the civilian attempt to bring the armed forces to justice. Faced with strong military hostility to being tried by civilians, the Alfonsín government decided not to pursue any further criminal charges. The passage in December 1986 of the so-called "Full Stop" Law (*Punto Final*), setting a final date for all charges to be lodged, and additionally establishing the principle of "due obedience" to superior orders as a valid defence (contrary to the Nuremberg principles), led by March 1987 to some 400 charges against some 250 military personnel being lodged to try to meet the deadline. The result was increasing tension, as a number of incidents, including a mass commemorating the "victims of subversion" attended by ex-President General Jorge Rafael Videla, testified to the fervent belief amongst the armed forces that their friends and comrades had done no wrong. At Easter Major Ernesto Barreiro failed to answer torture charges in court and took refuge at Córdoba, following which the soldiers at Campo de Mayo, led by Colonel Aldo Rico, "refused to obey their natural commanders" in protest at the government's policy of prosecuting those accused of crimes in the "dirty war". General Ernesto Alais, commander of the Second Army Corps at Rosario, was prepared to move against them but unable to raise more than 1,000 troops and was afterwards forced to resign. Talks between leading personalities culminated in mass rallies for democracy in which for the first time Radicals and Peronists combined with other groups to defend the new order, and the surrender of the rebels to the President in person announced on the evening of Easter Day ended the mutiny, though later two minor rebellions stirred provincial garrisons in the North.

Though all reports of deals were denied, and the army commander, General Héctor Ríos Ereñu, who had earlier been reported as describing the "war" against subversion as "totally just and legitimate", was replaced by General José Dante Caridi, who held that army personnel should answer to civilian courts, 15 of the 22 generals whose dismissal had been demanded by the insurgents were retired in the next few days and the Supreme Court "temporarily" halted all trials.

In 1989 the new civilian president, Dr **Carlos Menem**, went a stage further. Despite his own history as a prisoner of the military regime and strong opposition from the Mothers of the Plaza de Mayo and other human rights organizations, he sought to defuse the military issue by proclaiming an amnesty for 280 military officers and civilians, including 39 convicted of human rights offences, 57 terrorists, the three members of the Junta who fought the Falklands War and army rebels against the government of President Alfonsín. Following a new military revolt early in December 1990, he pardoned those remaining few senior military officers who had been successfully tried and sentenced (or, in the case of General Guillermo Suárez Mason, extradited from the United States but not yet tried) for human rights crimes during the "Dirty War", including General Jorge Videla, Admiral Emilio Massera, General Robert Viola and General Ramón Camps. Predictably the pardon stunned human rights activists and relatives of the thousands of victims and received only the "unrepentant ingratitude" of General Videla, who in an open letter to the Army Chief of Staff demanded an apology and "the restoration of military honour" for having "defended the nation against subversive aggression".

Mario Eduardo Firmenich, former leader of the Peronist guerrilla movement, the *Montoneros*, who was also freed, prudently said nothing.

Brazil. In **Brazil** reports of the systematic violation of human rights by military and naval intelligence organizations were almost exclusively confined to the period between 1968 and 1976 when they operated under the authority of the Fifth Institutional Act. The long gap between the suppression of the insurgent movements of that period and the reinstatement of civilian rule made it unlikely that these actions would be successfully prosecuted, and, with the death of **Tancredo Neves**, any hope there might have been that members of the armed forces would be brought to book died also. The new **Constitution**, finally agreed on Sept. 2, 1988 after 578 days of debate and formally proclaimed in Brasilia on Oct. 5, specifically rejected the so-called "national security doctrine" and outlawed torture, though under Article 148 the armed forces formally retained the power to intervene whenever law and order are deemed to be under threat.

Chile. The military *coup* of Sept. 11, 1973 was savage. Hawker Hunter fighters attacked the presidential Moneda palace with rockets. President Allende committed suicide with the palace in flames around him. Most of the people who had stayed with him to the bitter end were summarily executed. The military leaders behind the *coup* were obsessed by the idea of rooting out the "marxist cancer" identified with the Popular Unity coalition. Armed resistance to the *coup*, however, was minimal.

Hundreds of people were killed in the *coup* itself and immediately afterwards. Pinochet set up a secret police force answerable directly to him and ruled by decree from 1973 to 1990. For much of this period **Chile** was under a state of emergency. Torture, murder, disappearance, internment, exile, internal exile, imprisonment without trial, mass arrests, death threats and political blacklisting were all used by the government.

Killings and disappearances in Chile do not compare in number to those of **Guatemala** and **El Salvador**. They were, however, shocking in a country which up to 1973 had an exemplary record of respect for human rights and an ingrained tradition of legality. It was, however, the sense that terror, modulated according to the circumstances, was used deliberately as an instrument of government that provoked the outrage and international condemnation which isolated the Chilean government.

On March 4, 1991 President Aylwin officially acknowledged the violation of human rights when, with a catch in his throat, as president, he asked the victims of violations committed by the state and their relatives for forgiveness. He presented to the nation the report of the government's Commission on Truth and Reconciliation giving details of 2,279 people who were executed for political reasons, died under torture or were "disappeared" between September 1973 and March 1989. The report, impressive and horrifying in its detail, lists only clearly confirmed killings so its total is inevitably an underestimate. It gives no information on the far greater number of non-fatal cases of torture, arbitrary imprisonment and, in this context only, minor excesses of the regime.

The Commission's findings were based to a large extent on the Catholic Church's *Vicaría de Solidaridad* (Vicariate of Solidarity) which had filed 1,134 cases on murders committed between 1973 and 1988. These figures included not only political murders of members of *Unidad Popular* parties and suspected opponents of the military régime, but protesters shot down in demonstrations and people killed in staged armed "confrontations", a technique which replaced "disappearance" as a means of disposing of political enemies.

By the end of the 1970s the security forces had realized that forced disappearances transformed the victim's relatives into formidable human rights campaigners and provoked international disapproval. Detained people were simply shot down, often during hours of curfew, enabling the government to say that they were killed in an exchange of fire with the security forces. The *Vicaría de Solidaridad* received a total of 682 documented reports of "disappearance", not counting some 52 cases where the bodies of victims have been found and identified.

Tens of thousands of Chileans were sent into exile in the course of the dictatorship. Thousands more left because they were blacklisted or left destitute by the major recessions of 1975 and 1982. The active involvement of political refugees in human rights campaigns in every Western country was a constant problem for the Pinochet government. In 1976 the Chilean secret police used a car bomb to kill Orlando Letelier, Minister of Defence at the time of the *coup* and a former ambassador to Washington, in the heart of Washington D.C. because of his lobbying against the military government.

Since Patricio Aylwin became president, more common graves of people summarily executed after the *coup* have been found in the north of Chile. The Supreme Court, however, has ruled that the amnesty decree of 1978 prevents the authorities even from investigating these findings and determining who was responsible. President Aylwin has publicly criticized the judiciary for its less than enthusiastic defence of human rights under the dictatorship and has urged it to take up some of the cases reviewed by the Commission. General Pinochet angrily rejected the findings of the Commission for Truth and Reconciliation but Generals Matthei of the Air Force and Stange of the Carabineros, both of whom have less personal responsibility for the excesses of the early years of the military régime, gave it a cautious welcome.

Uruguay. In **Uruguay**, also, no effective action could be taken against those responsible for human rights violations during the 12 years of military rule. The civilian government of Dr Julio Sanguinetti took office on March 1, 1985. Within hours the new President had legalized left-wing political groups. On March 8 the Chamber of Deputies approved by 86 votes to five an Amnesty Bill covering 267 political prisoners. The 193 released on March 10 included Raúl Sendic, former Tupamaro leader, while 61 transferred to police custody pending review of murder charges included the founder of the Tupamaros, Jorge Manera Lluberas, and Antonio Mas Mas, who killed Dan Mitrione, the US police adviser, in 1970. However, though the President had reportedly reached an agreement with the commander of the army, General Medina, for the exemplary punishment of the worst human rights violations, it was not long before the armed forces too wanted a general amnesty (*Ley de Caducidad*).

The controversial bill, nicknamed like its Argentine counterpart, the "Full Stop" Law, led to fighting on the floor of the Chamber of Deputies before its passage on Dec. 22, 1986, thus averting a major political crisis and possible armed intervention. However widespread civilian opposition to what amounted to an amnesty for the majority of members of the armed forces accused of human rights violations during the military-backed governments of 1973–85 continued to manifest itself openly in 1987 and 1988 in unrest and moves to call a referendum on the issue. After long delays, however, the referendum, on April 16, 1989, confirmed the controversial law by 1,008,925 votes (57 per cent) to 770,221 (43 per cent), though the defeat of the ruling **Colorado Party** in the presidential elections that followed was attributed at least in part to their equivocal position on the issue.

Other countries. After the breakdown of the uneasy peace between government and guerrilla groups in **Colombia** in July 1985 serious breaches of human rights by both sides became a daily occurrence, and the government came under cold scrutiny for the reported excesses of the armed forces in countering the endemic violence which in the previous 25 years had killed an estimated 75,000 people. In the first quarter of 1987 alone 75 members of the security forces, 14 provincial politicians, some 70 alleged guerrillas and over 100 civilians died. In addition, 62 civilians were kidnapped, mostly in and around the capital, Bogotá. More than a hundred intellectuals fled the country after the proliferation of death lists which heralded the assassination on Aug. 25 of Dr Héctor Abad Gómez, Liberal president of the local human rights committee in Medellín.

In February 1986 the Congress of **Bolivia** ordered the trial, on charges of torture and murder, of former President Luis García Meza, who sensibly remained in hiding in the remote north-east. President García's government had between 1980 and 1981 been responsible for initiating the unchecked growth of the cocaine trade.

On Jan. 28, 1988 the Minister of Government and Police in **Ecuador**, Sr Luis Robles Plaza, was forced to resign. He had been accused of human rights abuses which, it was alleged, had been overlooked abroad on account of President León Febres Cordero's free market policies.

When in **Paraguay** in 1988 the Pope called for respect for human rights and political freedoms, the crowd gathered outside Asunción Cathedral were attacked by police with truncheons and many were injured. In response Archbishop Ismael Rolón cancelled a ceremony to commemorate the 451st anniversary of the founding of the city, a date, not altogether concidentally, chosen by General Stroessner for his inauguration to an eighth five-year term as President.

The most serious breaches of human rights by government or military officers in recent years, however, has undoubtedly been in **Peru**, where Ayacucho and parts of two other departments have been under martial law for several years. In 1988 Amnesty International confirmed that there had been a sharp increase in reported cases of torture and unlawful killing in the Andean emergency zone since the previous year. Since the insurgency began in 1980, government sources said that at least 11,500 and 15,000 were known to have died, and since 1982 at least 3,200 people were said locally to have "disappeared". The government, which had extended the state of emergency to cover six provinces and Lima itself, was also thought to be behind the emergence of a right-wing counter-terrorist group, the so-called Commando Rodrigo Franco. According to a Senate committee report, 3,198 people died violently in 1989 as a result of insurgent and death-squad activity, compared with 1,986 in 1988, making a total of some 15,800 since 1980.

The Caribbean. The Caribbean, with one of the most stable political and social environments in the world, not surprisingly has an exemplary human rights' record. From their colonial past, one dominated by England, have evolved government systems based on Westminster and parliamentary democracy. With very few exceptions, the maintenance of such systems, from the holding of free elections to ensuring the various checks and balances like the judiciary remain independent, has led to few human rights' abuses.

In fact, it is because the region is known for its human rights' record, as attested to by the United Nations, Freedom House and Amnesty International, that when the exceptional abuse occurs, it creates such a big impact. **Haiti** and **Cuba** in the wide Caribbean region are the two countries consistently cited for human rights' abuses. Neither shares the political make-up of the other Caribbean countries.

Cuba has been ruled by **Fidel Castro**, who overthrew the pro-American Batista régime, for decades. He adopted a style of politics aligned to the USSR. In the state system, freedom of expression, political organization and other expressed democratic freedoms were abolished. Dissenters were imprisoned or summarily executed. In the late 1980s, many were shipped to Miami in a massive clean-out of non-supporters of the Castro government.

Haiti, one of the world's poorest countries, has long been a nation exploited by rulers. The **Duvaliers**, father and son, (Papa Doc and Baby Doc) supported by vigilantes, the **Tontons Macoutes**, ravaged the country and viciously suppressed the human rights of Haitians. The overthrow of Baby Doc only replaced one brutal leader with another (Prospero Avril), but after attempts to hold democratic elections Jean-Bertrand Aristide, a liberationist priest, was sworn in as a popularly elected president on Feb. 7, 1991.

In the Caribbean Community (CARICOM) countries, the case of Grenada provides the most startling example of human rights' abuses, occurring first under former Prime Minister **Eric Gairy** and later under the short-lived **Maurice Bishop** régime, which overthrew Gairy in 1979. Gairy's popularity turned him into what amounted to be a dictator, although parliamentary elections were held at the constitutional times. But such was his hold on the country that for a long time he was able to perpetuate various atrocities.

Gairy was supported by a special unit answerable to him only known as the "Mongoose Gang". This group beat up political opponents of Gairy, many including Maurice Bishop were routinely imprisoned and there were killings. The Gairy atrocities led to his peaceful, popular overthrow while he was on a visit to the USA and the Marxist government of Bishop took over.

As Bishop moved his country from the depression of the Gairy reign, CARICOM countries reluctantly lent their support to the government, many insisting on the condition of future democratic elections. Jealousy of Bishop's popularity by members of his ruling council and Bishop's increasingly moderate posture in relations with regional governments led to a split. It culminated in his overthrow by Bernard Coard and the more militant faction, and in the resulting carnage Bishop and scores of followers were gunned down in cold blood. The December 1983 US-led intervention brought a halt to this chapter of human rights' abuses, with Coard and his supporters arrested, tried, and sentenced to death (later commuted).

The only other human rights' concern has been charges of election rigging in **Guyana** by the ruling People's National Congress which has dominated Guyana's politics, first under the late Forbes Burnham and now President Desmond Hoyte. The country has been widely criticized for supressing opposition voices such as the Catholic church by withholding newsprint. The biggest blot remains the death of university lecturer Dr. **Walter Rodney** in mysterious circumstances. Before his death by bomb, Rodney was regularly harassed and arrested.

Thus, human rights' abuses mainly relate to odd instances rather than any systematic suppression of people by governments. In all cases, people and other governments strongly resist and normally succeed in overturning any attempt at human rights' abuse or halting it. Attempts to introduce restrictive legislation on unionization and freedom of association, or any public order laws, have been successfully rejected in countries including Dominica, Antigua, Barbados and others.

In 1990, Antiguan journalist Tim Hector successfully took a case against his newspaper to the Privy Council after the Vere Bird government convicted him of publishing information detrimental to it. The media is regarded as a strong guardian of freedoms, and other attempts to muzzle journalists, as in St. Vincent and Grenada in recent years, have been met with widespread condemnation.

Human rights has also been on the agenda of CARICOM states, with countries and top politicians such as leader of the Barbados Labour Party opposition in Barbados Henry Forde, advocating that an exemplary human rights' record be a condition of membership.

With Caribbean countries firmly committed to liberal democratic forms of government, and more integration, along with the need to maintain stable political and social climates due to the dependence on tourism, there is no reason to suggest, the 1990 attempted *coup* in Trinidad and Tobago nothwithstanding (this has not led to any restriction of human rights), that the region will not remain at the top of the list of countries with outstanding human rights' records.

PARC, GG, MH

I

INFLATION. Very high annual rates of inflation have been a feature of Latin American economies for several decades. It is a measure of the extent to which they are taken for granted that when the government of General **Pinochet** in **Chile** succeeded in bringing the annual inflation rate down to double figures (i.e., below 100 per cent), it was hailed in some quarters as a major economic achievement. However Chile's 1973 figure of 365 per cent is by no means the largest recorded: in **Argentina** in 1984 inflation reached 688 per cent and in 1989 4,923 per cent. In **Bolivia** in 1985 it was over 16,000 per cent.

The cumulative effects are even more striking. In **Uruguay** even the relatively modest levels of inflation of the 1960s meant that between 1958 and 1967 the cost of living rose by some 14,000 per cent. The inability of successive governments to cope with declining living standards was a significant cause of the outbreak of the Tupamaro insurgency and the assumption of power by the armed forces in 1973. However under the five-and-a-half years tenure of the Radical government of **Raúl Alfonsín** in Argentina (1983–89) inflation totalled 614,801 per cent, there was a 65 per cent fall in real wages, and the national debt rose to over $65,000 million, military unrest remained largely rhetorical, though the government did in the end resign prematurely, owing to loss of public confidence.

In fact relatively high rates of inflation in Latin America are not at all a new phenomenon. In the mid-nineteenth century the depreciation of the Brazilian currency was so great that a new unit of a thousand *reis*, the *milreis*, became the norm. In the late nineteenth century, when the gold standard was almost universal, Chile successfully maintained a paper currency, but again only at the cost of a steady decline of its value which caused great irritation to foreign traders. The Chilean example highlights one of the reasons for inflation, that it enables governments to maintain high rates of borrowing with the assurance that the sum repaid will always fall well short of the sum borrowed.

The remedies for inflation are almost as controversial as the problem itself. **Mexico** adopted the gold standard in 1906, despite the fact that though it was the world's largest silver producer, it produced only small quantities of the more precious metal. The result was a sharp deflation, which in turn caused steep rises in the real price of bread, a contributory cause of the outbreak of the **Mexican Revolution** in 1910. In the 1920s several countries in the Caribbean region (Panama, Guatemala, El Salvador, Nicaragua, Honduras, Cuba and the Dominican Republic) tied their currencies to the US dollar, and in the post-Bretton Woods age Mexico was able to maintain a fixed parity with the dollar from 1954 to 1975, during which time it enjoyed historically high rates of growth. The financial excesses of the López Portillo era (1976–82) not only brought continued depreciation of the *peso* but a rate of borrowing which by 1982 had made the country a by-word for debt. Stabilization of the *peso* in 1988 was only possible because the country had been able to accumulate unusually large hard-currency reserves.

High rates of inflation are unpopular with lenders and so remain a major target of IMF-backed stablilization programmes, the effect of which is, however, to arrest economic development, increase unemployment, and bring misery to the poorer sectors of society. Not surprisingly, most Latin American government faced with the alternative of going to the IMF have sought to "muddle through", generally with unhappy results. One major exception was Bolivia, where the government of Victor Paz Estenssoro (1985–90) enforced a rigorous stabilization programme. When he took office inflation had reached an annual rate of 20,561 per cent. By 1989 it had fallen to 16.5 per cent, one of the lowest in Latin America, and a modest economic recovery continued. By mutual agreement, in December 1989 Argentina wrote off $800,000,000 of Bolivia's foreign debt against $300,000,000 owed by Argentina for Bolivian natural gas, after Brazil had permitted Bolivia to renegotiate $41,000,000 of its $380,000,000 debt to Brazil in exchange for a joint energy integration programme. However much of the success of the stabilization programme has been attributed to its ability to draw on large illegal balances generated by the cocaine trade developed by the military governments of the early 1980s.

Stabilization programmes of this type create immense political and social problems and are hard to apply over the long time-periods needed. The alternative is the the "heterodox shock" developed by the 40-year old Brazilian economist Francisco Lopes.

In **Brazil** itself, on Feb. 28, 1986, President **José Sarney** introduced the radical "Plan Tropical" or **Cruzado Plan** — its centrepiece being a new currency unit, the *cruzado*, worth 1,000 old cruzeiros. The Plan, imposed an immediate freeze on all prices, taxes and services, fixed the exchange rate at Cz13.80 to the US dollar, abolished indexation, increased salaries by 8 per cent across-the-board and initiated partial unemployment benefit for all workers who had been out of a job for at least a month. After the first day, when customers attacked shopkeepers who attempted to raise prices, the public were mobilized to police the scheme.

Initially the results were good. Inflation, 220 per cent in 1985 and rising in the first two months of 1986, was almost halted. A new record trade surplus in January was followed by import savings resulting from the unexpected fall in oil prices, boosting the economy further and terminating investment in the fuel alcohol programme. In a concession to labour, a modified form of indexation of wages was reintroduced in March, when inflation had fallen to zero. However, though inflation held steady for six months at 1 per cent a month and the trade surplus increased still further, the "inflationary psychosis" remained and a wave of strikes began accelerating in July and August.

The government launched on July 23 a three year plan for economic growth to be financed out of increased taxation on cars, fuel and foreign travel. Increasing governmental confidence was shown by radical cuts in its nuclear programme, refusal to sign any agreement with the IMF and Sarney's rejection of President Reagan's specious argument that Brazil was growing at the expense of the United States. Then the government introduced "corrective adjustments" to the Cruzado Plan, to avert shortages that had led Brazil for the first time in history to import coffee. The result was that the ruling coalition secured a sweeping victory in the elections held for the Constituent Assembly in November, but the Plan itself was destroyed.

The previous year, after the IMF decided to cut off further financial aid in March 1985, **Argentina**'s Minister of the Economy, Juan Sourrouille, in consultation with leading Argentine economists, had prepared a similar dramatic new economic initiative, which came into effect on June 14. Inflation, which had been 688 per cent to the end of 1984, had risen from an annualized rate of 800 per cent to over 1000 per cent. The centrepiece was the introduction of a new currency, the *austral*, hence its popular name, the Plan Austral, and the simultaneous introduction of comprehensive wage and price controls. By October inflation had dropped from over 30 per cent a month to 2 per cent, and the Government had demonstrated at the mid-term elections held on Nov. 3 that it had held on well to its public support. As in the Brazilian case a year later, however, the exigencies of politics were to undermine the success of the Plan after only seven months of effective operation, though inflation for the first half of 1986 was still well down, to 24.9 per cent. The first anniversary of the Plan was marked by a general strike and controls were further relaxed. Phase II of the Plan, which established new wage and price controls and sought to limit the unscheduled expansion of the money supply, brought a new general strike on Oct. 9. Although it had a mixed response, inflation was already rising, and by the second anniversary of the Plan the *austral* was already beginning to drop on the foreign exchanges.

One country whose experience has been very different, owing to a combination of very conservative fiscal policies, a strong export economy and rigorous exchange controls, is **Colombia**. Its inflation rate in 1988 climbed to 28.5 per cent, the worst for a decade, but with growth at 4 per cent its economic position remained relatively favourable, despite the effects of terrorist attacks on oil pipelines and banana plantations.

PARC

INSTITUTIONAL REVOLUTIONARY PARTY (Partido de la Revolución Institucional—PRI) (Mexico). The Institutional Revolutionary Party acquired its present name following a re-organization carried out by President Alemán in 1946. However the idea of an official party goes back to President Calles, who set up the National Revolutionary Party in 1929.

As presently constituted, the PRI is a party of affiliates. The main affiliated agencies are the CTM (the trade union confederation), the CNC (the peasant confederation) and the CNOP, which is an organization open to individual members. The CNC carries the least weight of the three, while both the CNOP and the CTM dispose of considerable powers of patronage. The PRI is, however, essentially subordinate to the government and (above all) the president. It serves as a patronage network and, to some extent, as a "ministry of elections". However Mexico still lacks an opposition party capable of mounting a serious national challenge; PRI candidates in some areas (notably the more urban ones) do face a serious challenge, but in other cases nomination is still tantamount to election.

There have been calls for a reform of the PRI to turn it into a members' party and reduce its character as a mechanism for distributing patronage. However the patronage itself has been too valuable for governments to give up lightly, and several projected attempts to reform the PRI have failed or been abandoned.

GP

INTELLECTUALS. Though South and Central America share a number of problems with the rest of the Caribbean area, one respect in which their historical background has been very different is that of education. Compulsory primary education was introduced in **Argentina** in the 1870s and **Costa Rica** in 1884, but for reasons both of élite suspicion and of cost was slow to spread to other parts of the continent. Hence today though literacy levels in the Southern Cone approximate to those in southern Europe, in the Andean countries and Central America adult illiteracy is still very common. In addition, though the early constitutions of most of the independent republics provided for universal male suffrage in accordance with the dominant liberal trends of the Independence period, by the mid-nineteenth century a conservative reaction had set in under which illiterates were excluded from the vote. In **Peru**, illiteracy became a disqualification in 1860; it was not until 1980 that illiterates were again admitted to the electoral rolls.

Not only does this mean that large sectors of the population are still disadvantaged when it comes to participation in the modern sector of society, but it also means that political power continues to be monopolized by a relatively small educated élite, including the **Armed Forces**. During the long years of military dictatorship in many of the countries it is therefore hardly surprising that a prominent role in opposition politics has historically been performed by those members of the intellectual élite who have gained distinction as writers or poets, since they were able to disguise their critique in fictional or other literary form (see **Literature**). However the tradition of dictatorship has had other, harmful, effects, causing historians to concentrate their efforts on the colonial or early national periods, rather than on recent times, encouraging mysticism rather than philosophy and producing sociological theorists rather than practical investigators. Even in such fields as medicine or veterinary science, the shortage of resources and the absence of a tradition of laboratory investigations, mean that university courses are strongly biased towards theoretical rather than practical knowledge, and in consequence many leading physicians and surgeons have completed their studies at universities in the United States or France.

The uncomfortable divide between theory and practice has been rationalized in various ways. Some, following the Uruguayan José Enrique Rodó, have argued that the theoretical is higher and finer than the merely material. As Rodó himself did in his *Ariel* (1900), many have also sought to draw a distinction on this basis between the spiritual basis of Hispanic culture and what they see as the gross materialism of the Anglo-Saxon, as represented by the United States. Given **Mexico**'s past history, it is not surprising that one of the most precise statements of this position should have come from the Mexican philosopher, Leopoldo Zea, in his *Magía y cibernética* (1959).

Mexico. Mexico has two internationally famous literary figures — Octavio Paz and Carlos Fuentes—together with a number of others who are nationally known and held in high regard. Indeed it is generally true that Mexican intellectuals enjoy more influence over policy than intellectuals in many other countries; this is partly because of the country's political stability and strong executive, and partly because of the role of Mexico's intellectuals in projecting the country's international image.

Until the mid-1960s most Mexican intellectuals were broadly supportive of the country's political order and impressed by the occasional left-wing gesture made by the authorities (for example their refusal to break relations with **Cuba** after the Revolution in that country). However the Tlatelolco massacre in 1968 shocked the intellectual community, who had never liked Díaz Ordaz very much in any case. Echeverría (1970–76) tried hard to win the intellectual Left back to supporting the system, but he was at best partially successful. Many intellectuals now preferred to be independent and outspoken rather than co-opted by the system.

Echeverría was the last president to seek to control the press closely (television is another matter). After 1977 several intellectual monthlies started up of which the most important were *Vuelta* (closely linked to Octavio Paz) and *Nexos* (which was closer to the intellectual Left). Moreover the political reform of 1977 made it far easier for parties of the Left to obtain registration; a number of well-known academics are associated with these parties and some of them have now served in Congress.

Despite the fact that most Mexican intellectuals identify with the Left, they have made few attempts to win a mass base in opposition to the system. Some of them have, however, supported the Left populism of **Cuauhtémoc Cárdenas**. Of greater importance has been the concern of intellectuals with rights issues such as police repression, torture and ballot rigging. After the **PRI** somewhat implausibly declared itself the winner in elections in Chihuahua in 1986 a number of intellectuals signed a circular letter complaining about fraud. Shortly afterwards there followed a new political reform which guaranteed the opposition a number of seats in state assemblies.

Today the main power enjoyed by intellectuals consists of their ability to influence foreign views of Mexico. Since these views are of potential economic significance to Mexico (they affect the investment climate), the Mexican government must take notice of them. However most intellectuals in Mexico are now more concerned with issues of freedom and the opportunity for self-expression than with promoting the kind of socialism that many of them would have supported a generation ago.

PARC, GP

INTER-AMERICAN SYSTEM. The idea of a permanent organization covering the whole of the Americas originated with **Simón Bolívar**, but it was US Secretary of State James G. Blaine who was responsible for the formal creation of the Inter-American system in calling the First Conference of American States at Washington at 1889 which formed the International Union of American States. The Second Conference did not take place until after the Spanish–American War. It was held in Mexico in 1901–2. At it delegates agreed that in future Conferences would be held every five years, and the Third and Fourth Conferences, therefore, were held at Rio de Janeiro in 1906 and Buenos Aires in 1910, the latter to coincide with the centenary of the start of independence. These early Conferences were primarily about the promotion of trade and cultural contacts, but in 1910 the organization's name was changed to the Union of American Republics and that of its principal organ to the Pan American Union. It was not until 1914 that the United States first invited other American states, the so-called ABC countries (Argentina, Brazil, Chile), to join it at a special conference at Niagara Falls, to take part in an exercise in regional peacekeeping by mediating in the conflicts of the Mexican Revolution. The conference broke up when it became apparent that the United States was primarily interested in securing its own objectives — an ominous sign of what was to come.

During the Great War no further meetings took place. Then for a time it looked as if the League of Nations would supersede any regional organization, so it was not until 1923 that the Fifth Conference was held at Santiago de Chile, where the name of the Union was changed again, to the Union of Republics of the American Continent. At this meeting the United States, which had not joined the League, threw its weight behind negotiations for the first Inter-American peace treaty, the Pan American Treaty for the Pacific Settlement of Disputes, usually known as the Gondra Treaty, after its sponsor, the then ex-President of Paraguay. In the next five years, however, the United States was to resume its intervention in the Caribbean, and the Sixth Conference, held at Havana in 1928, following a tour of Latin American states by President Coolidge, was marked by the first moves of Latin American delegates to try to establish the principle of non-intervention in their internal affairs. Its main achievement was to establish the Pan American Union on a formal Treaty basis, which, however, prohibited it from exercising the political functions it had gradually been assuming.

By the Seventh Conference in Montevideo in 1933 radical changes had taken place on both sides. In the United States, the election of Franklin D. Roosevelt had been followed by the formal declaration of the "Good Neighbor" policy. After the rise of Hitler in Europe, and the failure of the League to settle the Chaco War between **Paraguay** and **Bolivia** (1932–38). Latin American rulers once again sought the help of their powerful neighbour, and in 1936 a special meeting of the Pan American Union in Buenos Aires formally established the principle of consultation in case the peace of the continent should be threatened, and at the Eighth Conference held in Lima in 1938 all states adopted the Declaration of Lima reaffirming the sovereignty of the various states and their determination to defend themselves against "all foreign intervention or activities that might threaten them".

When war broke out in Europe in 1939 Roosevelt proclaimed the neutrality not just of the United States but of the Americas, establishing a so-called "Hemispheric Safety Belt" — a 320-km (200-mile) wide zone round the two American continents south of Canada, violation of which the United States would regard as an attack on itself — and at the Second Meeting of Consultation of the Foreign Ministers of the American States, held at Havana in 1940, the United States had little difficulty in obtaining support both for this action and for the establishment of a permanent Inter-American Peace Committee to concert action in the event of attack. At the end of the war the Inter-American Conference on Problems of War and Peace established a system of continental security for the member states.

It was on this basis that with the onset of the Cold War the United States broke with its traditions by sponsoring the Inter-American Treaty of Reciprocal Assistance of 1947 (*Tratado Interamericano de Ayuda Recíproca*—TIAR) known colloquially in the United States as "the **Rio Treaty**"). By this was established a formal military alliance against the possibility of attack from outside the hemisphere, putting the Declaration of Lima of 1938 into written form in a fashion intended to meet the new conditions. By a series of bilateral military agreements with a number of countries, starting with Brazil, the United States proceeded on this basis to set up a permanent alliance system for the Western Hemisphere, analogous to that which in 1949 was to be established for the North Atlantic Treaty nations, including Canada. Subsequently in 1948 the old Pan American Union was transformed into a new regional organization within the United Nations, the **Organization of American States** (OAS).

PARC

J

JAGAN, CHEDDI BHART. A former dentist, Cheddi Jagan came into prominence in British Guiana (later **Guyana**) with the victory of his **People's Progressive Party** in 1953. He was Premier for 133 days before the constitution was suspended; he was put under house arrest, but returned to office in 1957. He was again ousted after the violent racial crisis of 1963–64 and his agreement to the adoption of a system of proportional representation. As Guyana's opposition leader, he has veered between offering the government "critical support" and denouncing it as illegitimate. While at times under pressure from the Working People's Alliance and other opposition groups, he has maintained a strong power base among the mainly Indian sugar workers. In the late 1980s he trimmed his traditional marxist views to accommodate private sector involvement in Guyana's economy.

RP

JAMAICA. *Population*: 2,400,000 (mid-1988). *Area*: 11,000 sq km. *GDP*. US$3,220 million (1988). *GNP per capita*: $1,070 (1988). *Debt service as percentage of GNP*: 17.4 per cent. *Average annual rate of inflation* (1980–88): 18.7 per cent. *Defence spending*: $25,560,000 (1984–85). *Urban population (as percentage of total)*: 51. *Life expectancy*: 71 (men); 75 (women).

Geographical background. Jamaica is an island state in the central Caribbean with Cuba some 150 kilometres to the north and Haiti approximately 180 kilometres to the east. The island is relatively mountainous, but only 230 kilometres east to west and 80 kilometres north to south.

Socio–political background. Jamaica became an independent member of the Commonwealth in August 1962, with the British sovereign as head of state but represented through the office of the Governor-General, currently Howard Cooke. The legislature is composed of a popularly elected House of Representatives of 60 seats, and an appointed 21 member Senate.

Outline of political history. On Feb. 9, 1989 the **People's National Party (PNP)** was returned to government in a general election which gave **Michael Manley** the post of Prime Minister. The defeat of Edward Seaga's **Jamaica Labour Party (JLP)**, traditionally to the right of the PNP, which only secured 15 of the 60 seats in the quinquennially elected House of Representatives, represented an astonishing victory for the PNP since it had refused to contest the previous general election in 1983 on the grounds of inadequate electoral registers, failure to carry out electoral reform and the high levels of political intimidation and violence. Agreements between the two major parties prior to the 1989 election campaign defused much of the trouble traditionally experienced in such contests.

Manley has distanced himself from the policies of "democratic socialism" adhered to by the PNP in its last two terms of office between 1972 and 1980, and has largely accepted the agenda of liberal "free" market economics and governmental non-intervention. The pursuit of overt non-alignment is also missing from the new PNP government's foreign policy, although diplomatic relations have been restored with Cuba (they had been broken immediately upon Seaga's election in 1980) and in October 1990 a bauxite-and-pimento for Lada cars exchange was concluded with the USSR to be followed by possible joint venture contracts.

Outline of economic development. Attempts by the Manley administrations to widen the export base of the economy and diversify the range of markets were effectively reversed by the neo-liberalism of the Seaga governments which further concentrated the reliance upon the US and UK market (in 1987 origin of imports stood at 43.6 per cent and 6.5 per cent, and export market stood at 44 per cent and 14.6 per cent respectively). The **Caribbean Basin Initiative** announced by President Reagan in January 1984 giving preferential access for certain products to the US market has had only limited effect on the Jamaican economy (80 per cent of affected goods were already subject to preferential treatment) and was due to expire in 1995, but was extended permanently by the US Congress on Oct. 1, 1990.

Current economic situation. The current PNP government has inherited a substantial visible trade deficit caused by the JLP reliance upon external borrowing to finance imports for domestic development and growth. This corresponded with a decline in the proportional contribution of alumina and bauxite to export revenue. However whilst the visible trade balance has deteriorated over the 1980s it has partially been compensated for by the growth of tourism-derived earnings (now the single biggest foreign exchange earner) and expatriate remittances. Over 39 per cent of government expenditure goes to service Jamaica's external debt of $4,500 million and the reduction of the total debt has become one of the PNP's main economic targets. However this objective is hindered by devaluations of the Jamaican dollar which has been subject to a continued and steady devaluation—by 70 per cent between 1980–1989, and by a further 20 per cent since February 1989—obliging the government to switch to a free-floating exchange rate in September 1990. This is in keeping with the PNP's ideological shift to competitive deregulation throughout the economy. Despite this change continuing negotiations with the IMF for a renewed finance package have been jeopardized by the failure to meet conditions imposed in an earlier 15-month agreement. Although there is rapid growth in the economy — 38 per cent expansion in the bauxite and alumina sector alone during 1989, though overall GDP growth is at 4.6 per cent—the government has resisted any relaxation of deficit targets, in part to comply with IMF terms.

Prospects for development. In contrast to the last PNP government, Manley has dramatically improved relations with the USA, although this has not resulted in the restitution of economic aid to Jamaica cut during Congressional budget battles. Nevertheless, in crude growth terms the Jamaican economy is likely to remain buoyant due to large expansion in the refining, mining and tourism sectors of the economy and despite the substantial economic disruption caused by Hurricane Gilbert in 1988 from which many sectors of Jamaican society are still recovering.

JCJS

JAMAICA LABOUR PARTY (JLP). The Jamaica Labour Party was founded in 1943 by the charismatic trade union leader Alexander Bustamente following his break with the **People's National Party (PNP)**. Bustamente steered Jamaica through independence and the JLP remained in government until 1972. Following Bustamente's demise the JLP became a relatively more open party, but it was only in 1980 that the party under Edward Seaga was able to return to government on a programme of privatization, deregulation, an open economy, and close allegiance towards the **United States**. Although the JLP programme was radically different from that of the PNP in 1980, by the 1989 elections the JLP had succeeded in setting the political and economic agenda by which the PNP had to largely react and accommodate itself to.

There are signs that significant sectors of the party are now dissatisfied with the leadership of Edward Seaga due to his alleged authoritarianism and due to the scale of the 1989 election defeat.

JCJS

JUAREZ, BENITO. Benito Juárez (1806–72) was a leading Mexican Liberal in the nineteenth century. His chief claim to fame is that he led the armies which in 1867 overthrew the Emperor Maximilian whom the French had installed in Mexico.

Juárez was born in 1806 in the state of Oaxaca; he was of Indian descent and did not learn Spanish until his teens. He was educated in a Catholic seminary, but soon took up the study of law and later adopted political positions of marked anti-clerical bent. In 1847 he became governor of Oaxaca, and built up a local power base.

When the French sought to impose Maximilian in 1862, Juárez led the revolt and continued to fight despite the fact that the French army behind Maximilian initially appeared successful. Maximilian assumed the throne of Mexico in 1863. When French troops finally withdrew from Mexico, Juárez was able to capture Maximilian in 1867 and had him executed. Juárez then assumed a dominant position in national politics until his death in 1872 which left the way open for the 30-year dictatorship of Porfirio Díaz.

Although Juárez would today be considered progressive in terms of his anti-colonialism and anti-clericalism, he was supportive of Mexican capitalism. He showed no interest in communal Indian property rights and believed that land should be held individually. While Juárez is today seen as a hero figure and Porfirio Díaz as a villain, the two were politically closer than this suggests. Both believed in progress and property rights; neither in the communal or religious organization of society. However it was Juárez who led the fight against a foreign intervention and this explains his hero status.

GP

JUSTICIALISTA PARTY (Partido Justicialista — PJ (Argentina). Heir to the Peronist Party (Partido Peronista), it takes its name from the doctrine proclaimed by Juan Domingo Perón when first elected president of

Argentina in 1946: *Justicialismo*, from "*justicia social*"—"social justice". Strongly pro-labour and nationalistic, Peronism was also devoted to fostering, through state intervention, the growth of national industry. From its inception it has harboured a wide variety of political leanings, ranging from the revolutionary left to the extreme right.

Perón ran for the presidency in 1946 as the candidate of three parties: the Labour Party (*Partido Laborista*—PL) headed by union leaders Luis Gay and Cipriano Reyes, the Union of Civic Radical Renewal (*Unión Cívica Radical Renovadora*—UCRN), a breakaway faction of the **Radical Civic Union** (*Unión Cívica Radical*—UCR) led by Hortensio Quijano and John William Cooke, and the Independent Party (*Partido Independiente*—PI). Once Perón was elected, the three were merged, first under the name of Single Party of the Argentine Revolution (*Partido Unico de la Revolución Argentina*—PURA), then, in late 1946, as the Peronist Party. When women were given the vote by the 1949 constitution, a parallel Feminine Peronist Party (*Partido Peronista Femenino*—PPF) was created, led by Perón's second wife, María Eva Duarte de Perón, popularly known as Evita.

The military government which emerged from the 1955 *coup* which ousted Perón banned the Peronist Party and attempted to "de-peronise" the country. The Peronists regrouped under a new name, Popular Union (*Unión Popular*—UP), formally led by Juan Bramuglia. The UP was proscribed by the military when elections were called in 1958. From exile, Perón established an electoral alliance with the candidate of the Intransigent Civil Radical Union (Unión Cívica Radical Intransigente—UCRI), Arturo Frondizi. Once elected president with the help of the Peronist vote, Frondizi kept his part of the bargain, legalizing the UP. However, when in 1962 the UP candidate, Andrés Framini, won the governorship of Buenos Aires (the country's largest electoral district, Frondizi, under military pressure, annulled the elections. Shortly afterwards Frondizi was deposed and the Peronists found themselves again proscribed.

A left-wing faction broke away to form the Peronist Revolutionary Movement (Movimiento Revolucionario Peronista—MRP), which engaged in unsuccessful armed actions. The Peronists were barred from running in the 1963 elections, won by the candidate of the Unión Cívica Radical, Arturo Umberto Illia—who in power fostered the emergence of "neo-Peronist" parties. These successfully contested provincial elections until the legal reappearance, in the mid-1960s, of "orthodox" Peronism. The Peronists were again proscribed, together with all other parties, following the military *coup* which ousted Illia in 1966.

A new strand of revolutionary left-wing Peronism emerged in 1970, in the form of the *Montoneros* guerrillas. These earned themselves a considerable amount of popularity with their harassment of the military government. The mainstream Peronists reformed as the Justicialista Party and entered an alliance with several other minor parties, forming the Justicialist Front for National Liberation (*Frente Justicialista de Liberación Nacional*—Frejuli), to contest the elections called by the military for March 1973. The *Montoneros* and the left-wing Peronist Youth (*Juventud Peronista*—JP) provided much of the impetus for a campaign which culminated with the election of Frejuli candidate Héctor Cámpora, whose brief government was indeed seen as heavily influenced by the policies of the Peronist left.

Perón returned to Argentina, and Cámpora, after only two months in office, resigned. New elections were called for September 1973, amid increasingly violent confrontation between the right and left wings of Peronism. Elected president by a wide majority, Perón came down decisively in favour of the right wing. Perón died in July 1974 and was succeeded by his vice-president (and third wife), María Estela Martínez de Perón. Increasing violence and worsening economic situation led to her ouster by the military in 1976. Again the Peronists, with all other parties, were banned.

When elections were called in 1983, the Justicialista Party ran as the senior partner in another alliance, but for the first time ever in a free contest, lost to the UCR. A new split took place within the ranks of Peronism, between the "orthodox" and the new "renewalist" wing, headed by Antonio Cafiero and determined to make the party more visibly democratic. The "renewalists" won the leadership of the PJ, yet when President **Raúl Alfonsín** proved himself unable to pull the country out of an economic crisis, it was the more "orthodox" **Carlos Saúl Menem**, governor of La Rioja, who won the nomination as presidential candidate—and the elections held in 1989.

Once in power, Menem performed a volte-face, embracing radical free-market policies and striking an alliance with the small conservative parties (most notably the **Democratic Centre Union** (*Unión del Centro Democrático*—UCD) which had hitherto been the Peronists' most implacable enemies. This has created new strains within the PJ. The Peronist-controlled umbrella labour confederation, the General Confederation of Labour

(*Confederación General del Trabajo*—CGT), split into pro- and anti-Menem factions, and the PJ bloc in congress suffered even greater division.

EC

K

KUBITSCHEK DE OLIVEIRA, JUSCELINO. Kubitschek is generally, and rightly, regarded as one of the most successful and most popular presidents of **Brazil**. He accomplished as president most of what he wanted to do, and, despite attempts from the political right to prevent him taking office in January 1956, he handed over office peacefully to an elected, right-wing successor, **Jânio Quadros**, in January 1961. He was the first president to hand over office to an elected successor since Dutra in 1950, and the only directly elected civilian president, in the strict sense, to do so since Artur Bernardes, another *mineiro*, in 1924. No other directly elected president since Kubitschek has handed over power to a successor elected to that post. Despite, or, perhaps, because of such impeccable democratic credentials, Kubitschek was deprived of his political rights in June 1964, being the most eminent political victim of the recent *coup*.

Kubitschek was born in Diamantina, Minas Gerais, in 1902. His father, João César de Oliveira, had been a *garimpeiro*, a policeman and a tax inspector. His mother was a primary school teacher, whose uncle, João Nepomuceno Kubitschek, had been state senator in the constituent assembly in Minas Gerais in 1891 and Vice-President of the state from 1894 to 1898. Kubitschek's father died young, the family was poor, and only by working as a telegraphist was he able to study medicine in Belo Horizonte.

In 1930 Kubitschek supported the Liberal Alliance movement, which launched the candidatures of Vargas and João Pessoa, but then went to study urology in Paris, returning after the revolution of 1930. In December 1931, he married Sara Gomes de Lemos, whose family had extensive political connections in Minas Gerais and at national level. Kubitschek worked as a military doctor during the São Paulo revolt of 1932, when Minas sided with the Provisional Government of Vargas. During service in the south of Minas, he became friendly with Benedito Valadares, a federal official in the region.

On Sept. 5, 1933 the state governor of Minas, Olegário Maciel, the only pre-1930 state leader whom Vargas had allowed to continue in office, died. Out of the blue, but to avoid siding with one state faction or another, Vargas, in December, appointed Benedito Valadares as federal *interventor* in Minas Gerais, who immediately invited Kubitschek to be head of his Civil Household, (*Gabinete Civil*).

In April 1934, Kubitschek joined the Progressive Party (*Partido Progressista*—PP), of Minas Gerais, founded in February 1933, largely under the influence of Maciel and Valadares. In September 1934, Kubitschek became Secretary of the party and, in October, was elected as federal deputy with more votes than any other candidate in Minas, when Benedito Valadares was elected as state governor. He built up his political base in Minas Gerais, but his mandate as deputy ended, with the declaration of the *Estado Novo*, in 1937, when Valadares continued in office, now as interventor, in the state of which he had been elected governor. Kubitschek returned to medicine, but, in April 1940, was appointed by Valadares as mayor of Belo Horizonte.

For most of his time as mayor, Kubitschek continued to work as a doctor, but kept in direct personal touch with the *comités de bairro*, "neighbourhood committees", discussing their particular problems. He gave priority to improving the infrastructure of the city, especially roads, drains and water supply. One of his most spectacular and controversial projects was the development of the Belo Horizonte suburb of Pampulha, including a chapel in honour of St. Francis, designed by Oscar Niemeyer with frescoes by Cândido Portinari. The employment of these two outstanding Brazilian artists, accused of being Communists, sparked a row which lasted for 17 years, anticipating some of the controversy surrounding **Brasília**, including Niemeyer's eventual design for the Memorial JK, the memorial in honour of the capital's founder.

In March 1945, Kubitschek joined in the early efforts to create the Social Democratic Party (*Partido Social Democrático*—PSD) in Minas, working with his contacts in the *comités de bairro* to build up a strong party base at local level. In the elections of Dec. 2, 1945 as candidate for the PSD, he came in second place in his state for elections for the Constituent Assembly, which became the elected Congress after the promulgation of the new Constitution on Sept. 18, 1945. In 1948, he visited the USA and Canada, returning with the conviction that Brazil's full development was only possible through rapid and diversified industrialization. He continued to build up his political support, both in Minas and at federal level, and, in the elections of October 1950, which brought Vargas to the presidency, Kubitschek was elected as governor of Minas Gerais.

As governor, he vigorously developed a programme to diversify the agrarian and pastoral economy of Minas by developing its infrastructure and industrial base with emphasis on electrification, road building and air transport. He was able to attract public and private capital and international loans for his various projects, bringing electricity to different regions of the state, building 16 trunk roads, totalling 3,087 kilometres, and new airfields, raising the state total to 75. This greatly improved communications within the state and with its neighbours. He also gave stimulus to the fertilizer industry and provided support for a state refrigeration company, while also building health posts and schools and expanding the state system of higher education. This included two faculties of medicine, one of law and one of pharmacy and odontology.

The death of Vargas threw the whole political system into a crisis, but, eventually, Kubitschek emerged as the presidential candidate of the PSD, with Goulart as candidate for the Vice-President. Kubitschek was elected on Oct. 3, 1955 and, despite strenuous efforts by right-wing opponents, both civilian and military, to overturn the election results, he took office on Jan. 31, 1956.

As president, Kubitschek showed the same drive, energy and imagination which he had brought to Minas Gerais. He was determined to carry through his *Programa de Metas* (Programme of Goals) setting out his 30 basic aims, to which he added, in April 1955, the building of a new national capital. His whole presidency was marked by confidence, energy and a determined hope for the future, in marked contrast to the years of crisis and confrontation which both preceded and followed his term of office. Brasília was a symbol of all these hopes. There was a negative side, too, to the Kubitschek years, not always fully realized at the time [*see* Brazil], but his presidency marked, and still marks, a high note in national politics and development.

Kubitschek's most important political failure was not to be able to pass on the presidency to a candidate of his own party or of the Vargista alliance. The victory of Quadros in 1960 led to a major political crisis and, eventually, to the *coup* of 1964.

In 1961, Kubitschek was elected as senator for Goiás and voted against the restrictions imposed on the succession of Goulart. In 1964, he tried to persuade Goulart to take measures to avoid a *coup*. He, at first, tried to reach a working agreement, through the Social Democratic Party (*Partido Democrático Social*—PDS) with the *coup* leaders, but, on June 8, 1964 was deprived of his elected office and of his political rights, for 10 years.

From 1966 to 1968, Kubitschek joined in the attempt to offer opposition to the régime through the *Frente Ampla*, a broad opposition front, working with **Lacerda** and **Goulart**. This was suppressed in April 1968, after which Kubitschek effectively left political life. He was killed in a motor accident on Aug. 22, 1976. President Geisel ordered three days of mourning, but, in 1980, President Figueiredo vetoed a bill presented by **Tancredo Neves**, to cancel the actions taken against Kubitschek in 1964.

Some military leaders and civilians, supported by Sara Kubitschek, criticized, in 1981, features of Niemeyer's design for the *Memorial JK* in Brasília, where Kubitschek is buried, but they were overruled by Niemeyer, supported by public opinion. On Sept. 12, 1981, the day when Kubitschek would have been 79, the *Memorial* was inaugurated by his widow and by President Figueiredo. It has now become something of a national shrine and a major tourist attraction. During the years of *abertura* and redemocratization, Kubitschek and his *Memorial* became symbols of the resistance of civil society to the military régime and of hopes for a new democratic future for Brazil.

PF

L

LACALLE HERRERA, LUIS ALBERTO. Luis Alberto Lacalle Herrera has been President of **Uruguay** since March 1, 1990, when he formed a Council of Ministers with **Colorado Party** participation. Prior to his election he was a lawyer and a farmer, and director of the **National Party (Blancos)**. Born in 1945, he is the nephew of the Party's former leader, Luis Alberto de Herrera, and represents the "Herrerista" faction of the party. He was a consistent opponent both of the military government and of the amnesty law passed under his predecessor's government.

PARC

LACERDA, CARLOS. Lacerda was one of the most implacable and effective opponents of Vargas and the whole Vargista tradition in **Brazil**, in which he included Juscelino Kubitschek. He was a persistent advocate of a military-led *coup* to prevent his opponents taking office, being most successful in promoting the *coup* of 1964. He then found that he could not ride the tiger, ending, not as President of the Republic, which was his aim, but by being deprived of his political rights, after seeking an accommodation with those centre-left political leaders whom, previously, he had most bitterly opposed.

Born in 1914, Lacerda came from a political family, which had been involved in the revolts of 1922 and 1924. Two of his uncles were among the first leaders of the **Brazilian Communist Party**, and Lacerda, in his youth, was on the political left, nominating Luis Carlos Prestes as honorary president of the **ANL** in 1935. By 1939, he was a fierce critic of Communism and, through his political journalism, especially in the *Correio da Manhã*, a strong critic of Vargas. He joined the UDN, after its formation in May 1945, and, in 1946, began his column, "*Na tribuna da imprensa*", in the *Correio da Manha*. In December 1949, he gave this name, *Tribuna da Imprensa*, "Press Gallery", to his own newspaper, which became the voice of the UDN and the scourge of Vargas.

During Vargas' second government, from 1950 to 1954, Lacerda founded, in 1953, the *Clube da Lanterna*, the *Lantern Club*, deriving the name from Diogenes' search, lantern in hand, through Athens, looking for one just man. His fierce attacks on the Vargas government led to an attempt on Lacerda's life in August 1954, which was traced to Vargas' own family and palace guard. This also involved the killing of an air force officer. Lacerda worked closely with the leaders of the armed forces to put pressure on Vargas to resign, which resulted in the suicide of Vargas on Aug. 24, 1954.

Lacerda and other UDN leaders tried to prevent the election, then the inauguration, of **Kubitschek**, by military *coup*, if necessary. He already had tried, unsuccessfully, to postpone the Congressional elections of Oct. 3, 1954, when he, himself, was elected as federal deputy. To exclude Kubitschek, he recommended, in the Chamber, the suspension of the Constitution of 1946, and, in due course, was involved in a short-lived military adventure, on the cruiser, the *Tamandaré*, to oppose Kubitschek.

Ironically, it was the election of Kubitschek and the building of **Brasília** which gave Lacerda his only taste of high public office. He was elected as the first governor of the state of Guanabara, created to replace the former Federal District, virtually contiguous with the city of Rio de Janeiro, after the inauguration of Brasília in 1960. At the same time, he supported **Jânio Quadros** in his campaign for president, urging his nomination in the UDN convention, even though Jânio was not a party member. He believed that only Quadros could win the election for the UDN.

By August 1961, Lacerda had broken with Quadros, largely over the president's policy towards the USA and Cuba, especially when Quadros had decorated Ché Guevara. Lacerda had taken refuge in the Cuban embassy after the *Tamandaré* affair in November 1955, on his way to the USA, and was receiving United States' and Alliance for Progress money for his projects in Guanabara.

After the resignation of Quadros, Lacerda did all in his power to prevent the succession of **João Goulart** and became one of the main civilian conspirators urging a *coup*, together with other UDN governors. After the *coup*, of 1964, he was dismayed to find that the military leaders did not intend to hand over power to right-wing civilians, particularly Lacerda. His deep frustration led him to try to develop the *Frente Ampla*, the Broad Front, of opposition to the military régime. He had prolonged discussions with Kubitschek and Goulart, but a majority of the left were, understandably, suspicious of his change of heart. His overtures to the left, especially to Goulart, then lost support for Lacerda on the right, especially among the *linha dura*, or hard-line military, who always had been pro-Lacerda.

The final break came in 1967 and 1968, after Lacerda had become a vehement critic of the military government, addressing mass rallies on behalf of the *Frente Ampla*. In April 1968, Gama e Silva, the Minister of Justice, forbade all activities of the *Frente Ampla*. On Dec. 30, 1968, after Institutional Act No. 5, and after having been imprisoned, Lacerda was deprived of his political rights. He died, in Rio de Janeiro, on May 21, 1977.

Lacerda remains, as he lived, a controversial, enigmatic figure. He is regarded as an effective governor of Guanabara by his supporters, and as a ruthless administrator by his critics, chastized for callously "removing" *favelados* and sanctioning the murder of beggars, all to improve the "image" of the State. By some he is seen as a champion of democracy, against the *Estado Novo* and left-wing totalitarianism. Others judge him as an unscrupulous leader of the right, thwarted in his ultimate aim for power, and as a willing accomplice in the Cold War scheming for the United States.

PF

LATIN AMERICAN ECONOMIC SYSTEM (Sistema Económico Latino-americano — SELA). The Latin American Economic System was founded in 1975 at the instance of the Presidents of Mexico and Venezuela, to create a Latin American regional organization that would not be dominated by the United States and which would include Cuba. There are now 26 member states. Its purpose is to promote regional economic co-operation and development through study and discussion of specific problems. Decision-making is through regular annual conferences. The Secretariat is in Caracas, Venezuela.

PARC

LATIN AMERICAN INTEGRATION ASSOCIATION — LAIA (Asociación Latino-Americana de Integración — ALADI). Creation of a Latin American Free Trade Area—LAFTA (*Asociación Latino-Americana de Libre Comercio* — ALALC) was envisaged by the **Economic Commission for Latin America (ECLA)** as early as 1955. The formal organization, consisting of the states of South America together with Mexico, was created by the Treaty of Montevideo of 1960 which came into effect on June 1, 1961. However, because of the very different levels of economic growth of the member states it failed to achieve its objective of promoting intra-regional trade, and by 1980 only three per cent of all concessions had been made since the Treaty came into effect. By a second Treaty of Montevideo LAFTA was therefore reconstituted on Aug. 12, 1980 as the Latin American Integration Association — LAIA (*Asociación Latinoamericana de Integración* — ALADI), with the more limited purpose of protecting existing trade arrangements. Members are divided into three tiers: most-developed—Argentina, Brazil, Mexico; intermediate—Chile, Colombia, Peru, Uruguay, Venezuela and least developed— Bolivia, Ecuador, Paraguay. The permanent directive body of the organization is the Committee of Representatives, with representatives from each of the member states and a number of observers, subject to the overall direction of the Council of Ministers. The Secretariat has its offices in Montevideo, Uruguay.

PARC

LIBERAL PARTY (Partido Liberal — PL) (Colombia). The two traditional parties of **Colombia**, the Conservative Party and the Liberal Party, emerged in the 1840s and were able to mobilize both an electorate and armies in the battlefield. The parties were essentially loose coalitions of large landowners and merchants, with strong regional roots. The Liberals were clearly distinguished from the Conservatives mainly by their deep anti-clericalism, though in power they not only curtailed the power of the Church but also abolished slavery and attempted to reduce the power of central government by instituting a federal constitution. The stronger roots of the Conservative party in the rural areas gave that party electoral predominance well into the first decades of the twentieth century. The Liberals, however, drew the urban vote in the growing towns. In 1930 they reversed the Conservatives' in-built majority, and between 1934 and 1938 Alfonso López Pumarejo pushed through significant social reforms.

Though the Conservatives returned to power in 1946, fears engendered by their loss of support were amongst the factors leading to the outbreak of civil war (*La Violencia*) in 1948, following the assassination in Bogotá of the radical Liberal politician, Jorge Eliecer Gaitán. The Conservatives used their control of the state to attack Liberals and the Liberals raised guerrilla armies to attack Conservatives. The inter-party pact, the *Pacto de Sitges* (1957) restored peace between the parties by alternating the presidency between then and allocating public office and government jobs on the principle of parity. At the restoration of competitive elections in 1974 the Liberals were heavily in the majority, though they included Conservatives in their administrations until 1982. But the fact that the Liberal Party was still a coalition of interests meant that splits within it could still lose it elections. In 1982 it lost the presidency to the reforming Conservative Belisario Betancur Cuartas, but won it back in 1986. In 1988, when direct elections for municipalities were introduced, it lost the key prizes of the mayoralities of Bogotá. Currently the party remains split into three main factions, and the assassination of the former "New Liberal" Luis Carlos Galán has deprived it of its most promising younger figure.

JP

LIBERAL PARTY OF HONDURAS (Partido Liberal de Honduras–PLH). In the present century power in Honduras has alternated between the PLH (founded 1890) and the **National Party** (*Partido Nacional*–PN), except for their short-lived "pact of national union" (1971–1973). They have been involved in regimes of civilian, military and civilian–military coalition types.

The PLH won the 1981 and 1985 presidential elections (under Dr Roberto Suazo Córdova and José Azcona del Hoyo respectively) and half the seats in the 1985 elections to the national assembly (four more than the PN). Both the presidency and advantage in the assembly were lost in 1989 to the PN.

The PLH is divided up into tendencies. The main Liberal faction is the conservative *Rodista* tendency named after the party's former leader Modesto Rodas Alvarado who died in 1979. This faction dominated the election victories of 1981 and has since divided. The *suazocordovistas* include defeated presidential candidate of 1989, Carlos Flores Facussé, and would like closer links with the army; a faction loyal to Efraín Bú Girón; and *azconistas* who support the centre-right technocrat who won the presidency in 1985.

The left-of-centre Liberal People's Alliance (*Alianza Liberal del Pueblo*—ALIPO) was founded in 1978 and is itself composed of a merger between the Villeda Morales Movement (*Movimiento Villeda Morales*—MVM) and the Democratic Left (Izquierda Democrática—ID). ALIPO was in a minority at the 1981 party congress. In 1984 the Reina brothers of the Democratic Left split ALIPO by forming a separate faction under the name of the Revolutionary Democratic Liberal Movement (*Movimiento Liberal Democrático Revolucionario*—M-Líder) with Armando Aguilar Cruz as its General Secretary. (The Liberal Unity Front (*Frente de Unidad Liberal*—FUL) refused to attend the 1981 party convention after it was denied tendency status within the party.)

The PLH stands on a democratic, social reform and Central American integrationist platform but nevertheless has both conservative and radical currents.

LLP

LIBERATION THEOLOGY. The phrase "Liberation Theology" appears to have been first used by the Peruvian theologian Gustavo Gutiérrez in 1968. More precisely the phrase should be in the plural since there is no single theology of liberation, but a broad body of progressive theology which emphasizes a new type of presence of the **Church** in society, of the Church travelling with and being witness to the trials of the faithful and the fallen. Latin American theologians have been at the forefront of liberation theology and "praxis", in particular priests in the Jesuit and Franciscan orders, and as a consequence have been subject to the double trial of internal repression—for example the call went out in **El Salvador** in 1977 by the far-right "to be patriotic, kill a priest" and in 1989 six Jesuits were murdered by the army—and the opprobrium of the Vatican. Liberation theology remains not only the most dynamic theology in Latin America but also continues the terms of reference for other theological and Church developments.

JCJS

LITERATURE. Given the small size of the intellectual elite in South and Central America, and the historical prevalence of military dictatorship, it is hardly surprising that some of the most effective critics of their societies have been **intellectuals** who embodied their critique in literary or fictional form.

A few have even held high political office. An early example was Domingo Faustino Sarmiento in **Argentina**, who in *Facundo* (1845) disguised his criticism of Juan Manuel de Rosas as a commentary on the life and career of a regional caudillo of the inland province of La Rioja, who had the added advantage of being dead. After the fall of Rosas in 1853 he became a leading figure in the politics of the new republic and was elected President for the term 1874–80, making education a main theme of his presidency. In the twentieth century, one of the more surprising candidates was Dr Juan José Arévalo who, after 16 years in exile, during which he had published both political polemic and a number of textbooks on sociology and history, was recalled from his post at the University of Tucumán (where he had settled and become an Argentine citizen) to become President of his native **Guatemala**. Earlier, in his novel *Doña Bárbara* (1919), Rómulo Gallegos had embodied a critique of the dictatorship of Juan Vicente Gómez of **Venezuela** in fictional form. In 1948 he was elected President as candidate of the newly legalized **Acción Democrática (AD)**, but was overthrown within a few months by a military *coup*.

Many other writers have through the universal medium of the Spanish language had their main impact outside their own countries. Some, like Miguel Angel Asturias of **Guatemala**, have had to live much of their lives in exile, becoming in this way part of an international élite equally at home in many countries of the region as well as in Europe. Asturias drew on his early memories of the miasma of fear and suspicion engendered by the rule of Manuel Estrada Cabrera (President 1898–1920) in his *El Señor Presidente* (1946), but it served equally well as a critique of the recently overthrown dictatorship of Jorge Ubico or of Maximiliano Hernández Martinéz in neighbouring **El Salvador**. His great trilogy dealing with the interaction of people, maize and power in Central America, too, spoke to a wider audience than that of his native country. He was appointed Guatemalan Ambassador in Paris by the civilian government of Dr Julio César Méndez Montenegro (President 1966–70) and was awarded the Nobel Prize for Literature in 1967.

More recent literary defenders of **human rights** in the region have included A.P. Esquivel of **Argentina**, who was awarded the Nobel Prize for Peace in 1980 for his work, and Ernesto Sábato, who was chosen in 1983 by President **Raúl Alfonsín** to chair the Argentine National Commission on the Disappearance of Persons.

Conversely major events in the region have given rise to important literary works which in their turn have influenced the perception of those events. Outstanding in this regard was the long sequence of "novels of the **Mexican Revolution**" which starts with the country doctor Mariano Azuela's *Los de abajo* ("The underdogs") in 1916. Though it was already beginning to lose its initial impetus by the 1930s, at the fiftieth anniversary of the Revolution in 1960 there began a new series of attempts to re-evaluate where and how it had lost its way. In *La muerte de Artemio Cruz* ("The death of Artemio Cruz"—1962), the author, Carlos Fuentes, himself the child of a diplomatic family who, though educated in the United States, chooses to write in Spanish, re-examines the Revolution through the dying eyes of a General who has done well out of it and become one of the *nouveaux riches*.

The influence of "magical realism" on much recent literary work in the region does not necessarily make it less telling as a critique of society and its arrangements. Unlike the Mexican Revolution, the *violencia* in **Colombia** has not given rise to a school of novelists, but thousands of readers, world-wide, have come to see the country through the eyes of Gabriel García Marquez. The central event of *Cien años de la solitud* ("One Hundred Years of Solitude"), a massacre of demonstrators, may or may not have happened, and if it did happen, is now seen, not as it "actually" happened, but as the story of the book that renders it, but the point is made—this is a society in which the past and the present form a continuum and the optimism of those eager for change is constantly in conflict with powerful conservative forces which in the end are victorious.

PARC

LIVING STANDARDS. The 1980s, during which the entire region has suffered severely from the recession of 1981 and the ensuing debt crisis, have seen a general decline in living standards.

Statistics on the cost of living are much easier to calculate than those of **unemployment**, but the very high rates of **inflation**, and the continuing need to revise both prices and wages, makes comparisons across time problematic.

The indexation of wages, established in **Argentina** by **Juan Domingo Perón**, who also introduced the "thirteenth month" bonus or *aguinaldo*, became established practice also in Chile. Throughout most of South America in the post-World War II period policies were dominated by the influence of the developmental ideas of the **Economic Commission for Latin America** (ECLA), which called for state led growth, the management of the economy to avoid violent fluctuations, and social welfare programmes to eliminate the yawning gap between rich and poor. The most systematic attempt at such planning, backed by the power of the armed forces, occurred in **Peru** under the military government of General Velasco Alvarado between 1968 and 1975. However despite the success of such measures in achieving a measure of social welfare, they did not preclude social violence such as broke out in **Uruguay** at the end of the 1960s, and disillusion was in turn to fuel the revolt of **Sendero Luminoso** in Peru itself.

The military developmentalist régimes of the 1970s, influenced by free market ideologies, abandoned such measures, arguing (as classical developmental economists had done) that the benefits of faster growth would in time "trickle down" to the poorer members of society. In **Brazil**, where these neo-classical policies were pursued most consistently for a period of more than 20 years, statistics show that although the poorest 10 per cent did improve their standard of living in constant terms very slightly, the top 10 per cent improved theirs very substantially, leading to a widening of the gap between rich and poor which shows no sign of closing.

Living standards in the Caribbean are overall comparatively high, in a number of countries outstandingly so, with all countries fully satisfying the basic needs requirements of food, housing and education.

The region is still categorized as part of the so-called Third World. However, the standard of living exhibited throughout the region, Haiti and, recently, Guyana excepted, confound the rigidly held images conjured up by the Third World label.

Regional commitment to the basic needs priority areas has been, and still is, complemented by a steady build-up of infrastructural facilities. The level of advancement in this respect is dependent on the economic stability of respective countries, but all boast road networks, water-borne systems and electrical networks. Most also exhibit sophisticated communications networks.

In individual cases, such as Trinidad, with its motorways and city buildings, countries and some sectors of the population exhibit standards rivalling industrialized countries. Others including Bermuda and the Bahamas have constantly enjoyed living standards among the highest in the world. On a country-by-country basis, living standards generally surpass expectations, considering the dependent nature of Caribbean economies.

Much of the growth in living standards occurred during the late 1970s and 1980s. During this period, most countries enjoyed booming economies, with rapid expansion in tourism, in particular, and manufacturing, and per capita incomes grew accordingly. In 1987, Bermuda had the highest GNP per head in the world — US$22,540. The Bahamas had a GNP per head of US$10,280 in 1988 and Barbados a GNP per head of US$5,530 in 1987. Even the smaller countries with seemingly small GNPs have been able to enjoy comparatively high living standards, taken into consideration the smaller populations.

The growth of economies has not only been reflected in government raising living standards, but also in, most indicative, consumer spending and foreign travel by populations. In terms of electronic commodities, television sets, radio receivers and other paraphernalia, the Caribbean ranks top among African, Caribbean and Pacific countries. Bermuda and Barbados are examples which, taking the ratio of consumer electronics per population, surpass many industrial nations. One in four people owns a television and there is almost total ownership of radio sets.

Car sales, telephone ownership and travelling are all high. Such has been the spending that governments have had to take steps to stem outlays, by increasing taxes on cars and travel. Trinidad in the early 1980s was credited with carrying a great deal of Barbados' tourist industry, particularly in the crucial summer months, and is the country which has suffered most from overspending, both governmental and private.

The story of Trinidad, as told though its national form of expression, calypso, has gone from "Money Ain't No Problem" to "Capitalism Gone Mad" to "The Sinking Ship". The country has not been able to raise living standards commensurate with the growth in its economy, boosted by oil revenues, mostly because of massive spending on ill-conceived projects, and as income dropped, so have living standards, with the population unable to enjoy any of the many things they took for granted. House prices have soared, small-sized cars cost TT$80,000, there are restrictions on foodstuffs, the importation of goods and the export of currency. Devaluation has not helped either.

Guyana, among Caribbean Community (CARICOM) countries, provides the saddest tale of poor living standards. The country has been beset by a stagnant economy, rampant inflation, low productivity and unemployment. Even basic needs have been threatened by the decline in what is potentially the region's most productive country, one with vast untapped mineral wealth and large agricultural and forestry tracts.

Converseley, Barbados is the example held up of the increasing living standards of Caribbean countries. Its range of basic needs facilities are unmatched in the region, so is its network of infrastructural development in communications including airport and port facilities. These are complemented by cultural and sports centres. Salaries remain high and house and car ownership are priorities. More than 80 per cent have telephones, radio ownership is nearly 100 per cent and there is a television ratio of 1: 6.

Statistics do not convey the quality of life and standard of living enjoyed by Caribbean countries. For instance, Bermuda's housing stock surpasses that of most developed countries and, in the region escapes the wide gaps between rich and poor which are immediately evident in industrialized countries. From its economic profile, Trinidad would be expected to have an overall higher standard of living, but this is not the case.

Indications are that while standards of living will not enjoy rapid growth for some time, West Indians will continue to steadily improve their standards, more so once the world economy stabilizes. St. Lucia was able to produce a tax-free budget at the end of April 1991 even in a slow economic climate. Steps are being taken in Guyana and Trinidad to stimulate their economies while, if the present Aristide government survives, there is hope that Haiti will finally embark on the road of bringing the country into the modern age. At present nothing suggests that the region will not remain one of the outstanding areas in the world in respect of its living standards.

PARC, MH

LOME CONVENTION. The term "Lomé Convention" refers to the framework that regulates economic assistance and trade between the European Community (EC) and developing countries. The First Lomé Convention was signed at Lomé, Togo, in February 1975 and came into effect on April 1, 1976. It replaced the earlier Yaoundé Convention between the EC and its former colonial territories and the Arusha Declaration, and has since been replaced three times. Lomé II, signed in October 1979, came into effect in January 1981; Lomé III, signed in December 1984, came into effect on March 1, 1985, and Lomé IV, signed in December 1989, came into effect in March 1990 and unlike its predecessors will run for 10 years. Of the 68 African, Caribbean and Pacific (ACP) countries parties to Lomé IV, 15 are in the Caribbean: Antigua and Barbuda, Bahamas, Barbados, Belize, Dominica, The Dominican Republic, Grenada, Guyana, Haiti, Jamaica, St Kitts-Nevis, St Lucia, St Vincent and the Grenadines, Suriname and Trinidad and Tobago. The latest agreement increases the proportion of grants to loans in EC aid, though falling far short of that demanded by the ACP countries, and contains important provisions on sustainable development, support for ACP economies in the face of short-term economic fluctuations, action on debt imbalances, detailed provisions for technical co-operation, additional concessions on the access of ACP products to the Community, extension of provisions of the convention to minerals and metals in addition to agricultural products, simplification of the rules of origin and improvements to the system of stabilization of export prices (Stabex).

PARC

LOPEZ PORTILLO, JOSE. José López Portillo was President of Mexico 1976–82. He is not now generally regarded as having been a successful president. He does have certain achievements to his credit, but these relate for the most part to his early period in office. Unfortunately he is most remembered for mismanaging the economic problems which began to become apparent in 1981; as a result he presided over a full-scale economic crisis in which the government dramatically nationalized the banking system but nevertheless came close to international bankruptcy.

Before becoming president López Portillo served in a number of bureaucratic positions. Many of these were economic although López Portillo had no economics training, having trained instead as a lawyer. Nevertheless he served as Finance Minister under Luis Echeverría, (1970–76), to whom he had been personally close for many years. His nomination as presidential candidate in 1975 was seen as a surprise, but it was welcomed by the business community and conservatives generally. He appeared to promise a quieter government after the controversies of the Echeverría period.

At the beginning this promise appeared satisfied. López Portillo stopped the land redistributions which had been initiated in 1976. He negotiated an "Alliance for Production" with the private sector. He promised a rapid increase in oil production in order to resolve the public sector's financial problems. He also agreed a political reform with the Left, as a result of which a number of Marxist parties were afforded legal recognition.

The first half of his presidential term was on the whole successful. However after 1979 López Portillo began to believe that Mexico's oil boom had solved all of his government's economic difficulties. He once told an audience that "our problem is to manage abundance". As a result he began to ignore local problems and devoted his attention to a high profile "Third Worldist" foreign policy. However the economy began to weaken in 1981 as international interest rates rose and the price of oil fell back a little; the lack of appropriate official reaction worried investors who began to sell *pesos* and buy dollars. López Portillo made several half-hearted attempts to restore confidence, but finally lost patience and nationalized the banks without warning on Sept. 1, 1982.

The last few months of his presidency were of total economic crisis. The US government needed to find ways of rescuing Mexico from outright bankrupty, and it was clear that the foreign debt burden left by López Portillo's government would be a major constraint on the economy for years. Moreover there was a good deal of personal corruption in his administration, which might have been forgiven if the economy as a whole was going well but proved highly unpopular in the midst of economic crisis. In 1983 his successor, Miguel de la Madrid faced pressure to put López Portillo on trial for corruption, but he resisted. However the ex-president is still semi-disgraced.

GP

M

MADERO, FRANCISCO INDALECIO. Francisco Madero began the Mexican Revolution when he called for an uprising against Porfirio Díaz on Nov. 20, 1910. Madero was opposed to Díaz' constant re-election as president; he believed that an end to re-election would reduce the power of the state's political machinery and would therefore allow a more authentic democracy to flourish.

Madero was a well-mannered intellectual whose opposition to Díaz was initially underestimated. After he announced his rising, he suffered some severe military setbacks. However other forces joined him in opposition to the government, and Díaz' military machine soon disintegrated. Madero reached Mexico City in June 1911 and was quickly elected president.

Madero found it difficult to re-establish order after his triumph; his own rebellion was soon followed by others. However he faced greatest danger from conservative opponents of the Revolution who soon started plotting against him. These conservatives were helped by the US Ambassador in Mexico, Henry Lane Wilson. In February 1913 Madero was overthrown by General Victoriano Huerta and murdered.

Huerta was overthrown in his turn and, once the Constitutionalists led by Obregón and Carranza had finally triumphed, Madero came to be regarded as a Revolutionary hero. Nevertheless Madero's political liberalism was largely replaced later by other Revolutionary objectives such as land distribution. It is not clear how much he would have been at home in post-Revolutionary Mexico, though his descendants have tried to maintain his tradition.

GP

MALUF, PAULO SALIM. Since the late 1960s, Maluf has been one of the most prominent and ambitious right-wing politicians in **Brazil**, and, in recent years, one of the most frustrated. His wealth and power-base are centred in São Paulo, but he has made strenuous, and expensive, efforts to extend his influence and support, especially in São Paulo. He has been both mayor of the city of São Paulo (1969–71) and governor of the state (1979–1982). By contrast, in the six years up to the elections for governor in October/December 1990, he lost five elections.

Maluf was born in 1931, to a family of Lebanese origins, and, after graduating as a civil engineer, held important positions in several of the family firms. In 1967, he was appointed by the State Secretary of Finance, Antônio Delfim Neto, as head of the *Caixa Econômica Federal* (Federal Savings Bank) of São Paulo. In 1969, with the support of President Artur da Costa e Silva, he was nominated as mayor of São Paulo, even though the state governor, Abreu Sodre (1969–1971), opposed him.

He was very active in the building of roads and a network of schools at primary and secondary level. His flamboyant style was reflected in 1970, when he gave a motor car to every member of Brazil's winning World Cup team. In 1971, he became state Secretary of Transport, and in 1976, won 76 per cent of votes to become president of the *Associação Comercial* of São Paulo.

In 1977, he opposed early suggestions that the repressive *Institutional Act No. 5* of 1969, should be repealed, but later qualified his opposition. In 1978, he launched his candidacy for indirect election to the governorship of São Paulo, opposing ex-governor Laudo Natel, who had the support of President Ernesto Geisel. Maluf won an astonishing victory against the officially nominated candidate, taking office in March 1979, when Figueiredo started his presidency.

His victories against the odds brought charges of misuse of his great wealth, while the violent response to workers' or strikers' demonstrations strengthened his right-wing reputation. In May 1982, Maluf left the governorship, to be a PMDB candidate for federal deputy in the November elections, in which he won more votes than any other deputy in Brazil.

From 1982, he worked steadily to win the PMDB nomination in the indirect election to succeed Figueiredo. He spent large sums of money in building his political clientage, including the distribution of ambulances to poor *municípios* in the north-east, which angered the local power-brokers of both left and right. In 1984, having largely caused the split in the party, he easily won the Democratic Socialist Party (*Partido Democrático Social*—PDS) nomination, but was beaten by **Tancredo Neves** in the indirect election of January 1985.

In November 1988, Maluf suffered another defeat, when beaten by Luiza Erundina de Souza, of the **Workers' Party** (*Partido dos Trabalhadores*—PT) in the election for mayor of São Paulo, but, despite this setback, ran a very effective campaign for the federal presidency in

1989, especially through television. He also, clearly, had an eye on the election for governor in 1990, perhaps hoping to win in the first round on Oct. 3, not least because of his close ties to President **Collor de Mello**, for whom he was "best man" at Collor's wedding, and a political patron more generally.

Maluf's defeat in the second round of voting for governor, in December 1990, leaves a question mark over his political future. He is anything but a spent force, but now has an up-hill battle, both in São Paulo and at national level. His short-term political future, like that of the political right more generally, is bound up with that of President Collor de Mello and his government.

PF

MANLEY, MICHAEL. Prime Minister of **Jamaica**, 1972–80 and 1989–present, Michael Manley is the son of Norman Manley, co-founder of the **People's National Party** (PNP) and succeeded him as leader of the party and Leader of the Opposition in 1969. He was born in St Andrew in 1924 and educated at Jamaica College and the London School of Economics and Political Science. He then worked as a journalist before returning to Jamaica and holding posts in the National Workers Union, 1953–72. A member of the Senate between 1962 and 1967, he has been MP for Central Kingston since 1967. In his first two terms as Prime Minister his party sought to restructure Jamaica on socialist lines, but came to grief on its inability to meet IMF terms. In international affairs, he aligned himself with **Cuba**, which sent construction brigades to construct workers' housing and other projects, and incurred the suspicion and hostility of the United States. Since his return to power in 1989, Manley has pursued a much more cautious policy both at home and abroad. In addition to several books on politics, he is author of *A History of West Indies Cricket* (1988).

PARC

MAQUILADORA. The term *maquiladora*, in Spanish, means "mills of gold". It reflects the perception in Mexico that *maquiladora* plants are a kind of licence to print money.

The *maquiladora* sector of the Mexican economy was set up in 1967 after a visit to Mexico by Lyndon Johnson. This led to an agreement that Mexican and foreign-owned companies could operate along the Mexican border with the USA duty free (in relation to the Mexican tax system) as long as they exported all their products. The United States, meanwhile, agreed to let such products be imported with duty charged only on the proportion of the value added in Mexico; in other words all US products exported to Mexico for up-grading in the *maquiladora* sector would be allowed to be re-imported duty free. Subsequently the provisions of the programme have been extended to cover most of Mexico.

The *maquiladora* sector has grown very rapidly. Most companies are US-owned though Japanese firms are also present to an increasing degree. In 1968 some 11,000 workers were employed in the sector; by 1985 this had increased to 212,000, and employment more than doubled again, to 469,000, by mid-1990. The programme has, however, proved controversial with critics suggesting that it has done little more than provide an outlet for low-paid and unskilled Mexican labour. Certainly there are few linkages between *maquiladora* plants and the rest of the economy, but there are positive signs that at least some employers are taking seriously their role in training and upgrading the workforce. An increasing number of *maquiladora* plants now employ Mexican engineers and managers.

GP

MARTINIQUE. *Population*: 327,073. *Area*: 1,100 sq km. *GNP*: US$1,650 million. *Trade volume*: $1,479.5 million. *Top five trade partners*: France, Guadeloupe, French Guiana, USA, Venezuela. *Education spending (as a percentage of GNP)*: 13.3. *Birthrate*: 19.4 per 1,000. *Life expectancy*: 67 (men); 73 (women).

Geographical background. Martinique is an island in the Windward chain of the Lesser Antilles in the Eastern Caribbean, lying between Dominica and St Lucia. A French territory since the early seventeenth century, it remains a French overseas possession with the status of an overseas department (*département d'outremer*) and that of a region of France.

Socio–political background. Martinique was given departmental status in 1946, modified by the decentralization reforms introduced in the early 1980s. The French government appoints a Prefect (or Government Commissioner) to represent the French authorities. There is an elected 45-member General Council which has responsibility for local affairs. The members serve a six-year term, with about half of the seats coming up for election every three years. In 1974 Martinique was made a region of France. There is an elected 41-member Regional Council with the power to discuss wider economic and social policy. The island also elects four deputies and two senators to represent Martinique at the National

Assembly in Paris. French troops are stationed on the island.

Outline of political history. The conservatives have traditionally been stronger in Martinique than on Guadeloupe. Traditional social structures, favouring the locally born white élite, have reinforced the strength of the political right-wing on the island. However, this has been challenged since the 1960s by the growing strength of the left-wing alliance of parties, led principally by the Martinique Progressive Party (*Parti progressiste martiniquais*—PPM), led by the poet, activist and long-time mayor of Fort-de-France, Aimé Césaire. In the first direct elections to the Regional Council in 1983, the left-wing parties gained a small majority of seats and secured the presidency. In 1988 the left-wing parties gained a majority of the seats on the General Council for the first time, although they failed to secure the council's presidency. The majority of political opinion, motivated by the considerable economic and social advantages of continued French control, seeks greater autonomy from France, rather than independence. Pro-independence groups, often vocal and sometimes violent, have only gained limited support in elections, although the high abstention rate in elections also displays popular dissatisfaction with the current position. In October 1990 the PPM lost its control of the Regional Council when pro-independence groups succeeded in capturing nine seats in elections after fears had been expressed about the possibly damaging impact of the single European market on the Martiniquan economy.

Current economic situation. Martinique's economy remains strongly tied to that of France. Large amounts of French aid have given the country a good infrastructure and social benefits in line with those of mainland France. The result, however, has been to make the economy more dependent. The high level of imports and limited agricultural and manufacturing exports create a high balance-of-payments deficit, while Franch aid and government transfers disguise a large budget deficit. Agricultural production centres on sugar, bananas and other tropical fruits. The sugar industry has declined significantly and has largely been replaced by banana growing for export as the main agricultural activity. In recent years tourism has been developed and now provides an important source of income and of employment. The rate of unemployment is high, between 30 and 40 per cent, particularly among the younger age-groups, prompting emigration to France, compensated for by immigration by government officials from France.

LP

MEDIA.

The Press in South and Central America. Press freedom, a contentious issue in both South and Central America in the past, is less so today under democratic governments. However certain factors still shape the power and role of the press in society and politics. Newspapers are generally the private property of family-owned conglomerates with a wide range of economic interests. They are in general conservative socially and extremely partisan in their political affiliations. In foreign affairs, however, they take their lead from the international wire services, and in particular from those under US ownership. In return threatened proprietors have been able to count on the powerful support of the US Press against their own governments.

In 1951 President **Juan Domingo Perón** of **Argentina** created a *cause célèbre* when his government expropriated the opposition journal *La Prensa*, after a "spontaneous" strike by Peronist workers in reaction to its criticism of the regime. Response abroad, particularly in the United States, was swift and unfavourable, and the régime never recovered from the authoritarian image continually presented of its actions from then on. The oldest newspaper in Argentina, *La Nación*, did however survive as an opposition journal, and still exists, despite the press becoming a prime target both of the left under Isabel Perón and the right under the military governments of 1976–83, with the result that many outstanding journalists went into exile.

Similar condemnation by US press sources occurred after the closure of all opposition journals in **Cuba** after 1959, at the decision to nationalize newsprint in **Chile** under **Salvador Allende**, at the Peruvian military government's attempts to nationalize the press in 1973 and at the restraints imposed on the press in **Nicaragua** by the Sandinistas, though in this last case the very vocal opposition of the Chamorro-owned *La Prensa* was not only maintained but extensively quoted in support of the allegation that the press were not really free. Criticism of censorship by right-wing governments has, it is fair to say, not been so assiduous, despite its general prevalence in South and Central America well into the 1980s.

Control of the press takes a variety of forms. The requirement of prior submission to censorship was imposed in Brazil after 1967, in **Bolivia** in 1967, in Chile in 1973 and in **Uruguay** as late as 1983. Some countries, such as **Chile** and **Paraguay**, have constitutional restraints on press freedom; others, such as **Peru**, maintain control through emergency legislation. The military government of **Brazil** relaxed censorship in 1982 as part of its process of *abertura*, but maintained control over the press by informal means.

The main devices used for this purpose are on one hand the control of newsprint supplies, most of which have to be imported, and on the other according or withholding contracts for government advertising. Both these devices have been consistently used for many years to maintain the ascendancy of the ruling party in **Mexico**, though President Miguel de la Madrid abandoned the practice of paying monetary "wages" (bribes) directly to journalists.

In Guatemala, El Salvador, Panama and Haiti, tactics of control are more direct. Journalists who are overly critical can be and are physically attacked or killed.

Radio and television. Radio and television stations developed as offshoots of press interests, and though radio was well established throughout the region by the 1950s, the 1980s have been the decade of the television revolution. Though government departments remain the licensing authorities and grant concessions for radio and TV stations, control of these media is increasingly understood to have formidable political significance. Much of the output of the television stations, as in Europe, consists of dubbed versions of US serials such as *Dallas* and *Los Colby*. The major Spanish-language producer of such serials, or *telenovelas*, is the *Televisa* network of Mexico, though in recent years Spanish productions have been becoming increasingly popular also.

The question of control of other media by a press conglomerate was thrown into sharp relief by the role of the *Rede Globo*, owned by the *O Globo* newspaper syndicate, in the election of President **Fernando Collor de Mello** of **Brazil**. Collor, who had no political party and had acquired his reputation as a television presenter, leapt into prominence in the early stages of the campaign and soon surged ahead of his rivals. But in most countries, as in **Colombia**, rival networks are run by the main political parties.

Other than state control, as in **Cuba**, or state ownership, as with some Argentine channels before privatization, there are three alternative models. In most countries the state requires the TV companies as part of their contracts to allow some public service broadcasting. Other providers of radio and, increasingly, TV programmes are religious organizations and universities.

One of the more striking features of the past 20 years has been the far greater independence shown by the Mexican press. During the 1960s political control over the press was extensive and the bribing of journalists acquired the character of a system. There was even a special Mexican name for this bribery—*embute*.

Gradually, however, journalists struggled to become freer in their outlook and reporting. There remains press corruption, but this co-exists with high quality journalism. Of the daily newspapers, *Excelsior* is one of the most prominent. Its political coverage is extensive; it is generally aligned with the Institutional Revolutionary Party (*Partido Revolucionario Institucional*—PRI) but its columnists often take a markedly independent position. More pro-business is *El Financiero* which is in many respects modelled on the *Financial Times*. The major left-wing daily is *La Jornada*. There are also a number of other dailies at various levels of seriousness, but without any very distinctive character. Additionally there are many provincial newspapers, some of which are quite high quality.

Some of the best reporting is to be found in the more intellectual weeklies and monthlies — notably *Proceso*, *Vuelta* and *Nexos*. Circulation is relatively low, but readership includes much of the élites. *Proceso*, in particular, contains a good deal of serious reporting from a standpoint sympathetic to the Left opposition.

Indeed press influence in **Mexico** comes more from its élite readership than its access to the popular majority. As elsewhere in the world, the press has to compete with television. Moreover only a minority of Mexicans have had a secondary education; the potential circulation available to (for example) intellectual weeklies is limited. There is also the problem of price in what is still a poor country. Despite these limitations, however, press reportage has become a political factor of some significance; it has contributed to the gradual opening of Mexican political society.

The full range of media systems—press, radio, TV, satellite and cable—has been developed in the Caribbean. Outside the industrialized world and certainly in the so-called Third World, the Caribbean exhibits the most sophisticated range of media.

Media development has been seen as an aid to the whole independence process, and countries have moved from limited media and foreign control to radio and press, with high government and national ownership. There is heavy local and regional content in press and radio, and attempts are being made, with success, to incorporate more national and regional television programming. Thus, media in the Caribbean have changed as countries have, to become more reflective of regional concerns and culture.

The region adheres to the liberal democratic tradition of the media which, basically, holds that the media is an independent institution and a watchdog of government and guardian of freedoms. Thus attempts at muzzling journalists have been widely condemned thoughout the region. At various times Guyana, Grenada, Barbados, Jamaica and St Vincent among others have come under pressure from other Caribbean countries and respective national organizations for restricting media freedom, whether by revoking work permits, removing staff from posts, refusing newsprint to opposition-owned media, or seeking to monopolize media by restricting opposition voices.

Instances of blatant media interference are, however, not prevalent. The most celebrated case in recent years was the case of Tim Hector v. Antiguan government. Hector was prosecuted under a new law after he published findings of a US Senate hearing linking the Antiguan government to a murder cover-up. The case was taken through the range of Caribbean courts, with Hector eventually winning before the final court of appeal, the Privy Council of the UK, in early 1990.

Caribbean mass media date back to the early eighteenth century, with the introduction of the press medium as it then was in Jamaica. The Caribbean was among Britain's most prosperous colonies, and with a number of such governed in the Leeward and Windward Island groupings, the imperial power saw the need to communicate with its governors and through them to the people. The topography of the region aided press distribution and the literacy levels led to a demand for news and, from very early, the last third of the eighteenth century, indigenous newspapers.

Today every regional country is served with at least one daily newspaper, the vast majority having two. Among Third World countries, the Caribbean has the highest distribution of press per population. In 1985 the Bahamas had a ratio of 154: 1,000 with three dailies, Trinidad 149: 1,000 with four and Barbados 145; 1,000. Dailies are complemented by weekly and other publications. St. Lucia, for instance, has six regular newspapers.

The press remains the medium most reflective of local, national and regional issues. Some newspapers, including Jamaica's *Gleaner*, Barbados' *The Nation* and a range of papers from Trinidad —*Bomb*, *Express*—are available in other countries. The Nation Company launched a paper aimed at the eastern Caribbean islands, *OECS News*, but after a few years this was closed in 1989. Colour printing has been incorporated.

Electronic communication was introduced to the region in the 1930s with British cable systems. The real impetus came just before or after independence, concentrated between the decades of the 1960s and 1970s. Caribbean countries first established national radio stations along the lines of the British Broadcasting Corporation (BBC), through which to have a national voice and aid the education process with the transmission of health care and agricultural programmes.

Radio remains the most popular communication medium, with the majority of Caribbean countries possessing two national stations, one privately owned, and some countries many more. Barbados has two government-owned and four privately operated stations. In some countries—among which Antigua—there are specialist religious stations with limited broadcasts. Generally, regional stations cater to all areas of society with a range of music, news and current affairs, religious and cultural programming. A number of stations broadcast round the clock.

Again the Caribbean tops Third World countries in the level of radio receivers per population. In 1985 St. Lucia had 760 receivers per 1,000 inhabitants, Barbados 758 per 1,000, the Bahamas 531 and Dominica 506. Every country has more than a third of its population owning radio receivers.

Television was introduced in the 1960s, and by 1971 Barbados had the region's first colour service. This medium is the least heavily owned among Caribbean people, but is growing. Many countries, including Guyana, Montserrat, Dominica and St. Lucia are without national systems, but possess cable, while St. Vincent's lone television station is privately owned. Some eastern Caribbean countries are served by Barbados' lone station, CBC. Still, the region also heads Third World countries in the level of distribution of television sets.

Television programming is dominated by American films, as is cable and satellite. This has led to much talk of "cultural imperialism" and fears have been expressed about the impact of foreign programmes. No one has yet shown a correlation between foreign programming and social impact. In any event, this medium is still relatively new to some Caribbean countries. Antigua, Trinidad, Jamaica, Barbados and the Bahamas have managed between 20 and 40 per cent local programming. This percentage is likely to increase as steps are being made to produce more national and regional programming.

Regional media integration is undertaken mainly through two Barbados-based organizations, the Caribbean News Agency, (CANA), established in 1968 and the Caribbean

Broadcasting Union, (CBU), which became operational in 1970. CANA serves the press and radio, providing news reports and features, particularly on specialized subjects such as Trinidad's oil industry or meetings such as CARICOM summits and facilitates the easy distribution of reports from member countries to each other.

CANA, which has showed a profit in recent years, has had a significant impact on regional broadcasting. At the beginning of 1991, 15 radio stations subscribed to CANA's daily news programme, seven to its weekly *Sports Caribbean* presentation and six link to CANA's studio monthly for the phone-in and discussion programme *Caribbean Crossfire*. This programme allows people in participating countries to debate topical issues. Regional programmes *Business Report* and *Forging Ahead* are also produced daily.

The CBU had 28 members at the beginning of 1991, including 19 national broadcasting and nine private systems. Radio stations are linked twice weekly on *Horizons* and *Caribbean Link*. A major regional breakthrough has been Caribvision, started in 1987 betweeen Barbados, Jamaica, Trinidad and Curacao, through which nightly TV news is exchanged direct via satellite. The CBU also has a weekly spot on the USA's Cable News Network (CNN), allowing a five-minute feature on any subject.

In addition, there is bilateral co-operation between countries in respect of TV and radio. Trinidad's national carnival festival is transmitted in Barbados and Barbados has shown a series from Trinidad—Gayelle—and Jamaica, including the popular comedy Oliver At Large starring Jamaican Oliver Samuels.

Media development is underpinned by teaching programmes. The University of the West Indies (UWI) offers a one-year Mass Communications course at the Mona, Jamaica campus. The Caribbean Conference of Churches (CCC) undertakes regular training as well as the CBU, while countries have various training programmes. Journalist organizations conduct various seminars and regional meetings are held annually.

There will be future media development in the Caribbean, mostly in respect of television. Indications are that, with the region seeking ways of closer economic and political union, the media will become more oriented towards the Caribbean in all respects. The Nation company of Barbados is in the process of establishing a radio station in Jamaica, other companies have interests in countries other than their own and programme exchanges will increase.

Attitudes to the media should ensure that it remains aligned to liberal democratic traditions. It is also likely that television will become more regional and national, with fears of any cultural imperialism proving unfounded.

PARC/GP/MH

MENEM, CARLOS SAUL. Elected president of Argentina in 1989, to serve a six-year term. Carlos Saúl Menem, the son of immigrants from Syria, was born on July 2, 1930 in the north-western province of La Rioja. He pursued a career in law, graduating form Córdoba university at the age of 25, in the year a military *coup* put an end to a decade of elected Peronist rule. Menem joined the Peronist party the following year. He became involved in defending members of the predominantly Peronist trade unions, and in conspiracies to overthrow the military government. He was imprisoned for his part in one such uprising in 1956.

This background, and his cultivation of nationalistic and revolutionary rhetoric identified Menem with the left wing of Peronism, though through marriage into the Yoma clan Menem also became a leading member of the economic élite of La Rioja. He rose rapidly within the ranks of the provincial Peronist party: in 1963 he became party president, and in 1973 he successfully ran for governor.

When the military overthrew the government of María Estela Martínez de Perón in 1976, they classified Menem as among those with a "subversive" background, and imprisoned him. Released seven years later, he returned to politics and was again elected governor of La Rioja in 1983. In 1988, in contest with the "renewalist" faction that led the Peronist party, Menem won the nomination as candidate to the presidency—and in 1989 was elected president.

Once in office, Menem performed a virtually complete about-face, abandoning his old nationalistic and populist ideas and embracing radical free-market policies. He entered into an alliance with the conservative Unión de Centro Democrático (UCD) and chose his initial economic team from among representatives of big business. His first years in office followed a pattern similar to that of his predecessor, Raúl Alfonsín: a very high degree of popular support for a drastic adjustment programme which showed signs of initial success, followed by rapid disenchantment as the economic situation worsened, and by considerable popular opposition to Menem's decision to pardon the military leaders of the "dirty war" who were serving prison sentences.

EC

MEXICAN REVOLUTION. The Mexican Revolution began, it can be stated with precision, on Nov. 20, 1910. The ending of the Revolution cannot be identified with equivalent certainty, but most historians consider that the approval of the Mexican Constitution in 1917 ended the active phase of armed hostilities. The Revolution led to a great many deaths; possibly around 1,000,000 Mexicans died as the direct or indirect result of hostilities out of a total population of 14,000,000. While a number of political ideas were expressed by those who participated in the Revolution, those leaders most firmly identified with a cause (**Madero** and **Zapata**) ultimately failed to prosper.

Nevertheless, like all Revolutions, that in Mexico created a symbolism of national unity. This may have had little to do with the fighting itself, but was of great assistance to the Sonorans, and subsequently **Lázaro Cárdenas**, in their efforts to establish a new form of stable government. It is true that some of the extreme inequalities of power, particularly in southern Mexico, were tempered by the proconsular governors sent to rule provincial Mexico in the name of the Revolution. The Revolution also permitted considerable political mobility; post-Revolutionary Mexico was far less stratified by race or education than it was before.

Under President Cárdenas (1934–40) and to some extent in the 1960s, the Revolution came to be identified with the cause of social reform, in particular land redistribution. Moreover the rights of labour, though certainly circumscribed by official manipulation, were greater after the Revolution than they had been before. However perhaps the most important Revolutionary legacy was the creation of a far more effective Mexican state which has provided the country with over two generations of political stability. Revolutionary ideology also helped the new political élite to extend its control into those parts of rural Mexico where Indians still spoke their own languages and related to the dominant culture only through the Catholic **Church**. The Revolution was also highly anti-clerical, and there were major conflicts between Church and State during the 1920s and 1930s.

During the last decade or so, the authorities have significantly downplayed the ideological significance of the Revolution. They have instead asserted the system's democratic nature and the importance of effective economic management.

GP

MEXICO

General background. Population: 84,300,000 (1989). *Area*: 1,972,547 sq km. *GDP*: US$97,302 million. *Trade volume*: $28,897 million (1986). *Top five trade partners*: USA, Japan, Germany, Spain, France. *Defence spending*: $966,000,000. *Education spending (as percentage of GNP)*: 2.7. *Urban centres with population over 20,000*: 43. *Birthrate*: 33.5 per 1,000. *Life expectancy*: 50.5 (men); 53.5 (women).

The United States of Mexico, with its population of 84,300,000 (1989 estimate), is the most populous Spanish-speaking country in the world and the second most populous country in Latin America. By territory it is the third largest country in Latin America with an area of 1,958,201 sq km. However, despite the very considerable size of the country, the terrain itself is quite difficult. Over one half of the country is at an altitude of over 1,000 m; much of it is at over 2,000 m. Much of the national territory is either arid or semi-arid.

Mexican GDP *per capita* was in 1988 estimated to be $2,588. This places Mexico some way above the Latin American average, but poorer than the richest Latin American countries such as Uruguay and Venezuela. Income inequality is, however, very great and living standards for the poorest Mexicans are as low as almost anywhere else in Latin America despite the fact that the rate of literacy now approaches 90 per cent. The 1980s saw a considerable fall in levels of *per capita* income, in the order of 20 per cent; total GDP in 1989 was only slightly above its previous high point, reached in 1981 but the prospects for economic recovery during the 1990s are extremely good.

Total Mexican exports in 1989 amounted to $22,765 million; in that year Mexico ran a slight deficit on its trade account and a somewhat more substantial one on its current account. Long-term capital inflows more than bridged the gap. Since Mexico is an oil exporter, the export figure for 1990 is likely to be significantly higher. However, despite the importance of oil, manufacturing now accounts for more than one half of Mexican exports. This represents a considerable change from as recently as 1985 when oil amounted to more than 60 per cent of Mexican exports. Oil will have increased its relative share of Mexican exports somewhat during 1990, as a result of the Gulf crisis, but the trend during the last decade has been for manufacturing exports to show considerable dynamism. The third major exchange earner is tourism which has shown a gradual upward tendency. Over the past decade, and despite some severe economic problems, Mexico has succeeded in developing an increasingly sophisticated industrial economy.

Mexico's international economic position is

very closely tied up with that of the USA. The United States is by far Mexico's largest trading partner, taking 69.3 per cent of Mexico's exports during 1989 and supplying 68 per cent of its imports. Recent political changes have tended to reinforce this connexion; Mexico is presently negotiating a free trade agreement with the United States and the administration of President Salinas has made clear that it sees Mexico's long-term future in terms of ever closer economic relations with the rest of North America.

Trade statistics taken on their own do not reflect the importance to the Mexican economy of remittances from Mexicans working (in many cases illegally) in the United States; figures for investment flows also show the clearly dominant role of the United States. As a result of all this, Washington's attitude plays an important role in determining what happens to the Mexican economy. The Baker Plan of 1986 and the Brady Plan of 1989 are cases in point. Behind the United States, Japan is a distant second most important partner (taking 5.8 per cent of Mexican exports and supplying 4.5 per cent of its imports); President Salinas has been keen to increase Mexican trade with Japan, but his success so far has been limited. In fact Japan in 1989 accounted for a lower proportion of Mexican trade than it did in 1984; this is the result, mainly, of a fall in oil prices. Mexican trade with Japan is followed by trade with Germany, France and Spain. One noteworthy feature of Mexico's trade pattern is that there is very little trade with the rest of Latin America.

The serious setbacks suffered by the Mexican economy during the 1980s ensured that public spending on projects and programmes was cut back sharply during the 1980s, partly due to the policy of economic liberalization and partly to the imperatives of debt servicing. In 1990 total public spending was budgeted at around 40 per cent of GDP; however nearly one third of this was to be accounted for by debt service. Of the remainder, just under one half of the budget was devoted to infrastructural and investment spending. Of the remainder, health and labour was the major item followed by education. What this means is that Mexico spends a relatively low proportion of its GDP on education; in 1989 the figure was 15.1 per cent of total budgetary expenditure—which is under 5 per cent of GDP—though the figure was scheduled to rise to 16.9 per cent in 1990. There is significant private investment in education, particularly on the part of the Church, but the education/GDP ratio remains well below the 8 per cent which the UN recommends for developing countries with a high proportion of young people in the population. It is also important to note that educational policy in Mexico is not solely a budgetary matter. One important factor in the past has been that the teachers' union was controlled by a boss figure, and that many decisions pertaining to education (such as the recruitment of teachers) were taken for political rather than educational reasons. Now, however, the former head of the teachers union has been forcibly retired and there is a greater prospect that educational spending will prove more productive. Indeed President Salinas has been seeking to increase the relative importance of spending on education, but he has started from a low base line. Spending on education during 1990 was projected to increase by 39 per cent in real terms between 1989 and 1990. Defence spending is not of major consequence in Mexico. The proportion of the national budget devoted to "justice and security"—which includes the police as well as the military—was just 3.9 per cent in 1989, which is just short of 1 per cent of GDP. Unusually for Latin America, the Mexican military is not a serious force in either politics or society.

It is government policy to reduce the role of the public sector in state enterprise activities, though some state-owned companies such as the oil monopoly Pemex are considered too sensitive politically to touch. There has been some privatization in recent years, and the forthcoming privatization of the state telephone company and the banks will further reduce the role of the state in direct commercial operations. The government hopes that it will consequently be possible to increase spending on education and welfare services more rapidly in the future.

During the last 30 years, one of the main social changes in Mexico has been the growth of the cities. As recently as 1960 most Mexicans lived in the countryside; now nearly 70 per cent of the Mexican population is urban. This growth of urbanization has occurred in the context of a rapidly growing population as a whole; this doubled between 1940 and 1965 and has now almost doubled again. Mexico therefore has a very young population; according to some estimates, around one half of the population is aged 16 or less. However the birthrate has declined somewhat in the past fifteen years, and the rate of growth of population is now estimated at no more than 2.5 per cent. Life expectancy at birth is now estimated at 69.3 years, and has been increasing slowly during the last four decades. We do not yet know whether the economic setbacks of the 1980s have significantly altered this trend.

Geographical background. The physical geography of Mexico, while almost infinitely complex in detail, is largely defined by two mountain ranges which pass from the north of the country to the south. The mountains pass fairly close to the Pacific coast although there is a significant coastal plain on the Caribbean side of the country. Between the two ranges there is a plateau on which are located the major cities. The floor of the plateau first rises and then subsides as one moves south. It is 1,100 m at El Paso on the Texas border, but rises to 2,300 m at Mexico City before falling to around 1,500 m at Oaxaca.

One of the crucial limiting factors of Mexican geography is the relative absence of rainfall. Rainfall is relatively abundant only in the southern part of the country and then only close to the Caribbean or Pacific coasts. This shortage of water has had a major effect on patterns of human settlement within Mexico. The Amerindian population of Mexico tended to concentrate in the south, while the north has been of more recent settlement; the outlook of the north is less traditional in almost every way. Apart from the question of water, the altitude of the plateau also gives some protection from the heat which would otherwise be expected in a country most of which lies south of the Tropic of Cancer; the temperature is similarly mild except at very high altitude.

The ethnic composition of the population, like Mexico's geography itself, is simple in outline but complex in detail. Most Mexicans are *mestizo*—that is, of mixed European and Indian blood—although the nature of the mix will vary considerably. Some 5 per cent of the Mexican population considers itself pure white; many of these are descended from fairly recent migrants from Europe. Under 25 per cent of the population considers itself pure Indian. However *mestizaje* is a cultural as much as racial fact; it denotes a person with some background in both the Amerindian world and that of modern Mexico. Mexico also has a modest infusion of African, Arab and Chinese blood, but not on a large scale.

The vast majority of the population defines itself as Catholic although active religious observance is in slow decline. This decline has been the result of general changes in Mexican society rather than of public policy itself. The separation of **Church** and State, which is established by the **Constitution**, is however broadly supported; there is relatively little demand for distinctively Catholic politics in Mexico.

The Indian population itself divides into over 50 groups or sub-divisions; many of these have their own language. Particularly noteworthy are the Maya, who live in the south east of Mexico (and also in Guatemala and to some extent Honduras), and the Yaqui of the north west. Nevertheless there are today relatively few Indians without some knowledge of the Spanish language, which more than anything else defines *mestizaje*. Government policy during the 1920s and 1930s strongly supported the imposition of a single national identity, neither Spanish nor Indian but simply Mexican; aggressive efforts were made to extend education into the rural areas in order to promote this view of nationhood. Today official policy is strongly hostile to any form of racial discrimination, although some discrimination undoubtedly still exists. Nevertheless ethnicity is no longer a major factor in political self-identification.

Mexico is now predominantly an urban nation. **Mexico City**, with an estimated population in excess of 19,000,000 is by far the largest conurbation. The vast majority of positions in Mexico's public administration are based in the Federal District, and this is also a considerable industrial centre; the most important universities are also based there. Extensive government subsidies on food and transport has helped to raise living standards in the Federal District well above the Mexican average and have therefore acted as a magnet to further migration, despite the considerable difficulties facing migrants. Congestion and pollution are major problems within Mexico City despite the best efforts of government to deal with them.

However the recent tendency has been for medium-sized provincial cities—defined as having a population between 500,000 and 3,000,000—to grow faster than the Federal District itself. Moreover the spread of manufacturing into other urban areas has encouraged strong growth in these as well. Monterrey is particularly noteworthy as an example of an industrial city. Futhermore some of the towns on the Caribbean coast grew rapidly in response to the oil boom of the 1970s. During the 1980s the provincial cities appear to have avoided the worst of the economic difficulties which overtook Mexico City which suffered most from the cutbacks in public service and reductions in public sector salaries stemming from the debt crisis and recession. The northern cities, in particular, appear to have tied themselves more to the economies of Texas and California than to the central region of their own country. They tend in fact to run a current account surplus with the United States (due to the in-bond industries and US tourism) which then helps subsidize the poorer, southern, part of the country.

Indeed an inescapable fact of Mexican geography is the 2,400 km border which it shares with the **United States**. During the first half of the nineteenth century the United States took half of what was then Mexico's national territory. Over the past 50 years, however, the character of the south west of the United States has become increasingly Mexican due to northward migration. There has been a significant amount of legal migration to the United States, but much migration has been illegal — sometimes legalized retroactively as a result of amnesty laws. In any event Mexico's northern border exerts a considerable pull; there has also grown up a good deal of industry in border areas as a result of in-bond (***maquiladora***) plants which were set up by agreement between the two countries.

Mexico's southern border with **Guatemala** is less salient, although a number of Central American refugees fled to Mexico during the political troubles of the 1980s. Mexico's southern border is 885 km long, and separates countries whose relations have traditionally been unfriendly. (Mexico also shares a short border with **Belize**, but this is of less significance). In fact southern Mexico shares many of the characteristics of Guatemala; it is far poorer and less developed than the north of the country. There is a tourist trade, at least in the Yucatán and Oaxaca, but little else.

Socio–political background. Mexico has enjoyed the reputation of being one of the most politically stable of the Latin American republics. While its stability has appeared slightly more in question in recent years, there is no real sign of any impending breakdown; on the contrary the system has made, or at least not prevented, a number of gradual changes which have taken the sting out of many recent challenges.

The most important political institution in Mexico is the **presidency**. Mexican presidents serve for six years; they then leave office and have no possibility of returning to the presidency. However during their period in office their powers are so great as to be almost unlimited; Mexico has been described by one of its own scholars as "a six-year dictatorship." Perhaps the dictatorship (if there is one) last for around five and a half years rather than six, since the ending of the presidential term is marked by an interregnum in which neither the outgoing nor the incoming president is clearly in control. In fact Mexican presidents, though still extremely powerful, are perhaps slightly more accountable than was the case a generation ago. The press is better informed and far more outspoken than was once the case, and electoral provisions guarantee that opposition parties will be represented in Congress.

Presidential power is exerted mainly through the public administration. Cabinet government does not exist even in theory; members of the Mexican Cabinet are known as "Secretaries" rather than "Ministers" because it is their role to carry out presidential instructions rather than to make policy. Not every president will exercise power without referring to his advisers, but it has not been unknown for a Mexican president to surprise almost everybody by an arbitrary act of government. Some critics of the presidential institution have expressed the fear that presidents could become quite detached from reality, as a result of nobody in government daring to tell a Mexican president an unpalatable truth.

It is clear that presidents choose their Cabinets and there are virtually no restrictions on presidential choice; one past president offered a Cabinet post to his mistress. Similarly any cabinet member dismissed by the president has little or no recourse. The public sector as a whole is (with a very few exceptions) organized on a clientele system. However it is in point of fact impossible for any president to select the entire public administration—whose size runs into millions—so considerable patronage power does *de facto* devolve on members of the Cabinet, labour leaders and other influential figures. Moreover, since the next president is chosen from within the Cabinet, many Cabinet ministers will have some hopes of succeeding to the ultimate office.

One of the most common topics of political conversation in Mexico concerns who will be the next president. The choice matters a great deal because incoming presidents are not necessarily constrained to follow the policies of their predecessors; in fact these are quite often reversed, at any rate partially. However it is in the interests of the incumbent president not to make a clear choice too soon. He is instead likely to juggle with several possibilities in order to preserve his own freedom of manoeuvre. Although a potential president must be born in Mexico of parents who were also Mexican born, there are few other limist on whom the candidate may be. Essentially, at any rate until now, the outgoing president has enjoyed a virtual free choice; however a choice, once made, cannot be revoked—and more than one outgoing president has come to feel that he made a wrong decision.

The public sector has a role in developing the Mexican economy. However it also has a role in channelling public resources to Mexican society in a judicious way so as to reduce social conflict and increase public acceptance of the status quo — and, not least, support for the ruling Institutional Revolutionary Party (**Partido de la Revolución Institucional** — PRI). The federal government enjoys financial resources which are far more impressive than those available to state and local government. Thus although Mexico is notionally a federal republic, the actual exercise of power is very centralized. State governors are also answerable to the national president and can be removed without warning or explanation. Within their own states, however, state governors do enjoy a major patronage role.

The second most important institution in Mexico is the official party the PRI. The nominees of this party have won every presidential election, every state governorship but one and every Senate seat but four since it was first formed in 1929. It has also won the vast majority of seats in both national and local Congresses, and also the vast majority of municipalities. While formal electoral opposition is now significantly stronger than ever before, the PRI remains clearly the dominant party.

The PRI has little or no ideology. It has promoted candidacies of people whose political views have ranged across the whole spectrum. It operates, more than anything else, as yet another instrument of presidential power. Yet it is a formidable patronage machine, and it also appears to provide some kind of channel of integration between the ordinary citizen and the state.

Because the political system itself is so centralized, the real political competition centres around organized interests rather than narrowly defined political forces. The most important of these interests is the business community. The support of the private sector is necessary for any government to succeed with its economic policies. Indeed attempts by some previous Mexican governments to force the private sector to do their bidding did not succeed and have had to be reversed; it has been too easy for holders of capital to send their money abroad. For example, the government of **Carlos Salinas** has recently committed itself to privatizing precisely those banks which **José López Portillo** nationalized in 1982.

It is compulsory in Mexico for privately owned companies to join one of the government-approved employers' organizations, they are not forbidden from forming independent organizations of their own. These independent organizations, notably Coparmex, at times play a role which formal political opposition might play in more pluralist systems. Since 1987 regular negotiations between the government, organized labour and business associations has become institutionalized.

The intelligentsia also exerts considerable influence, largely because it helps to determine the international reputation of a particular Mexican government. This can be a factor of considerable economic significance as well, in view of the openness of Mexico to influences from the USA. Moreover the Mexican **press** is far more influential and outspoken than it was a generation ago although television still tends to be bland and uncritical of the authorities. There is also a close connexion between some Mexican intellectuals, part of the Mexican press and Left-wing opposition parties; although these parties do not enjoy any significant degree of executive power they do enjoy the necessary legal protection to enable them to make quite outspoken attacks on the government and its policies.

The influence of organized labour, though less, is still considerable. Fidel Velázquez has been head of the officially recognized Confederation of Mexican Workers (*Confederación de Trabajadores de México*—CTM) since 1947; he was born in 1900 and has survived in office for much longer than anybody expected. Under Fidel the CTM has enjoyed a vast power of patronage, although its direct influence on policy has been very much less.

Finally, while the United States government does not seek overt power over Mexico, its real influence is considerable. Indeed it is precisely because of this that the Mexican authorities have only a limited freedom of action in dealing with their own businessmen, intellectuals and opposition politicians; they cannot afford to risk too much US disapproval. Mexican governments certainly have pursued policies which they knew Washington would not welcome—notably during the oil boom years of the late 1970s—but they have rarely been able to persist in them for any length of time.

Outline of political history. Mexico acquired its identity as a colony of Spain. There were many Indian civilizations in Mexico prior to the arrival of Hernán Cortés. However the most prominent of the pre-Hispanic cultures, the Aztecs and the Maya, despite their warlike tradition could not stand against the horses, guns and wheels that the Spaniards brought to Mexico. Mexico remained under Spanish rule for three centuries. Mexico acquired its ethnic identity from the years of Spanish rule. It was at the beginning a country with a poor Indian majority and a small white population; political power remained tightly controlled by Spain, and each viceroy remained for an average of no more than four years. There was some ethnic mixing of blood, probably more after independence than before, and the vast majority of Mexicans now trace back their ancestry to both Spain and pre-Columbian America. Of those who do not, many are descended from more recent migrants from Europe. Some writers, most famously Octavio Paz, believe that this double-identity is a key to the outlook of most Mexicans. The "white" world, of Europe and the United States, came to be seen as a world of despoilers and conquerors, while the Indian world as vulnerable and backward. The result, it was said, is an ambivalence toward contact with the rich countries and its representatives; Mexicans want what this world has to offer, but are fearful of losing control and being hurt and humiliated as a result. There is perhaps less to this argument today than there once was. After all the current President of Mexico and much of his Cabinet have university degrees from the United States or Europe; they understand international politics and business as well as anyone and are unlikely to suffer from many deep ambivalences or feelings of inferiority. Nevertheless what is true is that there remains to this day in Mexico a broad rule (to which there are many individual exceptions) that wealth, position and light skin colour are inter-related. There is little overt racial prejudice, but much wealth and power in Mexico (as in any other society) is inherited and passed on through generations. The pattern of social stratification introduced by the Conquest to some extent still remains.

However it should not be thought that there is one Indian identity. At the time of the Conquest there were many Indian cultures and languages; this fact greatly assisted the Spaniards in consolidating their rule. Three hundred years of Spanish rule did not eradicate this plurality; some Indians, notably the Yaqui Indians of the north west of the country, remained effectively outside imperial authority during the whole period. In fact it was not until post-Revolutionary governments in the 1920s and 1930s sought to impose a form of national unity in cultural matters that the number of separate Indian languages seriously declined. Even today there remain hundreds of Indian dialects and a (by now) relatively small number of Mexicans do not speak Spanish at all.

After the Crown, the most important institution of Spanish Mexico was the Church. It did not take long before the conquerors decided that local Indians should be converted to the faith. By no means all of them resisted conversion. The cult of the Virgin of Guadeloupe, which developed after an apparition of a "dark" Virgin to one Juan Diego in 1531, provides a good example of the way in which a foreign religion was assimilated to local patterns of belief. Yet, despite some exceptions, the Church came to be associated in Mexico (as in the rest of Spanish America) with power, privilege and obscurantism. Early dissent was broken by the Inquisition, which was active in Mexico. However it remains true that one of the first leaders of the Independence movement was a parish priest, Miguel Hidalgo, whose rising began in 1810. Although he was captured and executed, the momentum of events continued until independence was won in 1820. However the early post-independence leaders were both Catholic and conservative. As a result most "progressive" thinking, from the 1820s until the very recent past, has been anti-clerical. However anti-clericals often did overlook the rectitude and strength of the Church's appeal to peasant Mexico; the Catholic legacy of the conquest was voluntarily accepted by many, probably most, Mexicans — and most Mexicans still consider themselves to be Catholics.

A final legacy of Spanish rule was a relatively backward economy. It was unfortunate for Mexico, as for other Latin American countries, that Spain suffered a process of economic decline which started in the seventeenth century. Spain increasingly saw the New World as a source of plunder rather than as an area to be developed. Thus although the Spanish rulers of Mexico appeared to have many advantages over the Pilgrim Fathers (in respect of climate, natural resources and earliness of settlement), the North Eastern states of the USA were by 1800 very much richer than Mexico. The disparity in *per capita* income level between newly independent Mexico and the USA was around four to one. The Spaniards did develop some export enclaves in Mexico, notably silver production, but by and large this abundant wealth of resources brought little material progress. When the United States became independent in 1783, it was already a "developed" country by the standards of its time; when Mexico became independent in 1821, it was clearly a poor country.

Mexico's war of independence was particularly protracted and brutal, and the divisions which it provoked prevented an early consolidation of a stable political order. It is certainly true that Spanish rule did not create the institutions which might have survived it; moreover Mexico itself was too fragmented and divided for institution-building to be effective, at any rate without the years of peace and stability that the weakness of its institutions and lack of consensus did so much to prevent. There was thus a vicious circle; lack of unity prevented the development of a stable political system which, in turn, induced further disunity. Nor did any of the competing factions or leaders prove sufficiently strong to impose order at the point of a gun. Instead the first half-century of Mexican independence was taken up with a series of civil wars. Even worse, the independent country lost Texas when the "Lone Star" state defected to the United States and a decade later it was deprived of around one-half of its total national territory following defeat by the United States in the war of 1846–47. Arizona, New Mexico, Nevada and California were all transferred to the United States. The effect of these continuing conflicts upon the Mexican economy proved disastrous, and Mexican *per capita* income had fallen by the early 1870s to approximately one fourteenth of that of the United States.

A key turning point occurred in the early 1860s when the French sought to turn Mexico into a semi-colony by imposing the rule of the Emperor Maximilian upon the country. At first things appeared to go well for Maximilian, although some patriotic resistance held out, but when France withdrew its forces to confront the threat posed by its Prussian neighbour Maximilian was left isolated. Maximilian's enemies, led by **Benito Juárez**, overthrew and executed the Emperor and ushered in the first period of stability since independence.

Juárez and his allies were Liberals who believed in a version of social reform. The famous Constitution of 1867 disestablished the Church, many of whose lands were expropriated by the "Reformists". The Liberals, moreover, stood for individual rather than collective ownership of property—a belief which had unfortunate consequences for those many Indians who continued to subsist on the basis of communal landownership. Independent Indian tribes in the northwest of the country were subdued by the Liberals at the end of the nineteenth century, in much the same way—though with greater brutality—as a similar process occurred north of the border.

The beginnings of serious economic growth in Mexico also dates back to the Liberal period, promoted to a large extent though the development of export agriculture (in the hands of a landowner class) and mining (in the hands, mainly, of foreign investors). This was an age of railway construction, foreign investment and—towards the end of the period—the growth of Mexico City. Some Mexicans did, indeed, become very rich. However the decline of communal landholding and the extension of landlord rights, had the effect, in the more populous south of Mexico, of creating a new serfdom for the Indian majority. In sum, while it is indisputable that there was considerable economic progress during this time, the distribution of income clearly worsened and patterns of social control became increasingly repressive and authoritarian.

The Liberals professed to believe in democratic principles and Constitutional government. However this belief gradually became corrupted and Juárez was succeeded, after a brief interregnum, by Porfirio Díaz who established a personal ascendancy over Mexican politics which only ended when the Revolution broke out in 1910. Porfirio Díaz believed that economic progress required authoritarian government. Indeed, in the less settled north of the country, the Porfirian period saw the first attempt to impose real state power upon people who were essentially frontiersman; it is not altogether surprising that these attempts were resisted.

In political terms, Porfirio Díaz ruled Mexico as though it were a personal machine. He nominated candidates for state governor; these were then imposed through rigged elections. He surrounded himself with a group of loyalists, who grew older alongside himself. Consequently there was no provision for bringing younger, more dynamic people into government and those who were left out of the state patronage machine resented the advantages accruing to those within it.

Eventually, therefore, Porfirio Díaz' enemies combined against him. In 1908 the dictator gave an interview with an American journalist, a Mr Creelman, in which he hinted that he might retire in 1910. Hopes were raised among those who wished to succeed him. When it became clear that Porfirio was not after all prepared to give up power in that year, Francisco Madero launched a revolt. Madero's slogan was *¡sufragio efectivo, no re-elección!*, which loosely translates as "honest elections and no boss rule". Madero was an idealistic figure who had not had been previously associated with politics but, despite being criticized at the time (and by some later historians) for unrealism, he pursued his Revolutionary ends with greater courage and tenacity than some other more highly regarded figures.

Madero launched his revolt on Nov. 20, 1910. At first he faced serious setbacks, but was eventually supported by some irregular forces in the north of the country — forces which perhaps opposed the Mexican state as much because it was a state as because it was a dictatorship. Díaz' forces soon began to crumble, and the dictator himself went into exile and died not long afterwards. Madero became president and the first, most benign, phase of the Mexican revolution was over.

The loosening of federal authority did, however, spawn a series of revolts which created major difficulties for Madero. One of the most important revolts was **Emiliano Zapata's** peasant movement in the southern state of Morelos. Zapata led an army in defence of the traditional communal rights of the Mexican peasantry, which were being threatened by advancing commercial agriculture and landlord power. In November 1911, after some unsatisfactory negotiations with Madero, Zapata proclaimed his Plan of Ayala which called for a new Revolution and a major land reform. From then until his assassination in 1919, Zapata was almost continuously in revolt against what was left of the Mexican state.

Madero's hold on power became increasingly tenuous, but the major threat he faced came from conservatives who wished to restore some kind of pro-business dictatorship. Early in 1913 Madero was overthrown and murdered by General Victoriano Huerta who sought to turn Mexico away from democracy, reform and mobilization. However Huerta's rule quickly proved unacceptable to the vast majority of Mexicans. Although Henry Lane Wilson, the US Ambassador to Mexico in early 1913, identified himself with Huerta, the incoming government of Woodrow Wilson also declared itself opposed to the dictator; the British government was prepared to accept Huerta but its ability to influence the course of events was limited. In the end, a broad coalition of Revolutionary forces combined against Huerta who was overthrown in July 1914.

There followed a period of intense and often confused fighting. However the armies of Venustiano Carranza and Alvaro Obregón ultimately triumphed. Once they had captured **Mexico City** they organized their supporters into a Constitutional Convention. This Convention produced the 1917 **Constitution**, which remains in force (though somewhat amended) to this day. It is perhaps ironic that the two most celebrated articles of the Constitution were somewhat peripheral to the major concerns of the majority of the delegates. These were Articles 27 and 123.

Article 27 asserted the right of the Mexican state to ownership of the wealth of the Mexican sub-soil. What this appeared to pose, in fact, was a challenge to the private oil and mining companies which had invested during the government of Porfirio Díaz. Article 27 was in some ways a throwback to the traditional Spanish attitude which vested ownership of the subsoil in the Crown and was quite different from the system prevailing in the United States according to which the owner of land also owned the soil beneath it. Porfirio Díaz, in order to expedite oil and mineral development, had legislated on the United States pattern; the Revolutionaries preferred an older and more nationalist path. It has been suggested by historians that Article 27 was part of an effort by the more educated supporters of Carranza to direct the Revolutionary energies which had been aroused during the upheavals toward a determined policy of nation-building. An assertion of Mexico's national identity, and a rejection of Anglo-Saxon liberalism, were central to this process. The educational and cultural policies of the Revolutionary leadership during the 1920s were part and parcel of the same process. However in the short run Article 27 complicated Mexico's relations with the United States; because of US opposition, Article 27 was never fully enforced despite the fact that the Mexican government did eventually expropriate the oil companies (through a quite different process) in 1938.

Article 123 emphasized the rights of urban labour. These had certainly not been much emphasized in the past. The government of Porfirio Díaz had crushed strikes, or at any rate permitted employers to do so, and the urban working class did not enjoy significantly better treatment from any of the early Revolutionary governments. Living standards in Mexico City fell disastrously in 1915 and 1916. However Carranza did use his control of Mexico City to recruit workers into his armies, and needed to offer something in return. When he did offer were, mainly, promises. However the Revolutionary Mexican state did build an alliance with labour, which it both controlled and protected; this was to become a political fact of great significance as urbanization and the relative importance of the trade unions increased.

Meanwhile the majority of Revolutionary delegates were primarily interested in the issues of land and religion. The Church emerged from the Revolution defeated. This was partly (as historians sympathetic to the Revolution have insisted) because the Church hierarchy had become associated with the reactionary and unpopular Huerta government. It was also partly (as historians sympathetic to the Church have argued) because the Church was the only genuinely national organization to survive the Revolution. As such it represented a potential threat to the monopoly of state power which the Revolutionaries wished to build up, and to the nation-building operation which they wished to undertake. Finally, and most cynically, the Church represented a considerable source of wealth which could be plundered. In any event, the 1917 Constitution asserted a clear division between Church and State and put a number of restrictions upon the operations of the Church.

Also crucial to the Revolutionaries was the issue of landownership. Patterns of landownership in Mexico were (and still are) very complex. Nevertheless there was in certain parts of Mexico a clear tension between the large-unit capitalist agriculture which Porfirio Díaz had encouraged and the more traditional claims of communal landholders and smaller farmers. Even where landownership itself was not especially contentious, the fact of growing landowner power during the "Porfiriato" was. Consequently there arose during the revolution various armies of *agraristas*, who had claims either upon local landowners or state governments, or both. All of these forces pressed for a radical change of land tenure law and a redistribution of land.

The drafting of the Constitution was only the first step in the long process of establishing a stable post-Revolutionary political order. The most basic problem was that of reconstituting some form of state authority. Despite the occasionally ringing tones of the 1917 Constitution, it remains true that the Revolutionaries themselves were a loose coalition of forces, held together largely through personal loyalties and only incidentally through political ideas. It was not long before one group, the so-called "Sonora dynasty", achieved political supremacy.

Alvaro Obregón and Plutarco Elias Calles, both prominent Sonorans, began during the 1920s to reconstruct a political machine, some of whose characteristics had their roots in the "Porfiriato". State funds were used to reward friends and punish enemies. When asked how he controlled the army, Obregón is said to have replied "I know of no General who can withstand a broadside of 50,000 *pesos*". The use of state revenues to co-opt potential dissidents has become a tried and tested part of the Mexican political system. Notwithstanding this fact, however, there were several armed risings during the 1920s which Obregón and Calles, with their increasingly-professional army, successfully defeated.

Calles replaced Obregón as President in 1924. Although Calles had served in Carranza's army, he was not a military leader in the same manner as Obregón. Calles was rather a brilliant political organizer who sought to expand the basis of Revolutionary government from the troop commanders to broader groups within Mexican society. One such group was Mexican labour; Calles became associated with the build-up of the first Mexican labour confederation (*Confederación Regional Obrera Mexicana*—CROM).

Calles was also determined to proceed with the secularization of Mexican society; he was a bitter enemy of the Catholic Church and his attitude led to a major peasant rising in the *Bajio* area of Mexico. This so-called *Cristero* movement continued until 1929 when a partial compromise was reached.

Calles and Obregón also attempted to impose a dominant national culture upon society. Under José Vasconcelos, Minister of Education under Obregón, there were major initiatives to develop rural education. The content of this education—atheistic and explicit on sexual education—was often bitterly resisted by local Catholics and a number of rural schoolteachers were murdered. Nevertheless rural education, road building, the use of radio and the setting up of the National University in Mexico City had a considerable impact in reducing regional differences. Moreover in parts of southern Mexico, where traditional élites appeared to have survived the Revolution, pro-consular governors were sent in to break up concentrations of landed power and confront the Church. In the *henequen*-producing state of Yucatán, for example, the power of the landlords was broken by a radical governor imposed by Mexico City.

The Mexican economy recovered surprisingly quickly from the Revolutionary conflict. Although the Revolutionaries were in general hostile to landed power, they did not take the same attitude to manufacturing enterprise; manufacturing boomed during the 1920s, as did the production of some minerals. A number of Revolutionary generals turned themselves into businessmen, with the support and encouragement of the state. Many members of this new group came to enjoy fortune as well as power.

In 1928 Calles supported the Presidential candidacy of Obregón, as he had agreed to do. However the assassination of Obregón at his victory banquet—by a religious fanatic, but possibly at the behest of Calles—created a new political crisis. Calles responded by calling for the creation of an official party into which all who supported the Revolution would be welcomed. Thus was formed the National Revolutionary Party (*Partido Nacional Revolucionario* — PNR), which has survived (despite two changes of name) as the dominant party to this day.

The official party served as a key centralizing influence. Elections were largely formalities, but nominations were very competitive; contending local interests therefore needed the *imprimatur* of Mexico City if they were to prevail. This enabled Mexico City to divide and rule. At the same time the electoral machinery gave the government the means to tolerate local powers which it did not wish to disturb. What this meant was that the central government could challenge local power holders at a time of its own choosing; when it did so, it almost invariably won. Thus the period between 1930 and 1960 was one in which political power came to centre almost completely on Mexico City.

After World War II the mechanism of the official party could also be used to re-base the ruling élite away from those generals who fought in the Revolution and toward civilian figures who knew how to run an economy and society in peacetime. Thus the official party, despite its democratic appearance, was an instrument more of rule than representation. Nor was it particularly designed to be able to compete with other parties. When faced with serious party political competition, it tended to respond by ballot rigging and other forms of notionally illegal behaviour.

After the death of Obregón and the setting up of the Revolutionary Party, Calles enjoyed a few years of ascendancy in Mexican politics. Barred from returning to the presidential palace, he endeavoured to rule indirectly through a series of weak figures who served out short presidential terms. Calles, meanwhile, manipulated the party machinery from behind the scenes. The full presidential term was lengthened from four years to six, but Mexico had four presidents (including Obregón) between 1928 and 1934. Calles' position changed, however, when Lazáro Cárdenas assumed the presidency at the end of 1934.

Cárdenas was born in 1895 in the state of Michoacán. He served in the Revolutionary army and remained loyal to Obregón and Calles after the Revolution; his military career was sound rather than spectacular. However Cárdenas managed to acquire a certain popular appeal in the early 1930s without ever opposing or appearing to pose a threat to Calles. When the Depression struck Mexico, many active supporters of the Revolutionary Party became disillusioned by the more conservative path which the government had followed after around 1927. Cárdenas' candidacy appeared to reflect these feelings, but not so abrasively that Calles became alarmed.

Once in the presidency, however, Cárdenas was determined to be his own man. Calles raised some public objections to Cárdenas' tolerance of (and even active support for) trade union militancy; there was a confrontation and Calles was forced into exile in 1936. Cárdenas therefore established one cardinal principle of Mexican politics, which has survived until this day; ex-presidents may seek to exert influence behind the scenes, but the president of the day has the final decision on all matters. No overt challenge to an incumbent president has succeeded since Cárdenas defeated Calles.

Under Cárdenas 20,000,000 hectares of land were expropriated, and there was considerable emphasis on offering budgetary support to strengthen the agricultural sector. Trade union organization was also encouraged and union militancy tolerated. However what was of greatest significance was not so much the reforms themselves as the relationship forged between these reforms and new organizations which were created to enforce them. Thus Cárdenas set up the **National Peasants Confederation** (*Confederación Nacional de Campesinos*—**CNC**), which subsequently became an official political machine—establishing a strong basis for the system in rural areas. Together with the main labour confederation, the CTM (which the government was careful to keep separate from the peasant organization), the CNC put state power on a new and far stronger basis. The reorganization of the official party in 1938 integrated the CTM and CNC directly into the renamed Mexican Revolutionary Party (the PRM).

Cárdenas also confronted the oil companies and expropriated them on March 18, 1938. The reason for the expropriation was that the companies had refused to implement a government-arbitrated wage award which they considered excessive. While the wage award was undoubtedly steep and may have been based on incorrect information, the companies' straightforward refusal to pay put Cárdenas in a very difficult position. He did not feel that he could afford to back down, while expropriation was nevertheless a hazardous course of action. He nevertheless decided to expropriate, in the knowledge that the Mexican economy would suffer in the short term.

Cárdenas was helped by the fact that he enjoyed particularly good relations with Josephus Daniels, the US Ambassador in Mexico, who was in turn highly throught of by President Roosevelt. However although Washington took only token reprisals, the companies themselves refused Cárdenas' offer of compensation and instead mounted a determined and effective boycott of Mexico. Mexico continued to produce some oil, but far less than prior to the expropriation, and industrial relations in the oilfields remained troublesome. As a result the balance of payments worsened and devaluation became inevitable.

By the end of Cárdenas' term in 1940, the urban middle class was becoming increasingly restive. They resented both the militancy and power of the CTM and the economic hardships resulting from the oil expropriation and the company boycott. Moreover the more conservative Revolutionary generals (many of whom had acquired substantial private interests of their own) were also unwilling to support continuing radicalism. The Spanish Civil War also encouraged disaffected right-wing interests to make representations against the government's Left-wing policies.

At the end of his term, therefore, Cárdenas sought to conciliate the middle classes while avoiding any threat to the political system as such. His main objective was to prevent a complete split in the official party ahead of the 1940 elections. To this end he nominated Manuel Avila Camacho — a young and relatively conservative figure — as his successor while preserving the appearance that Avila Camacho was actually the choice of the various organizations (trade union, peasant and individual) which constituted the official party. Although the disaffected Right forced a contest in these elections, massive official rigging made it appear that Avila Camacho had won overwhelmingly. His victory was quickly recognized by Washington.

Cárdenas is one of the most controversial figures in the whole of Mexican history; he also did more than anyone else to shape the present-day structure of Mexican politics. Sympathizers consider that he achieved the maximum of reform which was possible under the circumstances of the time. Whatever the shortcomings of his land reform, it was by far the most revolutionary in Latin America before the Cuban revolution; its effect on the distribution of income was also strong. The urban working class also benefitted from integration into the CTM. Real wages were higher in the late 1930s than they were to be for quite some time thereafter. Meanwhile Cárdenas accepted the need for religious toleration and managed to carry through his reforms with a minimum of violence. Furthermore the oil expropriation proved that the Mexican state was capable of safeguarding its essential interests in the face of powerful international challenges.

Cárdenas' critics, however, also have some valid arguments. For one thing Cárdenas left the economy in severe difficulty; inflation was rising and it had been necessary to devalue the *peso* in 1939. There could be no serious prospect of a resumption of private investment until the social mobilizations, and particularly the strike activity, of the Cárdenas period were brought under control. In 1940 Mexico was still a poor, mainly rural and mainly illiterate society with a short life-expectancy. If Cardenista policies of encouraging strikes and land seizures and expropriating foreign assets had continued after 1940 then it is likely that Mexico would have remained poor.

Cárdenas also has critics on the left who stress some of the authoritarian characteristics of his government. He allowed worker and peasant organizations to form, but deliberately kept them apart so that they did not become too powerful. In any case neither the CNC nor the CTM was truly independent; Cárdenas and his successors had ample powers to control both if they so wished. Cárdenas also extended state control over the last real independent regional fiefdoms which had held out from the Revolution. Moreover he made a personal choice of successor and ensured that electoral challenge to this successor did not prosper. Cárdenas was certainly no believer in liberal democracy. On the contrary he laid down many of the foundations for the extreme presidentialism which has been a characteristic of Mexican politics ever since.

The Mexican political system itself has changed only in detail since 1940; most of the political change which has taken place since 1940 has in fact occurred since 1975 and will be reviewed under current developments. What is of greatest interest during 1940–75 is the way in which policy, particularly development policy, changed and evolved to meet changing circumstances.

Cárdenas hoped in 1940 that Avila Camacho would continue with broadly similar "Revolutionary" policies but in a more moderate and less contentious form. What in fact happened was that the direction of policy became very much more conservative. One important reason for this was that the outside world was also changing; the United States became more conservative after around 1940, Mexican relations with the United States remained close; Mexico entered World War II in 1942 and sent a token squadron of fighter pilots into combat. From around 1947, however, the issue became anti-Communism rather than anti-Fascism. President **Miguel Alemán** (1946–52) eagerly exploited the change in world politics in order to force a break with the Mexican Left and bring organized labour under tighter political control. Washington continued to regard Mexico as an ally. Although Mexico did not follow US policy in every particular after 1947, its differences were carefully muted—at any rate until the brief but extravagant display of oil power at the beginning of the 1980s.

Meanwhile the Presidential institution became increasingly powerful. President Alemán reorganized the official party in 1946 and gave the party its present-day name of the Institutional Revolutionary Party (the PRI); a tighter official control was excercised through the official trade unions and peasant organizations. Post-*Cardenista* presidents also followed his precedent of hand-picking their successors and, where necessary, rigging the subsequent elections in order to guarantee victory. Almost all of them did, however, willingly follow the convention of stepping down quietly themselves once their term of office had ended. It does seem likely that Alemán considered the possibility of his own re-election, but was dissuaded by clear signs that other members of the political elite (including Cárdenas himself) would not accept such a development. Alemán's position may thereby have been weakened to the point that he did not have a fully free hand to choose his successor. There is, however, no doubt that every presidential selection since then has been made by the outgoing leader.

Historical turning points are often approximate, but the outbreak of World War II is widely seen as marking the beginning of a sustained period of industrial growth in Mexico. The effect of the War was to increase the level of inflation and depress sharply the level of real wages. Meanwhile both Cárdenas' agrarian reforms, and the effective abandonment of these reforms by his successors, had the outcome of increasing agricultural production. Mexican industry was therefore in a position to benefit from relatively low wages, increasing agricultural output and (again after 1940) soft loans from the USA. Industrial growth occurred at a high and sustained level during the period 1945–70.

With industrial growth came the growth of cities. The focus of Mexican politics moved from the countryside to the city, The Mexican middle class grew in size and self-confidence and by the end of the 1960s was expressing increasing frustration with the rigidity and authoritarianism of Mexican politics.

The direction of public policy was also to favour capital accumulation, provided only that the newly wealthy industrial and agricultural interests did not challenge the political order as such. Despite what has been asserted by some historians, it was not so much that the Revolutionaries forgot their principles and remembered their friends. It was more that a country with a rapidly rising population needed private investment if it was to find jobs for its people. Land reform was no longer the answer; private capital accumulation needed to take its place. Needless to say, this required a direction of policy which was considerably different.

The Mexico of a generation ago, therefore, was one in which industry and urbanization were growing rapidly; agriculture rather less so. Income inequalities were widening although the majority of Mexicans derived some benefit from the process of economic growth. Life expectancy and literacy indicators were steadily improving. Nevertheless there was little truly "Revolutionary" about this Mexico except for a rhetoric which did not entirely obscure the six-year dictatorship which the presidential office had become. The romantic if violent history of Mexico appeared to most policymakers as something which they should at all costs seek to avoid repeating. The era of adventure was over; the era of business was just beginning.

Recent developments—political. The political system was relatively stable during the 1940–65 period because it continued to draw strength from the Revolution and the land reforms of the Cárdenas period. These had enabled the system to construct, through the CNC and the PRI, a powerful and effective political machine in the rural areas. At the same time the thrust of economic policy was to draw resources from the rural areas and channel them into the cities. Mexican capitalists and the growing middle class benefitted from this direction policy, but both groups were at the same time denied the means of open political expression. Indeed while the economy advanced considerably between 1945 and 1970 the political system became increasingly centralized, restrictive and closed.

Meanwhile the central government increasingly controlled the various regions of Mexico. It did so in part by aggressively using its power to appoint and remove governors so as to undercut the influence of regional strongmen. Another factor was the increasing use of branches of the state bureacracy as sources of patronage which rivalled those of the elected authorities. Efforts to introduce more democracy into local and regional government were blocked and the ruling party increasingly operated merely as a "Ministry of Elections".

The political order was however disturbed by the student movement of 1968. By 1968 the urban middle class had grown significantly, and the Federal District had become the most important centre for pre-university and university courses. More profoundly, Mexico now had a majority of its citizens living in urban areas; the middle class had grown in numbers but the opportunities open to its younger members had not grown proportionately. The result was an undertone of insecurity and frustration behind the student revolt of 1968.

The student movement itself was suppressed. Troops fired on a student demonstration in October 1968, killing scores and perhaps hundreds of people. The repression was partly effective in the short term, although it did not prevent several thousand young Mexicans from resorting to insurgency in the early 1970s. However it also had the effect of persuading some very senior Mexican politicians that something had gone badly wrong with the country and that changes were needed. One such politician was Luís Echeverría who was Interior Minister in 1968, and so directly involved in the repression.

Thus when Echeverría succeeded Díaz Ordaz as president in 1970, he surprised many observers (not least Díaz Ordaz himself) by moving his government to the Left in order to try to co-opt student opposition. While opponents of the system who resorted to armed struggle were ruthlessly crushed, those who were prepared to compromise were offered inducements to come to terms with the system. The public sector was greatly expanded, and President Echeverría responded to the expressed misgivings of the private sector by launching a series of rhetorical attacks on the business community. Business responded to this unwelcome new climate by exporting capital: the result was economic crisis and devaluation in 1976.

The actual political system changed little during this time; instead Echeverría sought to use the conduct of economic policy to seek to rebalance the political order. In this he was partially, but by no means wholly succeessful. He was able to bring a younger generation of Left-leaning graduates into government, and appeared to increase the credibility of the system in the eyes of at least part of the generation of 1968. However there remained a current of Left-wing dissidence which resisted attempts at co-optation by Echeverría. Meanwhile business interests, which were between 1945 and 1970 largely happy to leave government to the political leaders, became increasingly alarmed and active. Finally Echeverría's efforts to use the economy for political purposes led to the development of an inflationary problem in Mexico for the first time for many years; there was no devaluation of the peso against the dollar between 1954 and 1976, but the 1976 devaluation was very heavy. Moreover Echeverría also resorted to foreign borrowing in order to avoid the need for tax increases; Mexico thus acquired a significant foreign debt. If it had not been for the fact that the Mexican state oil company made a number of major oil discoveries during 1972–74, the economic crisis of 1976 would have been far worse than it eventually proved.

Why did Echeverría break so sharply from the policies of Díaz Ordaz? One explanation comes from the pendulum theory of Mexican political behaviour. According to this, presidents who are seen as excessively left-wing or right-wing are likely to be implicitly repudiated by a move toward the centre or, on occasion, toward the other end of the spectrum on the part of their successors. Thus right-wing presidents such as Alemán (1946–52) and Díaz Ordaz (1964–70) were followed in the case of Alemán by a centrist (Ruiz Cortines) and in the case of Díaz Ordaz by a left-winger (Echeverría). Similarly left-wingers such as Cárdenas and Echeverría were followed by a move to the centre.

There is undoubtedly something to this analysis. However it should be noted that the theory deals only with movements from the trend of Mexican presidential politics; it does not explain what the trend actually is. What is considered to be the political centre today is not what it was 30 years ago. In order to understand political developments at a deeper level one needs to consider the effect of changes in Mexican society.

One obvious change has related to the relationship between the state and the most powerful social forces in Mexico. Social forces were themselves changing in character as the Mexican population became larger, more urbanized, better educated and somewhat more affluent. Moreover the memory of the turbulence and upheavals of Mexican politics prior to 1940 was fading by 1970; younger Mexicans were less appreciative of the values of order and gradual economic progress. They also wanted a freer and more equal society — things which the authorities found it difficult to concede. The impact of these demands was to upset the equilibrium on which Mexican politics rested and bring about changes which are still working through the system. Thus in the mid-1960s Mexico was politically quiet. The private sector and the Church were quiet because they were largely content with the way in which things were moving, while the Left was kept under political control. This relative quiescence had earlier been briefly disturbed by the Cuban Revolution but this did not have a decisive long-term impact on Mexico. However the student movement and the Echeverría presidency did have such an effect.

Echeverría was succeeded as President by José López Portillo in December 1976. It seemed at first as though López Portillo would seek to restore equilibrium to Mexican political society after the upheavals of the Echeverría period. López Portillo moved to reassure the private sector, which had been very shaken by Echeverría, and announced his intention to increase oil production sharply. He also offered a limited but real political reform.

The effect of this reform was to encourage opposition political parties to register and compete in elections; while it was clear that the official party would win the vast majority of electoral contests, a system of proportional representation was introduced into the Chamber of Deputies so that other parties were guaranteed one quarter of the seats no matter how well the official party did. Electoral opposition did exist in Mexico prior to 1977. The main opposition party, the pro-Catholic National Action Party (**Partido de Acción Nacional – PAN**), had registered as early as 1939. There was also a left-wing opposition party—the Popular Socialist Party (*Partido Popular Socialista*—PPS)—and another party, the Authentic Party of the Mexican Revolution (*Partido Auténtico de la Revolución Mexicana*—PARM), which was not entirely opposed to the government but was at least nominally separate from the official PRI; however neither the PPS nor the PARM was taken very seriously, although the PAN did have a real if limited base of its own. The law of 1977 encouraged the registration of a number of other parties — including the Mexican Communist

Party which later merged with some other left-wing groupings to form a Socialist party. The PRI, though still able to outpoll all of its rivals, now faced a more authentic electoral opposition on the Left as well as the Right.

The effects of this reform were very great in the long-term, but limited in the short. What was of greater immediate significance under López Portillo was the evolution of the Mexican economy. We have seen that Echeverría sought to co-opt dissidents by expanding the size of the public sector. It seemed for a time, however, as if López Portillo could afford to finance a larger, and still expanding, public sector by aggressively increasing oil exports. Oil production had begun to increase in late 1973 but it took some time for a true appreciation of the extent of Mexico's oil discoveries to sink home. When they did, Mexico enjoyed an intense new economic boom.

Unfortunately the resulting prosperity lulled President López Portillo into a false sense of security. He tried to continue many of the policies of the previous administration—expanding the public sector, extending subsidies indiscriminately and covering a growing public sector deficit with foreign borrowing. In addition he pursued an increasingly aggressive foreign policy which was closer to that of Cuba than the United States; López Portillo was an enthusiastic supporter of the Sandinista movement in Nicaragua. Eventually the private sector again began to lose confidence and started to export its capital. The government did not respond quickly enough to reduce its borrowings. The result was an economic crisis in 1982 which was even more serious than that of 1976. López Portillo became seriously alarmed at the resulting capital flight and nationalized the banks in a dramatic gesture on Sept. 1, 1982.

The events of 1982, and particularly the bank nationalization, imparted a shock to the system almost as great as the Tlatelolco massacre of 1968. This time, however, it was the propertied interests who were outraged. They had been somewhat alarmed by Echeverría, and after 1982 many businessmen came close to losing all confidence in their own political system. A second consequence of the economic crisis was to depress Mexican living standards for several years; the economy did not really recover until 1989. This, too, had major political implications. During the 1945–82 period, most Mexicans were enjoying improved living standards; the key indicators such as life expectancy, literacy rate, access to housing etc. all improved steadily during this time. After 1982 they went sharply, if temporarily, into decline. Consequently there was a growing willingness on the part of the Mexican electorate to detach their support from the official party in favour of one or other of the opposition electoral candidates. Finally many members of the political élite, including the incoming President Miguel de la Madrid, reached the conclusion that the direction of economic policy needed to be reversed; instead of using the public sector to lead the development process, it was necessary instead to return to a more market-oriented pattern.

The first political challenge which the government faced came from a stronger and more confident PAN. The incoming government of Miguel de la Madrid appeared at first to be willing to accept opposition victories in those (mainly northern) municipalities where they occurred; it remained the case that the PRI won most of the contested elections, but there was a swing in the opposite direction. However from late 1983 it became clear that the ruling party was willing to falsify election results in order to prevent the opposition from winning.

Meanwhile de la Madrid was faced with the even more difficult task of restoring a degree of confidence to the private sector. He began by filling his Cabinet with economically orthodox technocrats and adopted IMF-approved austerity policies during his first year in office. Nevertheless many businessmen either switched to supporting the opposition PAN or, more frequently, became increasingly outspoken at their unhappiness with the turn of events.

Economic recovery was slow to come. Clearly, 1983 was a year of recession, and the recovery which did take place in late 1984 proved to be unsoundly based; problems were already emerging when the economy was further set back by a major earthquake which struck in September 1985 and then by the sharp decline in international oil prices from the beginning of 1986. However in response to these increasing difficulties the de la Madrid government extended and deepened its commitment to policies of economic liberalism. Mexico entered the GATT in 1986, and began serious policies of privatization at around that time. Nevertheless Mexico came close to a financial collapse in the early part of 1986; it was at this point that Washington again intervened. US Treasury Secretary James Baker prepared a rescue package for the Mexican economy in return for an understanding that de la Madrid would continue with market-oriented policies. By this time the Mexican private sector was also beginning to be convinced that there would be no return to pre-1982 style "financial populism", and financial confidence in Mexico began slowly to improve.

Meanwhile, although the political system did

not change in any formal sense—it remained intensely presidential with little provision for popular input into government—the political atmosphere changed considerably. The tone of public debate became increasingly outspoken and critical. There was more controversy than ever around election processes. Some foreign observers began to express concern that Mexico's record of political stability might be under threat. The level of public confidence in the political authorities declined. De la Madrid was publicly booed at the opening of the World Cup in Mexico City in 1986.

In 1986 the PRI split seriously—for the first time since 1952. The dissident faction was led by Cuauhtémoc Cárdenas and Porfirio Muñoz Ledo. Cuauhtémoc Cárdenas was the son of the former President Cárdenas; he had himself enjoyed a moderately successful political career, serving as governor of the state of Michoacán. However his background, left-wing political views and lack of training in economics made it unlikely that he would rise further in the hierarchy. Porfirio Muñoz Ledo had been close to Echeverría, under whom he served as Minister of Labour and President of the PRI. Again, however, he was associated too much with the Left of the party to have serious chance of further advancement; his career within the existing system had almost certainly come to an end.

In August 1986 these two figures, supported by a number of others, set up the so-called "Democratic Current" within the PRI. There was a period in which it looked possible that there would be some kind of negotiated agreement between themselves and the PRI hierarchy, but at the end of 1987 the supporters of the Current formally left the PRI and mounted an independent challenge in the 1988 elections.

The Presidential elections of 1988 marked a further turning point in the evolution of the Mexican political system. They were more competitive and closely fought than any previous presidential elections. After the particularly flagrant rigging of elections in the northern state of Chihuahua in 1986, de la Madrid appears to have acknowledged that the PRI had gone too far in its attempt to preserve an electoral monopoly and that more competitive party politics had to be accepted. A new electoral law was presented in late 1986 which had the effect of introducing proportional representation into regional as well as national assemblies; this meant that the opposition was guaranteed some form of participation in all state assemblies in Mexico and its credibility was thereby enhanced. Additionally the wholesale rigging of the Presidential election was now made more difficult.

De la Madrid selected Carlos Salinas de Gortari as presidential candidate for the PRI. Salinas had been Minister of Planning and Budget under de la Madrid and one of the main architects of Mexican economic policy, particularly during 1986 and 1987; he was a brilliant technical economist with three higher degrees from Harvard. However he had conspicuously refused to build a base of support within the ruling party, and he did not have the charismatic appeal of some of his rivals for the nomination. De la Madrid evidently chose the man whom he believed would make the best president, not necessarily the best presidential candidate.

The right-wing PAN mounted a stronger challenge than in the past. The PAN had always enjoyed a real but limited base of support, mainly among middle class inhabitants of certain provincial towns in northern Mexico. It was thought unlikely that its support could fall below around 15 per cent but it had yet to make the breakthrough into real nationwide popularity. However the PAN had obviously picked up support from a wider section of the Mexican public after 1982 although the widespread nature of ballot rigging made it difficult to tell exactly by how much.

Meanwhile the Left was also strengthening its position. Ever since the 1977 political reform it had been part of the government's strategy to try to keep the Left divided. A large number of left-wing parties were therefore given official recognition; these included various Trotskyist groupings as well as orthodox Communists and more moderate Socialists. While the share of the vote received by the Left as a whole had increased somewhat, this fragmentation ensured that no left-wing party could do particularly well. However in 1988 the Marxist Left agreed to promote a single candidate, Heberto Castillo.

Even more serious was the candidacy of Cuauhtémoc Cárdenas which was sponsored by the PPS and the PARM. These had, until then, been seen as tame Left-wing parties which effectively supported the government. Cuauhtémoc had a powerful popular appeal, coming more from his name and background than from any great speaking ability. Shortly before the elections he was able to persuade Heberto Castillo to withdraw in his favour, and as the campaign progressed there were signs that he was becoming increasingly successful in attracting the votes of the disaffected and discontented.

When the votes were finally counted, the result appeared all-but-sensational. Between 1952 and 1988 Presidential candidates of the official party were either effectively unopposed or else they won with huge majorities; de la Madrid's 78 per cent of the vote, won in 1982, was relatively low. However it was clear even before the poll that Salinas' share of the vote would be considerably less than this; perhaps as low as 60 per cent. On election evening itself, early returns appeared to provide a severe shock for the system. Results were then delayed by a mysterious computer failure; government opponents began to assert that another fraud was being prepared. When the results were finally announced, Carlos Salinas was given a suspiciously neat 51 per cent of the vote; Cárdenas was given 32 per cent and Manuel Clouthier of the PAN 17 per cent. Cárdenas himself was convinced that he had in reality won the elections and that the PRI had stolen victory in the confused hours following the computer breakdown.

According to the official figures, Cárdenas had in fact carried the Federal District and several more states. For the first time the opposition had won Senate seats, in both the Federal District and in Michoacán. Moreover while the PRI continued to enjoy a majority in the Chamber of Deputies, its margin was down to a rather uncomfortable 260 seats as against 240 won by the opposition.

When President Salinas was inaugurated, therefore, he faced a stronger party-political opposition than ever before. Even if the official returns were accurate, he had won by a bare overall majority. Salinas himself indicated that he was prepared to accept the existence of a more pluralist party-political system than ever before although the official PRI continued to be in a majority. During 1989 a number of opposition victories were recognized in significant municipalities, and in June 1989 for the first time an opposition victory was recognized in a state governorship election—that of Baja California Norte where the candidate of the PAN was declared the winner.

Mexico is still short of being a full-scale democracy; there is still some electoral dishonesty and the relationship between the ruling party and the government is still very close. Nevertheless electoral competition is far more a feature of Mexican politics than ever before. Opposition parties are stronger and there is a greater willingness on the part of the authorities to accept that electoral pluralism should and does exist in Mexico.

Meanwhile President Salinas was faced with the fact that the official party itself was a far weaker force than it had been in the past. Reform of the official party had been intermittently on the political agenda for the previous 20 years, but nothing effective had been done. The problems with policies of reform were many. For one thing, the Mexican Constitution stipulates that elected office holders may not be re-elected. In some cases, such as municipal president and Deputy, the prohibition is on consecutive re-election; in other cases, such as President and state governor, the prohibition is on any kind of re-election. It is therefore difficult for political figures to make a career from elective office; they tend instead to alternate between positions of elected authority and posts in the federal bureaucracy. It is virtually impossible then for elected politicians to build up a reservoir of personal power along the lines of (for example) the repeatedly re-elected mayors of American cities or US Senators. What tends to happen instead is that the real sources of local and regional power—such as powerful local business interests—avoid direct political involvement but tend instead to manipulate the formal government; the federal government in Mexico City also does its share of such manipulation.

The PRI therefore finds it difficult to produce consistently high quality candidates for elected office. Instead power groups within the official party tend to press for the nomination of their own candidates, more as a reward for past loyalty than out of any belief that the candidates themselves are the most appropriate for the job in hand. However middle-class constituencies in northern towns (for example) are likely to object to the nomination of an ageing trade union leader to be their local federal deputy; indeed candidates sponsored by organized labour have done notably badly when faced by serious opposition challenge.

However while the PRI suffers from certain shortcomings as an electoral machine, it does have some advantages to the government in other ways. The loyalty of organized labour has played an important part in permitting Mexican industrialization to develop with reasonable smoothness. Indeed the official union confederation, the CTM, has played an active part in supporting incomes policies both in 1977 and again since 1987. It is likely that these have played a major part in bringing down the rate of inflation in Mexico. However what the leadership of the CTM wants in return for this support is to enjoy the power of patronage. An obvious arena for such patronage is that of elected office—but the bargain can only be sustained if the relatively unpopular figures which the CTM is likely to nominate can expect to be elected. This problem may gradually become less pressing as the CTM gradually weakens in the face of a more market-oriented economy, but for now the obstacles to reforming the official party are indeed great.

Another problem with the Mexican political system is that the relative lack of accountability within the federal bureaucracy and the official party tend to encourage corruption. There has always been a fairly thin line between the officially approved tactic of using state resources for patronage purposes in the interests of political stability, and outright malfeasance. The issue became even more serious when Echeverría expanded the number of state enterprises. These suffered from very poor accounting discipline and were undoubtedly used for private appropriation to a considerable extent. Moreover after the economic crisis of 1982 many Mexicans blamed official corruption for their own economic hardships; there can be little doubt that corruption was extensive under the presidency of López Portillo. Finally, during the 1980s, "ordinary" corruption was significantly overlaid by the increasing importance of the narcotics trade operating on Mexican soil.

It is true that De la Madrid announced an anti-corruption policy in 1983, but the extent of this was limited and it was not really followed up. President Salinas went much further. In February 1989 he ordered the arrest of the notorious oil-workers leader, Joaquín Hernández de Galicia (nicknamed "La Quina"), on corruption and murder charges. A number of other arrests followed, including that of Félix Gallardo who was the most wanted drug trafficker on the government's lists. The former head of de la Madrid's federal police was also arrested and charged with drug trafficking and the murder of a journalist who threatened to expose his operations.

There is one final point which should be considered here which relates to the politics of economic management. The structure of Mexican politics is essentially corporate, although employers' associations act with far more freedom than do labour organizations. Independent labour organizations have been tolerated, but militancy has generally been resisted.

Since late 1987 economic policy in Mexico has itself become explicitly corporatist. Government has negotiated a series of "Economic Solidarity Pacts" with the CTM and a range of employers' associations. This marked a major change in economic policy-making from the days of Díaz Ordaz and Echeverría, when employers' demands for open participation in decision making were rejected. Since 1987 both de la Madrid and Salinas have accepted that there is an employers' interest the expression of which need not be confined to the deferential use of official channels; employers' associations can now negotiate, directly across the table, with government. One of the main employers' demands, that of accelerating the rate of privatization, has largely been met. The CTM, similarly, has been able to ask for concessions in return for accepting wage restraint. These concessions have related to a limited range of price controls on government supplied products, and on such items as food. While it is too early to say whether these Economic Solidarity Pacts will become a permanent feature of Mexican policy-making, it is clear that they have been of considerable importance since 1987.

Outline of economic development. If one takes the past 50 years, Mexico has enjoyed a positive rate of economic growth. However this general trend was interrupted by serious economic instability during the 1970s and progress went into reverse during the 1980s. Very recently economic growth has re-started, although in 1989 and 1900 the rate was only slightly faster than the rate of population growth. The prospects for the rest of the 1990s are extremely promising. Moreover the rate of inflation, which rose through most of the 1970s and 1980s and reached a peak of 135 per cent in the autumn of 1987, has since been brought down and is now below 30 per cent and continuing to fall.

Between 1940 until around 1970 economic growth rested upon two major foundations. One of these was manufacturing, which grew at annual average rates of over 6 per cent. This rate of growth permitted steady increases in real wages although these grew less rapidly than output; profits therefore tended to rise very rapidly indeed. However despite its rapid growth, the contribution of manufacturing to the balance of payments was on the whole negative. Manufactured exports were relatively limited and did not make up for the imports of capital goods and technology which were necessary for continued expansion.

The second pillar of growth was Mexican agriculture. It is unusual, at least in Latin America, for agricultural growth to continue during a period of industrialization. Nevertheless this is what happened in Mexico. Some of this growth may have represented a recovery following on from the ending of Revolutionary conflicts and upheavals; some of it was due to the land reform itself. Much of it was however due to growing public spending, at any rate during the 1940s and 1950s, on roads and irrigation projects particularly in the northern part of the country. This is where a capitalist agriculture developed after the War, in contrast to the collectivist *ejidal* system which continued to operate in the poorer parts of the country. The *ejidal* system may also have had a positive effect by encouraging labour intensive techniques and the growing of food, whereas larger units often involved themselves in export projects.

However much of Mexico is difficult to farm effectively because of a shortage of water. Government spending on irrigation projects is subject to the law of diminishing returns; the most rewarding projects are developed first, and later projects are either more costly or less useful. Government investment in agriculture ceased to grow after around 1960 and agricultural output itself began to stagnate in the late 1960s. It has not significantly progressed since then although both the size of the population and its consumption of agricultural produce have increased considerably.

Thus, whereas the contribution of agriculture to the balance of payments was positive as recently as 1970, this has now ceased to be the case. Moreover as the agricultural trade surplus declined, Mexico was threatened by a tightening balance-of-payments constraint unless the manufacturing sector could somehow be persuaded to reduce its deficit. From the late 1960s government policy began to emphasize export promotion in manufacturing. An agreement between Presidents Díaz Ordaz and Lyndon B. Johnson led the United States to accept goods imported from Mexico under the so-called **maquiladora** programme. These imports would attract duty only on the value-added within Mexico. In other words raw materials, capital goods and technology exported from the United States into *maquiladora* factories could be re-imported duty free without quota or other limit. Conversely the Mexicans agreed to allow 100 per cent foreign ownership of *maquiladora* plants, in contrast to the rest of the industrial sector where various limitations were placed upon direct foreign investment. The Mexican authorities also sought to develop the tourist trade and pressed some big local manufacturing concerns (notably the car companies) to export more.

Even so manufactured exports did not increase very markedly before 1982. The most important single reason for this is that the Mexican government continued with a protectionist policy in respect of imports and, for this and other reasons, allowed the Mexican *peso* to become over-valued against the dollar. Rather than pursuing policies which would have prevented this, the authorities instead looked during the 1970s to two other sources of balance-of-payments support — oil exports and foreign borrowing.

Mexico had (and still has) rather a chequered oil history. There was an oil boom during 1910–20, followed by a period in which the industry declined. There was an acrimonious nationalization in 1938. The state oil company, Pémex, decided a few years after the nationalization that it would withdraw from foreign markets in order to avoid further political controversy. Pémex instead concentrated on the refining and petrochemicals sectors within Mexico, which were themselves growing rapidly; by the early 1970s, however, it had neglected exploration to the point of becoming a net oil importer.

From the late 1960s, oil exploration was once more emphasized. As a result Pémex made a number of major discoveries during 1972–74 and shortly afterwards began to increase production. In October 1974 a number of inspired articles appeared in the US press stating that Mexico had discovered a major source of crude oil and that this could act as a counterbalance to the power of OPEC. The Echeverría government reacted by playing down the significance of its oil reserves. Nevertheless Mexico became an exporter of oil on an increasing scale from the middle of 1975.

Under López Portillo the "oil card" was played with great enthusiasm. Production was rapidly expanded, Pémex spent heavily and oil money flooded into the country. It seemed for a time as though the balance of payments constraint on Mexican development had been definitively lifted. However in 1980 López Portillo took the decision to restrict oil output to around 2,700,000 barrels a day, which was a considerable figure but less than the head of Pémex, Jorge Díaz Serrano, had wanted. In 1981 the price of oil began to weaken and Mexico was slow to adjust its prices downwards; a good deal of potential revenue was thereby lost.

Since 1982 Mexico has remained an oil exporter, but production has been held at or just below 2,500,000 barrels a day. International oil prices were in slow decline during 1981–85, falling sharply at the beginning of 1986; they remained fairly low until the Iraqi invasion of Kuwait in August 1990. However although oil exports still provide a useful source of income, no government since 1982 has wanted to over-depend on oil exports. In fact the tendency has been to reduce investment in oil, partly because of suspicions about inefficiency, excessive union power and corruption within Pémex, and partly due to fears that any sharp increase in oil income might undermine the rest of the economy.

If the effect of the oil boom was quickly dissipated, the consequences of foreign borrowing were even more unsatisfactory. The Mexican government undertook relatively little foreign borrowing before around 1972, but after that year the total increased considerably. This was partly for balance-of-payments reasons, but there was another important factor as well. Echeverría, and later López Portillo, wanted to expand the role of the public sector in Mexico, so as to pursue various social and political objectives, but they feared that tax increases would lead to powerful opposition from the private sector. Borrowing appeared to offer an easy way out.

It is also worth noting that it became easier during the early 1970s for Latin American countries to borrow internationally. Although the banks only became genuinely eager to lend to Latin America after the petrodollar recycling projects began in 1974, international credit had already loosened considerably by 1972. Dollar inflation during the 1970s was higher than international interest rates, so that the rate of interest to borrowers appeared to be negative. Most Latin American countries took advantage of what they then believed were favourable terms and sharply increased their borrowing.

As in most other Latin American countries, the eventual result of this expansion of borrowing was a credit crunch. Mexico has the particular problem that, as a result of its long border with the United States, it cannot impose exchange controls. When the private sector or the middle class becomes worried about political or exchange risk, it is a simple matter to send capital abroad. In both 1976 and 1981–82 this capital outflow quickly reached torrential proportions and precipitated major economic crises.

The economic crisis of 1976 was quickly forgotten in the light of Mexico's oil boom. The crisis of 1982, however, had far more drastic effects; this is partly because it could not be dismissed as a "one off" and partly because López Portillo responded to it by moving to the Left and nationalizing the banks. A further factor is that after 1982, for reasons which related as much to Latin America as a whole as specifically to Mexico, further lending to Mexico has become unfeasible (for many years at any rate), and there was no quick way of expanding exports to fill the gap. Instead Mexico now had to service a debt swollen by the emergency borrowing undertaken in 1982 at historically high rates of interest while its oil revenues were falling in value. The debt had become a seriously damaging factor for the Mexican economy.

Between 1983 and 1989 Mexico serviced its debt in a reasonably reliable manner, but its efforts to negotiate better terms had little impact. Mexican nationalists who advocated a moratorium or repudiation of the debt were ignored. In 1989, however, Mexico was able to undertake a major debt reduction under the aegis of the Brady Plan, promoted by the US government. The details are very complex, but the overall result was to reduce Mexico's debt liabilities by around one third. The foreign debt remains a major problem, but is no longer an insuperable one.

The crisis of 1981–82, therefore, was in large measure a balance of payments crisis. However the extent of capital flight and the bank nationalization deepened the problem into a crisis of confidence. This was a serious matter in a country such as Mexico. Because of the confidence problem, even heavy cuts in real public spending did not significantly improve the government's financial position in the short run. The devaluation of 1986, which was largely forced by the collapse in oil revenues, made the position more difficult still.

The government's immediate policy response to this crisis was the orthodox policy of seeking to stabilize the economy at a lower level of activity. GDP fell by 5.3 per cent in 1983 and imports fell sharply; the trade balance greatly improved. When economic growth resumed in late 1984, it quickly became clear that the underlying difficulties remained unresolved: the recovery quickly pulled in more imports and further balance of payments problems threatened; when the price of oil collapsed in early 1986, it was obvious that no policy of fiscal expansion would be possible for many years to come. Instead the authorities had little choice but to take as much time as was necessary to achieve a radical market-oriented economic restructuring.

One policy response after 1982 which did succeed in the long-run was to promote the growth of other exports. The *maquiladora* sector, which had grown only slowly during the 1970s, became one of the leading sectors during the 1980s. The number employed in *maquiladora* plants increased from some 127,000 in 1982 to over 439,000 by the middle of 1990. Beyond the *maquiladora* sector itself, the authorities also began to adopt more liberal policies on foreign investment. Another initiative was tariff reduction which was pursued hesistantly in 1985 and then with far more vigour during 1986–87. As happened in other countries, a combination of devaluation and tariff reduction led to a strong export response. In 1989 manufacturing overtook oil as the leading Mexican export sector.

A further response was privatization. To the extent that this brought in money from abroad, it had a positive effect on the balance of payments; it also helped to alleviate the government's considerable financial difficulties both because of the direct increase in public revenue and because it was a confidence-boosting policy which reduced the rate of interest at which government could borrow. Privatization proceeded very slowly at first, but more rapidly from 1987 when the first significant measures were announced. In 1990 President Salinas announced the privatization of the banks — thereby directly reversing López Portillo's policy in 1982. It seems likely that much of the public enterprise sector will have been divested by the middle of the 1990s.

All in all the direction of policy since 1982 has been remarkably consistent despite some external shocks and the change of President in 1988. A long period of state-promoted growth and protectionism has given way to a free-market orientation. The result was a significant period of retrenchment and austerity, but the beginnings of sustained growth were achieved by the beginning of the 1990s.

These various changes have had a considerable impact upon the living standards of most Mexicans. The strength of Mexican agriculture during the 1940s and 1950s was positive in income distribution terms, but its weakness thereafter was negative. The high rural birthrate and the scarcity of land contributed toward sharply increasing income inequality after around 1955. The cities grew, and most people in urban areas enjoyed at least a slow increase in living standards, but many of those living in rural areas were left behind. Moreover the pattern of public spending and subsidy tended to increase the gap between country and city. Many of those living in rural areas responded to this situation by migrating either to the cities or, increasingly, to the United States.

Nevertheless, despite some undoubted worsening in the distribution of income, there is evidence that most Mexicans did benefit to at least some degree from the economic growth of the 1945–82 period. After 1982, however, almost all sectors of Mexican society suffered setbacks; real wages in urban areas fell by around one third, and the extent of rural poverty increased and deepened.

The still fragile economic recovery which began in 1989 will have different implications again. The Federal District, which was the chief beneficiary of the rise in public employment and subsidized public services, is likely to have lost out to some degree as a result of renewed fiscal orthodoxy. On the other hand, the increase in market-oriented policies is unlikely to be of much help to the rural poor; the government has sought to attract private investment into agriculture but with limited success. The chief beneficiaries of this renewed growth are likely to be in the north of the country, or in towns away from the Federal District where there is potential for growth in industry or tourism.

In some other respects, however, the momentum of "modernizing" social change has continued despite the economic cycle. The trend toward urbanization continued, though it is no longer the Federal District which shows the most rapid rate of growth. It is rather the state capitals in the more prosperous regions, and the north of Mexico as a whole, which have attracted the migrants. There has been a slow but continuing shift in economic power from the federal capital to the north of Mexico. The centralization of the Mexican economy, which played an important part in the centralization of Mexican politics, is now at an end.

Current economic situation. The Mexican economy is becoming increasingly integrated with that of the United States. President Salinas and President Bush are currently negotiating a free trade agreement between the two countries, on a model similar to that existing between the United States and Canada. Already almost all economic indicators show how closely the Mexican economy is integrated with its northern neighbour. The USA takes 69 per cent of Mexican exports (1989); it supplies 68 per cent of Mexican imports and it provides 87 per cent of foreign tourists to Mexico, and 63 per cent of direct foreign investment into Mexico.

On the one hand, this may be disadvantageous to Mexico. The United States economy is growing more slowly than those of Japan and Germany. On the other hand, lower Mexican labour costs should ensure that Mexican exports to the United States grow more rapidly than the United States economy itself. This was certainly the pattern with manufacturing industry during the 1980s. Between 1985 and 1989 the value of *maquiladora* exports to the United States increased from $1,268 million to $3,052 million. Given the absolute size of the United States economy, there is a virtually unlimited potential for *maquiladora* exports to increase further. To the extent that protectionist pressures grow within the United States, Mexico will be far better able to withstand them than will the countries of the Pacific Rim.

The Mexican authorities undoubtedly see manufacturing as the leading sector of their economy. Tourism, agriculture and oil are important but either do not have the same growth potential or (as in the case of oil) may have serious side-effects. Nevertheless they expect tourism, agriculture and other sectors to benefit from the more liberal attitude toward private investment in general and foreign investment in particular. The government is trying hard to get private companies to invest in agricultural projects, preferably in ways which co-operate with existing peasants and *ejidatarios* rather than supplanting them. A number of innovative ideas have been developed to try to encourage foreign investment into infrastructural activities such as road building.

One major problem during the 1980s which

now appears on its way to solution is that of public sector finances. By the end of 1983 Mexico had a vast foreign debt which appeared virtually impossible to service. The cost of debt service was such that, even after major cuts in real public sector programmes, the costs of paying interest was almost crippling. In order to service the debt, moreover, the Mexican government found it necessary to borrow in *pesos*; due to the perceived risk of devaluation and the general lack of private sector confidence, Mexican interest rates needed to be extremely high. For this reason, the government could not balance its books and therefore needed to borrow at very high rates of interest merely to pay the existing high interest on its existing borrowing. There was therefore a real danger, most manifest in 1986 and 1987, that inflation and interest rates would chase each other higher and higher.

It was largely for this reason that the *Pact of Economic Solidarity* was agreed in late 1987 between government, employers and unions. By cutting the headline rate of inflation, the government was able to reduce the nominal rate of interest. This then reduced the cost of its borrowings and improved the fiscal balance. The "virtuous circle" effect was that this further reduced the cost of government borrowing, and so on. Further reductions in domestic interest rates followed the debt reduction agreement reached between Mexico and the foreign banks under the Brady Plan. Accelerating the rate of privatization further improved the public sector financial position. After President Salinas publicly announced in May 1990 that he would denationalize the banks, real domestic interest rates fell to levels only slightly above those in the industrialized countries.

What this has meant is that the government, finding the cost of debt service far less than in the past, has once again been free to increase real spending on social programmes. Rather than, as in the 1970s, expanding the role of nationalized industries, President Salinas has concentrated on "welfare" programmes such as education, health and the direct relief of poverty. While there must still be some scepticism about the effectiveness of the Mexican bureaucracy, it is now undoubtedly true that public resources are being devoted to areas where there is most need for them.

The improvement in the public financial position holds out long-term encouragement for reducing the rate of inflation. However inflation has come down only slowly since 1988 mainly because the government has been determined not to stick with an inappropriate level of relative prices. In other words, there is some inflationary effect in the short term from increasing the domestic price of gasoline and taking other measures which will improve the public financial position in the long run and also the allocative efficiency of the Mexican economy. Once this has been done, there is every prospect that inflation will have been defeated and not merely suppressed.

Prospects for development. In sum, therefore, the prospects for the Mexican economy are extremely positive. This is an economy which now has a functioning "leading edge", in the shape of manufacturing exports to the rest of North America, and there is considerable potential for growth in many other areas. The public financial position is better than for a generation, and there is evidence that serious investment is at last being undertaken in education and infrastructure. While inflation is still higher than in most advanced industrial countries, it is being reduced and any reduction is likely to be permanent. The government is securely in office and will not change before late 1994; by then it is likely that a political consensus will have re-formed around the measures now being undertaken.

GP

MEXICO CITY. Mexico City (known in the vernacular as México, D.F.) has a population in excess of 18,000,000. It is in some ways an exciting metropolis and an interesting place in which to live. There are good art galleries, an excellent Museum of Anthropology and some excellent cuisine. It is also, however, an ecologist's nightmare.

One problem with Mexico City is the altitude. At just over 7,000 feet Mexico is not as high as some of the Andean cities, but nevertheless there is already a thinning of the oxygen layer. Moreover the mountains which surround the capital make it difficult for the atmospheric pollution over the city to clear; often it is instead blown back into the city itself. Consequently the quality of the air is often bad, with lead, ozone and other contaminants ever-present. Another problem is that the city, once sited on a lake, has now exhausted almost all locally-available supplies of water; water has to be piped into the city from long distance, and sewage has to be pumped out thus creating another health hazard in a part of the world where earth tremors are frequent.

Mexico City has grown rapidly during the century. When serious industrialization got underway, many plants were situated near the federal capital. There were very few planning controls and few attempts were made to resist the siting of even very dirty industrial processes near population centres. Subsequently Mexico City also became the chief beneficiary of the large expansion of the public sector after 1970. The vast majority of bureaucratic positions are in the federal capital.

Efforts to decentralize have so far been sporadic and half-hearted although the issue has at least reached the political agenda in a serious way. Efforts to reduce pollution include restrictions on the use of cars, further expansion of the city underground system (which already has 10 lines), and the shifting of some government offices out of Mexico City.

GP

MONROE DOCTRINE. The "Monroe Doctrine" is the name later given by his countrymen to a statement on US foreign policy made by President James Monroe in his seventh Annual Message to Congress on Dec. 2 1823. Although aimed at Europe it stated three principles which were to govern US foreign policy towards the emerging states of Latin America and their independence struggles: that there should be no further colonization on the American continents or attempt to recover colonies that had become independent (the "no colonization" principle); and that the USA would not interfere with existing colonies (the "non-interference" principle), but that any transfer of colonies between outside powers would be inacceptable (the "no transfer" principle).

These principles were stated in the following terms.

(1) "The American continents, by the free and independent condition which they have assumed and maintain, are henceforth not to be considered as subjects for future colonization by any European powers."

(2) "With the existing colonies or dependencies of any European power we have not interfered and shall not interfere."

(3) "We could not view any interposition for the purpose of oppressing them, or controlling in any other manner their destiny, by any other European power in any other light than as the manifestation of an unfriendly disposition towards the United States."

The idea of making a joint declaration to this effect had in fact initially been raised with Secretary of State John Quincy Adams by the British Foreign Secretary, George Canning, who was concerned that the French government might assist the Spanish to recapture their colonies and be rewarded by transfers of territory. Adams, who was also concerned at reports of Russian interest in California, decided instead to make a unilateral statement, knowing that the coincidence of British interests would ensure that it was upheld without the need to make any concessions to Britain in return. On hearing of the statement, however, Canning arranged for the publication of correspondence between him and the French Foreign Minister, the Prince de Polignac (the "Polignac Memorandum"), from which it became clear that the French, whatever their sympathies, had no intention of becoming involved in such a doubtful enterprise.

It was not until the Mexican War of 1846–48, when the United States became a continental power, that Monroe's message acquired its modern name, and became commonly confused with what was then known as "Manifest Destiny"—the belief that the United States was ultimately destined to stretch not only from the Atlantic to the Pacific, but from the North Pole to the Isthmus of Panama (or, according to some wilder spirits, Cape Horn). In the twentieth century the Doctrine was reinterpreted in the **Roosevelt Corollary** (1904) to justify the United States intervening in various Caribbean states to prevent or pre-empt European states doing so. After this had been abandoned under the Clark Memorandum of 1928 as costly and unproductive, the principle of non-intervention was effectively multilateralized, both by resolutions of successive Pan-American Conferences and by the Charter of the **Organization of American States**. Since however the Doctrine is not, as the USA would wish, a universally accepted principle of international law, but only a statement of principle of US foreign policy, it is accepted by other states only so far as they wish, as witness the alliance between **Cuba** and the Soviet Union after 1961.

PARC

MONTSERRAT. *Population*: 11,900 (1987). *Area*: 102 sq km. *GDP*: EC$129,500,000. *Trade volume*: EC$78,700,000. *Top five trade partners*: USA, UK, Canada, Antigua and Barbuda, St. Kitts (Christopher) and Nevis. Birthrate: 16.8 per 1,000.

Geographical background. A Leeward Island, Montserrat was colonized by the English in 1632 and administered as one of the Leewards from 1871 to 1956. As a member of the West Indies Federation, Montserrat got its Constitution in 1960. Britain retains responsibility for external affairs and security.

Socio–political background. Montserrat is headed by a Governor, has a seven-member Executive Council and a 12-member Legislative Council.

John Osbourne has been Chief Minister since November 1978, when his People's Liberation Movement (PLM) won all seven seats elected by the people.

Outline of political history. William Bramble was, however, the first local to dominate politics, from 1952 to 1970. His son, Austin Bramble, toppled him, becoming Chief Minister as head of the Progressive Democratic Party (PDP). The Bramble name was removed from active politics following the August 1987 elections when Austin lost his seat and announced his retirement. The PDP won one seat while the National Democratic Party, (NDP), formed in 1984, won two seats. One member subsequently resigned to become an independent.

Recent developments—political. Montserrat has suffered two political hiccups recently. In August 1986 there were island-wide strikes in support of an Anglican priest threatened with deportation for opposing plans to legalize gambling. This led to a no-confidence motion in John Osbourne in October. It was defeated.

More damaging has been the virtual dismantling of Montserrat's vibrant offshore services sector following British police investigations into the misuse of licences in 1989. Among the serious allegations was that banks were laundering funds from illegal activities. By the beginning of 1990, most licences were revoked, registration had been suspended, several people charged, including a former Attorney-General sentenced to nine months in March 1990, and there was a constitutional crisis over new provisions. Osbourne finally agreed to a transfer of the offshore sector responsibilities to the British authorities while the British government withdrew proposals that would allow it to impose laws in special circumstances.

Outline of economic development. The breakdown of offshore banking and the devastation of the island by Hurricane Hugo in September 1989 has slowed Montserrat's economic growth. The port, almost all housing and agriculture were destroyed, and the tourist industry hit hard.

Despite these setbacks, Montserrat is well developed economically, recording negligible unemployment in 1989. Tourism contributes some 30 per cent of GDP, with the island attracting a high quality niche market of retiring expatriates and foreigners who own villas.

Current economic situation. With a highly developed infrastructure, the island has become a data processing and computer centre. Electronics assembly is also important, accounting for more than 60 per cent of earnings.

Agriculture (4.3 per cent of GDP in 1987) remains an export earner. Limes, tomatoes and peppers are main exports, along with cattle. There is widespread subsistence farming, although some 24 per cent of the land area is covered by forests. Only some 2,000 people live in the capital Plymouth.

Montserrat has been able to maintain a social security system and comprehensive health care and education sectors. It is a member of the Organization of Eastern Caribbean States and CARICOM.

Prospects for development. It is estimated that the great damage caused by Hurricane Hugo will take at least until 1992 to correct. The construction industry is however benefitting, maintaining maximum levels of employment. With its infrastructure, and with new legislation governing offshore banking, it is expected that Montserrat will at least be able to again attain the 12.4 per cent growth in GDP it achieved in 1988, before Hurricane Hugo struck.

The issue of independence is also to be resolved. A referendum planned for 1990 came to nought in the wake of Hugo. John Osbourne seems determined to take Montserrat into independence although there is no popular support. With rebuilding the country the priority, and the need for financial support a necessity, Montserrat is likely to remain a British dependency for some years to come.

MH

MOVEMENT OF THE REVOLUTIONARY LEFT (Movimiento de la Izquierda Revolucionaria — MIR) (Bolivia). The MIR emerged in the late 1960s from young Christian Democrat and various left groupings in **Bolivia** to form a focus of opposition to **Hugo Bánzer's** *coup* of 1971. While an active force within the student movement, it remained clandestine during the "bánzerato". It contested the 1978 elections within the Democratic Popular Unity (*Unidad Democrática Popular*—UDP) alliance, and in the 1979 and 1980 elections the leader of the MIR, **Jaime Paz Zamora**, was the UDP's vice-presidential candidate. The party was once again forced underground by the military *coup* of July 1980 and lost eight of its leading members in January 1981 when the security forces attacked a house in which they were meeting. In October 1982 the UDP finally took office, although by January 1983 the party had resigned its six seats in Cabinet and opposed the government of **Hernán Siles** although Jaime Paz remained his vice-president. Such manoeuvring within

Congress only accentuated divisions within the party and during this period the MIR split into three antagonistic factions: MIR-Masas (masses), led by Walter Delgadillo; MIR-Bolivia Libre (Free Bolivia), a larger grouping around Antonio Araníbar; and the greater number who continue to support the personalistic politics of Jaime Paz in the MIR-Nueva Mayoría (New Majority). The pragmatism of this latter group has been vindicated by the outcome of the "Patriotic Accord" in which the MIR and the Nationalist Democratic Action party (*Acción Democrática Nacionalista*—ADN) share Cabinet posts under the presidency of Jaime Paz Zamora who took office in 1989.

CS

N

NATIONAL ACTION PARTY (Partido de Acción Nacional-PAN) (Mexico). *The Partido de Acción National*, is the oldest and still (on balance) the single strongest opposition party in **Mexico**. It was set up in 1939 by Gómez Marín, a Catholic intellectual who sought to use his party in order to change the climate of public opinion.

Even from the beginning there was a good deal of ballot rigging against the PAN. This is despite the fact that this party offered very little challenge at a national level. By 1960 its fortunes had significantly declined. Subsequently, however, it began a slow revival, though more as a vehicle for the occasional protest vote than because the electorate as a whole supported the PAN's variety of political Catholicism. The PAN was, however, relatively successful among the middle classes of various provincial towns—mostly though not exclusively in the north of the country.

Following the economic crisis and bank nationalization of 1982, the PAN appears to have increased its support considerably. It won municipal elections in a number of northern towns during 1983, as a result of which the **Institutional Revolutionary Party** returned to a policy of systematically rigging the ballot against it. In 1988 the PAN's presidential candidate, Manuel Clouthier, won just over 17 per cent of the vote at national level; the party probably suffered to some extent from the additional challenge to the system mounted by Cuauhtémoc Cárdenas from the Left. Nevertheless the party continued to poll well in certain towns, notably in Guadalajara where it won a clear majority of Congressional seats.

In 1989 the PAN finally won a governorship, in the state of Baja California Norte; this is the first time that the PRI has conceded defeat in a governorship election. However there is still no convincing evidence that the PAN is a serious challenger to the PRI at a national level.

GP

NATIONAL AUTONOMOUS UNIVERSITY (Universidad Nacional Autónoma de México-UNAM). During the 1920s and 1930s UNAM was considered to be one of the great Revolutionary achievements. It provided tangible evidence of the new regime's commitment to education, while providing something of material benefit from the still small but expanding metropolitan middle class. It was also a place from which a selected few from that minority of students supportive of the Revolution could be recruited into politics. During the past generation, however, UNAM has played a very different role. Its main problem is that it has become far too big. If one includes evening classes, there are some 400,000 students enrolled. Meanwhile government money has failed to keep pace with this expansion. It is still true that there are serious academics and good academic departments at UNAM, but there can be no doubt that there has been some deterioration in quality. Now most Mexican parents who can afford to do so send their children to the private universities and thence for post-graduate training abroad. As academic qualifications, particularly at post-graduate level from foreign universities, become increasingly important to advancement within the government so UNAM has less to offer an ambitious student who has the opportunity of going elsewhere.

Attempts by the university authorities to impose serious admission standards for entry into the UNAM have been strongly resisted by students; this issue sparked off considerable student unrest during 1986–87. Graduation standards, however, are somewhat higher than standards for admission with the result that a very high proportion of UNAM students do not proceed to graduation. Some of those who do can still find jobs outside with sufficient prospects to give them a chance of élite status. But the UNAM is no longer the place for gilded youth.

GP

NATIONAL LIBERATION ALLIANCE (Aliança Nacional Libertadora—ANL) (Brazil). The ANL was a mass movement, organized in 1935, as **Brazil**'s version of the Popular Front. The honorary leader of the ANL was nominated, on March 30, 1935, in a public rally in Rio de Janeiro, by a young law student Carlos **Lacerda**, later to be the most severe critic of Vargas, one of the conspirators behind the *coup* of 1964, and governor of the state of Guanabara. The man nominated was Luís Carlos Prestes, famed leader of the "Prestes Column" after 1924 and now a Communist, recently returned from Moscow.

The ANL sought to unite the left across the country, with fierce attacks on Brazil's foreign debts and the power of imperialist capitalism, but its main appeal was resistance to fascism. It also embraced a comprehensive reform programme, including an end to *latifundismo*, the system of large land-holdings, seeking rural as well as urban support. By July 1935 it claimed 400,000 members. Even allowing a quarter of this claim, represented a huge jump in left-wing mobilization at the national level.

The ANL seemed to offer promise of successful left-wing mobilization, urging much-needed reforms. Instead, it ended in disaster, following a series of ill-judged, unco-ordinated military risings, between Nov. 23–27, 1935 in Rio de Janeiro, Recife and Natal. These mostly sprang from local issues, but allowed the government to dramatize their significance as major "Communist" threats. The result was a massive wave of arrests and prison sentences, which, effectively, decimated the political left and made it impotent for the next decade.

PF

NATIONAL LIBERATION PARTY (Partido de Liberacíon Nacional—PLN) (Costa Rica). The National Liberation Party of **Costa Rica** from its inception was explicitly anti-communist, evolving out of the Social Democratic Party (*Partido Social Democrático*—PSD) in October 1951. The PSD had arisen victorious from the civil war and the defeat of the Popular Vanguard Party (*Partido Vanguardia Popular*—PVP) formerly the communists, and the National Republican Party (*Partido Republicano Nacional*—PRN).

The former had supported the latter party in the progressive social legislation prior to 1944. Whilst the PLN repressed PVP and labour organizations, José Figueres Ferrer (the party founder and first PLN president, 1953–58) developed an autocratic yet populist politics albeit within the democratic framework. The PLN's membership of the Socialist International has not prevented its hostility towards the governments of Arbenz in Guatemala, nor of the FSLN in Nicaragua; its outlawing of the PVP in Costa Rica, nor neoliberal leanings.

Since the late 1970s the PLN has been informed by a strengthening dedication to neoliberalism and a commitment, partly to satisfy IMF conditionality, to cut the public sector which it had done so much to develop (at the end of the 1970s, 20 per cent of employment was in the public sector). Following the presidency of Rodrigo Carazo Odio of the National Unity (*Unidad Nacional*, 1978–82) in which a singular foreign policy of non-alignment, as opposed to neutralism was pursued, the PLN government of Luis Alberto Monge (1982–86) reverted to a strongly anti-Nicaraguan, anti-Soviet position and one more amenable to IMF conditions. With the death of Figueres, the suspension of former president Daniel Oduber on drugs related dealings in June 1990 and the PUSC election victory, the face of the PLN looks set to change in the 1990s.

JCJS

NATIONAL PARTY (Partido Nacional—PN) (Honduras). Since its formation in 1923 the PN has contested power with the **Liberal Party of Honduras** (*Partido Liberal de Honduras*—PLH). After World War II it was first in power in 1957 and in 1965 the party held a majority of seats in the national assembly and supported the military candidate for the presidency who had overthrown the Liberal government of 1963. The party has been associated with large landed interests and likened to the civilian wing of the armed forces.

Following the crushing electoral defeat of 1981 the party divided into various factions. These were led by Ricardo Zúñiga (whose faction fought the 1981 election), Juan Pablo Urrutia, Mario Rivera López and Rafael Leonardo Callejas. The latter, a right-wing old-style *caudillo*, won the presidential election of November 1989 ending eight years of Liberal rule.

LLP

NATIONAL PARTY (Partido Nacional—PN or Blancos) (Uruguay). The National (or *Blanco*) Party originated as a federalist party of landowners, merchants and senior clergy supporting General Manuel Oribe in the *Guerra Grande* against the **Colorado Party** (1835–51). It was the only substantial opposition grouping during the 93 years of *Colorado* domination of Uruguayan politics after 1865. But in 1958 factional in-fighting in the Colorado Party, the defection of a factional leader to the National Party, and the maladministration and corruption associated with the Colorado-dominated government resulted in a sweeping *Blanco* victory. The death of Dr Luis Alberto de Herrera, the leader who had dominated the *Blancos* since the 1930s, the resulting division between the so-called *Eje* (Axis) and Ubedoxia factions, the continuing economic *malaise* and the desire to restore executive leadership gave the *Colorados* a majority in 1966 and elected General Oscar Gestido to the restored presidency. The main beneficiary of the association of the *Colorados* with the military and military-backed regimes of 1973–85, the *Blanco* leader Wilson Ferreira Aldunate, was however, arrested in 1984 on his return from exile and so deprived of the chance to contest the 1985 elections. He died before he had a second chance.

SAC

NATIONAL PEASANTS CONFEDERATION (Confederación Nacional de Campesinos — CNC) (Mexico). The CNC was set up under President **Lázaro Cárdenas.** It has continued in existence until this day, although it is not an especially radical or dynamic organization. It remains a significant source of patronage for rural Mexicans.

The dramatic period of land reform in Mexican history came to an end around 1940. There have been periods since then during which presidents have appeared to favour a renewed redistribution of land, notably under Adolfo López Mateos during 1959–60 and under Luís Echeverría during 1974–76. The CNC benefitted on both occasions. However most Mexican presidents, including all of those in office since 1976, have taken the view that land reform is no solution to rural poverty: the problems of rural over-population and low rural productivity have to be tackled in a different way. Moreover around three quarters of Mexico's population is now urban, so that agrarian questions do not have the relative importance which they did have during the heyday of the CNC in the 1930s.

Meanwhile the CNC itself is a very docile organization. It has been under effective governmental control at almost all times since 1940. What it has done has been to contribute to the government's political strength in rural areas by providing ready-made organization for the official party (of which the CNC is formally a part).

GP

NATIONALIST DEMOCRATIC ACTION PARTY (Acción Nacionalista Democrática — ADN) (Bolivia). The Nationalist Democratic Action Party was founded in 1979 by General Hugo Bánzer Suárez, former President of **Bolivia**, following his overthrow the previous year by his protégé, Air Force General Juan Pereda Asbún. With extreme Right views and the slogan "Peace, Order, Work", it evoked support from the business interests of Santa Cruz, as well as a surprising degree of enthusiasm among the rural peasantry. It won 13 Congressional seats in its first election in 1979, and in 1980 won 30 seats and 16 per cent of the poll in support of the former dictator. Over the next three years the size of its support and the fact that none of the traditional parties would enter into an electoral alliance with it led to extreme political instability and repeated military *coups*. In elections held in 1985 its support had climbed to 29 per cent, higher than any other party, in the inconclusive first round, but once more the rival parties combined to defeat it. By 1989 its support had fallen back to 22 per cent, behind that of the ruling **National Revolutionary Movement** (*Movimiento Nacional Revolucionario—MNR*), and Congress chose the third placed candidate, **Jaime Paz Zamora** of the **Movement of the Revolutionary Left** (*Moviemiento de la Izquierda Revolucionaria—MIR*) as the new President.

PARC

NATIONALIST REPUBLICAN ALLIANCE (Alianza Republicana Nacionalista—ARENA) (El Salvador). The National Republican Alliance (ARENA) of **El Salvador** was founded by ex-Salvadorean Army officer and landowner Major Roberto D'Aubuisson in September 1981, primarily as a response to the failure of the institutionalist National Reconciliation Party (Partido de Conciliación Nacional—PCN) to effect and ensure political control favourable to land-owning interests. ARENA is a party of the far-right, vehemently opposed to any liberal political reform although sympathetic to neo-liberal economics. Many of the party's patrons and sponsors have been associated with death-squad activity (including D'Aubuisson himself, who is widely believed to have ordered the assassination of Archbishop Oscar Romero in March 1980, amongst many others), although the current leader (and El Salvador's President) Alfredo Cristiani has sought to present ARENA as a more libertarian and less reactionary party in order to present an acceptable face particularly towards the United States of America. The old-guard of ARENA still maintain an effective veto on the government's ability to negotiate with the FMLN, particularly in view of the Assembly majority held by the party.

JCJS

NATIONALIST REVOLUTIONARY MOVEMENT (Movimiento Nacionalista Revolucionario — MNR) (Bolivia). Formed in 1941, the MNR participated in the populist government of Gualberto Villarroel (1943–46) and won the 1951 election, though was prevented by the military from taking office. In 1952 it was installed in power following a national insurrection and established its longstanding and widespread support for three key pieces of legislation: agrarian reform, nationalization of the mining sector, and universal adult suffrage. The wide spectrum of political interests within the MNR became more evident and more conflictive as faction leaders struggled over the line of succession for the presidency. In 1959 the first breakaway occurred as Walter Guevara Arce, on the right of the party, launched the Authentic Revolutionary Party (*Partido Revolucionario Auténtico*—PRA), while in 1963 Juan Lechín Oquendo, the trotskyist leader of the miners' union, established the Revolutionary Party of the Nationalist Left (*Partido Revolucíonario de la Izquierda Nacionalista*—PRIN). **Víctor Paz'** support for **Hugo Bánzer's** seizure of power in 1971 provoked **Hernán Siles** to form the Nationalist Revolutionary Movement of the Left (*Movimiento Nacionalista Revolucionario de Izquierda*—MNRI), and secured victory over his arch rival Paz in the elections of 1979 and 1980. While the MNRI largely disintegrated after it took power in 1982, the MNR of Víctor Paz not only remained united around its leader during its 1985–89 period in office, but went on to win the 1989 election with Gonzalo Sánchez de Lozada as its presidential candidate. Only the "Patriotic Accord" between **Jaime Paz Zamora** and Hugo Bánzer prevented the MNR from enjoying a further period of government.

CS

NETHERLANDS ANTILLES. *Population*: 280,000 (1989). *Area*: 993 sq km. *GDP*: US$1,452 million. *Trade volume*: $1,872 million. *Top five trading partners*: USA, Bahamas, Venezuela, Netherlands, Bermuda. *Life expectancy*: 58 (men); 65 (women).

Geographical background. The Netherlands Antilles comprise five islands (six before 1986) in the Caribbean Sea which are part of the Kingdom of the Netherlands. Curaçao, Bonaire (and before 1986 Aruba) lie in the Southern Caribbean, off the north coast of Venezuela. The official languages are Dutch and the local creole, Papiamento. St Maarten, St Eustatius and Saba are in the north-eastern Caribbean and are English-speaking. The islands represent Dutch colonial acquisitions in the seventeenth century. Slavery was abolished in 1868. The islands were granted internal autonomy in 1954.

Socio–political background. The Netherlands Antilles is a parliamentary democracy, with a two-tier system of representation at island and at federal level. The Netherlands appoints a governor who is responsible for the islands' defence and foreign affairs. A Dutch naval vessel and detachment of marines is stationed on the islands. The federal parliament (or Staten) consists of 23 elected members. Executive power is exercised by a Prime Minister and Cabinet. A minister plenipotentiary represents the Antilles in the Netherlands Cabinet. Each island has its own lieutentant-governor, elected island council and executive. Since 1986 Aruba has had its own governor, 21-member elected parliament and plenipotentiary minister.

Outline of political history. Strong island loyalties and the voting system used in the Netherlands Antilles have led to the development of island-based political parties and the formation of multi-party coalitions to reach the two-thirds majority in the Staten required to form a government. The existence of parties strongly supporting their own island interests, instead of that of the federation as a whole, has often paralyzed decision-making, as for example during the 1970s when the People's Electoral Movement (*Movimento Electoral di Pueblo*—MEP) campaigned for separate status for Aruba. The fortunes of individual political parties have also fluctuated over the years. Curaçao, as the seat of government and the largest island, has formed the basis of Netherlands Antilles governments. Whereas the Democratic Party was the bedrock of coalition governments in the 1960s and early 1970s, so this role was taken by the social democratic New Antilles Movement (*Movimento Antiyas Nobo*—MAN) in the late 1970s and early 1980s and by the centre-right National People's Party (*Partido Nashonal di Pueblo*—PNP) in the late 1980s. In September 1984 the PNP's leader. Maria Liberia-Peters, became the territory's first woman Prime Minister.

Recent developments—political. In 1986 the island of Aruba separated from the remainder of the Netherlands Antilles. The seats in the Staten were redistributed among the other islands, giving the smaller islands their own representation for the first time. In Aruba the MEP lost power to a four-party coalition, only returning to power in elections in 1989. Independence is still planned for Aruba in 1996, but consideration of the problems involved is likely to lead to a re-evaluation of the plans and a referendum.

The departure of Aruba failed to heal the differences between the remaining islands in the federation. During 1988 St Maarten, under the Democratic Party—St Maarten leader Claude Wathey, began agitating for separation from Curaçao and eventual independence. In 1987 Wathey had withdrawn his party's support from the coalition government led by the leader of MAN, Don Martina. The government subsequently collapsed in March 1988 after losing support over a plan to dismiss 1,400 public sector employees. A new coalition was formed in May, led by Liberia-Peters, with a one-member majority in the Staten.

Elections to the *Staten* in March 1990 led to the existing Liberia-Peters administration being reformed, comprising the PNP and the Workers' Liberation Front/Independent Socialists (*Frente Obrero di Liberashon/Soshal Independiente*—FOL-SI) from Curaçao; the Bonaire Patriotic Union (*Union Patriotico Bonairiano*—UPB) from Bonaire; the Democratic Party-St Eustatius; the Windward Islands Patriotic Movement (WIPM) from Saba, and the St Maarten's People's Alliance, but this time excluding Wathey's Democratic Party—St Maarten, which lost one of its seats. The opposition representation in the Staten comprised the Democratic Party-Curaçao, MAN, Nos Patria, and the Democratic Party—St Maarten. In September Liberia-Peters announced her intention to hold non-binding referenda on the issue of constitutional changes (*see Prospects for development*).

Outline of economic development. The economic development of the Netherlands Antilles during the twentieth century has been based principally on the refining and transhipment of petroleum, and more recently, on financial services. The discovery and exploitation of petroleum in Venezuela led to the construction of large refineries in Curaçao and Aruba in the early twentieth century, which developed to provide a major source of income and employment for the Netherlands Antilles. In 1985 Exxon closed the refinery on Aruba (a major shock to the economy just prior to Aruba achieving separate status) and later than year Shell announced the closure of the Curaçao refinery. The island government on Curaçao managed to keep the facility open by buying the plant for a nominal sum and leasing it to the Venezuelan state oil company Petróleos de Venezuela (PDVSA). The Venezuelan government, worried about possible instability on neighbouring Curaçao should the refinery close, agreed to intervene and has turned an initially loss-making plant into a profitable enterprise. Other enterprises connected with the oil industry, such as bunkering facilities and the dry dock in Curaçao, have also been forced to reorganize themselves since 1985.

The financial sector on Curaçao developed during the 1950s, taking advantage of tax treaties to create a "tax window" for US corporations to escape tax for investments in Europe through Eurobonds. In 1985 nearly half of Curaçao's government revenue was derived from financial services. In 1984 this lucrative source of income for the Antilles was threatened when the USA abolished withholding tax payable to non-residents. This was followed by the abolition of the dual tax treaty itself in 1985.

Current economic situation. The Netherlands Antilles economy continued to readjust to the decline in its two principal activities. Both the refining sector and financial services suffered greatly during the 1980s from the fall in the price of oil and from the end of the advantageous tax treaty with the USA, leading to a serious shortfall in income for the island governments. Unemployment on the islands increased. Wide-ranging austerity measures, including wage cuts for public servants, redundancies and reductions in public expenditure, have been a feature of government economic policy in the late 1980s, particularly on Curaçao where the island government has a large budget deficit estimated at NAF 196,800,000 in 1990. High levels of aid from the Dutch government have been important in supporting the government in Curaçao. Gross domestic product per head, which was measured as one of the highest in the region during the 1970s, has declined in real terms during the 1980s.

The financial sector has continued to provide revenue, however, from the many offshore banks and companies registered in Curacao, while ways have been sought to diversify into other areas. The government has also sought to ensure that the sector's good reputation is maintained. In February 1990 new regulations were passed by parliament to make it more difficult to launder money in the islands, including tighter controls on transactions and customer identification. A new free-trade zone was established in Willemstad to help boost manufacturing and exports.

Tourism is being developed on both Curaçao and Aruba to compensate for the decline in traditional revenue areas. Curaçao's former attraction as a shopping destination for Venezuelan visitors was dramatically ended in 1983 by the devaluation of the Venezuelan currency. Since 1986 the Aruban government has embarked on a large-scale hotel construction programme and the number of tourist arrivals has risen dramatically.

St Maarten, separated goegraphically and linguistically from Curaçao, has, in recent years, developed a vibrant economy based on tourism. The island has became a major tourist destination, particularly for visitors from the United States. Tourist arrivals reached 488,720 in 1989. Construction of hotels, casinos and duty-free shops has flourished unhindered by planning controls. This rapid explosion of growth has also led to an increase in crime and fears about the possible use of the island for drug trafficking, taking advantage of its customs-free status, and for the laundering of drug profits.

The three remaining smaller islands, Saba, St Eustatius and Bonaire, are constrained in development by their small populations, limited transport and tourist accommodation facilities. EC and Dutch aid has been provided for the expansion of the airports on Bonaire and St Eustatius.

Prospects for development. The future of the islands remains uncertain. The decision in 1990 of the Netherlands Minister for Antillean and Aruban Affairs, Ernst Hirsh Ballin, to seek a new "commonwealth" arrangement between the islands and the Netherlands, rather than push the islands towards independence, involves further compromises between the islands. The Dutch government has often viewed the islands as a liability, but has been worried by the example of Suriname's instability since its independence from the Netherlands in 1976. The commonwealth idea would have the advantage of ensuring the islands' political and economic stability, giving their citizens Dutch citizenship (thus stemming immigration), and allowing the islands access to the single European market post-1992. Such a relationship would, however, still have to overcome the rivalries and misgivings between the islands, with the larger islands unwilling to accept the burden of supporting their smaller and poorer neighbours. A division of the Antilles into two groups, as proposed by Hirsh Ballin, based on Curaçao in the south and St Maarten, would be unpopular with all groups. The larger islands care little about the smaller and poorer islands, especially as they contribute virtually nothing to the federal budget, while Bonaire, St Eustatius and Saba fear dominance at the hands of Curaçao and St Maarten.

LP

NEVES DE ALMEIDA, TANCREDO. In January 1985, Tancredo Neves was elected, indirectly, by an Electoral College, as the first civilian president of **Brazil** since the military *coup* of 1964 had ended the government of **João Goulart**. His election, as candidate of the Democratic Alliance, formed by the **Party of the Brazilian Democratic Movement** (*Partido do Movimento Democrático Brasileiro*—PMDB) and the PFL, a break-away group of the Social Democratic Party PDS, was greeted with enormous public enthusiasm and celebration. Tancredo's presidency, after 21 years of military-backed government, was seen as promising a new start, introducing a "New Republic". The cheering and celebration quickly died away, when, on the eve of his inauguration, scheduled for March 15, 1985, Tancredo Neves became ill. The whole nation watched in sorrow and compassion, until Tancredo died on April 22. This was the day when Brazilians remembered another *mineiro* hero, *Tiradentes*, Joaquim José de Silva Xavier, who had been born in the same town as Tancredo, and hanged in 1792, for leading an independence insurrection against the Portuguese.

In the long process of *abertura*, or political opening, Tancredo Neves had emerged as the ideal candidate of "conciliation", a quality which characterized the political tradition of Minas Gerais. He was a man of the centre, even to the right of centre, so acceptable to the conservative political class and the leaders of the armed forces. At the same time, he had remained true to his earlier allegiance to **Getúlio Vargas** and the PSD, had never compromised with the *coup* of 1964 and had immediately joined the Brazilian Democratic Movement *(Movimento Democrático Brasileiro*—MDB) after its formation in 1965.

Trancredo Neves was born in March 1910 in the colonial town of São João del Rey. He studied law in Belo Horizonte and, in 1930, supported the Liberal Alliance which brought Vargas to power. In 1933, he joined the Progressive Party (*Partido Progressista*—PP), formed by Olegário Maciel and others, in preparation for the Constitutent Assembly of 1934. He became *vereador*, or councillor, in São João del Rey in 1935, till the declaration of the *Estado Novo* in 1937.

Tancredo maintained close links with Benedito Valadares, Vargas' *interventor* in Minas Gerais, joining the PSD after its foundation on April 8, 1945.

In January 1945, Tancredo Neves was elected as state deputy, becoming deeply embroiled in the complex political struggles of Minas Gerais, until, in 1950, he was elected as federal deputy of the PSD, on the same day as **Juscelino Kubitschek** was elected as governor of Minas Gerais. In 1953, he was appointed as Minister of Justice by Vargas, remaining close to Vargas until his death in 1954. He then worked hard to help the election of Kubitschek as president in 1955. After various posts in banking in Minas Gerais, he became State Secretary of Finance in July 1958.

In 1960, Tancredo suffered the most disappointing set-back in his career, when he was beaten by Magalhães Pinto of the UDN in the election of state governor in Minas Gerais, when **Jânio Quadros** was also elected as Federal president, with Goulart as Vice-president. After Quadros' resignation, Tancredo Neves went to Montevideo to discuss with Goulart the "parliamentary" system, to which the military leaders had agreed, in order to avoid the real danger of civil war. Tancredo returned on Sept. 1, 1961, successful in his mission, and, next day, Congress approved Goulart's nomination of Tancredo as Prime Minister.

On Jan. 6, 1963, a plebiscite voted full presidential powers for Goulart, and, in February 1963, Tancredo was chosen as the leader of the Congressional majority formed by the PSD and the **Brazilian Labour Party** (*Partido Trabalhista Brasileiro*—PTB). He worked hard, but unsuccessfully, to persuade Goulart and others not to provoke a military-led reaction in 1964.

In 1965, when most representatives of the PSD in Minas Gerais joined the National Renovating Alliance (ARENA), Tancredo joined the opposition *bloc* of the MDB. He was re-elected as Federal deputy in 1966 and 1970. In 1974, he declined an invitation to be MDB candidate for the Senate, preferring to stay in the Chamber, playing a conciliatory rôle in internal disputes within the MDB. In 1978 he was elected Senator and, in 1979, with the renewal of the multi-party system, helped to found the Popular Party (*Partido Popular*—PP), together with a group of right-of-centre politicians and businessmen.

The party wanted, among other things, a Constitutent Assembly, revision of the National Security Law, and protection for small and medium-sized landholdings. Tancredo became president of the PP in June 1981, but, when faced, in November, with the regime's new electoral "package", including the *voto vinculado*, he urged the fusion of all opposition groups under one banner. The PP joined the PMDB and, in February 1982, Tancredo was elected as national vice-president of the party.

With the elections of November 1982, Tancredo became governor of Minas Gerais, an ambition he had long cherished, but as the process of *abertura* unfolded, he entered into negotiations with other politicians, including the president of the PMDB, **Ulysses Guimarães**, and prominent figures in the PDS, the government party, and military leaders, With Ulysses, he agreed that if the next election for president were direct, Ulysses would be candidate: if indirect, Tancredo. With the military leaders, he reached a secret pact that provided for the election for the Constituent Assembly not to be separate from that for Congress, so ensuring a more conservative assembly.

Excitement concerning the election of January 1985 was intense, right up to the day of voting, but, even as early as September 1984, there was evidence that the political interests behind the Democratic Alliance, of the PMDB and the PFL, had guaranteed Tancredo's victory. Otherwise, he would never have given up his long-coveted governorship of Minas Gerais.

Tancredo's death in March 1985 left confusion and many open questions. He would have brought to the presidency authority, legitimacy and strong party and Congressional support, none of which could be bequeathed to his successor, the Vice-President and former leader of the PDS, **José Sarney**. His death also deprived the process of *abertura* of its most skilful and respected candidate of conciliation.

PF

NEW BRAZIL PLAN. By the start of 1990, after the failure of **José Sarney**'s **Summer Plan** and Autumn Plan of 1989, it was clear to everyone in **Brazil** that the most urgent task facing the new president must be to curb inflation, **Fernando Collor de Mello** shared this view. His first act on taking office in March 1990, was to present a new stabilization package, which went far beyond any of its predecessors, both in its range and in its boldness of conception. This was the New Brazil Plan, often referred to as the Collor Plan. The new Plan sought to reduce corruption and tax evasion and to cut the size of the public sector, by eliminating various ministries, by reducing the number of public employees and by privatizing State enterprises. The measures also aimed to liberalize imports. It introduced, or reintroduced, another new currency, once again to be called the *cruzeiro*, together with a floating exchange rate.

The centrepiece of the package, which stunned all those affected, was a fierce liquidity squeeze. The Plan placed a limit of Cr 50,000 (about US$1,000) on bank and savings accounts withdrawals for 18 months, and a 20 per cent limit on withdrawals of funds tied up in the "overnight" market. It also de-indexed wages and imposed a whole series of new taxes on personal wealth, shares and gold holdings.

The target, in the public sector, was to translate a deficit of 8 per cent of GDP, projected earlier in the year, into a surplus of 1.2 per cent by the end of 1990. This would be financed by the privatization programme, tighter tax administration, increased revenues, especially from the tax on financial operations, and the ending of subsidies.

The proposal to sequestrate, even temporarily, some US$100,000 million, or, roughly, the equivalent of 30 per cent of Brazil's GDP, from bank and savings accounts and overnight deposits, was one which a leading left-wing politician said would have brought tanks onto the streets, had it been proposed by the left. Minister Cardoso de Mello, at the same time, was quick to point out that 90 per cent of Brazilians would not be affected by the measure, since they did not have funds which would be touched by the Plan. Collor, meanwhile, was able to derive credit from the fact that he was making those who previously had profited from inflation now pay for it.

The ending of inflation was not as easy a task as Collor seemed to think. By November 1990, it was again running at about 19 per cent a month, and still at around 20 per cent in February 1991. In that month the government imposed a freeze on prices and wages, in a new package of firm measures, Collor Plan II. This included a 47 per cent increase in fuel prices and up to 71 per cent on utility charges. A general reaction was that the new package marked the end of the New Brazil or Collor Plan. Still, it seemed, Brazilian inflation was resisting attempts at shock treatment.

PF

NEW PROGRESSIVE PARTY (Partido Nuevo Progresista — PNP) (Puerto Rico). Founded in 1968 as a successor to the Republican Statehood Party (*Partido del Estado Republicano*—PER), which had been led since 1952 by Luis A. Ferré, a businessman who favoured statehood. A split in the PPD allowed the PNP to win the governorship in 1968 and it held the post again between 1976 and 1984. The PNP is generally conservative and favours Puerto Rico becoming a state of the USA. The PNP has traditionally gained much of its support from the San Juan metropolitan area.

LP

NICARAGUA. *Area*: 119,000 sq km. *Population*: 3,700,000 (1989). *GDP*: US$2,967 million (1988). *Trade volume:* imports: $791,000,000 (1988). exports: $236,000,000 (1988); *Top five trade partners* (1988): exports: Canada, West Germany, Guatemala, Japan, USSR; imports: USSR, Cuba, Netherlands, Italy, Spain. *Defence spending*: $457,000,000 (1986). *Education spending*: $175,000,000 (1986). *Urban population (as percentage of total)*: 59.4 (1988). *Birthrate*: 41 per 1,000 (1988). *Life expectancy*: 62 (men); 65 (women) (1988).

Geographical background. Nicaragua has a long history of violence between warring political factions and autocratic rule. For over a century Nicaragua's strategic position on the Central American isthmus has provoked US intervention. Even today, with its huge lakes and river network, Nicaragua is seen as the most likely site of a sea-level canal between the Atlantic and Pacific oceans. A US expeditionary force was sent to Nicaragua in 1912 partly to ensure that the Panama canal would retain its monopoly on inter-oceanic shipping. This intervention led directly to the establishment of the Somoza family dictatorship which lasted from 1936 to 1979.

Outline of political history. On Feb. 25, 1990, against all expectations, the ruling **Sandinista** party, the **Sandinista Front for National Liberation** (*Frente Sandinista de Liberación Nacional*—FSLN) lost the presidential and general elections in Nicaragua. The president, **Daniel Ortega**, was beaten into second place by Sra Violeta de Chamorro, the widow of Pedro Joaquín Chamorro, a campaigning newspaper owner who had been murdered in January 1978 on the orders of the previous president and dictator, **Anastasio Somoza**.

The Sandinistas had been in power for over 10 years. They won power in 1979 in an insurrection against Somoza, whose family had ruled Nicaragua since 1936. They took their name from Augusto César Sandino, a guerrilla leader who had fought against the occupying American marine force in the late 1920s and early 1930s. Sandino was subsequently murdered on the orders of Anastasio Somoza, the father of the dictator ousted by the Sandinistas.

When they won power in 1979 the Sandinistas were supported by the right-wing opposition to the dictatorship which had earlier tried in vain to reach a negotiated solution with Somoza in order to forestall an outright revolutionary victory. After the Sandinista victory, the right moved into opposition. Many of them joined or became supporters of the contras, the guerrilla force armed and financed by the Reagan administration. Violeta Chamorro herself was a member of the first revolutionary junta. Her resignation in April 1980, was one of the first clear signs of the split between the Sandinistas and their right-wing allies.

The Sandinistas came to power determined not to repeat the mistakes of the Cuban revolution. Nevertheless there was a constant tension between their professed pluralism and their revolutionary socialist rhetoric. They did not resort to wholesale expropriation but constantly wielded the threat of confiscation against recalcitrant landowners and businessmen. The banks and foreign trade were nationalized, however, giving the government control over export agriculture—coffee, sugar, cotton and cattle.

The contras were initially former members of

Somoza's National Guard who fled to Honduras in 1979. In March 1981 the Reagan administration authorized the first CIA operations against Nicaragua. The ranks of the contras were subsequently swelled by peasants unhappy with the collective direction taken by the agrarian reform and by Miskito indians from the Atlantic coast angry at Sandinista high-handedness. By 1983 Sandinista policy was dominated by the contra war. Realizing that they had to have popular support if they were repel the contras, the Sandinistas tried to rectify early mistakes, modifying the agrarian reform to permit individual ownership of land and approving substantial autonomy for the Atlantic Coast. They maintained as far as possible the innovations in education and health which made a dramatic impact on the lives of ordinary people. Nevertheless there was also resentment against the arrogant, "we-know-best" attitude of so many government functionaries which told against them in the elections.

The Sandinistas' military campaign against the contras was successful and by 1987 they were, in military terms, a spent force. But by then the damage, human and economic, was done, and they still remained a threat. Estimates of war damage range from $1,500 million to $4,000 million. In 1987 defence took over 60 per cent of the national budget. In 1988 inflation reached 33, 000 per cent. Nicaragua was running an annual trade deficit of $600,000,000.

The measures taken by the Sandinistas to bring the money supply under control were extremely painful. There were dismissals throughout the public sector and goods which had long since vanished from the shops reappeared at unaffordable prices. GDP fell by 11.7 per cent (21.5 per cent *per capita*) between 1987 and 1990 to under $300 per head, putting Nicaragua on a par with Haiti, and unemployment and underemployment rose to 40 per cent. In the late 1980s the advances made in health and literacy were eroded by lack of resources. By the end of 1990 Nicaragua's foreign debt was $10,000 million.

Current developments — political. Chamorro's 14-party coalition, the National Opposition Union (*Unión Nacional Opositora* — UNO), including two Communist parties, was united only by opposition to Sandinista rule. Indeed, since winning power, the UNO parties have not been able to agree upon a new name for their coalition. Chamorro herself was chosen as the UNO candidate, not for her political skills, but because she was maternal figure widely seen as being above political strife, a devout traditional Catholic, the widow of an anti-Somoza martyr and because, as owner of the shrill opposition paper, *La Prensa*, she had impeccable anti-Sandinista credentials.

In an election with a turn-out of 86.3 per cent, Chamorro won 55 per cent of the vote to Ortega's 41 per cent. She inherited a country, however, which institutionally had been created anew by the Sandinistas: they had given Nicaragua a new constitution, a land reform, a new army, a police force and a fair electoral system. With their 40 per cent of the vote, the Sandinistas remain the largest single political movement in the country. Their 39 seats in the National Assembly, against the UNO's 51, are sufficient to block constitutional reform.

As part of the agreement ensuring a peaceful transfer of power to Chamorro on April 25, the army command structure, with General Humberto Ortega, Daniel Ortega's brother, as commander-in-chief, was to remain intact, while the size of the army was reduced drastically from over 80,000 to around 30,000. Though committed to defend the constitution, the armed forces, created by and loyal to the FSLN, will resist any concerted move against the Sandinistas by the new government. The chief negotiators of the agreement were Humberto Ortega and Antonio Lacayo, Violeta Chamorro's son-in-law, a pragmatic political moderate whose chief concern is revitalizing the Nicaraguan economy.

The election offered the Nicaraguans a clear choice: continuing war, scarcity and US hostility with the Sandinistas, tempered by a measure of national dignity, or an end to the war and the opening of the purse strings of the US treasury with Chamorro. The war did come to an end under Chamorro but her election brought only $350,000,000 in US aid into the country in 1990, much less than the $800,000,000 needed, on UNO's own calculations, to reactivate the economy.

Current economic situation. Throughout 1990 the Nicaraguan economy remained in crisis. Severe cuts in public expenditure caused hardship and unemployment but did not succeed in stabilizing the economy. Inflation to the end of October 1990 was 3,200 per cent compared to 1,700 per cent in all of 1989. The Sandinistas had been able to count on a steady inflow of aid, mainly from the Soviet bloc. With Central America now sliding down the international political agenda, there is no sign that the United States is prepared to underwrite the new Nicaragua in the same way. Now the Chamorro government is urgently seeking new sources of foreign aid.

Chamorro also faces the problem of satisfying the expectations of her followers, notably the demobilized contras who have returned penniless to Nicaragua. In the second half of 1990 the rank-and-file contras, mostly peasants from the central region of Nicaragua, took over public buildings and blocked roads to press for more generous treatment and for land. They also demanded the dismissal of Humberto Ortega as head of the army and the sacking of the interior minister and a large tract of territory as a "development pole", a virtual state-within-a-state. They are backed by the vice-president, Virgilio Godoy, and the big business association, the Superior Council for Private Enterprise (*Consejo Superior de la Empresa Privada*—COSEP), who want to rid Nicaragua of all traces of Sandinismo, and landowners returning from abroad who want their old estates back.

Prospects for development. The stability of Nicaragua now depends on the ability of Chamorro's moderate Cabinet, headed by Antonio Lacayo, to fend off the more extreme demands of Virgilio Godoy and COSEP. Ironically her staunchest allies in the attempt to halt the extreme polarization of Nicaraguan politics are the Sandinistas. If the threat of renewed civil war is averted, they stand a good chance of returning to power in the next elections in 1996.

GG

NICARAGUAN CANAL, PROPOSALS FOR. The waters of Lake Nicaragua and the San Juan River have been used to cross the isthmus since Spanish times and a route for an inter-oceanic canal was surveyed by US engineers in the early 1870s. Following its acquisition of the **Panama Canal Zone** the US government acquired sole rights to the rival route by the Bryan-Chamorro Treaty of 1914. A proposal to construct a sea level canal using nuclear explosives was mooted by Anastasio Somoza Debayle but strongly opposed by **Costa Rica** on environmental grounds.

PARC/SAC

NORIEGA, MANUEL ANTONIO. Manuel Antonio Noriega Moreno was Panama's chief of military intelligence (G-2) under General Torrijos, and in this capacity was both able to monitor domestic political events, and supply valuable information to the US Central Intelligence Agency (CIA). For this role he had been recruited by the then CIA Director George Bush. The agency paid Noriega a retainer of US$100,000 per annum, although Noriega claims to have received over US$11,000,000 from the CIA over 15 years. His involvement in illegal narcotics was, it is widely believed, known and tolerated by the Agency. Only when this became a political embarrassment, in the wake of the Iran–contra scandal, were connections severed, On June 7, 1987 Noriega's former second-in-command Col. Roberto Díaz Herrera revealed in public the extent of Noriega's involvement in narcotics trafficking. This initiated the process which led to his indictment in Florida courts on drug charges in February 1988, and his "arrest" formed a pretext for the US invasion of December 1989.

Noriega faces a range of narcotics-related charges in the USA as well as 16 charges in Panama ranging from extortion and fraud to murder. Bargaining is currently under way in the US courts over the defence evidence which could cause serious political damage to the US intelligence agencies, the Drugs Enforcement Agency and to President Bush himself in an exposé potentially more far-reaching than the Iran–contra case.

JCJS

O

OIL. Latin America contains two major oil producers, a number of more minor oil producers and several countries with little or no oil production. The region as a whole is a net exporter of oil; this has been the case since World War I and is likely to remain true for some time to come. Moreover, although significant discoveries have from time to time been made, the overall regional profile has changed relatively little over the past 50 years; Venezuela and Mexico are oil rich, most South American countries have some oil, most Central American and Caribbean countries do not. Over the past 20 years, the most important discoveries have been made in Mexico and Venezuela although significant finds have also been made in offshore Brazil and north-east Colombia. There is considerable potential for further oil exploration and it is likely that much more oil will be discovered in the region. However it is unlikely that any new discoveries will greatly modify the present-day position.

Venezuela is the most important oil producer in Latin America. Although it actually produces less oil than Mexico, its impact on world markets is far greater as a result of its relatively small population. Over 80 per cent of Venezuelan oil production is exported. Venezuela became a major oil exporter during the 1920s; the position was further reinforced by major new discoveries during the 1940s, 1950s and 1980s. In addition to conventional crude oil, Venezuela has a very large shale "oil belt" in the Orinoco region; if one considers the two together, then its oil potential is virtually limitless.

Venezuela was, however, one of the founder members of OPEC and has for many years followed a relatively conservative policy with regard to production of oil for export. Between the end of 1958 and the nationalization of the oil industry at the end of 1985, Venezuela pursued a policy of high taxation which caused the foreign companies to limit their oil exploration. Consequently production began to fall from the peak of just over 3,000,000 barrels per day (bpd) reached during the early 1970s.

Following the oil nationalization, exploration was stepped up and a number of significant discoveries were made. Before these could be transformed into higher production, OPEC agreed a policy of quotas, first informally and later formally. Venezuela adhered to its own quota although there was some frustration that this was set low. Iraq's invasion of Kuwait in August 1990 however gave Venezuela the opportunity to increase its output further, and it did so. Production rose from some 1,800,000 bpd to around 2,300,000 bpd.

Since nationalizing its oil, Venezuela has also invested heavily in refining and petrochemical production. The Venezuelan state company, PDVSA, is now one of the largest companies in the world; while its main field of operation is still the production and refining of oil, it also plays an important part in developing Venezuela's mineral and petrochemical industries. Moreover while production and refining are state monopolies, private investment is permitted in the petrochemicals sector and PDVSA is negotiating with several private companies in order to set up a liquified natural gas export terminal. There is some suggestion that foreign participation may be permitted in future refining ventures. In fact Venezuelan oil does in general need a lot of refining, since it tends to be of the heavy type while world demand is increasingly focusing on the lighter oil products such as gasoline. Another distinctive factor is that PDVSA has extended its operations internationally by purchasing shares in several European and United States companies. It has thus assured itself a guaranteed outlet for a proportion of its crude oil.

Mexico presently produces some 2,800,000 barrels daily. Around one half of this is consumed domestically, with the balance exported. Like Venezuela, Mexico has always been known to be potentially oil-rich. However oil exploration and production was de-emphasized after the nationalization of the industry in 1938. It was only toward the end of the 1960s that renewed emphasis was put on oil exploration, after it appeared that declining reserves were threatening Mexican self-sufficiency. This new exploration discovered vast new reserves and Mexico returned, at first reluctantly and later with enthusiasm, to the export market. Since the early 1980s Mexico has not sought to expand its oil industry further and it is now believed to be in slow decline, the result more of a lack of investment than of any geological problems.

In fact Mexico's oil industry has suffered from a number of political setbacks. During the 1970s rapid expansion of the industry went hand-in-hand with serious corruption; moreover the sudden emergence of Mexico as a major oil exporter did not protect that country from economic crisis in 1982. Although the oil industry itself may not have been at the root of the crisis, oil exports certainly did not offer an easy escape from other economic problems. Moreover the fact that most Mexican oil exports have gone to the United States has affected nationalist sensitivities in Mexico. Since 1982 Mexican governments have deliberately de-emphasized oil in the interest of allocating limited investment capital to other economic sectors. Weak international markets have reinforced this effect. Until some respite was offered by the oil price increases which followed the Iraqi invasion of Kuwait, there were serious concerns that Pémex, the state oil company, was becoming seriously decapitalized. However Mexican production did increase significantly in response to the embargo on Iraqi oil.

The oil boom period also created a number of problems in managing Pémex itself. Pémex is radically over-manned, mainly as a result of the strength of the oilworkers' union, in which all but a few hundred very senior managers are enroled. In January 1989 the oilworkers' union leader was arrested on corruption and homicide charges. While it is certain that union power is not what it once was, it remains probable that this is a sector with relatively weak management and strong labour. Moreover domestic prices were set low for many years, with Pémex being expected to earn enough in foreign exchange to compensate for this subsidy. Although some price increases have occurred since 1982, they have largely been offset by falls in international prices; it remains true that domestic oil prices in Mexico are set well below international levels. Finally Pémex acquired a considerable foreign debt during its years of expansion; this is further inhibiting its financial strength.

Pémex is a state monopoly, in a way which has traditionally been designed to appeal to Mexican nationalists; the state controls production, refining and "basic" petrochemicals. Since 1982 there have been a few very cautious moves to open up some sections of the petrochemicals industry to private capital, but there is as yet no serious suggestion of a major re-orientation of public policy so as to permit private capital to add to the dynamism of the sector as a whole.

In the rest of Latin America oil reserves are less abundant, although many countries are significant producers. Whether or not they are also exporters depends as much as anything else on their population. **Brazil** is the third largest oil producer in Latin America, but is an oil importer. However **Ecuador** which is the sixth largest producer is an exporter of oil and a member of OPEC.

One major oil bearing seam occurs just to the east of the Andes. Discoveries here have enabled **Colombia**, Ecuador and sporadically **Peru** to become oil exporters and have permitted a limited amount of production in **Chile** which is likely to remain a net importer. None of the Andean countries has a very large population and the actual volume of output is relatively small, ranging from some 130,000 bpd in Peru to 450,000 bpd in Colombia. Nevertheless the proportionate significance of oil is considerable; it is by far Ecuador's main export and is also rapidly becoming one of the main legal exports from Colombia. All of these countries have state oil companies which are responsible for some oil production, but private foreign investment is also present on a significant scale. In Colombia and Peru, however, foreign operations are sometimes the victims of attack from insurgents; in addition to political risk, oil company personnel are at some physical danger.

The policy choices facing those countries which do not have oil in abundance are naturally different from those facing Mexico and Venezuela. Because there is no danger of undermining their own market through overproduction, they can in fact sell as much as they can produce. Even Ecuador, which is a member of OPEC and in theory bound by quota decisions, in practice does not observe them very fully. Moreover in no Andean country (not even Ecuador) do oil exports amount to as much as one half of total exports. These republics do not have to worry excessively about the sometimes distorting effect which an abundance of oil can have on the rest of the domestic economy. On the other hand, each of these countries does find it necessary to accept foreign investment; this has entailed continuous and at times difficult bargaining between foreign companies and host governments. At times these relationships have become factors of major political significance. Foreign oil companies were nationalized in Peru in 1968 and Ecuador in 1976, although policy has not been consistently nationalist and the present-day trend has been for the Andean republics to welcome foreign investment on the right terms. For this reason, the trend has been for production to increase slowly across the Andean region as a whole.

On the Atlantic side, both Brazil and **Argentina** produce significant quantities of oil for domestic consumption. Both countries' industries are dominated by their state oil companies, Petrobrás and YPF respectively. In the case of Argentina oil production began when the state found oil in 1907, apparently by mistake when drilling for water. The state has continued to operate a considerable part of the Argentine industry although private capital has never been entirely excluded. Argentina is also one of the few Latin

American countries in which "private" does not invariably mean foreign; local private companies have at times been active in oil development. However the Argentine state oil company does not have a particularly good record; it is by no means one of the most efficient state oil companies in Latin America. Largely for this reason, in 1990 President **Carlos Menem** significantly reformed the Argentinian industry in the direction of private investment.

In Brazil it was again the state which first found oil. However in the Brazilian case this was as late in 1938; the discovery was the result of a deliberate policy of looking for oil at a time when foreign companies were more interested in Brazil as a source of sales for oil produced elsewhere. After World War II the Brazilian government deliberately set up Petrobrás with a refining monopoly in order to generate the funds necessary to explore Brazil properly; for many years such exploration proved very disappointing but an important offshore oil find in 1974 went some way towards vindicating Brazilian hopes. Private companies still operate in the distribution and petrochemical sectors and are, in theory, allowed to explore for oil; however the terms have not been very attractive and oil production remains essentially in the hands of the state. Meanwhile the state company Petrobrás has made use of its position in Brazil to emerge as a major industrial conglomerate company with a range of interests in minerals, trading and overseas oil operations.

There is less to report in the rest of the region. **Bolivia** has limited oil production, and a much more important reserve volume of gas which has emerged as Bolivia's largest legal export since the collapse of the tin market. Plans are presently being made to pipe some of this gas to Brazil; this will replace the ending of gas exports to Argentina scheduled for 1992. There is also slight oil production in **Guatemala** where the obstacles to development are political more than geological. Paraguay, Uruguay, most of Central America, and the Spanish-speaking Caribbean have to import all of their oil.

GP

Latin American Oil Production*

	1988	1989	1990
Mexico	2,866*	2,868	2,930
Venezuela	1,866	1,889	2,207
Brazil	567	604	639
Argentina	462	471	483
Colombia	378	407	451
Ecuador	316	292	289
Peru	151	139	136
Chile	27	22	20
Bolivia	17	19	18

**Source*: *Petroleum Economist* (adapted).
**Figures shown in 000 bpd.

ORGANIZATION OF AMERICAN STATES — OAS (*Organización de los Estados Americanos* — OEA). The Organization of American States was established by Charter as the first regional organization within the United Nations at the Ninth Inter-American Conference held at Bogotá in 1948. Its purpose is to further peace, security, mutual understanding and co-operation among the states of the Western Hemisphere. With the accession of Canada in January 1990 and the admission of Belize and Guyana in January 1991 it now has 35 members. Its main organ of consultation is the annual meeting of the General Assembly, a full-scale conference of Foreign Ministers held in different capitals. Its headquarters, where the Permanent Council sits and Meetings of Consultation of Ministers of Foreign Affairs are normally held, is in Washington, DC. The Permanent Council consists of representatives of each of the member states with the rank of Ambassador, the chair rotating among the representatives in alphabetical order, three months at a time. The current Secretary General is João Clemente Baena Soares of Brazil.

History. Originally the centrepiece of the Organization was to be the Conference itself, but the Tenth Inter-American Conference was delayed until 1954, when the fact that it was held in Caracas led to Costa Rica boycotting it. At it, under pressure from US Secretary of State John Foster Dulles, whose sole purpose in attending was to obtain a strong anti-communist resolution, delegates accepted a modified version, the Declaration of Solidarity for the Preservation of the Political Integrity of the American States against the Intervention of International Communism. Even then the *Declaration of Caracas* (as it is more commonly known) was passed without the support of either Mexico or Argentina.

The Eleventh Inter-American Conference, scheduled for Quito in 1958, was indefinitely postponed. Thereafter the major forum of the Organization became the regular meetings of Foreign Ministers. It was they who in 1960 voted sanctions against Trujillo in the Dominican Republic, while showing a clear reluctance to criticize **Fidel Castro's** regime in **Cuba**. The following year there was strong criticism of the abortive Bay of Pigs expedition and of the US role in it, though the use later in the year of US warships to drive the Trujillo family out of the Dominican Republic was tacitly condoned, and with an effective combination of pressure and inducement the Kennedy Administration succeeded in persuading the Organization to exclude Cuba and to impose a general embargo on Cuban trade; a decision subsequently reinforced by the Cuban Missile Crisis. After the Ninth Meeting of Consultation of Foreign Ministers in Washington in January 1964 only Mexico retained its links with Cuba and the embargo on Cuban trade established in 1962 was much strengthened. The unilateral American intervention in the **Dominican Republic** in 1965 placed an even greater strain on the Organization, and the USA secured a bare two-thirds majority for its action, the vote of the disputed government of the Dominican Republic being counted in its favour.

In 1970 the organization was reconstituted on its present basis by the Protocol of Buenos Aires, and the General Assembly, which met for its first regular session at San José, Costa Rica, in 1971, replaced the Inter-American Conferences and various councils. For many years it fulfilled a useful role in airing current political issues and through the work of its related agencies achieving important though less spectacular gains for Latin American co-operation. In 1979 the Inter-American Court of Human Rights was established with its seat in San José, but the Tenth General Assembly was unable to go beyond naming Argentina, Chile, El Salvador, Haiti, Paraguay and Uruguay as countries of "special concern" with regard to human rights when **Argentina** threatened to secede. Worse still since the **Falklands War** of 1982 open conflict between the United States and the majority of the Latin American states both over this issue and over US policy towards Central America has effectively stultified the political work of the Organization. It was as a result of this that the task of mediation in Central America was taken up by the *ad hoc* Contadora Group, made up of representatives of Mexico, Panama, Colombia and Venezuela.

Current political problems. The meeting of the sixteenth General Assembly in Guatemala City in 1986 was effectively paralyzed by the division between the United States and the Latin American majority on the issues of Central America and the **Falklands/Malvinas**. Britain's unilateral declaration of a fisheries conservation zone had prompted a request from Argentina for an emergency session of the Permanent Council, which in a compromise resolution unanimously adopted on Nov. 11 urged Britain and Argentina to resume negotiations over the sovereignty of the islands and to refrain from further actions that could upset "the already delicate existing situation". In supporting this, the United States Secretary of State, Mr George Shultz, was understood to have headed off a much more toughly worded resolution condemning the British action and reasserting Argentine sovereignty, while he concentrated his attack on **Nicaragua**, where, he said, there would be "civil war" until "genuine democracy" was restored. The resolution adopted by consensus on Nov. 14 calling on the Contadora Group and its co-sponsors "to persist in their efforts towards peace in Central America" was meaningless as long as the United States, through its allies Honduras and Costa Rica, was able, as it had consistently done in private, to frustrate talks with Nicaragua. An equally meaningless resolution on human rights was virtually the only other tangible outcome of the session. In effect the Falklands/Malvinas issue had served to deflect much criticism of the United States for its decision the previous month to resume overt aid to the contras in Nicaragua, and it was not until a week later that the disclosures began in Washington of earlier covert aid by the Administration.

In 1987, a year dominated by events in Central America, the OAS continued to maintain its less conspicuous role as a regional force for collaboration in a number of ways. A report published by the OAS in April warned of decreasing prospects for growth in the the economies of Jamaica, Trinidad and Tobago and Suriname owing to low world prices for alumina, bauxite and petroleum. The Permanent Council called for restraint when President Lusinchi of **Venezuela** complained in August that a Colombian warship had infringed his country's territorial waters in the Gulf of Venezuela and despatched troop reinforcements to the area. The Venezuelan foreign minister, Simón Alberto Consalvi, brushed aside Colombian proposals for mediation. The rejection of **Bolivia's** bid for access to the sea by Chile led the former to threaten to take its dispute to the OAS, but Chilean spokesmen made it clear that they would not recognize the Organization's jurisdiction.

The meeting of the seventeenth General Assembly held in Washington, DC, in November 1987 was dominated by President **Daniel Ortega** of Nicaragua, who in his first visit to that city since taking office scored a substantial propaganda *coup*. The release of more than 1,000 prisoners on the eve of his departure confirmed his acceptance of the Arias Plan. The initial refusal of Honduras to play its part in the peace process had been undermined by the finding in October of the

Inter-American Commission on Human Rights that at least 130 people had been abducted by the Honduran armed forces between 1981 and 1984. Hence when on Nov. 9, the Nicaraguan Foreign Minister, Fr. Miguel d'Escoto, trumped a tentative offer of direct talks from the United States by accepting it, the Honduran Foreign Minister, Carlos López Contreras, responded with an offer to ban the contras from Honduran soil and establish joint border verification.

Inevitably, in the early part of 1988, US attempts to force the resignation of General **Manuel Antonio Noriega** led to the OAS being drawn into the tragicomedy. At a Special Meeting of Consultation on Feb. 27, delegates invited to consider the crisis in Panama voiced support for President Delvalle but failed to vote either for the United States or for General Noriega. Following the decision of the United States Senate on June 26, which led to the recall of the Panamanian Ambassador and a diplomatic protest at US interference in **Panama's** internal affairs, an extraordinary session of the OAS convened at Panama's request resolved by 17 votes to one (the United States) that US activities in Panama constituted "unwarranted interference" in Panama's internal affairs. Fortunately the other work of the OAS and its related agencies went on despite its political paralysis. On Jan. 20 Honduras, the first Latin American government to be arraigned before the Inter-American Court of Human Rights, was held guilty of maintaining army death squads responsible for the "disappearance" of named civilians.

Following the annulment of the May 7, 1989 elections in Panama an extraordinary Meeting of Consultation of Foreign Ministers was held in Washington on May 17 which approved by consensus a resolution to send a delegation to Panama. An amendment specifically naming General Noriega, the Commander of the Panamanian Defence Forces, as responsible for "grave events and abuses" which had curtailed the right to free choice and curtailed human rights was carried by 20 votes to two (Panama and Nicaragua) with seven abstentions (Antigua and Barbuda, Bahamas, Dominica, Grenada, Peru, Suriname, Uruguay). The delegation led by the Secretary-General, João Baena Soares, visited Panama from May 23–27 and held talks with government and opposition parties, including General Noriega himself, but was unsuccessful in negotiating a resolution to the dispute.

A second Meeting of Consultation of the Foreign Ministers held in Washington, DC on July 19–20 called for a transitional government to be formed by Sept. 1, when the presidential term of the *de facto* head of state, Manuel Solís Palma, was due to expire and fresh elections to be held as soon as possible. The US demand for the resignation of General Noriega was not however accepted, and when the mediation mission delivered its report at a further Meeting of Consultation on Aug. 23–24 the US Deputy Secretary of State, Lawrence Eagleburger, denounced Panama in the strongest terms, stating that if power was not transferred by Sept. 1 "civilized nations" would have to declare the regime illegal. The Foreign Minister of Venezuela was subsequently dismissed for his strong line in support of the United States position. In the event the Bush Administration refused to recognize the interim government actually installed, broke off diplomatic relations and, in December, landed US troops to overthrow General Noriega. On Dec. 22 1990 a Meeting of Consultation "deeply deplored" the action and called for the immediate cessation of hostilites and beginning of negotiations, a resolution carried by 20 votes to 1 (that of the United States), with six abstentions (Antigua and Barbuda, Costa Rica, Honduras, El Salvador, Guatemala and Venezuela).

PARC

ORGANS OF PEOPLE'S POWER (Organos de Poder Popular—OPP) (Cuba). The Organs of People's Power were established in **Cuba** in 1976, after an experiment in Camagüey province, to reduce the centralization of decision-making and to encourage the democratization and localization of authority into municipal, provincial and national legislatures and administrations (albeit within the constraints of democratic centralism). Participation on the various levels of the OPPs was by popular election and represented the formal separation of public administration from the Party. The OPPs were approved by the 1975 PCC Congress and incorporated into the 1976 Constitution following a national referendum on Feb. 24, 1976. In October 1976 elections at the constituency level of municipality generated delegates (currently 10,740) for 169 municipalities whom in turn voted for the 14 provincial assemblies and the National Assembly (the highest legislative and administrative apparatus of the state). The National Assembly elects the Council of State from its own members, and the Council constitutes the national executive. **Fidel Castro** is currently President of the Council.

JCJS

ORTEGA, DANIEL. Daniel Ortega Saavedra (born 1944) is the oldest of three brothers, all of whom were early members of the **Sandinista National Liberation Front** in Nicaragua. The youngest brother, Camilo, was killed by the National Guard in 1978 in Masaya. The other brother, Humberto, was Minister of Defence in the Sandinista government and is now commander-in-chief of the armed forces.

Daniel Ortega spent seven years in prison before being freed in a prisoner-hostage exchange in 1974. He became a leader of the *Tercerista* faction of FSLN which advocated mass insurrection against the Somoza regime. Between 1979 and 1984 he held the post of chairman of the governing junta of the provisional government. He was elected president in November 1984. Ortega was regarded as a moderating and pluralist influence in the Sandinista government. After the electoral defeat in February 1990, however, there must be some doubt regarding his future as leader of the Sandinista movement.

GG

P

PACIFIC, WAR OF THE (Guerra del Pacífico). The War of the Pacific (1879–84) substantially altered the balance of power on the west coast of South America with consequences that are still important. The root cause was a territorial dispute between **Bolivia** and **Chile** over the southern boundary of Bolivia's coastal province of Antofagasta, where by a compromise Chileans had been admitted to work the nitrate fields. Following complaints about the taxation of its nationals, in February 1879 Chile seized the Bolivian port of Antofagasta and the surrounding coastline. **Peru** first offered to mediate and then, under a so-called "secret" Treaty of 1873 (which was already known to Chile), came to the aid of Bolivia. However by the end of 1880 Peru's fleet had been entirely destroyed and its own southern provinces of Tacna, Arica and Tarapacá had been annexed by Chile. In 1881 Chilean forces occupied Lima and in 1883 dictated a peace, the first *Treaty of Ancón*, by which Peru ceded Tarapacá and Chile occupied Tacna and Arica for a period initially supposed to be only 10 years.

Bolivia, otherwise relatively unscathed by war, lost its access to the sea, and gained a desire to regain it which had dominated its foreign policy ever since. In 1904 it abandoned its claim to Arica, which it had never exercised. Chile, which had not held the promised referendum on its future, in return admitted Bolivia's right to the Atacama Desert, most of which was in the hands of Peru, but agreed at the same time to construct and grant rights of transit for Bolivian products on the Arica–La Paz Railway, which was completed in 1912 and made the development of the tin mines possible. In 1928 the Bolivian section of the railway was handed over to the Bolivian government.

Peru retrieved Tacna in 1929 under the second Treaty of Ancón, which provides that no Chilean territory formerly belonging to Peru could be alienated to a third country (i.e. Bolivia) without Peruvian consent. Bolivia was thus driven to redouble its efforts to secure the Chaco, thus bringing on the **Chaco War**. It remains landlocked and dependent on access to the Pacific by the railway to Arica in Chilean territory, and has taken every opportunity up to and since the centenary of the war in 1979 both to regain direct access or seek alternative routes to the outside world, most recently by railway through Brazil. The government of Hugo Banzer made the most recent serious attempt to negotiate a corridor to the port of Arica, but the terms offered by General Augusto **Pinochet** were so tough that the negotiations were abandoned without success.

PARC/SAC

PANAMA. *Population*: 2,300,000 (mid-1988). *Area*: 77,000 sq km. *GDP* $5,490 million (1988). *Trade volume*: exports $2,352 million (1988); imports $2,815 million (1988). *Expenditure* (as percentage of total public expenditure): defence 5.9 (1988); education 15.6 (1988); health 16.7 (1988). *Urban population* (as percentage of total population): 54 (1988). *Percentage of population under the age of 14*: 35.9. *Infant mortality rate*: 22 per 1,000. *Life expectancy*: 70 (men); 74 (women).

Geographical background. The Republic of Panama is situated at the narrowest part of the Panamanian isthmus which forms the land bridge between the South and North American continents, where the shortest distance between the Atlantic and Pacific Oceans is a mere 65 kilometres. The southern border (with Colombia) province of Darien is largely tropical jungle and swamp. The central belt, marked by the Panama Canal and the major cities of Panama City and Colón at its southern and northern points respectively, contains the majority of the population. West of the Canal to the Costa Rican border the more mountainous Cordillera Central rises from the mainly agricultural provinces of Veraguas and Cocle.

Socio–political background. The population of Panama is predominantly mestizo (70 per cent) with an Afro-Caribbean and Indian community (21 per cent) and a small white population which effectively constitutes a ruling class. The most recent constitutional reforms (of April 1983) created a 67-member Legislative Assembly subject to election, by universal adult suffrage every five years. The President, also elected quinquenially, holds executive power. Of greater importance however in shaping the political development of the country have been the Panamanian Defence Forces (*Fuerzas de Defensa de Panamá*—FDP), local business and US Southern Command (SouthCom) located in US military bases around the Canal.

Outline of political history. Panama gained its sovereignty as a result of a secessionist war with

Colombia in 1903. The infant republic ceded "in perpetuity" to the United States what became the **Panama Canal Zone** through the Hay-Bunau-Varilla Treaty of 1904. By 1914 the transisthmian Canal had been built. At the same time Panama adopted the US dollar as the official currency (although renamed the Balboa). Although the protectorate status of Panama came to an end in 1936, the Canal Zone remained under US sovereign control until the **Panama Canal Treaties** of 1977 established a timetable for a process of transferring sovereignty of the Canal Zone to Panama by Dec. 31, 1999.

Insofar as Panamanian governments since 1904 appeared to challenge US strategic interests in the Canal they invited interference by the United States. Thus, of the nationalist governments of Arnulfo Arias (first elected in 1940) whose legal terms of office should have lasted 14 years, he only served 31 months. The *coup* of 1968, at first with US backing, brought Omar Torrijos Herrera to power whose radical Panamanian nationalism resulted in a curious mixture of autocratic corporatism, fervent nationalism and the formation of an openly transnational service economy. Although mysteriously killed in an air crash in 1981, Torrijos's successful negotiation of the Canal Treaties seemed finally to guarantee Panama's sovereignty and economic autonomy. The organizational basis of Torrijos' power lay in the National Guard (renamed and reorganized in 1983 into the FDP) and its associated political party created in 1979 the Democratic Revolutionary Party (*Partido Democrático Revolucionario*— PRD). In July 1983 **Manuel Antonio Noriega** became head of the FDP, and in his consolidation of political and economic power he oversaw the resignation of President Ricardo de la Esprlella in February 1984, the fraudulent election of Dr Nicolás Ardito Barletta in May 1984 and his resignation in September 1985, when he was replaced as President with Eric Arturo Delvalle, the unconstitutional removal of Delvalle in favour of Manuel Solís Palma in February 1988, and the nullification of the Presidential elections in May 1989 in which Guillermo Endara's Democratic Alliance of Civil Opposition (*Alianza Democrática de Oposición Cívica*—ADOC) is generally believed to have won. Ambiguous US support for Delvalle following his removal, and then US backing for Endara in the 1989 presidential elections thinly veiled US determination to oust Noriega himself from power.

Recent developments—political. On Dec. 20, 1989 26,000 US troops invaded Panama in order, as President Bush stated, to arrest Noriega, to safeguard the lives of US citizens and "to defend democracy" and "the integrity of the Canal Treaties". Between 4,000 and 7,000 people were killed of which 23 were US soldiers. Condemned by the Organization of American States, the invasion was followed by the appointment as President of Endara, who by refusing to hold fresh elections provoked the Group of Eight Latin American states to expel Panama in April 1990. The lack of a cohesive opposition to **ADOC** has frustrated the democratization of Panama.

Recent developments—economic. The efficacy of Noriega's fragmentation of the political opposition, the manner in which ADOC has monopolized post-invasion power and the erosion of Panamanian economic strength has left Panama in an unstable position. The economic foundations built by Torrijos in the form of the International Finance Centre (where over 200,000 companies and 110 banks had located), the Colón Free Trade Zone (second in the world only to Hong Kong), and international shipping have been severely compromised by the maladministration and corruption of the 1980s. Annual growth in GDP in the period 1965–80 averaged 5.5 per cent, compared with only 2.6 per cent between 1980–88. Of particular alarm for the economy in the 1980s, where international competition in services was severe, was that over the same periods growth in the service sector fell from 6 per cent per annum to 3.5 per cent per annum. In particular, widespread involvement of public officials in narcotics smuggling and the laundering of profits from narcotics trafficking have jeopardized international confidence in the integrity of the Panamanian tax haven, and has succeeded in drawing sharp pressure from the US Drug Enforcement Agency for Panamanian banks to remove secrecy laws.

Prospects for economic development. However, there is evidence of a slow recovery in banking confidence with average US dollar deposits in Panamanian banks up $1,400 million between December 1989 and June 1990, to total deposits averaging $15,000 million, still a long way below the pre-Noriega high of US$40,000 million. Due to the US economic blockade dating from 1987 Panama failed to service its external debt currently standing at $8,200 million, with arrears of about $450,000,000. In addition the United States has failed to fulfil commitments of $420,000,000 in aid for the post-invasion reconstruction, substantial parts being tied to the controversial Mutual Legal Assistance Treaty giving US agencies access to details of bank accounts held in Panama. Panamanian nationalist fears that the USA is intent on reneging on the terms of the

Panama Canal Treaties (evidenced, they claim, by the 1989 invasion) has undermined confidence in the ability of the Canal to provide substantial returns to Panama. Pre-invasion plans for the modernization and improvement of the Canal as well as Japanese-financed exploratory surveys for a sea-level Canal have now been placed in jeopardy. Losses from war damage have been variously estimated between $1,500 million and $2,200 million. In order to cut public expenditure the Endara government is pushing through rapid privatization programmes.

JCJS

PANAMA CANAL TREATIES, 1977. This series of treaties is critical to the future of **Panama**, and demands that the USA adheres to its terms is the only unifying bond in Panamanian politics. Signed by Omar Torrijos and Jimmy Carter on Sept. 7, 1977, they were approved by the slimmest of margins in April 1978 by the US Senate (68 to 32, with a two-thirds majority required). Strong opposition remains in the United States to the terms of the Treaties, which include: the complete transfer of sovereign authority by Dec. 31, 1999; the phased transfer of the management and operation of the Canal to Panama (the first Panamanian to head the Panama Canal Commission, Fernando Manfredo, took up his post on Jan. 1, 1990); the removal of all US military bases; the permanent neutrality of the Canal (although the USA reserves the right to "defend" its neutrality); the complete removal of US rights to interfere in the sovereign affairs of Panama. The ability and intent of both parties to keep to the letter and spirit of the Treaties has been compromised by the economic instability caused by the US blockade and invasion of 1989, and in Panama the Treaties are widely regarded to be in great jeopardy.

JCJS

PANAMA CANAL ZONE. The Panama Canal Zone was created as a result of an agreement between US Secretary of State John Hay and Phillipe Bunau-Varilla (a French citizen with major holdings in the Compagnie Universelle du Canal Interocéanique which held excavation rights for a transisthmian canal). Broadly the terms of the agreement were as follows: (i) Panama to cede in perpetuity to the United States a strip of territory 10 miles wide from Colón to Balboa, which would be treated as US sovereign territory, subject to US laws, US policing and (ii) free from Panamanian taxation. Furthermore, (iii) the USA reserved unlimited rights to deploy armed forces in Panama deemed necessary to deal with potential threats to Zone security; (iv) to purchase or exercise the "right of eminent domain" to acquire land, buildings, water, etc, regarded necessary for the operation of Zone activities. This Zone treaty was updated in 1936 by which parts (iii) and (iv) were dropped, and again in 1955 when the terms of (ii) were waived. Only with the **Panama Canal Treaties** of 1977 was the fundamental basis of Zone status revised and in 1979 the Zone ceased to exist, though the USA retains a garrison of 13,000 or so in the Canal area.

JCJS

PARAGUAY. *Population*: 3,900,000 (1988). *Area*: 406,752 sq km. *GDP*: US$5,909 million. *Trade volume*: $784,000,000 (1986). *Top five trade partners*: exports: Brazil, Netherlands, Argentina, Spain, Switzerland; imports: Brazil, USA, Japan, Argentina, UK. *Defence spending*: $65,000,000 (1.1 per cent of GNP). *Education spending (as percentage of GNP)*: 1.6 *Urban population as percentage of total (centres over 20,000)*: 32.2. *Birthrate*: 36.0 per 1,000 (1985). *Life expectancy*: 62.8 (men); (women) 67.5.

Geographical background. The Republic of Paraguay, a landlocked country bounded by Brazil, Argentina, and Bolivia, is divided into two parts by the River Paraguay, from which it takes its name. Eastern Paraguay, the original area of settlement where 95 per cent of the population live, consists of the western part of the Paraná Plateau, and is a well watered and fertile country with low hills, fine grassland and forest cover. Western Paraguay consists of the northern part of the Gran Chaco, a vast alluvial plain, covered with thin scrub and dry grass. Where water exists it tends to be strongly alkaline or salty, and population is extremely sparse. The capital, Asunción, lies on the eastern bank of the Paraguay at its confluence with the River Pilcomayo.

The climate is generally mild, between 10 and 21°C in winter and 26 to 37°C in summer, but hot winds from the Matto Grosso in Brazil and cold winds from the southern Andes can bring abrupt changes in temperature in a short space of time. Rain falls all the year round, annual rainfall in Eastern Paraguay ranging from 2,000 mm on the Brazilian frontier to 1,200 mm on the Paraguay River.

Socio–political background. Uniquely in South America, the first encounter of the indigenous Guaraní-speaking inhabitants of Paraguay with the Spaniards came not by conquest, but by the arrival of Jesuit missionaries, who founded

Asunción in 1537 and gathered the inhabitants into mission settlements (reductions). Would-be colonists were barred until in 1767 the King was persuaded to ban the Order, whereupon the missions were sacked and their inhabitants dispersed or enslaved. In 1776 nominal control over the region was transferred from Lima to Buenos Aires.

Asunción, which as a result lost its pre-eminence in the region, formed its own government in 1810, defeated an expedition from Buenos Aires and with the deposition of the last royal governor in 1811 became the first Spanish-speaking country in the Americas to achieve independence. Within three years its leader, José Caspar Rodríguez de Francia, known as "El Supremo", had been granted dictatorial powers, sealed the country off from the outside world and ruled as an enlightened but formidable despot (1814–40). His successor, Carlos Antonio López (1842–62), re-established trade with the outside world and built up the army which his son and successor, Francisco Solano López (1862–70), was to lead against the combined forces of Argentina, Uruguay and Brazil in the War of the Triple Alliance (1865–70). Nine tenths of the male population perished and Paraguay was forced to cede territory to both Brazil and Argentina.

Today some 95 per cent of the population is mestizo. Guaraní is spoken almost universally and both it and Spanish are recognized as national languages, though the latter is taught in the schools and is the main vehicle of instruction. Roman Catholicism is the official religion and the President must be a Catholic.

Under the Constitution of 1967 Paraguay is a presidential republic. The President who is directly elected for a five-year term and eligible for re-election has the power to dissolve the bicameral Congress, which consists of a Senate of at least 30 and a Chamber of Deputies of at least 60 members, both directly elected at the same time as the President. The Army totals some 12,000 officers and men, of whom some two-thirds are conscripts. The Navy, which numbers 3,150 personnel, has six river defence vessels and smaller patrol craft, with one marine regiment. The Air Force has eight combat aircraft and a staff of 1,400.

Outline of political history. Following the battle of Cerro Corá (1870) republican government and political parties emerged and in 1904 the Liberals seized power, inaugurating a generation of dominance which ended with the Chaco War of 1932–35. Paraguay conquered three quarters of the disputed northern Chaco from Bolivia, and retained most of it at the peace treaty, but Bolivia kept its oil fields and the Paraguayan part of the Chaco turned out to be worthless. The victorious military leader, General José Félix Estigarribia, elected president in 1939 as a Liberal, was killed in an air crash the following year. A series of military *coups* and counter-*coups* followed until in 1954 **General Alfredo Stroessner** seized power and was elected president. For the next 34 years General Stroessner ruled as an old-fashioned and paternalist Latin American military dictator, keeping control with the aid of the military, the police and the **Colorado Party**. When it became clear that his regime had outlived its usefulness, he was toppled in a military *coup* in 1989.

Recent developments—political. The crisis of the Stroessner regime came with the visit of Pope John Paul II to Asunción in May 1988. Although the Pope called pointedly for respect for human rights and political freedoms, the crowd gathered outside Asunción Cathedral were attacked by police with truncheons and many injured. In response Archbishop Ismael Rolón cancelled a ceremony to commemorate the 451st anniversary of the founding of the city, the date chosen by General Stroessner for his inauguration to an eighth five-year term as President.

General Stroessner had been re-elected for the seventh time on Feb. 14 that year in a ballot in which he was said to have received 1,186,693 votes or 88.6 per cent of those cast. He was received coldly when, against advice, he visited New York in July to address the United Nations, and 12 of his entourage attacked demonstrators so violently that one had to be taken to hospital. During the latter part of the year he was seen to be visibly failing. On Feb. 3, 1989 he was overthrown in a military *coup* in Asunción which left 17 dead. He was allowed to go into exile in Brazil but charges of corruption were brought against both him and his son, Gustavo, who was later extradited from Brazil.

The leader of the *coup*, **General Andrés Rodríguez**, was sworn in immediately as interim President. In presidential and congressional elections held on May 1 he won 74.18 per cent of the votes cast against seven other candidates, the next largest percentage of votes, 18 per cent, going to Domingo Laino of the **Authentic Radical Liberal Party** (*Partido Liberal Radical Auténtico*—PLRA), and the ruling *Colorados* automatically being allocated two thirds of the seats in both the Chamber of Deputies and the Senate. Free elections are promised for 1993.

Outline of economic development. Paraguay has no mineral wealth and the bulk of the population (some 50 per cent) work in agriculture, forestry and stockrearing. Very little of the available land—some 2 per cent—is cultivated. Trade unions have long been actively discouraged and incomes are low. In consequence many Paraguayans have emigrated—it is said that more live in Buenos Aires than in the whole of Paraguay. On the other hand substantial Brazilian immigration into the eastern border region adjoining the River Paraná which began in the late 1960s and was actively encouraged by the Stroessner government has aroused nationalist resentment and led to clashes.

Based originally on river transport, now in decline, Paraguay's slow communication system has impeded economic development. A single antiquated railway line, the Paraguayan Central Railway, links Asunción with Buenos Aires. The road system has been much improved in recent years and modern bridges link Paraguay with Brazil and Argentina, though the journey can be a tiresome one. There are also regular air services both by the national airline, Líneas Aéreas Paraguayas, and other carriers, from the international airport at Asunción to both countries.

With the stabilization of the currency in 1957, inflation, previously endemic, was brought under control, but accelerated in the 1970s, when Paraguay suffered from high world oil prices. Paraguay has no hydrocarbon reserves, but a vast potential for hydroelectric power. Hence following the success of the earlier Aracay scheme, the decision was taken to accept Brazil's 1964 annexation of the Salto de Guairá (Sete Quedas) and to build a giant dam and hydroelectric plant on the River Paraná at Itaipú. The project and associated activity stimulated growth averaging 10 per cent a year in the later 1970s. Unfortunately the fall in oil prices in 1982 meant that most of the generating capacity has only just been installed and Paraguay failed to benefit as had been hoped from the sale of power to Brazil's southern cities. Instead, its long-standing role as a major centre for smuggling of all kinds increased sharply, bringing about major distortions in the economy.

Current economic situation. In March 1990 it was reported that the target of 6 per cent growth in 1989 had been achieved and the public sector deficit had been reduced to zero by sharp spending cuts and an increase in tax revenues. Inflation to the end of November 1989 had been 28 per cent.

PARC

PARTY OF THE BRAZILIAN DEMOCRATIC MOVEMENT (Partido do Movimento Democrático Brasileiro—PMDB). The PMDB emerged from the restoration of the multi-party system in 1979. It was made up of most of the MDB, the broadly left-wing, anti-régime coalition, which had existed together with the National Renovation Alliance (*Aliança Nacional Renovadora*—ARENA), since 1965. The MDB had had some notable successes, particularly in the Congressional elections of 1974. Régime strategists of *distensão* and *abertura* now wanted to end a process by which votes for MDB were seen as virtually a referendum, not just on the government's performance, but on the régime itself. To retain its identity, the party now simply added the title of "party" to its old name.

Throughout the period of *abertura*, up to 1985, the PMDB remained a broad, heterogeneous coalition, united mainly by its opposition to the régime. After the New Organic Law of Political Parties, of December 1979, another, centre-left party which was founded was the Popular Party, (*Partido Popular*—PP). This included, among other former MDB leaders, **Tancredo Neves de Almeida**. After the régime introduced new electoral legislation in November 1981, in preparation for the vitally important elections of 1982, the PP merged with the PMDB. Tancredo Neves eventually was chosen as the party's presidential candidate, and elected, indirectly, in January 1985.

Under the presidency of **José Sarney**, from March 1985 to March 1990, the PMDB remained the main party of government, with the PFL, in the Democratic Alliance *(Aliança Democrática)*. By late 1985, severe strains were evident within the Alliance and between PMDB leaders and Sarney. The **Cruzado Plan** of February 1986 bound the president and party together, leading to the sweeping victory of PMDB candidates in the elections of November 1986, for Congress/Constituent Assembly.

For the rest of Sarney's presidency, relations between him and the PMDB deteriorated, though Sarney managed, by various means, to win right-wing support for his projects, including his fifth year in office. In 1988, came the long-expected split in the party, with the formation of the Party of Brazilian Social Democracy (*Partido da Social Democracia Brasileira*—PSDB) the "Tucanos", which deprived the PMDB of some of its most experienced leaders and intellectuals, especially in São Paulo.

As expected, the presidential election of 1989 was a disaster for the PMDB, despite the great respect in which the party's president, **Ulysses Guimarães** was held. After the Congressional election of October 1990, the PMDB still remains, numerically, the strongest party in Congress and its candidate for governor in São

Paulo, Luiz Antonio Fleury, won an important victory over **Paulo Maluf**. This was largely helped by the record of the out-going PMDB governor, Orestes Quércia, who now must be regarded as a major presidential candidate for the election of 1994. The PMDB, despite the bruising it has received in recent years, remains an important political force.

PF

PARTY OF BRAZILIAN SOCIAL DEMOCRACY (Partido da Social Democracia Brasileira—PSDB). The PSDB of **Brazil** was formed by a breakaway group from the **Party of the Brazilian Democratic Movement** (*Partido do Movimento Democrático Brasileiro*—PMDB) in July 1988. From the foundation of the PMDB, in the restructuring of the party system in 1980, a persistent question was how far this heterogeneous party of the opposition, building on its MDB origins, might survive intact, especially if ever it were to become a party of government.

The success of the opposition in the elections of November 1982 made these questions even sharper, since they led to a widespread collapse of morale in the pro-government **Social Democratic Party** (*Partido Democrático Social*—PDS) with many of its representatives alarmed at the régime's evident inability to deliver the vote and to guarantee their re-election. Some turned, therefore, to **Paulo Salim Maluf** as their new political patron, others sought cover in the PMDB, swelling the ranks of its right-of-centre membership. This incursion of conservative political refugees further alarmed the *auténticos*, the "authentic", more left-wing or radical elements in the PMDB.

The implosion of the PDS in 1984, and the formation of the Liberal Front Party (*Partido da Frente Liberal*—PFL) and the *Democratic Alliance*, brought more former PDS deputies and supporters into the PMDB. The death of President-elect **Tancredo Neves** and the accession of **José Sarney**, in 1985, increased still further the strains within the PMDB. The question, as Sarney took office, was not whether, but when, the split in the PMDB would occur.

It nearly came in late 1985, in the wake of the PMDB set-back in the municipal election in São Paulo. By January and early February 1986, important leaders of the PMDB were distancing themselves from Sarney and it seemed that a new breakaway party would be announced at any time. It was largely the efforts of the party leader, **Ulysses Guimarães**, which held it together: Ulysses urged the need of party unity, to guarantee the process of redemocratization. He was especially anxious that nothing should jeopardize the work of the Constituent Assembly, which was to put the seal on the process of *abertura* and mark the start of the new political era.

The dramatic announcement of the **Cruzado Plan** on Feb. 28 ended any immediate chance of a split in the PMDB. The Plan bound Sarney to the PMDB and the PMDB to Sarney. Together, they won a massive victory in the elections for Congress/Constitutent Assembly in November 1986.

The dismantling of the Cruzado Plan, and the subsequent unpopularity of Sarney and the PMDB, renewed pressures to split the party as did the growing tensions between the President and PMDB members of his government. Now, the general aim of the leadership was to preserve party unity until, at least, the promulgation of the new **Constitution**.

Eventually, the strains became too great, worsened by the increasingly evident corruption within the Congress/Constituent Assembly and, more particularly, the manipulation by Sarney of the *Centrão*, the large centre group, which contained many of the right-of-centre members of the PMDB in the Chamber. This manipulation reached scandalous proportions, especially over the question of the choice between a presidential and a parliamentary system of government, over the issue of agrarian reform, and, above all, over whether Sarney should be allowed a fifth year in office. It was the corruption and blatant use of patronage over this last question which eventually brought the long-expected split in the PMDB, in July 1988. The result was the formation of the PSDB, whose members quickly became known as the "*Tucanos*" (the "Toucans").

While, in part, the formation of the PSDB was a reaction to the clientelistic politics of large sections of the PMDB and to "*fisiologismo*", an unseemly scrabble for office, it also had a more positive dimension. The aim of the founders of the PSDB was to provide a modern, social-democratic party, to meet the needs and demands of Brazil's new democracy. The initial appeal was to the centre-left. The party began with a strong base in São Paulo, among some of the most prominent members of the PMDB. These included the former state governor, Franco Montoro, the two São Paulo senators, Mário Covas and Fernando Henrique Cardoso, and the former Finance Minister and distinguished economist., Luiz Carlos Bresser Pereira. It was a glittering leadership group, which now had to find a following.

The following has been slow to come. The PSDB has support in the academic and business community, but little in terms of trade union or working class base. It still has not put down roots. It is another party built from the top. It had no time to organize and field effective candidates for the municipal elections of November 1988, so it could attract attention, without having anything to lose.

In the direct elections for President, in 1989, PSDB strategists judged that Mário Covas might present a serious challenge to the candidates further to the left, **Lula** and **Brizola**, and might dominate the middle ground in the absence, at the start of the year, of a serious candidate of the right.

Covas was a widely respected candidate. Born in 1930, he first trained as an engineer, then was elected as federal deputy for São Paulo in 1962, for the Social Labour Party (*Partido Social Trabalhista* — PST). After the suppression of political parties in October 1965, he joined the MDB and was re-elected in 1966. He was deprived of his political rights, *cassado*, in January 1969, following *Institutional Act No. 5* and was out of politics till 1979. In 1982, he was again elected as federal deputy for São Paulo, for the PMDB, and, in May 1983, was appointed as mayor of São Paulo, at the time when mayors in capital cities still were not elected. After a successful term in office, he was elected as Senator for São Paulo in November 1986, and played an important role in the Constituent Assembly.

Despite the high regard in which he was held, Covas did not have the electoral success which many people had expected. He did not become the candidate of the business community, even in São Paulo, and offered insufficient appeal to the broad mass of the electorate. He was easily passed by Lula, Brizola and **Collor**. He and the PSDB then gave their support to Lula in the second round.

In the Congressional elections of October 1990 and in the elections for governors, PSDB candidates, despite their relatively high quality, again failed to win sufficient support. The party elected no governors and its representation in the Chamber fell from 60 to 37.

The paradox of the PSDB is that it contains some of the most able and highly respected politicians in Brazil and some of the country's leading social science theorists, men such as Fernando Henrique Cardoso and Luiz Carlos Bresser Pereira: but it has not yet found the key to popular appeal. Its programme is soundly constructed within the mould of social democracy and one of its principal aims is to provide the kind of modern party, free from clientelism and the widely condemned political vices of the past. Still, the electorate votes for other candidates.

Perhaps it is a matter of time, in the sense that the party is still very new and that its impact still remains to be felt. It is, also, still too confined to São Paulo, where its candidates face a formidable PMDB political machine led by Orestes Quércia, who left the governorship with his political position greatly strengthened. There is also the undoubted fact that the PSDB, built from the top downwards, is strong in leadership, but without a sufficient following or widespread political base.

The short-term future of the PSDB may be within a broad left of centre coalition, working with Brizola and the PDT and Lula and the **Workers' Party** (*Partido dos Trabalhadores* — PT) as well as with other parties. Such as combination, especially if Collor's policies should falter or fail, would be a formidable one. In such a combination, the skills and experience of the PSDB would be important, both in opposition and in government.

PF

PAZ ESTENSSORO, VICTOR. Víctor Paz Estenssoro, born in 1907, served as Minister of Finance of **Bolivia** under Villarroel (1943–46) and with his overthrow went into exile in Argentina. From here he won the 1951 election but was prevented from taking office by the intervention of the military. However, the National Revolution of 1952 overthrew the military and installed Paz, leader of the **Nationalist Revolutionary Movement (MNR)**, as president. Following the completion of his first term of office in 1956, Paz became Bolivian ambassador to the UK before returning for re-election to the presidency in 1960. Although Paz also won the 1964 election, he was displaced by a military *coup* some six months into his term and went into exile in Peru until 1971. He returned to support the regime of **General Hugo Bánzer** who had seized power that year, but was forced back into exile in 1973. Paz came second in the inconclusive presidential elections of 1979 and 1980 behind Siles, and was runner-up to Bánzer in the 1985 poll. Nevertheless, Congress confirmed Paz as president and his term of office (1985–89) was marked by a drastic austerity programme for economic recovery.

CS

PAZ ZAMORA, JAIME. Jaime Paz Zamora, born in 1939, the most successful of the post-Revolution generation of Bolivian politicians, was elected by Congress to the presidency of **Bolivia** in August 1989. This was the culmination of a pursuit for power which led him into an alliance with **Hugo Bánzer**, for many years his political enemy. As leader of the **Movement of**

the Revolutionary Left, a party with youthful, radical credentials, Jaime Paz stood as vice-presidential candidate for the Democratic and Popular Union (UDP) coalition alongside **Hernán Siles** in the elections of 1979 and 1980. It was during the election campaign of 1980 that Paz narrowly escaped death in a plane crash, a result of sabotage, in which four of his UDP colleagues were killed. With the retreat of the military in 1982, Paz became vice-president until his resignation in December 1984. With the breaking away of the left, Paz led his supporters towards the social-democratic right and, finally in 1989, into alliance with the ultra-conservative Nationalist Democratic Action (ADN) party with which it now shares power under his presidency.

CS

PEOPLE'S NATIONAL CONGRESS—PNC (Guyana). The ruling party in **Guyana** since 1964, the PNC was founded in October 1957 when a faction within the **People's Progressive Party** headed by **Forbes Burnham** merged with the United Democratic Party. Burnham became leader of the PNC, which drew its support principally from the Afro–Guyanese urban working and middle class. Originally strongly anti-communist, the PNC took power in 1964, and 10 years later declared itself a co-operative socialist party. It subsequently developed some of the characteristics of a communist party, including the use of government resources for party purposes under the 1974 Sophia Declaration, which held the party to be "paramount" over the government. The identification of party and state was formalized in 1975 by the creation of a joint office of the general secretary of the PNC and the Ministry of National Development. Schoolchildren, teachers and government employees were required to take part in PNC rallies, with government vehicles used to transport the participants, and in the 1980s, the annual Republic Day celebrations featured North Korean-style "mass games".

On the death of President Burnham in August 1985, President **Desmond Hoyte** became PNC leader. At the biennial congress of August 1989, he appointed the First Vice-President and Prime Minister, Hamilton Green, as deputy leader and Seeram Prashad as general secretary; the two posts had been held by Ranji Chandisingh, the Vice-President for National Development, whose ministry had been abolished in January, as part of a series of measures by Hoyte to disentangle the party functions from those of the state, in line with his adoption of free-market economic policies.

RP

PEOPLE'S NATIONAL PARTY—PNP (Jamaica). The PNP was created in **Jamaica** in 1938 following the extensive general strikes of that year, and constituted the first successful attempt at a broad party organization based on social democratic principles. Amongst others it was founded by the current Prime Minister's father Norman Manley and derived support from the fledgling Bustamente Industrial Trade Union (BITU). Following deep ideological splits in the 1940s, the rightist BITU split to form the **Jamaican Labour Party (JLP)**. The PNP, however, has enjoyed the substantial support of the Trades Union Council (TUC).

Michael Manley succeeded his father in the leadership of the PNP in 1969, and the 1972 election was primarily a contest over the PNP's competence to govern, and not over appeals to democratic socialism which developed largely from 1974 onwards. PNP attempts to nationalize the critical Jamaican bauxite industry, to extend health, education and social services to the majority of the population, as well as to pursue a vigorous non-aligned foreign policy were eventually undermined by the terms of International Monetary Fund loan conditionality and the fall in foreign exchange earnings to finance such programmes. Manley was defeated in elections he called in 1980.

Although the democratic socialist rhetoric and promises have substantially diminished in the run-up to, and following the February 1989 general elections, the PNP remains a social democratic party dedicated to the mitigation of the negative consequences of a transparent open economy in a liberalized global order. The current deputy Prime Minister, P. J. Patterson, is likely to succeed Manley as leader of the PNP in the near future following Manley's recent ill health.

JCJS

PEOPLE'S PROGRESSIVE PARTY—PPP (Guyana). The first political party formed in **Guyana** (then British Guiana), the PPP was founded in 1950 by a group led by **Cheddi Jagan** and his US-born wife, Janet, who were declared party leader and general secretary, respectively. Jagan is currently leader and general secretary, while his wife now edits the party newspaper, the *Mirror*. The PPP, which has traditionally held a marxist ideology and enjoyed close relations with the pre-Gorbachev Soviet leadership, had two periods in power before Guyana became independent, but has been in opposition since 1964. Its first spell in office in 1953 lasted only 133 days before it was dismissed by the Governor on the grounds that it had promoted communist subversion. After a split in 1955 which led to the creation of the **People's National Congress** led by **Forbes Burnham**, it again held office from 1957 to 1964, a period which ended in severe political and ethnic violence.

The PPP's main strength has been among the rural Indo–Guyanese population; Jagan is president of its affiliated trade union, the Guyana Agricultural Workers' Union, which organizes the majority of sugar workers. While the party still holds to its basic socialist position, PPP leaders indicated in late 1990 that it was preparing an electoral programme aimed at securing broad-based support, including economic policies which would give an active role to private business. The PPP, which had long accused the government and the PNC of rigging successive general elections, appeared to have the best chance in many years of mounting a strong opposition campaign in the 1991 election, after securing President **Desmond Hoyte's** agreement to electoral reform.

RP

PEREZ, CARLOS ANDRES. Carlos Andrés Pérez Rodríguez, Venezuelan statesman, was born at Rubio on Oct. 27, 1922, and educated at the Universidad Central de Venezuela. A devoted supporter of **Rómulo Betancourt**, to whom he was briefly private secretary in 1945, he entered the Chamber of Deputies in 1947, but went into exile in Costa Rica following the 1948 *coup* and between 1953 and 1958 was chief editor of the San José daily *La República*. Returning to the Chamber in 1958, his five-year term was interrupted by a brief spell as Minister of the Interior, 1953–64. In 1968 he became Secretary General of the **Democratic Action** party, (*Acción Democrática*). As President of Venezuela, 1974–79, he carried through the nationalization of the iron and steel industry in 1975 and of the oil industry in 1976. He was re-elected in 1988 and took office for an unprecedented second five-year term in 1989.

PARC

PERÓN, JUAN DOMINGO. President of **Argentina** 1946–55 and 1973–74, born on Oct. 8, 1895 the grandson of a Sardinian immigrant, Juan Domingo Perón chose a career as an officer in the army, where he distinguished himself mainly as a scholar, translator and author of books on military history and strategy, and a professor at the staff colleges of both the army and the navy.

After the death of his first wife, Aurelia Tizón, in 1938, Colonel Perón was posted as military attaché to Italy, with the mission of assessing the political situation in Europe. He was much impressed by what he saw in Germany, and particularly by the Fascist experience in Italy. Following his return to Argentina in 1940, he became one of the leaders in the work of the Unification Working Group (*Grupo Obra de Unificación*— GOU), the conspiratorial cabal of colonels who organized the military *coup* of 1943.

Within the military government, Perón, as head of the labour secretariat, built himself a following among the trade unions. His rise to war minister, then vice-president, and the growing prominence of his mistress (later second wife) María Eva Duarte (*Evita*) irked many among the military, who in 1945 forced him to resign and imprisoned him. A mass demonstration in October 1945 forced his release and became the platform for his successful candidacy in the 1946 elections.

His policies were a blend of pro-labour measures and the promotion of industrialization through protectionism and state intervention. His style of government was increasingly authoritarian, particularly after his re-election in 1951 and the death of *Evita* in 1952.

In 1955 Perón was ousted by a military *coup* and forced to flee into exile. For the following 18 years he directed his Peronist (later **Justicialist**) party from Madrid, out-manoeuvring a series of attempts to destroy it or turn it into "Peronism without Perón". After the Peronists won the elections in 1973, Perón returned to Argentina: new elections were called, and he was again elected President (with his third wife, María Estela Martínez, as vice-president). He presided over the violent split between the right and left wings of Peronism that became one of the causes of the "dirty war" of the mid-1970s, before dying on July 1, 1974.

EC

PERU. *Population*: 22,330,000 (mid-1990 estimate). *Area*: 1,285,216 sq km. *GDP*: 21,758.0 million (1988). *Trade volume*: exports US$3,540 million; imports $2,141 million (1989). *Top five trading partners*: USA, Japan, Germany, UK, Brazil. *Defence spending*: $702,000,000. *Education spending (as percentage of GNP)*: 2.7 (1988). *Urban population as percentage of total (centres over 20,000)*: 69.3 (1989 estimate). *Birthrate*: 25 per 1,000 (1990). *Life expectancy*: 62.7 (1989).

Geographical background. Peru possesses three main geographical zones — coast, highlands (*sierra*) and jungle (*selva*)—which together contain every climate found on earth. A desert that varies in width from 30 to 50 kilometres runs the length of Peru's Pacific coast. Thirty-six river valleys fed by rain from the Andes house the main cities that form the economic and political heart of the country. Irrigated agriculture produces sugar, cotton, rice, maize and other foodstuffs on what are the most technologically advanced farms in Peru. Inland the Andes rise majestically to over 4,000 metres, forming the backbone of the country. Within short distances a myriad of micro-climates exist that range from sub-tropical sugar cane valleys to bleak moorlands. Only 4.5 per cent of the *sierra* is arable land, whereas around 25 per cent comprises unimproved pasture. Agriculture is mainly geared towards cereal, potato, vegetable and livestock husbandry. Most of Peru's mines (copper, silver, lead, gold) are located in the *sierra*. Until 1940 approximately 65 per cent of Peruvians lived in the highlands, but large-scale migration to the coast has reduced this figure to 35 per cent. Today the coastal cities (Lima, Trujillo, Chiclayo, Arequipa, etc.) house 55 per cent of the population. To the east the Andes meet the tropical rainforest of the Amazon basin, which covers 65 per cent of Peru's superficie. Here most cultivable land and human settlement is located in the *ceja de selva* ("jungle's eyebrow"). These Andean foothills produce coffee, tea, palm oil, exotic fruits, and—importantly—coca. Peru's spectacular but difficult landscape has hindered economic development and political integration.

Socio-political background. As well as possessing an amazing topography, Peru is one of the most complex societies in Latin America. After Pizarro's defeat of the Inca Empire in the 1530s a small group of Spanish extraction exploited the colony for their own benefit, dominating a large indigenous population that never fully accepted their conqueror's right to govern and doggedly defended their own culture and traditions. Ethnic divisions have been reinforced by deep geographical and class cleavages. Spanish settlement and government was centred on the coast. The bulk of indigenous peasants lived in the highlands. Over the past three centuries Peru has had one of the most unequal social structures in Latin America: the *criollo* "oligarchy" owned the mines, *haciendas* (estates) and manufactories, it dominated commercial life and sustained its privileged position by ruthlessly squashing periodic challenges from below. In 1961 the wealthiest 1 per cent of the population received 30 per cent of national income; the top 5 per cent some 53 per cent of national income. Democracy has shallow roots. Until 1980 literacy and property qualifications excluded the majority from participating in what were more often than not "formal" elections characterized by widespread fraud or the vetoing of opposition parties. Between Independence from Spain in 1821 and 1980 the military occupied government for around 100 of the 160 years. From 1912 until 1985 no democratically elected government managed to avoid being ousted by a military *coup* before its term of office expired. For the majority of the population prior to 1950 the state signified taxation and conscription; they received little in the way of education, health provision or other benefits. Inefficiency and corruption in the judiciary and other branches of government encouraged alienation and mistrust among peasants and the urban poor. The elite also discouraged the lower classes from organizing, with the result that by the 1960s Peru possessed a more weakly developed civil society than Chile, Colombia or Venezuela.

Outline of political history. In an attempt to change this state of affairs and modernize the country, on Oct. 3, 1968 General Juan Velasco Alvarado launched a military takeover, so beginning a 12-year period of army rule that has proved a watershed in the socio–political life of twentieth century Peru. Velasco's period in office (1968–75) was unlike other military governments in Latin America at the time, although his policies, like theirs, were influenced by "national security" considerations. As part of his strategy to cut the power of the oligarchy, reduce inequality by widening ownership and control, so creating conditions for a more democratic society, Velasco implemented a thorough-going agrarian reform that effectively destroyed landlord power in the countryside. Almost 8,000,000 hectares were handed over to direct producers in co-operatives or on an individual basis. Industrialists were encouraged to invest and expand production. Some foreign enterprises in the extractive sector (mining, oil) were nationalized, along with the fishing industry, where domestic capital dominated. The state began to play a more interventionist role in the economy, administering agro-industrial enterprises, mines and investing in large-scale infrastructural projects (e.g. coastal irrigation schemes, road building, etc.). As a result, the state's contribution to GDP increased from 13 to 23 per cent between 1968 and 1975. At the social and cultural level efforts were made to further peasant integration into national life. Health care provision and educational opportunities expanded (between 1968 and 1980 secondary school enrolment increased from 15 per cent to 57 per cent—one of the highest in Latin America). The government attempted to introduce elements of industrial democracy into factories, providing profit-sharing incentives and seats on boards for workers. Peasant, trade union and shanty town organizations flourished. Many old elite families found themselves marginalized from power while new entrepreneurial groups emerged.

This experiment in military reformism from above came to an abrupt end in August 1975 when General Francisco Morales Bermúdez led a bloodless *coup* against a very sick General Velasco. During this "second phase" of military rule (1975–80) Morales responded to growing economic problems due to world recession, falling commodity prices and excessive foreign borrowing by implementing a succession of IMF designed "stabilization" programmes. These reduced the 1978 real minimum wage to only 55 per cent of its 1973 level. Deepening unemployment and hunger produced a strong response from labour and shanty town organizations that had grown in strength during the Velasco period. General strikes occurred in July 1977 and May 1978 that paralyzed Lima and other key cities. Miners, schoolteachers and other groups entered into prolonged confrontation with the Morales regime. The military reacted with widespread repression, but was unable to demobilize the population, whose demonstrations started to take on an overtly political complexion as demands for a return to democracy increased.

Faced from without by growing radicalism among the urban poor, and from within by deepening divisions inside the military as to how to control a potentially explosive political situation, in 1978 Morales Bermúdez instigated a controlled return to elected government with the holding of a poll for a Consituent Assembly—one indication of the degree of popular discontent being the 29.5 per cent of votes cast for the marxist left, hitherto an insignificant political force. The resultant Assembly was controlled, however, by an alliance between the populist Popular Revolutionary American Alliance (*Alianza Popular Revolucionaria Americana*—APRA), headed by its historic *caudillo* Víctor Raúl Haya de la Torre, and the rightist Popular Christian Party (*Partido Popular Cristiano*—PPC), under the leadership of lawyer Luis Bedoya. These parties succeeded in drafting a constitution that created a presidential system of government with a two-house congress, a second-round balloting system on the French model and, after considerable pressure and debate, enfranchised illiterates. Full elections were called for May 1980, the clear winner being Fernando Belaúnde and his Popular Action (*Acción Popular*—AP) party, who garnered 45.4 per cent of the ballot compared to second-placed APRA's 27.4 per cent. Belaúnde, who had been removed from office by General Velasco in 1968, was able to capitalize on widespread anti-military sentiment. He also profited from fears about APRA's authoritarian tradition and the poor image of APRA candidate Armando Villanueva (Haya de la Torre having died in 1979), factors that led many voters to support Belaúnde as the "lesser evil". Although organizations heavily influenced by the left, through their struggles against the Morales regime, had been the prime mover in forcing the military back to the barracks, in early 1980 Peru's left split into five different factions which resulted in a steep decline in support. This fell to a combined figure of 14.4 per cent of the national vote.

Belaúnde originally attained office in 1963 on the basis of a centre-left reformist programme that promised agrarian reform and modernization. His failure to deliver proved an important element in Velasco's decision to seize power in October 1968. Likewise, in his second term as president (1980–85) Belaúnde presided over an incompetent and corrupt government that made extravagant promises in the election campaign (such as 1,000,000 new jobs) but once in office did nothing to ameliorate the harsh living conditions endured by a majority of Peruvians. Although Belaúnde was a "developmentalist" by inclination he appointed an international banker, Manuel Ulloa, as his Finance Minister. Ulloa, surrounded by a team of young technocrats and bankers firmly in the neo-classical tradition, lowered tariffs with a view to increasing international competitiveness, attempted to expand raw material exports and embarked on a policy of continuous mini-devaluations through a crawling peg system to foment export promotion. Some denationalizations and cutting of subsidies on basic commodities occurred. To encourage foreign investment regulations governing profit remittance were relaxed. The policy ended in abject failure. Given that the government was opposed to raising revenue from taxing business or direct taxation, additional foreign loans were negotiated at a time when interest rates rocketed, leading to a sharp increase in foreign debt and the repayment ratio. In order to bridge the fiscal deficit taxes on domestic petroleum sales were increased at regular intervals. Inflation started to rise steeply (61 per cent in 1980, 125 per cent in 1983 and 163 per cent in 1985) and stabilization packages produced further declines in real wages, leading to deep recession. In 1983 GDP fell by a massive 12.3 per cent, unemployment grew to an extent that by mid-1984 only 30 per cent of the workforce was in full time employment (between 1980 and 1984 over 20 per cent of Peru's industrial workers lost their jobs) and the informal sector expanded to record proportions. The already miserable living standards of the majority fell to historically low levels: in 1983 real wages fell by 21.4 per cent and salaries by 15.9 per cent. Between 1980 and 1985 GDP fell in real terms at an annual average rate of 0.5%. In 1984 *per capita* income was $882, one of the lowest in Latin America. Official unemployment in 1985 stood at a record 12.4% and official underemployment (defined as those earning less than the minimum wage or working less than 20 hours per week) at 60 per cent. In reality the unemployment figures were far higher. Instead of providing 1,000,000 new jobs between 1980 and 1985, as promised in Belaúnde's election campaign, gross economic mismanagement resulted in some 400,000 jobs being lost and industry working at an average of only 59 per cent capacity.

Recent developments—political. The economic record of the Belaúnde administration was the poorest of any Peruvian government since the 1930s. Substantial declines in living standards were accompanied by increases in crime, social unrest and record levels of corruption on the part of political appointees in the state apparatus. During the first half of 1985 a power vacuum existed: faced with extensive public hostility the government practically ceased to function; fears were expressed regarding a possible "Beirutization" of Peru. Against this backdrop it was no surprise that support for the AP candidate in the April 1985 presidential election plummeted from the 45 per cent obtained in 1980 to 6 per cent, despite control of the state machine and support from powerful media interests. The PPC, who had been a coalition partner of AP (only leaving the government six months before the poll in order to save its skin), allied with a small rightist breakaway faction from APRA and managed to gain 10 per cent of the vote. As a result representation of AP and the PPC in congress was slashed: the number of AP deputies fell from 98 to 10 in the 1985–90 congress. Just as the April 1985 general election was a disaster for the Peruvian right, it provided an overwhelming victory for APRA, Peru's oldest and best organized political party that had been vainly attempting to gain office since the 1930s. Led by Alan García, a charismatic, youthful 36 year-old lawyer who successfully caught the electorate's mood in favour of change and energetically pushed a message of hope and national renewal, APRA garnered 53 per cent of the poll. It also managed to win a majority in both houses of congress, with a representation of 32 senators and 107 deputies. The left, most of which had coalesced after the 1980 debacle to found the United Left (*Izquierda Unida*—IU), came second with 25 per cent of the national vote and became the main opposition force in parliament, securing the election of 15 senators and 48 deputies.

Although APRA possessed no detailed policies on attaining office, the negative experience of several IMF-style stabilization packages since 1976 convinced García and his associates that orthodox monetarist strategies were inappropriate. The monetarist premise that inflation was demand-led was discarded on the grounds that most Peruvians lacked disposable income and the economy suffered from a lack of demand. It was argued that inflation was cost-induced owing to constant currency devaluations, strong inflationary expectations and high interest rates. A Keynesian-style reactivation strategy aimed at obtaining high growth rates, rising living standards, reduced inflation and a long-term restructuring of the economy in favour of national capital was consequently adopted. Upon becoming president on July 28, 1985 Alan García announced that payment of the foreign debt would be restricted to 10 per cent of export earnings, the money saved being directed towards internal investment. Prices of basic commodities and wages were raised, then frozen for 100 days so to lessen inflationary pressures. Subsidies would be channelled to producers to boost production and interest rates cut to encourage investment, especially in agriculture. The exchange rate was frozen with the aim of lowering inflation (the rising cost of imported food being particularly onerous to the poor) and providing stability for exporters. Tariffs were raised on selected items to protect national industry. On the political front the APRA administration, having waited 60 years to gain office, aimed to convert APRA into the "natural" party of government along the lines of the Mexican **Institutional Revolutionary Party**. A non-aligned foreign policy was adopted. Economic and political strategy was to be underpinned by a policy of *concertación*—co-operation between industry, labour and the state to pull Peru out of its social and economic crisis.

For two years the García administration seemed well on target to achieve its goals: in 1986 GDP rose by 9.5 per cent, followed by an equally impressive 7.8 per cent in 1987. Real wages grew by 14.4 per cent in 1986 and 8.7 per cent in 1987, the first significant increases since 1975. Employment expanded. By the end of 1986 industry was on average operating at 70 per cent capacity, well up on the 59 per cent of the previous year. Official inflation rates decreased from 163 per cent in 1985 to 78 per cent in 1986 and 86 per cent in 1987. The currency stabilized at an average 10.9 *intis* to the dollar in 1986 and 16.8 *intis* in 1987. After the disappointments of the Belaúnde years, this relative improvement in economic performance brought political rewards. President García's popularity in opinion polls published through 1986 and 1987 registered a remarkably high 70 to 80 per cent. In the local elections of November 1986 APRA candidates won control of most municipalities. Nationally APRA gained 48 per cent of the vote, followed by 31 per cent for IU. The right, represented by Bedoya's PPC, polled a mere 15 per cent despite spending heavily on propaganda. AP, deeply traumatized by the scale of its 1985 defeat, failed to compete.

Particularly pleasing for Alan García and APRA was its performance outside its traditional strongholds in northern Peru, the party's birthplace. In various speeches García referred to Peruvian society as a "pyramid" divided into four segments: (i) a relatively small "formal" and modern sector that constitutes the privileged Peru composed of the industrial and financial élite; (ii) the middle class and the organized working class in relatively stable employment; and the "informal" or underprivileged Peru composed of: (iii) the unemployed or underemployed shanty town inhabitants; and (iv) *campesinos* (land workers). Organizations controlled by the left, the main opposition force, influenced the latter groups. To expand APRA support among the "informal" urban poor, García launched public works programmes to provide them with a minimum wage. Preference when hiring was given to individuals expressing APRA sympathies, they were used on APRA projects and to disrupt rival campaign meetings at election time. Similar attempts to establish clientelage networks in the countryside were launched in 1986 when five *rimanacuys*, or mass dialogues, were held. At these events García met with village and peasant community leaders to discuss problems, the president promising technical aid and credit to the participants. His goal was to by-pass existing shanty town and peasant organizations dominated by the left, such as the Peruvian Peasants Confederation (*Confederación Campesina del Perú*—CCP). The manoeuvre appeared successful when APRA won IU strongholds in the highlands, including Cuzco and Puno, in the 1986 municipal elections. Likewise, in Lima APRA received a substantial shanty town vote to defeat the incumbent IU mayor Alfonso Barrantes by 38 to 34 per cent despite fielding a third-rate candidate. In addition to the improving economic situation. APRA's popularity owed much to the personality of Alan García. Whereas the "aristocratic" Belaúnde appeared aloof, bungling and unconcerned about the plight of the majority, García made a conscious effort to communicate with the populace via "*balconazos*" (speeches from the balcony of the presidential palace), television, as well as regular visits to markets and shanty towns. From the outset he strove to create an image of drive and authority, giving the impression that the power vacuum at the centre of the political system evident towards the end of the Belaúnde government had been filled. García also tried to create the impression that his administration was more caring and efficient than its predecessor.

The Achilles heel of the APRA government, however, remained Peru's precarious economic position. Although the heterodox economic strategy met with considerable short-term success, by early 1987 it was obvious that problems loomed on the horizon. To maintain the model on course to meet the target of a 6 per cent per annum growth rate from 1987 to 1990 substantial investment would be required, for some industries were already operating at full capacity. The increasing informalization of the economy meant that tax revenues had not risen as expected, leading to an increase in the public sector deficit (–2.4 per cent of GDP in 1985, –5.1 and –6.6 per cent in 1986 and 1987). Balance of payments problems also arose as producers diverted exports to the home market—the current account balance stood at $135,000,000 in 1985, –$1080 million in 1986 and –$1481 million in 1987. Non-gold currency reserves consequently fell from $1407 million in 1986 to $646,000,000 in 1987. Aware of the importance of investment to the success or failure of economic policy García held regular talks with the 14 industrial and financial groups that monopolize the Peruvian economy. They were offered price adjustments, tax incentives, the right to import capital goods at favourable exchange rates and other inducements to invest. Yet industrialists and financiers remained cautious owing to insecurity caused by the guerrilla insurgency of **Sendero Luminoso**, a mistrust of García's populist rhetoric and government price freezes, as well as concern regarding the political weakness of the right (in the November 1986 municipal elections the alternative to APRA remained IU). For a variety of reasons therefore many investment decisions were scaled-down, postponed or cancelled. Faced with what he interpreted as an investment strike by the oligarchy, on July 28, 1987 President García took an impetuous gamble, announcing the nationalization of the banks in his independence day speech, a move that severed the close links built up between the government and key sectors of the business community since 1985.

The bank nationalization policy was ill

thought-out and announced without consulting the party apparatus. It caused a political earthquake, providing an issue to enable the right to re-emerge as a serious actor on the political scene. Supported by AP, the PPC and most of the media, Thatcher-admiring novelist Mario Vargas Llosa organized a series of meetings in Peru's main coastal cities against what he called APRA "totalitarianism" and a supposed threat to the savings of small account holders. A lack of business confidence produced a collapse in investment and substantial capital flight (between August 1987 and August 1988 around $5,500 million left Peru). By the last quarter of 1987 it was obvious that the economic honeymoon was over: in December 1987 the currency was devalued by 50 per cent in an effort to foment exports and currency reserves. Production levelled off and as the government printed money inflation began to rise sharply, reaching 666 per cent in 1988 and 3,399 per cent in 1989. With García forced to enact the first of several draconian stabilization packages in September 1988 in a vain attempt to control inflation, GDP slumped by a massive −8.5 per cent in 1988 and −10.4 per cent in 1989, more than wiping out previous gains. The resultant fall in living standards produced a steep decline in popularity for García and APRA. City-wide protests and looting greeted the September 1988 adjustment, to be followed by bitter strikes and street disorders as workers struggled to defend their jobs and incomes. Strong rumours about a *coup* and the resignation of the president swept Lima in late 1988. Political and criminal violence escalated, the APRA government appearing as much out of control as Belaúnde had during his last year in office.

With Mario Vargas Llosa and his Liberty (*Libertad*) movement having cajoled the PPC and AP into an electoral coalition, the Democratic Front (*Frente Democrática*—FREDEMO), the APRA candidate Luis Alva understandably unpopular, and the legal Left having divided into two camps in 1989, it appeared certain that the renowned novelist would win the general election of April 1990. Amply supplied with funds from Peru's business community (especially the bankers) and openly backed by the most influential sectors of the mass media, FREDEMO candidates registered many victories in the November 1989 municipal elections. By January 1990 Vargas Llosa held a commanding lead in the opinion polls, with 48 per cent of preferences, well ahead of second-placed Alfonso Barrantes of the Socialist Left (*Izquierda Socialista*—IS) who registered 17 per cent support. The April 1990 election, however, produced a major surprise when agronomist Alberto Fujimori, presidential candidate of the Cambio-90 movement, attracted a meteoric increase in support during the last 10 days of the campaign to gain 24.6 per cent of the vote to 27.6 per cent for Vargas Llosa. APRA, who fought a strong unified campaign and used control of the state machine to full advantage, garnered only 19 per cent. In a repeat of the 1980 election, the candidates of the divided Left were regarded as a "wasted vote", IU receiving a derisory 6.9 per cent and IS 4 per cent.

Among the factors explaining the rapid decline in support for Vargas Llosa numbered widespread hostility to his extreme neo-liberal social and economic programme, especially the "shock" economic policy promised by FREDEMO; disgust at the large amount of money wasted by FREDEMO candidates on an avalanche of poor-quality advertising at a time when large sectors of the population were suffering from hunger and malnutrition; the *gringo pituco* ("rich white") image of the novelist, who also appeared to many electors as extremely arrogant and intolerant; effective anti-FREDEMO propaganda by the opposition, particularly APRA; a widely held feeling that Vargas Llosa was in the pocket of the bankers and the traditional *caudillos* of the Peruvian right, Fernando Belaúnde and Luis Bedoya; and last but not least, memories of the ineffective Belaúnde administration between 1980–85.

For his part, Fujimori profited from his image as a true independent at a time of great public cynicism and disillusion with all established political parties. Fujimori's no-nonsense modesty and popular perceptions of Japanese character traits (honest, diligent, efficient, technologically advanced, etc.) also widened his appeal among electors. As no candidate received the 50 per cent plus one valid vote necessary to secure victory in the first round, a second ballot between the two front runners took place on June 10, 1990. Assisted by votes from APRA and the Left, Fujimori won by a clear margin, obtaining 57 per cent to Vargas Llosa's 34 per cent, in spite of backing for the novelist from the hierarchy of the Catholic Church (alarmed by the presence of evangelicals in the Cambio-90 coalition), and racist attacks by desperate FREDEMO supporters (denounced by Vargas Llosa) on Fujimori's Japanese parentage.

The 1990 elections provided a severe jolt to Peru's political system and encouraged its fragmentation. FREDEMO, who appeared to have victory in its grasp, split amid bitter recrimination shortly after the June poll, as populist elements in AP blamed defeat on the political naivety and unrealistic monetarist zeal of economic liberals in *Libertad*. A majority of Vargas Llosa's *Libertad* movement are debating the idea of converting the organization into a political party with a rigid "Thatcherite" ideology to compete with AP and the PPC. The legal Left also remains deeply divided, personal animosities sharpened in the late 1980s making future unification problematic. APRA, although performing far better in the 1990 elections than many anticipated, contains serious internal schisms along personal and policy lines, conflicts that are likely to accentuate if Alan García decides to seek nomination as APRA's presidential candidate for 1995. In a deeply polarized society the 1990 elections indicated a massive rejection of "formal" political organizations and their leaders. The Peru of the largely white upper and middle class, heavily influenced by Europe and the USA, was rejected by a preponderantly Indian and mestizo majority who had had enough. Developments in Peruvian politics in 1990 illustrated that the gap between the "official" and the "real" Peru that General Velasco hoped to narrow remains as wide as ever.

Outline of economic development. From 1890 to 1940 Peru was more fortunate than most neighbouring countries in that it produced a wider range of export commodities (sugar, cotton, wool, minerals, some oil). Even in times of depressed international prices one item could usually be relied upon to receive a reasonable return. With the state heavily influenced by the agro-export oligarchy, over these decades Peru had one of the most open economies in Latin America. In the agrarian sector export crops were grown on modern plantations (sugar) and *haciendas* (cotton) employing wage labour and sharecroppers respectively. Wool was the chief export of highland agriculture, especially in the central and southern *sierra.* Around 70 per cent of the rural population lived on peasant smallholdings that cultivated subsistence crops but were also integrated into labour and commodity markets. Beginning in the 1890s, some industrial development occurred (textiles being the leading sector), but after 1920 growth stagnated, so that in 1940 a majority of the populace still earned their living from rural activities.

After World War II major socio-economic changes materialized. Large-scale rural–urban migration, chiefly from the highlands to the coast, took place stimulated by demographic increase, land fragmentation and falling living standards in the peasant economy. Lima grew in size from 500,000 inhabitants in 1940 to around 3,000,000 in 1968, other coastal cities registering important increases. To feed the expanding towns, sugar and cotton cultivation contracted (these two key crops accounted for only 11.2 per cent of Peru's exports in 1970, having been 50.5 per cent in 1950). The fishing industry (fishmeal and canning) boomed during the 1950s and 1960s to become the leading export sector. Overall, healthy export revenues in the post-war "long boom" helped GDP to increase by 4.5 per cent per annum between 1955–60, 6.7 per cent between 1960–65 and 4.4 per cent 1965–70. Although some expansion in the urban middle class took place, most of the benefits of this growth remained in the hands of the élite. Even so, important developments in manufacturing (chemicals, pharmaceuticals, vehicle assemble, food processing, electrical goods, etc.) led to significant shifts in the composition of GDP. Agriculture declined from 20.4 per cent of GDP in 1950 to less than 15 per cent in 1968. Manufacturing's share of GDP grew from 16.7 per cent in 1950 to 22.2 per cent in 1968. Since then the balance has stabilized: in 1989 agriculture accounted for 13.5 per cent of GDP, manufacturing 21.2, mining 10.5, commerce 13.2, services 35.2, construction 5.2 and fishing (which declined as a result of overfishing) 1.2 per cent. Output in the manufacturing sector expanded by 6 per cent a year in the 1950s and almost 11 per cent in the 1960s. Much of the growth was stimulated by foreign firms and investment. Production was typically capital intensive, concentrated on Lima and provided relatively little permanent employment, so despite quite rapid industrial growth the proportion of the economically active population employed in factory-based manufacturing stood at 4.5% in 1961, just over 5% in 1968 and 10.4% in 1989. Agriculture and fishing still account for 34.4% of employment (1989).

Current economic situation. Upon officially assuming the presidency on July 28, 1990, Alberto Fujimori inherited an economic shambles of terrifying proportions. After major falls in 1989 and 1990, GDP was forecast to decline by a further 8 per cent in 1990. Inflation was spiralling out of control: from slightly over 30 per cent a month in the first quarter of 1990, it touched 90 per cent in July 1990, equivalent to an annual rate of 221,000 per cent! The currency had undergone devaluation on a massive scale: from an average of 16.8 *intis* to the dollar in 1987, to 30,000 *intis* in April 1990 and *180,000* intis to the dollar by July 28, 1990. Manufacturing output and demand had plunged after the September 1988 adjustment: production falling by 32.9 per cent during the first quarter of 1989, after which recovery was weak. Living standards had suffered additional substantial erosion. An estimated 800,000 workers in Lima who had been employed in 1987 have reputedly lost their jobs as a consequence of the

1989–90 recession, most being compelled to swell the ranks of an ever expanding informal sector. Salaries had fallen by around 28 per cent in 1988 and wages by 27 per cent, trends that accelerated in 1989, when hyperinflation reduced real salaries by an incredible 50.8 per cent and wages by 45.7 per cent of their 1988 level. In real terms the minimum monthly wage declined by 51.7 per cent in 1989.

Confronted with such chaos, Fujimori wisely took drastic action early on into his presidency, even though he had been coy about stating his economic policy during the election campaign, preferring to allow Mario Vargas Llosa to take all the flak. On Aug. 8, 1990 the new Prime Minister, Juan Carlos Hurtado Miller, announced a stabilization package (the "Fujishock") that was even more severe than that envisaged by FREDEMO. Among the measures adopted included an elimination of all subsidies and price controls, the abolition of import controls, a maximum tariff of 50 per cent and a minimum tariff of 10 per cent, an increase in export taxes and a reduction in the legal reserve requirement for commercial banks from 80 to 60 per cent. Huge increases in gasoline prices were announced—up 3,000 per cent from 7 US cents a gallon to around $4.80 a gallon in August 1990. Basic items like bread, milk, noodles, sugar and cooking oil increased in price by seven times. The cost of medicine rose by an average 400 per cent. The minimum wage, however, only rose four times, to $125 per month. The Social Compensation Programme promised by the government to cushion the impact of the harsh economic measures among the poorest sectors of society got off to a slow start and functioned half-heartedly. The "shock" treatment reduced inflation in October and November 1991 to around 11 per cent a month. Unfortunately the likelihood is that inflation rates will gradually climb in 1991. Since 1976 successive Peruvian governments have implemented 29 stabilization programmes. Not one of them has worked. In another policy initiative, president Fujimori has shelved Alan García's 10 per cent ceiling on debt repayments and is attempting to reach agreement with the IMF in the hope that Peru's reinsertion into the international financial system will produce new loans and foreign investment. Peru's external debt stands at nearly $20,000 million and servicing it requires $2,000 million a year.

Prospects for development. Although the authorities are expecting a fall in inflation and a slight economic recovery in 1991—based on mining, construction, fishing and a growth in exports leading to higher reserves—the substantial drop in real wages signifies continued weak internal demand and poor sales for manufacturing industry. Overall, the development prospects of Peru remain extremely bleak.

LT

PETROLEOS MEXICANOS (PEMEX). The state oil company, Pémex, came into existence following the expropriation of all foreign-owned oil companies in **Mexico** on March 18, 1938. By choosing to make the oil expropriation a fundamental issue of national sovereignty, the Mexican authorities made it difficult to change policy and permit private investment to return to oil-related activities. Pémex still has a monopoly of oil exploration, production, refining and distribution; it also controls what are defined as "basic" petrochemicals. It may contract private companies for specific functions, but it may not cede control over the main decisions surrounding the industry.

Pémex has always been characterized by a strong labour union. This feature has its roots in the period immediately after the expropriation; most managers of the industry were foreign and were recalled by the expelled companies. The oil industry was largely kept going by its workers. The union was formed early and remained strong. Although the government purged Communists from union leadership positions in the late 1940s, it did not seek to control the union's affairs directly. Instead it permitted the emergence of strong "labour bosses" who supplemented their undoubted popularity through extra-legal sources of power such as financial inducements and sometimes direct physical force. However when the oilworkers' leader Hernández de Galicia ("La Quina") became too independent for Mexico City, President Salinas ordered in the army in February 1989 to ensure his arrest.

Pémex has the advantage that the Mexican subsoil has some huge oil reserves. During the 1970s Mexico turned from being an importer of oil to becoming a net exporter, although the process was accompanied by some scandalous corruption and a great deal of political controversy. Mexico remains a significant exporter of oil, with an output of some 2,500,000 barrels per day (bpd). Nevertheless the relative decapitalization of Pémex since the economic crisis of 1982 has left some doubt surrounding the capacity of the company to invest enough in the industry to sustain output at current levels. It does not help that gasoline prices are well below international levels.

President Salinas is considering ways of easing some of the restrictions on Pémex' commercial operations while retaining its existing legal position. One set of options being explored is for US banks to earmark some loans to Pémex for drilling, while foreign drilling contractors are brought in to do the work.

GP

PINOCHET UGARTE, AUGUSTO. General Augusto Ugarte Pinochet (born 1915) was made commander-in-chief of the Chilean army three weeks before the *coup* of 1973. He was not among the first *coup*-plotters but as head of the army he was *primus inter pares* of the four heads of the armed forces. After the *coup*, with characteristic ruthlessness and political cunning, Pinochet gradually established his ascendancy over the other members of the military junta and over the armed forces in general. He used the promotion system within the army to create a force personally loyal to him and ensured that the secret police, the DINA (*Dirección Nacional de Inteligencia*, replaced in 1976 by the CNI — *Centro Nacional de Informaciones*) reported directly to him.

General Pinochet wanted the 1980 constitution to make him president until 1997 but was persuaded to include the provision for a plebiscite in 1988 to approve a second eight-year term. The economic collapse of 1982 and a wave of bitter, massive protest drastically changed his prospects but, in 1980, at the height of a consumer boom, the plebiscite did not seem too great a risk. General Pinochet retains enormous, if declining, influence in public life: he can remain as commander-in-chief of the armed forces until 1993; he is a senator for life and a member of the National Security Council.

GG

POPULAR DEMOCRATIC PARTY (Partido Popular Democrático — PPD) (Puerto Rico). Founded in 1938 by Luis Muñoz Marín, the PPD led the campaign for greater autonomy for **Puerto Rico**, culminating in the granting of commonwealth status, and oversaw the industrialization of the 1950s and 1960s. The PPD has always had a strong hold on the legislature. In recent years the party has compaigned vigorously for the retention of Puerto Rico's current status and tax incentives.

LP

PRESIDENCY (Mexico). Mexico's political system is strongly presidential. There are fewer restraints, checks or balances on presidential power in Mexico than in almost any other political system. The ruling party invariably controls Congress and also the vast majority of state governorships and legislatures. The judiciary enjoys some independence but there is no tradition of judicial review as such.

The Mexican presidential term last six years. There is no re-election. However the tradition has been for many years that the outgoing president has chosen his successor; this situation can only exist for as long as the candidate of the ruling **Institutional Revolutionary Party** is guaranteed electoral victory. Such has been the case up to and including 1988; it remains to be seen what will happen in 1994. In any event the last year of the presidential term is a kind of *interregnum*, as attention shifts from the outgoing president to the incoming man.

The new president chooses his own Cabinet; one or two figures may be kept over from the previous administration, but no more than this. The president had the notional power to select the entire public administration, but in practice some of this will be sub-contracted to other power holders. To the extent that there are real limits on presidential power, these are likely to be imposed by the business community and — to an increasing but still limited extent — the formal political opposition.

A number of Mexican intellectuals believe that their system is too presidential, and that something should be done to limit the power of the chief executive. However presidential power emerged as a counterweight to the regional fiefdoms and political bosses who were so powerful in Mexico prior to around 1940. Many Mexicans prefer a strong central authority to the threat of lawlessness.

GP

PUERTO RICO. *Population*: 3,273,600 (1987). *Area*: 8,891 sq km. *GDP*: US$24,372 million. *Trade volume*: $30,398 million. *Top five trading partners*: USA, Dominican Republic, United States Virgin Islands, Venezuela, Japan. *Education spending (as percentage of GNP)*: 7.2 (1987). *Birthrate*: 19.4 per 1,000. *Life expectancy*: 70 (men); 77 (women).

Geographical background. The Commonwealth of Puerto Rico comprises the island of Puerto Rico, the fourth largest island in the Greater Antilles group in the Caribbean Sea, and a number of small offshore islands. A ridge of mountains, heavily forested, runs down the centre of Puerto Rico, with most of the human settlement in the coastal areas, particularly around the capital, San Juan. Population density is high. The area was inhabited by Arawak Indians prior to its discovery and colonization by Europeans in the sixteenth century. Claimed by Spain, Puerto Rico became a Spanish colony, developing a plantation economy based on the labour of imported African slaves. Slavery was abolished in 1873. Immigration from Europe and elsewhere in the Caribbean during the nineteenth century added to the ethnic mix. A local struggle for autonomy at the end of the nineteenth century was cut short by the capture of Puerto Rico by the Americans in 1898 during the US–Spanish War and its cession to the USA after the peace treaty.

Socio–political background. Puerto Rico is an "unincorporated territory" of the USA, styled as a state in "free association" with the USA. Puerto Ricans are US citizens, but do not have the right to vote in presidential elections or have representation at Washington, apart from an elected Permanent Representative who can speak in the House of Representatives, but who has no vote. Congress has the right to make laws apply to Puerto Rico and the appropriate federal departments are responsible for defence, currency, communications and foreign affairs. Puerto Rico enjoys internal self-government and elects a government to run the island. Elections are held every four years to elect a governor and the bicameral legislature, comprising a 27-member Senate and a 51-member House of Representatives. The Governor appoints a Cabinet of secretaries of state to assist him in the daily running of the government.

Puerto Rico is an important base for the US military. When Puerto Rico was acquired by the USA the strategic importance of the island as a naval base and as a guardian of the sea approaches to the vitally important Panama Canal was soon recognized. This has been augmented by the perceived threat to US interests in the region from Cuba since 1959. In 1981 Puerto Rico became a centre of the US Forces Caribbean Command as part of the Reagan administration's reorganization of strategic policy in the region and the US Navy base on the offshore island of Vieques was used for major naval exercises.

Outline of political history. Modern political development began in 1938, with the formation of the **Popular Democratic Party** (*Partido Popular Democrático*—PPD) and the introduction of full universal suffrage. The PPD, under the charismatic leadership of Luis Muñoz Marín, campaigned vigorously to break the island's cycle of poverty and colonial dependence. An elective governorship was introduced in 1947 and the first gubernatorial elections were won by Muñoz, who was re-elected at subsequent elections until his retirement in 1967. Muñoz was also instrumental in steering Puerto Rico towards commonwealth status, as opposed to statehood or independence, thereby giving it autonomy in internal affairs. Puerto Rico became a state in "free association" (*estado libre asociado*) with the USA in 1952, after the proposals had been endorsed by a referendum. A further plebiscite on the status issue was held in 1967, with 60.5 per cent favouring the existing commonwealth status and 30.5 per cent favouring statehood. However, dissension within the PPD weakened the party's chances in the 1968 election and the post of governor was won by Luís A. Ferré, leader of the pro-statehood **New Progressive Party** (*Partido Nuevo Progresista*—PNP).

Since then the PNP and PPD have alternated in power, although the PPD has usually maintained an advantage in elections to the legislature. The breakdown of the PPD hegemony led to the development of a competitive two-party system, divided principally on the status issue. The PPD regained the governorship in 1972 when a young lawyer and senator, **Rafael Hernández Colón** defeated Ferré. He, in turn, lost to the PNP candidate, **Carlos Romero Barceló**, mayor of San Juan, in 1976. Romero was re-elected in 1980, but his margin of victory was small, forcing him to abandon plans for a further plebiscite on the status issue. Romero's record in government, particularly over circumstances surrounding the Cerro Maravilla affair in which two pro-independence activists were shot dead by police in 1978, divided his party, leading to a breakaway faction led by Hernán Padilla Ramírez, mayor of San Juan, who contested the 1984 gubernatorial election against Romero. In the event Hernández Colón regained the governorship, securing 47.6 per cent of the vote to 44.5 per cent for Romero.

The US government argues that commonwealth status makes the alleged "colonial" status of Puerto Rico no longer an issue of debate, but this has not prevented continued discussion of the question by the UN Special Committee on Decolonization. The pro-independence movement in Puerto Rico consists of the Puerto Rican Independence Party (*Partido Independentista Puertorriqueño*—PIP), the pro-Cuban Socialist Party (*Partido Socialista Puertorriqueño*—PSP) and a number of small left-wing groups, many of whom have resorted to political violence. Many of the attacks by extremist nationalist groups have occurred on the US mainland, such as the attack on the US House of Representatives in 1954. More recently nationalist bombing incidents in Puerto Rico and the USA have been carried out by the Armed Forces of National Liberation (*Fuerzas Armadas de Liberación*

Nacional Puertorriqueña — FALN) and the Puerto Rican Popular Army (*Ejército Popular Boricua*—EPB or *Los Macheteros*).

Recent developments—political. Recent political developments have centred around the status issue, which re-emerged as an item for political debate after Governor Hernández announced his intention to seek a new vote on the issue during his inauguration address in January 1989. In the gubernatorial elections held in November 1988 Hernández had retained the governorship, but by a much narrower margin than had been predicted in earlier opinion polls. The PPD retained its majority in both the Senate and House of Representatives and also the post of Permanent Representative. The PNP candidate, Baltasar Corrada del Río, mayor of San Juan, was judged to have benefited from the support of the then Vice-President George Bush who visited the island during the Republican presidential primaries. Like most Puerto Rican elections, the status issue had officially not been part of the campaign, but it had been understood that the choice of administration would almost certainly have an impact on the issue.

The leaders of all three main political parties petitioned Congress early in 1989 and on Feb. 9, 1989 President Bush addressed a joint session of Congress and approved the concept of a referendum. Legislation was introduced into Congress to authorize the holding of a plebiscite. Intensive lobbying was conducted by the Permanent Representative, Jaime B. Fuster, and the representatives of the other parties, on the precise terms of the questions to be put to the Puerto Rican electorate. The subsequent hearings and arguments over the terms were closely watched with interest in Puerto Rico. The bill passed the House of Representatives in late 1990—but it remained unclear whether all the outstanding objections would be overcome in time for a vote during 1991.

The status issue prompts basic questions as to the role and identity of Puerto Rico and the Puerto Ricans. The choices of statehood, independence or commonwealth reflect fundamental questions about nationhood, American assimilation, cultural and linguistic differences, and the existence of a distinctive Puerto Rican identity. Independence may be the spiritual goal of the majority of the population, but political and economic realities argue strongly against it as a viable option. The main pro-independence party, the PIP, has in recent years only achieved about 5 per cent of the popular vote in elections and drawn much of its electoral support from intellectuals, but the PIP's leader and only senator, Rubén Berríos Martínez, has consistently been one of the most popular politicians on the island.

Popular support for the statehood option, favoured by the PNP, grew during the 1980s and opinion polls conducted in 1990 placed it above the commonwealth option. Statehood has also received the support of important politicians on the US mainland. The PNP's policy of maintaining links with both Democratic and Republican leaders has thus paid dividends. Whereas the PPD is associated with the liberal wing of the Democratic party, the PNP has cultivated both Republicans and yet also represents Democrats on the island. Both Romero and Corrada, a former Permanent Representative to Washington, are nominally Democratic Party leaders in Puerto Rico, but other leaders of the PNP have close links with the Republicans. Ronald Reagan and George Bush were both strong supporters of statehood and Bush received Corrada's endorsement during the 1988 presidential election campaign. Republican help has also been provided to the PNP in local elections. Proponents of statehood see incorporation as providing greater stability, opportunities for growth and investment and settling fears of political and economic inferiority.

The PPD has stood by the existing commonwealth status, claiming that it has provided unique benefits for the island over the past—something that would be lost if Puerto Rico became the 51st and poorest state of the USA. The PPD, however, has insisted that the *status quo* should be enhanced by allowing Puerto Rico greater autonomy in internal affairs to let it regulate its own trade and economic development free of interference from Congress. Similar proposals had been endorsed by the 1967 referendum, but the reforms were not introduced into Congress at that time. The need for greater economic autonomy was particularly brought home by attempts during the 1980s to remove the benefits to Puerto Rico accruing under Section 936 of the Internal Revenue Code.

In January 1990 Hernández appointed Antonio J. Colorado, formerly head of the Economic Development Administration, as his secretary of state. Colorado has been a key figure in the lobbying to retain Section 936. In February Hernández gave his state of the commonwealth address and announced his intention to privatize the Puerto Rico Telephone Company, which had been brought into state ownership in the 1970s during his first term as governor. He proposed that the $2,000 million anticipated from the sale should be invested in two trust funds to produce income for education and development projects. The plan aroused strong controversy, particularly from the trade unions, who organized a one-day strike in protest.

Outline of economic development. Puerto Rico's economic development in modern times has been based on "Operation Bootstrap", the name given to Governor Muñoz Marín's plan during the 1940s and 1950s for rapid industrialization and infrastructural development. In the colonial period the island had had a traditional agricultural economy, based on the production of sugar, coffee and tobacco by plantations and by small farmers. During the early years of US administration US corporations developed large sugar estates on the island, displacing many small farmers and increasing the dependency of Puerto Rico on a single crop. Social inequalities and poverty were exacerbated by the economic effects of these large absentee corporations and development was hampered during the 1930s by the Depression and the effects of hurricanes. Under Operation Bootstrap US companies were induced to come to Puerto Rico and aid in the island's development through government intervention, tax incentives and the attractive wage differentials between Puerto Rico and the mainland USA. In return Puerto Rico would benefit financially, employment would be created and some of the island's chronic poverty would be eliminated. The Puerto Rico Industrial Development Company (later the Economic Development Administration) was the main government agency charged with planning the development. Manufacturing industries such as pharmaceuticals, petrochemicals and electronics were encouraged to come to the island and today these industries predominate on the island. The industrialization was successful in transforming Puerto Rico's economy and annual growth rates between 1948 and 1973 averaged 6.9 per cent. The island's infrastructure became one of the best in the region.

Since the 1970s, however, the Puerto Rican economy has suffered from integration into the world economy and from the erosion of its historic advantages. Reliance on export industries, the US market, and on tourism has left the economy vulnerable to a downturn, particularly in the American domestic economy. The advantages Puerto Rico once enjoyed, such as in wage rates for example, have been eroded by lower rates in neighbouring countries such as the Dominican Republic or Haiti which also enjoy duty-free access into the USA for some goods under the **Caribbean Basin Initiative** (CBI). Rates of growth slowed to an annual average of about 2 per cent and to 0.2 per cent between 1980 and 1984. Industrialization also failed to solve many of the territory's deep-rooted problems, such as population growth and unemployment, and the economy became increasingly dependent on federal funds. Despite great advances, Puerto Rico's GDP *per capita* is still only about half of that of Mississippi, the poorest state in the Union.

Current economic situation. In the late 1980s the Puerto Rican economy experienced a period of sustained economic growth, with an average annual growth rate of 3.7 per cent in real terms between 1985 and 1989. An expansion in the number of companies setting up plants on the island resulted in more jobs and a fall in the rate of unemployment. Although an estimated $2,200 million of damage was caused by Hurricane Hugo in September 1989, it was anticipated that reconstruction activity would help maintain economic growth. Improvement in the industrial sector was noted particularly in the pharmaceutical industry, which employs 16,000 people and provides exports worth $4,000 million annually.

The centrepiece of the Puerto Rican economy in recent years has been the tax exemptions offered to companies under Section 936 of the Internal Revenue Code. Under Section 936 mainland US companies with affiliates in Puerto Rico can earn up to 100 per cent tax credits on their profits there. This provision came under intense attack from the US Treasury during the 1980s. In 1981 the tax credits cost the Treasury more than $1,300 million or 18 per cent of Puerto Rico's GNP. Intensive lobbying by Puerto Rico has, so far, staved off any abolition of Section 936. It has been estimated that loss of Section 936 would lead to the closure of about 25 to 30 per cent of Puerto Rico's industry. Opponents of statehood also argue that a similar event would occur if Puerto Rico became a state as the benefits were phased out over a period of years. In April 1990 the Congressional Budget Office published a report which claimed that adoption of statehood could cost Puerto Rico 100,000 jobs and 73 per cent of its investment from US companies by the end of the decade through the loss of tax incentives. The federal government has also tried to release 936 funds by stipulating that a proportion of them should be used for investment in other Caribbean countries under the terms of the Caribbean Basin Initiative (CBI) and its revision, CBI II, which came into effect in mid-1990. The island government seized on this as providing a way of ensuring 936's survival, but so far few twin-plant ventures have been created.

Tourism, although an important and visible source of income for the island, only accounts for about 6 per cent of GDP. During the late 1980s the state-managed Tourism Company was active in promoting Puerto Rico as a tourist destination.

This was necessary in part to counteract bad publicity resulting from the fire in the Dupont Plaza hotel in 1986 caused by arson, which led to the deaths of 97 people. San Juan International Airport has continued to develop as an important regional hub for air communications, and for longer distance links with the USA and Europe.

The upturn in the economy, however, masks continuing weaknesses. Puerto Rico's export-orientated industries remain heavily dependent on the US market and vulnerable to a recession in the mainland USA. Nearly 90 per cent of exports go to the USA, but the economy also requires the substantial importation of raw materials and capital goods to supply its industries. Labour intensive industries were also seen to be at a disadvantage from competition from countries with lower wages. The attempts to diversify Puerto Rico's economic base by using Section 936 funds for twin-plant ventures in the Caribbean has so far produced little of substance. Only 5 per cent of Puerto Rico's exports go to other Caribbean countries.

Puerto Rico's infrastructure, although highly developed, has also suffered from a high level of use. The public corporations running public utilities have come under increasing stress and produced a poorer service. The Aqueduct and Sewer Authority has had particular problems in providing an efficient water and sewerage supply and in 1989 Hernández announced investment of $1,000 million over a four-year period. Other infrastructural plans include a major road upgrading programme and two new plants for the electricity concern, *Autoridad Energía Eléctrica*, which would increase generating capacity by 17 per cent.

As for Puerto Rico's other problems, unemployment started rising in the 1970s, reaching 25 per cent of the labour force in 1983. By 1990 this figure had been reduced to 16 per cent, but this still masked widespread seasonal and underemployment. The burden of unemployment has also fallen heaviest on the younger age groups. Population pressures have continued to increase, although large-scale emigration to the urban centres of the USA has at least created a way out for many people and alleviated some of the pressure. Poverty and dependence on federal aid have increased. In 1981 56 per cent of the population received state assistance from the federal food stamp programme (nearly 10 per cent of the whole US food stamp budget). In 1983 federal aid equalled 32 per cent of GDP. This in itself has spurred on greater consumerism and dependence on the US market. Proponents of statehood point out that as a state the island would be entitled to receive US$3,600 million annually in Federal funds for Medicare and other social welfare programmes—well above the current $82,000,000 ceiling on such disbursements. Others contest that statehood would lead to "welfarism" and even greater dependency. Other problems that have received greater attention in recent years include corruption, drug trafficking and the growth in crime.

The problems of individuals have been matched by the financial problems of the commonwealth government. Puerto Ricans pay no federal taxes and federal customs receipts on foreign goods are returned to the island, yet the government has a serious budget deficit, totalling $200,000,000 in 1989, and a high burden of debt. Puerto Rico's external debt in 1989 totalled $12,000 million—one of the highest *per capita* figures in the world. State economic planning has led to a large proportion of the island's GDP being derived from the commonwealth budget. In the late 1980s this budget deficit was worsened by a revenue shortfall caused by the failure to introduce revenue-raising measures to compensate for the cuts in personal and corporate taxation that were to be introduced in stages over a five-year period. As a result Hernández was forced to postpone further cuts, much to the anger of some members of his party.

Prospects for development. The future of Puerto Rico is dependent on the settling of the status issue. Whichever way the people of Puerto Rico decide, the consequences of the vote will govern the direction of the state for the foreseeable future.

LP

Q

QUADROS, JANIO DA SILVA. When Jânio Quadros abruptly resigned the presidency of **Brazil** in August 1961, he precipitated a major political crisis, which later led to the military-backed *coup* of 1964. Quadros hoped that he would be recalled to office with enlarged executive powers. The call did not come, even from those politicians, civilian and military, who had strongly backed him in the election of 1960, as the main electoral hope of the right.

There were good reasons to think that Quadros' political career must now be finished and that he must remain discredited by the social and political forces he had so bitterly disappointed. Such a judgement appeared to be confirmed, when, on April 10, 1964 by decision of the Supreme Command of the Revolution, Quadros was stripped of his political rights, joining the early ranks of the *cassados*.

Reports of Jânio's political demise were greatly exaggerated. By 1968, he already was making public political statements, and was sent off, by order of the Minister of Justice, to Corumbá, Mato Grosso, his birthplace, for 120 days. In 1980, he joined the **Brazilian Labour Party** (*Partido Trabalhista Brasileiro* — PTB), and, eventually, was its candidate for the governorship of São Paulo in 1982. In 1985, he won an impressive victory to be elected as mayor of São Paulo and, as late as 1989, though protesting to the contrary, he was ready to take the field as candidate of the right in the direct presidential election. He is one of the most colourful and effective politicians in Brazil. He is also, by far, the one whose style and appeal most closely resembles that of the current president, **Fernando Collor de Mello.**

Quadros was born in Corumbá, which is now the capital of Mato Grosso do Sul, on Jan. 25, 1917 but his family soon moved to Curitiba, capital of Paraná. He was trained in law and set up a small practice in São Paulo, but also worked as a teacher. He stood for election as *vereador*, councillor, in 1947, for the Christian Democrat Party (*Partido Democrático Cristiano*—PDC) but was not elected. He was, however, one of those who was given a place made vacant by the cancellation of the mandates of **Brazilian Communist Party** (*Partido Comunista Brasileiro* — PCB) members by the Dutra government, so entered the São Paulo Municipal Chamber in 1948.

He made an immediate impact by campaigning against corruption in government, especially that of Adhemar de Barros, national leader of the Progressive Socialist Party (*Partido Social Progressista*—PSP) who headed and controlled a huge political machine, both urban and rural, in São Paulo. Quadros took up demands and protests from some of the poorest communities, which he regularly visited, and his strange appearance, wild looks and wilder hair, made him known throughout the city. In 1950, he was elected to the Legislative Assembly of São Paulo, still for the PDC, with more votes than any other candidate in the state.

Early 1953 brought the first election for mayor in São Paulo for 23 years, since the city was deprived of its municipal autonomy after the Revolution of 1930. Jânio became the candidate of the PDC and the Brazilian Socialist Party (*Partido Socialista Brasileiro*— PSB), opposing the entrenched power and wealth of eight parties, which controlled a radio network, newspapers and other media. His slogan was "*O tostão contra o milhão*", "The penny against the million", pointing up the difference in resources. With his ceaseless attack on corruption and maladministration, his symbol soon became a broom, which was to remain with him throughout his career. He was elected mayor by a large majority.

Now aged 36, Jânio's first action as mayor was to dismiss many state employees, cutting costs and ending perks. He would appear without warning in public offices. He issued his famous *bilhetinhos*, "little notes", demanding action, and he tightened up the city finances to such a degree as to balance the budget.

In the election for governor of São Paulo in 1954, the two principal candidates were Quadros and Adhemar de Barros. Quadros broke with the PDC after a disagreement, and put himself forward as a candidate without a party or a clearly defined programme. His campaign was marked by tumultuous meetings, where crowds waved brooms and held lighted candles, while Jânio, wild in gesture and appearance, promised honest government and an end to corruption. He won the governorship, with 660,264 votes against his nearest rival Adlemar de Barros, with 641,960.

Taking office, on Jan. 31, 1955 Quadros, at once, began to build up his career at national level, announcing that he would be a presidential candidate in the election scheduled for October 1955, then offering to withdraw in return for a series of agreements with the Café Filho government and with National Democratic Union

(*União Democrática Nacional*—UDN) leaders. These included extremely favourable financial conditions for São Paulo, which would allow Quadros to restructure the state finances, reducing the deficit inherited from his predecessors.

He left office in 1958 with a reputation strong enough to ensure the election of his chosen successor, Carlos Alberto de Carvalho Pinto, who had been responsible, first, for the city's, then for the state's finances under Quadros. Carvalho Pinto was the joint candidate of several parties, including the PDC and the UDN, but not of the PTB, for which, at the same time, Quadros was standing as candidate for election as federal deputy in Paraná. He was elected, with the highest proportional vote in the state, while not supporting the PTB candidate in São Paulo. It said much both for Quadros and for party labels.

Once elected as federal deputy, Quadros left for Europe, without attending Congress, returning only on Sept. 21, 1959, which, again, was indicative of his respect for Congress. By then efforts already were well developed to project him as presidential candidate in 1960, supported by the Jânio Quadros Popular Movement (*Movimento Popular Jânio Quadros*—MPJQ). He won the backing of several parties, including the PDC, but the most important, after much contention and recrimination, was that of the UDN. This was due, almost entirely, to the efforts of **Carlos Lacerda**, who saw in Quadros the man who might win for the right against the joint forces of the PDS and PTB. They were supporting Marshall Lott, who, as Minister of War, had guaranteed the succession for **Juscelino Kubitschek**. Lacerda saw the election of Quadros as paving the way for his own ascent to the presidency. On Oct. 3, 1960 Quadros won 48.26 per cent of the total vote. Goulart was elected as Vice-President.

In his short term in office, Quadros continued to apply the basic policies which he had developed in São Paulo, especially austerity in government finances, including an attack on inflation by cutting subsidies. He again tried to streamline government and cut the numbers of public employees. He introduced a multiple exchange rate, and provided incentives to exports. He introduced a credit and wage squeeze, and took a hard line with wage demands, strikes and the unions, despite his earlier public identification with the problems of the poor and the working class. His "independent foreign policy" was partly linked to the need to find new markets for Brazilian exports: but all this came to a sudden end with his resignation in August 1961.

After his loss of political rights in 1964, Quadros turned to literature and painting, but, especially after the start of *abertura*, began to urge the need for a Constituent Assembly and a strong democracy, including a "district vote" and votes for illiterates. With the reorganization of the party system in 1979, he moved towards the PTB, joining the party in 1980. He then made overtures to the Popular Party (*Partido Popular*—PP), holding discussions with its leaders, including **Tancredo Neves**, suggesting the fusion of the PP and PTB. When party coalitions for the elections of 1982 were forbidden by the régime, Quadros left the PTB, recommending a new single party of united opposition.

In August 1981, returning from England, he tried to join the PMDB, but there was strong reaction against him and his application was rejected by the regional executive committee in São Paulo, by 13 votes to two, one of the two votes being that of Orestes Quércia, later to be a successful PMDB governor of the state. Brizola then invited Quadros to join the Democratic Labour Party (*Partido Democrático Trabalhista*—PDT), but he refused. He rejoined the PTB and stood as its candidate for governor in 1982. He came third. It was only the second electoral defeat in his whole career.

Quadros' chequered relations and flirtations with various parties in these years reflect the inchoate nature of the party system after 1979 and his own casual attitude to party labels. His strength was in his direct appeal to the electorate, as he again showed, in November 1985, when he defeated the strongly favoured PMDB candidate, Fernando Henrique Cardoso, to become mayor of São Paulo for a second time. The victory of Quadros gave a boost to the political right, which had spent lavishly to support him, partly in order to deliver a blow to the PMDB at national level. Quadros' time in office was generally regarded as successful, in attempting, once again, to provide sound, honest government and an efficient administration attentive to the needs of the city.

Right up to the end of 1988, and even into 1989, Quadros was seen as perhaps the strongest candidate of the right with enough electoral appeal to stand against Brizola, but his health was failing and, in the event, the challenge was taken up by a new champion of the right, **Fernando Collor de Mello**, whose style, lack of party backing and, right until he took office, lack of distinct programme, fitted completely the picture of Quadros three decades earlier. He, too, offered an attack on corruption and inefficiency and a promise of sound finance and reforms in government. He even discussed with Quadros the possibility of taking over his symbol, the broom.

Quadros' main weakness was his lack of party and congressional support, even a disdain and dislike of party and congressional politics. He thought he could stand alone, but could not. It will be interesting to see how far the historical parallels stretch.

PF

R

RADICAL CIVIC UNION (Unión Cívica Radical—UCR) (Argentina). Formed in 1891 as a breakaway faction of the Civic Union (*Unión Cívica*), the UCR is usually depicted as the party which gave political expression to **Argentina's** emerging middle classes. Its first leader, Leandro Alem, and his successor, **Hipólito Yrigoyen**, campaigned for an end to the electoral fraud through which the conservative oligarchy kept itself in power. Recourse to armed insurrection, though unsuccessful, helped achieve that objective in 1912, with the passage of the 1912 Sáenz Peña electoral law. The UCR began to contest provincial and legislative elections in 1912, and in 1916 their candidate, Yrigoyen, won the presidency.

The UCR again won the elections in 1922, but led by the candidate of the "anti-personalist" faction, Marcelo T. de Alvear, who opposed Yrigoyen's highly personal conduct of the party and government, and was willing to countenance a degree of co-operation with the conservatives. The pendulum swung back again in 1928, when Yrigoyen was elected for a second presidential term, which was cut short by a military *coup* in 1930.

The division between personalists and anti-personalists was not healed until 1940, only to re-emerge in a different guise in 1945, when a faction calling itself the Movement of Intransience and Renewal (*Movimiento de Intransigencia y Renovación*—MIR), led by Ricardo Balbín and Arturo Frondizi, unsuccessfully opposed the "unionist" leadership's decision to strike an alliance with the conservatives to run against **Juan Domingo Perón**. One faction of the party, the Radical Civic Renewal Union (*Unión Cívica Radical Renovadora*) even broke away to support Perón's candidacy. By 1951 the MIR had become the dominant force in the party, and ran a Balbín– Frondizi slate, unsuccessfully, against the Peronists.

Following the ouster and proscription of the Peronists, a deeper split took place. Opposing Frondizi's quest for an electoral alliance with the Peronists, Balbín broke away and formed the People's Radical Civic Union (*Unión Cívica Radical del Pueblo*—UCRP), while the faction headed by Frondizi renamed itself Intransigent Radical Civic Union (*Unión Cívica Radical Intransigente*—UCRI). The 1958 elections were won by Frondizi, with the UCRP running against him and later acting as the main opposition party in congress.

Frondizi was ousted by the military in 1962, and when elections were called in 1963, with the Peronists banned, UCRP candidate Arturo Umberto Illia was the victor (with UCRI candidate Oscar Alende coming second). Illia was then himself ousted by the military in 1966—two years after the UCRI had suffered another rift; a majority faction led by Frondizi breaking away to form the Movement for Integration and Development (*Movimiento de Integración y Desarrollo*), the minority under Alende retaining the party name.

When elections were called in 1973, the UCRP gained the right to the old party name, *Unión Cívica Radical*, and once again fielded the veteran Balbín as presidential candidate—losing to the Peronists. In those elections the MID supported the Peronists, and the UCRI, renamed the Intransigent Party (*Partido Intransigente*—PI), joined a left-wing coalition, the Revolutionary Popular Alliance (*Alianza Popular Revolucionaria*—APR). By this time a rising force within the party was the Renewal and Change (*Renovación y Cambio*) movement founded in 1972 by **Raúl Alfonsín**.

Alfonsín succeeded Balbín (who died in 1982) as party leader, and in 1983 he was elected president. A worsening economic situation eroded Alfonsín's popularity, and was the chief factor in the defeat of the UCR in the elections held in 1989—indeed it led to Alfonsín cutting short his mandate by half a year.

EC

REGIONAL ORGANIZATIONS. *See* **Andean Pact, Caribbean Community and Common Market (CARICOM), Central American Common Market (CACM), Latin American Integration Association (LAIA), Latin American Economic System, Organization of American States (OAS)**. On the early history of regional organisation *see* **Inter-American System**. On regional economic development *see* **Economic Commission for Latin America and the Caribbean (ECLAC)**. *See also* **Lomé Convention**.

RESOURCES. South America is rich in natural resources. Apart from petroleum and natural gas (see **Oil**), mineral deposits of significant commercial value include:

Alumina: Jamaica, Brazil, Suriname, Guyana; also Haiti, Dominican Republic, Venezuela.
Barium: Mexico.
Beryllium: Brazil.
Chromium: Cuba.
Coal: Brazil, Chile, Colombia, Mexico, Venezuela.
Copper: Chile, Peru, Mexico; also Brazil, Ecuador, Panama (inactive).
Diamond: Brazil, Guyana, Venezuela.
Emerald: Colombia; also Brazil.
Fluorite: Mexico.
Gold: Bolivia, Brazil, Chile, Mexico; also Colombia, Costa Rica, Dominican Republic, Ecuador, Nicaragua, Suriname.
Iron ore: Brazil, Venezuela, Mexico, Chile, Peru; also Argentina, Chile, Colombia, Guatemala, Trinidad.
Lead: Argentina, Bolivia, Honduras, Mexico, Peru.
Manganese: Brazil, Chile, Mexico.
Molybdenum: Chile.
Nickel: Cuba; Guatemala (inactive).
Nitrates: Chile.
Silver: Mexico, Peru, Chile, Bolivia, Argentina, Dominican Republic, Honduras; also Colombia, Costa Rica, Venezuela.
Sulphur: Mexico.
Tin: Brazil, Bolivia, Peru, Argentina.
Uranium: Argentina, Brazil.
Zinc: Argentina, Bolivia, Brazil, Ecuador, Honduras, Mexico, Peru.

PARC

REVOLUTIONARY DEMOCRATIC FRONT (Frente Democrático Revolucionario — FDR) (El Salvador). The Revolutionary Democratic Front of **El Salvador** was established on April 18, 1980 from the unification of thc CRM and the Salvado rean Democratic Front (*Frente Democrático Salvadoreño*—FDS). The CRM itself was composed of the mass organizations which had developed from the mid-1970s onwards, namely the Popular Revolutionary Bloc (*Bloque Popular Revolucionario* — BPR), the United People's Action Front (*Frente de Acción Popular Unificada*—FAPU), the Popular Leagues—28th February (*Ligas Populares—28 de Febrero*—LP-28), and the National Democratic Union (*Unión Democrática Nacionalista*—UDN). This co-ordination represented the final rejection of the claims by the junta to mediate the crisis and indeed of the rump of the PDC to play a useful role. It was consequently a recognition of the absence of a "middle way" advocated by **José Napoleón Duarte**, and the necessary precondition of a political coalition spreading from the centre to the far left which could purposefully and effectively unite with the armed struggle conducted by the Farabundo Martí Front for National Liberation (*Frente Farabundo Martí para la Liberación Nacional*—FMLN). The FDR is currently headed by Guillermo Ungo and Ruben Zamora and since November 1980 formally allied itself with the FMLN, and negotiates as an equal partner with the FMLN.

JCJS

RIO DE JANEIRO. On Jan. 1, 1502 the Portuguese captain, Gonçalo Coelho, sailed into what now is known as Guanabara Bay, in which was to be set the city of Rio de Janeiro. He thought the bay was the mouth of a large river, hence the name "River of January". The site was first settled, not by the Portuguese, but the French, under Admiral Villegaignon in 1505. The French were defeated in a naval battle in January 1567 and, with the exception of a further short period of French control in 1710 to 1711, the city remained Portuguese. With the growth of the mining economy in Minas Gerais, Rio de Janeiro became the major outport and, in 1763, took over from Salvador da Bahia as **Brazil**'s capital.

In 1808, the arrival of the Portuguese king, Dom João VI and his court, fleeing from Napoleon's army, largely transformed the small capital city of less than 60,000 people. The court stayed for 13 years, till Dom João returned to Portugal in 1821, but Rio continued as the capital of the Empire, and as the centre of the nation's political life, until the inauguration of **Brasília** in 1960.

One of the most lasting benefits of the court's arrival was the work of a series of painters, who left an unrivalled record of the city and its inhabitants in the early nineteenth century. The most famous is Jean Baptiste Debret, a court painter who stayed for 15 years, then, on his return to Paris, published his perceptive account of Brazil, accompanied by superb paintings, now available in his *Viagem pitoresca e histórica ao Brasil*. Another nineteenth century pictorial record was made by Johann Moritz Rugendas, whose work, sadly, was scattered in the 1920s, but some of which survives in *Viagem pitoresca através do Brasil*.

Other artists, too, such as Thomas Ender and the English painter, Lieutenant Chamberlain, portrayed life in nineteenth century Rio de Janeiro. Their work was then complemented by the magnificent photographs of Marc Ferrez, whose work from 1865 to 1918 is contained in the beautiful volume *O Rio Antigo de fotógrafo Marc Ferrez*. He shows Rio de Janeiro on the eve of its most elegant period of development, after Oswaldo Cruz had rid it of yellow fever. By the 1920s, it must have been, both in its natural setting, its buildings, its avenues and gardens, all woven along Guanabara Bay, one of the most beautiful capital cities in the world.

The natural setting of Rio is, indeed, one of breathtaking beauty, with the city spread along a chain of crescent beaches, backed by steep mountains. Guanabara Bay is one of the world's great natural harbours, stretching inland for about 24 kilometres, studded with islands, and now spanned by an elegant motor bridge, leading to the city of Niteroi and to the northern parts of the state of Rio de Janeiro.

The entrance to the bay is dominated by the *Pão de Açúcar*, the "Sugar Loaf" mountain. In the ridge of mountains, many still richly wooded, immediately behind the city, is the *Corcovado*, the Hunchback. On the summit, at 710 metres, is the famous statue of Christ the Redeemer, with arms outstretched, built in 1931 and floodlit by a system personally designed by Marconi, in the same year. The statue of Christ overlooks the city and the bay, and the beautiful mountain range and beaches on the other side, leading up to Cabo Frio, the "Cold Cape". In these jagged "Organ Mountains", always changing colour in the view from Corcovado, across the blue and green waters of the bay, is the *Dedo the Deus*, the up-pointed "Finger of God".

In the mountains fringing the northern zone of the city is the *Pico de Tijuca*, Tijuca Peak, at 1,012 metres, with views along all the southern beaches, including Copacabana, Ipanema, Leblon and, further on, to Barra de Tijuca, Recreio dos Bandeirantes and a beautiful area of mangrove swamps, now a military zone. Below *Pico de Tijuca*, in the northern zone, is the Maracanã football stadium, scene of Brazil's many triumphs and fierce clashes between rival local teams, especially Flamengo and Fluminense.

Further to the north, is the *Baixada Fluminense*, a mainly industrial zone, made up of the four *municípios* of Duque de Caxias, Nova Iguaçú, Nilópolis and São João de Meriti, home to almost 3,000,000 people. The *Baixada* has the reputation of being one of the most violent areas in the world. It reproduces, on the outskirts of Rio de Janeiro, social indices closer to those of north-east Brazil than to the developed south-east. In the four *municípios* of the *Baixada*, infant mortality, in late 1986, was 120 per 1,000, and a dreadful 90 per 1,000 babies up to one year. At that same time, 45 per cent of the children had no schools to which they might go. Fifty-five per cent of the economically active population earned less than 2.5 minimum wages, namely, about US$142. Forty-five per cent of homes had no water supply. Only 35 per cent of dwellings had any rubbish collection. There were virtually no sewers at all. The inhabitants of the *Baixada* commonly travelled long hours on the crowded Central Railway, or by bus, to the city centre for daily, or irregular, work. Life for most of them was, and remains, very hard.

Clearly visible from the Corcovado, is also the *Sambódromo*, now the centre for the carnival procession. This was built by **Leonel Brizola**, at the beginning of his term as governor from 1983 to 1987, and also serves, for the rest of the year, as one of the CIEPs, Integrated Centres for Popular Education, commonly known as *Brizolões*. Many of the people who provide the glorious spectacle of the carnival procession, with its dazzling costumes, pounding music and endless movement, come from the *Baixada Fluminense*, or from the almost 500 *favelas*, or shanty-towns, which creep up and, sometimes, almost cover, the hills and vacant plots in and around the city.

By 1983, when Brizola became governor, *favelados*, people living in these areas of informal, self-help housing, made up about 33 per cent of the population of the city. Over the last two decades, the urban population of Rio de Janeiro had grown by 50 per cent, but the *favela* population by 300 per cent. Taken together, the *favelas* of Rio are now, equivalently, the third largest city in Brazil. Twenty years ago, the *carioca* population, people living in Rio de Janeiro, was 3,600,000, with about 600,000 living in *favelas*, a ratio of non-*favela* to *favela* population of 80 to 20. By 1983, the ratio was 67 to 33 per cent and it is estimated that, by the mid-1990s, there may be about the same number, around 5,500,000, in each group.

The city of Rio de Janeiro is now the capital of the state of that name. Till 1960, with the inauguration of Brasília, it was the federal district, then became the state of Guanabara. In 1974 it again was "fused" with the state of Rio de Janeiro, with Faria Lima appointed as governor, taking office in March 1975. There is still an unresolved tension between the municipality, or the city and the state, which became particularly acute after 1987, when the state governor and the mayor were of different political parties.

Meanwhile, the city of Rio de Janeiro continues to be beautiful, and not just in its natural setting. Its people, despite, too often, the burden of poverty and deprivation, bring vitality, colour and humour to their daily lives and to the popular culture of the city, through its music, food and football, and on beaches where men, women and children, of all classes, colours and creeds, mix freely.

Rio de Janeiro still holds a special place in the hearts of Brazilians, even if it no longer is the nation's capital. It is still the *cidade maravilhosa*, the "marvellous city".

PF

RIO TREATY. The Rio Treaty, properly the Inter-American Treaty of Reciprocal Assistance (*Tratado Inter Americano de Assistência Recíproca — TIAR*) was signed at the International Conference of American States at Rio de Janeiro in 1947 and subsequently ratified by all member governments. It established a joint security framework to protect the Western Hemisphere from attack from outside, declaring that "an armed attack by any State against an American State shall be considered as an attack against all the American States" and pledges each state "to assist in meeting the attack". It also allows for collective defence in cases of attack from within the hemisphere, including internal disturbance or subversion, though in this case the Treaty merely requires the signatories to consult on possible common measures. The Treaty has been invoked on 11 occasions, the first by **Costa Rica** against **Nicaragua**.

PARC

RIOS MONTT, EFRAIN. Gen. Efraín Ríos Montt joined the Guatemalan army in 1943 and rose rapidly through the ranks, training in counter-insurgency at US military schools at Fort Gulick, Panama and Fort Bragg, North Carolina. He became army Chief-of-Staff under Arana Osorio and was chosen as the FNO coalition candidate for the 1974 election which was fraudulently won by Kjell Laugerud of the Democratic Institutional Party (*Partido Institucional Democrático*—PID). Ríos Montt conducted the most repressive of counter-insurgency campaigns, *Victoria '82* and *Firmeza '83* after having led a military *coup* on March 23, 1982 against the fraudulently elected PID candidate Aníbal Guevara, and directed the heaviest period of repression and human rights abuses in Guatemalan history. He was ousted by Gen. Oscar Mejía Victores, on Aug. 8, 1983.

As a fundamentalist evangelical Christian Ríos Montt has been a major contributor to the mass conversions of Guatemalans through the 1980s, particularly by his own "Church of the Word" sect.

Ríos Montt was a favourite contender for the Nov. 11, 1990 presidential elections but was disqualified under Article 186 of the Constitution which prevents leaders of military *coups* from contesting presidential elections. It was quite likely that had he been permitted to be a candidate he would have become president. His "No venta" (No sale) party gained 11 congressional seats in the November 1990 elections.

JCJS

RODNEY, WALTER. One of the key figures in establishing the "black power" movement as an influence in Caribbean politics in the 1970s, Walter Rodney was a leading opponent of the government of **Guyana** as an executive member of the Working People's Alliance. He was killed by a bomb explosion in June 1980, aged 38. A history graduate of the University of the West Indies with a doctorate from London, he was barred from Jamaica in 1968 after six months' lecturing at the UWI's Mona campus, during which he had developed links with Rastafarian groups in the Kingston ghettoes. The ban sparked off riots in which three people were killed and US$2,000,000 in damage was caused. His most influential work, *How Europe Underdeveloped Africa*, was written during a subsequent six years at the University of Dar-es-Salaam.

RP

RODRIGUEZ, GEN. ANDRES. Gen. Andrés Rodríguez, President of **Paraguay** since 1989, seized power in a *coup* on Feb. 3, 1989 and was elected constitutional president on May 1. A career soldier, he had risen to become second-in-command of the armed forces, father-in-law to the son of his predecessor, **General Alfredo Stroessner** and one of the richest men in Paraguay. Latterly however he had emerged as leader of the "traditionalist" faction of the ruling Colorado Party opposed to the succession of his son-in-law, and the *coup* was precipitated by a move to transfer him from command of the First Army to the formal post of Defence Minister.

PARC

ROMERO BARCELO, CARLOS. Born in 1932, Romero studied law before becoming involved in politics for the New Progressive Party (PNP) of **Puerto Rico**. He was mayor of San Juan between 1969 and 1976, before serving as governor between 1976 and 1984. A fierce champion of statehood for Puerto Rico, his administration was partisan, replacing opposition party holders from office, but also creating divisions within his own party. After his election defeat in 1984 he retired as party leader, but remains deeply involved in politics.

LP

ROOSEVELT COROLLARY. The Roosevelt Corollary to the **Monroe Doctrine** was a response of the United States to the growing practice of European powers intervening by force to ensure that independent countries in the Caribbean met their international financial obligations. President Theodore Roosevelt reasoned that if, under the Monroe Doctrine itself, the USA could not afford to let the European powers intervene (as they had done in Venezuela in the previous year), then the United States would have to intervene for them, and within a decade and a half several countries (especially Panama, Nicaragua, Honduras, Cuba, the Dominican Republic and Haiti) had effectively become American protectorates.

Roosevelt's Annual Message to Congress of Dec. 6, 1904 had stated: "Chronic wrongdoing . . . may in America, as elsewhere, ultimately require intervention by some civilized nation, and in the Western Hemisphere the adherence of the United States to the Monroe Doctrine may force the United States, however reluctantly, in flagrant cases of such wrongdoing or impotence, to the exercise of an international police power".

PARC

ROSAS, JUAN MANUEL DE. Juan Manuel Ortiz de Rosas was born of an aristocratic family in Buenos Aires in 1793 but grew up on the pampa. In the course of a turbulent youth he gained a reputation for his skill in the *gaucho* pursuits of riding, etc., and became a successful rancher and businessman. Following the fall of Riviadavia, he assumed the role of leader of the Federalists (the supporters of provincial autonomy) and was elected Governor of Buenos Aires in 1829 for a three-year term during which time he formed an alliance with the Provinces of Entre Ríos, Santa Fe and Corrientes. He then took command of the Desert Campaign of 1833–34 and used his *gaucho* skills to conquer and to make peace with the Indian tribes to the south. In 1835 he was recalled to the governorship, and granted the rigorous dictatorship he had requested. Backed by a formidable party, the Popular Restoration Society (*Sociedad Popular Restauradora*) and its armed wing the *Mazorca*, organized by his wife Doña María de la Encarnación Escurra de Rosas, he instituted a reign of terror against his real or imaginary enemies in which thousands died. All had to wear the Federal colour (red) and display it on their houses and his portrait, draped in red, was displayed even on church altars; the light blue of the unitarians was forbidden on pain of death. Having failed to recapture **Uruguay** for Buenos Aires he went on to incur the opposition of European powers and in 1852 a coalition of his provincial enemies with them overthrew him at the Battle of Monte Caseros. Taking refuge on a British warship, he spent the last 25 years of his life in exile in Southampton and died at Burgess Street Farm, Swaythling, in 1877, and was buried in the Old Cemetery, Southampton. Latterly, he has been acclaimed by the Peronists as the effective maker of modern **Argentina**, even though against his will. His body was flown to Buenos Aires in 1989 and reinterred in Recoleta Cemetery in the presence of the President of the Republic, Dr **Carlos Menem**, and other high dignitaries.

PARC

S

ST KITTS AND NEVIS. *Population*: 44,000 (1987). *Area*: 261.6 sq km (St Kitts: 168.4; Nevis: 93.2). *GDP*: EC$183,400,000 (1986). *Trade volume*: EC$290,000,000 (1987). *Top five trade partners*: USA, UK, Trinidad and Tobago, Canada, Japan. *Defence spending*: EC$90,000 (1985). *Education spending (as percentage of GNP)*: 15. *Birthrate*: 23 per 1,000.

Socio–political background. St Kitts and Nevis is an independent federation still officially known as St. Christopher and Nevis. It is headed by Dr Kennedy Simmonds, leader of the People's Action Movement (PAM) which in coalition with the Nevis Reformation Party (NRP), both formed in 1970, has ruled since the February 1980 general elections. Prime Minister since independence on Sept. 19, 1983, Dr Simmonds has dominated politics in St Kitts and Nevis as Robert Bradshaw and the Labour Party, formed in 1932, did from 1967–1980.

The Concerned Citizens Movement (CCM) is currently the only other representative party apart from the PAM and NRP. There are however three other registered political organizations — the People's Democratic Party (PDP); Progressive Liberal Party (PLP) and United National Movement (UNM).

St Kitts has an 11-seat elective National Assembly and is allowed up to four senators if the Attorney-General is nominated. The Nevis Island Assembly has five elected and three nominated members. A three-man Nevis Island Administration, headed by a Premier, has sole responsibility for affairs of Nevis. The St Kitts and Nevis constitution also allows Nevis to opt out of the federation. To effect this Nevis must present detailed proposals for its own constitution to the Assembly six months before the proposed date of seceding, must gain Assembly passage and support in a referendum of two-thirds of the public.

Outline of political history. The issue of separation has dominated much of the history of St Kitts and Nevis. St Kitts became the first British colony in the Caribbean in 1623. Nevis was added in 1628 and Anguilla was joined in 1816. St Kitts–Nevis–Anguilla was administered as a member of the Leeward Islands, obtained a constitution in 1960 along with other Leewards and in February 1967 became an associated state.

The country was led by Robert Bradshaw of the Labour Party which was formed to fight for independence. Anguilla however rejected government from St Kitts three months after the grouping achieved associated status. In 1971 it reverted to what, in effect, was British dependent status. Despite strong protests from St Kitts, Anguilla was allowed to separate in December 1980, a status not formally recognized by St Kitts (*see* **Anguilla**).

Bradshaw and the Labour Party won elections in 1971 and 1975, each time with seven of the then nine seats. Separation again became an issue from 1970, this time centred on Nevis. The two Nevis seats at both elections were won by PAM and NRP — parties advocating a break with St Kitts, the NRP winning both in 1975. Ironically, those who had fought for independence along with the Labour Party, were unable to savour the achievement when it finally came. Bradshaw died in May 1978, his replacement Paul Southwell, who had been Chief Minister until 1966, died in May 1979 and Lee Moore, who succeeded Southwell, lost his seat at the June 1984 elections and again in March 1989.

A coalition of PAM and the NRP broke the 30-year hold of the Labour Party on St Kitts and Nevis. Labour won four seats and 58 per cent of the vote, but a new government was formed under Dr Simmonds on the strength of PAM's three seats and the NRP's two representing Nevis. Independence, scheduled under Labour for June 1980, was suspended. A new White Paper on independence, featuring greater autonomy for Nevis, was presented in 1982 and approved. The Labour Party, always in the forefront of independence moves, refused to support the proposals, mainly on the ground that Nevis was given disproportionate power. It called for elections before independence. This was rejected by the government, and the disagreements over the proposed new constitution led to arson attacks in 1982 and industrial unrest in 1983. The Labour Party boycotted celebrations after St Kitts and Nevis became independent in September 1983.

Current developments—political. PAM and the NRP won decisive victories in elections since independence. At the last elections in March 1989, the PAM retained its six seats, Labour two while the CCM won a Nevis seat from the NRP, which now holds two. In recent years only drug trafficking allegations have plagued the government, which initiated an anti-drug trafficking campaign in 1989.

Outline of economic development. The Simmonds government has won high marks for management of the economy which is agricultural based and sugar dominated. St Kitts and Nevis had a GNP per head of US$2,770, in 1988, attributed to growth in tourism.

In 1987 agriculture accounted for 9.4 per cent of GDP and some 30 per cent of employment. Sugar and sugar products accounted for some 39 per cent of export earnings in 1988. Other important crops are root crops, with sea-island cotton and coconuts the main products on Nevis. Diversification is a priority, and there have been attempts to grow coffee and rice.

Tourism, which contributed 9.4 per cent to GDP in 1987 is increasingly important. Manufacturing comprises the production of sugar by-products, electrical components assembly and garment making. This sector accounted for 14.7 per cent of GDP in 1987.

Current economic situation. At the end of 1988, St Kitts and Nevis had a budget surplus of EC$800,000. Inflation was low, but there was 10 per cent unemployment, despite labour shortages in agriculture. The future of the country is however much tied to the performance of the agricultural sector, especially sugar.

St Kitts and Nevis has considered entering wider political union, but insisted on the inclusion of its Leeward Island neighbours and especially the Virgin Islands, where some 10,000 St Kitts and Nevis citizens now live. There have been no moves recently for wider political union or any secession of Nevis from St Kitts. The country remains a member of the OECS and CARICOM.

MH

ST LUCIA. *Population*: 142,344 (1987). *Area*: 616 sq km. *GDP*: US$86,100,000. *Trade volume*: $335,800,000. *Top five trade partners*: UK, USA, Trinidad and Tobago, Japan, Canada. *Urban centres with a population of over 20,000*: Castries. *Birthrate*: 28 per 1,000. *Life expectancy*: 67 (men); 74 (women).

Geographical background. St Lucia is a Windward Island with volcanic ridges, *Les Pitons*, and a typical Caribbean climate. Temperatures average 25°C. Rainfall varies from nearly 5,000 millimetres in mountains to 1,500 millimetres in lower regions.

Socio–political background. A Commonwealth country, St Lucia is governed by the United Workers' Party (UWP), headed by Prime Minister John Compton. The UWP won nine seats in the 17-member House of Assembly at the last general elections on April 6, 1987. It failed to increase this number at another election on April 30, held to give the UWP a stronger mandate. A defection from the St Lucia Labour Party (SLP) in June increased the UWP's majority. The Progressive Labour Party (PLP) is the other registered party. There is also an 11-member Senate.

Outline of political history. St Lucia experienced 14 changes of control, with battles through the seventeenth century between the indigenous Carib people and the French, before becoming a British colony in 1814. It became a part of the Windward Islands administrative system, joined the West Indies Federation, 1958–62, gained its constitution in January 1960, became an associated state in 1975 and became independent on Feb. 22, 1979.

Representative government was introduced in 1924, but the first elections under adult suffrage were held in 1951. These were won by the SLP which governed until 1964 when it was defeated by the then new UWP. John Compton, in line with the changing status of St Lucia, became its first Chief Minister, Premier and Prime Minister. His stay in the latter post was short-lived, as the SLP won elections in July 1979, five months after elections, and Allan Louisy became Prime Minister.

The post-independence period of St Lucia has been marked by constant political upheaval. This began in February 1980 when the SLP appointed Boswell Williams Governor-General in place of Sir Arthur Lewis. The unpopular decision led to 12 SLP House members calling for the resignation of Louisy and the installation of George Odlum, then Deputy Prime Minister.

The stand-off ended in April 1981 when Odlum and three other SLP members voted with the opposition against the SLP's budget. The "rebel" four subsequently formed the PLP and Winston Cenac was appointed Prime Minister in May. Despite a one-man majority, Cenac refused to call new elections and the budget was approved.

Cenac won by a vote of one a no-confidence motion in September, but was forced to resign in 1982 after the government proposed legislation changing MPs' expenses, a move met with almost total disapproval, strikes and, finally, a general strike.

The UWP won the elections in May 1982 and in December Boswell Williams was removed and Sir Arthur Lewis reappointed Governor-General. Attempts by the SLP and PLP to unite to form more effective opposition were rejected by the SLP, which won eight seats in the April 1987 elections won by the UWP. Cenac however defected, adding to the nine seats won by the UWP.

Current political situation. The second reign of the UWP has not translated into quieter political times in St Lucia. From 1987 Compton's government has had strained relations with the Catholic church over the introduction of casino gambling, given the go-ahead in 1989.

Charges of police corruption led to the dismissal of the Commissioner and three others, along with stronger drug trafficking legislation in November 1988. The Minister of Communications, Works and Transport also resigned in 1989 following allegations of corruption.

Government assumption of control of the vital banana industry in October 1988 has led to wide and continuous protests. Initially, control was for a year but was extended to July 1990. The 1988 St Lucia Banana Growers' Association (SLBGA) conference was cancelled by the government and the directors fired.

Outline of economic development. Bananas dominate St Lucia's economy. Exported mainly to the UK, the crop accounted for more than 55 per cent of export earnings in 1988. Other agricultural produce—coconuts, citrus, spices—are important. In 1989, agriculture contributed 14.5 per cent to GDP and it employs nearly one-third of the workforce.

Tourism, mainly from the USA and UK, is vital. The sector contributed some 20 per cent to GDP in 1988. Manufacturing, through "free trade" zones, based on the production of garments, electronic parts assembly and packaging is being encouraged.

St Lucia attained a GNP per capita of US$1,540 between 1986 and 1988. As at March 31, 1989, the country had a public debt of EC$113,700,000 of which only EC$29,000,000 was owed abroad. However, unemployment remained high at 30 per cent.

Current economic situation. The Compton government is committed to investing in tourism by boosting infrastructure and manufacturing. Alternative crops to bananas have been experimented with as the government attempts to reduce the lopsided dependence on this crop. In early 1990 there was a dispute with the Dominican Republic after it sold bananas to the UK, and it is feared that with the single European market soon to emerge, the country's protected status under the **Lomé Conventions** will be weakened.

St Lucia is now committed to political union with Grenada, Dominica and St Vincent, although it remains a member of CARICOM and the OECS. With high unemployment and a high birthrate, the future is one envisaged in the context of wider economic and political union.

MH

ST VINCENT AND THE GRENADINES. *Population*: 115,000 (1988). *Area*: 239 sq km. *Trade volume*: EC$405,448 million. *Top five trade partners*: USA, UK, Trinidad and Tobago, Canada, Japan. *Defence spending*: EC$8,100,000 (1987–88). *Education spending (as percentage of GNP)*: 17.3. *Birthrate*: 23.7 per 1,000.

Geographical background. Part of the Windward Islands, St Vincent and the Grenadines are a group of 34 islands, the biggest of which are St Vincent, Bequia, Mustique, Union Island and Canouan. All share the typical Caribbean temperatures, but rainfall ranges from 3,850 mm in the mountainous, volcanic regions of St Vincent to 1,450 mm in the smaller islands. St Vincent features Mt Soufrière, an active volcano which devastated the country in the early eighteenth century and again in 1902. It further erupted in 1971 and 1979. The islands are also distinguished by their "Black Carib" population, a hybrid of original Carib people and African slaves.

Socio-political background. St Vincent and the Grenadines is administered from Kingstown, St Vincent. An independent Commonwealth country, it is led by James "Sonny" Mitchell of the New Democratic Party (NDP), which won all 15 seats in the enlarged House of Assembly at the May 1989 elections. Mitchell, an agronomist, represents his island Bequia. There are three other active political parties—the St Vincent Labour Party (SVLP), Movement for National Unity, (MNU) and the United People's Movement (UPM).

Outline of political history. The road of St Vincent's current stable position had had its share of problems. Against the wishes of both the French and Vincentians, the island became a British colony in 1773, and was administered as a Windward Island until 1959. Elections under adult suffrage were first held in 1951, the island was a member of the 1958–62 West Indies Federation and gained its own constitution and separate governing system in January 1960.

The first problem came over whether St. Vincent should become an Associated State as most of the Windwards and Leewards did in 1967. Elections in 1966 failed to give a clear-cut mandate as the ruling People's Political Party, (PPP) only got a one-seat majority. New elections were held in May 1967, with the SVLP and

Milton Cato replacing the PPP and Ebenezer Joshua. The country finally moved to associated status on Oct. 27, 1969.

Both the SVLP and PPP won six seats at the April 1972 elections in an enlarged House, with James Mitchell, a former SVLP Minister, winning as an independent. He joined forces with the PPP, with himself as Premier and Joshua as Deputy. Joshua resigned in September 1974 citing policy differences and a no-confidence motion in the Mitchell government was carried. The SVLP won 10 seats in the resulting December elections and the PPP two. Milton Cato therefore became the country's first Prime Minister after independence on Oct. 27, 1979.

Cato again won the December 1979 elections, winning 11 seats. This period was one of upheaval for St Vincent. Just three days after elections, an uprising on Union Island had to be put down by force, with help from various Caribbean countries. In May 1981, an umbrella group called the Committee in Defence of Democracy was formed to protest against legislation governing essential services, public order and labour relations. Following a general strike in June, the legislation was withdrawn.

Recent developments—political. The Working People's Party (WPP) was formed in 1980, the United People's Movement (UPM) in 1979 and the Movement for National Unity, (MNU), following a split from the UPM, in 1982. Cato sought to exploit opposition confusion by calling an early election in July 1984. Mitchell's NDP won with nine seats and the SVLP was soundly beaten, with five ministers losing their seats. Cato resigned, to be succeeded by Hudson Tannis, but he was killed in a plane crash and the leadership of the SVLP was handed to Vincent Beache.

Mitchell's government came under pressure in 1987 when it forced the National Broadcasting Corporation to feature government news. A senior news editor was moved in 1988, causing consternation in the region. Despite this, Mitchell won 66 per cent of the votes in the May 1989 election, winning all seats.

The NDP has maintained popularity with new economic measures and especially land reform, giving numerous small farmers the chance to own their own land in the crucial banana industry. Mitchell has also been in the forefront of political union with other countries and is pursuing the Regional Constituent Assembly with St Lucia, **Grenada** and **Dominica**. Although a member of the OECS and **CARICOM**, St Vincent has also sought to increase relations with countries outside the regional grouping, particularly the **Dominican Republic** and **Venezuela**.

Outline of economic development. Agriculture dominates St Vincent's economy, with bananas the main export, almost totally to the UK and regional countries, particularly Barbados and Trinidad and Tobago. In 1987 agriculture contributed some 21 per cent to GDP, which averaged seven per cent in the 1980s. In 1988 GDP was US$130 million and agricultural output increased steadily in the last decade, achieving 24 per cent growth in 1988.

Current economic situation. Banana production is susceptible to weather and volcanic conditions, and the Mitchell government has encouraged diversification. Bananas accounted for 37 per cent of all export earnings in 1988 and agriculture more than 80 per cent of export revenue. St Vincent remains the top producer in the world of arrowroot starch. Other major crops are root crops, plantains and spices.

Manufacturing is based around garment production and electronic parts assembly, and more and more, the manufacture of tennis racquets. The latter earned 11 per cent of exports in 1988, when the sector added 16 per cent to GDP.

Tourism is based on yacht travel through the islands, some 3,500 in 1987, and rich expatriates who own property on the islands. Mustique is especially 'well-heeled', with residents including Princess Margaret of the UK.

Prospects for development. The St Vincent government had planned tourism expansion as a means of boosting employment. Unemployment is high, reaching 45 per cent of the workforce in 1989. With the coming in 1992 of the single market in the EC, it is becoming increasingly important to reduce the dependency on bananas. This is the main reason why the Mitchell goverment sees a stable future in forming a unitary state with other islands.

MH

SALINAS DE GORTARI, CARLOS. Carlos Salinas de Gortari, President of **Mexico**, was inaugurated in December 1988 and his term will end at the end of November 1994. Carlos Salinas is a good example of the new type of technocratic leader who has limited political experience but considerable educational achievement. He studied for a number of years of Harvard where he acquired two Masters degrees and a PhD. He returned to Mexico to work in a relatively lowly position in the Finance Ministry. When his superior, Miguel de la Madrid, was moved to the Planning and Budgeting Ministry, Salinas followed. His ascent through the bureaucracy was then extremely rapid. When de la Madrid became

President in 1982, Salinas was given the Planning Ministry; he was then 34 years old.

Salinas remained as Secretary of Planning and Budgeting until his nomination as candidate of the PRI in October 1987. He played a crucial part in the making of economic policy under de la Madrid, particularly after the resignation of Jesús Silva Herzog as Finance Minister in June 1986. Salinas was originally considered to be less of an economic liberal and more of a consolidationist than de la Madrid; by 1986, however, he appears to have come round to that view that a fundamental restructuring of the Mexican economy was necessary.

When de la Madrid nominated him as presidential candidate, Salinas had little political base of his own. This is perhaps part of the reason why the PRI's share of the vote fell substantially in 1988. Another reason is that Salinas, more than de la Madrid, seems willing to accept at least some election results which are unfavourable for the ruling party. As President, Salinas has followed broadly the same economic policies as did de la Madrid. These are essentially pro-free market and free-trade though there are formal negotiations with labour and employers' associations on certain issues relating to wages and prices. On other matters, however, Salinas has been notably more adventurous. He has made a real effort to check corruption and the abuse of power at several levels of Mexican government; several political bosses influential in the previous administration have either been gaoled or had their influence removed. Conversely Salinas has been more conciliatory towards opposition parties and somewhat more sympathetic to pluralism in general.

GP

SAN ANDRES ARCHIPELAGO. The island group of San Andrés, Providencia, and the cays of Roncador, Quitasueño and Serrana, lies in the Caribbean some 180 km east of Nicaragua and 480 km north of Colombia, and is an important tourist area and free port. The group has, since independence, formed part of the territorial possessions of **Colombia**, but has been claimed by **Nicaragua** on the grounds of their proximity. In 1928 the Nicaraguan government renounced their claim by the Guerra–Meneses Treaty, and in 1972 the United States government recognized Colombian sovereignty and returned to Colombia the cays originally occupied during the American Civil War. However on Feb. 4, 1980 the Sandinista government declared the 1928 treaty void unilaterally on the ground that at the date of signature Nicaragua had been occupied by the **United States**, but subsequently agreed to bilateral talks on the issue. In 1986 alarm at Nicaraguan statements led to the Colombian government flying troops and sending warships to the islands, but no further problems arose.

PARC

SAN MARTIN, JOSE DE. José de San Martín is revered as the Liberator of the South of Hispanic America as **Simon Bolívar** is of the North. He was born in the province of San Juan, Argentina, in 1778 and for 20 years served in the armies of Spain before returning in 1812 to aid his countrymen. At the declaration of independence at Tucumán in 1816, San Martín was assigned command of the southern armies, and in a bold departure from the original plan of attacking the Spanish armies in Upper Peru (now **Bolivia**), he assumed the governorship of Cuyo, and in January 1817 led his troops from Mendoza over the Andes into **Chile** by the northern passes of Uspallata and Los Patos without the loss of a single soldier or piece of baggage. Taking the Spanish by surprise, he broke their resistance at Chacabuco (Feb. 12, 1817) and a year later destroyed their authority completely at Maipó, traditionally known in Argentina as Maipú (April 5, 1818). Refusing the post of supreme dictator of Chile in favour of the Chilean O'Higgins, he proceeded to recruit and train forces for the attack on **Peru** in 1820. Though following his success in capturing Callao he entered Lima accompanied by only a single *aide-de-camp* to attend the declaration of independence by its own citizens on July 28, 1821, he was soon chosen as protector of Peru. His troops together with those of Bolívar's lieutenant Antonio José de Sucre combined at the battle of Pichincha (May 1822) to free Quito, which however Bolívar then annexed to New Granada. At Guayaquil on July 26, 1822 San Martín and Bolívar finally met, but recognizing that South America was not big enough to hold them both and that his task was now finished, San Martín surrendered his supreme authority in Peru and returned to Buenos Aires. From there he went into exile in France, where he died at Boulogne-sur-Mer in 1850. In 1880 his ashes were repatriated to Buenos Aires and buried in state in the Cathedral precinct, though as a Mason he was denied the right to lie in consecrated ground. A man of outstanding character, whose devotion to independence was unquestionable, today he is honoured as the greatest of Argentines and an eternal flame burns in his honour.

PARC

SANDINISTA NATIONAL LIBERATION FRONT (Frente Sandinista de Liberación Nacional—FSLN) (Nicaragua). The Sandinista National Liberation Front was founded in **Nicaragua** in 1961 by Carlos Fonseca, Silvia Mayorga and Tomás Borge, as one of a number of Latin American guerrilla movements inspired by the **Cuban Revolution**. It took its name from a Nicaraguan national hero, General Augusto Sandino, who took up arms to resist the **United States'** intervention of 1926, and eluded all attempts to capture him. After the US withdrawal he was assassinated on the orders of the elder Anastasio Somoza. The FSLN's early years were a series of setbacks and defeats at the hands of the younger Somoza's National Guard, leading to a division on strategy into three factions. However, after the earthquake of Dec. 23, 1972 which devastated Managua, Somoza's flagrant profiteering and misappropriation of relief aid alienated the majority of the upper and middle classes, including the Church and the Conservative Party. As it became clear to them that Somoza could only be dislodged by force, many threw their support behind the FSLN, and the assassination of the Conservative journalist Pedro Joaquín Chamorro in January 1978 marked the outbreak of insurrection which was savagely suppressed. The FSLN-led coalition finally took power on July 19, 1979 after two months of all-out fighting, and formed a provisional government, from which some of the non-Sandinista members withdrew in 1980.

In power, the FSLN adopted a tripartite party structure reflecting its three factions. Membership of the nine-person National Directorate, with three members from each faction, remained unchanged for 11 years. Ministries allotted to National Directorate members became fiefdoms, often following their own policies. Their main achievements were agrarian reform and imaginative and far-reaching health, education and social welfare programmes. In 1985 their leader, **Daniel Ortega Saavedra**, was elected President in a free and fair election which a boycott by several opposition parties failed to disrupt.

From 1982 onwards, however, the Sandinista government had to devote substantial resources to combatting the US-sponsored "contras", and after 1984 a combination of the US economic boycott of the country, damage to coffee plantations and other civilian targets from guerrilla attack, and lack of co-ordination and excessive reliance on bureaucratic controls, devastated the vulnerable and dependent Nicaraguan economy, leading to hyperinflation, shortages and an endemic black market. In the 1990 elections Ortega was defeated by the candidate of the 13-member National Opposition Alliance (UNO), Violeta Chamorro, the widow of Pedro Joaquín Chamorro, who since then has ruled with the support of the Sandinista commander of the armed forces, Ortega's brother, Comandante Humberto Ortega.

GG

SARNEY, JOSÉ. José Sarney Costa, President of **Brazil** 1985–90, had greatness thrust upon him, in March 1985, through the death of president-elect, **Tancredo Neves**. As late as June 1984, he was still president of the **Social Democratic Party** (*Partido Democrático Social*—PDS), the party of the military-backed régime. In that month he broke with the party, in a dispute with **Paulo Maluf** and his supporters, and, later, was chosen as the candidate for Vice-President within the Democratic Alliance. Sarney's succession to the presidency owed much to the support of **Ulysses Guimarães**, president of the **Party of the Brazilian Democratic Movement** (*Partido do Movimento Democrático Brasileiro*—PMDB) who, above all, was anxious to guarantee the process of redemocratization and the accession of a civilian president. At the same time, the new president was viewed with hostility or suspicion by many people in the PMDB, and with scarcely less resentment by many in the PDS, who regarded him as a turncoat. His lack of personal, party and Congressional support made him, ironically for the first civilian president since 1964, heavily dependent on the backing of the leaders of the armed forces.

Sarney was born in April 1930, his name being José Ribamar Ferreira de Araújo Costa. His father was Sarney de Araújo Costa. Throughout the state, Sarney's son became known as "Zé de Sarney", short for "José, son of Sarney". In 1965, he legally adopted the name José Sarney Costa.

He became involved in regional politics, at first with the PDS and the most prominent political boss of Maranhão, Senator Vitorino Freire. In 1958, he joined the UDN, heading its regional directorate in Maranhão until 1965, when the parties were suppressed by *Institutional Act No. 2*.

Sarney was elected as federal deputy in 1958, with the support of the United Oppositions (*Oposições Coligadas*), made up of the National Democratic Union (*União Democrática Nacional*—UDN), the Christian Democrat Party (*Partido Democrático Cristão*—PDC), and the Republican Party (*Partido Republicano*—PR). In Congress, he joined the Nationalist Parliamentary Front (*Frente Parlamentar Nacionalista*). From 1959 to 1960, he was Vice-Leader of the UDN in the Chamber.

In 1960, Sarney joined a group within the UDN which wanted to respond to a range of demands within society, defining itself as modernizing and reformist, under the heading of the *Bossa Nova* group, seeking a political parallel to the new wave in Brazilian popular music. The general tone of the *Bossa Nova* group was a left-of-centre, reformist commitment, partly inspired by social teaching within the Catholic church. The main thrust of the group was to adjust the old anti-Vargista UDN to the changing circumstances of the 1960s, showing care and concern for social problems and support for **Jânio Quadros**, "nationalist" policies, including anti-trust laws, curbs on the remittance of profits, defence of mineral rights, change in income tax laws and an attack on inflation. The *Bossa Nova* group continued even after the resignation of Quadros in 1961.

In October 1962, Sarney was re-elected to Congress and, in April 1963, was one of the signatories of the manifesto of the *Bossa Nova* in Curitiba, in the national convention of the UDN. This manifesto, presented by a close associate of Quadros, José Aparecido de Oliveira, marked a sharp break with the traditional UDN. It sought reforms in banking and tax, in the agrarian system and in the urban area. It demanded an independent foreign policy and supported the *Plano Trienal* of the **Goulart** government, accepting some of the platform of the **Brazilian Labour Party** (*Partido Trabalhista Brasileiro—PTB*). Up to the *coup* of 1964, Sarney adopted a liberal position, rejecting any idea of a repressive régime.

Despite this liberal stance and his apparent support for Goulart's "basic reforms", Sarney was enthusiastic in his backing of the post-1964 régime. In October 1965, he easily won election as governor of Maranhão, against Vitorino Freire's candidate, Renato Archer, who was to remain one of Sarney's principal political rivals. The election owed much to the support of President Castello Branco. Sarney was able to attract substantial investment to Maranhão for infrastructure projects, including a major bridge over the São Francisco river and the building of the port of Itaquí.

In 1970, he left the state government and was elected as Senator for Maranhão, still proclaiming his liberal principles, first under Médici, then under Geisel. He repeatedly expressed his support for Geisel's "*distensão*", political relaxation, arguing that economic development was incompatible with political underdevelopment. Throughout 1977 and 1978, he joined in the debate on the reconstruction of political parties. He also advised President Figueiredo, who nominated him, in 1979, as national president of **ARENA**. He said that he wanted to turn ARENA into a modern party on social-democratic lines.

By late July 1979, Sarney had given up the idea of a two-party system. He supported the political amnesty and the overall opening of the political system, as reflected in a lecture in the National War College (*Escola Superior de Guerra*—ESG) in September entitled: "The Analysis of Political Parties". This was part of the background to the régime's restoration of the multi-party system, which led to the creation of the PDS as the main party of support for the miltary-backed régime. On Feb. 28, 1980 Sarney was elected as president of the PDS, by the provisional national executive of the party. Much of his energy went into the programme to restructure the party system, seeking an accommodation with the Popular Party (*Partido Popular*—PP) but also with **Brizola** and the Democratic Labour Party (*Partido Democrático Trabalhista*—PDT) and Lula and the PT.

In 1981, Sarney was charged by Figueiredo to take stock of the PDS throughout the country and to see how sufficient support might be mobilized to guarantee a victory for the régime in the choice of Figueiredo's successor. His report was generally sombre, recommending various devices, including the extension of the system of *sublegenda*, or transferable vote, for virtually all offices. The PDS, if not desperate, was extremely anxious about its ability to control the political and electoral process, a concern which was more than justified after the Riocentro bombing incident, on April 30, 1981 and the resignation of General Golbery do Couto e Silva, in August.

Sarney helped to shape the electoral "package" of November 1981, which introduced the *voto vinculado*, but this, and other measures, introduced in 1982, were not enough to stop the victory of the opposition in the elections of November 1982. The PDS never really recovered from the 1982 elections, which led directly to the implosion of the party in 1984, largely caused by internal pressures and rivalries, the most evident of which centred round Maluf. In June 1984, Sarney broke with the PDS and, by March 1985, was President of Brazil.

The high-point of Sarney's presidency, as far as he was concerned, was from the end of February 1986, when he announced the **Cruzado Plan**, to late November 1986, basking in his own and the PMDB's success in the elections for Congress/Constituent Assembly. Its most negative feature, in terms of Brazil's real interests, was the vote in Congress to allow Sarney five years in office, and the manner in which this vote was achieved. The vote was partly determined by the fear among military leaders and some members of the PMDB, that an election in 1988 would certainly be won by Leonel Brizola. (*See* also **BRAZIL**).

The fact remains that Sarney's fifth year in office was a misfortune both for himself and the country. Policy-making was virtually paralyzed, as the government, and all involved with it, had to tread water, whether in terms of the foreign debt, the internal debt, or any other area of policy formation. At the end, Sarney and his government lacked credibility and legitimacy. He was a stopgap president who stayed too long.

PF

SENDERO LUMINOSO (Shining Path) (Peru). In May 1980 the Peruvian Communist Party — Shining Path (*Partido Comunista del Perú—Sendero Luminoso*—PCP–SL) launched a "protracted people's war" with the aim of overthrowing the Peruvian state and establishing a social order akin to that of China during the 1950s and 1960s. The Maoist PCP-SL's activity commenced in the highland department of Ayacucho and has gradually extended over much of the *sierra*: in 1981 the government declared a state of emergency in six provinces; by December 1989 this figure had grown to 56 out of 181 provinces housing over 50 per cent of the population. The PCP–SL is active in 18 of Peru's 24 departments. At first the counterinsurgency campaign was entrusted to the police force, who were unable to cope with the task, so the army took over responsibility in 1983.

Prior to 1984 most guerrilla actions took place in the highlands, but since then Lima and other coastal cities have seen increased activity (car bombs, blackouts, the burning of factories, selective assassinations, etc.). In the Upper Huallaga alley in Huánuco department, the PCP–SL reputedly levies taxes on cocaine smugglers to finance its operations. The civil war has been both bitter and bloody. Since 1980 approximately 20,000 people have been killed, with few prisoners taken on either side. The armed forces, unable to successfully infiltrate the PCP–SL's tightly organized cell structure, has been consistently involved in human rights abuses, especially against the Andean peasantry. Periodic massacres in peasant villages have occurred in the hope that a few *Senderistas* and their sympathizers will number among the victims. In 1986 the armed forces killed over 300 *Sendero* prisoners in three Lima prisons. For its part, *Sendero* have acted ruthlessly against the civil defence groups established by the military. As part of the organization's strategy of removing the presence of the Peruvian state from the countryside and establishing "liberated areas" in the highlands, the PCP–SL has assassinated district governors, departmental prefects, state functionaries and elected representatives. They have also killed peasant leaders, trade unionists and politicians who are members of IU. Between July 1989 and April 1990 the PCP–SL suffered a number of reverses in the Upper Huallaga valley, Puno, Cañete, Lima and other locations, but rapidly falling living standards have ensured a steady flow of recruits to the organization.

Another organization, the Tupac Amaru Revolutionary Movement (*Movimiento Revolucionario Tupac Amarú*—MRTA), began guerrilla actions in 1984. More Guevarist in orientation, the MRTA operates in Lima, the high jungle area of Huánuco and San Martín departments, as well as the central highlands. In July 1990 MRTA leader Víctor Polay and 47 other members tunnelled their way out of the "high security" Miguel Castro prison in Lima.

In January 1990 a group split from the pro-Moscow Communist Party to form the Patriotic Liberation Front (*Frente Patriótica de Liberación* — FPL) and commenced guerrilla activity. The FPL is far less important than the PCP–SL or the MRTA.

To date the civil war has resulted in damaged estimated at $15,000 million and shows no sign of abating. President Fujimori has responded to the situation by attempting to forge close ties with the military, appointing an army general as Minister of the Interior. The insurgency introduces an important source of instability into the political system and may well provoke a military *coup*. At present, however, the generals are holding back, one important reason being that they know the PCP–SL would welcome a *coup* so to further polarize society.

LT

SILES ZUAZO, HERNAN. Son of President Hernando Siles (1926–30) and one of the founders of the Nationalist Revolutionary Movement (*Movimiento Nacionalista Revolucionario* — MNR) of **Bolivia**, Siles was the leader of the 1952 uprising and was sworn in as interim president pending the return from exile of the party leader **Víctor Paz Estenssoro**. He served as Vice-President 1952–56 and as President 1956–60, and remained in exile for much of the period 1964–78. Having broken with the MNR over Víctor Paz' support for **Hugo Bánzer's** *coup* in 1971, Siles led the Nationalist Revolutionary Movement of the Left (*Movimiento Nacionalista Revolucionario de la Izquierda* — MNRI) in the Democratic and Popular Unity (*Unidad Democrática Popular*—

UDP) coalition in three successive elections. However, the results of 1978 were annulled because of fraud, those of 1979 gave Siles victory but without an overall majority and led to an interim President, while the 1980 elections resulted in a clear victory though he was prevented from taking office by a military *coup*. Siles finally took up his mandate in 1982, presiding over economic collapse and his own political isolation, and was forced to curtail his term of office by calling elections in 1985.

CS

SOCIAL CHRISTIAN UNITY PARTY (Partido de Unidad Social Cristiana—PUSC) (Costa Rica). The Social Christian Unity Party of **Costa Rica** was founded in December 1983 out of the National Unity (*Unidad Nacional*), the Republican Party (*Partido Republicano*), the Christian Democratic Party (*Partido Demócrata Cristiano*), the Democratic Renewal Party (*Partido Renovación Democrática*) and the Popular Unity (*Unión Popular*). Initially a general conservative alliance it became more influenced and dedicated to neo-liberalism over the 1980s. But as the **PLN** moved in similar directions, the appeal of the PUSC at the 1990 elections lay in the fact that it had been untarnished by government and it claimed that it could manage the economy more competently than the PLN. Ideological differences are not substantial, and whilst the PUSC urged the breaking of diplomatic relations with **Nicaragu**a in 1986 and was hostile to the foreign policy of Oscar Arias it has quietly continued the arbitration role set out by the latter. Its claims to greater management competence have already been questioned by opinion polls which indicated that 30 per cent of respondents were unhappy with the first three months of PUSC government (compared with 11 per cent for the PLN government in 1986).

JCJS

SOCIAL CONSERVATIVE PARTY (Partido Social Conservador–PSC) (Colombia). The Conservative Party of **Colombia**, which has disputed power with the **Liberal Party** since the 1840s, adopted its present name in July 1987. The Conservatives had been split for many years, and their choice in 1986 of the unpopular right-wing candidate Alvaro Gómez Hurtado, opposed by the more moderate faction led by ex-President Misael Pastrana Borrero, lost them the election. Despite the change of name, they remain split and their deep crisis was clearly reflected in the May 1990 elections when their official presidential candidate came fourth in the poll, after the Liberal winner, a candidate, Gómez Hurtado, who had left the PSC to form his own movement, the Movement of National Salvation, and a party, Democratic Alliance–M–19, of ex-guerrillas new to the electoral scene.

JP

SOCIAL DEMOCRATIC PARTY (Partido Democrático Social—PDS) (Brazil). After the return to multi-party government in **Brazil** in 1979, the PDS became the dominant party of the régime, the main home for former members and supporters of the National Renovation Alliance (*Aliança Renovadora Nacional* — ARENA), which had lasted since 1965, and for the political right more generally.

In a series of political stratagems, or *casuismos*, the architects of the "slow, gradual and secure" "relaxation" of political controls tried to strengthen the electoral chances of the PDS. One such device was the *voto vinculado* for the elections for governors. Congress, and regional and local offices in November 1982. This requirement that a voter should choose a member of the same party for every office was generally successful, except in Rio de Janeiro, where Brizola and the PDT were elected, partly as a result of the *voto vinculado*: but the elections still represented a severe setback for the PDS.

The 1982 elections showed PDS support, as previously for ARENA, to come mainly from the poorer and more backward areas of Brazil, where clientelistic politics were still relatively strong. The opposition was successful in the industrial heartlands and in regions responsible for substantial agrarian-based contributions to GDP. The results induced a degree of panic in some PDS members of Congress, who feared, with reason, for their re-election. Looking for someone who could save the party, many deputies turned to **Paulo Salim Maluf**.

As President Figueiredo refused to indicate an official presidential candidate throughout 1984, the strains in the party became increasingly severe, with several candidates canvassing support. This crisis came to a head with the resignation of José Sarney as president of the PDS in June. Maluf won the party nomination, but lost the indirect election in January 1985, to **Tancredo Neves**, candidate of the Democratic Alliance (*Aliança Democrática*—AD) made up of the Party of the Brazilian Democratic Movement (*Partido do Movimento Democrático Brasileiro*—PMDB) and a break-away group from the PDS, the Liberal Front Party (Partido da Frente Liberal—PFL).

The death of Tancredo Neves, brought to the presidency the former leader of the PDS, **José Sarney**. Party fortunes seemed to recover in November 1985, when **Jânio Quadros** defeated Fernando Henrique Cardoso in the election for mayor of São Paulo, but slumped again after the **Cruzado Plan**, of 1986, as seen in the elections of November, when the PMDB won every elected governorship but one.

The PDS acted as an effective conservative lobby in the Constituent Assembly and they had a strong presidential candidate in 1989 in Paulo Maluf, who also had an eye on the elections for governor in October/December 1990. The party did less badly than many people had expected in the Congressional elections of October 1990, winning 40 seats in the new Chamber as compared with a previous 32. Maluf, on the other had, was beaten in São Paulo, his fifth electoral defeat in six years, at a cost which, even he, must scarcely dare to calculate.

The PDS is likely to continue as a right-wing party, with support from the business community and landowners , but with a much diminished role by comparison with the days of the military-backed régime.

PF

SOMOZA, ANASTASIO. The Somoza dynasty began with Anastasio Somoza García (1896–1956) and ended with his younger son, Anastasio Somoza Debayle (1925–1979). Anastasio Somoza García was a quick-witted, English-speaking member of a minor political family who endeared himself to the US occupying forces in the late 1920s. When they left Nicaragua in January 1933, he was made Chief of the National Guard. Recognizing the realities of power in Central America, both he and his sons sought to make themselves useful to successive US governments. Somoza made himself president in 1936. He was assassinated by the poet Rigoberto López Pérez in 1956.

Somoza was succeeded by his elder son Luis, while Anastasio Somoza Debayle remained as Chief of the National Guard. There was a puppet civilian government between 1963 and 1967 after which Anastasio Somoza became president. His greed alienated the majority of the upper and middle classes which had profited from 20 years of rapid economic growth from 1950 to the early 1970s. His flagrant profiteering and misappropriation of relief funds after the earthquake of Dec. 23, 1972 caused an international scandal. When he fled Nicaragua in July 1979, Somoza was said to be the owner of about 20 per cent of the agricultural land in Nicaragua and to have a personal fortune of some US$900,000,000. Somoza was killed by an Argentine guerrilla group in Paraguay in September 1980.

GG

SPORT. Millions around the world who have no other interest in the region know of the many great sporting heroes that South and Central America have produced. Though football is the most universal, because the basic requirements are so few that they are available even to the poorest children, many other sports are also played and followed, including some which are peculiar to the region such as the Mexican game of *Jai-Alai*, cousin of the Basque game *pelota*, and the Argentine *pato*, which has been described as "basketball on horseback".

Football. Association Football (known commonly but wrongly in the USA as "soccer") is a national obsession in South and Central America, notably in **Argentina**, home of Diego Maradona, and **Brazil**, the land of the great "Pele". It was however Uruguay which despite its small size was host to and the first winner of the World Cup (*Copa Mundial*) in 1930. Argentina, the runner-up in 1930, acted as host to the competition in 1978 under the military government, anxious to show the world (despite the facts of the "dirty war") that "Argentines are human and right", and **Mexico** did so in 1986, when Argentina were helped on their way to their second victory by the "hand of God" (and the brain of Maradona). Mexico itself did not come out of the occasion as well as it had hoped. The celebrated "Mexican wave" was seen round the world but the President was booed at the opening ceremony, in the first major evidence of the rising political unrest which was to boost the candidacy of **Cuauhtémoc Cárdenas**.

It was a disputed decision in the third qualifying round for the World Cup of 1970 that sparked the so-called "Football War" of 1969 between **El Salvador** and **Honduras**, and in the same year thousands perished in **Peru** by the unlucky accident that they were indoors watching the national team on television when an earthquake sent the city of Yungay sliding into a river. Happily, largely as a result of the formidable precautions taken to avert it, violence at football matches is not a major problem in South America, though the traffic congestion caused by the victorious fans of Boca Juniors or River Plate is.

Baseball. Countries where the United States has been predominant are exceptions to the general popularity of football, and in **Cuba**, the **Dominican Republic**, **Haiti**, **Nicaragua** and

Panama, baseball takes its palace, and Haiti is, in fact, a major exporter of baseballs. In 1962 US observers deduced the presence of Soviet instructors in Cuba from the fact that they were playing football and not baseball.

Athletics. The political disturbances leading up to the "Tlatelolco massacre" in Mexico in 1968 distracted attention from the very real success of the Olympic Games, where in the high altitude spectacular new records were established in field events. The lack of resources for advanced training facilities and the dominant influence of the United States and Eastern Europe probably explains the relatively small impact the region has made in athletics competitions at top international levels, despite the keen competition in the quadrennial Panamerican Games. A major exception is Cuba, where as with other Communist countries substantial resources were put into sports facilities and training for athletes of international standing, and sport used as a diplomatic way of gaining friends and influence among world youth. Mexico and Brazil have also produced world champions in track and field events.

Boxing. Latin Americans dominated the list of both WBC and WBA champions in the 1980s except in the heaviest weights, where the United States is virtually unchallenged. WBC champions during the decade included W. Benitez and W. Gomez of Puerto Rico (Light-Middle and Super-Bantam), A. Arguello of Nicaragua (Light), R. Limon, S. Sanchez and L. Pintor of Mexico (Super-Feather, Feather and Bantam), P. Cardona of Colombia (Fly) and H. Zapata of Panama (Light Fly).

Cycling. **Colombia**, which geographically makes the Alps look like a row of sandcastles, seems a particularly unsuitable place for the national obsession, cycle racing, but not surprisingly those who have been able to achieve success in the Andes have come in recent years to make their mark in the Tour de France and other major competitions in Europe.

Lawn Tennis. Tennis is widely popular among members of the middle classes in Latin America. In 1976 **Chile** reached the finals of the Davis Cup but went down to Italy 4–1. Guillermo Vilas of **Argentina** became a national hero when he won the US Masters in 1974, and Gabriela Sabatini, who first reached the top 10 ratings in 1986, has helped maintain the country's reputation. María Bueno of Brazil won the Ladies' Singles Championship at Wimbledon in the early 1960s.

Polo. Originating from the Indian sub-continent, polo was introduced by the British, but the *estancias* of Argentina have long produced the world's best polo players, who play on the world circuit throughout the year and at the National Open championship held in Buenos Aires in November.

Motor racing. It was the Argentine Juan Fangio who was the first driver from the region to achieve world standing and international fame in motor racing in the 1960s, but in the late 1980s it was the Brazilian Ayrton Senna who dominated the Formula One circuit and the Brazilian Grand Prix is now one of the fixtures of the international year.

Caribbean. Caribbean countries, concerned with raising living standards, particularly post-independence, have not concentrated on the development of sport. Spending on sport is less than one per cent of GDP and across the region is private-sector driven, through sponsorship. Thus, only the so-called More Developed Countries (MDCs), have sports facilities of reasonable standards, and on a region level, competition is concentrated in **Barbados**, **Jamaica**, **Trinidad**, **The Bahamas** and **Guyana**.

The very low priority of sport in the development process and allocation of resources has, however, not hampered the expression of sport in the Caribbean. The full range of sports are played to some degree, football, athletics, golf, tennis, netball, bodybuilding and watersports among the most popular. Played impromptu in communities and organized along club, national and regional lines, sport plays a central, uniting role in the region, and Caribbean countries, individually and as a group, have achieved international successes disproportionate to governmental interest and commitment of resources.

In all respects, participation, organization and support, cricket dominates sport in the region and nothing, not religion nor politics, is as uniting and central to the people of the Caribbean as cricket. Unsurprisingly, the main facilities are cricket oriented, although, in the main, privately developed. Throughout the region there are club competitions at various levels, schoolboy competitions and inter-campus cricket of the University of the West Indies. The major tournament is the annual regional competition among Barbados, the current champions and the country with the best record, and Trinidad, Jamaica, Guyana, the Windward Islands and the Leeward Islands.

For 22 years the competition was sponsored by the oil company Shell Antilles (Caribbean) Ltd. It is now sponsored by the Jamaican-based Red Stripe, and has evolved to its current participants, the match championship series and a knock-out competition sponsored by Geddes-Grant. The

Windward and Leewards at one time entered the competition as a single team, but now compete separately. In 1990, the Leewards won the championship for the first time. The competition regularly attracts packed audiences of more than 20,000. The annual Northern Telecom Youth Tournament is also followed with great interest.

The pride of the Caribbean is the West Indies cricket team, to which any cricketer who plays in the regional competition is eligible, and in world cricket the West Indies team is supreme. The team has dominated the international game in the last two decades and its success has led to a growing interest in places including Canada and the USA where cricket is not played to any appreciable degree in comparison with other sports. The West Indies team has literally demolished every other cricketing nation with a combination of vastly superior fast bowling, batting and all-round playing. It has not lost a Test series in recent memory, not at home since 1973, and very few other encounters.

Along the way, the West Indies have given the world most of its all-time great cricketers. There has been the famed three Ws, all Barbadians – the late Sir Frank Worrel, (knighted in 1964, whose image graces the Barbados five dollar bill,) Everton Weekes and Clyde Walcott. Wes Hall and Charlie Griffith, also of Barbados, formed one of the great bowling partnerships. Former captain Clive Lloyd and Lance Gibbs (Guyana), current legendary captain Viv Richards (Antigua), and the world's all-time best opening partnership of Desmond Haynes and Gordon Greenidge are all in the annals of cricketing history.

Even among this array of Caribbean talent, one cricketer is revered. Celebrated as "the grestest cricketer on earth or Mars", Barbadian Sir Garfield Sobers is acclaimed as the person who, more than anyone else, brought a new dimension to the game. Not only did he embody the spirit that so unites the Caribbean around cricket, but he brought a new style and record-setting prowess to the game which was not see before or has not seen since Sir Gary retired in 1974.

He entered the West Indies as a teenager, as an all-rounder, but mastered every bowling, fielding and batting position. At 21, in 1958, Sir Garth, as he is popularly known, scored an unbeaten 365 not out in Jamaica, an innings halted by invading fans. It remains the highest individual score ever achieved. He established numerous records in his career from 1954–1974 which included captaincy of the West Indies and 93 test matches. One memorable record saw him become the first player to score six "sixes" in an over.

Knee problems brought Sir Gary's career to an end and while some of his records have been overtaken, no one has matched his elegance on the cricket pitch. He was knighted in 1975, Her Majesty Queen Elizabeth II performing the ceremony at the Garrison Savannah in Barbados instead of at Buckingham Palace—the first person to be so knighted in a break from tradition—as a tribute to Sir Garfield's exploits. He has since taken up golf, leading Barbados in regional tournaments, coaching and promoting sporting links for the Board of Tourism.

In terms of participation, football is second to cricket. Shell has switched sponsorship to this sport and in 1989 a regional tournament was inaugurated, contested between both English and French-speaking countries. The 1990 finals in Trinidad between Martinique, Barbados, Jamaica, St Vincent, Grenada and the host country were disrupted by the July 28 attempted *coup* by the Jamat al Muslimeen. Shell has however pledged its continued support and further interest in football has been engendered by the success of Trinidad and Tobago in the World Cup competition. The country narrowly failed to go to the Italian 1990 World Cup finals by a one goal defeat in Trinidad by the USA.

Netball is the top female sport with many countries competing internationally. Trinidad has been outstanding, winning the competition in the mid-1980s when it hosted the world tournament. An annual regional tournament is held. Jamaica won in 1990 with 12 teams competing in Kingstown, Jamaica. Trinidad was absent, serving a one-year international ban.

Trinidad has also for most of the past decade been the centre of athletics through the Texaco Games. There is regional competition at junior levels through the bi-annual CARIFTA Games, last held in 1990 in Barbados, the Central American and Caribbean (CAC) Games and teams compete in the Commonwealth and Olympic Games.

Trinidad has produced the Olympic sprint champion Hasley Crawford but Jamaica remains the country which has produced the most prominent sporting figures in athletics. Merlene Ottey is the world's current female sprint champion, and Don Quarry was outstanding in world competition throughout the mid-1980s. At the 1990 CAC games in Mexico, eight CARICOM countries participated among 29. They won 36 medals with Jamaica contributing 14, including four golds.

Both Trinidad and Tobago and Jamaica have produced world champions in boxing. Leslie "Tiger" Stewart won the light heavyweight title and Jamaica's Mike McCallum remains one of the longest holders of a world title in the middle weight division.

Many countries and the region have had international success in bodybuilding. Barbados has been dominant in this sport, achieving international success with sportsmen such as Loftus Roach, Al Beckles, Earl Maynard and Patrick Nicholls. There are a range of local and regional tournaments, the biggest of the latter being the Central American and Caribbean championships, last held in Curação in 1990. This was marred by the first incidences of positive drug testing, with five divisional winners found in breach of regulations—two from Trinidad and Curaçao each and one from Barbados.

Golf is steadily developing. The regional competition is the Caribbean Amateur Golf Championships, in which the Organization of Eastern Caribbean (OECS) countries compete as one team. Jamaica has won the Hoerman Cup seven times, winning at home in 1990. In recognition of the sport's growing popularity, a new tournament for women, the George Teale Memorial Trophy, was introduced in 1990 with Barbados the first winners.

The OECS are also making strides in tennis, in preparation for competing in the regional section of the Davis Cup in 1991. The regional competition is the Commonwealth Caribbean tournament, with the men's teams cup the Brandons trophy with the women's the Phillips trophy. A new singles' tour for both men and women was introduced in 1990.

Windsurfing and surfing are two of the region's fastest growing sports. Barbados has hosted numerous international surfing meets, in 1990 the world windsurfing championships and in January 1991 the World Cup sailing meet. The region has had some notable successes in this area. Basketball is also fast growing, with Trinidad dominating the regional competition, winning in the last four years.

Sports such as hockey, table tennis and volley ball are also popular. A number of other sports including road tennis, distance road running and indoor sports such as darts and dominoes are well supported.

For the forseeable future, sport will remain at the bottom of the list in the allocation of finances. However, the hosting of competitions has led to a development of facilities in various countries and an increasing link with tourism, in the areas of sailing and marathon running as well as cricket, is leading to small but gradually increasing inputs into this sector by governments. Barbados is now completing a world-standard sports facility and attempts have been made to establish an international motor racing circuit. Much depends on the strength of the economies of the regional countries, and apart from the dominance of cricket, the trend will be that individual excellence in areas such as bodybuilding, surfing, boxing and athletics will continue to characterize sport in the Caribbean.

PARC, MH

STROESSNER, GEN. GUSTAVO. Gustavo Stroessner Mattiauda, President of **Paraguay** 1954–89, was born in Concepción in 1912, son of a German immigrant father and a Paraguayan mother, and became a career soldier. As a lieutenant in the Chaco War of 1932–38 he was decorated with the Silver Star for bravery, and thereafter pursued a successful if not distinguished military career until the civil war of March 1947 brought the **Colorado Party** to the fore. Chosen as the official Colorado candidate and so the sole candidate for the 1954 elections, once in power he banned both the Liberals and the **Febrerista Party**, and imposed a state of siege, which, with only one very brief interval, was to be in place for the next 34 years. In 1958 Stroessner's mandate was renewed by plebiscite, and despite the constitutional prohibition on re-election he was not challenged in 1963. In 1967 the Constitution was amended to allow him to be legally re-elected to a fourth term in 1968.

During the course of Stroessner's presidency, Paraguay underwent a major economic transformation. His decision to accept Brazil's *fait accompli* in 1964 annexing the hydroelectric resources of the Paraná River and agreeing to develop the Itaipú project with Brazil was a realistic one which brought considerable benefits. It lessened Paraguay's long-standing dependence on Argentina and on the profits of smuggling, though Brazilian settlement in Eastern Paraguay also bred nationalist resentment. By the 1980s however his formerly austere military dictatorship had become corrupt as well as old-fashioned and he was unlucky enough to outlive its era.

PARC

SUMMER PLAN. By late 1988, the **Sarney** government of **Brazil** was generally discredited and in disarray. The president had managed to defeat a proposal in the Constituent Assembly to introduce a parliamentary form of government and had exerted sufficient pressure on Congress to win for himself a fifth year in office. The vote in favour of this reflected the influence of the armed forces and a general fear that a direct presidential election in 1988 would be won by **Leonel Brizola**.

November 1988 had also seen defeat for the government and the ruling **Party of the**

Brazilian Democratic Movement (*Partido do Movimento Democrático Brasileiro*—PMDB) in the elections for mayor and growing pressure and opposition from the trade unions over wages. This led to an attempt, once again, to reach a "social pact" between the government, employers and workers. There was also a new source of opposition, from the Party of Brazilian Social Democracy (*Partido da Social Democracia Brasileira*—PSDB) which had been formed by dissident members of the PMDB, mainly occasioned by the venality and corruption shown in winning the vote in favour of Sarney's fifth year in office.

There was also the serious threat of hyperinflation. The monthly rate for December 1989 was a shade under 28 per cent, with the rate for the year at just under 1,000 per cent. Politicians of the left feared that hyperinflation might cause such disruption that the direct elections for president, scheduled for November 1989 might be cancelled. The Minister of War, General Leônidas Pires Gonçalves, and others on the right, feared, by contrast, that hyperinflation could lead to a walk-over for the left in that election. He, consequently, was one of those who urged the introduction of yet another "package", in addition to the **Cruzado Plan** of February 1986, the Cruzadinho in July of that year, Cruzado II in November, and the Novo Cruzado or Bresser Plan in June 1987.

Already, even when the "social pact" was being worked out in early November, there were rumours that the Minister of Finance, Maílson da Nóbrega, was preparing another Plan which would undercut the "pact". Unlike the tight secrecy which had surrounded the Cruzado Plan, this new package, already, was being widely discussed, so that, as in the case of the Bresser Plan, people were able to prepare for it, by, for instance, putting up prices in preparation for a price freeze. On Jan. 15, 1989, Sarney, again in a television speech, revealed the Summer Plan, echoing the Spring Plan (*Plan Primavera*), already adopted in **Argentina**.

Its central features were to chop three zeros off the *cruzado*, as had been the case with the cruzeiro in 1986, producing a new *cruzado*, devalued by 16.38 per cent, to introduce a credit squeeze, to freeze prices on about 170 essential items, for an initial period of 45 days, and to end indexation, especially for wages and salaries. This was to be done by abolishing the Standard Price Reference (*Unidade de Referência de Preços*—URP). This meant, in effect, a return to collective bargaining, perhaps the single most controversial feature of the Plan.

To reduce public spending, it was proposed to sell, or deactivate, at least 14 state enterprises and to close six ministries, or incorporate them into others. For the same reason, up to 90,000 state employees were to be sacked.

Adverse reaction to the Summer Plan came from the trade unions, the business community and industry, including Petrobrás, which complained that the Plan set the domestic price of oil at the equivalent of US$14 per barrel, when world prices were much higher. Despite such criticism, the Summer Plan had an immediate impact on inflation. Rapid price increases, to anticipate the government intervention, pushed up the monthly rate for January 1989 to 70.28 per cent, but in February it was only 3.6 per cent and 6.01 in March: then it began a renewed climb, to 24.83 per cent in June and, in July, 29.0, a shade higher than for the previous December, before the Summer Plan was introduced.

By April 1989, it was clear that the *Summer Plan* was running out of steam and that, unlike 1986, there was no chance of leaving adjustments till after the November elections. On April 19, following the seasons, the government introduced the Autumn Plan.

The economy, again, was to be indexed, to take account of rising inflation, with the Minister of Finance, Mailson da Nóbrega, admitting that they had underestimated the "inflationary culture" of Brazilians. A new version of the National Treasury Bond (*Obrigação do Tesouro Nacional*—OTN), the old basis for indexation, was introduced, which, eventually, were called National Treasury Bonds (*Bônus do Tesouro Nacional*—BTN). One aim here was to provide a government-controlled index, instead of the United States' dollar, which had started to act as an unofficial one. The underlying fear was a "dollarization" of the economy, such as had happened in Argentina.

The price freeze was ended, but not entirely. Prices could be readjusted every three months, and some wage increases were allowed, but could not be passed on to the consumer in further price increases, if they were lower than the Consumer Price Index (*Indice de Preços ao Consumidor*—IPC). There was to be an initial rise in wages and salaries of 13.58 per cent. The new *cruzado* was devalued by 3.02 per cent, the first shift in the official exchange rate since the Summer Plan.

No-one was happy with the new package. Employers' leaders complained that prices would still be controlled, while wages would be negotiated. Union leaders protested, with the Workers' Central Union (*Central Unica dos Trabalhadores* — CUT) threatening a general strike for May 1989. A prominent economist and

Federal Deputy, José Serra, said that re-indexation was necessary. He believed that the *Summer Plan* had broken the expectation of monthly inflation, but at a very high price. He calculated that the strategy had doubled the public deficit, which, on a conservative calculation, might rise from NCz$ (New cruzados) 40,000 million to NCz$80,000 million by the end of the year. Such a rise was completely out of line with targets to reduce the deficit, previously agreed with the IMF.

It was now apparent that any really effective measures to deal with inflation and other underlying problems facing the economy, such as the fiscal deficit, and the internal and foreign debts, would have to wait until the country had a new, directly elected president, endowed with new legitimacy and credibility.

PF

SURINAME. *Population*: 429,000 (mid-1990). *Area*: 163,000 sq km. *GNP per capita*: US$2,460 (1988). *Trade volume*: exports: $394,700,000 (1988); imports: $386,400,000 (1988). *Urban population as percentage of total*: 65.2. *Life expectancy*: 67. *Adult literacy*: 80.2 (1980).

Geographical background. The Republic of Suriname, which gained its independence from The Netherlands in 1975, is bounded on the west by Guyana, by Brazil in the south and by French Guiana in the east. Suriname's Atlantic litoral forms its northern definition, as well as being the most populous area of this tropical state.

Socio–political background. Ethnically and religiously diverse, reflecting Suriname's history as a slave colony followed by indentured labour, the population is composed of Creoles (32 per cent), East Indian (35 per cent), Indonesian (10 per cent), Bosneger (10 per cent) and Amerindian and Chinese (both 3 per cent). Moreover, 42 per cent of the population are Christian, 27 per cent are Hindu and 20 per cent are Muslim, in addition to which five main languages are spoken as well as numerous Bosneger and Amerindian languages.

Outline of political history. The resumption of constitutional government in 1987, following the suspension of the original independence Constitution in February 1980 during an army *coup*, placed legislative authority in a quinquennially elected 51-seat National Assembly. Until a new army *coup* on Dec. 24, 1990, executive powers were held by President Ramsewak Shankar, who was elected by the National Assembly. The Front for Democracy and Development (FDD) coalition of three, largely ethnic-based parties, secured 40 of the 50 seats in the 1987 Assembly elections, with four seats going to the leftist Palu group, three to the army-backed National Democratic Party, and three to Pandawa Lima (PL). Substantial *de facto* power had remained in the hands of Lt.-Col. Desi Bouterse, the army commander who succeeded in capturing power following the 1980 *coup* and institutionalized his rule through the National Military Council.

Recent developments—political. The 1990 *coup* followed Bouterse's resignation on Dec. 23, but *coup* leaders immediately re-appointed him. Tensions between the army and the government had been sharpest in their relationship with the numerous guerrilla groups, particularly towards the Surinamese Liberation Army (SLA), or Jungle Commando, led by Ronnie Brunswijk. (Suriname can claim to have the highest proportion of guerrilla groups to total population of any state in the world, a reflection of this heterogeneous society). On many occasions since 1987 government attempts at negotiations and cease-fire agreements had been undermined by the army's deep reluctance to treat with the guerrillas. The Korou Agreement of July 1989 between Brunswijk and the Government was ratified by the National Assembly but jeopardized by what were widely regarded as army-inspired insurrection and sabotage amongst Bosneger and Amerindian dissidents. Finally after face-to-face talks with both Bouterse and Shankar, Brunswijk was arrested by the army during talks in March 1990 when he was nominally immune from arrest. The army's excesses resulted in the National Assembly curbing the army's policing powers for the first time in April 1990. The assertion of growing civil control over the army may have provoked the Christmas *coup*. The army had been more successful during 1990 in dislodging rebel forces from several key positions, particularly in the economically valuable centres of Moengo and Langetabbetje, and this combined with Brunswijk's temporary decision to seek exile in the Netherlands seemed to indicate an end to the civil war. There is growing evidence that substantial sections of the army are involved in the trafficking of drugs, particularly into the Netherlands, and that curbs on army activities by the Shankar government were jeopardizing such activities, thereby contributing to the *coup*.

Outline of economic development. The 1980 *coup* and the widespread and apparently intractable nature of the civil war have damaged both Suriname's foreign relations and its economy. Following extensive human rights' abuses in 1982 both the Netherlands and the United States suspended crucial economic and developmental aid to the country (aid grants fell from SG172,960,000 in 1982 to a low of SG1,400,000 in 1985). Apart from humanitarian and closely tied aid following the return to constitutionalism in 1987, it has only been in 1989 and 1990 that there have been small signs (e.g. programme aid, cultural and air traffic agreements) that aid would be resumed in full from the Netherlands.

A concerted sabotage campaign by rebel forces, beginning in 1986, severely damaged Suriname's bauxite and alumina industry upon which it relies for some 76 per cent of its foreign exchange earnings. The combination of the suspension of aid plus marked decline in foreign earnings had resulted in large and unbridgeable government deficits which stood at 23.4 per cent of GDP in 1988. However, sharp reductions in imports (resulting in rationing of certain essential goods) and increases in alumina and aluminium production (as opposed to raw bauxite) in which Suriname receives a greater income from added value combined with increases in world prices during 1988 has resulted in a more manageable trade balance. Notwithstanding this, foreign exchange reserves are precarious (down to one week's import coverage in mid-1989) and are likely to remain so until full Dutch and US aid is restored. Official development aid is particularly important since those in government employment constitute some 40 per cent of the labour force, with total unemployment of the order of 35 per cent, and investment by the public authorities therefore continues to remain critical to the economy. Private foreign investment, particularly in the mining sector, has been severely curtailed by the civil war, where mining and processing facilities were subject to frequent guerrilla attacks. Market agriculture, which employs approximately 17 per cent of the labour force, is concentrated in the production of rice, bananas (principally for export), palm oil, sugar and citrus fruits. Despite Suriname's small population, but because 95 per cent of its land surface is tropical forest and due to the sporadic nature of agricultural development, the country is a net importer of food stuffs. Without careful and long-term planning this weakness will continue, a condition made more likely in the wake of the *coup*.

Current economic situation. Once again, though, the 1990 *coup* has totally undermined the process of the normalization of Suriname's external relations and in particular over the restoration of critical development aid. Repeated charges from Bouterse and government officials that rebel groups were being given safe haven and indeed support from French Guiana placed great strain on relations with France. The matter has been further complicated by the constant flow of refugees from eastern Suriname — the heart of Jungle Commando activities—into French Guiana. Only with a credible ceasefire and guarantees of freedom from army reprisal will the 12,000 refugees be able to return under United Nations High Commission for Refugees (UNHCR) plans currently under negotiation.

Prospects for development. The disintegration of the rebel movements in Suriname during 1990 plus the government's demonstration of will to control the army more effectively had given reason for cautious optimism for more prosperous and stable years for Suriname in the 1990s than at any time since independence. The re-establishment of direct army control, despite promises of new elections, effectively reverses four years of the slow process of democratization of Suriname.

JCJS

T

TECHNOCRATS. The Mexican system of public administration is clientelistic. Moreover although party competition exists in theory, the PRI until 1988 was seriously challenged only in certain regions. In consequence, there has been a tendency over the past generation to downplay the importance of political control and organization and to stress more thoroughly the importance of economic management. As a result, the top ranks of government have been filled increasingly by trained economists and to a consistently lesser extent by holders of local or regional office. It may be that the government's need to cope with a more active opposition since 1988 will lead to more value being put on the tasks of political management; in any event, it is overwhelmingly likely that the top administrative positions will be filled by trained economists for the forseeable future.

The last president of Mexico to have significant electoral experience was Díaz Ordaz (1964–70) who served as senator from the state of Puebla. His successor, Echeverría, did not serve in an elected position prior to the presidency but he had served for 12 years in that most political of all government departments, *Gobernación*. Echeverría's successor, López Portillo, had no real political experience before becoming president (except for his service in administrative positions relating to economic management); neither did Miguel de la Madrid or Carlos Salinas de Gortari.

A similar picture emerges if one takes Salinas de Gortari's first Cabinet. All of the economics ministries are filled by men with degrees from US universities; it is in these ministries that the most important policy decisions are made. It is true that there are more "political" figures in his Cabinet than there were in the Cabinet of de la Madrid, but the shift of balance has been only very slight.

GP

TELEVISA. In **Mexico**, as in other parts of the world, television is the most important medium of mass communication. Although some television channels in Mexico are government-owned, the most influential channels are owned by the private sector company Televisa. In the early 1980s, Televisa was said to enjoy over 95 per cent of the ratings.

Televisa emerged as the result of a combination between the owners of three independent television channels — the O'Farrill family, the Azcarraga family and the Alemán family. Subsequently it expanded into cable television, importing many programmes directly from the United States. Televisa has produced a somewhat bland image; its politics are effectively pro-system, and it has little truck with artistic or social experiments. It success lies in its ability to market popular programmes such as soap operas, sports programmes and imported US films.

Televisa has always been unpopular with a section of the Mexican Left. Part of the reason for this relates to the normal clash in many societies between high and low culture; the problem is particularly acute in Mexico where low culture (jeans, soap operas) tends to be approving of the United States and capitalism while high culture is nationalist. The Left has also feared the political influence exerted by Televisa, not so much through any overt propaganda but through a more subtle colouring of the values and assumptions of viewers. More recently there was criticism that Televisa's coverage of the 1988 elections was unfairly biassed toward the government. Nevertheless, although there was some possibility during 1970–82 that public policy would move against Televisa, this no longer appears at all likely.

GP

TONTONS MACOUTES. The Tontons Macoutes (literally, "uncle bogey-men"), were a "militia", or rather a group of thugs, organized under Dr. **François** ("Papa Doc") **Duvalier** to support and defend his regime in **Haiti**. In return, they were generally allowed to support themselves through petty extortion and protection rackets. At one stage they were led by the notorious Mme Adolphe, wife of the Minister of Health. They remained available to the regime of "Baby Doc" and have survived the fall of his government as a freelance terrorist body available to other prospective authoritarian leaders, latterly Roger Lafontant.

JKB

TOURISM (CARIBBEAN). Rapid growth in the last two decades has brought tourism to the fore as the Caribbean's largest single industry. In 1989, the region received 10,850,000 stay-over visitors and 6,710,000 cruise ship passengers, with gross expenditure estimated at US$7,800 million; further increases were expected for 1990, for the ninth successive year.

For many countries in the region, tourist earnings in hard currency offset persistent trade deficits. In 1989, the industry provided employment for approximately 325,000 people, and the number of hotel rooms was estimated at 118,500, an increase of 46 per cent since 1980.

During the decade, stay-over arrivals increased by 58 per cent, and visitor expenditure by 106 per cent. The number of cruise ship visitors increased over the period by 86 per cent. The United States provided 58 per cent of all arrivals in 1989; however, visitors from the US declined in number in the late 1980s, with a buoyant European market providing the main growth in the industry.

The two leading Caribbean destinations have traditionally been **Puerto Rico** and the **Bahamas**, which respectively attracted 2,260,000 and 1,580,000 stayover visitors in 1989. In third place was the **Dominican Republic**, with 1,300,000—virtually double the 1985 figure of 660,200. An ambitious tourism development programme in the Dominican Republic in the last two decades has seen the number of hotel rooms increase from 1,200 in 1972 to 3,400 in 1980 and to an estimated 21,000 in 1989, the largest number of any Caribbean country.

The Dominican tourism industry has also become the largest single earner of foreign exchange in the country, with net earnings of US$429,000,000 in 1988 outweighing the trade deficit of $358,000,000. By contrast, ferronickel exports, in a year of exceptionally high prices, earned $309,000,000, and sugar brought in only $142,000,000, compared with $300,000,000 in 1984. Gross visitor expenditure in 1989 was about $675,000,000, and is expected to increase to somewhere between $750 and $800,000,000 in 1990.

The Dominican Republic offers a particularly dramatic example of the growth of the tourist industry, but nearly all Caribbean countries have shown sustained growth during the 1980s. Exceptions are **Trinidad and Tobago**, which has traditionally focused its economic development strategy on oil-based industry and only recently devised a tourist development plan; **Guyana**, affected by economic difficulties combined with poor infrastructure and transport links; and Haiti and **Suriname**, both of which have been grappling with prolonged political instability.

Measured by thousands of stay-over arrivals, other major destinations in 1989 were **Jamaica** (715), St Maarten (504), **US Virgin Islands** (492), **Barbados** (461), **Bermuda** (416), Aruba (344), **Martinique** (312), **Cuba** (310) and **Guadeloupe** (255). For many islands, the annual total of visitor arrivals outnumbers the resident population; for example, the **Cayman Islands**, with a population of 25,000, received 210,000 stay-over visitors in 1989, and the **British Virgin Islands** (population 12,000) received 176,000.

Some caution, however, must be observed in interpreting tourism statistics. Several Caribbean countries include visiting nationals resident overseas in their total of visitor arrivals; in the case of the Dominican Republic, an estimated 300,000 of the 1989 total of 1,300,000 were in this category. While such visitors contribute by bringing foreign exchange into the country, they are more likely to stay with relatives and eat in their houses, rather than bringing business to hotels and restaurants.

Likewise, statistics based on occupancy reports from hotels are liable to include business travellers as well as holiday-makers, while some countries will roughly equate air arrivals with stay-over tourists.

The traditional focus of Caribbean tourism remains the beach holiday. However, intensified international competition in the industry has led to the development of large hotel complexes offering sports, excursions, night clubs and luxury restaurants, conference facilities, shopping and in some cases casino gambling.

Certain countries have a specific attraction to offer tourists, such as Trinidad's carnival, and a few small islands, notably Dominica, are making an effort to promote a more selective approach to tourism, encouraging small groups to make botanical or bird-watching visits.

A striking features of the 1980s was the rapid growth of the cruise ship business, which has in turn led to ambitious development plans being produced in several countries for the city areas surrounding cruise terminals. Since cruise ship calls involve large numbers of passengers disembarking for relatively brief periods, the associated development tends to concentrate heavily on the opportunities to extract the maximum revenue from the visitors during this time: souvenir stalls, duty-free shops, bars and fast-food cafeterias are the norm, together with slickly presented guided tours of "heritage" areas such as the old city of San Juan in Puerto Rico.

The increase in cruise ship business has not been without problems. Hoteliers in some countries have complained that disproportionate resources are being devoted to promoting a form of tourism which, because of the short length of stay, produces much less revenue *per capita* than stay-over tourism. Grievances by residents include the congestion caused by the presence of cruise ship visitors in crowded town centres, together with the tawdriness of the souvenir business. Conversely, cruise passengers often complain of harassment by vendors and hustlers of various kinds.

On one side or the other, these tensions sometimes lead to a reduction in cruise ship calls. In 1988, the cruise liner operators imposed a virtual boycott of Kingstown in St Vincent, reducing calls to nine in comparison with 114 the year before, following complaints of harassment and poor facilities. Conversely, the Bermuda government imposed a limit on cruise ships calls in the 1990 summer season, in order to reduce the number of passengers being landed.

The friction over the cruise ship trade has a parallel in a continuing debate within the Caribbean about the role of tourism in the region. While it is generally recognized that tourism has become established an an important and even fundamental sector in national economies throughout the Caribbean, a number of doubts remain.

One area of concern has to do with the externally dependent nature of the business. Caribbean countries can find their tourist trade declining without warning because of factors beyond their control: economic recession in one or more of the countries of origin (principally the United States, Canada, Britain and continental Europe); exchange rate fluctuations; changes in holiday fashion; competition from other destinations; increases in air fares or a reduction in air services, such as the closure of Eastern Airlines' routes in 1989.

Tourists may also be put off by reports of political unrest or by the effects of hurricanes, even when the chosen destination may remain unaffected by any problems.

These difficulties can be confronted, but at a price. Expensive promotion campaigns are required to offset declining business in a given market or to open up new business in another. Most Caribbean governments have recognized the benefits of attracting tourists from a diverse range of countries, rather than being dependent on one market; however, their ability to do so is often limited by the difficulty of securing the appropriate air services.

Lack of language skills is a further problem in opening up new markets. With Spanish, English, French and Dutch as official languages in the Caribbean (and Creole and Papiamento widely spoken as everyday languages), many islands have found it natural to seek tourist business in countries with which they share a language.

In addition to the externally related problems, the industry has to cope with certain domestic issues affecting its position. Regional tourism officials have identified one of these difficulties as an ingrained feeling in Caribbean society that service equals slavery, an emotive issue in a region where a majority of the population are descended from slaves.

One manifestation of this association of tourism with colonial domination is a degree of indifferent and surly service to visitors. In the Bahamas, for example, surveys have shown poor service as a consistent cause of dissatisfaction among tourists, and the Prime Minister, Sir Lynden Pindling, has frequently upbraided the industry for failing to improve in this respect. As an expression of his concern for the future of tourism in the Bahamas, Pindling took over the Tourism portfolio in September 1990, spending some days working in roles such as hotel bellboy or laundryman.

Other complaints aired by visitors and residents alike include a range of social ills associated with tourism or offering a threat to tourists, including crime and harassment of tourists, prostitution, high rates in certain countries of HIV infection, and the destruction of distinctive local cultures. Economically, it is often argued that tourism furthers the import of extra-Caribbean consumption patterns and, consequently, consumer goods, despite efforts to encourage hotels to use more local produce.

Allied to these problems are anxieties about the effects of mass tourism on the environment. In several Caribbean countries, a debate is under way about how far tourist development can go before it destroys the natural beauty which is the original attraction for the tourist, and a number of governments have adopted building codes aimed at preventing over-development of large hotels and the whittling away of public access to beaches. However, tourism has helped encourage the preservation and restoration of historic sites in several countries.

The increase in the economic importance of the tourist industry has been accompanied by a concentration of hotel ownership in the hands of the major international chains, which have been responsible for the majority of new projects during the 1980s. Smaller enterprises are more often locally owned, and some of the larger hotels remain in local hands. A programme adopted by the Seaga government in **Jamaica**, and continued by the following government of Prime Minister **Michael Manley**, has seen the sale of a number of state-owned hotels into private ownership, with Jamaican capital involved in several of the purchases.

It is evident, however, that international hotel companies proposing hotel development in smaller islands exert a good deal of economic weight, which can lead to governments overcoming environmental hesitations for the sake of the revenue and employment opportunities expected from the schemes.

Relations between governments and private sector representatives in the Caribbean tourist industry have indeed not always followed a smooth course. Government-sponsored tourist boards, responsible for international promotion of the industry, have frequently been criticized for waste and inefficiency, and the private sector has persistently complained of tourism being given a low priority by many governments. Hoteliers in Barbados and other countries, for example, have complained that tax relief on imported inputs favours manufacturing industry but not tourism.

In an effort to co-ordinate regional tourist strategies, a Caribbean Tourism Organization (CTO) was formed in January 1989 through a merger of two existing regional bodies. The CTO groups government and private sector, and regional tourism ministers form its governing council. A separate organization, the Caribbean Hotel Association, represents hoteliers' interests.

The two organizations agreed in October 1990 to work together on a joint marketing project; to improve public awareness about the value of tourism, with the aim of improving the quality of service offered by the industry; to improve the standards of hotels and other facilities; and to discuss transport needs with airlines serving the region.

While there is undoubted scope for further expansion of the industry, some countries have started to recognize that arrivals cannot be expected to continue to increase indefinitely. Barbados, for instance, indicated in 1987 that a ceiling of between 400,000 and 450,000 stay-over arrivals was being considered, with the aim of pursuing "quality rather than quantity"; however, arrivals subsequently increased beyond the ceiling, as even more ambitious targets were announced.

The competitive building of large hotels on even very small islands such as Anguilla and Nevis could, if taken to its logical conclusion, lead to considerable over-capacity in the region as a whole. While a substantial increase in trade is expected as a result of the emergence of the European single market in January 1993, established operators in the region were showing some concern in 1990 at the prospect that Cuba—hitherto a relatively minor competitor and as yet not a CTO member—might succeed in substantially increasing its tourist potential. This could bring considerable turmoil into an industry which is already sensitive to its vulnerability in a competitive world market.

RP

TRINIDAD AND TOBAGO. *Population*: 1,235,400 (1988). *Area*: 5,128 sq. km. (Trinidad: 4,828 sq km., Tobago: 300 sq km.). *GDP*: US$3,800 million (1989). *Trade volume*: US$2,375 million (1989). *Top five trade partners*: USA, UK, Germany, Canada, Japan. *Defence spending*: TT$180 million (1985). *Education spending (as percentage of GNP)*: 13.7. *Urban centres with a population of over 20,000*: Port-of-Spain: 59,200; San Fernando: 33,600, Arima: 29,000 (1988). *Birthrate*: 27 per 1,000.

Geographical background. The Republic of Trinidad and Tobago, a status achieved in Aug. 1, 1976 while remaining a Commonwealth country, lies in the Caribbean immediately off the coast of Venezuela. It has one of the Caribbean's most developed economies on a foundation laid by Dr Eric Williams, who dominated the country with his People's National Movement (PNM) until his death in March 1981.

Socio–political background. Conversely, the country epitomizes much of the mismanagement and "squandermania" that has afflicted some Caribbean countries. In the 1980s, Trinidad and Tobago has slid from literally propping up the economies of less-rich Caribbean countries to instituting widespread wage freezes, spending cuts, foreign exhange restrictions and devaluations. Strikes have plagued the country and despite its stability, various upheavals have taken place.

Outline of political history. On July 27, 1990, Trinidad and Tobago became the focus of world attention when a black Muslim group, the Jamaat al Muslimeen, led by Yasin Abu Bakar, seized Prime Minister A.N.R. Robinson and members of Cabinet, citing unfair practices, harsh economic measures and reckless spending by the government in the face of unemployment, including erecting a statue to an obscure worker.

Some 114 members of the rebel group occupied Red House, the Republic's Parliament, taking 43 hostages, including employees of the national Trinidad and Tobago Television (TTT). The group, which had a series of clashes with authorities, many of which went before the courts, squat on a self-contained community on the outskirts of the capital Port-of-Spain.

The Muslimeen surrendered after five days. Prime Minister Robinson was shot in the leg and a number of people died after being caught in gun battles. The group is facing numerous charges, including treason. On March 28, 1991 it was reported that the group's lawyer, Farouk Hosein, had taken their case for dismissal of all charges to the Privy Council. The group argued that they were pardoned as a condition of laying down their arms.

The attempted *coup* came 20 years after the Republic's other major uprising. In April 1970 followers of the US-inspired Black Power movement led widespread, violent protests over weeks against unemployment among the black population and foreign presence in the economy. A *Public Order Act* was quickly introduced, and a state of emergency declared. However, part of the army mutineed; this was put down after three days and major participants were later imprisoned.

The Seventies proved to be a boon to the Republic of Trinidad and Tobago on the strength of high oil prices. Dr Williams embarked on a programme of nationalization, which saw the country taking over or holding majority shares in financial and productive sectors of the economy, while establishing a number of state organizations such as Caroni (sugar) and Trinidad and Tobago Oil Company (TRINTOC). In addition, there was massive industrialization, especially at Point Lisas, including an iron and steel complex, petrochemicals and fertilizer plants.

While Dr Williams remained above the constant opposition alliances and charges against his party, the growth of the Trinidad economy under his leadership also led to widespread mismanagement and unbridled spending by Trinidadians.

One minister embezzled millions, fleeing to Miami, USA and then to Toronto, Canada. Millions more were poured into a new racing complex, subsequently scrapped, and a housing project which did not realize one single house despite sucking up more than TT$100,000,000. By 1984, faced with falling oil prices and failure in other sectors of the economy, the PNM, headed by George Chambers, who replaced Dr Williams after the latter's death in 1981, was forced to introduce harsh policies and faced countrywide protests and violent strikes, particularly in the oil areas. It was this predicament which led to IMF involvement in April 1990 and forced the Muslimeen to attempt to seize power in Trinidad and Tobago's darkest period to date.

Trinidad became a British colony in 1802, after ownership by Spain. Tobago, a British colony since 1814, was added in 1888, and Trinidad and Tobago remained a joint colony until independence on Aug. 31, 1962.

Trade unionism has always been forceful in Trinidad and led to political organization. Dr Williams formed the PNM in 1956, winning the September elections to the Legislative Council. The country joined the West Indies Federation in 1958, gaining full internal self-government in 1959. Trinidad and Tobago withdrew from the Federation after Jamaica seceded in 1961, ensuring the collapse of the regional union, an event marked by Dr Williams's famous words, "one from 10 leaves zero".

Despite the 1970 uprising, the PNM won all 36 seats at the May 1971 elections and moved Trinidad and Tobago to republican status. At elections in September 1976, the PNM won 24 seats. The United Labour Front (ULF), a union-fronted party, won 10 seats with the two Tobago seats going to the Democratic Action Congress (DAC).

In 1980, Tobago was allowed limited autonomy and its own House of Assembly. Williams' death in March 1981 left a void in the PNM, filled with the election of George Chambers, surprisingly, as Prime Minister. At elections in November, the PNM added two more seats for a total of 26. Despite banding together as the Trinidad and Tobago National Alliance, opposition parties, the ULF, DAC and the Tapia House Movement only won two seats. The party which impressed was the Organization for National Reconstruction (ONR), headed by former PNM minister Karl Hudson-Phillips.

Unseating the PNM become an opposition priority, leading to closer ties, and the PNM suffered its first ever electoral defeat in the August 1983 local elections when opposition parties, known as the Accomodation, won 66 of 120 council seats. The ONR and the National Alliance joined as the National Alliance for Reconstruction, (NAR) in August 1984. In November the DAC won elections to the Tobago House in September 1985, DAC leader Robinson was elected head of the NAR, and the four parties merged as the NAR in February 1986.

This was the combination which finally broke the PNM's domination of Trinidad and Tobago politics. Fuelled by unrest at the PNM's harsh economic policies, the NAR swept the December 1986 elections, winning 33 seats and 66 per cent of the vote. Chambers was among the PNM members who lost their seats and Patrick Manning became leader of the three-man opposition.

Current developments—political. The NAR's victory failed to alleviate in any way the Republic's parlous economic position, and in-fighting added to its problems. In June 1987 Tapia House Movement *alumni* announced they were leaving the alliance. In November a former ULF member, the Minister of Public Works and Settlements, was dismissed. In February 1988, more than 100 NAR members met to discuss leadership and direction. This was seen by Robinson as a move to remove him, and subsequently two cabinet members and a junior minister, all former members of the ULF, were dismissed. Led by Basdeo Panday and representing the East Indian community, they were expelled from the NAR in October 1988 and subsequently formed the United National Congress (UNC) in April 1989.

The NAR's woes have centred on the sluggish Trinidad and Tobago economy and the attempted *coup* only added to the country's troubles. Import controls were imposed in the 1980s, causing problems within **CARICOM**, especially Barbados. Wages were cut, the Trinidad currency devalued and in April 1990 the IMF agreed to assist the country's ailing economy. Unemployment stood at 22.4 per cent in 1989.

Outline of economic development. The petroleum industry is vital to Trinidad and Tobago's economy and falling oil revenues, and the failure of many industrial plants, have contributed to the decrease in GNP and GDP especially in the last half of the '80s. In 1988 GNP stood at US$3,350 per head while GDP decreased by some six per cent between 1980 and 1987.

In 1986, the petroleum industry accounted for 25 per cent of GDP, 42 per cent of government revenue and 80 per cent of export revenue. Trinidad has the biggest natural asphalt reserves in the world and also its substantial natural gas fuels electricity, manufacturing and the country's two oil refineries.

There are a range of industrial products, from cement to petrochemicals to drink manufacturing. In 1988 this sector contributed 42.3 per cent to GDP and employed some 28 per cent of the population. Manufacturing has however declined, with failures in iron and steel products and vehicle assembly.

Tourism is relatively small, some 200,000 visitors annually, but the third foreign exchange earner. This sector has been targetted for development, with government upgrading airport facilities in Trinidad and Tobago and port facilities in Tobago.

Agriculture remains important, principally sugar, coffee, cocoa and citrus. There is also widespread vegetable farming for local production. This sector employed 13 per cent of the population in 1988 when it contributed 4.7 per cent.

Current economic situation. A rise in oil prices would greatly assist the economy of Trinidad and Tobago. The test of the NAR government, however, is to restore the standards of living in the country and reduce unemployment while curbing waste. A number of public corporations have been restructured, with subsidies reduced. It is going to be a long and hard road for the Republic, for unions have been keeping up pressure to at least restore cut incomes. Teachers, who up to April 1991 were each owed TT$50,000, were on strike.

How well the NAR copes will probably affect their fortunes at the next general elections, due in December 1991. In addition to the 36-member House of Representatives there is a 31-member Senate. The Tobago House of Assembly has 12 elected members and three members appointed by the majority party.

MH

TUPAMAROS (Movimiento de Liberación Nacional — MLN). The National Liberation Movement of **Uruguay**, commonly known as the Tupamaros, was a revolutionary movement established in 1962 under the leadership of Raúl Sendic Antonaccio, many of the members of which were the children of the political élite. In the late 1960s it adopted an urban guerrilla strategy characterized both by skilled tactics, as when very large numbers of arrestees were freed at a time, and by psychological warfare, as when the President's income tax returns were published. Its political wing, the *Frente Amplio* (Broad Front), led by Gen. Liber Seregni, emerged in the elections of 1971. Following the military takeover in 1973 large-scale arrests, detention and torture, however, broke the back of the movement, though the *Frente Amplio* survived. Sendic died on April 28, 1989 in Paris from the effects of his torture by the military authorities following his capture in September 1972. Sentenced to death, later commuted to 45 years' imprisonment, he had been pardoned by President Sanguinetti in 1985.

PARC

TURKS AND CAICOS ISLANDS. *Population*: 8,700 (1988). *Area*: 430 sq km. *GDP*: US$62,100,000. *Trade volume*: $40,400,000. *Birthrate*: 25.5 per 1,000.

Geographical background. The Turks and Caicos Islands consist of a number of low-lying islands in the Caribbean Sea to the south-east of the Bahamas and to the north of Haiti. They were first settled by Europeans collecting salt in the late seventeenth century. They became a British possession and were a dependency of Jamaica between 1874 and 1962. On Jamaica's attainment of independence they became a separate British dependency, receiving their own Governor in 1972.

Socio–political background. Under the terms of the 1988 Constitution the Governor is responsible for defence, security and foreign affairs. Executive power in other matters is in the hands of the Executive Council, comprising three appointed members, the Chief Minister and four of the elected members from the Legislative Council. The Governor serves as the Executive Council's chairman. Legislative power is held by the Legislative Council, comprising 13 members elected from multi-member constituencies, three ex-officio members and three nominated members. The Chief Minister is the member with the support of the majority of elected members.

Outline of political history. A sentiment for independence from Britain had built up in the islands during the 1960s and 1970s and in 1980 the British government agreed to grant independence if the ruling People's Democratic Party (PDM) won the general election to be held that year. However, following the death in an accident of the Chief Minister, the PDM lost the election to the opposition Progressive National Party (PNP), which favoured continued dependent status.

Recent developments—political. The PNP were returned to power in 1984, but in 1985 the Chief Minister, Norman Saunders, and two other party members, were arrested in the USA after an operation by the Drug Enforcement Agency working in co-operation with the British authorities. The relative isolation of the islands and their position on the route for drug trafficking between South America and the USA led to their use as a refuelling point by light planes used by drug smugglers. Local politicians and officials were bribed to turn a blind eye to these activities. Saunders was found guilty of drug conspiracy charges and sentenced to eight years' imprisonment. In 1986 direct rule was imposed by the Governor, Christopher Turner, after the publication of a Royal Commission report into arson and corruption which severely criticized the Chief Minister, Nathaniel Francis, and other politicians. A new constitution was granted in 1988, prior to elections in March 1988. Proportional representation was introduced in the hope that it would provide a more balanced representation in the Legislative Council, but in the event 11 of the 13 seats were won by the PDM whose leader, Oswald Skippings, became Chief Minister.

Outline of economic development. Traditionally the economy of the Turks and Caicos Islands was based on salt production, but this ceased in the 1960s. Poor soils and low rainfall have limited agricultural production, while relative isolation, poor transport and infrastructure have combined to hinder the islands' development. The closure of the last US military base on the islands in 1983 led to the loss of rent equal to 10 per cent of revenue. In response to this the British government during the 1980s attempted to help the islands' development by promoting tourism as the only viable means of providing jobs and income. The British government has succeeded in helping the islands to become self-financing in recurrent expenditure, but still provides capital aid to help with much-needed infrastructural development. In 1988–89 there was a recurrent budgetary surplus of nearly $500,000 and for 1989–90 British development aid was increased considerably, to £24,000,000, compared with £5,000,000 for the previous year.

Current economic situation. Tourism grew rapidly during the 1980s, boosted by the completion of an international airport on Providenciales and the construction of major hotel complexes on that island. The rapid growth of the tourism and construction sectors has led to an influx of illegal migrant workers, mostly from Haiti and the Dominican Republic, who may comprise as much as 10 per cent of the population. This reliance on tourism leaves the economy vulnerable to the threat of a downturn caused by a fall in tourist arrivals, but so far numbers have continued to increase dramatically, adding to the high GDP growth rates of over 20 per cent recorded during the 1980s. The other focus of development during the 1980s has been the offshore financial sector. The financial sector has concentrated on the registration of offshore companies, with some trust and specialized insurance business, aided by the use of US currency on the islands. In the aftermath of the Coopers & Lybrand report of 1989 into the offshore financial sectors of British Caribbean dependencies, regulation and supervision has been strengthened. Over 4,000 offshore companies were registered in the islands by the mid-1980s, but the unfavourable publicity surrounding the drug and corruption scandals limited potential expansion, although the total in 1989 stood at over 6,500.

LP

U

UNEMPLOYMENT. South and Central American states suffer from two endemic economic and social problems: unemployment and underemployment. It is probably no coincidence that statistics on unemployment for the region are exceptionally difficult to obtain and of very doubtful value. Even in **Mexico** in the late 1980s estimates of those unemployed and underemployed varied from 6,000,000–18,000,000, the official *Banco de México* figure for 1988 being some 17 per cent. In **Brazil**, the most complex and diverse economy of South America, the only reasonably reliable figures for unemployment are those for the area of Greater Rio de Janeiro, and even there the evidence of the shanty-towns is that both unemployment and underemployment are very high indeed. In the cash-crop economies of the Caribbean area, such as **Guatemala** and **Honduras**, recession affects even the subsistence sector, since it curtails the opportunities to supplement the family income by seasonal work on coffee or cotton plantations.

The region as a whole was hard hit by the recession of 1981, as a result of which all countries underwent a substantial rise in unemployment and underemployment in the official sector in 1982 and 1983. Much of the measurable urban unemployment was the immediate result of the decline of the tertiary sector which by that time made up about half of all urban employment in the region. This decline was in turn consequent on the slow-down in primary production and manufacturing industry. An important result was the sideways shift into the informal economy which resulted in the steep increase of the production of exports of cocaine and other narcotic drugs (*see* **Drugs**) in **Bolivia**, **Peru** and **Colombia**.

Throughout the rest of the decade, as production continued to lag and production levels sank back to the levels prevailing in the early 1970s, the number and plight of the unemployed was compounded by the variety of stabilization plans attempted by governments such as those of **Argentina**, Brazil and Mexico. Though with official encouragement new jobs became available, the vast majority were very low-paid jobs held in the main by women (*see* **Women's Issues**), producing for the export market on behalf of large foreign-owned corporations. The situation was particularly bad in Central America and especially in Guatemala, where by 1986 plantation owners facing a huge demand from hungry workers and backed by the ruthless power of the armed forces were able to pay well below the legal minimum wage and get away with it.

Caribbean. Unemployment poses one of the biggest problems for Caribbean countries, many of which constantly face double digit levels of unemployment. This has persisted despite countries significantly raising standards of living and increasing employment avenues for their respective populations.

Very few countries, mostly smaller islands such as Anguilla, St. Kitts-Nevis and Montserrat have relatively low unemployment levels. Not only do these countries enjoy small population levels, but large numbers of people go abroad to work. With immigration restrictions being tightened by traditional countries, USA, Canada and the UK, to which West Indians emigrate, this option has not for some time been a safety net for larger countries, which also have higher birth rates and, in many cases, are faced with harsher job losses in times of recession, crop failure, natural disaster or even government mismanagement.

A number of factors, some interlocking, have been responsible for the more than 10 per cent levels of unemployment in the Caribbean, a figure which is as high as 30 per cent in St. Lucia and 42 per cent in St Vincent. First, the move away from agriculture, along with mechanization, has led to many jobs lost in this sector, too many to be absorbed in other areas of economies which have for most of their development had agricultural-based and labour-intensive farming, particularly in the sugar cane industry.

The shift of Caribbean countries into service and light industries, with the vagaries in sectors like the tourist industry, has not led to the widespread, sustained employment originally envisaged. In the late 1970s and up to the mid-1980s, Caribbean countries benefited from the growth in the electronics and clothing industries, but subsequent recession in these areas has led to cutbacks and massive job losses in the region. The closure of Intel Corp. in Barbados was one such instance, making some 1,000 unemployed. Allied to this is the comparatively high wage rates in the region compared with places like Mexico. Thus the labour intensive electronics assembly industries have been moving out of many Caribbean countries.

Tourism, the major employer in the region, has

led to high levels of employment in countries such as the Bahamas, Bermuda, Jamaica and Barbados. This, too, can be very seasonal and dependent on a number of uncontrollable variables, the most important being the level of economic stability of source countries. The decline of the British economy since 1989 has had a negative effect on travel from that country, a main source, to the Caribbean. The Kuwait crisis of 1990–91 has also had its effect as core, high spenders curtailed travel.

Caribbean countries have relatively young populations and are faced every year with levels of up to 10,000 new people, mostly school leavers, entering the work force. The reality is that despite gradual, in some cases rapid, growth in the 1980s, Caribbean countries, dependent as they are on external forces, are unable to maintain the levels of growth required to cope with existing workforces, far less accommodate new entrants to the job market.

The changing economies and economic growth of Caribbean countries have also had their own negative effect on employment. Most countries have at least doubled per capita incomes in the 1980s, and allied with higher education levels, have led to populations turning their backs on certain jobs. Thus, Barbados imported workers to assist in harvesting the sugar industry in the late 1970s, there is a labour shortage in St. Kitts-Nevis despite 10 per cent unemployment, and Bermuda and the Bahamas have large proportions of foreign workers in their tourist industry, and in the case of Bermuda, police force.

Even countries with comparatively sophisticated mixed economies and high levels of industrialization such as Trinidad remain susceptible to high unemployment. The boom period in Trinidad ended in the mid-1980s, as the country's oil revenues fell, heavy manufacturing failed and exports dropped as receiving countries underwent economic pressure. Massive forced unemployment was only avoided as unions traded salary cuts for job security. Nevertheless, unemployment reached unprecedented levels, some 22 per cent in 1989.

Governments have tried various means of stimulating economic growth to combat unemployment, from infrastructural programmes to retraining. New areas of economic activity such as offshore business are, however, not high employment generating areas. Also, with emphasis among the Caribbean traditional support countries shifting to the Middle East and Eastern Europe, and the coming of the unitary European market in 1992, it is unlikely that the region will benefit from widespread investment, leading to new industries. More likely is that governments will have to seek ways of maximizing indigenous resources to ease unemployment, such as embarking on canning industries as an extension of fruit and crop production.

The future will be more a case of trying to hold unemployment levels to, say, 10 per cent, while providing social security facilities to assist those unemployed. Some countries have already implemented variations of unemployment benefit.

Whatever, it is unlikely that the very low levels of unemployment which characterized the region in the 1950s and 1960s when countries were in their early development stages will ever be attained in the future. The make-up of the economies, and the dependency on foreign forces whether for exports, investment or tourism mean unemployment in the Caribbean will continue to fluctuate in double digits, becoming lower with better economic management and stable world economies and higher with recession, poor forward planning and economic mismanagement. Any country with less than this figure will be doing exceptionally well.

PARC, MH

UNITED STATES–CUBAN RELATIONS. The dominant positions which US enterprise had achieved within the Cuban economy prior to 1959 were immediately and uncompromisingly overturned with the revolution. The wholesale nationalization without compensation of agricultural holdings, public utilities, energy industries and financial services provoked the rapid deterioration in Cuban–US relations. The first major response of the US government was to impose a blockade and then a comprehensive trade embargo on Cuba thereby cutting off Cuba's major export market and principal source of imports in one move. The attempted counter-revolutionary invasion at the Bay of Pigs on April 17, 1961 confirmed the uncompromising hostility of the Kennedy administration and set the terms of future relations.

The Cuban Missile Crisis of October 1962 was essentially a Soviet–American crisis which happened to be acted out around Cuba: the resolution of the crisis by Khrushchev and Kennedy was carried out without Castro's participation. The major consequence of the US embargo has been the extremely high economic costs placed upon Cuba in the form of lost markets (the USA itself and those of US allies), higher trading costs in transportation and insurance premiums, and the costs of defence against an ever-present and close threat. There is evidence from the 1960s of assassination attempts on Castro by the American

Central Intelligence Agency (CIA) along with acts of economic sabotage. The general relationship between the two countries is not likely to change in the immediate future.

JCJS

UNITED STATES OF AMERICA

Geographical background. With one-fifth of its coastline on the Gulf of Mexico, the continental United States of today dominates the economic and political life of the Caribbean Basin. The Caribbean is, in a hackneyed phrase, the United States' "back yard". From a strategic point of view, the area has increasingly come to be seen by policy-makers in Washington as a liability. Yet policy towards it, and by extension towards South America, with which the United States also regards itself as having a special relationship, has developed over many decades, piecemeal, and lacks consistency.

A significant distinction exists in international politics between the Caribbean Basin system and that of South America. Until recently the State Department had no single definition of the term "Caribbean", the widest definition including both mainland and island states, whether independent or not, between **Mexico** in North America and **Colombia**, **Venezuela** and the Guianas in South America. The area concerned is very large, and, to put it in perspective, it may he helpful to remember that the distance between Washington and St George's, **Grenada** is about the same as that between Moscow and London.

By extension the countries of South America have often been regarded as specially close to the United States. However for much of their history they have impinged relatively little on world politics, and the United States has taken very little account of them. They form in many respects a self-contained system of their own, joined though it is to the Caribbean world by the "hinge states", Colombia and Venezuela. Nor are they particularly close to the United States—Buenos Aires is about the same distance from Southampton or Le Havre as it is from New York.

Socio–political background. In many respects the United States is so unlike a European country that it could be regarded as a Latin American state that happens to speak English. As long as it was seen as the first among equals it was seen in many South American countries, notably **Argentina** and **Brazil**, as a role model to be admired and copied. The change in their perceptions came with the Spanish–American War of 1898, which marked the emergence of the rapidly industrializing United States as a world power, and was first embodied in *Ariel* (1900), a critique of US materialism by the Uruguayan José Enrique Rodó.

The term "Latin America" has a meaning only in a negative sense. Historically it has referred to 20 countries, 18 of which spoke Spanish, one Portuguese and one French. The same experience that united them is shared both with the United States and with the English and Dutch-speaking states in the Caribbean that have become independent only in the last 30 years. All have experienced colonization. All have, at one time or another, formed part of an empire ruled from Spain (Portugal and its empire was united with the Crown of Spain from 1582–1640).

Outline of early history. Because of later events, it is generally assumed in the United States and in Europe that the United States had a natural tendency to expand westwards. In fact, British settlement on the east coast of North America began in Newfoundland in 1497 and spread southwards, as is shown in the names of the settlements themselves: Virginia (named after Elizabeth I), the Carolinas (Charles I) and Georgia (George II).

The founders of the United States believed that they were creating nothing less than "a new order of the ages" in the Western Hemisphere. They owed their own independence at least in part to their alliance with royalist France (1777), but their belief that the future lay in distancing themselves as far as possible from warring Europe was embodied in Washington's Farewell Address (1797). His view: "It is our true policy to steer clear of permanent alliances with any portion of the foreign world" became the first plank of an emerging US foreign policy, in which the infant Republic expressed its intention not to interfere with Europe and its hope that Europe would no longer intervene in the Americas.

With the purchase of Louisiana by Thomas Jefferson in 1803 the United States simultaneously removed the threat of further French expansion and secured direct access to the Caribbean through the port of New Orleans. Jefferson was also the first US President to interest himself in **Cuba**, but an offer to purchase the island from the Spanish crown was turned down, and, with the beginnings of unrest on the mainland, Congress in 1808 passed the No Transfer Resolution, expressing opposition to any transfer of territory in the Americas between European powers, which might impel them to help Spain reconquer its colonies. Together a promise of non-interference with existing colonies and a statement of opposition to any fresh colonization in the hemisphere, the no transfer principle subsequently was embodied in 1823 in the definitive view of US relations with the rest of the world, the **Monroe Doctrine**.

Meanwhile the United States had rounded out its southern frontier by two brief campaigns to annex Florida from Spain before it could become independent as Mexico did in 1822. The following year, Stephen Austin obtained permission for his followers to settle in Texas, which was then the northern part of the Mexican state of Coahuila. Soon the English-speaking settlers were in a majority in Texas. In 1836 it seceded from Mexico and for a time was an independent republic, before asking for and receiving annexation to the United States in 1845. In the war that followed, known in the United States as the Mexican War and in Mexico as the War of 1847, Mexico lost over half its national territory to the United States. Within weeks gold had been discovered in California and the great California Gold Rush had started.

It was this that gave the United States its first strategic interest in Central America, when Commodore Vanderbilt organized a shipping route to California by way of the San Juan River and the waters of Lake Nicaragua. But interest in this region was to be cut short for a generation by the American Civil War. Though even after the war the Grant Administration tried tentatively to buy Cuba (from Spain) and the **Dominican Republic** (from its own inhabitants), further expansion in that direction would have meant strengthening the power of the South and Congress would not accept this. It was not until 1898 that a fresh outbreak of insurrection in Cuba led to US intervention and to the Spanish–American War.

US intervention in the Caribbean. As a result of the war the United States acquired **Puerto Rico** and gave Cuba its independence, though under terms (the "Platt Amendment") which made it a virtual protectorate. It also had had a sharp lesson in the strategic desirability of constructing an inter-oceanic canal. Two routes were available: the Nicaraguan route and that across the Isthmus of Panama at Darien, and Congress chose the latter. Negotiations were, however, held up as the government of Colombia sought to negotiate better terms for the sale of its interest in the shortest route, across the Isthmus of Panama. This was solved by a "spontaneous" revolt in Panama City. **Panama** proclaimed its independence, which was immediately recognized by the United States. As the government of Panama signed away in perpetuity its rights over a 10-mile wide strip of land on either side of the proposed canal, the Colombians could do nothing to stop it. Construction of the canal began in 1904 and it was opened 10 years later, three days after the outbreak of the Great War.

Theodore Roosevelt did not conceal his role; in his re-election campaign in 1904 he declared proudly: "I took Panama". But he and his successors were soon to find that becoming an imperial power brought problems as well as rewards. The new Canal had to be defended, and the sea routes leading to it kept clear. And the many surviving possessions of European powers in the Caribbean made them potential rivals, while the smaller independent states of the region continued to offer provocation when they suffered involuntary changes of government and defaulted on their debts. With the Press becoming militant, Roosevelt responded to the popular mood, and in 1904 enunciated what was to become known as the **Roosevelt Corollary** to the Monroe Doctrine, which claimed that, since the United States could not countenance intervention by others, it would have to intervene itself, if necessary acting as a trustee for the European powers.

On this basis the President of the Dominican Republic was persuaded in 1905 to make official the unofficial arrangement the USA had been operating since 1900 over Dominican customs duties—the government's chief source of revenue. More than half the revenues were confiscated for distribution to creditors. The reasoning was that by removing the chief prize of political revolution from contention in this way, stability of governments could be increased and the risk of foreign intervention eliminated. Things did not go quite as planned: President Morales himself was overthrown in 1906, and his successor, Ramón Cáceres, who assented to a Treaty in 1907 which re-established US financial trusteeship, was assassinated in 1911. But the trusteeship lasted in one form or another down to 1940.

Roosevelt is famous for his use of the African proverb "Speak softly and carry a big stick", and the phrase "the big stick" suggests the use of force. Wisely however Roosevelt himself was slow to use force. Though in 1906 he did answer the call of the Cuban government and sent troops there to re-establish orderly government, no further armed intervention took place during his Presidency, though US marines remained in Cuba and anti-Americanism became a dominant theme of Cuban politics.

In Central America Roosevelt's Secretary of State, Elihu Root, encouraged states to settle their disputes though a Central American court created in 1907, the first such international body for the peaceful resolution of disputes. But William Howard Taft, President 1909–1913, took a different tack, trying to avoid the pretext for European intervention in the region by substituting

American capital investment for European. This policy, known as "Dollar Diplomacy", annoyed the Europeans without solving the problem. Matters came to a head in **Nicaragua** where US intervention assisted in the fall of the nationalistic dictator José Zelaya, but fell short of providing a satisfactory successor government. Eventually in 1912 US Marines were landed and Nicaragua became a virtual American protectorate. The policy was continued by Woodrow Wilson, President 1913–21, when by the Bryan–Chamorro Treaty of 1913 the United States finally acquired the rights to the rival Nicaraguan canal, which however it had no intention of building.

With the outbreak of the Great War in 1914 intervention was stepped up. When its President fled in despair troops were sent to the Dominican Republic, which became a new protectorate. In 1915, when the president of **Haiti** was torn to pieces in the streets of Port-au-Prince, US forces landed there too, and another protectorate came into existence. In 1914 Woodrow Wilson intervened in Mexico to try to root out a dictator; in 1916 a punitive force under General Pershing (the Pershing Expedition) was sent into Northern Mexico, where all central government had broken down, to capture "Pancho" Villa and bring him to justice for his raid on Columbus, New Mexico. It was withdrawn in 1917 shortly before the United States itself entered the European War. In the same year, fearing a German invasion of Denmark which fortunately never took place, the United States bought the Danish Virgin Islands, now an American tourist resort. Finally, between 1917 and 1919 the United States exercised such pressure on the military ruler of **Costa Rica**, Fernando Tinoco, that he was forced to resign.

Other imperial powers in the region acquiesced in the new US dominance for two reasons. Firstly, they had no alternative, and secondly the United States was, regardless of the Monroe Doctrine, emerging as a force in European politics. The entry of the USA into the War was reluctant, but its status as an Associated Power protected the colonies of the victorious British and French empires in the Caribbean for a generation. The Dutch, who had been neutral, kept their possessions also. For the first time in 300 years there was no transfer of territory in the region at the end of a European War.

By the end of the Great War American investment everywhere in the region was already shaping national economies into complementarity with that of the United States, and in the 1920s the four northern states of Central America (**Guatemala**, **El Salvador**, **Honduras**, Nicaragua) joined Panama in linking their currencies to the dollar. Meanwhile a single large corporation, the United Fruit Company, with the "Great White Fleet" of banana boats and with International Railways of Central America as a subsidiary, was emerging under the leadership of Samuel Lee Zemurray as largest landowner and greatest financial power in each of these states, while Costa Rica, whose large number of small landowners gave it a very different sort of economy, became no less dependent on the US market for sales of its coffee.

Meanwhile in the protected states the US position was getting increasingly complicated. Calvin Coolidge (President 1923–29) chose not to oppose, and in consequence the USA was to be blamed for the rise to power of General Gerardo Machado y Morales, who dominated Cuban politics from 1925 to 1933. Under his dictatorship a new generation came to adulthood fired with nationalist fervour and a hatred both of the regime and of the United States, whose intervention in Haiti and the Dominican Republic, however well intentioned, provoked very similar reactions among the educated élite there.

The United States maintained its "Legation Guard" of marines in Managua until 1925, when they were withdrawn as an economy measure. Immediately revolt broke out, and the USA returned to supervize new elections. Since the US troops did not then leave the country, a dissident Liberal General, Augusto Sandino, took to the hills. An outstanding military leader who defied all attempts of the US occupation forces to capture him, Sandino did not come down from the hills until the Americans had gone. In the meanwhile he had built a substantial peasant-based nationalist movement. Despite his later importance as a nationalist hero to the Sandinistas of 1978–79, it does not appear, however, that he personally had very strong views on social reform. A traditional liberal, he fought to free his country from foreign domination and believed that once a democratic order was established people would be able to choose for themselves.

In Panama the construction of the mighty Canal made the US presence very conspicuous. The forces stationed in the Canal Zone for its protection were inevitably from the outset a major force in Panamanian politics, and their role an active one. US intervention took place in 1908, 1912 and 1916 to guarantee the outcome of the Presidential elections. As in Cuba the 1920s saw a massive influx of US investment, and a government newly aware of its insecurity sought in addition to revise the 1903 Treaty to give the United States airport facilities, radio communications and the right to joint control of all military operations in Panama in the event of war.

Even before the onset of the Great Depression,

concern was already growing in Washington at the extent of US involvement abroad. When Franklin D. Roosevelt was elected President (1933–45), he lost no time in proclaiming a new deal for Latin America, the "Good Neighbor" policy. By 1934 all US troops had been withdrawn. But the consequences were not at all what Roosevelt had intended. Within two years a new generation of dictators had seized power, with the support of the very National Guard forces the United States had trained and which they had hoped would uphold democracy: Jorge Ubico in Guatemala, Maximiliano Hernández Martínez in El Salvador, Tiburcio Carias Andino in Honduras, the Somozas in Nicaragua, Jorge Batista in Cuba and Rafael Leonidas Trujillo in the Dominican Republic. These were the dubious allies that were the first to spring to the aid of the United States when it was attacked by Japan in December 1941.

The war was the first practical test of the **Inter-American System**. Rather to their surprise the Mexicans found themselves fighting on the same side as the United States. Brazil went further, sending an expeditionary force to assist the allies on the ground in Italy. Even Argentina was persuaded to enter the war in its last days so that it could become a member of the new world order, the United Nations.

The single most important influence on post-war Latin America has been the emergence of the United States as a global superpower. The groundwork for the future relationship between the United States and Latin America was laid in 1945 at a Special Conference of the American States held at Chapultepec Castle, overlooking the City of Mexico: full conferences every four years, with annual meetings of Foreign Ministers when no conference was due. Resolutions reaffirmed the commitment of the American States to peace and the principle of non-intervention.

In September 1947 at Rio de Janeiro the United States broke with Washington's tradition of avoiding "entangling alliances" and signed the Inter-American Treaty of Reciprocal Assistance ('the **Rio Treaty**'). The following year, the Pan American Union was transformed into a new regional organization within the United Nations called the **Organization of American States (OAS)**. Its Charter, it turned out, although it enshrined the principle of non-intervention, was in practice to allow the United States a measure of freedom within the hemisphere that it did not and could not have had elsewhere.

In fact under Dwight D. Eisenhower (President 1953–61) the United States supported the reformist governments in **Bolivia**, Venezuela and Costa Rica, and at first looked benignly on the **Cuban Revolution**. But in 1954 it resumed the practice of intervention, though in a clandestine fashion, when the CIA created a secret force of "exiles" to overthrow the government of Jacobo Arbenz in Guatemala, which was thought to be coming under Communist influence. In 1961, under John F. Kennedy (President 1961–63), a similar ruse was used to try to overthrow **Fidel Castro**, when he sought to ally himself with the Soviet Union and called for revolution throughout the hemisphere. The failure of the landings at the Bay of Pigs was however very largely redeemed when as a result of the Cuban Missile Crisis of October 1962 the Soviet Union agreed to withdraw the missiles if the United States promised not to invade Cuba again. Other Latin American governments, fearful of the risk to their own peoples, joined with the United States in isolating Cuba from the OAS and from the inter-American system. Meanwhile Kennedy's decision to sponsor programmes of counter-insurgency training for Latin American officers both in the United States and in the Canal Zone had strengthened the capacity of their armed forces. In 1965 the United States intervened openly in a civil war in the Dominican Republic, landing marines to protect civilian lives and forestall a left-wing take-over. This time the United States had considerable difficulty in persuading the OAS to back its actions. But with the death of Che Guevara in Bolivia in October 1967 any threat to the security of the continent from Cuban-style guerrillas was clearly at an end.

When the far left shifted to a strategy of urban guerrilla warfare, the United States stepped up assistance to both police and armed forces, and in 1968 a series of military *coups* began which were to place most of South and Central America under military dictatorship. The election in Chile in 1970 of a Marxist president, **Salvador Allende**, presented a new problem and led to a new pattern of response. As it did with the elected government of **Michael Manley** in Jamaica, the government of President Nixon (1969–74) took a series of measures to "destabilize" Allende's government through a financial and trade boycott. The true extent of US complicity in the *coup* that overthrew Allende in 1973, and in the repression unleashed subsequently by the Pinochet dictatorship, is still to be fully resolved, but by 1976 it was universally believed throughout Latin America that the United States was conniving at the most appalling atrocities in the name of democracy.

Recent developments—political. Though the administration of Jimmy Carter (President

1977–81) was to go down to defeat as a result, it concluded more than 20 years of negotiation and relieved the United States of its biggest embarrassment by signing and securing the passage through the Senate of the **Panama Canal Treaties** of 1977. Under these the USA gave up at once most of its special rights in the Canal Zone, four-fifths of which reverted to Panama, and accepted joint operation of the Canal until it became Panamanian on Dec. 31, 1999. Though often obstructed by his subordinates, President Carter also reaffirmed support for human rights as a fundamental plank of US policy in Latin America, as well as in Eastern Europe, where in the end the issue of human rights was to be decisive in the sudden end of the Cold War in 1989.

Though the circumstances that led to the fall of the Somozas in Nicaragua and of Gairy in Grenada were peculiar to those areas, the outbreak of a fresh guerrilla campaign in El Salvador in 1980 was regarded by the administration of Ronald Reagan (President 1981–89) as a signal to reject the Carter emphasis on human rights and embark on a crusade to "roll back the frontiers of Communism". While in fact the whole of South America was to return to democratic government during the rest of the decade it was not with the help of the United States. Instead the Reagan Administration withheld criticism of the right-wing governments of Guatemala and El Salvador and initially looked to two of the worst of the South American military dictatorships, those of Argentina and Chile, to help El Salvador and to train a new clandestine force, the so-called "contras", to overthrow the government of Nicaragua. In the Caribbean heavy financial support was given to the Seaga government in **Jamaica**, Grenada was isolated and in the **Grenadian Intervention** (1983) military forces sent in to end left-wing rule, and subsequently steps taken to built up military strength in the Eastern Caribbean. The disclosure that arms had been sold to Iran to fund the contras (the "Iran-contra scandal") however destroyed much of their effectiveness, and in the end it was war-weariness and the destruction of the Nicaraguan economy that led to the defeat of the Sandinista government in free elections in 1990.

Outline of economic development. At Chapultepec in 1945 two divergent tendencies became apparent. The United States, mindful of what it had spent, was concerned primarily about the restoration of its pre-war trade position. In institutional terms it saw the creation of the United Nations as the major guarantor of peace for the future, and expected the other states of the hemisphere to share this view. The Latin Americans, believing that by their support they had a claim on the financial help of the world's richest country, wanted funds for economic development. No action followed and once the Cold War had begun, the United States was for the time being concerned only with securing its strategic position.

The price of the Inter-American Treaty of Reciprocal Assistance for the Latin Americans, however, was some visible move towards economic co-operation, and early in 1948 the United States sponsored the creation of an **Economic Commission for Latin America and the Caribbean (ECLAC)** to study the problems of the region and make recommendations. But at the Inter-American Conference at Bogotá the idea of a Marshall Plan for Latin America was rejected by none other than Secretary of State George Catlett Marshall himself. European recovery, he argued, in the mode of the then generally accepted "trickle down" theory of development, was of first priority and in due course would ensure the development of Latin America also. The United States had established the Point Four programme to foster private investment in the region. The consequence of this was of course to increase Latin American suspicion of US motives, while the economist Raúl Prebisch and his colleagues on ECLAC were already in the process of demonstrating that the trickle down theory did not work.

It was not until 1958 that the hostile reception accorded to him during his tour of South America convinced Vice President Nixon that a major economic initiative was needed in the region if revolution was to be averted. In the wake of the Cuban Revolution, President Kennedy persuaded Congress to establish and fund a programme for Latin American economic development which he called the Alliance for Progress (*Alianza para el Progreso*), but this far-sighted initiative soon succumbed to the Johnson administration's need for funds for his anti-poverty programme and for Vietnam. Hence all but a fraction of the US government money spent on aid to Latin America between 1952 and 1979 took the form of military aid, and this had the effect of arresting further social change by strengthening the most conservative governments of the region.

Current economic situation and prospects for development. After 1973, with concern in world financial circles about the need to recycle the increased profits of the Middle Eastern oil states, billions of petrodollars poured into Brazil, Mexico and other Latin American economies. With the onset of the debt crisis in 1983 Latin American economic development effectively came to an end for the rest of the decade, while the high exposure of the US banking system to Latin America meant that official encouragement to private enterprise to continue to invest in South America was largely ignored, though under President Reagan's **Caribbean Basin Initiative** US investment in the Caribbean area increased significantly. Consequently Latin America has lagged badly in development, particularly as compared with the so-called "tiger" economies of South-East Asia and its peoples face lean times in the decade of the 1990s, unless as called for by the Brady Plan, proposed by President Bush's Secretary of the Treasury in 1989, they can be relieved of the crushing burden of debt inherited from their predecessors.

PARC

UNITED STATES VIRGIN ISLANDS. *Population*: 106,000. *Area*: 354.8 sq km. *Birthrate*: 20.6 per 1,000.

Geographical background. The United States Virgin Islands comprise three main islands (St Croix, St Thomas and St John) and a number of small uninhabited islets lying in the north-eastern Caribbean, to the east of Puerto Rico.

Socio–political background. The islands were first settled by Europeans in the seventeenth century and by the mid-eighteenth century had become a Danish colony. The islands were sold to the USA in 1917 and placed under the jurisdiction of the Navy Department. In 1931 responsibility was transferred to the Department of the Interior. Inhabitants of the US Virgin Islands are US citizens but do not have the right to vote in presidential elections and only have a non-voting delegate to Congress. There is a 15-member elected Senate and an elected governor and deputy-governor, who serve for terms of four years.

Outline of political history. Politics in the United States Virgin Islands has been conducted by affiliates of the political parties on the US mainland. In 1974, however, Cyril E. King of the Independent Citizen's Movement, an offshoot of the Democratic Party, was elected governor. On his death he was succeeded by his deputy, Juan Luis, who served until 1986 when he was defeated by the Democratic Party candidate, Alexander Farrelly. There is little support for independence from the USA and referenda on other possible status alternatives have failed to produce a decisive majority in favour of a particular option. The most recent referendum was in 1981, but plans for a new referendum in November 1989, with a choice of six options between statehood and full independence, were postponed after Hurricane Hugo. In February 1990 Farrelly announced his intention to seek associate membership of the Organization of East Caribbean States (OECS).

Outline of economic development. The islands' economy is based on principally tourism. In 1989 tourism provided 70 per cent of non-oil revenues. St Thomas in particular has become a popular duty free centre for cruise ships and there is major tourist construction and development on St Thomas and St Croix. Governor Farrelly has expressed his wish to reduce some of the dependence on tourism, particularly in the light of experiences after the damage caused to the islands by Hurricane Hugo in September 1989. Reports in US papers stressed civil disorder and looting on St Croix in the aftermath of the hurricane. The hurricane caused damage estimated at US$1,000 million for all three islands and a temporary dislocation to the tourist industry and loss of government revenue.

Per capita income in the United States Virgin Islands is higher than in neighbouring islands, at about $8,000, and unemployment is low. The population includes a sizeable proportion of migrant workers from other Caribbean countries and retirees and others from the mainland USA. Most of the labour force works for the government, but heavy industry was attracted to St Croix in the 1960s with the creation of the Amerada Hess refinery (with a capacity of up to 750,000 barrels per day) and the Martin Marietta alumina plant. During the 1980s the heavy industry sector suffered, first from the closure of the alumina plant (although there are plans to refurbish and reopen it by 1991) and then from a drop in refining operations caused by the low price of petroleum. Tax incentives similar to those on Puerto Rico have attracted a wide range of enterprises to the Virgin Islands, including watch manufacture, electronics and pharmaceuticals. During the 1980s light industrial parks have been set up on St Croix. In November 1989 successful lobbying ensured the rejection by President Bush of a petition from the Timex Corporation for the duty-free entry of watch movements which would have threatened the watch industry on St Croix.

Current economic situation. The refund of US excise taxes on rum imported from the Virgin Islands (although the islands no longer grow sugar cane) under Section 221 of the Internal Revenue Code provide an important source of government revenue. The large budget deficit which Farrelly inherited from the previous administration was sharply reduced by the introduction of strict financial controls, but the effects of Hurricane Hugo (even allowing for substantial federal assistance) were expected to produce a deficit of about $40,000,000. In October 1990 Farrelly estimated government expenditure for the fiscal year 1990–91 at $496,000,000.

LP

URUGUAY. *Population*: 3,100,000 (1987). *Area*: 177,508 sq km. *GDP*: US$4,962 million. *Trade volume*: $1,958 million. *Top five trade partners*: exports and imports: USA, Brazil, Germany, Argentina, Canada. *Defence spending*: $134,000,000 (2.7 per cent of GNP). *Education spending (as percentage of GNP)*: 2.6. *Urban population as percentage of total (centres over 20,000)*: 66.1. *Birthrate*: 17.7 per 1,000 (1985). *Life expectancy*: 66.4 (men); 73.0 (women).

Geographical background. Situated between the River Uruguay and the Atlantic on the north bank of the Río de la Plata, the rolling and well watered plains of the southern part of the Eastern Republic of the Uruguay form an extension of the Argentine pampa. Low ranges of hills to the north share the characteristics of Brazil, from which Uruguay is separated only by the Rivers Cuareim and Yaguarón. Temperatures range between an average 10°C in winter and 23°C in summer, making Punta del Este the most popular seaside resort in South America. Montevideo, the capital, where three-fifths of the population lives, has seven fine beaches of its own.

Socio–political background. The present population of Uruguay is almost entirely of European descent, the native Charrua Indians having been wiped out early in the Spanish colonial period. Some 60 per cent of the modern population is of Spanish and some 30 per cent of Italian descent; the official language is Spanish but the spoken language has been affected by Italian influences. Church and State have been separated, and religious freedom is guaranteed by the Constitution. About two-thirds of the population regard themselves as practising Catholics, and there is a substantial Protestant minority.

Under the Constitution of 1966, as amended by the National Constituent Assembly in 1985, Uruguay is a presidential republic. Executive power is vested in a president directly elected for a five-year term. Congress, also directly elected for a five-year term, has two houses: the Senate with 30 members and the Chamber of Deputies with 99. The electoral system, the "double simultaneous vote", is unique. Candidates in each party (*lema*) may run under any of a number of rival *sub-lemas*, the winner being the candidate of the sub-lema with the most votes. The country is divided into 19 Departments each governed by the *intendente municipal* of its departmental capital with the aid of an elected *junta departmental*. The all-volunteer army now numbers 18,800 men organized in four military regions. The Navy has three frigates, a corvette, 2 offshore patrol vessels and smaller craft, and numbers 4,400 personnel including the naval air service and a naval infantry batallion. The Air Force numbers 3,000 personnel; its 110 aircraft are mainly intended for counter-insurgency purposes.

Outline of political history. The *Banda Oriental* (Eastern Bank) of the Uruguay was annexed by Brazil following the declaration of independence of the United Provinces (now Argentina), but fought for its independence of both (1828) under the leadership of José Artigas. After a chaotic history in the nineteenth century, **José Batlle y Ordóñez** established the foundations of a modern welfare state and sought to eradicate militarism by his advocacy of the collegiate system of government. Under the "First *Colegiado*" (1918–33) the president's powers were restricted by the creation of a Council of State to share power. Under the "Second *Colegiado*" (1952–67) the Council of State ruled alone, its presidency circulating annually among the six members of the majority party.

However low economic growth and falling urban living standards brought about both the restoration of the presidency and the emergence of the **Tupamaros**, a left-wing urban guerrilla group whose revelations of corruption among the élite helped discredit democracy. In 1973 President Bordaberry dissolved Congress and the military, who thus became the effective rulers of the country, established a military and police state, seeking to root out subversion by arbitrary arrest, detention and the use of torture. The refusal of the civilians to accept this state of affairs at referendum, however, brought the restoration of constitutional government in 1985, though the decision of the Army to arrest the Nationalist leader, Wilson Ferreira Aldunate, on his return from exile, meant that victory went by default to the Colorado candidate, Julio María Sanguinetti Cairolo.

Faced with widespread labour unrest, in 1986 President Sanguinetti sought and obtained a broad-based National Accord to retain democratic government and used his veto to help pass the austerity budget blocked by the opposition parties in Congress. However in the latter part of the year opposition criticism focused on Sanguinetti's commitment to the Army to amnesty all army officers for human rights violations. In September

Congress rejected the proposed amnesty bill brought forward by his **Colorado Party**; in November it also rejected a proposal by the opposition **Nationalist Party (Blancos)** to amnesty all but 38 against whom proceedings had already started, and with the armed forces on their guard and no party enjoying an overall majority the controversial "Full Stop" Law (Punto Final) led to fighting on the floor of the Chamber of Deputies before its passage on Dec. 22, thus averting a major political crisis and possible armed intervention. However widespread civilian opposition to what amounted to an amnesty for the majority of members of the armed forces accused of human rights violations during the military-backed governments of 1973–85 continued to manifest itself openly in the first months of 1987 in unrest and moves to call a referendum on the issue. A mass demonstration by workers' organizations on May 1 was followed by a rally in Montevideo on May 20 calling for an inquiry into the assassination in Argentina of Sr Zelmar Michelini and Sr Héctor Gutiérrez Ruiz, and despite wage concessions, a general strike was called for Nov. 10.

During 1988 the promised referendum on the military amnesty law was postponed, so politically the most significant development was that the former guerrilla movement, the Tupamaros, abandoned the way of armed struggle to re-enter democratic politics by way of the "third force" party, the Broad Front (*Frente Amplio*). The *Frente* itself, however, was in disarray following remarks by its leader, General Liber Seregni, accusing the ruling *Colorados* of governing unconstitutionally. On April 16, 1989 the country's thirteenth referendum confirmed by 1,008,925 votes (57 per cent) to 770,221 (43 per cent) the "Full Stop" law (Ley de Caducidad) promulgated in December 1986. The result, which confirmed amnesty to all police and military personnel guilty of violations of human rights between 1973 and 1985, was hailed by President Julio María Sanguinetti as "the end of the transition in Uruguay". On Nov. 14 the electorate gave its final verdict on his administration, however, when by a large majority the leading candidate of the *Colorado* Party, Jorge Batlle, was defeated in the presidential elections by Senator **Luis Lacalle** a 48-year old lawyer and farmer, of the opposition Nationalist (*Blanco*) Party, who unlike his Colorado opponents had consistently opposed both the military government and the amnesty law. General Liber Seregni Mosquera, president of the left-wing *Frente Amplio*, came third but the fact that his party carried Montevideo strengthened calls for a coalition between the two major parties.

Recent developments—political. On March 1, 1990 President-elect Luis Alberto Lacalle was sworn in as President, following meetings with regional Presidents and a six-day official visit to the United States, during which he also met officials of the IMF and creditor banks. By including four members of the opposition Colorado Party in his Cabinet he obtained cross-party agreement on a "social truce" and support for an economic plan to combat inflation.

Outline of economic development. Uruguay has been fortunate to enjoy excellent river transport, and with the assistance of the British-built railways established itself as a major exporter of high quality beef, as well as lamb, wool, hides and skins, at the end of the nineteenth century. It was on this prosperous agricultural base that the Batllista structure of social welfare was established.

The railways were nationalized after 1945 when the long-term decline of the beef industry had just begun. Meanwhile attempts to develop alternative industries led to a considerable level of import-substitution in textiles, rubber, glass etc., but were hampered by lack of natural resources—though there are small deposits of manganese, iron, lead, copper and gold, the country's only mineral of commercial significance is marble. There are no known oil deposits though about half the country's power supply comes from hydro-electric plants on the Río Negro. Hence the closure of the European market to imported beef in 1965 and the oil shocks of the 1970s accelerated a serious economic crisis marked by high levels of inflation and increasing indebtedness and the military belief that they could improve matters proved unfounded. Uruguay's *per capita* GNP, once among the highest in South America, declined remorselessly. Only tourism, which had emerged as a major revenue earner to become the mainstay of the post war economy, continued to grow.

Current economic situation. The Sanguinetti administration inherited from its military predecessors a disastrous economic situation. Inflation in 1985 had been 83 per cent and the country was more heavily in debt than ever. Agreement was however reached on a rescheduling package covering $1,760 million of Uruguay's $5,500 million foreign bank debt, signed on July 10, 1986. In June the President visited the United States, but his complaint that the United States' subsidies were harming Uruguayan beef was dismissed by President Reagan who said that they were a necessary weapon in a US trade war with Europe.

Closer integration with Argentina, foreshadowed by the Declaration of Colonia in 1985, was consolidated by the signature of the Act of Montevideo with President **Alfonsín** on May 26, 1987, which envisaged construction of a bridge between Colonia and Buenos Aires, co-operation on problems involving the Salto Grande hydro-electric complex and the control of hoof and mouth disease, and harmonization of truck loading limits, immigrations procedures, port operations and telephone communications. However although the country benefitted from the general improvement in world trade in 1988 and 1989, the overall situation remained difficult.

Prospects for development. On July 2, 1990 Sr Enrique Braga, the new Economy and Finance Minister, reported that the IMF had agreed a standby credit of US$150,000,000 over 18 months, and on July 17 creditor banks agreed terms for the government to buy-back US$1,000 million or some 60 per cent of its medium-term debt.

PARC

V

VARGAS, GETULIO DORNELLES. Vargas made a deeper, more persistent impression on the pattern of **Brazil's** development than any other politician in the history of the country. Almost four decades after his death, people still take sides for or against the man, his policies and an identifiable political legacy. The *coup* of 1964 and the régime which came to power through it were both a direct reaction to Vargas and *trabalhismo*.

In the presidential elections of 1989, different candidates still claimed his mantle, and in those for governor, in October and November 1990, the strong support for **Leonel Brizola** and the **Democratic Labour Party** (*Partido Democrático Trabalhista*—PDT) was a vote for the broad Vargista tradition.

Despite his importance and the length of his time in power, from 1930 to 1945, and from 1950 till his death in 1954, Vargas remains an enigmatic, much disputed, figure, less clear-cut and definable than most of his contemporaries. He has not yet found an adequate biographer and the generalized interpretations of him are too often coloured by his political opponents, both before and after his death.

The enigmatic image mainly reflects the man, who remained an enigma, unscrutable and unpredictable, even to some of his close associates, which partly explains his political success and endurance. The passion and emotion occasionally broke through, as was seen in the manner of his death, but he was mainly characterized by calm and measured calculation in his political dealings, which allowed him to survive as one of the masters of conciliatory politics, while also knowing when confrontation was required. Vargas is said to have been guided by the principle of never making an enemy who later could not be made a friend: only one example of his conciliatory style was when, within months of the São Paulo revolt against him in 1932, he opened a major avenue in São Paulo, named to commemorate the start of the revolt on July 9.

One of the least satisfactory of the common characterizations of Vargas is that which presents him as an irresponsible or, even, unprincipled "populist", an image which is drawn almost entirely from his last four years in office, but which does not best explain his actions even then and owes too much to his critics.

Vargas as the would-be tribune of the people, aiming to establish a "trade union state", allegedly on the model of Perón, was how his enemies particularly wished him to be seen by 1945, a charge which, again, was to be levelled at Goulart both before and after he took office in 1961. By 1945, this picture was beginning to replace the earlier one imposed on Vargas, of being an authoritarian, *caudilho* in the *gaúcho* tradition, the stock accusation of his "liberal" critics, especially in São Paulo.

There are, in fact, various Brazilian politicians on whom the label of "populist" or would-be tribune, could more easily be fixed, Adhemar de Barros, for example, or Lacerda or **Quadros**. It is certainly true that Vargas had a marked authoritarian streak and came from a tradition in Rio Grande do Sul of strong central government. The *Estado Novo*, it is also true, brought serious abuses in terms of repression, censorship and authoritarianism, but these should be set in the perspective both of Vargas' career as a whole and of later experience of worse political repression, condoned, if not directed, by some of his critics.

Looking at Vargas' career as a whole, there is no doubt about the importance of his formation in, and inheritance from, Rio Grande do Sul. Vargas always looked forward, kept on learning from experience and was skilled at adapting to changing circumstances and demands. At the same time, his drive to centralize Brazil throughout the 1930s, to strengthen and develop the powers and machinery of the federal state clearly reflected, though they were not simply determined by, his *gaúcho* heritage.

Vargas was born, not as he generally claimed, in 1883, but in 1882 in São Borja, on the southern border with Argentina, so that he already was a seasoned, experienced politician, forged in one of the fiercest traditions in Brazil, when he came to power in 1930. Both his grandfathers had fought in the struggles of the nineteenth century and his father had a distinguished record in the Paraguayan War, from which he emerged a lieutenant-colonel. In the bloody civil war in Rio Grande do Sul from 1893 to 1895, between "republicans" (*chimangos*) and the "federalists" (*maragatos*), the two sides of Vargas' family, the Vargas and Dornelles, supported different camps. With the victory of the Republicans, the Rio Grande Republican Party (*Partido Republicano Rio-Grandense*—PRR), became dominant in the state, first under Júlio de Castilhos, then under Borges de Medeiros. Vargas' father, Manuel, was a local PRR political chief. He was promoted to colonel by President Floriano Peixoto and to brigadier-general by President Prudente de Morais.

Vargas initially aimed at a military career, but then read law and effectively began his involvement with the PRR in 1907, together with a group of students who were to remain important throughout his subsequent career. Some of them joined him in government in 1930, while others, such as Eurico Gaspar Dutra and Góes Monteiro, later to become leaders of the armed forces, both supported and opposed Vargas in the years ahead.

In 1909, Vargas was elected to the state assembly, which, under the Constitution of the state of Rio Grande do Sul, had very limited powers in relation to the executive. It only met for three months of year to vote a budget and examine state government accounts. After a prolonged disagreement with Borges de Medeiros, he returned to the Assembly, advocating party co-operation during World War I and expressing scepticism about the effectiveness of parliaments for solving the most serious problems affecting the lives of nations.

In 1922, Vargas, with the PRR, joined a movement of opposition, articulated by Rio Grande do Sul, Bahia, Pernambuco and the state of Rio de Janeiro, against the official presidential candidate of São Paulo and Minas Gerais, Artur Bernardes. Bernardes was elected and was hostile to the opposition states, a lesson not lost on Vargas in 1929 and 1930. Vargas was elected as federal deputy in 1923, but immediately was caught up in the fierce civil war in Rio Grande do Sul in that year, in which, among others, Brizola's father was killed.

In 1924, he was again elected as federal deputy and supported President Bernardes in his suppression of the *tenente* revolt in São Paulo and his campaign against the Prestes Column. In 1925, he was part of a committee, proposed by Bernardes, to study reforms to be introduced in the Constitution of 1891, largely with a view to strengthening the power of the central government in relation to the states. In May 1926, he became a member of the Finance Committee of the Chamber, till the end of his mandate in November.

President Washington Luís, on taking office in November 1926, appointed Vargas as his Minister of Finance, to link Rio Grande do Sul to the powerful *café com leite* political alliance of São Paulo and Minas Gerais. Vargas told Borges de Medeiros that he was not sufficiently qualified, but was persuaded to take the job. As Minister of Finance, for little over a year, he helped to introduce Washington Luís' successful programme of financial stabilization, including the monetary reform approved by Congress in December 1926. This included a return to the gold standard and a flexible exchange policy, which both favoured exports and protected national industry.

By the treaty of Pedras Altas, which ended the 1923 civil war, Borges de Medeiros could not continue for another term as president of Rio Grande do Sul, but as head of the PRR he could nominate his candidate. In August 1927, he chose Vargas, who was also supported by the main opposition party, as the ideal candidate of conciliation. Elected as president of Rio Grande do Sul in November 1927, Vargas, coming, himself, from both sides of the political divide, committed himself to bringing peace to his state.

Very few accounts of Vargas pay sufficient, if any, attention to his career before 1930, preferring to jump at once into his years of national government. With typical caution, Vargas was a most reluctant revolutionary in 1929 and 1930. His experience in Rio Grande do Sul underlined the horrors of civil war and his time as Minister of Finance for Washington Luís, a very proper *paulista* businessman, was scarcely the springboard for revolution. The combination of the international financial crash and the political crisis, in which São Paulo tried to keep control of the economy, brought the confrontation which Vargas had hoped to avoid and, in due course, the end of the "Old Republic" in 1930.

Rather than see him as an ambitious, authoritarian *caudilho* or irresponsible "populist", it is better to recognize in Vargas a shrewd, mature politician, drawing on his experience in Rio Grande do Sul, to provide the greater centralization and stronger state control of the economy which he, and others, believed the country required. He needed all his skill to carry the country through the shock-waves of the Great Depression, which ended hopes for a rapid diversification of the coffee economy. He was able to reconcile civilian and military demands within the creation of a stronger state and, through the Estado Novo, respond to the pressures of industrialists and others, especially in São Paulo, who were anxious to develop Brazil's industrial economy and financial base.

At the same time, right from the first days of the Revolution of 1930, through Lindolfo Collor and his successors, he was able to draw on Rio Grande do Sul's other tradition of *trabalhismo*, modifying it to meet the requirements of an increasingly urban, industrial society. This was not just a political ploy, responding to pressures, as the *Estado Novo* began to give way to demands for change. Nor was his attempt to restructure the party system, in creating the **Brazilian Labour Party** (*Partido Trabalhista Brasileiro* — PTB) and the **Social Democratic Party** (*Partido Democrático Social*—PSD).

Vargas' second term in government, from 1950 to 1954, was consistent with his declared intentions before he was removed from office in 1945. It brought to a head all the issues which were to face Brazil's political economy over the next four decades. His government offered, overall, a positive and coherent response to them, in terms of a democratic political system and an economy committed to reconstruction and much needed measures of distribution and social reform. His enemies, both at home and abroad, bitterly attacked both Vargas and his *trabalhista* programme, which also sought to reconcile participation in the international economy with due protection for Brazil's proper national interests.

No-one, nearly four decades after his tragic death, has yet offered more effective replies to the issues which Vargas identified. His political programme, not "populist", but, broadly one of social democracy, may still offer the best solution for Brazil's development in the 1990s.

PF

VATICAN. The Vatican, under the Papacy of John Paul II, has sought to exercise a more comprehensive control and is committed to a greater centralization and monopoly of theological authority over the national churches than at any time since the Second Vatican Council (October 1962–December 1965). Not only is the Latin American Church under-represented in the College of Cardinals (of the 158 Cardinals only 23 come from Latin America although Latin Americans constitute close to 45 per cent of all Roman Catholics) but also in the major bureaucratic and theological positions. Efforts have been made to "de-politicize" the Church and remove the temptations of secular pursuits associated with the Latin American priesthood since Vatican II. Thus in response to the holding of political office by four priests in the Nicaraguan government of the Sandinista National Liberation Front (*Frente Sandinista de Liberación Nacional*—FSLN) the Pope invoked new Canon Laws promulgated on June 25, 1983 of which Canon Law 285 forbids priests from participating in trade unions, political parties or exercising civil power.

In order to counter the further rise and spread of liberation theology the Brazilian theologian Leonardo Boff was summoned in September 1984 to the Sacred Congregation of the Doctrine of the Faith, headed by Cardinal Joseph Ratzinger. Boff's work on liberation theology, *Church: Charisma and Power*, was condemned as "endangering the sound doctrine of the faith" and he was ordered to remain silent for a year. Papal documents such as "A certain instruction on certain aspects of the theology of liberation" (Sept. 3, 1984) and "Instruction on Christian freedom and liberation" (April 5, 1986) have further criticized such developments in the Latin American Church.

JCJS

VELASCO IBARRA, JOSE MARIA. The dominant figure of **Ecuador** in the middle third of the twentieth century was Dr José María Velasco Ibarra. Historically, he was a transitional figure, a conservative professor of law from a devout family of the sierra, who became a populist demagogue appealing to the semi-literate masses, especially those recently arrived in the country's cities. He was the only major Ecuadorean politician to be able to draw votes almost equally from the sierra and the coast, although in his later campaigns the coastal share in his vote became progressively larger.

President five times (1933–35, 1944–47, 1952–56, 1960–61, and 1968–71), he completed only one term, in the 1950s, during years made prosperous by Ecuador's banana boom. His appeal was based partly on his skills as an orator, appealing to the deepest emotional wellsprings of his auditors, and partly because as President he delivered concrete short-term benefits in classic pork-barrel style. Innocent of any knowledge of economics, or perhaps even of accounting, Velasco would spend everything in the treasury and more on public works projects; finally realizing no money was left, he would arbitrarily impose austerity measures and violently repress the ensuing protests, until the coalition against him grew to include a preponderance of the political forces, which would induce the military to stage a *coup* to remove him. Yet such was the magic of his charisma, that hardly had he been overthrown to general popular acclaim, than his support again began to grow. Personally honest and austere, spare in person, espousing the noblest ideals while his blindness to grubby realities led to general disaster, he seemed an incarnation of Don Quixote.

MCN

VENEZUELA. *Population*: 18,300,000 (1987). *Area*: 912,050 sq km. *GDP*: US$48,000 million (1987). *Trade volume*: $18,652 million (1986). *Top five trade partners*: exports: USA, Germany, Cuba, Canada, Japan; imports: USA, Germany, Japan, Italy, France. *Defence spending*: $682,000,000 (1.4 per cent of GNP) (1986). *Education spending (as percentage of GNP)*: 6.6.

Urban population as percentage of total (centres over 20,000): 67.0 (1985). *Birthrate*: 29.0 per 1,000 (1985). *Life expectancy*: 67.8—66.7 (men); 72.8 (women) (1988).

Geographical background. Venezuela occupies the centre of the north coast of South America, extending along a coastline of some 3,500 km. The national territory also covers 72 offshore islands in the Caribbean of which the largest, Isla Margarita, forms, with its adjacent islands, the State of Nueva Esparta; the rest being federal dependencies with their administrative capital on the island of Los Roques.

There are four main geographic divisions, but climatically the main division is by height. The main area of settlement, where 90 per cent of the population lives, is on the sub-tropical north-western and north-eastern plateaux, both low extensions of the Andes mountain chain, where temperatures range from 10°C to 25°C. In the higher mountains in the temperate zone, between 2,000 and 3,000 m, vegetation is sparse and scrubby and in the cold zone, or *páramo*, above 3,000 m, few plants can survive. The highest peak in the country, Pico Bolívar (5,000 m), and several others in the Sierra Nevada de Mérida, are perpetually covered with snow.

In the north-west on the Colombian frontier lies the tropical lowland basin of Lake Maracaibo, centre of the oil industry, where annual temperatures range between 24°C to 35°C. To the south-east lie the vast *Llanos del Orinoco*, or upland plains of the river basin of the 1,600 mile long Orinoco, which drains four-fifths of the country, and is linked by a natural channel to the Río Negro and so to the Amazon. The *Llanos* are rich and lush during the rainy season (May to October) but dry for the rest of the year. The *llaneros*, or cowboys of this region, were the major source of **Bolívar's** troops. South-east of the Orinoco lies the almost unpopulated Guyana Highlands. Venezuela claims the Essequibo region of **Guyana**, which forms a natural extension of this region, as part of its national territory.

Socio–political background. Venezuela, with a mean population density of only 13.5 per sq km., is one of the most sparsely populated countries in the Americas, but the concentration of its population in the northern uplands means that it is also highly urbanized. The bulk of the population (65 per cent) are of mestizo (mixed Spanish and Amerindian) blood, 21 per cent European, 7 per cent African and 7 per cent Amerindian. The national language, Spanish, is almost universally spoken. Some 75 per cent of the population are Roman Catholic, but the Constitution of 1961 establishes the right to free practice of other faiths.

Constitutionally Venezuela is a Presidential Republic. The president is directly elected by the people for a five-year term, and is eligible for re-election only after an interval of 10 years. He is chief executive and commander-in-chief of the armed forces, and appoints and presides over the Council of Ministers. There is no vice-president. The legislature is bicameral and is directly elected at the same time as the president. The Senate consists of 49 elected members, two directly elected from each state and two from the Federal District; additional senators represent minorities and ex-presidents of the republic sit ex-officio. The Chamber of Deputies is apportioned by population, subject to the provision that each state must have at least two representatives.

There are 20 states, a Federal District, where the capital Caracas, is situated, two federal territories and 72 federal dependencies. State government is in the hands of a governor, appointed by the President, and an elected legislature. The powers of the states are limited by the Federal constitution.

Since 1964 the armed forces have been generally believed to have renounced political activity and accepted the role of a modern professional force in support of elected civilian government. In 1989 their numbers totalled 70,500 including National Guard forces. Some 18,000 of these were conscripts, serving for two years (two-and-a-half years in the Navy) on a selective basis. The Army was 34,000 strong and was organized in a Headquarters command (including the Presidential Guard Regiment), a cavalry division and three regional infantry divisions. The Navy, 10,000 strong including naval air service, marines and coastguard, operated 6 missile-carrying frigates and three conventional submarines, as well as coastal patrol craft. The Air Force, 5,000 strong, had one air group of Canberra bombers, and three air groups of interceptors (F-5A, F 5-D, Fl6A/B, and Mirage III and V). The National Guard (*Fuerzas Armadas de Cooperación*) engage in internal security and customs duties, using light patrol craft and light aircraft.

Outline of political history. Before what is now Venezuela was first discovered by Christopher Columbus on Aug. 1, 1498 it was extensively populated by Carib and Arawak Indians. Its modern name, which means "little Venice", was given to it by Alonso de Ojeda when he sighted Carib huts built on stilts in the water of the Gulf of Venezuela in the following year.

European settlement began under a grant in 1528 from Charles V to the German banking firm of the Welsers, whose brutality to the native population led to the rescinding of their grant in 1546. The native Indians fought off Spanish colonization until 1580, when a smallpox epidemic put an end to their resistance. Thereafter the area was ruled as part of the Spanish Empire until the victory of the colonists led by **Simón Bolívar** at the Battle of Carabobo on June 24, 1823 brought the end of the war, initiated by Francisco de Miranda's declaration of independence on July 5, 1811.

Venezuela's history in the nineteenth century was extremely turbulent, and stability was established only when the then dictator, Cipriano Castro, sailed for Europe in 1908 to seek medical treatment, leaving the country in the hands of an uneducated soldier from the State of Táchira, Juan Vicente Gómez. Gómez immediately seized power and ruled the country as an autocrat until his death in 1935. Under him British, Dutch and US companies turned the country into a major oil-producing nation, and the forces emerged which were to transform the country into a model liberal democracy after World War II.

The foundation of **Acción Democrática (AD)** in 1945 by **Rómulo Betancourt** was followed by the country's first true elections in 1947. However the successful AD presidential candidate, the eminent novelist Rómulo Gallegos, was deposed after only eight months in a *coup* led by Marcos Pérez Jiménez, whose new dictatorship, sustained by a modern secret police apparatus, fell to a popular uprising in 1958. Following the success of this rising, by the Pact of Punto Fijo the leaders of the three main political parties agreed to work together to defend democracy, respect the electoral process and collaborate in government. Thereupon Betancourt himself was chosen as President (1959–64) in free elections supervised by the armed forces. Since then political power has peacefully passed between the AD and the rival Christian Socialists, organized as the **Committee for Independent Political Electoral Organization** (*Comité de Organizacion Política Electoral Independiente*)—COPEI). A guerrilla movement which organized in Venezuela in the early 1960s in imitation of the Cubans failed to make headway and subsequently became the first such movement in the region to be converted into a regular left-wing political party as the Movement to Socialism (*Movimiento al Socialismo*—MAS).

That it did not is largely owing to the appeal of a later AD president, **Carlos Andrés Pérez** (1964–69), a dynamic populistic leader with widespread appeal to the urban masses—in 1950 only 31.5 per cent of Venezuelans lived in cities of more than 20,000 inhabitants, by 1971 the proportion was 60.4 per cent. Enjoying the political advantages of a relatively united party and an overall majority in Congress, CAP (as he was known to the public) carried through not only the nationalization of the iron and steel industry but anticipated the end of the concessions by carrying through the long-awaited nationalization of the oil industry in 1976. The 13 existing companies were each given new names and placed under the control of the overall state organization now known as Petróleos Venezolanos (PDVSA).

Though petroleum wealth has funded three decades of democracy in Venezuela, it has not been without its problems. The guerrillas of the 1960s were not overcome without the vigorous use of force, and outbreaks of unrest since have at times been harshly dealt with. In addition, both the wealth of oil and, more recently, that generated by Venezuela's position on the trail of cocaine from the Andes to the markets of North America has had a corrupting influence, and accusations of corruption have been directed at the highest political leaders.

Such accusations is fact have been standard practice at Venezuelan elections and CAP's party succumbed at the end of his first term to the Venezuelan electorate's tendency to reject the incumbent government. His COPEI successor, Dr Luis Herrera Campins, was left to deal with the debt crisis, when the high spending and free wheeling days of the oil boom came to an abrupt end in the early 1980s. It was he who took the potentially fateful decision not to renew the agreement with Guyana under which Venezuela's claims to most of its territory had been suspended since 1966. Dr Jaime Lusinchi and the AD, who were successful in defeating ex-President Caldera and the COPEI in 1983, not only had the initial task of debt rescheduling but faced increasing problems as oil prices sagged in the mid-80s. By mid-1988 Venezuela was the only Latin American country apart from Colombia paying both interest and capital on its national debt, but the government, despite a series of austerity programmes, faced a new balance-of-payments deficit and was unable to get new credit.

Recent developments — political. In October 1987 President Lusinchi's efforts to prevent the re-nomination of 66-year old ex-President Carlos Andrés Pérez as candidate of the ruling AD in 1988, failed when labour leaders rejected his preferred but colourless nominee, the former Minister of the Interior, Octavio Lepage. With the President discredited by intra-party bickering, accusations of corruption against high level appointees and the decision of the central committee of the party to drop the president's secretary and alleged mistress, Blanca Ibáñez, from its list of candidates, "CAP" ran well ahead of his party in the Presidential elections of Dec. 4 and broke two decades of regular alternation between the two main parties. With 3,879,024 votes (52. 91 per cent) to 2,963,015 (40.42 per cent) for his 48-year old COPEI rival, Eduardo Fernández, who was handicapped by divisions within his own party, he secured a decisive victory and became the first Venezuelan President to be re-elected. Teodoro Petkoff Maleo, former guerrilla and leader of the *Movimiento al Socialismo* ran third with 200,479 votes (2.73 per cent) and of the 20 other candidates none exceeded one per cent and all together totalled only 288,869 votes (3.94 per cent of the poll).

At the same time the AD lost its absolute majority of the Chamber of Deputies, where MAS, running in alliance with the Movement of the Revolutionary Left (*Movimiento de la Izquierda Revolucionaria*—MIR), fared much better. The outcome was:

Party	*Chamber*	*Senate*
AD	97	23
COPEI	67	22
MAS	18	3
New Democratic Generation	6	1
La Causa R	3	–
Others	10	–
Ex-officio	–	3
Total	201	52

The elections were overshadowed to some extent by two incidents which cast doubt on the long-standing stability of Venezuela's armed forces. Tanks surrounded the presidential palace, Miraflores, while President Lusinchi was attending the meeting of the Group of Eight in Uruguay, and a commander and a captain were arrested when they returned to barracks. A week later, troops, who had in recent years established a number of bases in the border area, fired on and killed 16 fishermen on the Colombian border who were mistaken for guerrillas. What was more difficult to explain was why they then published photographs of the bodies with guns and explosives next to them.

Sr Pérez, who gained over 52 per cent of the vote as against 33 per cent for his rival, the remainder being divided between some 21 minor party candidates, in his victory statement promised to build on the work of Sr Lusinchi, seek a "social pact" and "re-programme" payments on the country's foreign debt, then standing at $30,200 million. Within days he had left for the Middle East for a "study tour" and conversations with OPEC heads of state, a sign that he would lend his considerable weight as a democratic socialist of international standing to the task of creating a common Latin American front on the debt issue. On Jan. 1, 1989 the outgoing government declared a debt moratorium.

Corruption in government continues to be a problem and the former Minister of the Interior and Development, José Angel Cliberto, was stripped of parliamentary immunity on Jan. 27, 1990, but when the Supreme Court dismissed charges against several former ministers, riots again broke out in Caracas and other cities.

Outline of economic development. Before 1914, when oil was first produced in commercial quantities, Venezuela's economy, like that of Colombia its neighbour, depended on the export of coffee and, to a lesser extent, cocoa; the main export crops introduced towards the end of the nineteenth century. Until the 1920s the country was predominantly agricultural, and economic activity was primarily directed towards the growth of subsistence crops and cattle and goat rearing. Behind the export economy the traditional ranching culture of the plains still survived. But since 1930 when Venezuela became the world's first major oil exporting nation, oil has dominated all else.

Reinvestment of the proceeds of the oil industry gave Venezuela rapid economic growth in the 1950s and 1960s, and high rates of growth and a general increase in the standard of living was again achieved between 1974 and 1978. The recession of 1979–81, however, hit the country hard. The resulting slump in world demand for petroleum brought a steep decline in revenues and the urgent need to cut back spending in the public sector. GDP contracted by 1.7 per cent in 1980 and 0.3 per cent in 1981. After a slight improvement in 1982, the sudden collapse of oil prices and the ebbing of confidence which marked the onset of the debt crisis was followed by further sharp contraction, by 5.6 per cent in 1983 and 1.7 per cent in 1984. With more than a third of the working population employed in that sector and dependent on state revenues, unemployment rose sharply, from some 7 per cent of the employed population in 1982 to over 20 per cent in 1984. For the rest of the 1980s the ability of the economy to expand was severely restrained by the heavy burden of debt service.

Some 14 per cent of the workforce work in agriculture, 23 per cent in manufacturing industry, and more than a third in the public sector.

However the number employed in the petroleum industry is very small indeed, not more than 50,000.

Transport. Historically the main means of bulk transport within the national territory has been by water. The Orinoco and its tributaries provide a natural network of more than 16,000 km of waterways. Coastal navigation is in the main by ships of the state-owned Venezuelan Navigation Company, and substantial investment has taken place to make the port of La Guaira, which serves Caracas and the surrounding region, one of the most modern in the Caribbean. Maracaibo is the main port for the oil industry, and Puerto Ordaz, on the navigable section of the River Orinoco, for the export of iron ore.

Because of its mountainous terrain, Venezuela was unable to benefit much from the railway era, and today only some 490 km of railway operate, mainly in the northern states of Lara, Miranda, Carabobo, Aragua, and Yaracuy. The only passenger service is the 268 km of track between Barquetismo and Puerto Cabello. Mineral railways are significant for the transporation of iron ore.

In 1981 there was a total of 62,449 km of roads, but much of the country is still served only by dirt tracks, and only 22,975 km have been asphalted, though Caracas is linked by all-weather roads not only to all major cities in Venezuela but also with the borders of Colombia and Brazil.

There is an extensive internal network of passenger air services centred on Caracas's Maiquetía Airport, and Simón Bolívar International Airport handles a full range of international services to the rest of the Americas and to Europe.

Petroleum. On Aug. 29, 1975 President Carlos Andrés Pérez signed the Oil Industry Nationalization Act, rescinding all concessions to private companies with effect from Dec. 31 of that year. At that time Venezuela was the world's third largest producer and the only substantial oil exporter outside the Middle East and three foreign corporations produced 90 per cent of its output: Creole Petroleum, a subsidiary of Exxon; Shell of Venezuela, a subsidiary of Royal Dutch-Shell, and Mene Grande Oil, a subsidiary of Gulf Petroleum. There were also 18 other smaller companies, all but two subsidiaries of foreign corporations, and altogether some 23,000 people then worked in the industry.

Under the 1975 Act the foreign concessionaries were replaced by a single state holding company, Petroleum of Venezuela (Petrovén or PDVSA), established in September 1975 with an initial capitalization of $465,000,000 and 16 state-owned operating companies. Substantial compensation, in excess of $5,000 million, was paid, some three-quarters of which was in tax-free, 6 per cent five-year bonds, redeemable only in Venezuela oil, and interim arrangements made for the sale of oil at standard prices to the former operating companies for a period of two years.

Most of Venezuela's oil production comes from the western part of the country and about half from the floor and eastern shore of Lake Maracaibo. Substantial reserves of heavy-grade crude in the Orinoco tar belt in the east of the country, estimated at 70,000 million barrels, have long been known but are unlikely to be extensively exploited unless a substantial rise in world prices occurs.

Production began in 1914 and climbed steeply until it reached a peak in 1970, which by coincidence was the last in which Venezuela was the world's largest oil exporter. Initial exploration was carried out by a variety of overseas companies, but in the 1920s, in response to pressure from the US government of the day, American companies came to monopolize 95 per cent of Venezuelan production and by 1941 Venezuela was not only the world's largest exporter of petroleum but had become also the second largest producer after the United States. From the beginning government policy was "to sow the oil" (*sembrar el petróleo*), in other words, to invest the proceeds of the industry for the future development of the country. When in 1942 heavy Allied tanker losses forced cutbacks in production, the government successfully renegotiated terms with the main concession-holders making Venezuela became the first country to obtain a division of profits on a 50–50 basis, so setting the benchmark for post-War agreements. Further revisions of terms in favour of Venezuela were facilitated by the fact that after 1948 the USA became a net oil importer and Venezuela its nearest and best source of supply, and financed in effect by the US government, which allowed US companies substantial tax concessions on their overseas operations. This however did not stop the Eisenhower administration imposing an oil quota on Venezuela in 1959, at a time when prices were already being driven down on the world market. Though in the 1950s and 1960s Venezuela was the richest Latin American country in terms of *per capita* GDP, the effects of excessive dependence on the export of a single commodity were already taking their toll.

In response Venezuela, under the AD government of President Betancourt, sought support in united action and became a founder member of the Organization of Petroleum Exporting

Countries (OPEC) in 1960. When OPEC was successful in obtaining a substantial increase in prices in 1973, Venezuela in line with its fellow members immediately implemented a policy of conservation and production gradually cut back to prolong the life of the existing fields as far as possible. Prior to the "oil shock" there had been concern that new emission-control legislation in the USA would work against Venezuelan oil with its relatively high sulphur content, but the decision of the Nixon administration to scrap the legislation worked in its favour also and reaction to the nationalization measure was muted. Since nationalization there has been a dramatic increase in the country's proven oil reserves, which are now estimated at some 58,000 million barrels. However although production has yet to return to 1970 levels at the present rate even these very substantial resources would be exhausted in only 40 years. Meanwhile Venezuela has been accepting reduced petroleum production quotas under agreement with its fellow OPEC members. At the same time not only have there been vigorous efforts to find new fields, but increasing attention has been given to the development of techniques of secondary recovery from existing wells.

Among OPEC countries, Venezuela has by far the largest refining capacity. It has 12 refineries with a combined capacity of some 1,300,000 barrels per day (bpd) and exports more than 800,000 bpd of refined products, mainly in the form of fuel oil, to the United States. Further expansion of refinery capacity has been hampered by the government decision to seize some $6,000 million of foreign exchange from PDVSA in 1982, and the decision of Exxon to close its refinery on the Dutch island of Aruba in 1985 had an adverse effect on Venezuela's exports.

Venezuela is also rich in natural gas, and the use of gas has formed an increasingly important part of development strategy. Proven reserves are estimated at 1,500,000 million cubic metres, enough to last for nearly a century at current rates. Exploitation and development have since 1971 been the responsibility of *Corporación Venezolano de Petróleo*, a subsidiary of PDVSA, the policy of which has been to pipe gas into the main industrial centres in order to liberate petroleum for export.

Electrical energy. Venezuela is fortunate in possessing vast potential for the development of hydroelectric power. Two-thirds of the country's consumers are supplied from the Guri Dam on the River Caroní, built by the state development corporation Venezuelan Corporation of Guayana (*Corporación Venezolana de Guayana*—CVG) with financial help from the International Bank for Reconstruction and Development (IBRD). Rural electrification and the construction of smaller plants across the country was carried out by another state agency, Electric Administration and Development (CADAFE) founded in 1959. But until their nationalization at the end of 1975 most of the generating companies were in private hands.

Other minerals. Venezuela is potentially very rich indeed in minerals, but as yet only a small proportion of those that are known to exist have been exploited. Economically most significant are iron ore, bauxite, coal, gold, silver and diamonds.

The country has vast deposits of high grade iron ore, with the main centres at Cerro Bolívar (some 90 km north of Ciudad Bolívar, formerly Angostura), Altamira and El Pao. Reserves were estimated at 2.5 billion tons in 1974. Two foreign-owned corporations, Iron Mines of Venezuela, a subsidiary of Bethlehem Steel, and the Orinoco Mining Company, a subsidiary of US Steel, between them turned the country into the world's tenth largest producer with an output of 26,400,000 tonnes in 1974, almost all of which was exported. In line with its policy of economic nationalism, the first government of President Carlos Andrés Pérez nationalized the iron industry with effect from Jan. 1, 1975, and vested it in the Orinoco Ferrominerals Company (*Ferrominero Orinoco*). Since then the effects of nationalization, the prevailing depressed market for steel and US moves to restrict entry into its home market have led to a steep decline in exports and cutbacks by the state steel corporation, *Siderúrgica del Orinoco* (Sidor).

Venezuela is now known to possess very large deposits of coal, mostly in the State of Táchira, but historically these have contributed little to economic growth and production in 1984 was only 45,000 tonnes.

With generous hydroelectric power available, Venezuela was well placed to develop the production of aluminium, which is now the country's second largest export, though accounting for only some 10 per cent of the total. Production is in the hands of two state-owned corporations, Alcasa and Venalum, and the Interalumina refinery at Puerto Ordaz, which commenced operations in 1983, is the largest in Latin America. At the same time the country has been found to have substantial bauxite deposits at Los Pijiguaos, where proven reserves exceed 500,000,000 tonnes. Production began in 1986 with the aim of creating a fully integrated aluminium industry.

There is significant production of both gold and diamonds, but the bulk of it is smuggled out of the country and so contributes much less than it should to the nation's prosperity.

Manufacturing. The major manufacturing industries, steel and aluminium, are in state hands. The motor vehicle industry in the 1980s suffered sharp cutbacks as a result of excessive competition between the many foreign-owned companies operating in the country and declining demand in the internal market, and underwent extensive rationalization. Other manufacturing plants are relatively small and exist exclusively to serve the internal market.

Agriculture. Agriculture is the most neglected sector of the Venezuelan economy, and suffers from a combination of underinvestment, poor management and excessive orientation towards an export economy. At the beginning of the 1980s this sparsely populated country imported some 40 per cent of its food, and though it produced such essentials as maize, wheat, sugar, and vegetable oils, it imported much of its needs from abroad. In 1984 the Lusinchi government started a 10-year development programme to try to reach self-sufficiency in these areas. Under it, tariff barriers to imports were raised and new provision made for rural credit. In addition a substantial programme of irrigation has been undertaken. But agriculture benefitted most from the devaluation of the *bolívar* in 1983 and the introduction of a multi-tier exchange rate which made the traditional cash crops, coffee and cocoa, much more competitive on the world market and encouraged a substantial increase in livestock exports.

Only some 20 per cent of the country's land area is at the moment employed for agricultural purposes. Of that, three-quarters is under pasture, and in the 1980s the main growth area in agriculture has been in stock-raising and dairy production. Yet the country is also a substantial importer of animal feed and even of livestock, while the smuggling of cattle across the frontier into Colombia, where they fetch higher prices, results in a significant loss to the economy.

A limited degree of land reform took place in the 1970s, as a result of which approximately 150,000 familes were resettled on large estates or on unused land.

Tourism. Venezuela's tourist potential is spectacular but is largely undeveloped. As well as the normal attractions of a Caribbean country, sun, sea and sand, it has formidable mountain ranges, unspoilt jungle and the world's highest waterfall, Angel Falls (979m.) However since Venezuelans normally go abroad for their own holidays, being used to a strong currency, the country has a substantial deficit on its tourist account.

The debt question. Since the onset of the debt crisis in 1983 the heavy indebtedness built up in the 1970s in the expectation of continuing high oil revenues has been a major problem confronting successive Venezuelan governments. A combination of high US interest rates, excessive short-term borrowing, a negative balance of payments and a massive flight of capital combined to frustrate the standard remedy of austerity and cuts in public sector expenditure. The disbursed foreign debt had risen from $16,300 million in 1978 to $35,100 million in 1982, and at first efforts to reschedule the short-term debt and so contain its further growth were quite successful, the debt standing at $35,900 million at the end of 1986.

However by that time substantial new fields in the North Sea and in Alaska had come on stream, and the rescheduling agreement signed on Feb. 26, 1986, of some $21,200 million of public sector foreign debt, was from the first threatened by the fall in oil prices, which was estimated to cost Venezuela more than $5,000 million in lost oil revenues during the year. On April 23, the government invoked the "contingency clause" in its agreement with foreign bank creditors. A new 21-point emergency programme announced by President Jaime Lusinchi on July 17 included import controls, a 93 per cent devaluation of the *bolívar*, and rationalization of taxation. But the conversion of some $7,000 million of private sector debt into government bonds rallied bank lenders, who had already granted a 2-year moratorium on the debt principal. In October the government proposed a new plan to postpone debt payments and link the rate of repayment to oil prices. But given the country's substantial reserves, debtors were hesitant and in November the government made the rescheduled downpayment of $750,000,000 on time.

Despite this, the measures failed both to control rising inflation or to reassure the private sector. For the first time for many years, in addition, the threat of social unrest appeared after the murder of an engineering student in Mérida sparked off two days of rioting which caused an estimated $2,000,000 worth of damage, and which subsequently spread to students in the capital. President Lusinchi blamed subversives, but in the aftermath of the Iran-contra scandal in the United States cancelled as potentially provocative the Andean Pact visit of President Reagan scheduled for May. The offer on May Day 1987 of worker banuses and a price freeze was opposed by both FEDECAMARAS (the employers' organization) and the Venezuelan Workers Confederation (CTV), which wanted the bonus treated as salary, and fears grew of a new round of inflation.

In 1988, an election year, the state of the economy was the major talking point. President Lusinchi, faced with a soaring debt standing at some $30,200 million at year end, sagging oil prices and a falling currency, sent a top-level team to Washington for talks with foreign bankers on the basis of a package of austerity measures such as might be recommended by the IMF. Venezuela, which had been meeting its obligations on both capital repayments and interest in full, unlike most other Latin American states, was unable to obtain a satisfactory arrangement with its creditors. Later following the Finance Minister's presentation to Congress of a budget based on absurdly over-optimistic assumptions, the government turned to the much more risky course of seeking to raise US$1,000 million through discounting future receipts of the state oil corporation PDVSA.

Current economic situation. The anti-inflationary plan announced by President Carlos Andrés Pérez when he took office for the second time in February 1989 has serious and unforeseen consequences. The sharp price rises in essential services, designed to reduce national dependence on oil, led to three days of spontaneous rioting in the capital, Caracas, in which 300 died and over 2,000 were wounded when the Army mobilized over nine battalions to restore order. Similar riots occurred in provincial areas.

Over the next year patient negotiation both with the country's creditors and with the government of the United States bore fruit, and on March 20, 1990 the Planning Minister, Miguel Rodríguez, signed in New York an agreement to restructure debts totalling US$20,500 million with an option for the government to "buy in" debt at a discount. The agreement was the fourth to be concluded under the initiative of US Treasury Secretary Nicholas Brady, known as the "Brady Plan", and was the first to promise a real reduction in the burden of debt.

Prospects for development. Excellent, if the debt burden can be kept under control in face of continued demands and high world interest rates.

Foreign policy. The foreign policy of Venezuela since the restoration of democratic government in 1958 has been characterized by a broad consensus between the two major political parties, a tendency for successive presidents to try to establish distinctive achievements within that consensus, and, in consequence both of this and the relative difficulty of domestic policy-making, an increasingly high profile for foreign policy on the presidential agenda.

Betancourt's policy, previously enunciated in AD publications, was to withhold recognition from dictatorships of both the left and the right — the so-called "Betancourt Doctrine". Having narrowly survived an assassination attempt from the right, and with his government challenged in the countryside by rural guerrillas inspired by Fidel Castro, he took a strong line against the Cuban Revolution. In mid-1960 the URD, previously a leading contender for power, took the fateful decision to withdraw from the ruling coalition over the question of its Cuban policy; by the time it returned to government under Raúl Leoni, Betancourt had played a leading role in the drive to exclude Cuba from the Western Hemisphere system.

Increased participation in international affairs came with the change of government in 1969. Venezuela had been slow to take on an active role in sub-regional organizations, though it had joined the Latin American Free Trade Area (LAFTA) in 1966. But its initial attitude towards the Andean Pact was suspicious, given that in effect it would be becoming that organization's banker, and it was Rafael Caldera who overrode internal business opposition in order to push through the decision to join. It was Caldera who took the bold step to restore diplomatic relations with the Soviet Union and even to make overtures towards Cuba, moves which were the tangible sign of the administration's distrust of the United States, whose economic policies, they believed, were actively detrimental to Venezuelan interests. Soon Venezuela was supplying Cuba with oil, while the oil that the USSR had previously sent to Cuba (at huge cost in transport) went to Spain instead. Under the banner of "ideological pluralism" Caldera had effectively reversed the Betancourt Doctrine, establishing closer links not only with democracies but also with the military governments of Brazil and Bolivia. However Venezuela's decision to join the Andean Pact coincided with the withdrawal of Pinochet's Chile.

The election of Carlos Andrés Pérez coincided with a new consciousness of economic power stemming from the dramatic increase in oil revenues, and Venezuela emerged as a possible leader of the Third World in seeking a New International Economic Order. Together with President Luis Echeverría of Mexico President Pérez took a leading role in setting up the **Latin American Economic System** (*Sistema Económico Latino-Americano*—SELA), and in the process extended relations with Cuba and aligned himself with General Omar Torrijos of Panama, both in renegotiating the position of the Panama Canal, and in affording material and moral assistance to the *Sandinista* insurgents in **Nicaragua**.

President Herrera's outspoken anti-communism gave him some sympathies with the incoming Reagan Administration in the United States, and the hostile reaction of Cuba when many of its citizens took refuge in the Venezuelan Embassy cooled relations sharply. Yet Herrera did not accept the State Department line on Nicaragua uncritically, and the outbreak of the **Falklands War** was seen in Caracas as a major betrayal by the United States of the principles of hemispheric solidarity it had so long espoused. Venezuela aligned itself openly and vociferously with Argentina, the more easily since the previous year an unsuccessful meeting with Forbes Burnham had led to a sharp escalation of the war of words over Venezuela's claim to some two-thirds of the national territory of **Guyana**, based on the tendentious argument that the existing boundary line, frozen for 12 years under the Protocol of Port-of-Spain of 1970, had been established by British "imperialism". Hence as US intervention in Central America deepened, Herrera refused to endorse it and aligned himself instead with the Presidents of Mexico, Panama and Colombia in the Contadora Plan to seek the pacification of Central America by negotiation and the early withdrawal of United States forces from the region. Though the Contadora initiative was ultimately to founder on the rock of US intransigence, it paved the way for the Arias Plan and the decision of the Central American presidents to take responsibility for their own countries. Venezuela's bargaining position in world affairs had meanwhile been seriously eroded by its evident inability to escape the debt crisis, and though with the return of President Pérez to power in 1989 links with international social democracy were again renewed, Venezuela remained unquestionably part of the world capitalist system and became a full member of the General Agreement on Trade and Tariffs (GATT) on Sept. 8, 1990.

PARC

VENEZUELA–COLOMBIA BOUNDARY DISPUTE. The land frontier between **Venezuela** and **Colombia** was settled by the arbitration of the Queen Regent of Spain in 1893 and by the transfer from Colombia to Venezuela of the uninhabited islets of Los Monjes in 1952. The present dispute, which dates from 1965, concerns only delimitation of the maritime zone in the Gulf of Venezuela (which Colombia terms the Gulf of Guajira). Unfortunately, owing to the considerable petroleum potential of the region this has not proved easy, though both sides have from the beginning been committed to a peaceful resolution of the dispute.

The decision in 1987 of President Virgilio Barco Vargas of Colombia to invoke the 1939 bilateral Treaty of Non-Aggression followed the rejection by President Jaime Lusinchi of an offer for direct negotiations on the two countries' conflicting claims, thus leaving Colombia without a remedy. An attack by ELN guerrillas from Colombia on a Venezuelan National Guard patrol in June of the same year further exacerbated feeling, and led to the dismissals of the Minister of Defence and of the chief of staff of the armed forces. Then in mid-August President Lusinchi, claiming that a Colombian warship had entered Venezuelan territorial waters in the Gulf, dispatched a substantial air, land and sea force to the region. Though the intention was clear, to use Venezuela's superior force to back its disputed claims, the Venezuelan refusal to accept mediation brought condemnation from the **Organization of American States**.

Following the change of government in Venezuela, President Carlos Andrés Pérez met President Barco on February 28, 1989 at the Urena border bridge and agreed to a joint commission chaired by the former Spanish Prime Minister, Sr Adolfo Suárez Gómez, to resolve the issue.

PARC

W

WEST INDIES FEDERATION. The short-lived West Indies Federation was created in 1958. Its purpose was to provide a structure which would enable the British island territories to gain independence as a substantial economic and political unit, able to hold its own in the regional context. It collapsed in 1961 when **Jamaica**, the largest of the British island territories, sought and was granted independence.

PARC

WOMEN'S ISSUES. Spanish is the language that has given the world the word *machismo* (from "*macho*", meaning literally "a he-mule") to designate aggressive masculinity. However many recent studies have confirmed what even male anthropologists already knew, that historically a disproportionate share of agricultural work in South America and the Caribbean has been and is carried out by women (an exception being the work of the cane fields in **Cuba** and other sugar-producing countries, originally performed by slaves). In the endemic economic crisis which has afflicted virtually the whole of South and Central America in the 1980s, women have been in the front line, managing the strategies by which the vast majority of poorer households seek to survive the onset and continuation of poverty.

Feminist movements in Latin America, therefore, have tended to be driven by the needs of the poorer and more deprived members of society. They gained a major impetus from the Conference of International Women's Year held in Mexico City in 1975, which in turn led in 1979 to the signing of the UN *Convention on the Elimination of All Forms of Discrimination Against Women*. Where there is political activism, women have been playing an increasingly important role in it.

Access to education. Women are doubly disadvantaged by the widespread illiteracy of South and more particularly Central America, since they are still much less likely than their brothers to benefit from what schooling is available. Furthermore the statistics on the number of children in school tend to be misleadingly optimistic, since few children in rural areas of Mexico are likely to have actually attended school for more than two years. Hence functional illiteracy (the inability adequately to understand and to communicate in the written language) is all-pervasive, and leads to serious disadvantage in terms of understanding one's legal rights. Since illiterates were excluded from the vote in **Peru** until 1980 and in **Brazil** until 1985, women were therefore also more likely to be denied political rights.

The right to vote and to participate in democratic government. Women first obtained the vote in Latin America in 1929 in **Ecuador**. This date compares favourably with that for the achievement of adult female suffrage in Britain (1928). Brazil and Uruguay followed suit in 1932, Cuba in 1934, and **El Salvador** in 1939. In other countries, however, women did not get the vote until after World War II had further loosened traditional attitudes: in **Venezuela** in 1947, in Chile in 1949, and in Mexico not until 1953. In **Argentina**, though "Evita" Perón played a major role in her husband's first government, women gained the vote in 1947. But though she organized women for Perón in 1951 through the Women's Peronist Party, the armed forces blocked her nomination for the post of Vice-President, leading to her celebrated renunciation speech. Since then women have made considerable progress in electoral politics, though since registration is voluntary, women are significantly less likely to register than men, except in Argentina and **Uruguay**. They have also become candidates for office. However as in the United States, and as indeed with male politicians in their own countries, many of the pathfinders were assisted by their family connections. Thus the first woman to be chosen to lead a political party in Latin America was and is Senator María Eugenia Rojas de Moreno, leader of the right-wing Popular National Alliance (*Alianza Nacional Popular*—ANAPO) in **Colombia**, daughter of its founder, the former dictator General Gustavo Rojas Pinilla. Evidence from **Chile**, where before 1973 men's and women's votes were counted separately, shows that women tended to vote for more right-wing candidates than men; their support in 1970 for Jorge Alessandri rather than Radomiro Tomic was a contributory factor to the election of **Salvador Allende**. In Argentina in 1988 the two most important women in politics were the deputies Adelina d'Alessio de Viola and María Julia Alsogaray, both of the liberal rightist, upper middle-class, **Democratic Centre Union** (*Union del Centro Democrático*—UCD) led by the father of one of them, Alvaro Alsogaray. When the Radical government established a department to protect women's rights, it was unable to appoint a member of its own party to the post.

The first woman to become President of a Latin American state (and the world's first woman executive president) was María Estela ("Isabel") Martínez de Perón, who was elected vice-president of **Argentina** in 1973 and succeeded her husband as President on his death on July 1, 1974. The first woman to run for President and to be elected in her own right was Violeta Barrios de Chamorro in **Nicaragua**, who was the widow of the leading critic of the Somoza regime, Pedro Joaquín Chamorro, whose assassination in 1978 had sparked the Nicaraguan Revolution.

Equality before the law. As in Europe the achievement of equal rights for women has taken a long time and is still far from complete. One of the first areas in which women were able to achieve formal equality was in the sphere of the professions (medicine, law etc.), but though by 1980 some 39 per cent of university students in Argentina were women and under the government of Dr **Raúl Alfonsín** there has been a vigorous programme encouraging open entry to the University of Buenos Aires, entry into the professions remains very much a prerogative of the élite and is far from representative of the position of women as a whole.

By the 1950s women in **Mexico** and **Chile** were increasingly evident in executive level positions, but their numbers in proportion to the whole remained limited and women were significantly disadvantaged in getting access to such positions if they came from any but the top social strata. Yet it was still possible to say that there was little if any significant movement for women's equality in South or Central America. Women in the Hispanic (and to a lesser extent the Luso–Brazilian) tradition were seen as having being concerned with the private sphere of the family and home and being "non-political". From the 1960s on, however, women, influenced by the "new feminism", have been seeking more substantial changes in the social and political structures that affect their lives and those of their families, and in the 1970s there was growing evidence, well-documented of increasing female participation in the work of trade unions and peasant confederations in, for example, **Peru** and Ecuador, where traditional Quechua notions of equality of partners within the home did not distinguish between the public and private sphere. In the 1980s women have been increasingly active in urban social movements in Brazil.

Legislation, however, cannot cope with what is probably the fundamental cause of male dominance within Hispanic society, the upbringing of male children, who are still accorded a degree of respect and admiration that at worst perpetuates patriarchy and at best does nothing to fit them for the egalitarian world of the future.

Revolutionary equality. Critics on the left have long argued that what was needed if women were to gain effective equality was total structural change in society. Accordingly major attempts to change social attitudes through structural change have been associated with revolutionary movements and can be seen both in programmes such as those of the **National Liberation Party** (*Partido de Liberación Nacional*—PLN) in **Costa Rica** or **Democratic Action** (*Acción Democrática*—AD) in Venezuela, and more spectacularly in the politics of revolutionary change and violence. Left-wing revolutionary movements such as those of the Cuban Revolution, the government of **Salvador Allende** in **Chile**, the Sandinista regime in Nicaragua and the Bishop government of **Grenada**, have all welcomed women to their ranks and accorded them a leading role in the revolutionary struggle. However though in each of these cases women made substantial gains, not all of them have proved to be as complete or as permanent as was at first hoped.

In Cuba the post-revolutionary government has laid great stress on the importance of mobilizing women for the cause, such that women serve alongside men in the armed forces. However at present few hold senior command positions, reflecting the move away from the original concept of a guerrilla force. Government policy from the outset reflected a formal commitment to the ideal of equality for women comrades. However its symbolism (beards, cigars etc.) was from the outset soaked in *machismo* and Cuba is a classic example of a socialist state that is criticized by feminists for not only not having eliminated gender inequality, but for policies which have in some ways left women worse off than before.

Up to 1970 planning was driven by the idea of need, latterly by the Stalinist principle of "to each according to their work". The building and staffing of child day-care centres was seen as fulfilment of the promise of equality to women, liberating them for other forms of productive work than child-rearing, and certainly the programme has been effective and has been maintained at a substantial level during the financial crisis of the 1980s. But the practical effect of this has been, critics say, simply to add the roles of full-time wage worker and political activist to the traditional ones of housewife and mother. There is an exceptionally large proportion of women in the Cuban National People's Power Assembly, but significantly very few in the higher reaches of an executive that has been becoming increasingly militarized since 1970. Only two of the 31 members of the Council of State are women, and only one of the 44 Ministers.

In Nicaragua, women participated in greater numbers than in any recent revolution in the region. They made up 30 per cent of the combat forces, and in 1979 the women's organization of the **Sandinista National Liberation Front** (*Frente Sandinista de Liberación Nacional*—FSLN), AMPRONAC, had over 8,000 members. A leading hero of the Revolution was "Commander Two" (Dora María Tellez), who led the seizure of President Somoza's palace in 1978. The FSLN had committed themselves strongly to equality as a goal from their beginnings in 1969, but many women who became activists did so because of Somoza's betrayal of the relief operations after the Managua earthquake of 1973.

Once in power, while believing that women can only attain true equality in a socialist society, the FSLN proclaimed the "unconditional equality of all Nicaraguans without distinction of race, nationality, creed or sex" and undertook practical steps to ameliorate their position as far as possible pending that outcome: banning media exploitation of women as sex-objects, enforcing equal pay and labour laws and amending existing practice in the direction of greater equality before the law. However again in 1985 only one of the 22 senior ministers was a woman, and the implementation of this programme was uneven. It remained easier, for example, for men than for women to obtain a divorce on the grounds of adultery. The Family Law (*Ley de Alimentos*) of 1982 was ineffective, and the majority of women continued to remain near the bottom of the income pyramid.

In Grenada the male members of the New Jewel Movement (NJM) were taken aback, after their seizure of power in 1979, to discover the strength of women's support for the Revolution, one of the first acts of which was to abolish "sexual exploitation"—the granting of scholarships etc. in return for sexual favours. The first National Women's Conference of Grenada in June 1979 was followed by the mass mobilization of women through the National Women's Organization (NWO), led by Phyllis Coard, in support of an extensive and continuing programme of according women equality throughout the whole range of work and social relationships.

Control of their own lives and property. Despite formal equality, Latin American practice has been slow to recognize the independence of wives from their husbands. However even in Argentina the nineteenth century liberal tradition places the control of marriage in the hands of the state rather than the Church, and a divorce law went through Congress within days of the Papal visit to Buenos Aires in 1987.

The restrictions of formal marriage, however, have long since ceased to matter much to the large numbers of couples who have not gone through any ceremony of marriage. In Mexico more than half of all children born are born to parents living together outside formal marriage.

Control of their own bodies. Given the preponderance of men in all legislative assemblies in South America, laws on matters relating to women are still effectively made by men, to the point that an overwhelmingly male body legislates to control women's fertility. In addition, there is strong opposition from the **Church** not only to abortion, but to birth control in any practicable form. Pope John Paul II in particular has been much more outspoken in condemning contraception than in condemning torture. This opposition, however, has not prevented Latin American women gaining some degree of control over their own fertility, since the degree of secularization in some countries is such that means of contraception are easily available and little notice is taken of periodic pronouncements by the hierarchy against the practice. The first World Congress of Planned Parenthood was held in Santiago de Chile as early as 1968. However economic conditions have in many parts of the region effectively restricted access to contraception to the better off. The Church's failure to distinguish between contraception and abortion has made it opposition to the latter much less effective than might have been expected; though opposition is vocal, legal abortion is now widely available.

Equality at work. So great is the presumption that women's primary role is to bear children, however, that women are still legally seen as primarily responsible for parenting. Hence despite such equal rights legislation as exists they still are liable to lose their jobs when they have children and if they are re-employed it is on much less favourable terms.

Equal pay for equal work. There is no question, however, but that women not only are much less well paid than men, but that the economic trends of the 1970s and 1980s have made their position worse. If in the past middle-class women accepted the primacy of their menfolk, it was within the assumptions of a society in which their first sign of success for a man was that he employed servants and his wife and daughters did not have to do the household chores. In Argentina in the 1980s an increasing number of middle-class women have been taking up paid work, but this seems to be seen both by them and their husbands as a temporary expedient detracting from their "proper" role and it does not seem to be accompanied with any real acceptance of the principle of conjugal equality. A recent International Labour Organization (ILO) survey of working men and women in Greater Buenos Aires showed that women not only were expected to undertake housework in addition to their paid occupation, but that in consequence they worked on average 90 hours a week compared with 40.3 hours for men.

PARC

WORKERS' PARTY (Partido dos Trabalhadores—PT) (Brazil). The PT emerged from a series of strikes in the late 1970s. These grew out of the "new unionism", a movement which sought to break with the old "corporatist" trade unions under the control of the Ministry of Labour. The strikes were mainly directed by metalworkers' leaders in the "ABC" industrial cities of São André, São Bernardo and São Caetano. The most prominent leader was **Luís Inâcio da Silva**, or "Lula".

The metalworkers' strike, which began in March 1979, was a direct challenge to the régime, to employers and the labour laws. It established Lula as a major political actor at national level. Apart from São Paulo, there were strikes in Rio de Janeiro and Belo Horizonte, and a total of over 400 strikes between January and October 1979, most of them coming in the first months of the Figueiredo government.

The experience of the 1979 strike, and of government reaction to it, quickened debate on the formation of an authentically working-class party, built from the "bottom up", rather than being state-directed, or imposed from above. These discussions had been preceded by an attempt, mainly by São Paulo intellectuals, in 1977, to form the Popular Democratic and Socialist Party (*Partido Popular Democrático e Socialista*—PPDS).

The principal founders of the PT were Lula, Jacó Bittar and Olívio Dutra, all trade unionists, who allowed a rather grudging, suspicious acceptance of intellectuals and students. After the restoration of multi-party politics in 1979, the union leaders seized the opportunity to form a PT *bloc*, with five federal deputies and one senator from the former "authentic" (*auténtico*), or more radical, faction of the old Brazilian Democratic Movement (*Movimento Democrático Brasileiro* — MDB). This allowed provisional registration with the Supreme Electoral Tribunal (*Tribunal Superior Electoral* — TSE), and representation in Congress.

By 1981 the PT had six deputies, but was involved in a dispute over a three-year prison sentense imposed on Lula and 11 other union leaders, under the National Security law, for their part in strikes in São Paulo in 1980. In 1982, the Supreme Military Court (*Tribunal Militar Superior*— TMS), declared them eligible to stand in the important elections of November 1982.

Despite the short time available, the PT managed to win registration for the 1982 elections in every state, depending on local voluntary help. Its performance was severely hit by the *voto vinculado*, but it elected six federal deputies from São Paulo, one from Rio de Janeiro, and one from Minas Gerais, plus state deputies, and *vereadores*, local councillors, mostly in São Paulo state. Lula came fourth in the election for governor of São Paulo, again hindered by the *voto vinculado*, but overshadowed by the **Party of the Brazilian Democratic Movement** (*Partido do Movimento Democrático Brasileiro*—PMDB) and its candidate, Franco Montoro.

In the direct elections for mayor in 1985, the PT won in Fortaleza, the capital of Ceará, with María Luiza Fontenelle, and finished second or third in many cities throughout Brazil. In Goiânia, for example, its candidate won 40 per cent of the vote. The PT claimed an increase of 87 per cent over its 1982 vote, with 11 per cent of the national total, nearly as much as that of the two right-wing parties, the Social Democratic Party (*Partido Democrático Social*—PDS) (4 per cent) and the Liberal Front Party (*Partido da Frente Liberal*—PFL) (9 per cent) combined. This had been achieved despite the PT's refusal to accept electoral coalitions.

In the elections of November 1986 which reflected the continuing, though already waning, popularity of the **Cruzado Plan**, the PT, like other parties, was eclipsed by the success of the PMDB. It still did relatively well, so that its representation grew from six federal deputies in July 1986 to 16 by February 1987. The PT vote in 1986 showed how far voting in 1982 had been affected by the *voto vinculado*, which no longer applied.

In the municipal elections in November 1988, the PT, like the PDT, benefitted from the deepening unpopularity of **José Sarney** and the PMDB. It joined in denouncing the corruption of the Sarney government and the venal response of some PMDB deputies to Sarney's efforts to manipulate the Constitutent Assembly. It had a major victory in São Paulo, where Luiza Erundina de Souza, a woman from the north-eastern state of Paraíba, without the full support of the PT leaders in São Paulo, won election for mayor, against the massive wealth and patronage of the former mayor and state governor, **Paulo Maluf**. The PT also won the other major industrial cities (the "ABC") of São Paulo state, together with Pôrto Alegre, capital of Rio Grande do Sul, and Vitória, capital of the state of Espírito Santo. It came second in both Rio de Janeiro and Belo Horizonte. The PT was now established as a party with genuinely national, popular appeal, and not just for the working class.

The successes of 1988, largely deriving from the energy and enthusiasm of grass-roots membership, and given further support from left-wing church groups, made Lula a leading presidential candidate for 1989, together with **Brizola**. In the first round of voting, on Nov. 15, Collor won 28 per cent of the national vote, Lula just over 16 per cent and Brizola well over 15 per cent. In the second round, on 17 December, **Fernando Collor de Mello** won 42.75 per cent and Lula 37.86. The difference between the two candidates was less than the number of blank and spoilt votes (4,024,339).

In the wake of the 1989 presidential election, the PT showed signs of slackening morale and internal division, which many observers thought were unwarranted. Lula decided not to stand for re-election to Congress in October 1990. The PT still remains the party of the left most firmly rooted in the working-class movement and the "new unionism", with strong links to the radical Church, including its "Base Groups" and to "popular" movements within civil society. It also draws on strong intellectual elements to provide a coherent analysis of Brazil's social and economic problems and their wider, international context. These include some of Brazil's and Latin America's most respected and distinguished social scientists, such as Prof. Florestan Fernandes (now also a federal deputy).

The programme so far defined by the PT is not extremely radical. It strongly favours social and economic reforms, including some measure of agrarian reform, which explains its support in regions such as Acre, among the rubber tappers. It demands a greater measure of social justice and more equitable distribution of wealth and opportunities. It is generally pragmatic on economic policy, on issues such as the foreign debt. It has a strong commitment to protection of the environment and has support across class boundaries.

In the Congressional elections of October 1990, the PT did much better than many observers had predicted. It doubled its representation in the Chamber of Deputies from 17 to 35. Together with the PDT, it offers the main challenge to the government and programme of Collor de Mello, as the most obvious civilian alternative in goverment, should his programme falter.

PF

Y

YOUTH. With 42 per cent of its population under the age of 17, the youthfulness of the population of **Brazil** reflects the fact that in the 1980s it increased at the rate of more than 2 per cent a year. Between 1981 and 1986, however, the population of **Nicaragua** increased even faster, at an average rate of 3.6 per cent a year, the highest in the hemisphere and in the world. Even without the relentless opposition of the Reagan Administration and the **United States**, therefore, the Sandinista government would have encountered formidable difficulties, in a country already looted by **Anastasio Somoza** and devastated by civil war, in making good on its promises to provide health and education for all, and it is a measure of its success that two of the worst scourges of the region were effectively eliminated.

Such a rapid rate of population growth however means a short political memory, and the election of President **Collor** in Brazil by an electorate few of whom were even born when the last free elections for President took place in 1960, was only the latest occasion on which success in elections has gone to the plausible populist with an attractive appearance and personality, but with nothing much in the way of a political programme. Those who were surprised at the youth of the new President of **Mexico** in 1988, who at 39 was little over half the age of the outgoing President of the United States, probably did not realize that he was twice the age of well over half of those voting for him. For such an electorate, the grind of long-term political and economic planning has little appeal, and the simplicities of those who argue that all can safely be left to the free market find easy acceptance. In any case the politicians of the region tend to see population not as a problem, but as a resource, and, furthermore, as the one resource that left to itself will increase of its own accord.

Unfortunately matters are not so simple, and a very youthful population presents two sorts of economic problems not found in the older stable economies of Europe or North America. The first is the narrowness of the tax base. With a smaller proportion of the population in productive work, it is correspondingly more difficult to extract the resources needed to maintain modern educational and social welfare systems. The second is the number of people for whom resources have to be made available. With proportionately far more consumers for these services, the sheer physical problem of constructing, staffing and maintaining schools, colleges, clinics and hospitals is much greater.

The commitment of Caribbean countries to youth is concentrated in two main areas—education and health. These two sectors usually account for the bulk of total public expenditure, often as much as 20 per cent in each case.

Post-independence, education has been seen as the first priority, a means of developing populations and ensuring that future generations are equipped with skills in the range of areas to allow the small island countries to compete. The education process was also seen as a means of countries controlling their own destinies by elevating nationals to positions of authority in all aspects of society. Educated societies are seen as part of the wealth of countries, which, apart from Jamaica, Trinidad and Guyana, lack mineral resources to any significant degree.

Thus, even though the region has evolved sophisticated education systems, spending on this sector remains high. The Bahamas, for instance, allocated 22 per cent of total spending to education in 1987, St Kitts 15 per cent, Trinidad 13.7 per cent and Barbados, highly regarded for its range of education facilities, 19.1 per cent in 1988–89.

There are high school ratios to population. Montserrat, with a population of some 12,000 has 13 primary schools and two secondary and Antigua with some 79,000 people has 43 primary and 15 secondary. Anguilla, with only 7,000 people, has introduced a comprehensive education system. Not surprisingly, literacy levels are high, with Barbados having a 98 per cent functional literacy rate, one of the highest in the world.

All countries have free education systems, through to secondary school, and education is compulsory, generally, between the ages of five and 16. Primary and secondary schools are complemented by vocational training centres, technical colleges and, for the region, there is the University of the West Indies, with three campuses in Jamaica, Barbados and Trinidad.

Various youth programmes are organized through schools. These range from sports, to cadets, scouts and guide programmes. International schemes such as the Duke of Edinburgh Award Scheme are also linked to schools and programmes such as Junior Achievement, increasingly popular, are aimed at exposing the youth to the world of business at early stages.

High spending on health care is also aimed at providing wide-ranging medical care to citizens, with special provisions for the young. Caribbean countries, with birth rates as high as 25 per 1,000, have populations with a high youth profile. Most countries have programmes which provide free medical and dental care for school children up to the secondary level.

Apart from health and education, there are no consistent programmes for youth development in the region. Countries have embarked on programmes with varying degrees, mostly minimal, of success. Trinidad and Tobago developed the Best Village cultural programme in the 1970s as a means of channelling youth into constructive activity and this has been one of the most successful programmes aimed at youth.

Some countries have national youth councils which receive government support and intermittently, attempts are made at regional youth congresses. These moves have not, so far, been sustained. Even though some governments allocate youth portfolios, not a lot has been accomplished in determining programmes for youth or establishing youth forums.

One plan constantly mooted in various forms involves attachment to military forces, the idea being that young people would acquire skills, do national service and acquire the discipline that comes with being involved with armed forces. This has fallen flat as most countries view the military with much scepticism.

In the forseeable future it is likely that the emphasis will continue on education and health. Governments will also provide facilities for recreation, but will allow young people to organize themselves in whatever areas and forge ahead with programmes they deem fit with minimal government direction.

PARC, MH

YRIGOYEN, HIPOLITO. President of **Argentina** 1916–22 and 1928–30, Hipólito Yrigoyen (often also spelt Irigoyen) was born on July 12, 1852. Together with Leandro Alem, he was one of the founders of the Radical Civic Union (*Unión Cívica Radical*—UCR), of which he became the leader in 1896. He led the party's campaign for clean electoral procedures against an entrenched conservative oligarchy which systematically resorted to fraud to remain in power. The campaign, which included a series of abortive armed uprisings, succeeded in securing the passage of the Sáenz Peña law, embodying the electoral reforms.

When elections were held in 1916, Yrigoyen won by an overwhelming majority. Though his first administration is often remembered for the "Tragic Week" of 1919, when strike action was violently repressed, this was an exception rather than the rule in a period of relative peace on the labour front, and of considerable economic progress.

In 1922 Yrigoyen was succeeded by Marcelo Torcuato de Alvear, leader of the "antipersonalist" wing of the UCR, which favoured accommodation with the conservatives. In 1928, at the age of 76, Yrigoyen was again elected president. In the second term he appeared increasingly out of touch with reality, and unable to cope with the impact of the worldwide economic depression. In September 1930 he was deposed by a military *coup*, an event usually described as marking the beginning of the era of military intervention in Argentine politics.

Yrigoyen died poor but still very popular, on July 3, 1933.

EC

Z

ZAPATA, EMILIANO. Emiliano Zapata was born, it is generally agreed, on Aug. 8, 1879 in the state of Morelos, just to the south of Mexico City. In the early part of the twentieth century there was acute tension in this area between the Indian holders of communal lands, and the expanding sugar-growing plantations which were owned by capitalists with connexions in Mexico City. These tensions prompted a rising by the *campesinos*, led by Zapata, which broke out in 1910. Under normal circumstances a revolt of this kind would be crushed. However by coincidence Zapata revolted at around the same time as **Madero**, and the Madero revolt destroyed the power of the Mexican state.

However relations between Zapata and Madero broke down as the latter refused to agree to the land redistribution demanded by Zapata. Zapata issued a plan of his own, the Plan of Ayala, calling for land reform and a new Revolution to secure it. For the next eight years, Zapata's forces were in almost constant conflict with the authorities in Mexico City, first Huerta and then Carranza. However while Zapata proved unable to exert much influence outside Morelos—he did briefly capture Mexico City but was soon forced to withdraw—he did enjoy extensive popular support within the state. After several years of fighting, Carranza's General Pablo Gonzalez was able to set a trap for Zapata and arrange for his assassination in 1919.

Zapata had little or nothing in common with the Revolutionary leaders who rebuilt the Mexican state after 1917. Nevertheless the 1917 Constitution did provide for land reform—and extensive land redistribution did take place during the 1930s. Communal landholdings, *ejidos*, are still common in Mexico although they are in some degree of crisis for economic reasons. Zapata, meanwhile, is officially a hero of the Revolution.

GP

GENERAL INDEX

CENTRAL AMERICA AND THE CARIBBEAN